CW00536867

The

Wine

Region

Atlas

ISTVAN BARCZIKAY

The
Wine
Region
Atlas

The Wine Region Atlas
by Istvan Barczikay

Edited and indexed by the author
Art direction and book design by the author

Cover illustrations and ephemera courtesy of the author

The information in the book (up to date, as of August 2022) is true and complete to the best of my knowledge.

ISBN 978-1-3999-3039-0

Contents

Introduction	6
What is in the atlas?	7
Map of Europe	8
World map	9
France	10
Alsace	23
Lorraine	37
Jura	38
Bugey	39
Savoie	40
Champagne	42
Burgundy	44
Beaujolais	87
Lyonnais	88
Rhône	89
Provence	95
Languedoc	96
Roussillon	97
South West France	98
Bordeaux	99
Loire Valley	108
Corse	114
Italy	115
Valle d'Aosta	122
Piemonte	123
Lombardia	136
Trentino-Alto Adige	137
Veneto	138
Friuli-Venezia Giulia	139
Liguria	140
Emilia-Romagna	141
Toscana	142
Marche	145
Umbria	146
Lazio	147
Abruzzo	148
Molise	149
Puglia	150
Campania	151
Basilicata	152
Calabria	153
Sicilia	154
Sardegna	155
Spain	156
Galicia	159
Castilla y León	160
La Rioja	161
País Vasco	162

Aragón	162
Catalonia	163
Valencia	165
Murcia	165
Castilla- la Mancha	166
Madrid	166
Extremadura	166
Andalucia	167
Balearic Islands	170
Canary Islands	171
Cava	172
Portugal	173
DOC of Portugal	176
Terras Madeirenses	177
Açores	178
Germany	179
Ahr	187
Mittelrhein	188
Mosel	189
Rheingau	190
Nahe	191
Rheinhessen	192
Pfalz	193
Hessische-Bergstrasse	194
Franken	195
Baden	196
Württemberg	197
Saale-Unstrut	198
Sachsen	199
Austria	200
Niederösterreich, Wien	203
Burgenland, Steiermark	205
Hungary	206
Tokaj	213
Switzerland	228
Greece	232
Mainland	235
Isands	236
Canada	237
British Columbia	240
Ontario	241
Québec	242
Nova Scotia	243
Usa	244
States of Usa	247
California	248
Oregon, Idaho	255
Washington	256
Other States	257

Chile	261
Argentina	264
The North	267
La Rioja Argentina	268
Mendoza	269
Center, Patagonia, Atlantic	270
South Africa	271
Geographical Units and regions	273
Outside of the 5 regions	274
Coastal Region	275
Australia	279
Western Australia	282
South Australia	283
Victoria	284
New South Wales, Queensland	285
New Zealand	286
Lebanon	289
Israel	289
Slovenia	290
Croatia	290
Romania	291
Czech Republic	292
Slovakia	292
Turkey	293
Bulgaria	293
Moldova	293
Cyprus	293
Ukraine	293
Russia	293
Serbia	294
Bosnia & Herzegovina	294
Montenegro	294
Albania	294
North Macedonia	294
England	295
Luxembourg	295
Belgium	295
Georgia	296
Armenia	296
Azerbaijan	296
China	297
Japan	297
Brazil	298
Uruguay	298
Index	299
About the Author	306

Introduction

I have dedicated two years curating this atlas stemmed from my love of wine. Years ago, I began studying wine as a way to enhance my experience in hospitality. In my meticulous studies, I discovered a gap in my educational experience, a collection of maps to assist in identifying, locating, and educating. So I went to work putting this atlas together.

As far as I believe, having a collection of maps dedicated to wine is an advantage for enthusiasts, from hobbyist to professional. It can assist those looking to expand their knowledge by helping them enjoy wine while understanding the geography from which they derive. This is the benefit of an atlas focused only on wine.

This atlas is more than a collection of maps. It provides valuable information essential to wine culture, up to date as of August 2022. Included is information regarding classification systems, leading wine producing countries, information on regions, sub-regions, important towns and villages, as well as respected vineyards and chateaux.

This comprehensive atlas will allow readers to identify wine locations and identify the features of a particular region and wine. It will help expand knowledge by revealing geographical features, wine classifications, neighboring regions, and lead to the discovery of similar wines.

I have loved the challenge of curating this collection of wine related maps. I hope that my passion for this world shines through the pages to those just starting on their own wine journeys, or those who are looking to expand their already extensive knowledge of the art.

If you love wine, this book is for you.

Istvan Barczikay

What is in the atlas?

The following list contains highlighted items in RED that are neither part of the index nor represented on a map [yet].

FRANCE
17 Regions
367 AOC
- 51 Grand Cru vineyards of Alsace
- 33 Grand Cru vineyards of Burgundy
17 Grand Cru villages of Champagne
42 Premier Cru villages of Champagne
61 Growths of the Médoc 1855 Classification
27 Châteaux of the Sauternes 1855 Classification
16 Châteaux of the Graves 1953 Classification
82 Châteaux of the St-Émilion 1955 Classification
- 4 Premier Grand Cru Classé A
- 14 Premier Grand Cru Classé B
- 64 Grand Cru Classé
655 Premier Cru vineyards of Burgundy
1878 Lieux-dit of Burgundy
74 IGP

ITALY
20 Regions
76 DOCG
332 DOC
170 MGA vineyards of Barolo DOCG
66 MGA vineyards of Barbaresco DOCG

SPAIN
17 Regions
2 DOCa (DOQ in Catalan)
69 DO
24 Vino de Pago

PORTUGAL
14 Regions
31 DOC

GERMANY
13 Anbaugebieten
41 Bereichen
164 Grosslagen
418 Grosse Lagen
330 Erste Lagen

AUSTRIA
9 Regions
17 DAC
95 Erste Lagen (1ÖTW)

HUNGARY
6 OFJ
32 OEM
27 Villages of Tokaj OEM
415 Vineyards of Tokaj OEM

SWITZERLAND
6 Regions
26 Canton
62 AOC
- 27 AOC cantonale
- 13 AOC regionale
- 22 AOC locale

GREECE
9 Regions
21 OPAP
12 OPE

CANADA
10 Provinces
3 Territories
9 BC VQA
5 VQA
7 CVQ
4 WANS

USA
50 States
262 AVA [Hawaii – 1 AVA]

CHILE
35 DO
- 6 Regions
- 17 Sub-Regions
- 8 Zones
- 4 Areas

ARGENTINA
103 IG
- 5 Regions out of 2 IG
- 14 Provinces out of 11 IG
- 2 DOC
- -64 Departments
- 24 Districts

SOUTH AFRICA
6 Geographical Units
5 Regions
30 Districts
97 Wards

AUSTRALIA
116 GI
- 1 Country
- 8 States
- 1 Super Zone
- 28 Zones
- 64 Regions
- 14 Sub-Regions

NEW ZEALAND
18 GI
- 11 Regions
- 7 Sub-Regions

LEBANON - 4 Regions - 4 Sub-Regions

ISRAEL - 6 Regions - 15 Sub-Regions

SLOVENIA - 3 Regions - 9 Sub-Regions

CROATIA - 4 Regions - 12 Sub-Regions

ROMANIA - 12 Regions - 33 DOC

CZECH REPUBLIC - 2 Regions - 6 Sub-Regions

SLOVAKIA - 6 Regions

TURKEY - 4 Regions - 4 Sub-regions

BULGARIA - 5 Regions

MOLDOVA - 3 IGP

CYPRUS - 5 OEOΠ

UKRAINE - 5 Regions

RUSSIA - 5 Regions

SERBIA - 2 Regions - 20 Areas

BOSNIA & HERZEGOVINA - 6 Regions

MONTENEGRO - 2 Regions

ALBANIA - 4 Regions

NORTH MACEDONIA - 3 Regions

ENGLAND - 6 Regions

LUXEMBOURG - 1 Region - 2 AOC

BELGIUM - 2 Regions - 7 AOC

GEORGRIA - 10 Regions

ARMENIA - 11 Regions

AZERBAIJAN - 3 Regions

CHINA - 8 Regions - 6 Sub-Regions

JAPAN - 4 Regions

BRAZIL - 6 Regions

URUGUAY - 6 Regions - 15 Departments

WINE-PRODUCING COUNTRIES

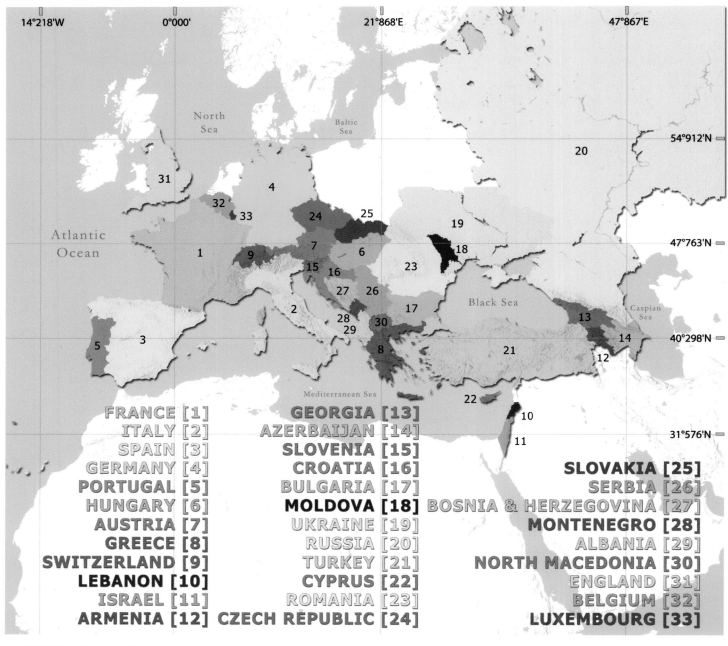

FRANCE [1]
ITALY [2]
SPAIN [3]
GERMANY [4]
PORTUGAL [5]
HUNGARY [6]
AUSTRIA [7]
GREECE [8]
SWITZERLAND [9]
LEBANON [10]
ISRAEL [11]
ARMENIA [12]

GEORGIA [13]
AZERBAIJAN [14]
SLOVENIA [15]
CROATIA [16]
BULGARIA [17]
MOLDOVA [18]
UKRAINE [19]
RUSSIA [20]
TURKEY [21]
CYPRUS [22]
ROMANIA [23]
CZECH REPUBLIC [24]

SLOVAKIA [25]
SERBIA [26]
BOSNIA & HERZEGOVINA [27]
MONTENEGRO [28]
ALBANIA [29]
NORTH MACEDONIA [30]
ENGLAND [31]
BELGIUM [32]
LUXEMBOURG [33]

Body of Water

| Mi | 0 | 547 | 1093 | 1640 | 2187 |
| Km | 0 | 880 | 1760 | 2640 | 3520 |

WINE-PRODUCING COUNTRIES

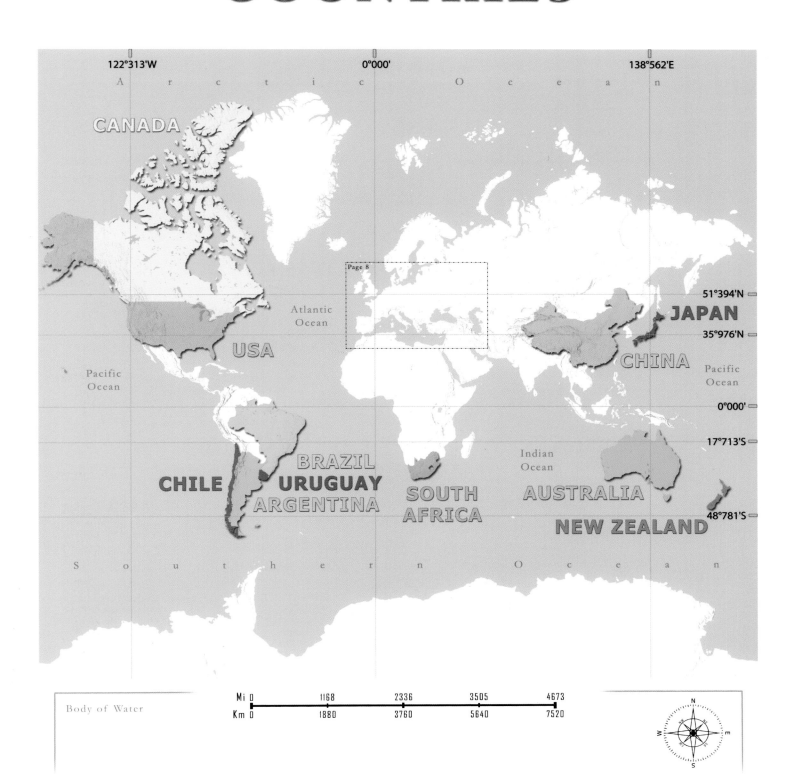

CANADA

51°394'N

JAPAN

35°976'N

CHINA

USA

Atlantic Ocean

Pacific Ocean

Page 8

Pacific Ocean

0°000'

17°713'S

Indian Ocean

BRAZIL

CHILE   URUGUAY

ARGENTINA

SOUTH AFRICA

AUSTRALIA

NEW ZEALAND

48°781'S

A r c t i c   O c e a n

S o u t h e r n   O c e a n

122°313'W

0°000'

138°562'E

Body of Water

| Mi 0 | 1168 | 2336 | 3505 | 4673 |
| Km 0 | 1880 | 3760 | 5640 | 7520 |

CLASSIFICATION SYSTEM
Regulated by the INAO [Institut National de l'Origine et de la Qualité]
AOC [Appellation d'Origine Contrôlée = Controlled Designation of Origin]
IGP [Indication Géographique Protégée = Protected Geographical Indication
   = Vin de Pays]
VIN DE FRANCE = VdT [Vin de Table = table wine]

17 Regions

367 AOC
including
51 Grand Cru vineyards of Alsace with AOC designation
33 Grand Cru vineyards of Burgundy with AOC designation [including Chablis]

17 Grand Cru villages of Champagne

42 Premier Cru villages of Champagne

61 Growths of the Médoc 1855 Classification

27 Châteaux of the Sauternes 1855 Classification

FRANCE

16 Châteaux of the Graves 1953 Classification
[revised in 1959]

82 Châteaux of the Saint-Émilion 1955 Classification
[amended in 1958, latest update 2012]
4 Premier Grand Cru Classé A
14 Premier Grand Cru Classé B
64 Grand Cru Classé [list only]

655 Premier Cru vineyards of Burgundy
[including Chablis]

1878 Lieux-dit of Burgundy [list only]

74 IGP [list only]

Alsace [53]

	VILLAGE	AOC	EST.		VILLAGE	AOC	EST.
		ALSACE / VIN D'ALSACE	1962				
		CRÉMANT D'ALSACE	1976				
GC	Marlenheim	STEINKLOTZ	1992	GC	Bennwihr, Sigolsheim	MARCKRAIN	1992
GC	Dahlenheim, Scharrachbergheim	ENGELBERG	1992	GC	Sigolsheim	MAMBOURG	1992
GC	Bergbieten	ALTENBERG DE BERGBIETEN	1983	GC	Kientzheim, Sigolsheim	FÜRSTENTUM	1992
GC	Wolxheim	ALTENBERG DE WOLXHEIM	1992	GC	Kientzheim	SCHLOSSBERG	1975
GC	Molsheim	BRUDERTHAL	1992	GC	Ammerschwihr	KAEFFERKOPF	2007
GC	Barr	KIRCHBERG DE BARR	1983	GC	Katzenthal, Ammerschwihr	WINECK-SCHLOSSBERG	1992
GC	Mittelbergheim	ZOTZENBERG	1992	GC	Niedermorschwihr, Katzenthal	SOMMERBERG	1983
GC	Andlau	KASTELBERG	1983	GC	Ingersheim, Katzenthal	FLORIMONT	1992
GC	Andlau	WIEBELSBERG	1983	GC	Turckheim	BRAND	1983
GC	Andlau, Eichhoffen	MOENCHBERG	1983	GC	Wintzenheim	HENGST	1983
GC	Nothalten	MUENCHBERG	1992	GC	Wettolsheim	STEINGRUBLER	1992
GC	Blienschwiller	WINZENBERG	1992	GC	Eguisheim	EICHBERG	1983
GC	Dambach-la-Ville	FRANKSTEIN	1992	GC	Eguisheim, Wettolsheim	PFERSIGBERG	1992
GC	Kintzheim	PRAELATENBERG	1992	GC	Hattstatt, Voegtlinshoffen	HATSCHBOURG	1983
GC	Rodern, Saint-Hippolyte	GLOECKELBERG	1983	GC	Gueberschwihr	GOLDERT	1983
GC	Bergheim	ALTENBERG DE BERGHEIM	1983	GC	Pfaffenheim, Westhalten	STEINERT	1992
GC	Bergheim	KANZLERBERG	1983	GC	Rouffach, Westhalten	VORBOURG	1992
GC	Ribeauvillé	GEISBERG	1983	GC	Westhalten, Soultzmatt	ZINNKOEPFLÉ	1992
GC	Ribeauvillé	KIRCHBERG DE RIBEAUVILLÉ	1983	GC	Orschwihr	PFINGSTBERG	1992
GC	Ribeauvillé	OSTERBERG	1992	GC	Bergholtz, Guebwiller	SPIEGEL	1983
GC	Hunawihr	ROSACKER	1983	GC	Guebwiller	KESSLER	1983
GC	Zellenberg	FROEHN	1992	GC	Guebwiller	KITTERLÉ	1983
GC	Riquewihr, Zellenberg	SCHOENENBOURG	1992	GC	Guebwiller	SAERING	1983
GC	Riquewihr	SPOREN	1992	GC	Wuenheim	OLLWILLER	1983
GC	Beblenheim	SONNENGLANZ	1983	GC	Thann, Vieux-Thann	RANGEN	1983
GC	Mittelwihr, Beblenheim	MANDELBERG	1992				

SUB-REGION	AOC	EST.	SUB-REGION	AOC	EST.
Lorraine [2]					
Toul	CÔTES DE TOUL	1998	Moselle	MOSELLE	2011
Champagne [3]					
	CHAMPAGNE	1936		ROSÉ DES RICEYS	1947
	COTEAUX CHAMPENOIS	1974			
Loire Valley [53]					
	CRÉMANT DE LOIRE (ANJOU-SAUMUR & TOURAINE)	1975	Touraine	TOURAINE	1939
	ROSÉ DE LOIRE (ANJOU-SAUMUR & TOURAINE)	1974	Touraine	BOURGUEIL	1937
Pays Nantais	MUSCADET	1937	Touraine	ST-NICOLAS DE BOURGUEIL	1937
Pays Nantais	MUSCADET SEVRE-ET-MAINE	1936	Touraine	CHINON	1937
Pays Nantais	MUSCADET COTEAUX DE LA LOIRE	1936	Touraine	TOURAINE NOBLE-JOUÉ	2001
Pays Nantais	MUSCADET CÔTES DE GRANDLIEU	1994	Touraine	VOUVRAY	1936
Pays Nantais	COTEAUX D'ANCENIS	2011	Touraine	MONTLOUIS-SUR-LOIRE	1938
Pays Nantais	GROS PLANT DU PAYS NANTAIS	2011	Touraine	CHEVERNY	1993
Pays Nantais	FIEFS VENDÉENS	2011	Touraine	COUR-CHEVERNY	1993
Anjou-Saumur	ANJOU	1936	Touraine	VALENÇAY	2004
Anjou-Saumur	CABERNET D'ANJOU	1964	Touraine	COTEAUX DU LOIR	1948
Anjou-Saumur	ROSÉ D'ANJOU	1957	Touraine	JASNIÈRES	2001
Anjou-Saumur	ANJOU VILLAGES	1991	Touraine	COTEAUX DU VENDÔMOIS	2001
Anjou-Saumur	ANJOU-COTEAUX-DE-LA-LOIRE	1946	Central/Upper Loire	ORLÉANS	2006
Anjou-Saumur	SAVENNIÈRES	1952	Central/Upper Loire	ORLÉANS-CLÉRY	2006
Anjou-Saumur	SAVENNIÈRES COULÉE DE SERRANT	2011	Central/Upper Loire	COTEAUX DU GIENNOIS	1998
Anjou-Saumur	SAVENNIÈRES ROCHE AUX MOINES	2011	Central/Upper Loire	POUILLY-FUMÉ	1937
Anjou-Saumur	COTEAUX DU LAYON	1950	Central/Upper Loire	POUILLY SUR LOIRE	1937
Anjou-Saumur	QUARTS DE CHAUME "GRAND CRU"	1954	Central/Upper Loire	SANCERRE	1936
Anjou-Saumur	BONNEZEAUX	1951	Central/Upper Loire	MENETOU-SALON	1959
Anjou-Saumur	COTEAUX DE L'AUBANCE	1950	Central/Upper Loire	QUINCY	1936
Anjou-Saumur	ANJOU VILLAGES BRISSAC	1998	Central/Upper Loire	REUILLY	1937
Anjou-Saumur	SAUMUR	1936	Auvergne / Central France	CHÂTEAUMEILLANT	2010
Anjou-Saumur	SAUMUR-CHAMPIGNY	1957	Auvergne / Central France	SAINT-POURÇAIN	2009
Anjou-Saumur	COTEAUX-DE-SAUMUR	1962	Auvergne / Central France	CÔTES D'AUVERGNE	2011
Anjou-Saumur	HAUT-POITOU	2011	Auvergne / Central France	CÔTES ROANNAISES	1994
			Auvergne / Central France	CÔTES DU FOREZ	2000
Burgundy [86]					
	BOURGOGNE	1937	Côte d'Or/Côte de Nuits	CÔTE DE NUITS-VILLAGES	1937
	BOURGOGNE ALIGOTÉ	1937	Côte d'Or/Côte de Nuits	MARSANNAY	1987
	BOURGOGNE PASSE-TOUT-GRAINS	1937	Côte d'Or/Côte de Nuits	MARSANNAY ROSÉ	1987
	CÔTEAUX BOURGUIGNONS	2011	Côte d'Or/Côte de Nuits	FIXIN	1936
	BOURGOGNE MOUSSEUX	1943	Côte d'Or/Côte de Nuits	GEVREY-CHAMBERTIN	1936
	CRÉMANT DE BOURGOGNE	1975	Côte d'Or/Côte de Nuits	RUCHOTTES-CHAMBERTIN Grand Cru	1937
Grand Auxerrois	IRANCY	1999	Côte d'Or/Côte de Nuits	MAZIS-CHAMBERTIN Grand Cru	1937
Grand Auxerrois	SAINT-BRIS	2003	Côte d'Or/Côte de Nuits	CHAMBERTIN-CLOS DE BÉZE Grand Cru	1937
Grand Auxerrois	VÉZELAY	2017	Côte d'Or/Côte de Nuits	CHAMBERTIN Grand Cru	1937
Grand Auxerrois	PETIT CHABLIS	1944	Côte d'Or/Côte de Nuits	LATRICIÉRES-CHAMBERTIN Grand Cru	1937
Grand Auxerrois	CHABLIS (INCL 1ER CRU)	1938	Côte d'Or/Côte de Nuits	CHAPELLE-CHAMBERTIN Grand Cru	1937
Grand Auxerrois	CHABLIS GRAND CRU	1938	Côte d'Or/Côte de Nuits	GRIOTTE-CHAMBERTIN Grand Cru	1937

Region	Appellation	Year	Region	Appellation	Year
Côte d'Or/Côte de Nuits	CHARMES-CHAMBERTIN Grand Cru	1937	Côte d'Or/Côte de Beaune	CHOREY-LÈS-BEAUNE	1937
Côte d'Or/Côte de Nuits	MAZOYÈRES-CHAMBERTIN Grand Cru	1937	Côte d'Or/Côte de Beaune	BEAUNE	1936
Côte d'Or/Côte de Nuits	MOREY-SAINT-DENIS	1936	Côte d'Or/Côte de Beaune	POMMARD	1936
Côte d'Or/Côte de Nuits	CLOS DE LA ROCHE Grand Cru	1936	Côte d'Or/Côte de Beaune	VOLNAY	1937
Côte d'Or/Côte de Nuits	CLOS ST-DENIS Grand Cru	1936	Côte d'Or/Côte de Beaune	MONTHÉLIE	1937
Côte d'Or/Côte de Nuits	CLOS DES LAMBRAYS Grand Cru	1981	Côte d'Or/Côte de Beaune	AUXEY-DURESSES	1937
Côte d'Or/Côte de Nuits	CLOS DE TART (M) Grand Cru	1939	Côte d'Or/Côte de Beaune	SAINT-ROMAIN	1947
Côte d'Or/Côte de Nuits	CHAMBOLLE-MUSIGNY	1936	Côte d'Or/Côte de Beaune	MEURSAULT	1937
Côte d'Or/Côte de Nuits	BONNES MARES Grand Cru	1936	Côte d'Or/Côte de Beaune	BLAGNY	1937
Côte d'Or/Côte de Nuits	MUSIGNY Grand Cru	1936	Côte d'Or/Côte de Beaune	PULIGNY-MONTRACHET	1937
Côte d'Or/Côte de Nuits	VOUGEOT	1936	Côte d'Or/Côte de Beaune	CHEVALIER-MONTRACHET	1937
Côte d'Or/Côte de Nuits	CLOS DE VOUGEOT Grand Cru	1937	Côte d'Or/Côte de Beaune	BIENVENUES-BÂTARD-MONTRACHET Grand Cru	1939
Côte d'Or/Côte de Nuits	VOSNE-ROMANÉE	1936	Côte d'Or/Côte de Beaune	MONTRACHET Grand Cru	1937
Côte d'Or/Côte de Nuits	ECHÉZEAUX Grand Cru	1937	Côte d'Or/Côte de Beaune	BÂTARD-MONTRACHET Grand Cru	1937
Côte d'Or/Côte de Nuits	GRANDS-ECHÉZEAUX Grand Cru	1937	Côte d'Or/Côte de Beaune	CHASSAGNE-MONTRACHET Grand Cru	1937
Côte d'Or/Côte de Nuits	RICHEBOURG Grand Cru	1936	Côte d'Or/Côte de Beaune	CRIOTS-BÂTARD-MONTRACHET Grand Cru	1939
Côte d'Or/Côte de Nuits	LA ROMANÉE (M) Grand Cru	1936	Côte d'Or/Côte de Beaune	SAINT-AUBIN	1937
Côte d'Or/Côte de Nuits	ROMANÉE-CONTI (M) Grand Cru	1936	Côte d'Or/Côte de Beaune	SANTENAY	1936
Côte d'Or/Côte de Nuits	ROMANÉE-SAINT-VIVANT Grand Cru	1936	Côte d'Or/Côte de Beaune	MARANGES	1989
Côte d'Or/Côte de Nuits	LA GRANDE RUE (M) Grand Cru	1992	Côte Chalonnaise	BOUZERON	1998
Côte d'Or/Côte de Nuits	LA TÂCHE (M) Grand Cru	1936	Côte Chalonnaise	RULLY	1939
Côte d'Or/Côte de Nuits	NUITS-SAINT-GEORGES	1936	Côte Chalonnaise	MERCUREY	1936
Côte d'Or/Côte de Beaune	CÔTE DE BEAUNE	1937	Côte Chalonnaise	GIVRY	1946
Côte d'Or/Côte de Beaune	CÔTE DE BEAUNE-VILLAGES	1937	Côte Chalonnaise	MONTAGNY	1936
Côte d'Or/Côte de Beaune	PERNAND-VERGELESSES	1936	Mâconnais	MÂCON	1937
Côte d'Or/Côte de Beaune	ALOXE-CORTON	1938	Mâconnais	MÂCON-VILLAGES	1937
Côte d'Or/Côte de Beaune	CHARLEMAGNE Grand Cru	1937	Mâconnais	POUILLY-FUISSÉ	1936
Côte d'Or/Côte de Beaune	CORTON Grand Cru	1937	Mâconnais	POUILLY-LOCHÉ	1940
Côte d'Or/Côte de Beaune	CORTON-CHARLEMAGNE Grand Cru	1937	Mâconnais	POUILLY-VINZELLES	1940
Côte d'Or/Côte de Beaune	LADOIX	1937	Mâconnais	SAINT-VÉRAN	1971
Côte d'Or/Côte de Beaune	SAVIGNY-LÈS-BEAUNE	1937	Mâconnais	VIRÉ-CLESSÉ	1999

Beaujolais [11]

	Appellation	Year		Appellation	Year
	BEAUJOLAIS	1937		CHIROUBLES	1936
	SAINT-AMOUR	1946		MORGON	1936
	JULIÉNAS	1938		RÉGNIÉ	1988
	CHÉNAS	1936		CÔTE DE BROUILLY	1938
	MOULIN-À-VENT	1936		BROUILLY	1938
	FLEURIE	1936			

Lyonnais [1]

	Appellation	Year
	COTEAUX DU LYONNAIS	1984

Jura [6]

	Appellation	Year		Appellation	Year
	CÔTES DU JURA	1937		ARBOIS	1936
	CRÉMANT DU JURA	1995		CHÂTEAU-CHALON	1936
	MACVIN DU JURA	1991		L'ÉTOILE	1937

Bugey [2]

	Appellation	Year		Appellation	Year
	BUGEY	2009		ROUSSETTE DU BUGEY	2009

Savoie [4]

	Appellation	Year		Appellation	Year
	CRÉMANT DE SAVOIE	2015		ROUSSETTE DE SAVOIE	1973
	VIN DE SAVOIE	1973		SEYSSEL	1942

Bordeaux [40]

Region	Appellation	Year	Region	Appellation	Year
	BORDEAUX	1936	Entre-Deux-Mers	CADILLAC	1973
	BORDEAUX SUPÉRIEUR	1943	Entre-Deux-Mers	LOUPIAC	1936
	CRÉMANT DE BORDEAUX	1990	Entre-Deux-Mers	STE-CROIX-DU-MONT	1936
	CÔTES DE BORDEAUX	2009	Entre-Deux-Mers	CÔTES DE BORDEAUX-ST-MACAIRE	1937
Left Bank/Médoc	MÉDOC	1936	Entre-Deux-Mers	BORDEAUX HAUT-BENAUGE	1936
Left Bank/Médoc	HAUT-MÉDOC	1936	Entre-Deux-Mers	ENTRE-DEUX-MERS HAUT-BENAUGE	1937
Left Bank/Médoc	SAINT-ESTÈPHE	1936	Entre-Deux-Mers	GRAVES DE VAYRES	1937
Left Bank/Médoc	PAUILLAC	1936	Right Bank	BLAYE	
Left Bank/Médoc	SAINT-JULIEN	1936	Right Bank	CÔTES DE BLAYE	1936
Left Bank/Médoc	LISTRAC	1957	Right Bank	CÔTES DE BOURG/BOURG/BOURGEAIS	1936
Left Bank/Médoc	MOULIS	1938	Right Bank	FRONSAC	1937
Left Bank/Médoc	MARGAUX	1954	Right Bank	CANON-FRONSAC	1939
Left Bank/Graves	GRAVES	1937	Right Bank	LALANDE-DE-POMEROL	1936
Left Bank/Graves	GRAVES SUPÉRIEURES	1937	Right Bank	POMEROL	1936
Left Bank/Graves	PESSAC-LÉOGNAN	1987	Right Bank/Saint-Émilion	SAINT-ÉMILION	1936
Left Bank/Graves	CÉRONS	1936	Right Bank/Saint-Émilion	SAINT-ÉMILION GRAND CRU	1954
Left Bank	SAUTERNES	1936	Right Bank/Saint-Émilion	MONTAGNE-SAINT-ÉMILION	1936
Left Bank	BARSAC	1936	Right Bank/Saint-Émilion	ST-GEORGES-SAINT-ÉMILION	1936
Entre-Deux-Mers	ENTRE-DEUX-MERS	1937	Right Bank/Saint-Émilion	LUSSAC-SAINT-ÉMILION	1936
Entre-Deux-Mers	PREMIÉRES CÔTES DE BORDEAUX	1997	Right Bank/Saint-Émilion	PUISSEGUIN-SAINT-ÉMILION	1936

South-West [32]

Region	Appellation	Year	Region	Appellation	Year
Dordogne	BERGERAC	1936	Dordogne	SAUSSIGNAC	1982
Dordogne	CÔTES DE BERGERAC	1936	Dordogne	CÔTES DE DURAS	1937
Dordogne	MONTRAVEL	1937	Garonne	CÔTES DU MARMANDAIS	1990
Dordogne	HAUT-MONTRAVEL	1937	Garonne	BUZET	1973
Dordogne	CÔTES DE MONTRAVEL	1937	Garonne	BRULHOIS	2011
Dordogne	ROSETTE	1946	Garonne	FRONTON	1975
Dordogne	PÉCHARMANT	1946	Garonne	SAINT-SARDOS	2011
Dordogne	MONBAZILLAC	1936	Garonne	GAILLAC	1938

Garonne	GAILLAC PREMIÈRES CÔTES	1938		Béarn / Pays Basque	BÉARN	1975
Garonne	COTEAUX DU QUERCY	2011		Béarn / Pays Basque	JURANÇON	1936
Garonne	CAHORS	1971		Béarn / Pays Basque	IROULÉGUY	1970
Gascogne	SAINT-MONT	2011		Other	CORRÈZE	2017
Gascogne	MADIRAN	1948		Other	ENTRAYGUES-LE FEL	2011
Gascogne	PACHERENC-DU-VIC-BILH	1948		Other	ESTAING	2011
Gascogne	TURSAN	2011		Other	MARCILLAC	1990
Gascogne	FLOC DE GASCOGNE	1990		Other	CÔTES DE MILLAU	2011

Rhône [31]

	CÔTES-DU-RHÔNE	1937		Southern Rhône	VINSOBRES	2006
Northern Rhône	CÔTE-RÔTIE	1940		Southern Rhône	RASTEAU	1944
Northern Rhône	CHÂTEAU-GRILLET	1936		Southern Rhône	CAIRANNE	2016
Northern Rhône	CONDRIEU	1940		Southern Rhône	GIGONDAS	1971
Northern Rhône	SAINT-JOSEPH	1956		Southern Rhône	VACQUEYRAS	1990
Northern Rhône	HERMITAGE	1937		Southern Rhône	BEAUMES-DE-VENISE	2005
Northern Rhône	CROZES-HERMITAGE	1937		Southern Rhône	MUSCAT DE BEAUMES-DE-VENISE	1945
Northern Rhône	CORNAS	1938		Southern Rhône	CHÂTEAUNEUF-DU-PAPE	1936
Northern Rhône	SAINT-PÉRAY	1936		Southern Rhône	LIRAC	1947
Northern Rhône	COTEAUX DE DIE	1993		Southern Rhône	TAVEL	1936
Northern Rhône	CLAIRETTE DE DIE	1942		Southern Rhône	VENTOUX	1973
Northern Rhône	CRÉMANT DE DIE	1993		Southern Rhône	LUBERON	1988
Northern Rhône	CHÂTILLON-EN-DIOIS	1975		Southern Rhône	DUCHÉ D'UZÈS	2013
Southern Rhône	CÔTES-DU-RHÔNE VILLAGES	1966		Southern Rhône	COSTIÈRES DE NÎMES	1986
Southern Rhône	CÔTES DU VIVARAIS	1999		Southern Rhône	CLAIRETTE DE BELLEGARDE	1949
Southern Rhône	GRIGNAN-LES-ADHÉMAR	1973				

Provence [9]

	BELLET	1941			PALETTE	1948
	CÔTES DE PROVENCE	1977			COTEAUX D'AIX-EN-PROVENCE	1985
	COTEAUX VAROIS EN PROVENCE	1993			PIERREVERT	1998
	BANDOL	1941			LES BAUX-DE-PROVENCE	1995
	CASSIS	1936				

Languedoc [21]

	LANGUEDOC	1985			MINERVOIS-LA LIVINIÈRE	1999
	MUSCAT DE LUNEL	1943			MUSCAT DE SAINT-JEAN-DE-MINERVOIS	1949
	PIC SAINT-LOUP	2017			CABARDÈS	1999
	MUSCAT DE MIREVAL	1959			MALEPÈRE	2007
	MUSCAT DE FRONTIGNAN	1936			LIMOUX	1938
	TERRASSE DU LARZAC	2014			CRÉMANT DE LIMOUX	1990
	CLAIRETTE DU LANGUEDOC	1948			CORBIÈRES	1985
	PICPOUL DE PINET	2013			CORBIÈRES-BOUTENAC	2005
	FAUGÈRES	1982			LA CLAPE	2015
	SAINT-CHINIAN	1982			FITOU	1948
	MINERVOIS	1985				

Roussillon [9]

	CÔTES DU ROUSSILLON	1977			MUSCAT DE RIVESALTES	1956
	CÔTES DU ROUSSILLON VILLAGES	1977			COLLIOURE	1971
	GRAND ROUSSILLON	1957			BANYULS	1936
	MAURY	1936			BANYULS GRAND CRU	1962
	RIVESALTES	1936				

Corse [4]

	VIN DE CORSE	1976			PATRIMONIO	1968
	MUSCAT DU CAP CORSE	1997			AJACCIO	1971

17 Grand Cru villages of Champagne

VILLAGE	SINCE	SUB-REGION	ZONE	SIZE	EXPOSURE	CH%	PN%	PM%
SILLERY	1911	Montagne de Reims	Grande Montagne Reims NE	91.9	NE	58	33	9
PUISIEULX	1911	Montagne de Reims	Grande Montagne Reims NE	18.8	SE	32	53	15
BEAUMONT-SUR-VESLE	1911	Montagne de Reims	Grande Montagne Reims NE	28.5	N	15	84	1
MAILLY-CHAMPAGNE	1911	Montagne de Reims	Grande Montagne Reims NE	285.9	N	9	88	3
VERZENAY	1911	Montagne de Reims	Grande Montagne Reims NE	418	W-N-E	14	85	1
VERZY	1911	Montagne de Reims	Grande Montagne Reims NE	407.8	N	22	77	1
LOUVOIS	1911	Montagne de Reims	Grande Montagne Reims S	41.1	S	18	82	-
BOUZY	1911	Montagne de Reims	Grande Montagne Reims S	377.8	S	12	87	1
AMBONNAY	1911	Montagne de Reims	Grande Montagne Reims S	385.3	S	19	81	-
TOURS-SUR-MARNE	1911	Vallée de la Marne	Grande Vallée de la Marne E	52.5	S	28	72	-
AŸ	1911	Vallée de la Marne	Grande Vallée de la Marne E	367	S	8	89	3
CHOUILLY	1985	Côte des Blancs	Côte des Blancs N	522.5	W-S-E	98	1	1
OIRY	1985	Côte des Blancs	Côte des Blancs N	88.4	Flat	99	-	1
CRAMANT	1911	Côte des Blancs	Côte des Blancs N	350.9	SW-SE, E flat	100	-	-
AVIZE	1911	Côte des Blancs	Côte des Blancs N	267.9	360	100	-	-
OGER	1985	Côte des Blancs	Côte des Blancs N	403	360	100	-	-
LES-MESNIL-SUR-OGER	1985	Côte des Blancs	Côte des Blancs N	433.8	360	100	-	-

VILLAGE	SUB-REGION	CH%	PN%	PM%	VILLAGE	SUB-REGION	CH%	PN%	PM%
BEZANNES	Montagne de Reims	100	-	-	TROIS-PUITS	Montagne de Reims	9	32	59
CHAMERY	Montagne de Reims	29	28	42	VAUDEMANGE	Montagne de Reims	83	17	-
CORMONTREUIL	Montagne de Reims	50	50	-	VILLERS-ALLERAND	Montagne de Reims	18	30	52
COULOMMES-LA-MONTAGNE	Montagne de Reims	21	14	65	VILLERS-MARMERY	Montagne de Reims	98	2	-
ÉCUEIL	Montagne de Reims	12	76	12	AVENAY-VAL-D'OR	Vallée de la Marne	13	77	10
JOUY-LÈS-REIMS	Montagne de Reims	15	29	56	BISSEUIL	Vallée de la Marne	63	30	7
LES MESNEUX	Montagne de Reims	5	33	61	CHAMPILLON	Vallée de la Marne	20	49	31
PARGNY-LÈS-REIMS	Montagne de Reims	4	19	77	CUMIÈRES	Vallée de la Marne	19	54	27
SACY	Montagne de Reims	13	49	38	DIZY	Vallée de la Marne	37	39	23
SERMIERS	Montagne de Reims	9	22	69	HAUTVILLERS	Vallée de la Marne	22	45	33
VILLE-DOMMANGE	Montagne de Reims	12	30	58	MAREUIL-SUR-AŸ	Vallée de la Marne	9	83	7
VILLERS-AUX-NŒUDS	Montagne de Reims	16	53	31	MUTIGNY	Vallée de la Marne	7	81	13
VRIGNY	Montagne de Reims	9	20	71	PIERRY	Vallée de la Marne	32	18	50
BILLY-LE-GRAND	Montagne de Reims	65	35	-	BERGÈRES-LÈS-VERTUS	Côte des Blancs	97	3	-
CHIGNY-LES-ROSES	Montagne de Reims	18	24	58	CUIS	Côte des Blancs	96	-	4
LUDES	Montagne de Reims	17	31	52	GRAUVES	Côte des Blancs	91	2	7
MONTBRÉ	Montagne de Reims	12	48	40	VERTUS	Côte des Blancs	91	9	-
RILLY-LA-MONTAGNE	Montagne de Reims	24	39	37	ÉTRÉCHY	Côte des Blancs	100	-	-
TAISSY	Montagne de Reims	38	26	36	VAL-DES-MARAIS	Côte des Blancs	100	-	-
TAUXIÈRES-MUTRY	Montagne de Reims	16	79	5	VILLENEUVE-RENNEVILLE	Côte des Blancs	99	1	-
TRÉPAIL	Montagne de Reims	90	10	-	VOIPREUX	Côte des Blancs	99	1	-

GROWTH	CHÂTEAU	SECOND WINE	GROWTH	CHÂTEAU	SECOND WINE
St-Estèphe					
Second	MONTROSE	La Dame du Montrose	Fourth	LAFON-ROCHET	Les Pélerins de Lafon-Rochet
Second	COS D'ESTOURNEL	Les Pagodes de Cos	Fifth	COS LABORY	Le Charme Labory
Third	CALON-SÉGUR	Le Marquis de Calon-Ségur (as of '13)			
Pauillac					
First	LAFITE ROTHSCHILD	Carruades de Lafite	Fifth	GRAND-PUY DUCASSE	Prélude a Grand-Puy Ducasse
First	MOUTON ROTHSCHILD (1973)	Le Petit Mouton	Fifth	GRAND-PUY LACOSTE	Lacoste-Borie
First	LATOUR	Les Forts de Latour	Fifth	LYNCH-BAGES	Echo de Lynch-Bages (as of '07) (3rd) Pauillac de Lynch-Bages (as of '09)
Second	PICHON-LONGUEVILLE BARON	Les Griffons de Pichon Baron (as of '12) Les Tourelles de Longueville (as of '83)	Fifth	CROIZET-BAGES	La Tourelle de Croizet-Bages
Second	PICHON-LONGUEVILLE COMTESSE DE LALANDE	Réserve de la Comtesse	Fifth	HAUT-BAGES-LIBÉRAL	La Chapelle de Bages
Fourth	DUHORT-MILON	Moulin de Duhart	Fifth	LYNCH-MOUSSAS	Les Hauts de Lynch-Moussas
Fifth	PONTET-CANET	Les Hauts de Pontet-Canet	Fifth	D'ARMAILHAC	none
Fifth	BATAILLEY	Lions de Batailley (as of '15)	Fifth	PÉDESCLAUX	Fleur de Pédesclaux (as of '07)
Fifth	HAUT-BATAILLEY	Château La Tour l'Aspic	Fifth	CLERC-MILON	Pastourelle de Clerc-Milon (as of '09)
St-Julien					
Second	LÉOVILLE-BARTON	Réserve Léoville-Barton	Third	LANGOA BARTON	Château Lady Langoa
Second	LÉOVILLE-LAS CASES	Le Petit Lion du Marquis de Las Cases	Fourth	ST PIERRE SEVAISTRE	none
Second	LÉOVILLE-POYFERRÉ	Pavillon de Poyferré	Fourth	TALBOT	Connétable de Talbot
Second	GRUAUD-LAROSE	Sarget de Gruaud-Larose (as of '81) (or Larose de Gruaud)	Fourth	BEYCHEVELLE	Amiral de Beychevelle
Second	DUCRU-BEAUCAILLOU	La Croix de Beaucaillou	Fourth	BRANAIRE-DUCRU	Duluc de Branaire-Ducru
Third	LAGRANGE	Les Fiefs de Lagrange			
Margaux					
First	MARGAUX	Pavillon Rouge 1906 (3rd) Margaux du Margaux	Third	DESMIRAIL	Initial de Desmirail Château Fontanrey (French market)
Second	RAUZAN SÉGLA	Ségla	Third	D'ISSAN	Blason d'Issan
Second	RAUZAN GASSIES	Gassies (as of '09)	Third	KIRWAN	Charmes de Kirwan
Second	LASCOMBES	Chevalier de Lascombes	Third	PALMER	Alter Ego (as of '98)
Second	DURFORT-VIVENS	Vivens or Le Relais de Durfort-Vivens Jardin de Durfort (Chinese market)	Third	GISCOURS	La Siréne de Giscours
Second	BRANE CANTENAC	Le Baron de Brane	Fourth	POUGET	Antoine Pouget
Third	CANTENAC-BROWN	Brio de Cantenac-Brown	Fourth	PRIEURÉ LICHINE	Confidences de Prieuré-Lichine (as of '08)
Third	BOYD-CANTENAC	Jacques Boyd	Fourth	MARQUIS DE TERME	Les Gondats de Marquis de Terme
Third	FERRIÉRE	Les Remparts de Ferriére	Fifth	DAUZAC	Aurore de Dauzac '14 (3rd) La Bastide-Dauzac
Third	MALESCOT ST-EXUPÉRY	La Dame de Malescot	Fifth	DU TERTRE	Les Hauts du Tertre
Third	MARQUIS D'ALESME-BECKER	Marquise d'Alesme			
Haut-Médoc					
Third	LA LAGUNE	Moulin de la Lagune	Fifth	CAMENSAC	La Closerie de Camensac
Fourth	LA TOUR CARNET	Les Douves de La Tour Carnet	Fifth	CANTEMERLE	Les Allées des Cantemerle
Fifth	BELGRAVE	Diane de Belgrave			
Graves					
First	HAUT-BRION	(R) Le Clarence de Haut-Brion (as of '07) (W) La Clarté de Haut-Brion (as of '09)			

27 Châteaux of the Sauternes 1855 Classification

CHÂTEAU	COMMUNE	SECOND WINE	CHÂTEAU	COMMUNE	SECOND WINE
Premier Grand Cru [1]			**Deuxième Cru [15]**		
D'YQUEM	Sauternes	none	D'ARCHE	Sauternes	Prieuré d'Arche
Premier Cru [11]			FILHOT	Sauternes	none
LA TOUR BLANCHE	Bommes	Les Charmilles de La Tour Blanche	LAMOTHE DESPUJOLS	Sauternes	Les Tourelles de Lamothe
LAFAURIE-PEYRAGUEY	Bommes	La Chapelle de Lafaurie	LAMOTHE GUIGNARD	Sauternes	L'Ouest de Lamothe Guignard
CLOS HAUT-PEYRAGUEY	Bommes	Symphonie de Château Clos Haut-Peyraguey	DE MALLE	Preignac	Château de Sainte-Héléne
RAYNE VIGNEAU	Bommes	Madame de Rayne	ROMER	Fargues	none
RABAUD-PROMIS	Bommes	Promesse de Rabaud-Promis	ROMER DU HAYOT	Fargues	none
SIGALAS-RABAUD	Bommes	Lieutenant de Sigalas, (formerly Cadet de Sigalas)	DE MYRAT	Barsac	none
GUIRAUD	Sauternes	Petite Guiraud (as of '09) (formerly Le Dauphin de Ch Guiraud)	DOISY DAÈNE	Barsac	none
SUDUIRAUT	Preignac	Castelnau de Suduiraut	DOISY DUBROCA	Barsac	La Damoiselle de Doisy
RIEUSSEC	Fargues	Carmes de Riessec / Clos Labère (shorter aging, older wood)	DOISY VÉDRINES	Barsac	La Petite Védrines
COUTET	Barsac	Chartreuse de Coutet	BROUSTET	Barsac	Les Charmes de Château Broustet
CLIMENS	Barsac	Cyprés de Climens	NAIRAC	Barsac	none
			CAILLOU	Barsac	Les Erables du Caillou
			SUAU	Barsac	none

16 Châteaux of the Graves 1953 Classification [revised in 1959]

CHÂTEAU	SECOND WINE	COMMUNE	COLOR
HAUT-BRION	(R) Le Clarence de Haut-Brion (as of '07) / (W) La Clarté de Haut-Brion (as of '09)	Pessac	Red / White (since 1960)
PAPE CLÉMENT	Le Clémentin du Pape Clément (as of '86) (3rd) Le Prélat du Pape Clément / (4th) PC4 '18 - blend of '00 '05 '10 '15	Pessac	Red / White (since 2010)
HAUT-BAILLY	La Parde de Haut-Bailly	Léognan	Red
CARBONNIEUX	La Tour Léognan	Léognan	Red / White
DOMAINE DE CHEVALIER	l'Espirit de Chevalier	Léognan	Red / White
DE FIEUZAL	l'Abeille de Fieuzal	Léognan	Red
D'OLIVIER	La Seigneurerie d'Olivier	Léognan	Red / White
MALARTIC LAGRAVIÉRE	La Réserve de Malartic (formerly Sillage de Malartic)	Léognan	Red / White
LATOUR-MARTILLAC	Lagrave-Martillac	Martillac	Red / White
SMITH HAUT LAFITE	Les Hauts de Smith	Martillac	Red
COUHINS	Couhins la Gravette	Villenave	White
COUHINS LURTON	none	Villenave	White
BOUSCAUT	Les Chênes de Bouscaut	Cadaujac	Red / White
LA MISSION HAUT-BRION	La Chapelle de la Mission Haut-Brion	Talence	Red / White (since 2010)
LA TOUR HAUT-BRION	none	Talence	Discontinued. Final Vintage 2005
LAVILLE HAUT-BRION	none	Talence	Discontinued. Final Vintage 2005

82 Châteaux of the Saint-Émilion 1955 Classification [amended in 1958, latest update 2012]

CHÂTEAU	SECOND WINE	CHÂTEAU	SECOND WINE
Premier Grand Cru Classé A [4]			
AUSONE	Chapelle d'Ausone	ANGÉLUS (2012)	Carillon d'Angélus
CHEVAL BLANC	Le Petit Cheval	PAVIE	Arômes de Pavie (as of '05) (formerly Château Tour Simard)
Premier Grand Cru Classé B [14]			
BEAUSÉJOUR	Croix de Beauséjour	CANON	Croix Canon (as of '12) (formerly Clos de Canon)
BEAU-SÉJOUR BÉCOT	Tournelle de Beau-Séjour Bécot	LA GAFFELIÉRE	Clos La Gaffeliére
BÉLAIR MONANGE	none	LA MONDOTTE	none
CLOS FOURTET	Closerie de Fourtet	FIGEAC	Petit Figeac (as of '12) (formerly La Grange Neuve de Figeac)
LARCIS DUCASSE	Murmure de Larcis Ducasse	TROPLONG MONDOT	Mondot
PAVIE-MACQUIN	Le Chênes de Macquin	TROTTE VIEILLE	La Vieille Dame de Trotte Vieille
CANON LA GAFFELIÉRE	Côte Mignon la Gaffeliére	VALANDRAUD	Virginie de Valandraud

Grand Cru Classé [64]

CHÂTEAU	CHÂTEAU	CHÂTEAU	CHÂTEAU
L'ARROSSÉE	DASSAULT	GRAND PONTET	PEBY FAUGÉRES
BALESTARD LE TONNELLE	DESTIEUX	GUADET	PETIT FAURIE DE SOUTARD
BARD HAUT	LA DOMINIQUE	HAUT SARPE	DE PRESSAC
BELLEFONT BELCIER	FAUGÉRES	JACOBINS	LA PRIEURÉ
BELLEVUE	FAURIE DE SOUCHARD	COUVENT DE JACOBINS	QUINAULT L'ENCLOS
BERLIQUET	DE FERRANDE	JEAN FAURE	RIPEAU
CADET-BON	FLEUR CARDINALE	LANIOTE	ROCHEBELLE
CAP DE MOURLIN	FLEUR MORANGE	LARMANDE	ST GEORGES CÔTE PAVIE
LE CHATELET	FOMBRAUGE	LAROQUE	CLOS SAINT MARTIN
CHAUVIN	FONPLEGADE	LAROZE	SANSONNET
CLOS DE SARPE	FONROQUE	LA MADELAINE	LE SERRE
LA CLOTTE	FRANC MAYNE	LA MARZELLE	SOUTARD
LA COMMANDERIE	GRAND CORBIN	MONBOUSQUET	TERTRE DAUGAY (QUINTUS)
CORBIN	GRAND CORBIN DESPAGNE	MOULIN DU CADET	LA TOUR FIGEAC
CÔTE DE BALEAU	GRAND MAYNE	L'ORATOIRE	VILLEMAURINE
LA COUSPAUDE	LES GRANDES MURAILLES	PAVIE DECESSE	YON FIGEAC

33 Grand Cru vineyards of Burgundy [including Chablis]

AOC	VINEYARD	SIZE	AOC	VINEYARD	SIZE
Chablis	CHABLIS GRAND CRU	99.79	Vosne-Romanée	ECHÉZEAUX	37.69
Gevrey-Chambertin	RUCHOTTES-CHAMBERTIN	3.3	Vosne-Romanée	GRANDS-ECHÉZEAUX	9.14
Gevrey-Chambertin	MAZIS-CHAMBERTIN	9.1	Vosne-Romanée	RICHEBOURG	8.03
Gevrey-Chambertin	CHAMBERTIN-CLOS DE BÉZE	15.39	Vosne-Romanée	LA ROMANÉE (M)	0.85
Gevrey-Chambertin	CHAMBERTIN	12.93	Vosne-Romanée	ROMANÉE-CONTI (M)	1.81
Gevrey-Chambertin	LATRICIÉRES-CHAMBERTIN	7.35	Vosne-Romanée	ROMANÉE-SAINT-VIVANT	9.44
Gevrey-Chambertin	CHAPELLE-CHAMBERTIN	5.48	Vosne-Romanée	LA GRANDE RUE (M)	1.65
Gevrey-Chambertin	GRIOTTE-CHAMBERTIN	2.69	Vosne-Romanée	LA TÂCHE (M)	6.06
Gevrey-Chambertin	CHARMES-CHAMBERTIN	12.24	Aloxe-Corton Pernand-Vergelesses	CHARLEMAGNE (CURRENTLY NOT IN USE)	
Gevrey-Chambertin	MAZOYÉRES-CHAMBERTIN	18.58	Aloxe-Corton Pernand-Vergelesses Ladoix	CORTON	93.90R
Morey-Saint-Denis	CLOS DE LA ROCHE	16.9	Aloxe-Corton Pernand-Vergelesses Ladoix	CORTON-CHARLEMAGNE	51.20W
Morey-Saint-Denis	CLOS ST-DENIS	6.62	Puligny-Montrachet	CHEVALIER-MONTRACHET	7.36
Morey-Saint-Denis	CLOS DES LAMBRAYS	8.84	Puligny-Montrachet	BIENVENUES-BÂTARD-MONTRACHET	3.69
Morey-Saint-Denis	CLOS DE TART (M)	7.53	Puligny-Montrachet Chassagne-Montrachet	MONTRACHET (LE MONTRACHET IN CHASSAGNE)	4.01
Morey-Saint-Denis Chambolle-Musigny	BONNES MARES	1.5	Puligny-Montrachet Chassagne-Montrachet	BÂTARD-MONTRACHET	6.12
Chambolle-Musigny	MUSIGNY	10.86	Chassagne-Montrachet	CRIOTS-BÂTARD-MONTRACHET	1.75
Vougeot	CLOS DE VOUGEOT	50.59			

655 Premier Cru vineyards of Burgundy [including Chablis]

BANK	VINEYARD	COMMUNE	SINCE	BANK	VINEYARD	COMMUNE	SINCE
Chablis AOC [40]							
Left	BEAUROY (U)	Chablis (Poinchy)	1938	Left	CHAUME DE TALVAT (U)	Courgis	1978
Left	TROËSMES	Beine	1938	Left	CÔTE DE JOUAN (U)	Courgis	1938
Left	CÔTE DE SAVANT	Beine	1938	Left	LES BEAUREGARDS (U)	Courgis	1978
Left	CÔTE DE LÉCHET (U)	Chablis (Milly)	1938	Left	CÔTE DE CUISSY	Courgis	1938
Left	VAU DE VEY (U)	Beine	1938	Right	FOURCHAUME (U)	La Chapelle Vaupelteigne	1938
Left	VAUX RAGONS	Beine	1978	Right	L'HOMME MORT	Maligny	1938
Left	VAU LIGNEAU (U)	Beine	1978	Right	VAUPULENT	La Chapelle Vaupelteigne	1938
Left	VAILLONS (U)	Chablis	1938	Right	CÔTE DE FONTENAY	Fontenay-prés-Chablis	1938
Left	LES LYS	Chablis	1938	Right	VAULORENT	Chablis (Poinchy)	1938
Left	SÉCHER	Chablis	1938	Right	BERDIOT (U)	Chablis (Fyé)	1978
Left	LES ÉPINOTTES	Chablis	1938	Right	CÔTE DE VAUBAROUSSE (U)	Chablis (Fyé)	1938
Left	CHATAINS	Chablis	1938	Right	LES FOURNEAUX (U)	Fleys	1938
Left	RONCIÉRES	Chablis	1938	Right	MOREIN	Fleys	1938
Left	BEUGNONS	Chablis	1938	Right	CÔTE DE PRÉS-GIROTS	Fleys	1938
Left	MÉLINOTS	Chablis	1938	Right	MONTÉE DE TONNERRE (U)	Chablis (Fyé)	1938
Left	MONTMAINS (U)	Chablis	1938	Right	CÔTE DE BRÉCHAIN	Chablis (Fyé)	1938
Left	FORÊTS	Chablis	1938	Right	PIED D'ALOUP	Chablis (Fyé)	1938
Left	BUTTEAUX	Chablis	1938	Right	CHAPELOT	Chablis (Fyé)	1938
Left	VOSGROS (U)	Chichée	1938	Right	MONT DE MILIEU (U)	Fleys	1938
Left	VAUGIRAUT	Chichée	1938	Right	VAUCOUPIN (U)	Chichée	1938

VINEYARD	VINEYARD	VINEYARD	VINEYARD	VINEYARD
Fixin [6]				
ARVELETS	CLOS DU CHAPITRE (M)	CLOS NAPOLÉON (M)	HERVELETS	LE MEIX BAS
CLOS DE LA PERRIÉRE (M)				
Gevrey-Chambertin [26]				
AU CLOSEAU	CLOS DES VAROILLES (M)	CRAIPILLOT	LE BOSSIÉRE (M)	LES CORBEAUX
AUX COMBOTTES	CLOS DU CHAPITRE (M)	EN ERGOT	LA PERRIÉRE	LES GOULOTS
BEL AIR	CLOS PRIEUR	ESTOURNELLES-SAINT-JACQUES	LA ROMANÉE (M)	PETITE CHAPELLE
CHAMPEAUX	CLOS SAINT-JACQUES	FONTENY	LAVAUT SAINT-JACQUES	PETITS CAZETIERS
CHAMPONNET	COMBE AU MOINE	ISSARTS (M)	LES CAZETIERS	POISSENOT
CHERBAUDES				
Morey-Saint-Denis [20]				
AUX CHARMES	CLOS SORBÉ	LE VILLAGE	LES CHENEVERY	LES MILLANDES
AUX CHESEAUX	CÔTE ROTIE	LES BLANCHARDS	LES FACONNIÉRES	LES RUCHOTS
CLOS BAULET	LA BUSSIÉRE (M)	LES CHAFFOTS	LES GENAVRIÉRES	LES SORBÉS
CLOS DES ORMES	LA RIOTTE	LES CHARRIÉRES	LES GRUENCHERS	MONTS LUISANTS
Chambolle-Musigny [24]				
AUX BEAUX BRUNS	LES AMOUREUSES	LES CHARMES	LES FUÉES	LES NOIROTS
AUX COMBOTTES	LES BAUDES	LES CHATELOTS	LES GROSEILLES	LES PLANTES
AUX ÉCHANGES (M)	LES BORNIQUES	LES COMBOTTES	LES GRUENCHERS	LES SENTIERS
DERRIÉRE LA GRANGE	LES CARRIÉRES	LES CRAS	LES HAUTS DOIX	LES VÉROILLES
LA COMBE D'ORVEAU	LES CHABIOTS	LES FEUSSELOTTES	LES LAVROTTES	
Vougeot [4]				
CLOS DE LA PERRIÉRE (M)	LE CLOS BLANC (M)	LE PETITS VOUGEOTS	LES CRÂS	

Vosne-Romanée [14]

AU-DESSUS DES ALCONSORTS	AUX RAIGNOTS	EN ORVEAUX	LES CHAUMES	LES ROUGES
AUX BRULÉES	CLOS DE RÉAS (M)	LA CROIX RAMEAU	LES GAUDICHOTS	LES SUCHOTS
AUX MALCONSORTS	CROS PARANTOUX	LES BEAUX MONTS	LES PETITS MONTS	

Nuits-Saint-Georges [41]

AUX ARGILLAS	EN LA PERRIÉRE NOBLOT (M)	AUX VIGNERONDES	LES PORRETS-SAINT-GEORGES	CLOS DE FORÊTS SAINT-GEORGES (M)
AUX BOUDOTS	LA RICHEMONE	CHAINES CARTEAUX	LES POULETTES	LES PRULIERS
AUX BOUSSELOTS	LES ARGILLIÉRES	CHÂTEAU GRIS (M)	LES PROCÉS	LES SAINTS-GEORGES
AUX CHAIGNOTS	LES CAILLES	LES CROTS	CLOS ARLOT (M)	LES TERRES BLANCHES
AUX CHAMPS PERDRIX	LES CHABŒUFS	LES DAMODES	CLOS DE LA MARÉCHALE (M)	LES VALLEROTS
AUX CRAS	AUX MURGERS	LES DIDIERS (M)	CLOS DES ARGILLIÉRES	LES VAUCRAINS
CLOS DES GRANDES VIGNES (M)	AUX PERDRIX	LES HAUTS PRULIERS	CLOS DES CORVÉES (M)	RONCIÉRES
CLOS DES PORRETS-SAINT-GEORGES (M)	AUX THOREY	LES PERRIÉRES	CLOS DES CORVÉES PAGETS	RUE DE CHAUX
CLOS SAINT-MARC (M)				

Aloxe-Corton [14]

CLOS DES MARÉCHAUDS (M)	LA MARÉCHAUDE	LES FOURNIÉRES	LES MOUTOTTES	LES VALOZIÉRES
CLOS DU CHAPITRE	LA TOPPE AU VERT	LES GUÉRETS	LES PAULANDS	LES VERCOTS
LA COUTIÉRE	LES CHAILLOTS	LES MARÉCHAUDES	LES PETITES LOLIÉRES	

Pernand-Vergelesses [8]

CLOS BERTHET (M)	EN CARADEUX	LES FICHOTS	VERGELESSES	VILLAGE DE PERNAND (M)
CREUX DE LA NET	ILE DES VERGELESSES	SOUS FRÉTILLE		

Ladoix [11]

BASSES MOUROTTES	HAUTES MOUROTTES	LA MICAUDE (M)	LE ROGNET ET CORTON	LES GRÊCHONS ET FOUTRIÉRES
BOIS ROUSSOT	LA CORVÉE	LE CLOU D'ORGE	LES BUIS	LES JOYEUSES
EN NAGET				

Savigny-Lés-Beaune [22]

AUX CLOUS	BASSES VERGELESSES	LES HAUTS JARRONS	LES MARCONNETS	LES TALMETTES
AUX FOURNEAUX	BATAILLÉRE (M)	LES HAUTS MARCONNETS	LES NARBANTONS	LES VERGELESSES
AUX GRAVAINS	CHAMP CHEVREY (M)	LES JARRONS	LES PEUILLETS	PETITS GODEAUX
AUX GUETTES	LA DOMINODE	LES LAVIÉRES	LES ROUVRETTES	REDRESCUL (M)
AUX SERPENTIÉRES	LES CHARNIÉRES			

Beaune [42]

A L'ECU	CLOS DES AVAUX	LES AIGROTS	LES GRÉVES	LES TEURONS
AUX COUCHERIAS	CLOS DES URSULES (M)	LES AVAUX	LES MARCONNETS	LES TOUSSAINTS
AUX CRAS	CLOS DU ROI	LES BOUCHEROTTES	LES MONTREVENOTS	LES TUVILAINS
BELISSAND	CLOS SAINT-LANDRY (M)	LES BRESSANDES	LES PERRIÉRES	LES VIGNES FRANCHES
BLANCHES FLEURS	EN GENÊT	LES CENTS VIGNES	LES REVERSÉS	MONTÉE ROUGE
CHAMPS PIMONT	EN L'ORME	LES CHOUACHEUX	LES SCEAUX	PERTUISOTS
CLOS DE L'ECU (M)	LA MIGNOTTE	LES EPENOTES	LES SEUREY	SUR LES GRÉVES
CLOS DE LA FEGUINE (M)	LE BAS DES TEURONS	LES FÉVES	LES SIZIES	SUR LES GRÉVES-CLOS SAINTE-ANNE (M)
CLOS DE LA MOUSSE (M)	LE CLOS DES MOUCHES			

Pommard [28]

CLOS BLANC	LA CHANIÉRE	LES BERTINS	LES CROIX NOIRES	LES PÉZEROLLES
CLOS DE LA COMMARAINE	LA PLATIÉRE	LES BOUCHEROTTES (M)	LES FREMIERS	LES POUTURES
CLOS DE VERGER	LA REFÉNE	LES CHANLINS-BAS	LES GRANDS EPENOTS	LES RUGIENS BAS
CLOS DES EPENEAUX (M)	LE CLOS MICOT	LES CHAPONNIÉRES	LES JAROLIÉRES	LES RUGIENS HAUTS
DERRIÉRE SAINT-JEAN (M)	LE VILLAGE	LES CHARMOTS	LES PETITS EPENOTS	LES SAUSSILLES
EN LARGILLIÉRE	LES ARVELETS	LES COMBES DESSUS		

Volnay [29]

CARELLE SOUS LA CHAPELLE	CLOS DE LA CHAPELLE (M)	CLOS DU VERSEUIL (M)	LE RONCERET	LES MITANS
CHAMPANS	CLOS DE LA ROUGEOTTE	EN CHEVRET	LE VILLAGE	PITURES DESSUS
CLOS DE L'AUDIGNAC	CLOS DES 60 OUVRÉES (M)	FRÉMIETS	LES ANGLES	ROBARDELLE
CLOS DE LA BARRE (M)	CLOS DES CHÊNES	FRÉMIETS-CLOS DE LA ROUGEOTTE (M)	LES BROUILLARDS	SANTENOTS
CLOS DE LA BOUSSE-D'OR (M)	CLOS DES DUCS (M)	LA GIGOTTE	LES CAILLERETS	TAILLE PIEDS
CLOS DE LA CAVE DES DUCS (M)	CLOS DU CHÂTEAU DES DUCS (M)	LASSOLLE	LES LURETS	

Meursault [19]

BLAGNY	LA JEUNELLOTTE	LES CAILLERETS	LES RAVELLES	PORUSOT
CHARMES	LA PIÉCE SOUS LE BOIS	LES CRAS	LES SANTENOTS BLANCS	SOUS BLAGNY
CLOS DES PERRIÉRES (M)	LE PORUSOT	LES GOUTTES D'OR	LES SANTENOTS DU MILIEU	SOUS LE DOS D'ANE
GENEVRIÉRES	LES BOUCHÉRES	LES PLURES	PERRIÉRES	

Monthélie [15]

CLOS DES TOISIÉRES (M)	LE CHÂTEAU GAILLARD	LE MEIX BATAILLE	LES CHAMPS FULLIOTS	LES RIOTTES
LA TAUPINE	LE CLOS GAUTHEY	LE VILLAGE	LES CLOUS	LES VIGNES RONDES
LE CAS ROUGEOT	LE CLOU DES CHÊNES	LES BARBIÉRES	LES DURESSES	SUR LA VELLE

Auxey-Duresses [9]

BAS DES DURESSES	CLOS DU VAL	LES BRÉTERINS	LES ECUSSAUX	REUGNE
CLIMAT DU VAL	LA CHAPELLE	LES DURESSES	LES GRANDS CHAMPS	

Puligny-Montrachet [17]

CHAMP CANET	CLOS DE LA MOUCHÉRE (M)	LE CAILLERET	LES DEMOISELLES	LES PUCELLES
CHAMP GAIN	HAMEAU DE BLAGNY	LES CHALUMAUX	LES FOLATIÉRES	LES REFERTS
CLAVAILLON	LA GARENNE	LES COMBETTES	LES PERRIÉRES	SOUS LE PUITS
CLOS DE LA GARENNE	LA TRUFFIÉRE			

Saint-Aubin [30]

BAS DE VERMARAIN À L'EST	EN MONTCEAU	LE CHARMOIS	LES CORTONS	PITANGERET
DERRIÉRE CHEZ EDOUARD	EN REMILLY	LE PUITS	LES FRIONNES	SOUS ROCHE DUMAY
DERRIÉRE LA TOUR	EN VOLLON À L'EST	LES CASTETS	LES MURGERS DES DENTS DE CHIEN	SUR GAMAY
ECHAILLE	ES CHAMPS	LES CHAMPLOTS	LES PERRIÉRES	SUR LE SENTIER DU CLOU
EN CRÉOT	LA CHATENIÉRE	LES COMBES	LES TRAVERS DE MARINOT	VIGNES MOINGEON
EN LA RANCHÉ	LE BAS DE GAMAY À L'EST	LES COMBES AU SUD	MARINOT	VILLAGE

Chassagne-Montrachet [55]

ABBAYE DE MORGEOT	EN CAILLERET	LA GRANDE MONTAGNE	LES CHENEVOTTES	LES PETITES CLOS
BLANCHOT DESSUS	EN REMILLY	LA MALTROIE	LES COMBARDS	LES PLACES
BOIS DE CHASSAGNE	EN VIRONDOT	LA ROMANÉE	LES COMMES	LES REBICHETS
CAILLERET	EZ CRETS	LA ROQUEMAURE	LES EMBAZÉES	LES VERGERS
CHAMPS JENDREAU	EZ CROTTES	LES BAUDINES	LES FAIRENDES	MORGEOT
CHASSAGNE	FRANCEMONT	LES BOIRETTES	LES GRANDES RUCHOTTES	PETINGERET
CHASSAGNE DU CLOS SAINT-JEAN	GUERCHÉRE	LES BONDUES	LES GRANDS CLOS	TÊTE DU CLOS
CLOS CHAREAU	LA BOUDRIOTTE	LES BRUSSONNES	LES MACHERELLES	TONTON MARCEL (M)
CLOS PITOIS (M)	LA CARDEUSE	LES CHAMPS GAIN	LES MURÉES	VIDE BOURSE
CLOS SAINT-JEAN	LA CHAPELLE	LES CHAUMÉES	LES PASQUELLES	VIGNE BLANCHE
DENT DE CHIEN	LA GRANDE BORNE	LES CHAUMES	LES PETITES FAIRENDES	VIGNE DERRIÉRE

Santenay [12]

BEAUREGARD	CLOS DES MOUCHES	GRAND CLOS ROUSSEAU	LA MALADIÉRE	LES GRAVIÉRES-CLOS DE TAVANNES
BEAUREPAIRE	CLOS FAUBARD	LA COMME	LES GRAVIÉRES	PASSETEMPS
CLOS DE TAVANNES	CLOS ROUSSEAU			

Maranges [7]

CLOS DE LA BOUTIÉRE (M)	LA FUSSIÉRE	LE CLOS DES ROIS	LE CROIX MOINES	LES CLOS ROUSSOTS
CLOS DE LA FUSSIÉRE (M)	LE CLOS DES LOYÉRES			

Rully [23]

AGNEUX (M)	CLOUX	LA RENARDE	MARISSOU	PRÉAUX
CHAMPS CLOUX	GRÉSIGNY	LE MEIX CADOT	MOLESME	RABOURCÉ
CHAPITRE	LA BRESSANDE (M)	LE MEIX CAILLET (M)	MONTPALAIS	RACLOT
CLOS DU CHAIGNE	LA FOSSE	LES PIERRES	PILLOT	VAUVRY
CLOS ST JACQUES (M)	LA PUCELLE	MARGOTÉS		

Mercurey [31]

CLOS DU CHÂTEAU DE MONTAIGU (M)	CLOS VOYENS	LA LEVRIÉRE	LES COMBINS	LES PUILLETS
CLOS DE PARADIS	GRAND CLOS FORTOUL (M)	LA MISSION (M)	LES CRÊTS	LES RUELLES (M)
CLOS DES BARRAULTS	GRIFFÉRES (M)	LE CLOS DU ROY	LES CROICHOTS	LES SAUMONTS
CLOS DES GRANDS VOYENS (M)	LA BONDUE	LE CLOS L'EVÊQUE	LES FOURNEAUX	LES VASÉES
CLOS DES MYGLANDS (M)	LA CAILLOUTE (M)	LES BYOTS	LES MONTAIGUS	LES VELLEY
CLOS MARCILLY (M)	LA CHASSIÉRE	LES CHAMPS MARTIN	LES NAUGUES	SAZENAY
CLOS TONNERRE				

Givry [37]

A VIGNE ROUGE	CLOS MARCEAUX (M)	EN VEAU	LE MÉDENCHOT	LES COMBES
CHAMP NALOT	CLOS MAROLE	LA BRÛLÉE	LE PARADIS	LES GALAFFRES
CLOS CHARLÉ	CLOS SALOMON (M)	LA GRANDE BERGE	LE PETIT PRÉTAN	LES GRANDES VIGNES
CLOS DE LA BARAUDE	CLOS-SAINT-PAUL (M)	LA MATROSSE	LE PIED DU CLOU	LES GRANDS PRÉTANS
CLOS DU CELLIER AUX MOINES	CLOS-SAINT-PIERRE (M)	LA PEITE BERGE	LE VIGRON	PETIT MAROLE
CLOS DU CRAS LONG	CRAUZOT	LA PLANTE	LES BOIS CHEVAUX	PIED DE CHAUME
CLOS DU VERNOY	CRÉMILLONS	LE CHAMP LALOT	LES BOIS GAUTIERS	SERVOISINE
CLOS JUS	EN CHOUÉ			

Montagny [49]

CHAMP TOIZEAU	LE CLOUZOT	LES COÉRES	LES PAQUIERS	MONTCUCHOT
CHAZELLE	LE VIEUX CHÂTEAU	LES COMBES	LES PERRIÉRES	MONTORGE
CORNEVENT	LES BASSETS	LES COUDRETTES	LES PIDANCES	SAINT-YTAGES
CREUX DE BEAUX CHAMPS	LES BEAUX CHAMPS	LES CRABOULETTES	LES PLATIÉRES	SAINTE-MORILLE
L'EPAULE	LES BONNEVEAUX	LES GARCHÉRES	LES RESSES	SOUS LES FEILLES
LA CONDEMINE DU VIEUX CHÂTEAU	LES BORDES	LES GOURESSES	LES TREUFFÉRES	VIGNE DU SOLEIL
LA GRANDE PIÉCE	LES BOUCHOTS	LES JARDINS	LES VIGNES DERRIÉRE	VIGNES COULAND
LA MOULLIÉRE	LES BURNINS	LES LAS	LES VIGNES DES PRÉS	VIGNES SAINT-PIERRE
LE CLOS CHAUDRON	LES CHANIOTS	LES MACLES	LES VIGNES LONGUES	VIGNES SUR LE CLOUX
LE CLOUX	LES CHAUMELOTTES	LES MAROQUES	MONT LAURENT	

Pouilly-Fuissé [22]

AU VIGNERAIS	EN SERVY	LE CLOS DE SOLUTRÉ	LES CRAYS	LES VIGNES BLANCHES
AUX BOUTHIÉRES	LA FRÉRIE	LE CLOS REYSSIER	LES MÉNÉTRIÉRES	POUILLY
AUX CHAILLOUX	LA MARÉCHAUDE	LES BRULÉS	LES PERRIÉRES	SUR LA ROCHE
AUX QUARTS	LE CLOS	LES CHEVRIÉRES	LES REISSES	VERS CRAS
EN FRANCE	LE CLOS DE MONSIEUR NOLY			

Irancy [67]
Adroit de Veaudilien, Adroit du Val Suzeau, Bas de la Grande Côte, Boudardes, Bouguéelle, Chérelle Est, Chérelle Ouest, Côte Charmois Ouest, Côte du Moutier, Croix Rouge, Crot Chabout, Envers du Val des Noyers, Envers du Val Suzeau, Grenouillères, Haut Champreux, Haut de Boudardes, Hautes Charmois, La Bergère, La Bouysarde, La Cave, La Comme, La Croix Buteix, La Croizette, La Grande Côte Est, La Grande Côte Ouest, La Voie de Girard, La Voie des Vaches, Le Dessus du Vau Falleau, Le Haut du Val des Noyers, Le Haut du Val Suzeau, Le Paradis, Les Babuttes, Les Bâtardes, Les Beaux Monts, Les Bégnaux, Les Bessys, Les Cailles, Les Chandeliers, Les Courgilliers, Les Grandes Vignes, Les Hauts de Charmois, Les Marteaux, Les Mazelots, Les Mères, Les Petits Creux, Les Rez, Les Ronces, Les Sous le Bois, Les Traces, Les Tremblas, Les Veaux Lâchés, Mouroux, Palotte, Poncelles, Pré Monsieur, Renouel, Sous les Petits Creux, Trou Mombart, Vallée de Coigny, Vau Pavée Est, Vauregniers, Veauchassy, Veauliaux, Veaupessiot, Vodon, Voie d'Auxerre, Voie de Cravant

Saint-Bris [2]   Sur Mouroux, Sur Veaupiary

Côte de Nuits-Village [116]
Au Chapeau, Au Clos Bardot, Au Clou, Au Leurey, Aux Boulardes, Aux Boutoillottes, Aux Brûlées, Aux Cases, Aux Cheminots, Aux Clous Virey, Aux Courottes, Aux Fauques, Aux Guillandes, Aux Herbues, Aux Langres, Aux Montagnes, Aux Petits Crais, Aux Prés, Aux Quartiers, Aux Vignois, Belle-Vue, Bois de Laranche, Champs de Vosger, Champs Pennebaut, Champs Perdrix, Clémenfert, Créole, Crétevent, En Beauregard, En Chantemerle, En Chenailla, En Clomée, En Combe Roy, En Coton, En Créchelin, En Fontenelle, En l'Olivier, En la Botte, En Tabeillion, En Vireville, Es Bonnemaines, Ez Polleuses, Fixey, La Berchère, La Cocarde, La Combe Assole, La Combe de la Damoda, La Croix Blanche, La Croix Violette, La Damoda, La Dominode, La Julbigne, La Mazière, La Montagne, La Mouille, La Place, La Platerre, La Prétière, La Sorgentière, La Toppe Citeau, La Vionne, Le Bas du Mont de Boncourt, Le Clos, Le Clos de Magny, Le Clos des Langres, Le Creux de Sobron, Le Creux Sobron, Le Fourneau, Le Meix au Maire, Le Meix Fringuet, Le Poirier Gaillard, Le Réchaux, Le Rozier, Le Vaucrain, Le Village, Les Basses Chenevières, Les Boudières, Les Carrés, Les Chaillots, Les Champs des Charmes, Les Champs Tions, Les Chazots, Les Chenevières, Les Clos, Les Crais, Les Crais de Chêne, Les Echalais, Les Entre Deux Velles, Les Essards, Les Fondements, Les Fourches, Les Foussottes, Les Germets, Les Gibassier, Les Grandes Vignes, Les Herbues, Les Loges, Les Mogottes, Les Monts de Boncourt, Les Ormeaux, Les Perrières, Les Petits Crais, Les Plantes du Bois, Les Portes-Feuilles, Les Retraits, Les Ruisseaux, Les Tellières, Les Treuilles, Les Vignes aux Grands, Les Vignottes, Meix Trouhant, Pommier Rougeot, Préau, Queue de hareng, Saint Seine, Vignois

Marsannay [78]
Au Champ Salomon, Au Champ St-Etienne, Au Larrey, Au Potey, Au Quartier, Au Ravry, Au Ronsoy, Aux Genelières, Aux Grands Bandeaux, Aux Herbues, Aux Journaux, Aux Nagelottes, Bas des Longeroies, Champs Perdrix, Clos de l'Argillère, Clos du Roy, Dessus des Longeroies, En Batayart, En Blungey, En Champy, En Charrière, En Clémongeot, En Combereau, En Grand Bois, En la Croix St-Germain, En la Malcuite, En la Montagne, En la Poulotte, En la Verde, En Monchenevoy, En Mormain, En Pilleul, En Sampagny, En Varangée, En Verdot, Es Clos, La Bretignère, La Chaire à Dieu, La Charme aux Prêtres, La Combe du Pré, La CombeVaulon, La Croix de Bois, La Friche, La Morisotte, La Plantelle, La Pucine, La Quenicière, Le Boivin, Le Clos de Jeu, Le Désert, Le Dixme, Le Grand Poirier, Le Moisereau, Le Parterre, Le Petits Puits, Le Poiset, Le Village, Les Clos, Les Crais, Les Cras, Les Creux Banots, Les Echezeaux, Les Etalles, Les Favières, Les Finottes, Les Grandes Vignes, Les Grasses Têtes, Les Herbues, Les Mogottes, Les Ouzeloy, Les Plantes, Les Portes, Les Récilles, Les Vaudenelles, Les Vignes Marie, Plante Pitois, Saint-Jacques, Vignes Blanches

Marsannay Rosé [36]
Au Corcaron, Au Larrey, Aux Avoines, Aux Crais, Aux Longues Pièces, Aux Nagelottes, Aux Perches, Aux Platières, Bargard, Champ Taignerot, Champforey, En Auvonne, En la Brouade, En la Caillée, En la Corrière, En Latte, En Lavaux, En Leautier, En Méchalot, En Pévenelle, En Vigne Ribaude, Es Barres, La Bretignère, La Champagne Haute, La Combe, La Combe Pévenelle, La Combe Vaulon, La Pointure, La Terrasse, La Varangée, Le Boivin, Le Charon, Le Village, Les Combottes, Les Plantes, Les Plantes du Dessus

Fixin [53]
Aux Boutoillottes, Aux Brûlées, Aux Cheminots, Aux Herbues, Aux Petits Crais, Aux Prés, Aux Vignois, Champs de Vosger, Champs Pennebaut, Champs Perdrix, Clémenfert, En Chenailla, En Clomée, En Combe Roy, En Coton, En Créchelin, En l'Olivier, En Tabeillion, Fixey, La Cocarde, La Croix Blanche, La Place, La Sorgentière, La Vionne, Le Clos, Le Poirier Gaillard, Le Réchaux, Le Rozier, Le Village, Les Basses Chenevières, Les Boudières, Les Champs des Charmes, Les Champs Tions, Les Chenevières, Les Clos, Les Crais, Les Crais de Chêne, Les Echalais, Les Entre Deux Velles, Les Fondements, Les Foussottes, Les Germets, Les Gibassier, Les Herbues, Les Mogottes, Les Ormeaux, Les Petits Crais, Les Portes-Feuilles, Les Tellières, Les Treuilles, Les Vignes aux Grands, Meix Trouhant, Pommier Rougeot

Gevrey-Chambertin [65]
Au Prunier, Au Vellé, Aux Corvées, Aux Echezeaux, Aux Etelois, Baraques, Billard, Carougeot, Champ, Champ Franc, Champerrier du Bas, Champerrier du Dessus, Champs-Chenys, Charreux, Chazière, Chéseaux, Clos Prieur-Bas, Combe de Lavaux, Combes du Bas, Combes du Dessus, Craite-Paille, Creux Brouillard, Croix des Champs, En Champs, En Dérée, En Pallud, En Songe, En Vosne, Es Murots, Grandes Rayes, Grands Champs, Jouise, La Bossière, La Brunelle, La Burie, La Justice, La Marie, La Nouroy, La Platière, Le Carré Rougeaud, Le Créot, Le Fourneau, Les Cercueils, Les Champs Perriers, Les Crais, Les Croisettes, Les Epointures, Les Evocelles, Les Gueulepines, Les Jeunes Rois, Les Journaux, Les Marchais, Les Seuvrées, Meix des Ouches, Meix-Bas, Mévelle, Pince-Vin, Pressonnier, Puits de la Baraque, Reniard, Roncevie, Sylvie, Tamisot, Vignes Belles, Village

Morey-Saint-Denis [23]
Bas Chenevery, Clos des Ormes, Clos Solon, Corvée Creuille, En la Rue de Vergy, En Seuvrey, La Bidaude, Larrey Froid, Le Village, Les Brâs, Les Champs de la Vigne, Les Cognées, Les Crais, Les Crais-Gillon, Les Herbuottes, Les Larrets, Les Pertuisées, Les Porroux, Les Sionnières, Monts Luisants, Pierre Virant, Rue de Vergy, Très Girard

Chambolle-Musigny [33]
Aux Croix, Derrière le Four, La Combe d'Orveau, La Taupe, Le Village, Les Argillières, Les Athets, Les Babillères, Les Barottes, Les Bas Doix, Les Bussières, Les Chardannes, Les clos, Les Clos de l'Orme, Les Condemennes, Les Cras, Les Creux Baissants, Les Danguerrins, Les Drazey, Les Echezeaux, Les Fouchères, Les Fremières, Les Gamaires, Les Guérippes, Les Herbues, Les Jutruots, Les Mal Carrées, Les Maladières, Les Mombies, Les Nazoires, Les Pas de Chat, Les Porlottes, Les Sordes

Vougeot [1]
Le Village

Vosne-Romanée [26]
Au-Dessus de la Rivière, Aux Champs Perdrix, Aux Communes, Aux Genaivrières, Aux Jachées, Aux Ormes, Aux Raviolles, Aux Réas, Aux Saules, Bossières, Champs Goudins, La Colombière, La Croix Blanche, La Montagne, Le Pré de la Folie, Les Barreaux, Les Beaux Monts Hauts Rougeots, Les Chalandins, Les Damaudes, Les Jacquines, Les Violettes, Maizières Basses, Maizières Hautes, Porte-Feuilles ou Murailles du Clos, Vigneux, Village

Nuits-Saint-Georges [34]
Au Bas de Combe, Au Chouillet, Aux Allots, Aux Athées, Aux Barrières, Aux Croix Rouges, Aux Herbues, Aux Lavières, Aux Pertuis Maréchaux, Aux Saints-Jacques, Aux Saints-Juliens, Aux Tuyaux, Belle Croix, En la Perrière Noblot, La Charmotte, La Petite Charmotte, Le Coteau des Bois, Les Argillats, Les Brûlées, Les Chaliots, Les Charbonnières, Les Charmois, Les Damodes, Les Fleurières, Les Hauts Poirets, Les Hauts Pruliers, Les Longecourts, Les Maladières, Les Plateaux, Les Poisets, Les Topons, Les Vallerots, Plantes au Baron, Tribourg

Côte de Beaune [7]
Dessus des Marconnets, La Grande Châtelaine, Les Mondes Rondes, Les Monsnières, Les Pierres Blanches, Les Topes Bizot, Montbatois

Pernand-Vergelesses [13]
Au Village, Clos de Bully, Derrière Frétille, Es Larret et Vignes Blanches, Le Devant des Cloux, Les Boutières, Les Noirets, Les Pins, Les Plantes des Champs et Combottes, Sous le Bois de Noël et Belles Filles, Sous les Cloux, Sur Frétille, Sur Herbeux

Aloxe-Corton [15]
Boulmeau, La Boulotte, La Toppe Marteneau, Les Boutières, Les Brunettes et Planchots, Les Bruyères, Les Caillettes, Les Citernes, Les Combes, Les Crapousuets, Les Cras, Les Genevrières et le Suchot, Les Morais, Les Petits Vercots, Les Valozières

Ladoix [38]
Bas de Naget, Bois de Gréchon, Bois de Naget, Bois des Toppes, Buisson, Champ Pussuet, Clos des Chagnots, Clos Royer, La Blancharde, La Butte, La Combe, La Corvée Basse, La Huchotte, La Mort, La Rangie, La Toppe d'Avignon, Le Bois d'Herbues, Le Clou, Le Seuriat, Les Barres, Les Briquottes, Les Buis, Les Carrières, Les Chagnots, Les Chaillots, Les Champs Rammés, Les Combottes, Les Forêts, Les Issards, Les Lièvrières, Les Madonnes, Les Mamées, Les Ranches, Les Toppes Coiffées, Les Vris, Sur les Forêts, Sur les Vris, Vigne Adaim

Savigny-lés-Beaune [29]
Aux Champs Chardons, Aux Champs des Pruniers, Aux Fourches, Aux Grands Liards, Aux Petits Liards, Aux Pointes, Dessus de Montchenevoy, Dessus les Gollardes, Dessus les Vermots, Ez Connardises, Grands Picotins, Guetottes, Le Village, Les Bas Liards, Les Bourgeots, Les Godeaux, Les Gollardes, Les Goudelettes, Les Petits Picotins, Les Peuillets, Les Pimentiers, Les Planchots de la Champagne, Les Planchots du Nord, Les Prévaux, Les Ratausses, Les Saucours, Les Vermots, Moutier Amet, Roichottes

Chorey-lés-Beaune [22]
Aux Clous, Champs Piétant, Confrelin, La Maladérotte, Le Grand, Le Grand Saussy, Les Beaumonts, Les Bons Ores, Les Champs Longs, Les Closeaux, Les Crais, Les Grandes Rêpes, Les Pertuisotes, Les Petites Rêpes, Les Ratosses, Petits Champs Longs, Pièce du Chapitre, Plantes des Plantes, Poirier Malchaussé, Saussy, Trot Garnier, Tue-Boeuf

Beaune [26]
Au Renard, Chaume Gauffriot, Dessus des Marconnets, Fb de Bouze, La Blanchisserie, La Creusotte, Le Foulot, Les Beaux Fougets, Les Bons Feuvres, Les Chardonnereux, Les Chilènes, Les Epenottes, Les Levées et les Piroles, Les Longes, Les Maladières, Les Mariages, Les Paules, Les Pointes de Tuvilains, Les Prévoles, Les rôles, Les Vérottes, Longbois, Lulunne, Montagne Saint Désiré, Montée Rouge, Siserpe

Pommard [33]
Chaffaud, Clos Beauder, Derrière Saint-Jean, En Boeuf, En Brescul, En Chiveau, En Mareau, En Moigelot, La Chanière, La Combotte, La Croix Blanche, La Croix Planet, La Levrière, La Plante aux Chèvres, La Vache, Le Bas des Saussilles, Le Poisot, Les Chanlins-Bas, Les Chanlins-Hauts, Les Combes Dessous, Les Cras, Les Lambots, Les Noizons, Les Perrières, Les Petits Noizons, Les Riottes, Les Tavannes, Les Vaumuriens-Bas, Les Vaumuriens-Hauts, Les Vignots, Rue au Porc, Trois Follots, Village

Volnay [24]
Beau Regard, Cros Martin, En Vaut, Ez Blanches, Ez Echards, La Bouchère, La Cave, La Gigotte, Le Village, Les Aussy, Les Buttes, Les Combes, Les Famines, Les Grands Champs, Les Grands Poisots, Les Jouères, Les Lurets, Les Pasquiers, Les Petits Gamets, Les Petits Poisots, Les Pluchots, Les Serpens, Paux Bois, Sur Roches

Monthélie [24]
Aux Fournereaux, Danguy, La Combe Danay, La Goulotte, La Petite Fitte, Le Meix de Mypont, Le Meix de Ressie, Le Meix Garnier, Les Champs Ronds, Les Crays, Les Darnées, Les Gamets, Les Hauts Brins, Les Jouènes, Les Longères, Les Mandènes, Les Plantes, Les Rivaux, Les Romagniens, Les Sous-Courts, Les Sous-Roches, Les Toisières, Monthelie, Sous le Cellier

Auxey-Duresses [36]
Auxey-Duresses, Creux de Borgey, Creux de Tillet, Derrière le Four, En Polianges, En Saussois, La Canée, La Chateille, La Jonchère, La Macabrée, La Montagne du Bourdon, La Ruchotte, Largillas, Le Larrey des Hoz, Le Moulin Moine, Le Pain Haut, Le Plain de Lugny, Le Porolley, Les Boutonniers, Les Closeaux, Les Cloux, Les Crais, Les Fosses, Les Grandes Vignes, Les Hautés, Les Heptures, Les Hoz, Les Lavières, Les Riames, Les Rondières, Les Vireux, Nampoillon, Pain Perdu, Sous la Velle, Sous le Marsain, Sur Melin

Saint-Romain [16]
Au Bas de Poillange, Combe Bazin, En Chevrot, En Gollot, En Poillange, L'Argillat, La Croix Neuve, La Périère, Le Dos d'Ane, Le Jarron, Le Marsain, Le Village Bas, Le Village Haut, Sous la Velle, Sous le Château, Sous Roche

Meursault [53]
Au Moulin Judas, Au Moulin Landin, Au Murger de Monthélie, Au Village, Clos de la Barre, Clos des Mouches, En Gargouillot, En l'Ormeau, En la Barre, En Marcausse, La Barre Dessus, Le Bois de Blagny, Le Buisson Certaut, Le Cromin, Le Limozin, Le Meix sous le Château, Le Meix Tavaux, Le Pré de Manche, Le Tesson, Les Casse-Têtes, Les Chaumes, Les Chaumes de Narvaux, Les Chevalières, Les Clous Dessous, Les Clous Dessus, Les Corbins, Les Criots, Les Durots, Les Forges, Les Gorges de Narvaux, Les Grands Charrons, Les Gruyaches, Les Luchets, Les Magny, Les Malpoiriers, Les Meix Chavaux, Les Millerands, Les Narvaux Dessous, Les Narvaux Dessus, Les Pellans, Les Pelles-Dessous, Les Pelles-Dessus, Les Perchots, Les Petits Charrons, Les Peutes Vignes, Les Rougeots, Les Santenots Dessous, Les Terres Blanches, Les Tillets, Les Vignes Blanches, Les Vireuils Dessous, Les Vireuils Dessus

Blagny [3]
Le Bois de Blagny, Le Trézin, Les Ravelles

Puligny-Montrachet [26]
Au Paupillot, Brelance, Champ Croyon, Corvée des Vignes, Derrière la Velle, La Rousselle, La Rue aux Vaches, Le Trézin, Le Village, Les Aubues, Les Boudrières, Les Charmes, Les Enseignères, Les Grands Champs, Les Houlières, Les Levrons, Les Meix, Les Nosroyes, Les Petites Nosroyes, Les Petits Grands Champs, Les Reuchaux, Les Tremblots, Meix Pelletier, Noyer Bret, Rue Rousseau, Voitte

Chassagne-Montrachet [46]
Blanchot Dessous, Bouchon de Corvée, Champ Derrière, Champs de Morjot, Clos Bernot, Dessous les Mues, En Journoblot, En l'Ormeau, En Pimont, Fontaine Sot, La Bergerie, La Canière, La Canotte, La Goujonne, La Platière, La Têtière, Le Clos Reland, Le Concis du Champs, Le Parterre, Le Poirier du Clos, Les Battaudes, Les Benoites, Les Beuttes, Les Chambres, Les Charnières, Les Chaumes, Les Chênes, Les Encégnières, Les Essarts, Les Grandes Terres, Les Houillères, Les Lombardes, Les Masures, Les Meix Goudard, Les Morichots, Les Mouchottes, Les Perclos, Les Pierres, Les Plantes Momières, Les Voillenots Dessous, Plante du Gaie, Plante Saint Aubin, Pot Bois, Puits Merdreaux, Sur Matronge, Voillenot Dessous

Saint-Aubin [22]
Au Bas de Jorcul, Bas de Vermarain à l'Ouest, Champ Tirant, En Choilles, En Goulin, En Jorcul, En l'Ebaupin, En Vermarain à l'Est, En Vesveau, Gamay, La Fontenotte, La Traversaine, Le Banc, Le Banc de Monin, Le Puits, Les Argillers, Les Castets, Les Pucelles, Les Travers de chez Edouard, Les Vellerottes, Sous les Foires, Tope Bataille

Santenay [34]
Bellefon, Bieveaux, Botaveau, Clos Genet, Comme Dessus, Croix Sorine, Derrière les Crais, En Aiguisey, En Boichot, En Charron, En Foulot, En Gatsulard, La Cassière, La Comme, La Plice, Le Chainey, Le Haut Village, Le Village, Les Brâs, Les Champs Claudes, Les Charmes Dessous, Les Charmes Dessus, Les Cornières, Les Crais, Les Hâtes, Les Pérolles, Les Potets, Les Prarons-Dessous, Les Prarons-Dessus, Les Saunières, Les Vaux Dessus, Saint-Jean, Sous la Fée, Sous la Roche

Maranges [29]
A la Croix de Bois, Au Chêne, Aux Artaux, Borgy, En Buliet, En Crevèche, La Tête de Fer, Le Bas des Loyères, Le Bas du Clos, Le Bourg, Le Chamery, Le Clos, Le Goty, Le Plain, Le Saugeot, Les Aubuzes, Les Meurées, Les Plantes, Les Regains Nord, Les Regains Sud, Les Varennes, Sous les Roseaux, Sur la Rigole, Sur la Rue des Pierres, Sur la Verpillère, Sur le Bois Nord, Sur le Bois Sud, Sur le Chêne, Vigne Blanche

Bouzeron [21]
En Rabeutelot, L' Hermitage, La Digoine, La Epoube, La Fortune, La Tournelle, Le Bois de Foiret, Le Bourg, Le Champ des Crots, Le Feulin, Les Bouchines, Les Boyottes, Les Clous, Les Corcelles, Les Cordères, Les Fias, Les Louères, Les Pertuzots, Les Seurrées, Sous le Bois, Vers le Petits Puits

Rully [29]
Bas de Vauvery, Bas des Chênes, Brange, Chaponnière, Chatalienne, Chêne, Cloux Louvrier, Crays, En Thivaux, En Vésignot, Fromange, La Barre, La Billeraine, La Chaume, La Crée, La Curasse, La Gaudine, La Martelle, Le Truyer, Les Cailloux, Les Gaudors, Meix de Pellerey, Montmorin, Moulin à Vent, Plante Moraine, Plantenay, Rosey, Varot, Villerange

Mercurey [78]
Bourg Bassot, Bourg-Neuf, Chamirey, Champ Ladoy, Champ Pillot, Champ Roin, Clos Château de Montaigu, Clos des Hayes, Clos Fortoul, Clos Rochette-Mauvarennes, Creu de Montelons, En Boussoy, En Grillot, En Pierre Milley, En Theurot, Es Montelons, Etroyes, Garnerot, La Brigadière, La Charmée, La Chiquette, La Corvée, La Creuse, La Croix Rousse, La Perrière, La Pillotte, La Plante Chassey, Le Bois Cassien, Le Bourg, Le Clos la Marche, Le Clos Laurent, Le Clos Rond, Le Closeau, Le Crêt, Le Fourneau, Le Meix de la Guinarde, Le Meix Foulot, Le Meix Frappé, Le Puits Brintet, Le Saut Muchiau, Les Bacs, Les Berlands-Framboisière, Les Bois de Lalier, Les Bosebuts, Les Bussières, Les Caraby, Les Caudroyes, Les Chaumellottes, Les Chavances, Les Cheneaults, Les Creux, Les Marcoeurs, Les Montelons, Les Montots, Les Morées, Les Morins, Les Murgers, Les Mussiaux, Les Noiterons, Les Obus, Les Plantes, Les Pronges, Les Rochelles, Les Varennes, Les Vaux, Les Vignes Blanches, Les Vignes d'Orge, Les Vignes de la Bouthière, Les Vignes des Chazeaux, Les Villeranges, Meix Adenot, Mipont Château, Ropiton, Sarrazine, Touches, Vigne de Maillonge, Vignes du Chapître

Givry [29]
Brusseaux de Charron, Champ la Dame, Champ Pourot, Chanevarie, Clos de la Brûlée, En Chenève, Gauron, La Corvée, La Feusée, La Pièce, La Pierre, La Putin, La Ridette, La Vernoise, Le Paradis, Les Faussillons, Les Fontenottes, Les Galaffres, Les Grognots, Les Mureys, Les Plants Sont Fleuris, Les Vignes Rondes, Meix Saint-Antoine, Mortières, Tambournette, Teppe des Chenèves, Varange, Vauvry, Virgaudine

Montagny [40]
Cruzille, Davenay, La Corvée, La Groule, La Pallue, La Tillonne, Le Corbeau, Le Creux de la Feuille, Le Curtil, Le May, Le May Cottin, Le May Morin, Le Recurleron, Le Reuilly, Les Beaucons, Les Betaux, Les Brus, Les Chazelles, Les Cloux, Les Corbaisons, Les Crets, Les Dazés, Les Echeliers, Les Guignottes, Les Joncs, Les Marais, Les Pendars, Les Plantats, Les Préaux, Les Prés, Les Rougereaux, Les Thilles, Les Varignys, Les Variniers, Les Vignes Sous l'Eglise, Montagny, Prés Berceaux, Sous les Roches, St Vallerin, Vignes Dessous

Mâcon-Villages [18]
Bossu, En Beaux, Le Château de Chaintré, Le Clos, Le Moulin à l'Or, Le Poisard, Les Barbiers, Les Buissonats, Les Champs Bardes, Les Champs Chetiers, Les Jonchayes, Les Landes, Les Pérelles, Les Perrières, Les Prés de Savy, Les Serreuxdières, Les Terres de Savy, Les Terres Pelletier

Pouilly-Fuissé [174]
A la Chaneau, A la Cotonne, A la Croix Bonne, Au Bois Billon, Au Bourg, Au Bucherat, Au Buchot, Au Chapal, Au Clos, Au Gaulia, Au Gros Bois, Au May, Au Métertière, Au Moule, Au Peloux, Au Sauge, Au Suif, Aux Charmes, Aux Combes, Aux Concizes, Aux Coreaux, Aux Grands Champs, Aux Morlays, Aux Murs, Aux Plantés, Aux Prats, Aux Vignes Dessus, Barvay, Beauregard, Bois Dayer, Bois de Lacroix, Bois des Fousses, Bois du Molard, Bois Lafaye, Bois Sansonnet, Bois Seguin, Champ Potard, Champ Ruy, Clos de la Maison, Clos Gaillard, Combe Poncet, Derrière la Maison, En Bertillonne, En Bonnard, En Buland, En Buterie, En Carmentrant, En Cenan, En Champ Roux, En Charmont, En Chatenay, En Chauffaille, En Courtesse, En Larzille, En Nanche, En Ouche, En Pomard, En Pragne, En Recepey, En Ronchevat, En Rontenoux, En Rousselaine, En Tancul, En Tillier, En Vallée, L'Arse, La Barrière, La Baudotte, La Bergerie, La Brétande, La Bucharlatte, La Cadole, La Carrière, La Chardette, La Chattière, La Corège, La Côte, La Croix Pardon, La Dépendaine, La Folle, La Gorge au Loup, La Grange Murger, La Grouillère, La Mouille, La Petite Bruyère, La Roue, La Ruère, La Teppe Charpy, La Terre Jeanduc, La Toule, La Truche, La Verchère, La Vigne des Verchères, Lamure, Le Bois des Taches, Le Carron, Le Champ Rocher, Le Grand Pré, Le Haut de Savy, Le Martelet, Le Moulin, Le Nambret, Le Plan, Le Repostère, Le Routé, Le Sabotier, Le Sang Clos, Les Belouzes, Les Bois Denis, Les Chardonnets, Les Chataigniers, Les Chevaux, Les Combettes, Les Condemines, Les Courtelongs, Les Creuzettes, Les Croux, Les Fourneaux, Les Gerbeaux, Les Grandes Terres, Les Guilloux, Les Insarts, Les Jettes, Les Longues Raies, Les Murgers, Les Piasses, Les Plessis, Les Prâles, Les Préauds, Les Prés Hauts, Les Prouges, Les Quarts, Les Robées, Les Rontets, Les Rossins, Les Scélés, Les Séries, Les Terres du Perret, Les Travers, Les Verchères, Les Verchères de Savy, Les Vernays, Les Vieilles Plantes, Les Vignes des Taches, Long Poil, Maison du Villard, Mont Garcin, Petite Croix, Petites Bruyères, Pierre Lotey, Plan de Bourdon, Pré de Vaux, Pré des Aires, Solutré, Sous le Four, Sur la Rochette, Sur les Moulins, Vergisson, Vers Agnières, Vers Châne, Vers Faux, Vers la Croix, Vers la Roche, Vers Pouilly, Vers Saint Léger, Vignes de la Fontaine, Vignes de la Hys, Vignes de la l'Eau, Vignes de la Roche, Vignes Derrière, Vignes des Champs, Vignes du Riat, Vignes Mottin, Vignes sur la Fontaine

Pouilly-Loché [8]
Au Bûcher, Aux Barres, Aux Scellés, En Chantonne, La Colonge, Les Mûres, Les Quatre Saisons, Loché

Pouilly-Vinzelles [11]
Aux Bourgeois, Château Bardon, Château de Vinzelles, Les Bois Préaux, Les Buchardières, Les Longeays, Les Petaux, Les Quarts, Les Verchères, Pré du Château, Sency

Saint-Véran [187]

A la Côte, A la Croix, Au Bois, Au Bois de Fée, Au Brûlé, Au Champ Palisse, Au Château, Au Clos, Au Cota, Au Grand Bussière, Au Grand Champ, Au Mont, Au Pommier, Aux Barons, Aux Bulands, Aux Champs Lière, Aux Colas, Aux Correaux, Aux Crays, Aux Essertos, Aux Grandes Vignes, Aux Jean des Moitiers, Aux Plantées, Aux Tilles, Aux Vessats, Aux Voisins, Bandonneau, Bayeux, Bossu, Bouteaux, Champ Meunier, Champ Rond, Chaponière, Chevigne, Clos de la Maison, Clos de la Maison Neuve, Clos Devant, Croix de Montceau, Croix de Vareilles, En Arène, En Avonne, En Beauvoir, En Bergeron, En Chailloux, En Charlures, En Chatenay, En Coland, En Combe, En Crébin, En Crèche, En Dougi, En Faux, En Gréfet, En Marmouille, En Messie, En Monchanin, En Paradis, En Réfort, En Rousseau, En Surigny, En Terre Noire, En Varenne, Ez Marzes, Ez Quarts, Grande Vigne, Janichon, Jully, L'Epinglier, L'Essard, La Barrière, La Boisserole, La Bonde, La Bounode, La Bruyère, La Combe, La Côte, La Côte Rotie, La Cour des Bois, La Croix Rouge, La Cuisse à la Vache, La Dinde, La Feuillarde, La Foudrole, La Grande Bruyère, La Grange aux Buis, La Grevette, La Louve, La Maison Rouge, La Planchette, La Platière, La Rapie, La Roche, La Tambourte, La Verchère, Le Clos, Le Clos des Poncetys, Le Clouzat, Le Colombier, Le Crouze, Le Grand Clos, Le Haut de la Roche, Le Partisselle, Le Poisard, Le Pré des Vaux, Le Vallon, Le Vernay, Le Village, Les Belouzes, Les Bergades, Les Bois, Les Brosses, Les Cailloux, Les Carettes, Les Carrales, Les Caves, Les Chaillouxx, Les Chantoux, Les Chanuettes, Les Charmonts, Les Chataigniers, Les Chatenay, Les Chênes, Les Colanges, Les Colongettes, Les Combes, Les Condemines, Les Copines, Les Corgedaux, Les Cornillaux, Les Crais, Les Cras, Les Crays, Les Creux Bertoux, Les Dimes, Les Dougys, Les Farquets, Les Fournaises, Les Grands Champs, Les Grands Dougis, Les Granges, Les Jacobins, Les Jonchets, Les Jyrondelles, Les Maillettes, Les Maléchals, Les Mauvetys, Les Molards, Les Morats, Les Mûres, Les Népesses, Les Nonjelettes, Les Partouts, Les Peiguins, Les Perrelles, Les Perrières, Les Perriers, Les Personnets, Les Philiberts, Les Plantes, Les Platrières, Les Pommards, Les Poncétys, Les Quatre Poiriers, Les Rochats, Les Rochettes, Les Rollins, Les Sables, Les Sablons, Les Saussemales, Les Serreuxdières, Les Souches, Les Spires, Les Valanges, Mont de Milly, Mont de Milly ou les Liats, Mont-St-Pierre, Montceau, Pré de la Verchère, Pré Jaux, Saint-Claude, Terre de la Maison, Vers la Croix, Vers la Maison, Vers le Bois, Vers le Champ, Vigne Blanche, Vigne de la Fontaine

Viré-Clessé [114]

A Baclot, A Jean Benoit, A l'Agremat, Au Buc, Au Chêne Monet, Au Coin, Au Pattin, Au Sorbier, Aux Châtaigneraies, Aux Cochets, Aux Donzarts, Aux Fargettes, Aux Grandes Plantes, Aux Mares, Aux Mécolans, Aux Ménards, Aux Nièvres, Aux Plantés, Aux Prêtres, Basse Ecole, Berthoud, Boulaise, Bréchen, Breillonde, Breuron, Champ Choley, Champ de Long, Champ du Mur, Champ Rond, Chanron, Chapelle Saint Trivier, Chapotin, Châtenet d'en Haut, Chaudron et Fond Dru, Clessé, Cray, Derrière chez Petit, Derrière la Forêt, En Brenillon, En Chavanne, En Chazelle, En Collonge, En Combe, En Fillon, En Fontenay, En Gelé, En Greppe, En Grévoux, En Long Champ, En Pélouzan, En Pommetin, En Roally, En Rozande, En Tinture, En Vercheron, Gandine, Gouvre, Grands Crays, Jean Large, L'Elit, L'Epinet, La Barre, La Bussière, La Catoire, La Combe, La Côte, La Croisette, La Forêt, La Forétille, La Mâsure, La Montagne, La Perrière, La Plaine, La Troupe, La Verchère, La Verpaille, Le Bois Noquet, Le Chapitre, Le Château, Le Clou, Le Crêt, Le Creuseromme, Le Mont Châtelaine, Le Virolis, Les Chailloux, Les Foretilles, Les Gros Buissons, Les Poiriers, Les Portes, Les Prés du Buc, Les Rapillères, Les Thibaudes, Les Vignes de Cray, Margillien, Petite Condemine, Petits Crays, Pignot, Pont de Veau, Quarts, Quintaine, Raverettes, Rousset, Rue du Mur, Sous la Bussière, Sous la Friche, Sous la Montagne, Sous les Plantes, Sous Mont, Sur l'Orme, Sur le Chêne, Sur le Mont, Tronche Fourrie, Vers Laizé, Viré

Saint-Amour [12]

Côte de Besset, Les Champs Grillés, Le Clos de la Brosse, Le Clos de Guillons, Le Chatelet, Le Clos des Billards, Les Bonnets, Le Mas des Tines, Vers l'Eglise, En Paradis, La Folie, Le Clos du Chapître

Juliénas [8]

Les Capitans, La Bottière, Les Paquelets, Les Chers, Les Mouilles, Vayolette, Fouillouses, Beauvernay

Chénas [2]

Les Brureaux, Clos des Blémonts

Moulin-à-Vent [85]

La Bruyère, Les Gros Vosges, Maisons neuves, La Grande Charrière, Les Michelons, Le Moulin à Vent, Champagne, Champs de Cour, Les Deschamps, Le Carquelin, Le Mont, Le Plantier de Fabre, Les Pinchons, Les Bruyères des Thorins, Les Seignaux, Les Dégollets, Les Thorins, Morperay, La Tour du Bief, La Galletière, Les Vérillats, Les Fromenteaux, Le Vieux Bourg, La Teppe, Les Vierres Manins, Petit Brenay, Les Prés Ouverts, En Brenay, Les Pérelles, La Pierre, Les Moriers, Moulin Lure, Les Philibons, En Reclaine, La Delatte, Bois Pondevaux, La Roche, Les Bûches, Le Petit Morier, Les Brussellion, Bois Maréchaux, Les Fargets, Les Rouchaux, Les Gimarets, Les Combes, Les Seignes, Bois Combe, Les Moussières, Les Petits Bois, Les Millettes, Les Grenériers, La Bruyère, Les Burdelines, Les Guillattes, Les Graiairiers, Les Amandilliers, Le Fonds de Morier, Le Bief, En Morier, Les Blancs, Champ Poirier, Les Caves, Les Maitairiers, Chassignol, Les Michauds, La Coudrière, Les Ecorchés, Deschanes, La Ranche, Les Joies, Les Garniers, La Dîme, Les Condemeines, Rochegrès, Le Venet, La Rochelle, Les Burdins, Rochenoire, Petites Caves, Terre du Thé, Les Rats, Les Brasses, Les Champs de Cour, Les Hantes, Les Grolliers

Fleurie [13]

Les Côtes, Le Bon Cru, La Roilette, Les Moriers, Les Roches, Les Garants, Poncié, Montgenas, La Chapelle de Bois, La Madone, Grille-Midi, Champagne, La Joie du Palais

Chiroubles [2]

La Grosse Pierre, Les Côtes

Morgon [6]

Douby, Les Charmes, Côte du Py, Grand Cras, Corcelette, Les Micouds

Régnié [2]

Grange-Charton, La Plaigne

Côte de Brouilly [2]

L'Héronde, L'Ecluse

Brouilly [1]

Pisse-Vieille

74 IGPs [3 levels] [list only]

Regional (8)

ATLANTIQUE [Bordeaux, Dordogne, Charentais]	FRANCHE-COMTÉ [Haute-Saône, Doubs, Territoire de Belfort departments and the majority of the Jura]
CHARENTAIS [Charente and Charente-Maritime departments]	MÉDITERRANÉE [Provence, Corsica]
COMTÉ TOLOSAN [South-West]	PAYS D'OC [Languedoc-Roussillon]
COMTÉS RHODANIENS [Rhône Valley, Beaujolais, Savoie]	VAL DE LOIRE [Loire Valley]

Departmental (28)

ALPES-DE-HAUTE-PROVENCE	CALVADOS	GARD	ILE DE BEAUTÉ [CORSICA]	PUY-DE-DÔME
ALPES-MARITIMES	COTEAUX DE L'AIN	GERS	ISÈRE	SAÔNE-ET-LOIRE
ARDÈCHE	CÔTES DE MEUSE	HAUTE VALLÉE DE L'AUDE	LANDES	VAR
ARIÈGE	CÔTES DU LOT	HAUTE-MARNE	PAYS D'HÉRAULT	VAUCLUSE
AUDE	CÔTES DU TARN	HAUTE-VIENNE	PAYS DES BOUCHES-DU-RHÔNE	YONNE
AVEYRON	DRÔME	HAUTES-ALPES		

Zonal (38) [located in the department of ...]

AGENAIS [Lot-et-Garonne]	COTEAUX DE TANNAY [Nièvre]	MONT CAUME [Var]
ALPILLES [Bouches-du-Rhône]	COTEAUX DES BARONNIES [Drôme]	PÉRIGORD [Dordogne, Lot]
CÉVENNES [Gard]	COTEAUX DU CHER ET DE l'Arnon [Cher]	SABLE DE CAMARGUE [Hérault, Gard, Bouches-du-Rhône]
CITÉ DE CARCASSONNE [Aude]	COTEAUX DU PONT DU GARD [Gard]	SAINT-GUILHEM-LE-DÉSERT [Hérault]
COLLINES RHODANIENNES [northern Rhône Valley region]	CÔTES CATALANES [Pyrénées-Orientales]	SAINTE-MARIE-LA-BLANCHE [Côte-d'Or]
CÔTE VERMEILLE [area of Banyuls and Collioure AOCs]	CÔTES DE GASCOGNE [Gers]	TERRES DU MIDI [Aude, Hérault, Gard, Pyrénées-Orientales]
COTEAUX D'ENSÉRUNE [Hérault]	CÔTES DE LA CHARITÉ [Nièvre]	THÉZAC-PERRICARD [Lot-et-Garonne]
COTEAUX DE BÉZIERS [Hérault]	CÔTES DE THAU [Hérault]	URFÉ [Loire]
COTEAUX DE COIFFY [Haute-Marne]	CÔTES DE THONGUE [Hérault]	VALLÉE DU PARADIS [Aude]
COTEAUX DE GLANES [Lot]	HAUTE VALLÉE DE L'ORB [Hérault]	VALLÉE DU TORGAN [Aude]
COTEAUX DE L'AUXOIS [Côte-d'Or]	LAVILLEDIEU [Tarn-et-Garonne]	VICOMTÉ D'AUMELAS [Hérault]
COTEAUX DE NARBONNE [Aude]	LE PAYS CATHARE [Aude, Ariège]	VIN DES ALLOBROGES [Savoie, Haute-Savoie]
COTEAUX DE PEYRIAC [Aude, Hérault]	MAURES [Var]	

REGIONS OF FRANCE [17]

WALES

Celtic
Sea

ENGLAND

NETHERLANDS

London

2°546'E

Dortmund

51°089'N

Brussels

GERMANY

BELGIUM

Koblenz

English
Channel

LUXEMBOURG

CHAMPAGNE

Paris

LORRAINE

Strasbourg

ALSACE

Munich

LOIRE VALLEY

Nantes

BURGUNDY

47°794'N

JURA

Innsbruck

AUSTRIA

Nevers

Lausanne

SWITZERLAND

ALPS

BUGEY

BORDEAUX

Bay of
Biscay

LYONNAIS

SAVOIE

45°572'N

Lyon

BEAUJOLAIS

MASSIF
CENTRAL

ALPS

Turin

SOUTH WEST
FRANCE

RHÔNE

ITALY

Ligurian
Sea

APENNINES

Toulouse

CORSE

León

PYRÉNÉES

PROVENCE

LANGUEDOC

ROUSSILLON

Rome

SPAIN

Barcelona

Mediterranean
Sea

41°365'N

Tyrrhenian
Sea

Body of Water

COUNTRY — · — · —

City ■

LAND FEATURE

Mi 0   62.14   124.27   186.41   248.55

Km 0   100   200   300   400

ALSACE
TOTAL AOC [53]
GENERIC AOC [2]
GRAND CRU VINEYARDS / AOC [51]
Alsace Communale [13]

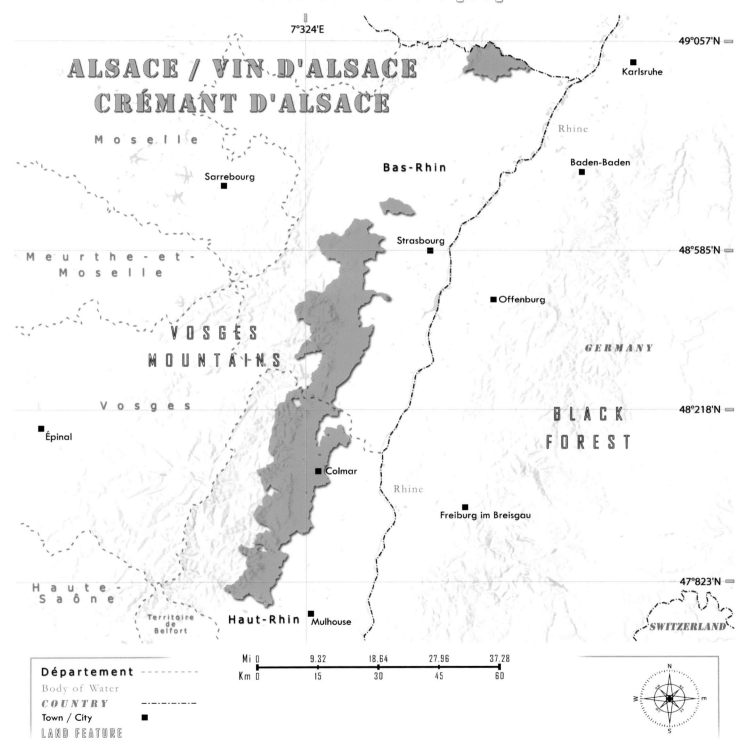

ALSACE / VIN D'ALSACE
CRÉMANT D'ALSACE

Moselle

Bas-Rhin

7°324'E

49°057'N

Karlsruhe

Rhine

Baden-Baden

Sarrebourg

Meurthe-et-Moselle

Strasbourg

48°585'N

Offenburg

VOSGES
MOUNTAINS

GERMANY

Vosges

48°218'N

BLACK
FOREST

Épinal

Colmar

Rhine

Freiburg im Breisgau

Haute-Saône

47°823'N

Territoire
de
Belfort

Haut-Rhin

Mulhouse

SWITZERLAND

| Mi 0 | 9.32 | 18.64 | 27.96 | 37.28 |
| Km 0 | 15 | 30 | 45 | 60 |

Département - - - -
Body of Water
COUNTRY —··—··—
Town / City ■
LAND FEATURE

ALSACE
Alsace Communale [13]

ALSACE
GRAND CRU VINEYARDS / AOC [51]

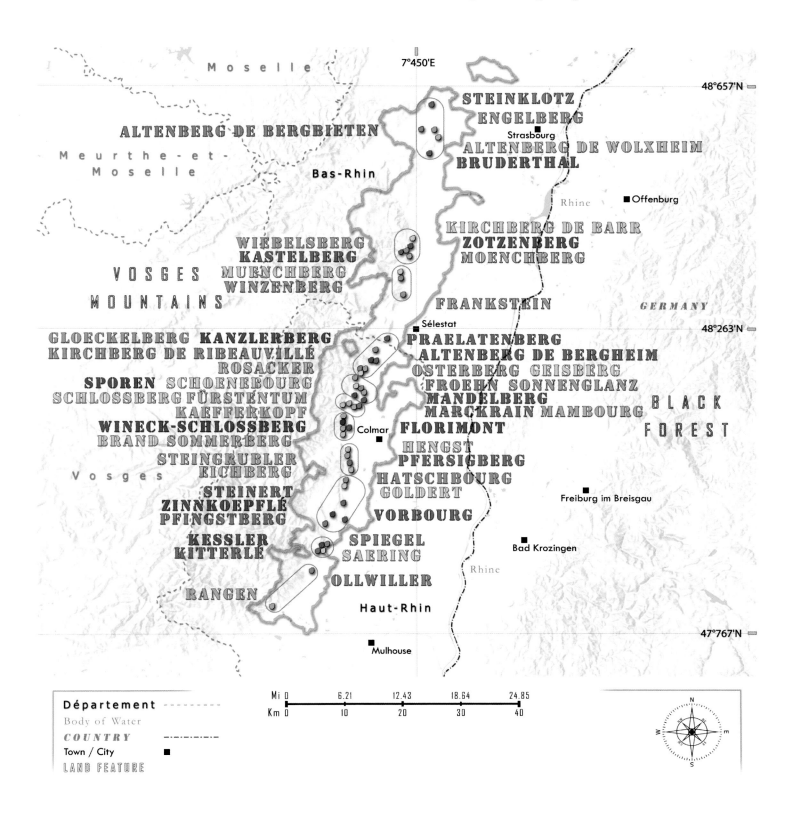

Moselle

7°450'E

48°657'N

STEINKLOTZ
ENGELBERG

ALTENBERG DE BERGBIETEN

Strasbourg

Meurthe-et-
Moselle

ALTENBERG DE WOLXHEIM
BRUDERTHAL

Bas-Rhin

Rhine

Offenburg

KIRCHBERG DE BARR
ZOTZENBERG
MOENCHBERG

WIEBELSBERG
KASTELBERG
MUENCHBERG
WINZENBERG

VOSGES
MOUNTAINS

FRANKSTEIN

GERMANY

Sélestat

48°263'N

GLOECKELBERG KANZLERBERG
KIRCHBERG DE RIBEAUVILLÉ
ROSACKER
SPOREN SCHOENEBOURG
SCHLOSSBERG FÜRSTENTUM
KAEFFERKOPF
WINECK-SCHLOSSBERG
BRAND SOMMERBERG
STEINGRUBLER
EICHBERG

PRAELATENBERG
ALTENBERG DE BERGHEIM
OSTERBERG GEISBERG
FROEHN SONNENGLANZ
MANDELBERG
MARCKRAIN MAMBOURG

BLACK
FOREST

Colmar

FLORIMONT
HENGST
PFERSIGBERG
HATSCHBOURG
GOLDERT

Vosges

Freiburg im Breisgau

STEINERT
ZINNKOEPFLÉ
PFINGSTBERG

VORBOURG

Bad Krozingen

KESSLER
KITTERLÉ

SPIEGEL
SAERING

Rhine

OLLWILLER

RANGEN

Haut-Rhin

47°767'N

Mulhouse

Mi 0   6.21   12.43   18.64   24.85
Km 0   10   20   30   40

N
W   E
S

Alsace
Grand Cru Vineyard AOC

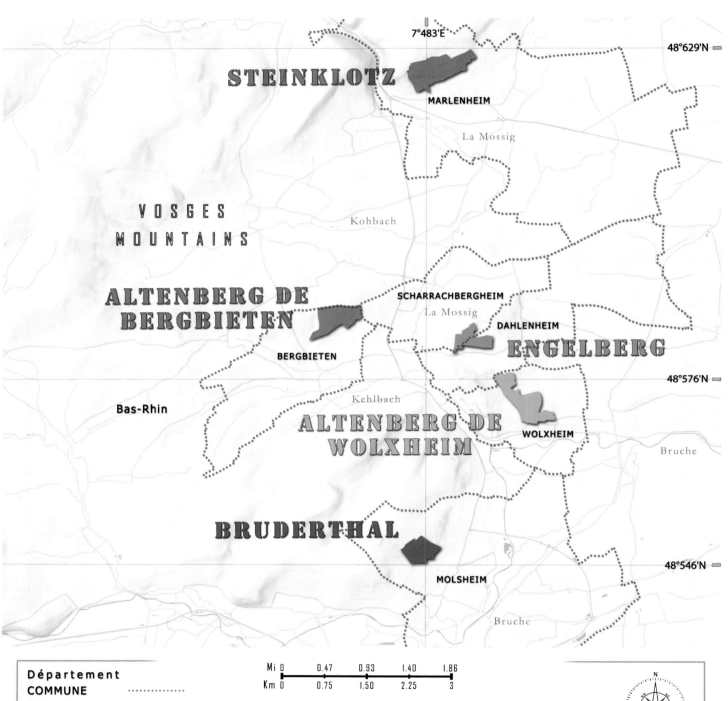

7°483'E

48°629'N

STEINKLOTZ

MARLENHEIM

La Mossig

VOSGES
MOUNTAINS

Kohbach

SCHARRACHBERGHEIM

ALTENBERG DE
BERGBIETEN

La Mossig

DAHLENHEIM

ENGELBERG

BERGBIETEN

48°576'N

Bas-Rhin

Kehlbach

ALTENBERG DE
WOLXHEIM

WOLXHEIM

Bruche

BRUDERTHAL

48°546'N

MOLSHEIM

Bruche

Département
COMMUNE   ·············
Body of Water
LAND FEATURE

Mi 0	0.47	0.93	1.40	1.86
Km 0	0.75	1.50	2.25	3

France

Alsace
Grand Cru Vineyard AOC

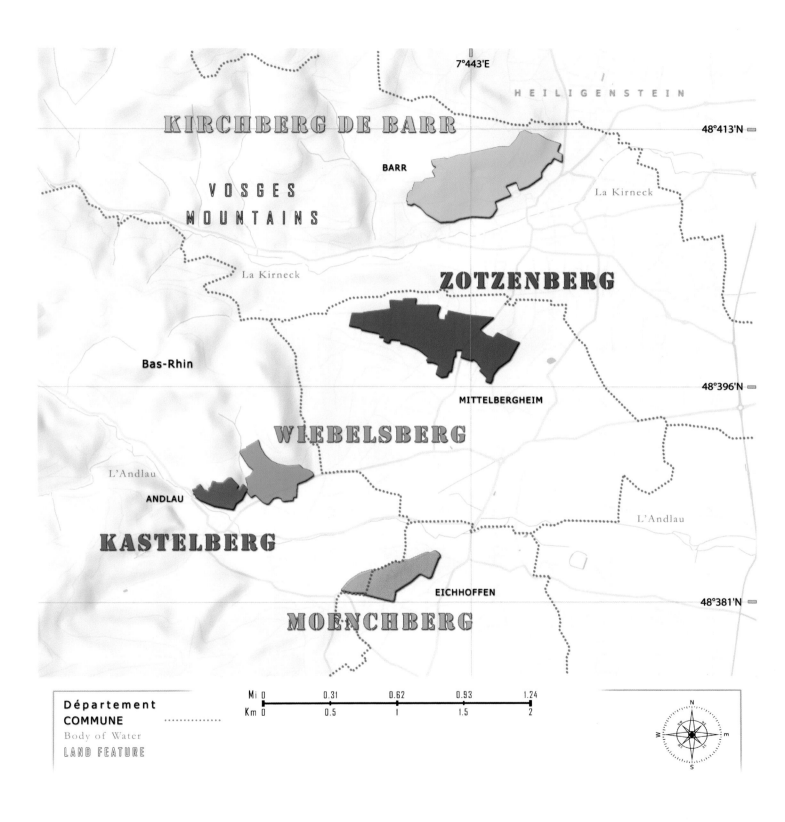

Alsace
Grand Cru Vineyard AOC

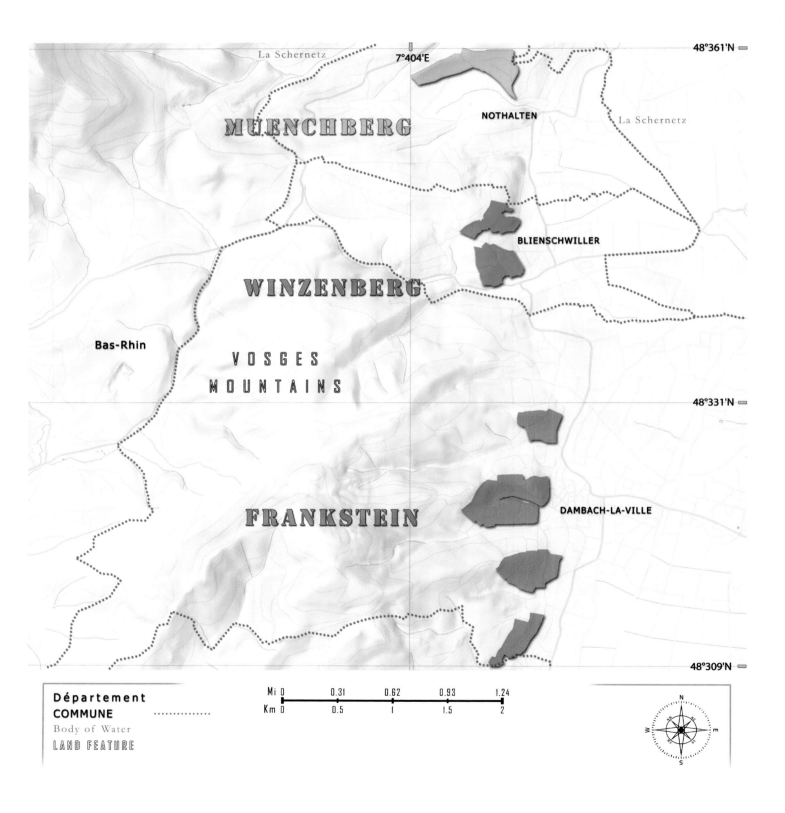

La Schernetz

7°404'E

48°361'N

MUENCHBERG

NOTHALTEN

La Schernetz

BLIENSCHWILLER

WINZENBERG

Bas-Rhin

VOSGES
MOUNTAINS

48°331'N

FRANKSTEIN

DAMBACH-LA-VILLE

48°309'N

Département
COMMUNE ·············
Body of Water
LAND FEATURE

Mi 0   0.31   0.62   0.93   1.24
Km 0   0.5   1   1.5   2

Alsace
Grand Cru Vineyard AOC

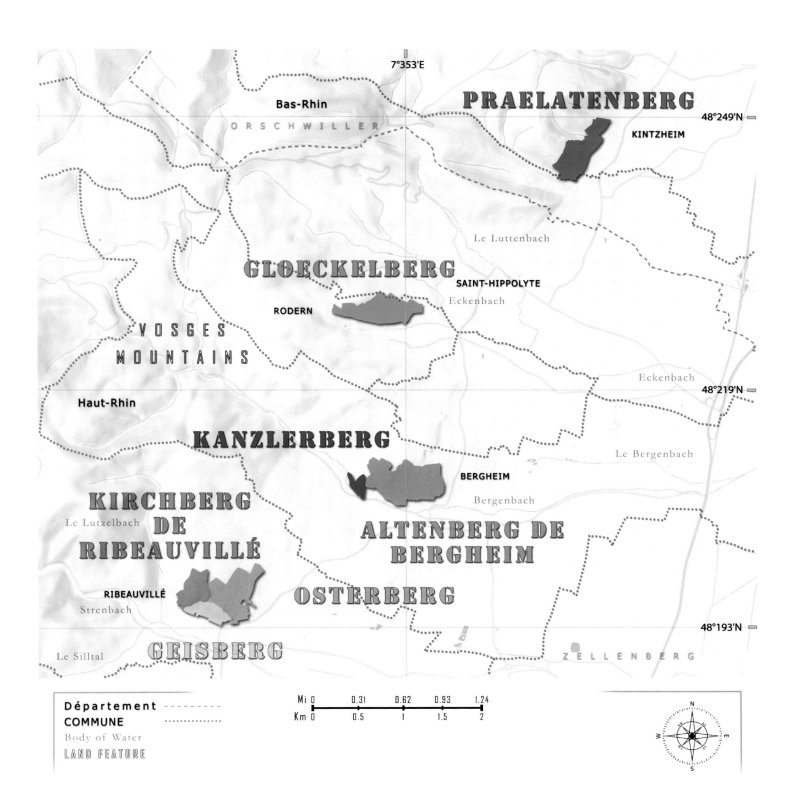

7°353'E

Bas-Rhin

ORSCHWILLER

PRAELATENBERG

48°249'N

KINTZHEIM

Le Luttenbach

GLOECKELBERG

SAINT-HIPPOLYTE

Eckenbach

RODERN

VOSGES

MOUNTAINS

Eckenbach

48°219'N

Haut-Rhin

Le Bergenbach

KANZLERBERG

BERGHEIM

Bergenbach

KIRCHBERG
DE
RIBEAUVILLÉ

Le Lutzelbach

ALTENBERG DE
BERGHEIM

RIBEAUVILLÉ

OSTERBERG

Strenbach

48°193'N

Le Silltal

GEISBERG

ZELLENBERG

Département - - - - - - - -
COMMUNE · · · · · · · · · · ·
Body of Water
LAND FEATURE

| Mi | 0 | 0.31 | 0.62 | 0.93 | 1.24 |
| Km | 0 | 0.5 | 1 | 1.5 | 2 |

Alsace
Grand Cru Vineyard AOC

ROSACKER

RIBEAUVILLÉ

VOSGES MOUNTAINS

HUNAWIHR

Haut-Rhin

SCHOENEBOURG

ZELLENBERG

FROEHN

48°185'N

7°324'E

SONNENGLANZ

48°165'N

RIQUEWIHR

Sambach

Le Lauenbach

SPOREN

BEBLENHEIM

Sambach

MANDELBERG

Le Hagelgraben

MITTELWIHR

48°149'N

Département
COMMUNE
Body of Water
LAND FEATURE

Mi 0   0.31   0.62   0.93   1.24
Km 0   0.5   1   1.5   2

N
W   E
S

Alsace
Grand Cru Vineyard AOC

RIQUEWIHR

7°292'E

Sambach

VOSGES
MOUNTAINS

Le Hagelgraben

SCHLOSSBERG

MITTELWIHR

48°149'N

FÜRSTENTUM

Haut-Rhin

MARCKRAIN

48°144'N

BENNWIHR

KIENTZHEIM

MAMBOURG

48°133'N

SIGOLSHEIM

Weiss

Le Walbach

AMMERSCHWIHR

Mi 0		0.31	0.62	0.93	1.24
Km 0	0.5	1	1.5		2

Département
COMMUNE ....
Body of Water
LAND FEATURE

Alsace
Grand Cru Vineyard AOC

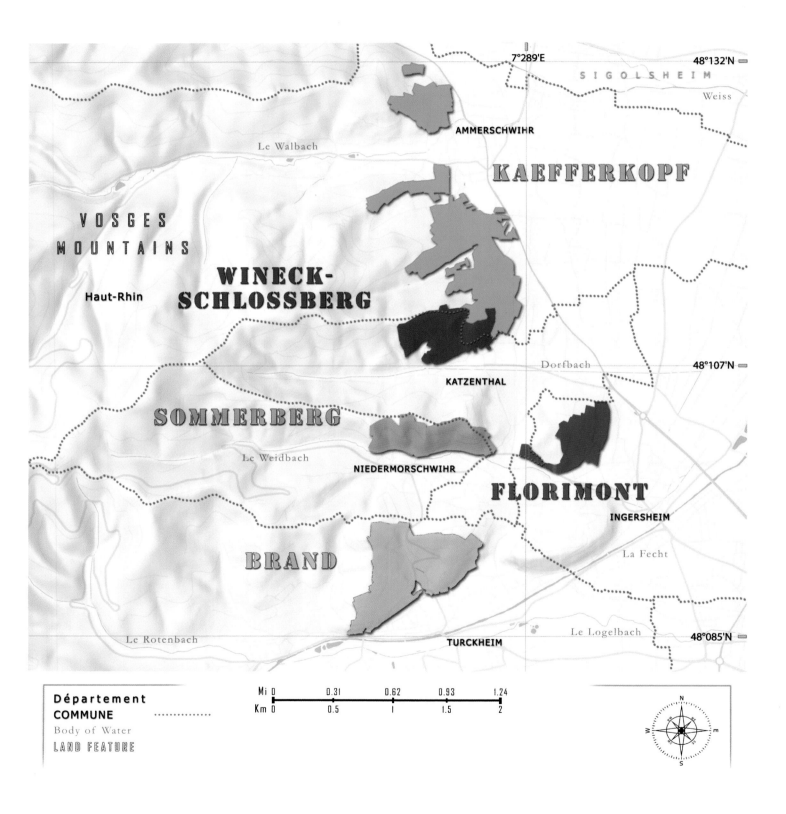

Alsace
Grand Cru Vineyard AOC

7°296'E

WINTZENHEIM

COLMAR

48°067'N

HENGST

VOSGES
MOUNTAINS

STEINGRUBLER

Haut-Rhin

WETTOLSHEIM

48°049'N

PFERSIGBERG

EGUISHEIM

HUSSEREN-
LES-
CHÂTEAUX

EICHBERG

Le Langgraben

48°027'N

HERRLISHEIM-PRÈS-
COLMAR

VŒGTLINSHOFFEN

Département
COMMUNE ....
Body of Water
LAND FEATURE

| Mi | 0 | 0.31 | 0.62 | 0.93 | 1.24 |
| Km | 0 | 0.5 | 1 | 1.5 | 2 |

Alsace
Grand Cru Vineyard AOC

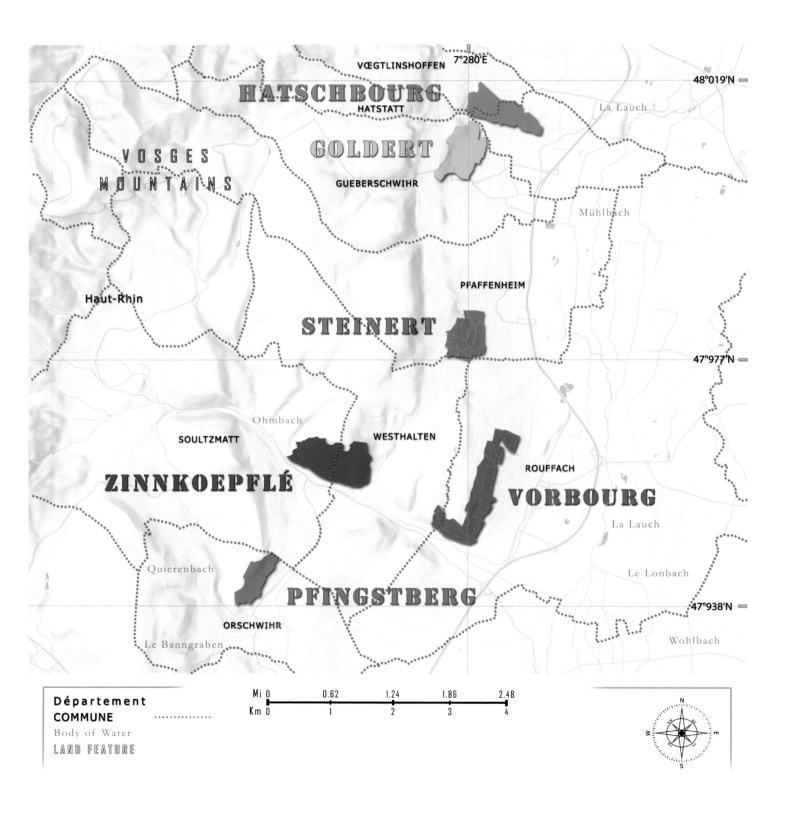

Département
COMMUNE
Body of Water
LAND FEATURE

Mi 0   0.62   1.24   1.86   2.48
Km 0   1   2   3   4

France

Alsace
Grand Cru Vineyard AOC

7°231'E

Le Banngraben

Quierenbach

VOSGES
MOUNTAINS

47°922'N

La Lauch

SPIEGEL

KESSLER

BERGHOLTZ

Haut-Rhin

47°910'N

GUEBWILLER

SAERING

KITTERLÉ

La Lauch

47°896'N

Rimbach

Rohrgraben

Département
COMMUNE ....
Body of Water
LAND FEATURE

| Mi 0 | 0.31 | 0.62 | 0.93 | 1.24 |
| Km 0 | 0.5 | 1 | 1.5 | 2 |

Alsace
Grand Cru Vineyard AOC

7°156'E

Rimbach

47°873'N

WUENHEIM

Wuenheimerbach

OLLWILLER

VOSGES
MOUNTAINS

Haut-Rhin

47°838'N

La Thur

RANGEN

47°809'N

THANN

La Thur

VIEUX-THANN

Département
COMMUNE
Body of Water
LAND FEATURE

| Mi 0 | | 0.62 | 1.24 | 1.86 | 2.48 |
| Km 0 | 1 | 2 | 3 | 4 |

LORRAINE

AOC [2]

LUXEMBOURG
6°041'E

49°473'N

■ Merzig

GERMANY

Saar

■ Thionville
Moseille

■ Verdun

Metz ■ **MOSELLE**

49°114'N

Meuse

Moselle

Moselle

■ Dieuze

Saint-Mihiel ■

Meurthe-et-Moselle

Moselle

CÔTES DE TOUL

Nancy ■

Toul

Meurthe

Moselle

48°551'N

Mi	0	5.59	11.18	16.78	22.37
Km	0	9	18	27	36

Département — — —
Body of Water
COUNTRY — · — · —
Commune / City ■

JURA
TOTAL AOC [6]

GENERIC AOC [3]
OTHER AOC [3]

Subzone of Arbois AOC [1] ———

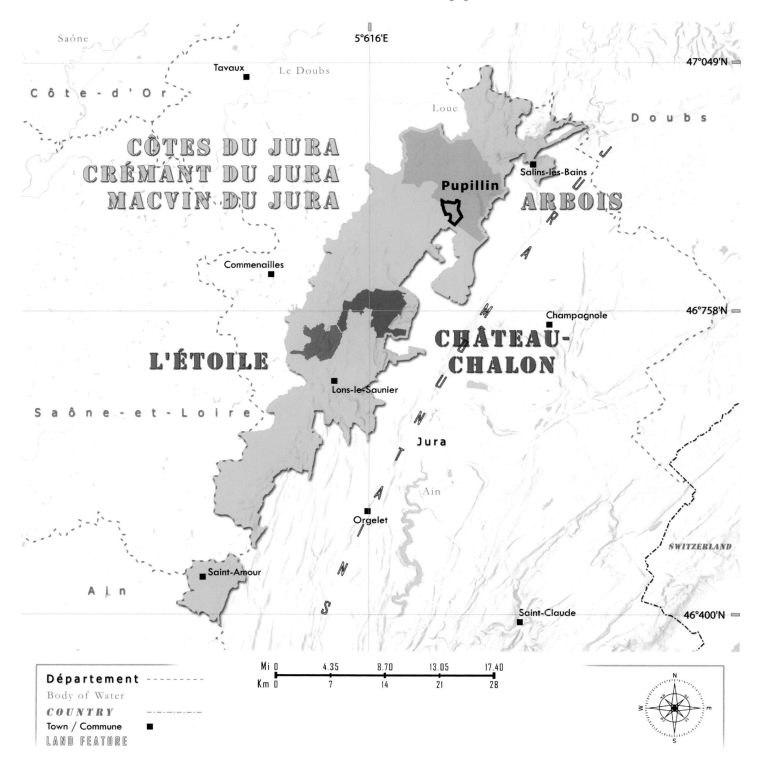

Saône

Tavaux

Le Doubs

5°616'E

47°049'N

Côte-d'Or

Loue

Doubs

CÔTES DU JURA
CRÉMANT DU JURA
MACVIN DU JURA

Salins-les-Bains

Pupillin

ARBOIS

J
U
R
A

Commenailles

Champagnole

46°758'N

L'ÉTOILE

CHÂTEAU-CHALON

Lons-le-Saunier

M
O
U
N
T
A
I
N
S

Saône-et-Loire

Jura

Ain

Orgelet

SWITZERLAND

Saint-Amour

Ain

Saint-Claude

46°400'N

| Mi | 0 | 4.35 | 8.70 | 13.05 | 17.40 |
| Km | 0 | 7 | 14 | 21 | 28 |

Département - - - - - - -
Body of Water
COUNTRY — · — · —
Town / Commune ■
LAND FEATURE

France

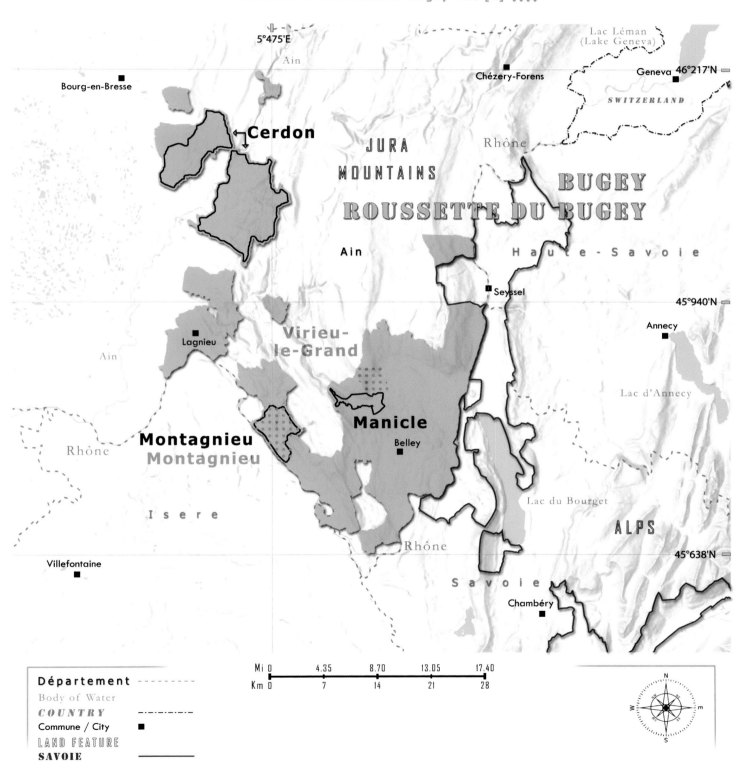

BUGEY

TOTAL AOC [2]

GENERIC AOC [2]

Subzone of Bugey AOC [3] ——
Subzone of Roussette du Bugey AOC [2] ::::

5°475'E

Ain

Lac Léman
(Lake Geneva)

Chézery-Forens

Geneva 46°217'N

SWITZERLAND

Bourg-en-Bresse

Cerdon

JURA
MOUNTAINS

Rhône

BUGEY

ROUSSETTE DU BUGEY

Ain

Haute-Savoie

Seyssel

45°940'N

Annecy

Lagnieu

Virieu-
le-Grand

Lac d'Annecy

Ain

Manicle

Montagnieu
Montagnieu

Belley

Rhône

Isere

Lac du Bourget

ALPS

Rhône

45°638'N

Villefontaine

Savoie

Chambéry

Mi 0   4.35   8.70   13.05   17.40
Km 0   7   14   21   28

Département ----------
Body of Water
COUNTRY —·—·—·—
Commune / City ■
LAND FEATURE
SAVOIE ————

N
W   E
S

SAVOIE

TOTAL AOC [4]

GENERIC AOC [3]
OTHER AOC [1]

Subzone of Roussette de Savoie AOC [4] ———
Denomination of Vin de Savoie AOC [16]

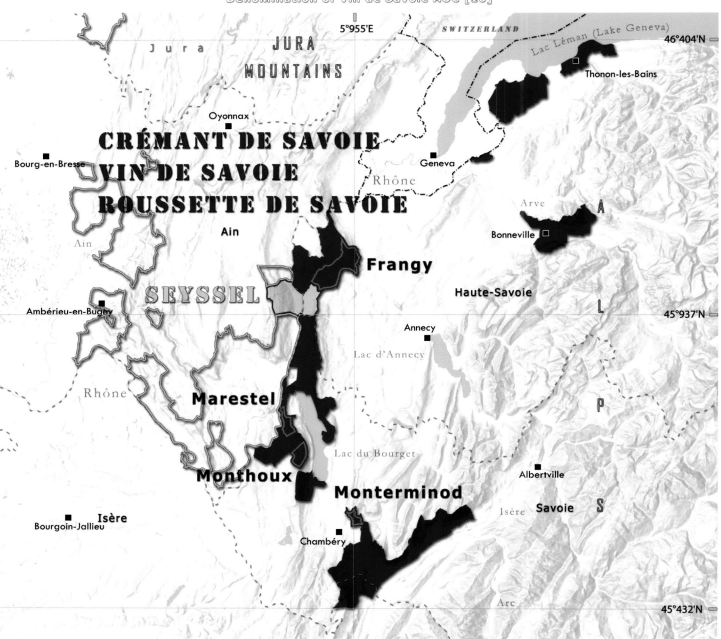

SWITZERLAND

Lac Léman (Lake Geneva)   46°404'N

5°955'E

JURA
MOUNTAINS

J u r a

Thonon-les-Bains

Oyonnax

CRÉMANT DE SAVOIE
Bourg-en-Bresse
VIN DE SAVOIE
Geneva
ROUSSETTE DE SAVOIE
Rhône

Arve   A

Ain

Bonneville

Frangy

L

Ain

SEYSSEL   Haute-Savoie

Ambérieu-en-Bugey   45°937'N

Annecy

Rhône   Lac d'Annecy

Marestel   P

Lac du Bourget

Monthoux

Monterminod

Albertville

Isère   Savoie   S

Isère

Bourgoin-Jallieu   Isère

Chambéry

Arc   45°432'N

Mi 0   5.59   11.18   16.78   22.37
Km 0   9   18   27   36

Département --------
Body of Water
COUNTRY — · — · —
Commune / City ■
LAND FEATURE
BUGEY
JURA

SAVOIE

Denomination of Vin de Savoie AOC [16]

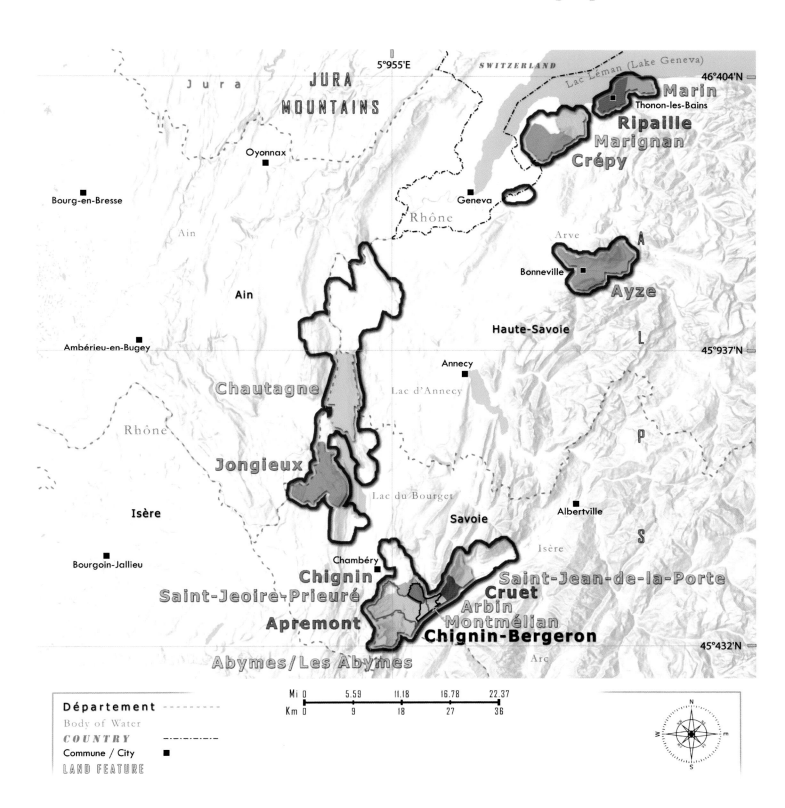

Jura

JURA MOUNTAINS

SWITZERLAND

Lac Léman (Lake Geneva)

46°404'N

Marin

Thonon-les-Bains

Ripaille

Marignan

Crépy

Oyonnax

Bourg-en-Bresse

Geneva

Rhône

Ain

Ain

Arve

A

Bonneville

Ayze

Haute-Savoie

L

Ambérieu-en-Bugey

45°937'N

Chautagne

Annecy

Lac d'Annecy

Rhône

P

Jongieux

Lac du Bourget

Albertville

S

Isère

Savoie

Isère

Bourgoin-Jallieu

Chambéry

Chignin

Saint-Jean-de-la-Porte

Saint-Jeoire-Prieuré

Cruet

Arbin

Apremont

Montmélian

Chignin-Bergeron

45°432'N

Abymes/Les Abymes

Arc

Département
Body of Water
COUNTRY
Commune / City ■
LAND FEATURE

| Mi 0 | 5.59 | 11.18 | 16.78 | 22.37 |
| Km 0 | 9 | 18 | 27 | 36 |

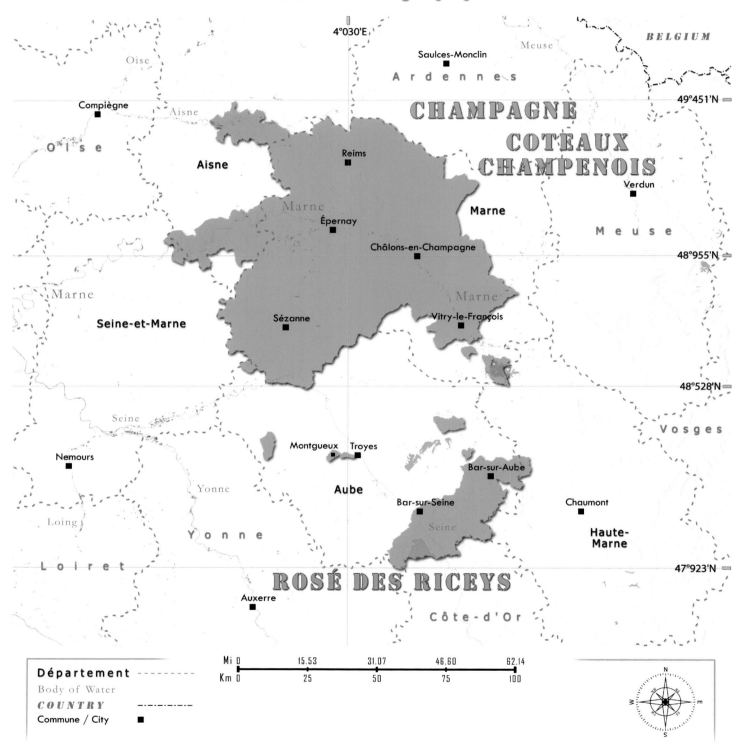

CHAMPAGNE
TOTAL AOC [3]

GENERIC AOC [2]
OTHER AOC [1]

Grand Cru Villages [17]

4°030'E

BELGIUM

Meuse

Saulces-Monclin

Ardennes

49°451'N

Compiègne

Oise

Aisne

CHAMPAGNE

Oise

Aisne

COTEAUX
CHAMPENOIS

Reims

Verdun

Marne

Marne

Meuse

Épernay

Châlons-en-Champagne

48°955'N

Marne

Marne

Sézanne

Vitry-le-François

Seine-et-Marne

48°528'N

Vosges

Seine

Montgueux   Troyes

Nemours

Yonne

Aube

Bar-sur-Aube

Loing

Bar-sur-Seine

Chaumont

Yonne

Seine

Haute-
Marne

Loiret

47°923'N

ROSÉ DES RICEYS

Auxerre

Côte-d'Or

| Mi | 0 | | 15.53 | | 31.07 | | 46.60 | | 62.14 |
| Km | 0 | | 25 | | 50 | | 75 | | 100 |

Département - - - - - - -

Body of Water

COUNTRY - · - · - · -

Commune / City ■

N
W · E
S

CHAMPAGNE
Grand Cru Villages [17]

Montagne de Reims [9]
Vallée de la Marne [2]
Côte des Blancs [6]

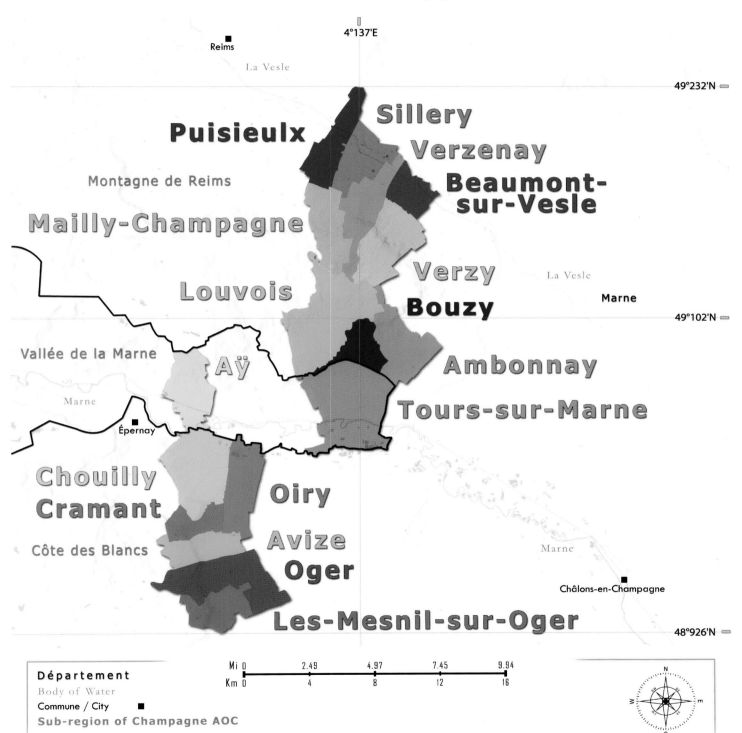

Reims

La Vesle

4°137'E

49°232'N

Puisieulx

Sillery

Verzenay

Montagne de Reims

Beaumont-
sur-Vesle

Mailly-Champagne

Verzy

La Vesle

Louvois

Bouzy

Marne

49°102'N

Vallée de la Marne

Aÿ

Ambonnay

Marne

Tours-sur-Marne

Épernay

Chouilly
Cramant

Oiry

Côte des Blancs

Avize
Oger

Marne

Châlons-en-Champagne

Les-Mesnil-sur-Oger

48°926'N

| Mi 0 | 2.49 | 4.97 | 7.45 | 9.94 |
| Km 0 | 4 | 8 | 12 | 16 |

Département
Body of Water
Commune / City ■
Sub-region of Champagne AOC

BURGUNDY
TOTAL AOC [86]

GENERIC AOC [6]
Sub-regions of Burgundy - AOC [80]

Montargis

5°042'E

48°056'N

Auxerre

Langres

Yonne

Grand Auxerrois [6]

Loire

Saône

Sancerre

Côte d'Or

47°324'N

Dijon

BOURGOGNE

Côte de Nuits [34]

BOURGOGNE ALIGOTÉ

Beaune

Côte de Beaune [28]

Nevers

CRÉMANT DE BOURGOGNE

Côte Chalonnaise [5]

BOURGOGNE MOUSSEUX

Chalon-sur-Saône

Saône

46°673'N

CÔTEAUX BOURGUIGNONS

Ain

SWITZERLAND

Saône-et-Loire

BOURGOGNE PASSE-TOUT-GRAINS

Lac Léman (Lake Geneva)

Mâconnais [7]

Mâcon

Allier River

Rhône

Roanne

Loire

Lac du Bourget

MASSIF

45°807'N

Clermont-Ferrand

CENTRAL

Rhône

Lyon

Rhône

| Mi | 0 | 15.53 | 31.06 | 46.60 | 62.13 |
| Km | 0 | 25 | 50 | 75 | 100 |

Département ---------
Body of Water
COUNTRY — - — - —
Town / City ■
LAND FEATURE

Bourgogne AOC
Subzone of Bourgogne [14]

5°042'E

48°056'N

Montargis

Côte Saint-Jacques

Tonnerre

Côtes d'Auxerre

Auxerre

Langres

Epineuil

Yonne

Chitry

Coulanges-la-Vineuse

Loire

Côte d'Or

Dijon

Saône

Sancerre

Montrecul

47°324'N

Le Chapitre

Hautes Côtes de Nuits

Côte d'Or

Hautes Côtes de Beaune

Nevers

La Chapelle Notre-Dame

Côtes du Couchois

Beaune

Côte Chalonnaise

Chalon-sur-Saône

Saône

46°673'N

Moulins

Saône-et-Loire

Ain

SWITZERLAND

Allier River

Mâcon

Roanne

Loire

Rhône

45°807'N

Clermont-Ferrand

MASSIF CENTRAL

Rhône

Lyon

Rhône

Rhône

JURA MOUNTAINS

Mi	0	15.53	31.06	46.60	62.13
Km	0	25	50	75	100

Département - - - - - - - - -

Body of Water

COUNTRY — — — — —

Town / City ■

LAND FEATURE

Grand Auxerrois
AOC [6]

Joigny

Saint-Florentin

Yonne

3°802'E

47°962'N

Tonnerre

CHABLIS
GRAND CRU

Auxerre

CHABLIS
(INCL 1ER CRU)

SAINT-BRIS

PETIT CHABLIS

47°695'N

Yonne

Montbard

IRANCY

Avallon

VÉZELAY

47°428'N

Département ----------
Body of Water
City / Commune ■

Mi 0	15.53	31.06	46.60	62.13
Km 0	25	50	75	100

N
W   E
S

Chablis AOC
Premier Cru Vineyards [40]
COMMUNE OF CHABLIS [17]
Petit Chablis AOC
Chablis Grand Cru AOC

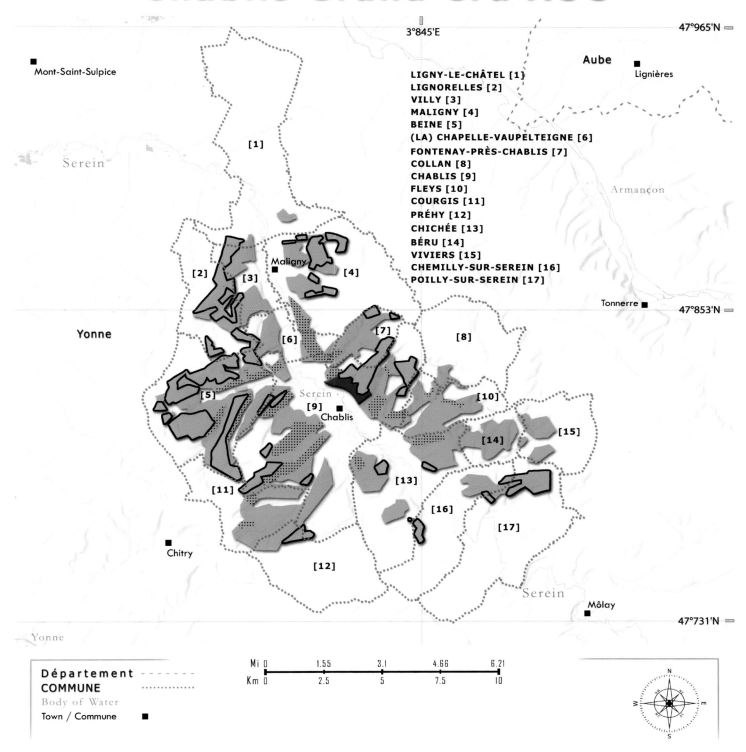

47°965'N

3°845'E

Aube

Lignières

Mont-Saint-Sulpice

LIGNY-LE-CHÂTEL [1]
LIGNORELLES [2]
VILLY [3]
MALIGNY [4]
BEINE [5]
(LA) CHAPELLE-VAUPELTEIGNE [6]
FONTENAY-PRÈS-CHABLIS [7]
COLLAN [8]
CHABLIS [9]
FLEYS [10]
COURGIS [11]
PRÉHY [12]
CHICHÉE [13]
BÉRU [14]
VIVIERS [15]
CHEMILLY-SUR-SEREIN [16]
POILLY-SUR-SEREIN [17]

Serein

Armançon

Maligny

[1]

[2]   [3]   [4]

Yonne

[6]   [7]   [8]

Tonnerre

47°853'N

[5]   Serein   [10]

[9]
Chablis

[15]

[14]

[11]   [13]

[16]

[17]

Chitry

[12]

Serein

Môlay

47°731'N

Yonne

Département – – – – – –
COMMUNE   ············
Body of Water
Town / Commune   ■

Mi 0   1.55   3.1   4.66   6.21
Km 0   2.5   5   7.5   10

Chablis AOC
PREMIER CRU UMBRELLA VINEYARDS [17]
Premier Cru Vineyards [23]

VILLY

MALIGNY

3°805'E

Serein

Yonne

47°859'N

LIGNORELLES

L'Homme Mort

FONTENAY-
PRÈS-CHABLIS

COLLAN

(LA) CHAPELLE-
VAUPELTEIGNE

FOURCHAUME

Côte de
Fontenay

BEAUROY

Troësmes

Vaupulent

Vaulorent

BERDIOT

CÔTE DE
VAUBAROUSSE

Côte de Savant

Côte de
Bréchain

Morein

LES
FOURNEAUX

BEINE

CÔTE DE LÊCHET

VAU DE VEY

MONTÉE DE
TONNERRE

Pied
d'Aloup

47°817'N

VAU
LIGNEAU

CHABLIS

Les Lys

Sécher Chapelot

Côte des Prés-Girots

FLEYS

MONT DE MILIEU

VAILLONS

Chatains

Les
Épinottes

Vaux Ragons

Beugnons

BÉRU

Mélinots

MONTMAINS

VAUCOUPIN

Roncières

Vaugiraut

Butteaux

Forêts

VOSGROS

COURGIS

Serein

CHEMILLY-SUR-SEREIN

CHAUME DE
TALVAT

CÔTE DE JOUAN

Côte de Cuissy

CHICHÉE

47°767'N

LES BEAUREGARDS

POILLY-
SUR-SEREIN

PRÉHY

Département
COMMUNE ....
Body of Water
Chablis Grand Cru ///////

Mi 0   0.62   1.24   1.86   2.48
Km 0   1   2   3   4

CHABLIS GRAND CRU AOC

Lieux-dits
7 official
1 unofficial

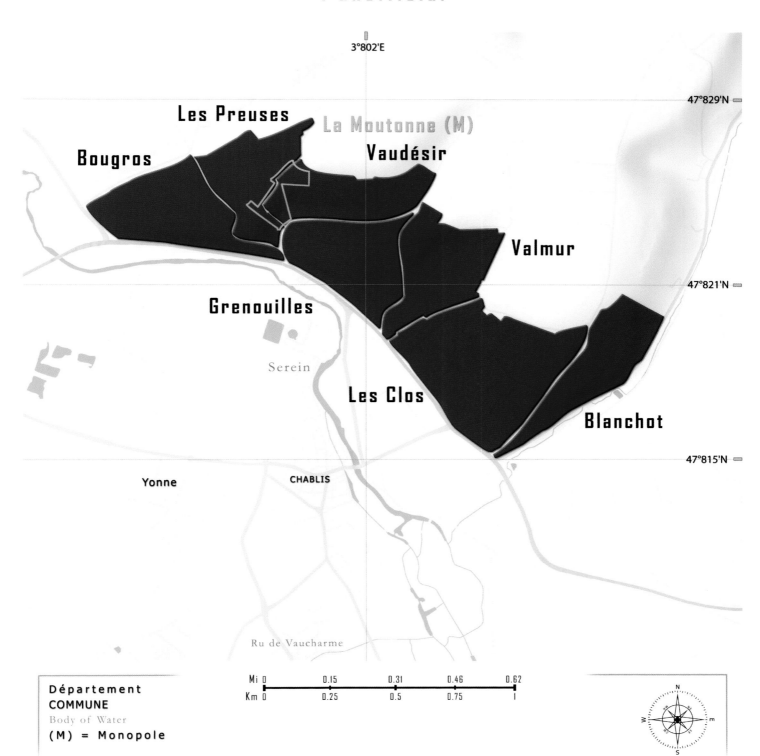

3°802'E

47°829'N

Les Preuses

La Moutonne (M)

Bougros

Vaudésir

Valmur

47°821'N

Grenouilles

Serein

Les Clos

Blanchot

47°815'N

Yonne

CHABLIS

Ru de Vaucharme

Mi 0   0.15   0.31   0.46   0.62
Km 0   0.25   0.5   0.75   1

Département
COMMUNE
Body of Water
(M) = Monopole

Côte de Nuits
AOC [34]

Fixin AOC
Premier Cru Vineyards [6]

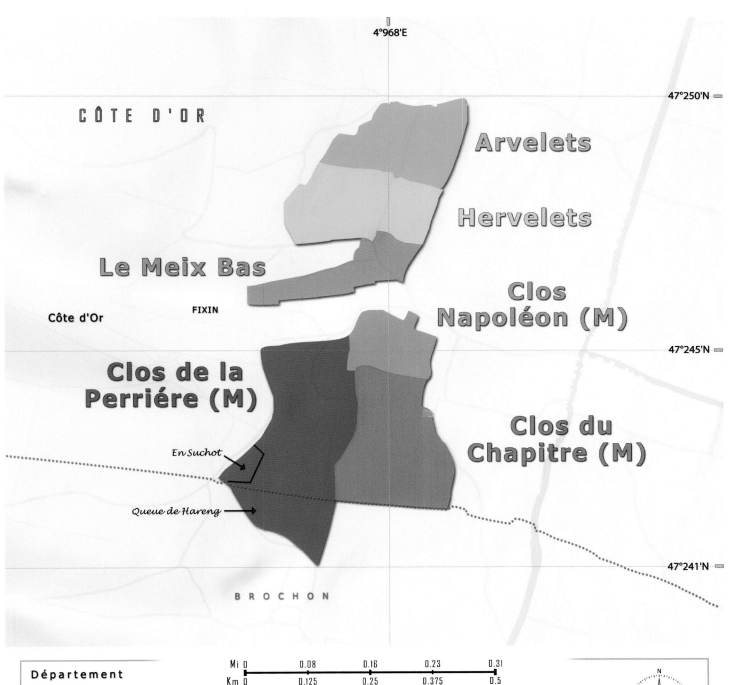

CÔTE D'OR

Arvelets

Hervelets

Le Meix Bas

Côte d'Or

FIXIN

Clos Napoléon (M)

Clos de la Perriére (M)

Clos du Chapitre (M)

En Suchot

Queue de Hareng

BROCHON

47°250'N

47°245'N

47°241'N

4°968'E

Département
COMMUNE
Body of Water
Lieu-dit
(M) = Monopole
LAND FEATURE

Mi 0   0.08   0.16   0.23   0.31
Km 0   0.125   0.25   0.375   0.5

Gevrey-Chambertin AOC

GRAND CRU VINEYARDS [9]
Premier Cru Vineyards [26]

BROCHON

47°235'N

CÔTE D'OR

Les Goulots

Champeaux

Combe Au Moine

Petits Cazetiers

Estournelles-
Saint-Jacques

Les Cazetiers

Poissenot

Clos Saint-Jacques

La Romanée (M)

Clos Du Chapitre (M)

La Bossiére (M)

Craipillot

Clos Des Varoilles (M)

Fonteny

GEVREY-CHAMBERTIN

Lavaut Saint-Jacques

Les Corbeaux

Champonnet

Au Closeau

Issarts (M)

47°221'N

RUCHOTTES-CHAMBERTIN

La Perriére

MAZIS-CHAMBERTIN

Clos Prieur

Cherbaudes

Bel Air

Petite Chapelle

En Ergot

CHAMBERTIN-CLOS DE BÉZE

CHAPELLE-CHAMBERTIN

Côte d'Or

Les Gémeaux

CHAMBERTIN

GRIOTTE-CHAMBERTIN

La Boïse

CHARMES-CHAMBERTIN

MAZOYÉRES-CHAMBERTIN

LATRICIÉRES-
CHAMBERTIN

La Manssouse

Aux Combottes

MOREY- SAINT-DENIS

47°204'N

Mi 0   0.16   0.31   0.47   0.62

Km 0   0.25   0.5   0.75   1

Département
COMMUNE
Body of Water
Lieu-dit
(M) = Monopole
LAND FEATURE

Morey-Saint-Denis AOC

GRAND CRU VINEYARDS [4+1]
Premier Cru Vineyards [20]

La Manssouse

GEVREY-CHAMBERTIN

47°207'N

CÔTE D'OR

CLOS DE LA ROCHE
Monts Luisants [1]
Les Genavriéres [2]
Les Froichots [3]
Les Mochamps [4]
Les Fremiéres [5]
Les Chabiots [6]

Monts Luisants

Aux Charmes

Aux Cheseaux

Les Genavriéres

Les Chaffots

Clos des Ormes

CLOS ST-DENIS
Les Chaffots [7]
Calouère [8]
Maison Brûlée [9]

Les Charriéres

Les Faconniéres

Les Millandes

Côte Rotie

Les Chenevery

47°199'N

CLOS DES LAMBRAYS
Les Bouchots [10]
Meix Rentier [11]

Le Village

La Riotte

Les Gruenchers

Les Blanchards

Clos Baulet

Côte d'Or

Clos Sorbé

MOREY-SAINT-DENIS

CLOS DE TART (M)

Les Sorbés

BONNES-MARES
(SHARED)

Les Ruchots

La Bussiére (M)

CHAMBOLLE-MUSIGNY

47°192'N

| Mi 0 | 0.16 | 0.31 | 0.47 | 0.62 |
| Km 0 | 0.25 | 0.5 | 0.75 | 1 |

Département
COMMUNE ....
Body of Water
Lieu-dit _____
(M) = Monopole
LAND FEATURE

Chambolle-Musigny AOC

GRAND CRU VINEYARDS [1+1]
Premier Cru Vineyards [24]

4°957'E

MOREY-SAINT-DENIS

47°194'N

BONNES-MARES
(SHARED)

CÔTE D'OR   Les Véroilles

Les Sentiers
Les Baudes
Les Fuées   Les Lavrottes
Les Noirots
Derriére la Grange   Les Gruenchers
Les Groseilles
Les Cras   Aux Beaux Bruns
CHAMBOLLE-MUSIGNY   Les Carriéres   Aux Échanges (M)   47°186'N
Les Chatelots   Aux Combottes
Les Feusselottes   Les Combottes
Les Chabiots   Les Plantes
Les Borniques   Les Charmes

FLAGEY-
ECHÉZEAUX

Les Hauts Doix

Côte d'Or   Les Amoureuses

La Combe d'Orveau   MUSIGNY
Les Petits Musigny
La Combe d'Orveau

47°174'N

VOUGEOT

FLAGEY-ECHÉZEAUX   Vouge

Mi 0   0.16   0.31   0.47   0.62
Km 0   0.25   0.5   0.75   1

Département
COMMUNE   ....
Body of Water
Lieu-dit   —————
(M) = Monopole
LAND FEATURE

Vougeot AOC

GRAND CRU VINEYARD [1]
Premier Cru Vineyards [4]

CHAMBOLLE - MUSIGNY

4°958'E

47°178'N

CÔTE D'OR

Les Petits Vougeots

GILLY-
LÈS-
CÎTEAUX

Clos de la Perriére (M)

Le Clos Blanc (M)

Les Crâs

Vouge

VOUGEOT

47°173'N

CLOS DE VOUGEOT

Côte d'Or

47°167'N

FLAGEY - ECHÉZEAUX

Mi 0   0.12   0.24   0.36   0.48
Km 0   0.2   0.4   0.6   0.8

Département
COMMUNE   ················
Body of Water
(M) = Monopole
LAND FEATURE

Vosne-Romanée AOC

GRAND CRU VINEYARDS [8]
Premier Cru Vineyards [14]

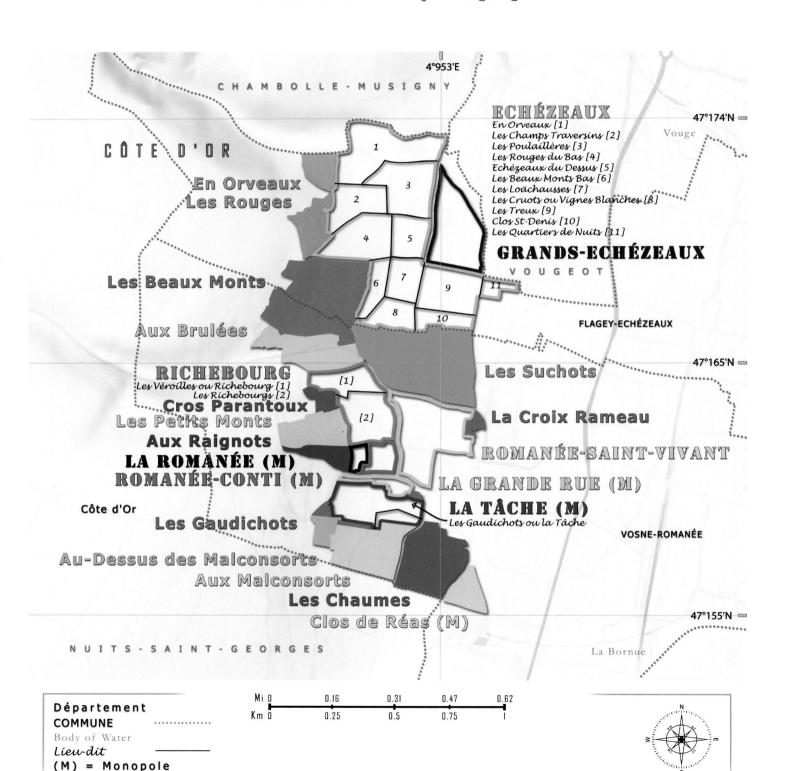

CHAMBOLLE - MUSIGNY

4°953'E

47°174'N

Vouge

CÔTE D'OR

En Orveaux
Les Rouges

ECHÉZEAUX
En Orveaux [1]
Les Champs Traversins [2]
Les Poulaillères [3]
Les Rouges du Bas [4]
Echézeaux du Dessus [5]
Les Beaux Monts Bas [6]
Les Loächausses [7]
Les Cruots ou Vignes Blanches [8]
Les Treux [9]
Clos St-Denis [10]
Les Quartiers de Nuits [11]

GRANDS-ECHÉZEAUX
V O U G E O T

Les Beaux Monts

Aux Brulées

FLAGEY-ECHÉZEAUX

47°165'N

RICHEBOURG
Les Véroilles ou Richebourg [1]
Les Richebourgs [2]
Cros Parantoux
Les Petits Monts
Aux Raignots
LA ROMANÉE (M)
ROMANÉE-CONTI (M)

Les Suchots

[1]

[2]

La Croix Rameau

ROMANÉE-SAINT-VIVANT

LA GRANDE RUE (M)

Côte d'Or

Les Gaudichots

LA TÂCHE (M)
Les Gaudichots ou la Tâche

VOSNE-ROMANÉE

Au-Dessus des Malconsorts
Aux Malconsorts

Les Chaumes
Clos de Réas (M)

47°155'N

N U I T S - S A I N T - G E O R G E S

La Bornue

Mi 0   0.16   0.31   0.47   0.62
Km 0   0.25   0.5   0.75   1

Département
COMMUNE ....
Body of Water
Lieu-dit ————
(M) = Monopole
LAND FEATURE

Nuits-Saint-Georges AOC
Premier Cru Vineyards [41]

NUITS-SAINT-GEORGES (NORTH) [12]
NUITS-SAINT-GEORGES (SOUTH) [17]
PREMEAUX-PRISSEY [12]

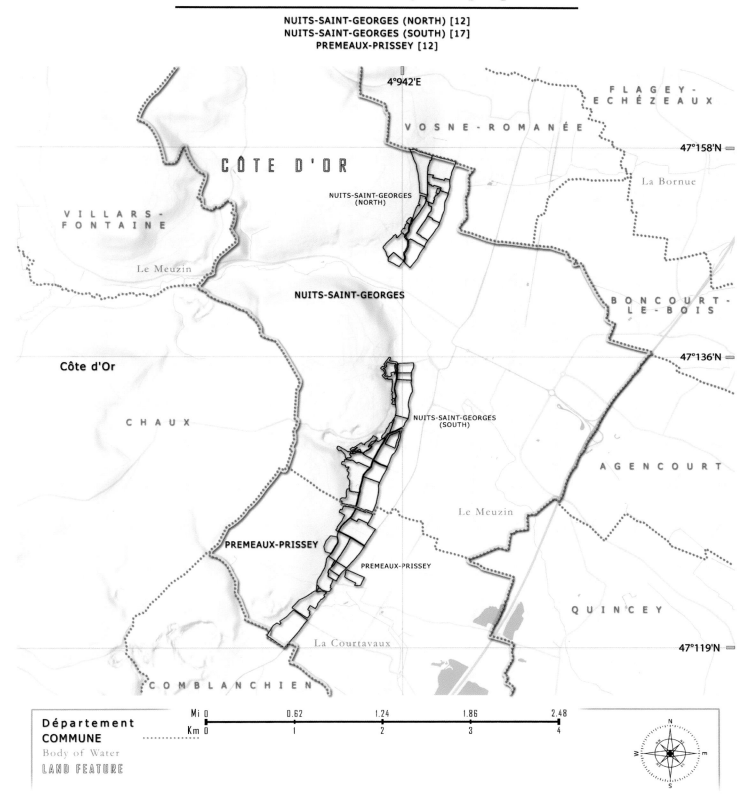

FLAGEY-ECHÉZEAUX

4°942'E

VOSNE-ROMANÉE

47°158'N

CÔTE D'OR

La Bornue

NUITS-SAINT-GEORGES (NORTH)

VILLARS-FONTAINE

Le Meuzin

NUITS-SAINT-GEORGES

BONCOURT-LE-BOIS

47°136'N

Côte d'Or

CHAUX

NUITS-SAINT-GEORGES (SOUTH)

AGENCOURT

Le Meuzin

PREMEAUX-PRISSEY

PREMEAUX-PRISSEY

QUINCEY

47°119'N

La Courtavaux

COMBLANCHIEN

| Mi | 0 | 0.62 | 1.24 | 1.86 | 2.48 |
| Km | 0 | 1 | 2 | 3 | 4 |

Département
COMMUNE
Body of Water
LAND FEATURE

Nuits-Saint-Georges (north)
Premier Cru Vineyards [12]

4°949'E

VOSNE-ROMANÉE

CÔTE D'OR

47°158'N

Les Damodes

Aux Boudots

Aux Cras

La Bornue

NUITS-SAINT-GEORGES
(NORTH)

La Richemone

Côte d'Or

Aux Murgers

Aux Chaignots

47°151'N

En la Perriére Noblot (M)

Aux Champs Perdrix

Aux Vignerondes

Aux Thorey

Aux Argillas

Aux Bousselots

47°145'N

Le Meuzin

Département
COMMUNE ················
Body of Water
LAND FEATURE
(M) = Monopole

| Mi | 0 | 0.12 | 0.24 | 0.36 | 0.48 |
| Km | 0 | 0.2 | 0.4 | 0.6 | 0.8 |

Nuits-Saint-Georges (south)
Premier Cru Vineyards [17]

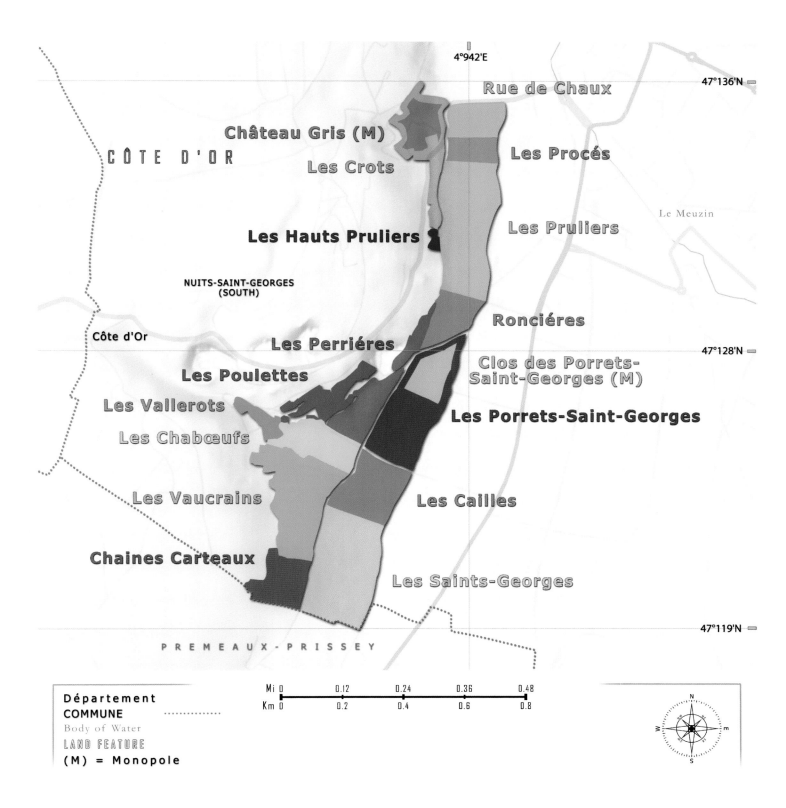

47°136'N
4°942'E
Rue de Chaux
Château Gris (M)
CÔTE D'OR
Les Crots
Les Procés
Le Meuzin
Les Hauts Pruliers
Les Pruliers
NUITS-SAINT-GEORGES (SOUTH)
Ronciéres
Côte d'Or
47°128'N
Les Perriéres
Clos des Porrets-Saint-Georges (M)
Les Poulettes
Les Vallerots
Les Porrets-Saint-Georges
Les Chabœufs
Les Vaucrains
Les Cailles
Chaines Carteaux
Les Saints-Georges
47°119'N
PREMEAUX-PRISSEY

Département
COMMUNE
Body of Water
LAND FEATURE
(M) = Monopole

Mi 0   0.12   0.24   0.36   0.48
Km 0   0.2   0.4   0.6   0.8

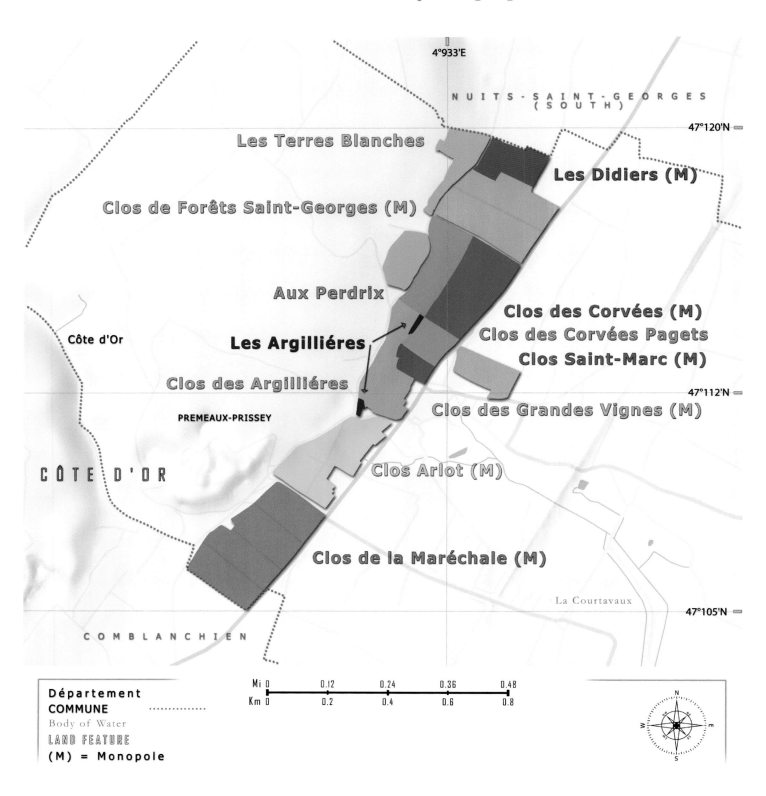

Nuits-Saint-Georges
(Premeaux-Prissey)
Premier Cru Vineyards [12]

4°933'E

NUITS-SAINT-GEORGES
(SOUTH)

47°120'N

Les Terres Blanches

Les Didiers (M)

Clos de Forêts Saint-Georges (M)

Aux Perdrix

Clos des Corvées (M)

Les Argilliéres

Clos des Corvées Pagets

Clos Saint-Marc (M)

Côte d'Or

Clos des Argilliéres

47°112'N

PREMEAUX-PRISSEY

Clos des Grandes Vignes (M)

CÔTE D'OR

Clos Arlot (M)

Clos de la Maréchale (M)

La Courtavaux

47°105'N

COMBLANCHIEN

Département
COMMUNE
Body of Water
LAND FEATURE
(M) = Monopole

Mi 0   0.12   0.24   0.36   0.48
Km 0   0.2   0.4   0.6   0.8

Côte de Beaune

AOC [28]

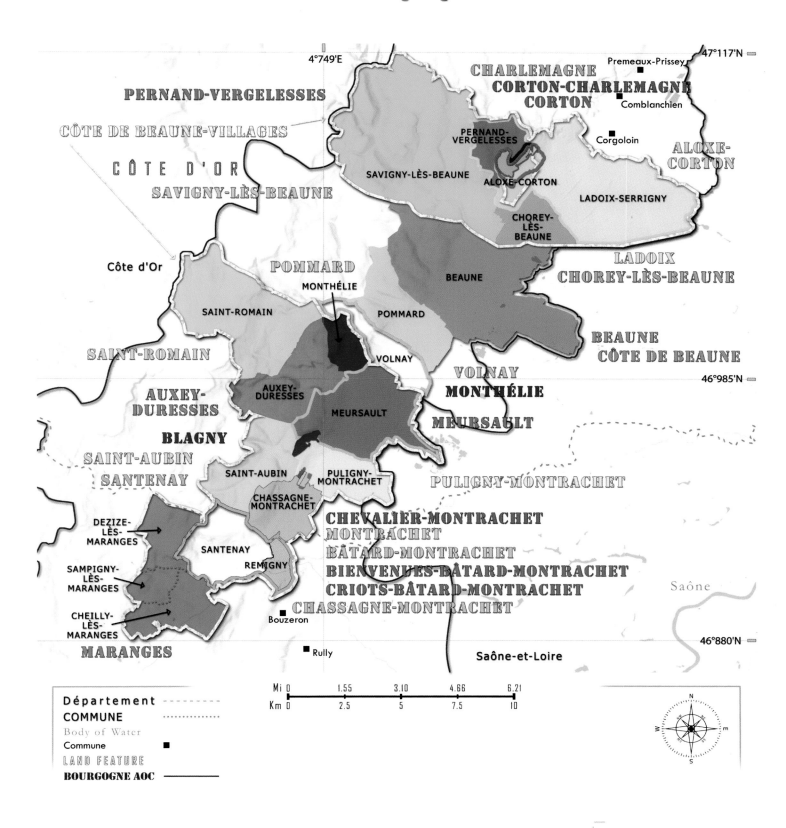

The Hill of Corton
GRAND CRU VINEYARDS [3 SHARED]
Premier Cru Vineyards [33]

Aloxe-Corton [14]
Pernand-Vergelesses [8]
Ladoix [11]

CÔTE D'OR

4°866'E

Côte d'Or

CORGOLOIN

Les Grêchons et Foutriéres LS

LADOIX-SERRIGNY

47°086'N

Les Buis LS

En Naget LS

La Corvée LS

Le Clou d'Orge LS

Sous Frétille PV

Hautes Mourottes LS

Basses Mourottes LS

Clos Berthet (M) PV

Le Rognet et Corton LS

La Micaude (M) LS

Village de Pernand (M) PV

Les Joyeuses LS

PERNAND-VERGELESSES

Bois Roussot LS

En Caradeux PV

En Charlemagne [1]
Le Charlemagne [2]
Les Pougets [3]
Les Languettes [4]
Le Corton [5]

Les Moutottes AC

Les Petites Loliéres AC

1

5

La Coutiére AC

Creux de la Net PV

CHARLEMAGNE

2

CORTON-CHARLEMAGNE

4

La Toppe au Vert AC

Clos des Maréchauds (M) AC

47°072'N

CORTON

3

La Maréchaude AC

Les Fichots PV

Les Maréchaudes AC

Les Paulands AC

Les Valoziéres AC

La Lauve

Les Chaillots AC

Les Fourniéres AC

Clos du Chapitre AC

Les Guérets AC
Les Vercots AC

47°062'N

Ile des Vergelesses Vergelesses PV PV
Vergelesses

ALOXE-CORTON

Les Échances

SAVIGNY-LÉS-BEAUNE

CHOREY-LÉS-BEAUNE

Mi 0   0.16   0.31   0.47   0.62
Km 0   0.25   0.5   0.75   1

Département
COMMUNE ....
Body of Water
Lieu-dit ————
(M) = Monopole
LAND FEATURE

Savigny-lès-Beaune AOC
Premier Cru Vineyards [22]

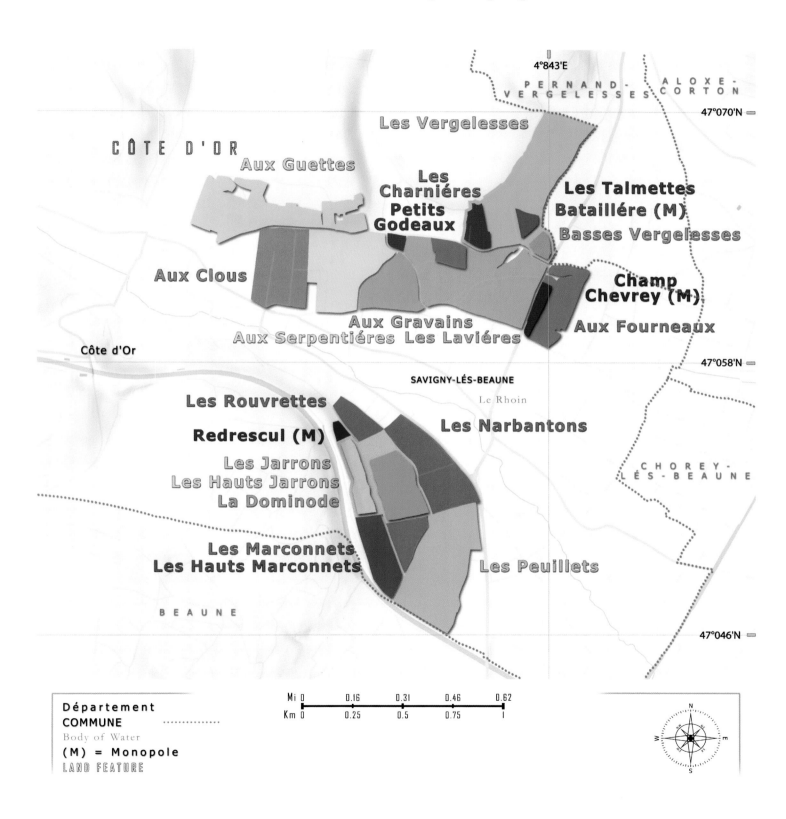

4°843'E

PERNAND-VERGELESSES

ALOXE-CORTON

47°070'N

Les Vergelesses

CÔTE D'OR

Aux Guettes

Les Charniéres

Petits Godeaux

Les Talmettes

Bataillére (M)

Basses Vergelesses

Aux Clous

Champ Chevrey (M)

Aux Gravains

Aux Serpentiéres   Les Laviéres

Aux Fourneaux

Côte d'Or

47°058'N

SAVIGNY-LÉS-BEAUNE

Le Rhoin

Les Rouvrettes

Les Narbantons

Redrescul (M)

CHOREY-LÈS-BEAUNE

Les Jarrons
Les Hauts Jarrons
La Dominode

Les Marconnets
Les Hauts Marconnets

Les Peuillets

BEAUNE

47°046'N

Département
COMMUNE ....
Body of Water
(M) = Monopole
LAND FEATURE

Mi 0   0.16   0.31   0.46   0.62
Km 0   0.25   0.5   0.75   1

N

Beaune AOC
Premier Cru Vineyards [42]

S A V I G N Y - L É S - B E A U N E

4°817'E

47°049'N

Le Rhoin

Les Marconnets

C Ô T E   D ' O R

En L'orme

Les Perriéres

Clos de l'Ecu (M)

Blanches Fleurs

A l'Ecu

Clos du Roi

Les Féves

En Genêt

Les Bressandes

Les Cents Vignes

Les Toussaints

Les Gréves

BEAUNE

Sur les Gréves-Clos Sainte-Anne (M)

Sur les Gréves

47°032'N

Aux Coucherias

Clos de la Feguine (M)

Le Bas des Teurons

Montée Rouge

Aux Cras

La Mignotte

Les Teurons

Côte d'Or

Clos des Avaux

Les Seurey

Champs Pimont

Clos de la Mousse (M)

Les Sizies

Les Reversés

Pertuisots

Les Sceaux

Les Aigrots

Belissand

Clos des Ursules (M)

Les Avaux

Les Tuvilains

Clos Saint-Landry (M)

Les Montrevenots

Les Chouacheux

Les Vignes Franches

Le Clos des Mouches

Les Boucherottes

La Bouzaise

Les Epenotes

47°013'N

P O M M A R D

Mi 0   0.31   0.62   0.93   1.24

Km 0   0.5   1   1.5   2

Département

COMMUNE   ....

Body of Water

(M) = Monopole

LAND FEATURE

Pommard AOC
Premier Cru Vineyards [28]

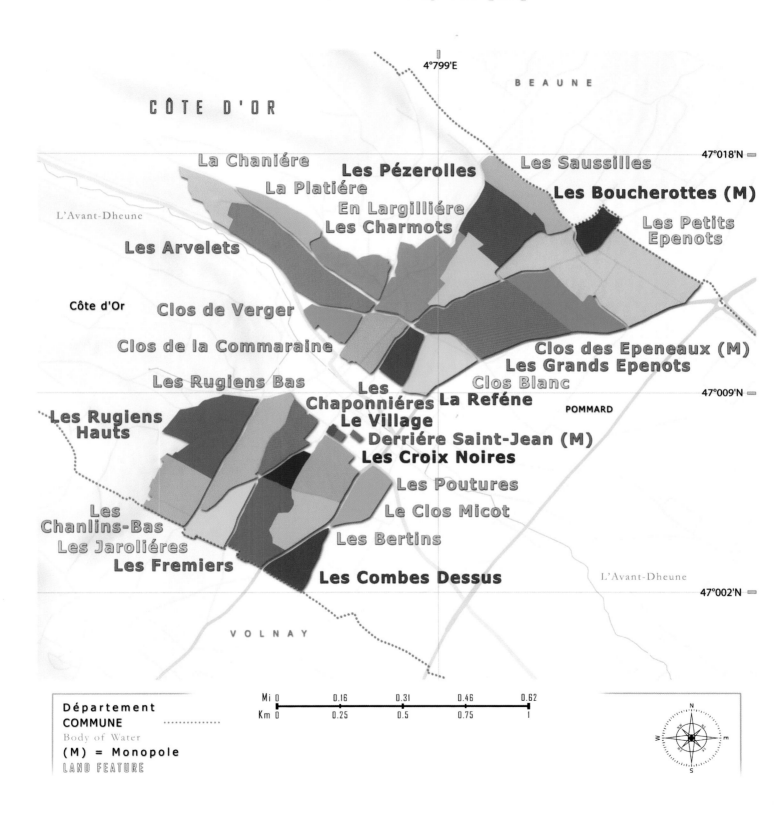

CÔTE D'OR

BEAUNE

4°799'E

47°018'N

La Chaniére
Les Pézerolles
Les Saussilles
La Platiére
Les Boucherottes (M)
L'Avant-Dheune
En Largilliére
Les Charmots
Les Petits Epenots
Les Arvelets
Clos de Verger
Côte d'Or
Clos de la Commaraine
Clos des Epeneaux (M)
Les Grands Epenots
Les Rugiens Bas
Clos Blanc
47°009'N
Les
Chaponniéres
La Reféne
POMMARD
Le Village
Les Rugiens
Hauts
Derriére Saint-Jean (M)
Les Croix Noires
Les Poutures
Le Clos Micot
Les
Chanlins-Bas
Les Jaroliéres
Les Bertins
Les Fremiers
L'Avant-Dheune
Les Combes Dessus
47°002'N

VOLNAY

	Mi 0	0.16	0.31	0.46	0.62
	Km 0	0.25	0.5	0.75	1

Département
COMMUNE ....
Body of Water
(M) = Monopole
LAND FEATURE

N
W   E
S

Volnay AOC
Premier Cru Vineyards [29]

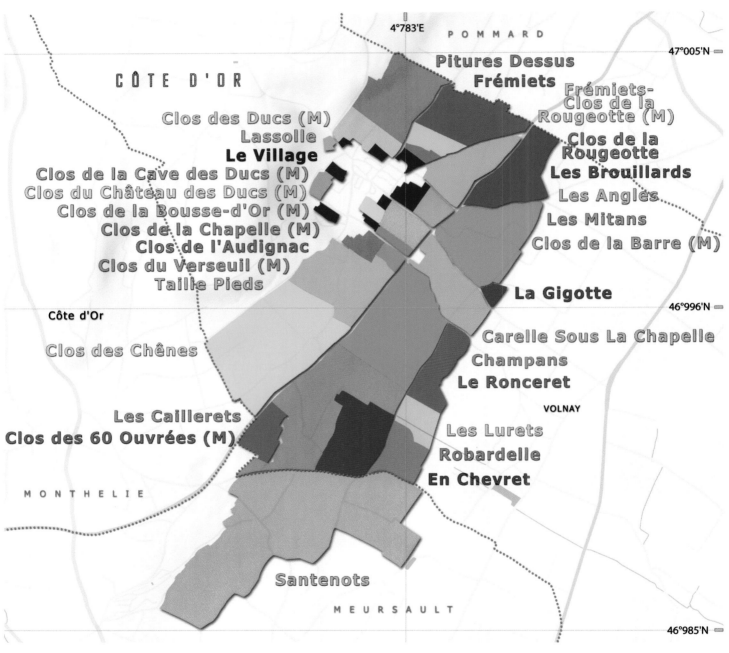

POMMARD

47°005'N

CÔTE D'OR

Pitures Dessus
Frémiets

Frémiets-
Clos de la
Rougeotte (M)

Clos des Ducs (M)
Lassolle
Le Village

Clos de la
Rougeotte

Clos de la Cave des Ducs (M)
Clos du Château des Ducs (M)
Clos de la Bousse-d'Or (M)
Clos de la Chapelle (M)
Clos de l'Audignac
Clos du Verseuil (M)
Taille Pieds

Les Brouillards
Les Angles
Les Mitans
Clos de la Barre (M)

La Gigotte

46°996'N

Côte d'Or

Carelle Sous La Chapelle
Champans
Le Ronceret

Clos des Chênes

VOLNAY

Les Caillerets
Clos des 60 Ouvrées (M)

Les Lurets
Robardelle
En Chevret

MONTHELIE

Santenots

MEURSAULT

46°985'N

| Mi 0 | 0.16 | 0.31 | 0.46 | 0.62 |
| Km 0 | 0.25 | 0.5 | 0.75 | 1 |

Département
COMMUNE ....
Body of Water
(M) = Monopole
LAND FEATURE

Meursault AOC
Premier Cru Vineyards [19]

MEURSAULT (NORTH) [5]
MEURSAULT (SOUTH) [14]

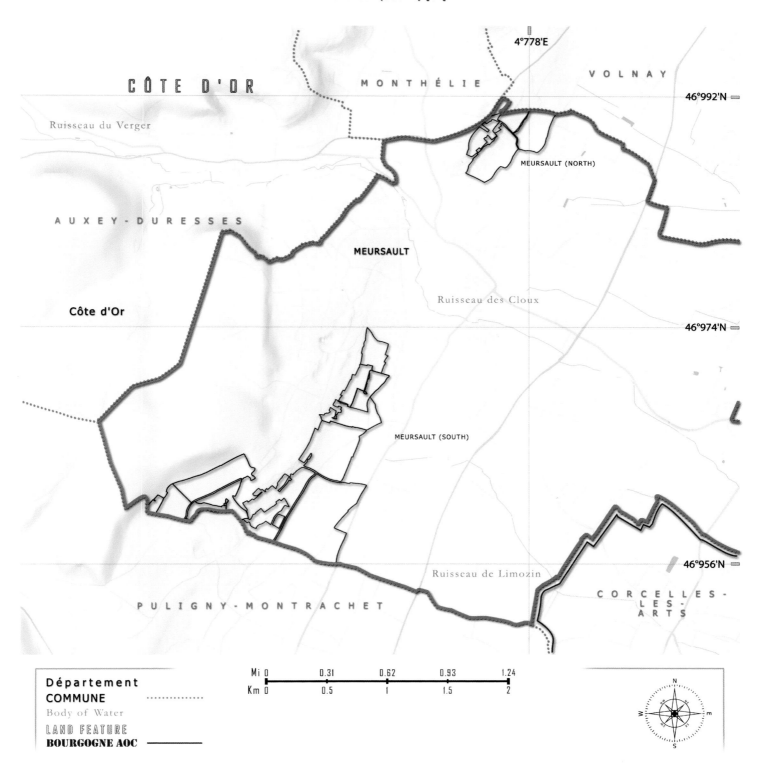

CÔTE D'OR

MONTHÉLIE

VOLNAY

4°778'E

46°992'N

Ruisseau du Verger

MEURSAULT (NORTH)

AUXEY-DURESSES

MEURSAULT

Côte d'Or

Ruisseau des Cloux

46°974'N

MEURSAULT (SOUTH)

CORCELLES-
LES-
ARTS

46°956'N

Ruisseau de Limozin

PULIGNY-MONTRACHET

| Mi 0 | 0.31 | 0.62 | 0.93 | 1.24 |
| Km 0 | 0.5 | 1 | 1.5 | 2 |

Département
COMMUNE
Body of Water
LAND FEATURE
BOURGOGNE AOC

Meursault (north)
Premier Cru Vineyards [5]

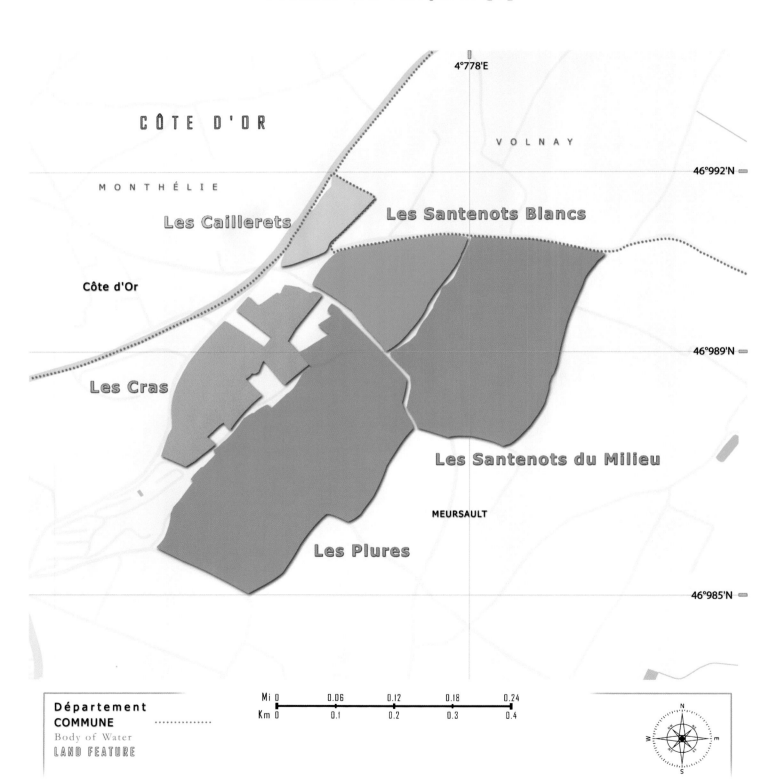

4°778'E

CÔTE D'OR

VOLNAY

46°992'N

MONTHÉLIE

Les Caillerets

Les Santenots Blancs

Côte d'Or

Les Cras

46°989'N

Les Santenots du Milieu

MEURSAULT

Les Plures

46°985'N

Département
COMMUNE
Body of Water
LAND FEATURE

Mi 0   0.06   0.12   0.18   0.24
Km 0   0.1   0.2   0.3   0.4

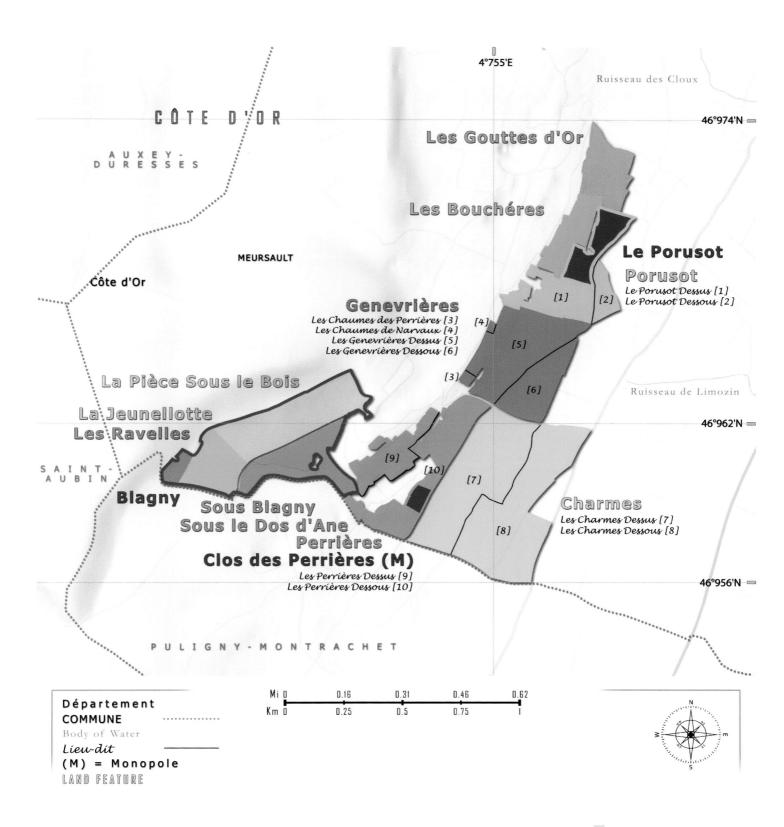

Meursault (south)
Premier Cru Vineyards [14]

4°755'E

Ruisseau des Cloux

46°974'N

CÔTE D'OR

AUXEY-
DURESSES

Les Gouttes d'Or

Les Bouchéres

MEURSAULT

Le Porusot

Porusot

Le Porusot Dessus [1]
Le Porusot Dessous [2]

Côte d'Or

Genevrières

Les Chaumes des Perrières [3]
Les Chaumes de Narvaux [4]
Les Genevrières Dessus [5]
Les Genevrières Dessous [6]

[1]

[2]

[4]

[5]

La Pièce Sous le Bois

[3]

[6]

Ruisseau de Limozin

La Jeunellotte
Les Ravelles

46°962'N

SAINT-
AUBIN

[9]

[10]

Blagny

Sous Blagny
Sous le Dos d'Ane
Perrières

[7]

Charmes

Les Charmes Dessus [7]
Les Charmes Dessous [8]

Clos des Perrières (M)

Les Perrières Dessus [9]
Les Perrières Dessous [10]

[8]

46°956'N

PULIGNY-MONTRACHET

Département
COMMUNE
Body of Water
Lieu-dit
(M) = Monopole
LAND FEATURE

Mi 0   0.16   0.31   0.46   0.62
Km 0   0.25   0.5   0.75   1

N
W E
S

Monthélie AOC
Premier Cru Vineyards [15]

VOLNAY

CÔTE D'OR

Les Barbiéres

46°997'N

Les Riottes

Le Clou
des Chênes

Les Clous

Sur la Velle

Côte d'Or

Le Meix Bataille

Les Vignes Rondes

46°993'N

Le Cas Rougeot

Le Village

Le Château Gaillard

Le Clos Gauthey

La Taupine

Les Duresses

MONTHÉLIE

Les Champs
Fulliots

Clos des Toisiéres (M)

46°989'N

AUXEY-DURESSES

MEURSAULT

Ruisseau des Cloux

4°766'E

Département
COMMUNE ·············
Body of Water
LAND FEATURE

| Mi 0 | | 0.12 | | 0.25 | | 0.37 | | 0.5 |
| Km 0 | | 0.2 | | 0.4 | | 0.6 | | 0.8 |

Auxey-Duresses AOC
Premier Cru Vineyards [9]

4°756'E

CÔTE D'OR

MONTHÉLIE

Climat Du Val

Clos Du Val
Reugne
La
Chapelle

Les Duresses

46°991'N

Côte d'Or

Bas des Duresses

46°989'N

Les Ecussaux

Les Bréterins

Les Grands Champs

AUXEY-DURESSES

46°986'N

Ruisseau des Cloux

MEURSAULT

Département
COMMUNE
Body of Water
LAND FEATURE

Mi 0   0.08   0.16   0.23   0.31
Km 0   0.125   0.25   0.375   0.5

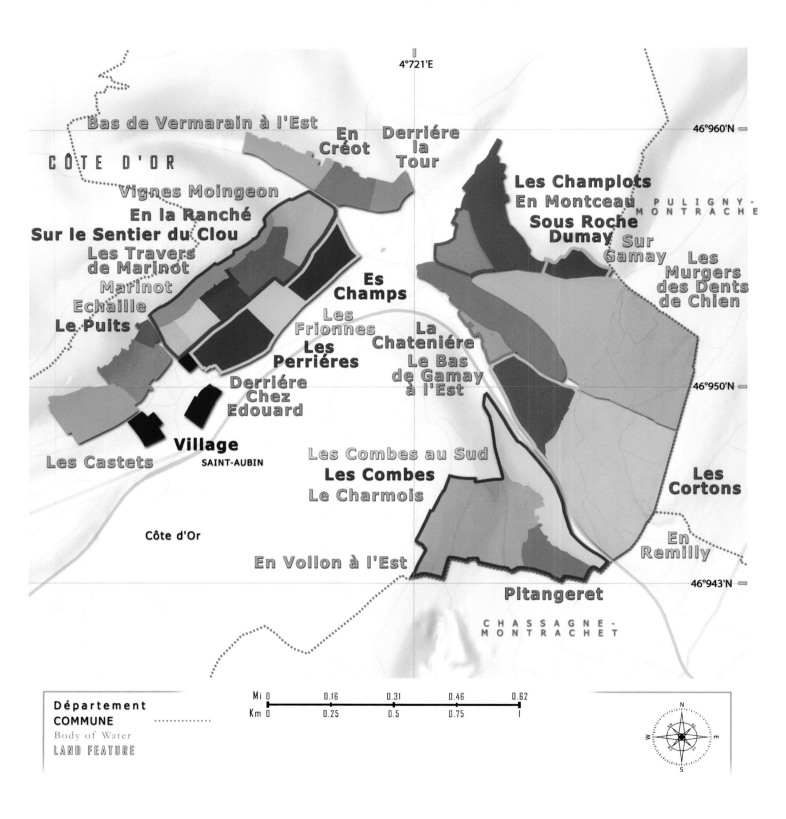

Saint-Aubin AOC
Premier Cru Vineyards [30]

4°721'E

Bas de Vermarain à l'Est

En Créot

Derriére la Tour

46°960'N

CÔTE D'OR

Les Champlots

En Montceau

PULIGNY-MONTRACHE

Vignes Moingeon

En la Ranché

Sous Roche Dumay

Sur le Sentier du Clou

Les Travers de Marinot

Sur Gamay

Les Murgers des Dents de Chien

Marinot

Es Champs

Echaille

Le Puits

Les Frionnes

La Chateniére

Les Perriéres

Le Bas de Gamay à l'Est

Derriére Chez Edouard

46°950'N

Village

SAINT-AUBIN

Les Combes au Sud

Les Castets

Les Combes

Le Charmois

Les Cortons

Côte d'Or

En Remilly

En Vollon à l'Est

46°943'N

Pitangeret

CHASSAGNE-MONTRACHET

Département
COMMUNE
Body of Water
LAND FEATURE

Mi 0   0.16   0.31   0.46   0.62
Km 0   0.25   0.5   0.75   1

Puligny-Montrachet AOC

GRAND CRU VINEYARDS [2+2]
Premier Cru Vineyards [17]

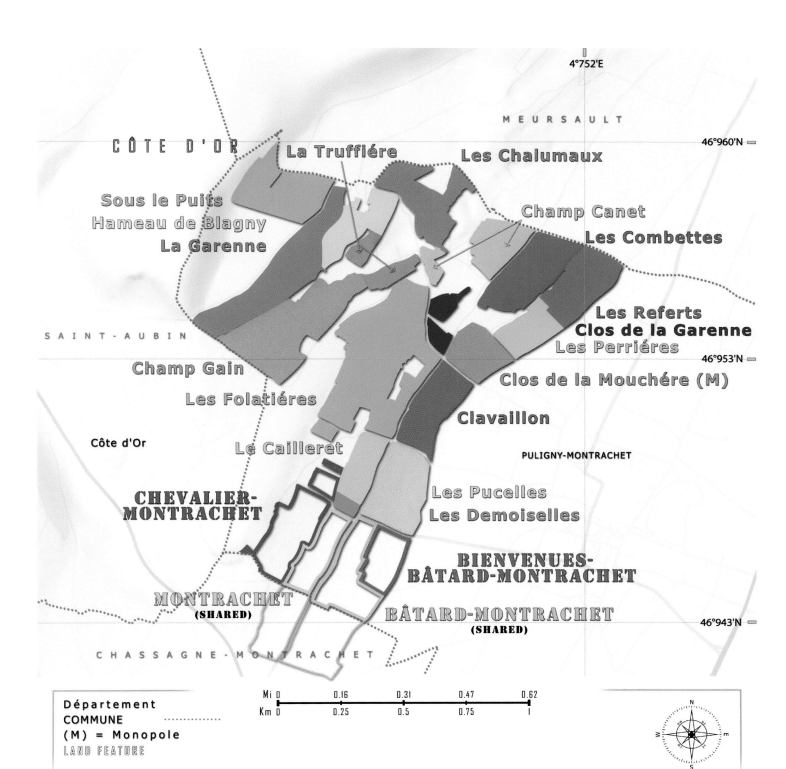

MEURSAULT

CÔTE D'OR

46°960'N

La Truffiére

Les Chalumaux

Sous le Puits
Hameau de Blagny
La Garenne

Champ Canet

Les Combettes

Les Referts
Clos de la Garenne

SAINT-AUBIN

Les Perriéres

46°953'N

Champ Gain

Clos de la Mouchére (M)

Les Folatiéres

Côte d'Or

Clavaillon

Le Cailleret

PULIGNY-MONTRACHET

CHEVALIER-
MONTRACHET

Les Pucelles
Les Demoiselles

BIENVENUES-
BÂTARD-MONTRACHET

MONTRACHET
(SHARED)

BÂTARD-MONTRACHET
(SHARED)

46°943'N

CHASSAGNE-MONTRACHET

4°752'E

Département
COMMUNE   ·················
(M) = Monopole
LAND FEATURE

| Mi 0 | 0.16 | 0.31 | 0.47 | 0.62 |
| Km 0 | 0.25 | 0.5 | 0.75 | 1 |

Chassagne-Montrachet AOC

GRAND CRU VINEYARDS [1+2]

Premier Cru Vineyards [55]

CHASSAGNE-MONTRACHET (NORTH) [25]
CHASSAGNE-MONTRACHET (SOUTH) [30]

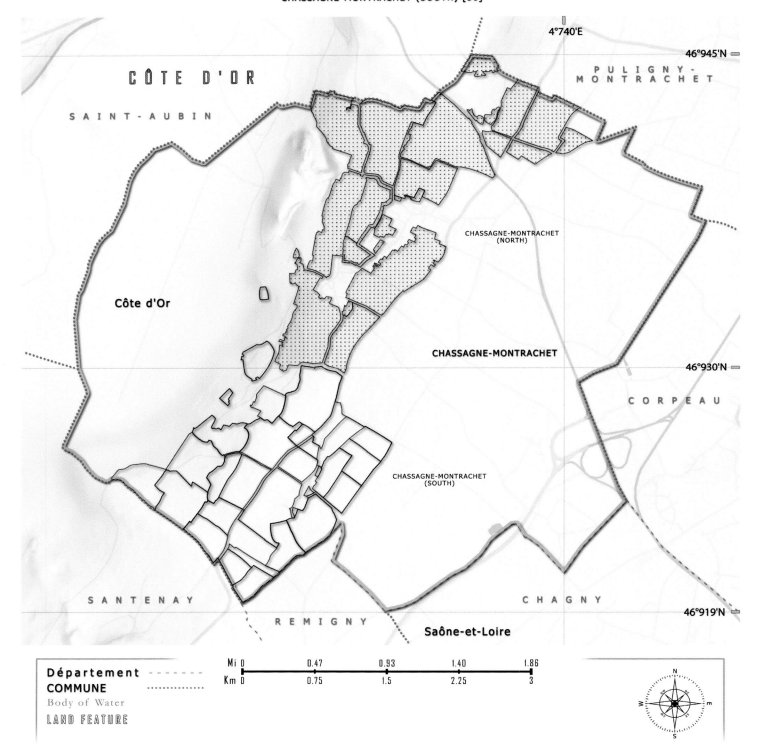

4°740'E

46°945'N

PULIGNY-MONTRACHET

CÔTE D'OR

SAINT-AUBIN

Côte d'Or

CHASSAGNE-MONTRACHET
(NORTH)

CHASSAGNE-MONTRACHET

46°930'N

CORPEAU

CHASSAGNE-MONTRACHET
(SOUTH)

SANTENAY

CHAGNY

46°919'N

REMIGNY

Saône-et-Loire

| Mi 0 | 0.47 | 0.93 | 1.40 | 1.86 |
| Km 0 | 0.75 | 1.5 | 2.25 | 3 |

Département - - - - - -
COMMUNE ·············
Body of Water
LAND FEATURE

Chassagne-Montrachet (north)
GRAND CRU VINEYARDS [1+2]
Premier Cru Vineyards [25]

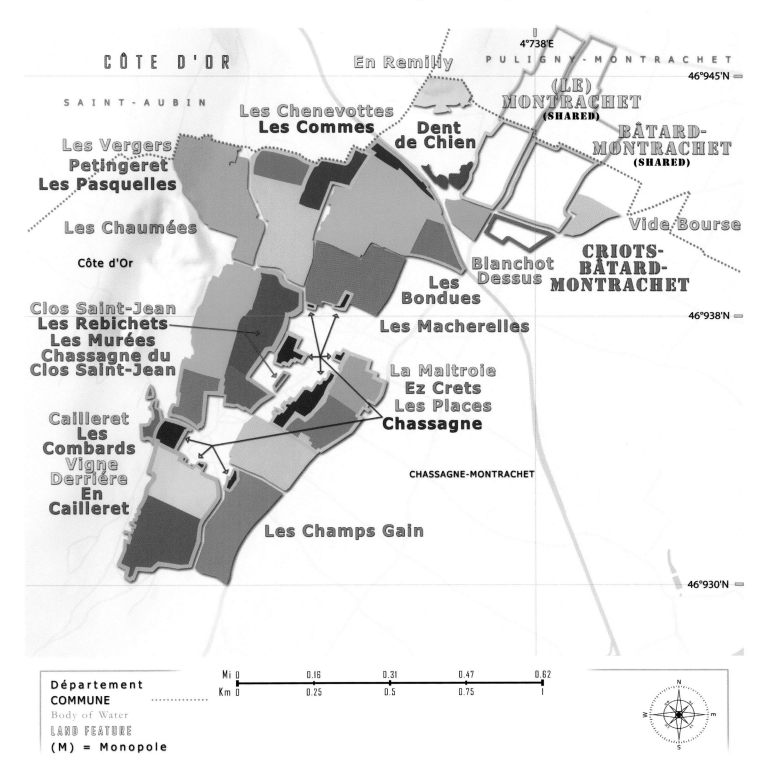

CÔTE D'OR

En Remilly

PULIGNY-MONTRACHET

4°738'E

46°945'N

SAINT-AUBIN

Les Chenevottes
Les Commes

Dent
de Chien

**(LE)
MONTRACHET
(SHARED)**

**BÂTARD-
MONTRACHET
(SHARED)**

Les Vergers
Petingeret
Les Pasquelles

Les Chaumées

Côte d'Or

Clos Saint-Jean
Les Rebichets
Les Murées
Chassagne du
Clos Saint-Jean

Vide Bourse

**CRIOTS-
BÂTARD-
MONTRACHET**

Blanchot
Dessus

**Les
Bondues**

Les Macherelles

46°938'N

La Maltroie
Ez Crets
Les Places
Chassagne

Cailleret
Les
Combards
Vigne
Derrière
En
Cailleret

CHASSAGNE-MONTRACHET

Les Champs Gain

46°930'N

Mi 0   0.16   0.31   0.47   0.62
Km 0   0.25   0.5   0.75   1

Département
COMMUNE ....
Body of Water
LAND FEATURE
(M) = Monopole

Chassagne-Montrachet (south)
Premier Cru Vineyards [30]

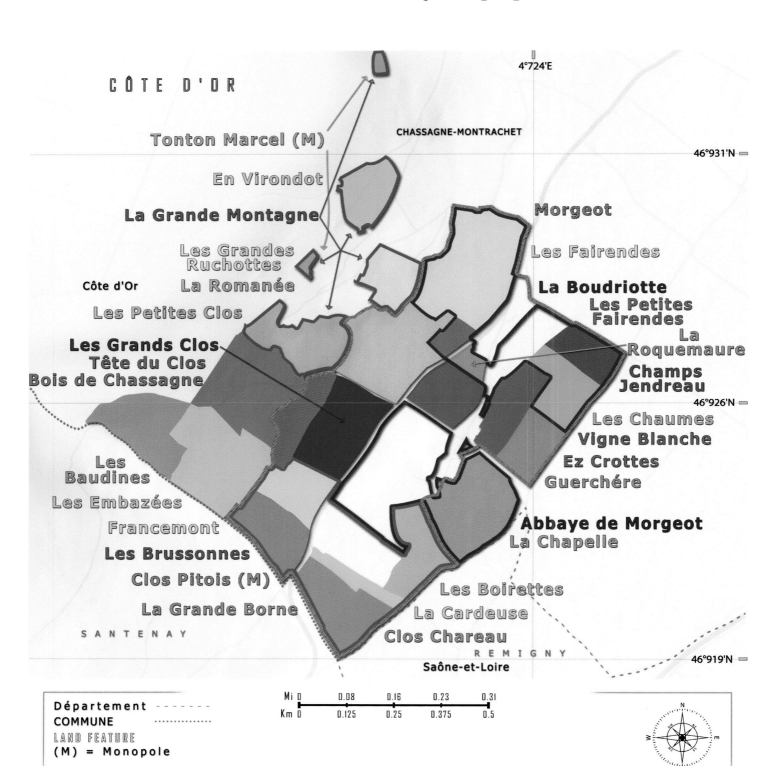

CÔTE D'OR

CHASSAGNE-MONTRACHET

4°724'E

46°931'N

Tonton Marcel (M)

En Virondot

La Grande Montagne

Morgeot

Les Grandes Ruchottes

Les Fairendes

Côte d'Or

La Romanée

La Boudriotte

Les Petites Clos

Les Petites Fairendes

Les Grands Clos

La Roquemaure

Tête du Clos

Champs Jendreau

Bois de Chassagne

46°926'N

Les Chaumes

Vigne Blanche

Les Baudines

Ez Crottes

Les Embazées

Guerchére

Francemont

Abbaye de Morgeot

Les Brussonnes

La Chapelle

Clos Pitois (M)

La Grande Borne

Les Boirettes

SANTENAY

La Cardeuse

Clos Chareau

REMIGNY

46°919'N

Saône-et-Loire

| Mi 0 | 0.08 | 0.16 | 0.23 | 0.31 |
| Km 0 | 0.125 | 0.25 | 0.375 | 0.5 |

Département - - - - - -
COMMUNE ·············
LAND FEATURE
(M) = Monopole

Santenay AOC
Premier Cru Vineyards [12]

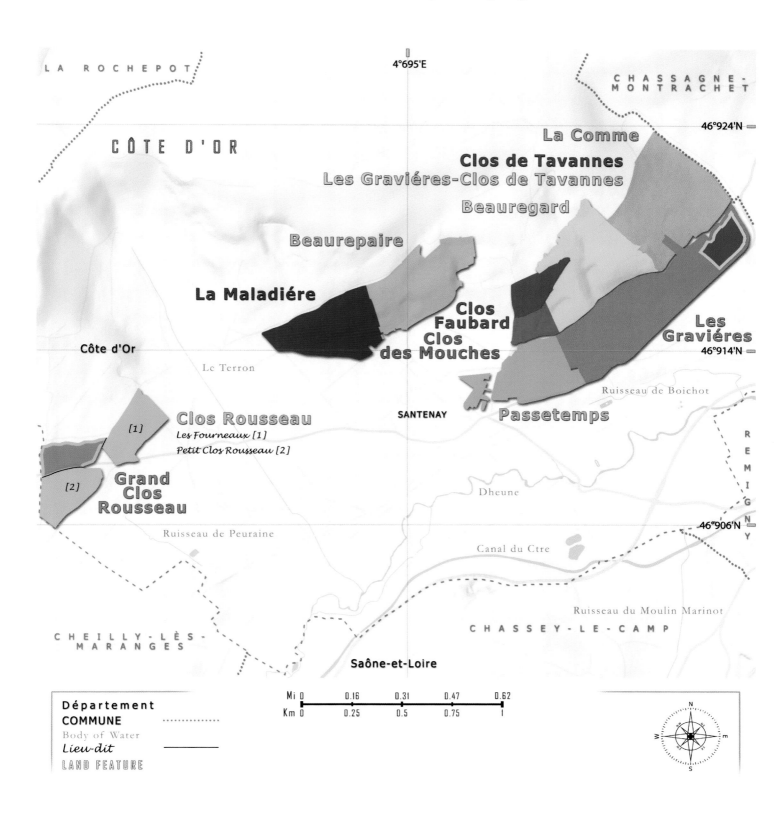

LA ROCHEPOT

CHASSAGNE-MONTRACHET

CÔTE D'OR

4°695'E

46°924'N

La Comme

Clos de Tavannes

Les Graviéres-Clos de Tavannes

Beauregard

Beaurepaire

La Maladiére

Côte d'Or

Le Terron

Clos Faubard
Clos des Mouches

Les Graviéres

46°914'N

Ruisseau de Boichot

SANTENAY

Passetemps

Clos Rousseau

Les Fourneaux [1]
Petit Clos Rousseau [2]

[1]

Grand Clos Rousseau

[2]

R E M I G N Y

Dheune

46°906'N

Ruisseau de Peuraine

Canal du Ctre

CHEILLY-LÈS-MARANGES

Ruisseau du Moulin Marinot

CHASSEY-LE-CAMP

Saône-et-Loire

Département
COMMUNE
Body of Water
Lieu-dit
LAND FEATURE

Mi 0	0.16	0.31	0.47	0.62
Km 0	0.25	0.5	0.75	1

Maranges AOC
Premier Cru Vineyards [7]

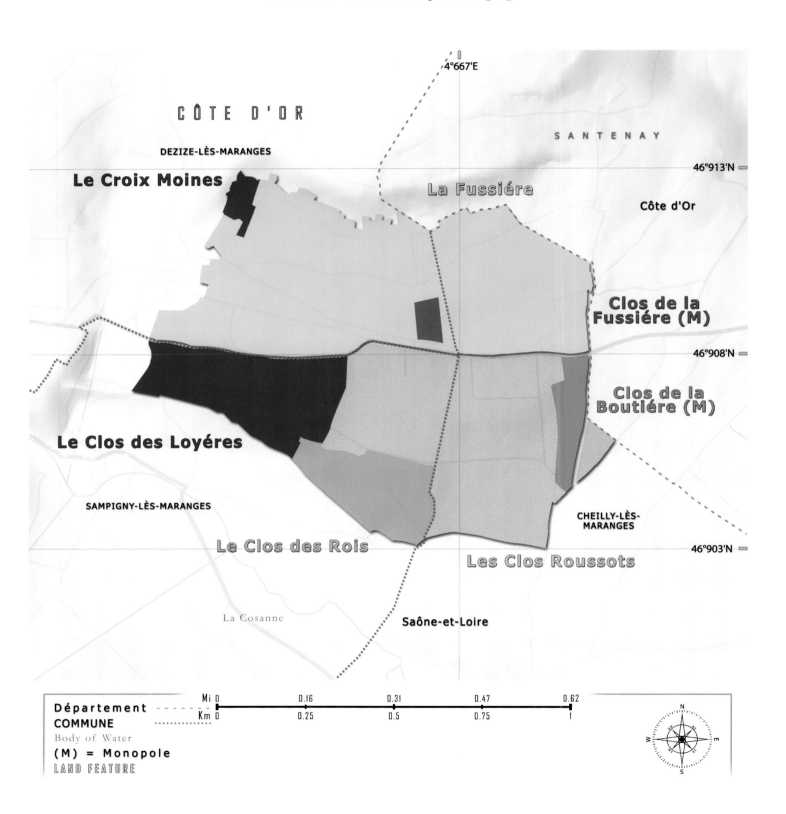

CÔTE D'OR

SANTENAY

DEZIZE-LÈS-MARANGES

Le Croix Moines

La Fussiére

Côte d'Or

46°913'N

Clos de la Fussiére (M)

46°908'N

Clos de la Boutiére (M)

Le Clos des Loyéres

SAMPIGNY-LÈS-MARANGES

CHEILLY-LÈS-MARANGES

Le Clos des Rois

46°903'N

Les Clos Roussots

La Cosanne

Saône-et-Loire

4°667'E

	Mi 0	0.16	0.31	0.47	0.62
Département					
COMMUNE	Km 0	0.25	0.5	0.75	1
Body of Water					
(M) = Monopole					
LAND FEATURE					

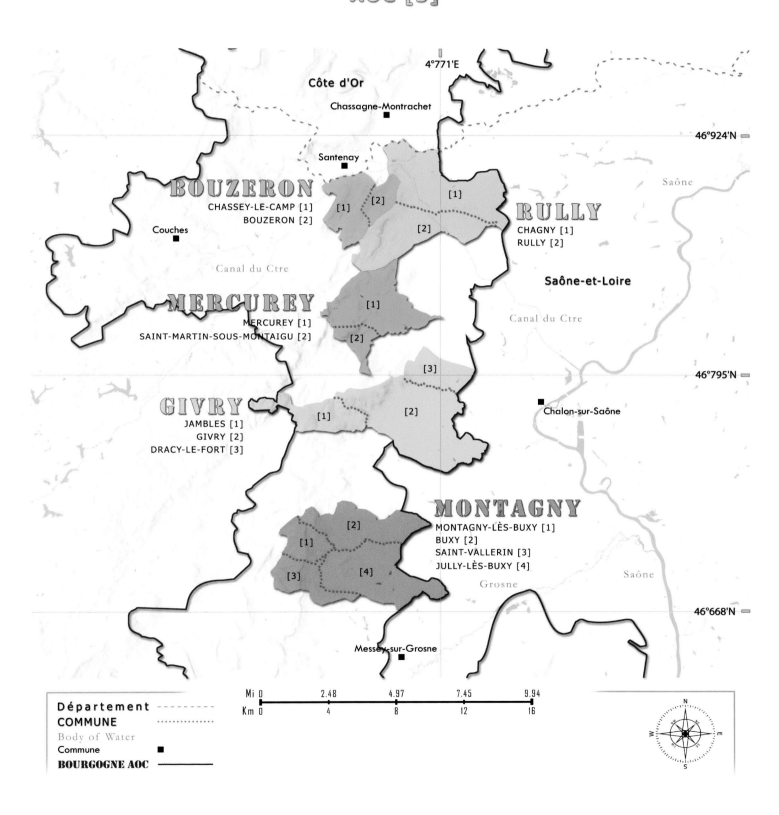

Côte Chalonnaise
AOC [5]

Côte d'Or

Chassagne-Montrachet

4°771'E

46°924'N

Santenay

Saône

BOUZERON
CHASSEY-LE-CAMP [1]
BOUZERON [2]

Couches

RULLY
CHAGNY [1]
RULLY [2]

Canal du Ctre

Saône-et-Loire

MERCUREY
MERCUREY [1]
SAINT-MARTIN-SOUS-MONTAIGU [2]

Canal du Ctre

46°795'N

GIVRY
JAMBLES [1]
GIVRY [2]
DRACY-LE-FORT [3]

Chalon-sur-Saône

MONTAGNY
MONTAGNY-LÈS-BUXY [1]
BUXY [2]
SAINT-VALLERIN [3]
JULLY-LÈS-BUXY [4]

Saône

Grosne

46°668'N

Messey-sur-Grosne

Mi	0	2.48	4.97	7.45	9.94
Km	0	4	8	12	16

Département - - - - - -
COMMUNE ·············
Body of Water
Commune ■
BOURGOGNE AOC ———

Rully AOC
Premier Cru Vineyards [23]

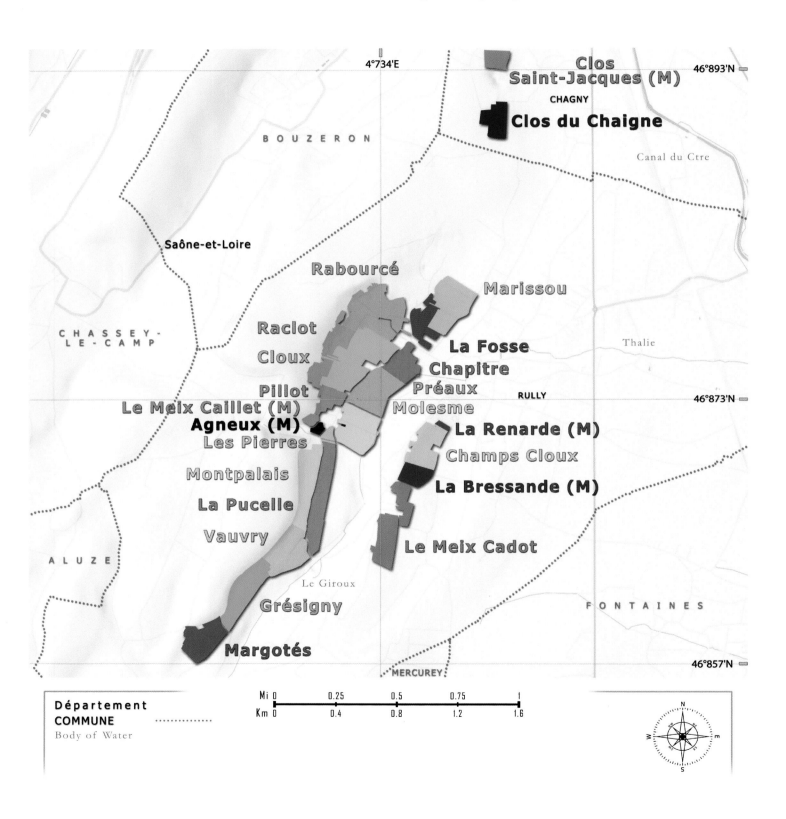

Clos
Saint-Jacques (M)

46°893'N

CHAGNY

Clos du Chaigne

Canal du Ctre

BOUZERON

Saône-et-Loire

Rabourcé

Marissou

CHASSEY-
LE-CAMP

Raclot

Cloux

La Fosse

Chapitre

Thalie

Pillot

Préaux

RULLY

46°873'N

Le Meix Caillet (M)

Molesme

Agneux (M)

La Renarde (M)

Les Pierres

Champs Cloux

Montpalais

La Bressande (M)

La Pucelle

Vauvry

ALUZE

Le Meix Cadot

Le Giroux

FONTAINES

Grésigny

Margotés

46°857'N

MERCUREY

Département					
COMMUNE	....				
Body of Water					

Mi 0   0.25   0.5   0.75   1
Km 0   0.4   0.8   1.2   1.6

Mercurey AOC
Premier Cru Vineyards [31]

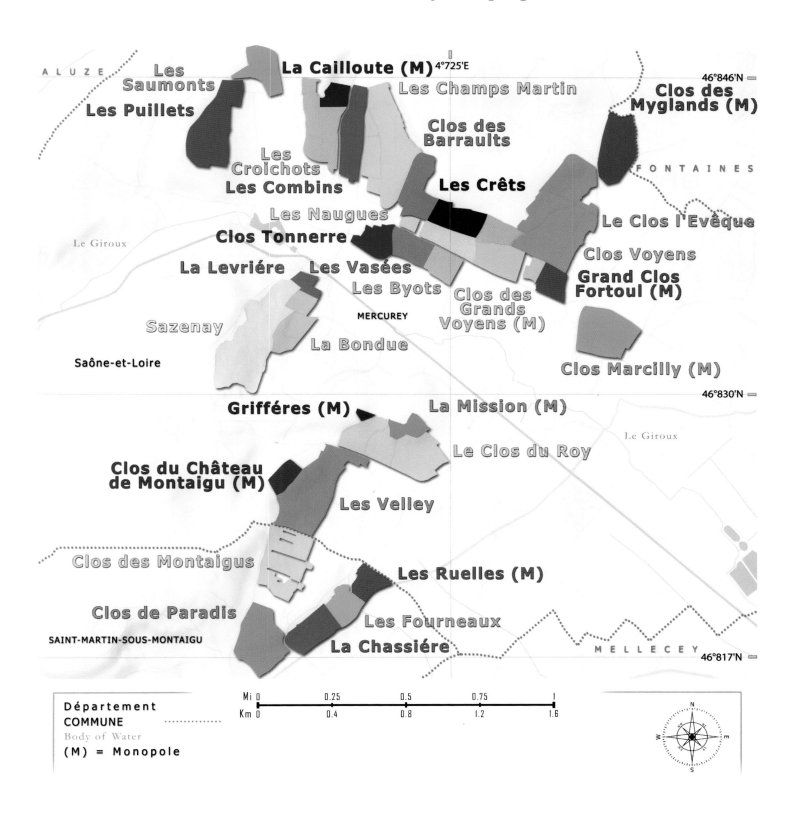

Les Saumonts
Les Puillets
La Cailloute (M) 4°725'E
Les Champs Martin
Clos des Myglands (M)
ALUZE
Clos des Barraults
FONTAINES
Les Croichots
Les Combins
Les Crêts
Les Naugues
Le Clos l'Evêque
Le Giroux
Clos Tonnerre
Clos Voyens
La Levriére
Les Vasées
Grand Clos Fortoul (M)
Les Byots
Clos des Grands Voyens (M)
Sazenay
MERCUREY
La Bondue
Clos Marcilly (M)
Saône-et-Loire
46°830'N
Grifféres (M)
La Mission (M)
Le Clos du Roy
Le Giroux
Clos du Château de Montaigu (M)
Les Velley
Clos des Montaigus
Les Ruelles (M)
Clos de Paradis
Les Fourneaux
SAINT-MARTIN-SOUS-MONTAIGU
La Chassiére
MELLECEY
46°817'N

Département
COMMUNE ....
Body of Water
(M) = Monopole

Mi 0   0.25   0.5   0.75   1
Km 0   0.4   0.8   1.2   1.6

Givry AOC
Premier Cru Vineyards [37]

Le Champ Lalot

Clos Jus

46°795'N

SAINT-DENIS-DE-VAUX

DRACY-LE-FORT

Clos du Cellier Aux Moines

Les Combes

Champ Nalot

En Veau

Le Pied de Chaume

Petit Marole

Clos Marole

La Brûlée

Les Bois Chevaux

Clos Charlé

Saône-et-Loire

Servoisine

Clos-Saint-Pierre (M)

GIVRY

Clos-Saint-Paul (M)

Clos Salomon (M)

Le Petit Prétan

Les Bois Gautiers

Les Grands Prétans

En Choué

Les Galaffres

46°779'N

Clos de la Baraude

A Vigne Rouge

Le Paradis

Le Vigron

Les Grandes Vignes

Le Pied du Clou

La Grande Berge

Clos Marceaux (M)

La Plante

JAMBLES

Clos du Vernoy

La Matrosse

Le Peite Berge

Crauzot

Le Médenchot

Clos du Cras Long

Crémillons

46°767'N

Ruisseau de Jambles

SAINT-DÉSERT

Montagny AOC
Premier Cru Vineyards [49]

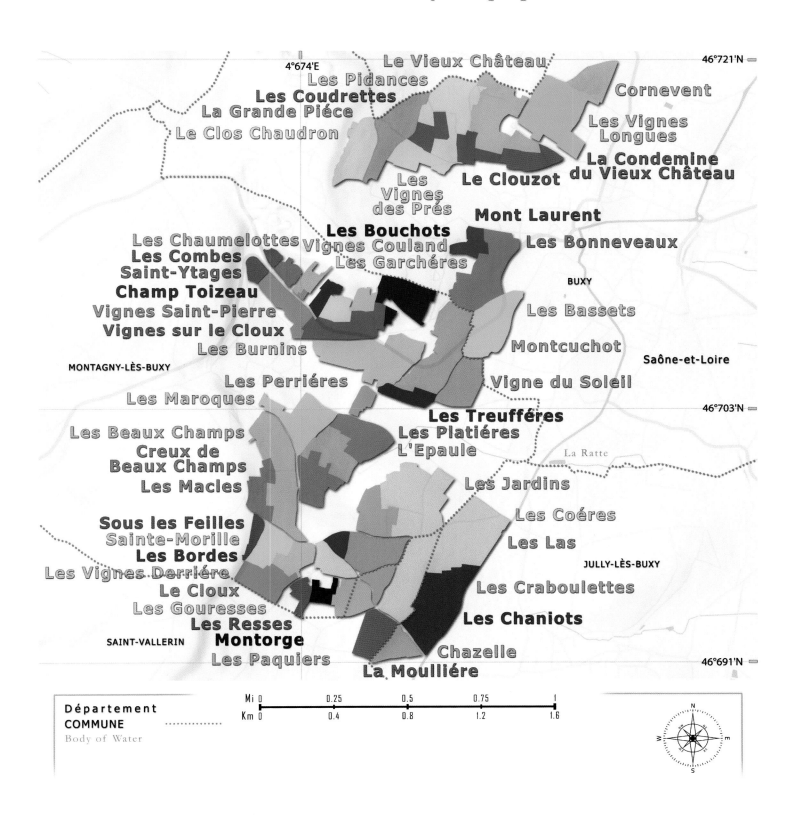

Le Vieux Château

46°721'N

4°674'E

Les Pidances

Les Coudrettes

Cornevent

La Grande Piéce

Le Clos Chaudron

Les Vignes Longues

Les Vignes des Prés

Le Clouzot

La Condemine du Vieux Château

Mont Laurent

Les Chaumelottes

Les Bouchots

Vignes Couland

Les Bonneveaux

Les Combes

Les Garchéres

Saint-Ytages

BUXY

Champ Toizeau

Les Bassets

Vignes Saint-Pierre

Montcuchot

Vignes sur le Cloux

Saône-et-Loire

Les Burnins

MONTAGNY-LÈS-BUXY

Les Perriéres

Vigne du Soleil

46°703'N

Les Maroques

Les Beaux Champs

Les Treufféres

Creux de Beaux Champs

Les Platiéres

L'Epaule

La Ratte

Les Macles

Les Jardins

Sous les Feilles

Les Coéres

Sainte-Morille

Les Bordes

Les Las

Les Vignes Derriére

JULLY-LÈS-BUXY

Le Cloux

Les Gouresses

Les Craboulettes

Les Resses

Les Chaniots

Montorge

SAINT-VALLERIN

Chazelle

Les Paquiers

46°691'N

La Moulliére

Département

COMMUNE

Body of Water

Mi 0   0.25   0.5   0.75   1

Km 0   0.4   0.8   1.2   1.6

Mâconnais

AOC [7]
Geographic Designations of Mâcon AOC

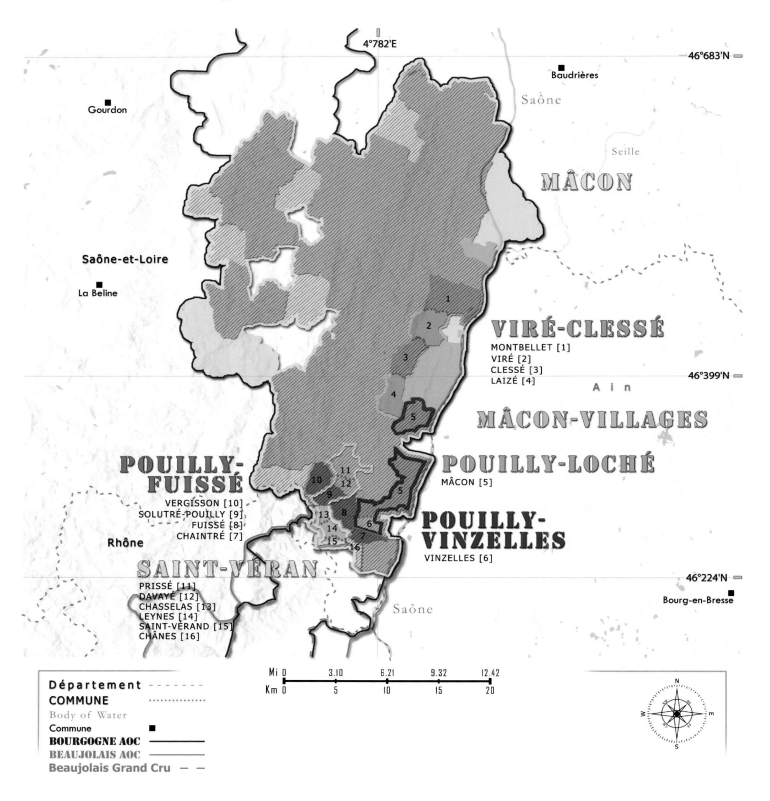

4°782'E

46°683'N

Baudrières

Saône

Seille

Gourdon

MÂCON

Saône-et-Loire

La Beline

VIRÉ-CLESSÉ

MONTBELLET [1]
VIRÉ [2]
CLESSÉ [3]
LAIZÉ [4]

46°399'N

A i n

MÂCON-VILLAGES

POUILLY-LOCHÉ

POUILLY-
FUISSÉ

MÂCON [5]

VERGISSON [10]
SOLUTRÉ-POUILLY [9]
FUISSÉ [8]
CHAINTRÉ [7]

POUILLY-
VINZELLES

Rhône

VINZELLES [6]

SAINT-VÉRAN

PRISSÉ [11]
DAVAYÉ [12]
CHASSELAS [13]
LEYNES [14]
SAINT-VÉRAND [15]
CHÂNES [16]

46°224'N

Bourg-en-Bresse

Saône

Mi 0   3.10   6.21   9.32   12.42
Km 0   5   10   15   20

Département - - - - -
COMMUNE ....
Body of Water
Commune ■
BOURGOGNE AOC ——
BEAUJOLAIS AOC ——
Beaujolais Grand Cru — —

Mâcon AOC

Geographic Designation [27]

COMMUNE OF THE GEOGRAPHIC DESIGNATION [73]

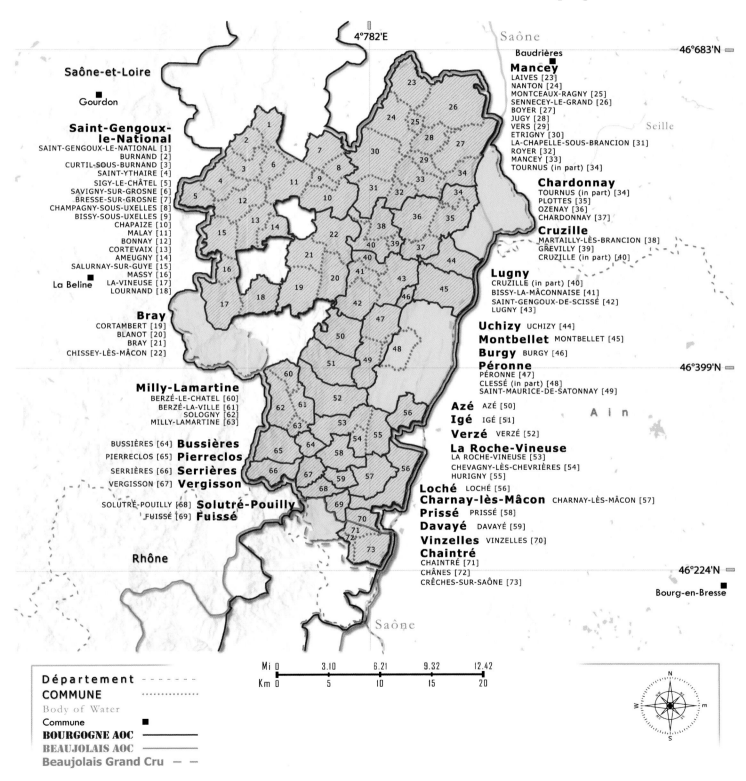

Saône-et-Loire

Gourdon

Saint-Gengoux-le-National
SAINT-GENGOUX-LE-NATIONAL [1]
BURNAND [2]
CURTIL-SOUS-BURNAND [3]
SAINT-YTHAIRE [4]
SIGY-LE-CHÂTEL [5]
SAVIGNY-SUR-GROSNE [6]
BRESSE-SUR-GROSNE [7]
CHAMPAGNY-SOUS-UXELLES [8]
BISSY-SOUS-UXELLES [9]
CHAPAIZE [10]
MALAY [11]
BONNAY [12]
CORTEVAIX [13]
AMEUGNY [14]
SALURNAY-SUR-GUYE [15]
MASSY [16]
LA-VINEUSE [17]
LOURNAND [18]

La Beline

Bray
CORTAMBERT [19]
BLANOT [20]
BRAY [21]
CHISSEY-LÈS-MÂCON [22]

Milly-Lamartine
BERZÉ-LE-CHATEL [60]
BERZÉ-LA-VILLE [61]
SOLOGNY [62]
MILLY-LAMARTINE [63]

BUSSIÈRES [64] **Bussières**
PIERRECLOS [65] **Pierreclos**
SERRIÈRES [66] **Serrières**
VERGISSON [67] **Vergisson**

SOLUTRÉ-POUILLY [68] **Solutré-Pouilly**
FUISSÉ [69] **Fuissé**

Rhône

Baudrières

Mancey
LAIVES [23]
NANTON [24]
MONTCEAUX-RAGNY [25]
SENNECEY-LE-GRAND [26]
BOYER [27]
JUGY [28]
VERS [29]
ETRIGNY [30]
LA-CHAPELLE-SOUS-BRANCION [31]
ROYER [32]
MANCEY [33]
TOURNUS (in part) [34]

Chardonnay
TOURNUS (in part) [34]
PLOTTES [35]
OZENAY [36]
CHARDONNAY [37]

Cruzille
MARTAILLY-LÈS-BRANCION [38]
GREVILLY [39]
CRUZILLE (in part) [40]

Lugny
CRUZILLE (in part) [40]
BISSY-LA-MÂCONNAISE [41]
SAINT-GENGOUX-DE-SCISSÉ [42]
LUGNY [43]

Uchizy UCHIZY [44]
Montbellet MONTBELLET [45]
Burgy BURGY [46]
Péronne
PÉRONNE [47]
CLESSÉ (in part) [48]
SAINT-MAURICE-DE-SATONNAY [49]

Azé AZÉ [50]
Igé IGÉ [51]
Verzé VERZÉ [52]
La Roche-Vineuse
LA ROCHE-VINEUSE [53]
CHEVAGNY-LÈS-CHEVRIÈRES [54]
HURIGNY [55]

Loché LOCHÉ [56]
Charnay-lès-Mâcon CHARNAY-LÈS-MÂCON [57]
Prissé PRISSÉ [58]
Davayé DAVAYÉ [59]
Vinzelles VINZELLES [70]
Chaintré
CHAINTRÉ [71]
CHÂNES [72]
CRÊCHES-SUR-SAÔNE [73]

Bourg-en-Bresse

Département - - - - - -
COMMUNE ....
Body of Water
Commune ■
BOURGOGNE AOC ————
BEAUJOLAIS AOC ————
Beaujolais Grand Cru — —

| Mi 0 | 3.10 | 6.21 | 9.32 | 12.42 |
| Km 0 | 5 | 10 | 15 | 20 |

Pouilly-Fuissé AOC
Premier Cru Vineyards [22]

SERRIÈRES

VERGISSON

PRISSÉ

Petite Grosne

Les Crays   **Sur la Roche**

46°313'N

CHARNAY-LÈS-MÂCON

En France

La Denante

La Maréchaude

DAVAYÉ

Saône-et-Loire

Au Vignerais

La Frérie
En Servy

Aux Bouthiéres

Aux Chailloux

Le Clos de Solutré

SOLUTRÉ-POUILLY

Pouilly
Les Reisses

Vers Cras

Petite Grosne

46°285'N

Les Brulés

Les Ménétriéres

Les Vignes Blanches

Le Clos

FUISSÉ

MÂCON

CENVES

Les Perriéres

CHASSELAS

Le Gointrond

Arlois

VINZELLES

Le Clos de Monsieur Noly

Aux Quarts

Ruisseau de Prétu

LEYNES

PRUZILLY

Le Clos Reyssier

Les Chevriéres

CHAINTRÉ

46°252'N

SAINT-VÉRAND   CHÂNES

Département
COMMUNE
Body of Water

Mi 0 — 0.5 — 1 — 1.5 — 2
Km 0 — 0.8 — 1.6 — 2.4 — 3.2

BEAUJOLAIS
TOTAL AOC [11]

GENERIC AOC [1]
CRU VINEYARDS / AOC [10]
Commune of Beaujolais-Villages [38]

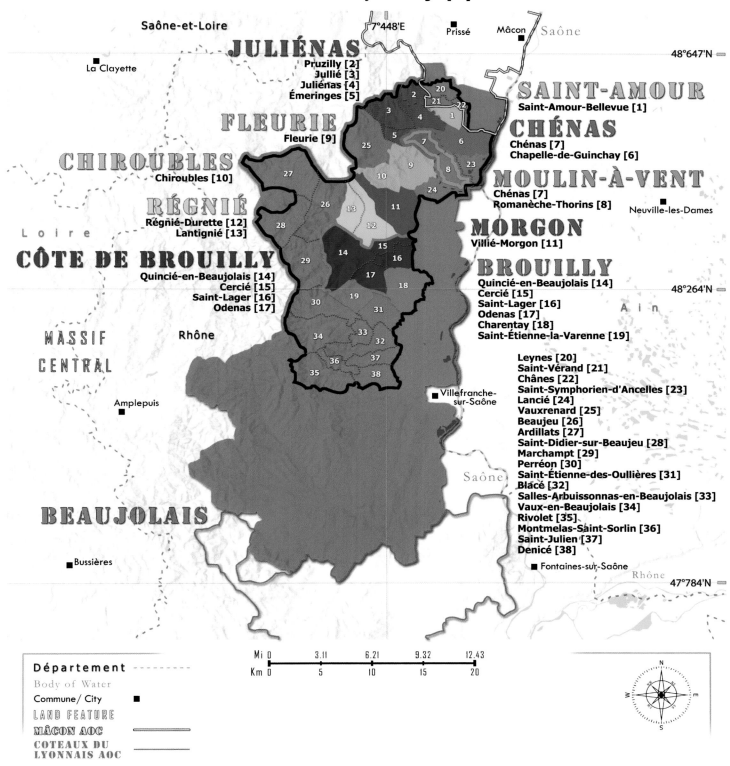

Saône-et-Loire

La Clayette

7°448'E

Prissé Mâcon Saône

48°647'N

JULIÉNAS
Pruzilly [2]
Jullié [3]
Juliénas [4]
Émeringes [5]

FLEURIE
Fleurie [9]

CHIROUBLES
Chiroubles [10]

RÉGNIÉ
Régnié-Durette [12]
Lantignié [13]

CÔTE DE BROUILLY
Quincié-en-Beaujolais [14]
Cercié [15]
Saint-Lager [16]
Odenas [17]

Loire

MASSIF CENTRAL

Amplepuis

Rhône

SAINT-AMOUR
Saint-Amour-Bellevue [1]

CHÉNAS
Chénas [7]
Chapelle-de-Guinchay [6]

MOULIN-À-VENT
Chénas [7]
Romanèche-Thorins [8]

Neuville-les-Dames

MORGON
Villié-Morgon [11]

BROUILLY
Quincié-en-Beaujolais [14]
Cercié [15]
Saint-Lager [16]
Odenas [17]
Charentay [18]
Saint-Étienne-la-Varenne [19]

48°264'N

A i n

Leynes [20]
Saint-Vérand [21]
Chânes [22]
Saint-Symphorien-d'Ancelles [23]
Lancié [24]
Vauxrenard [25]
Beaujeu [26]
Ardillats [27]
Saint-Didier-sur-Beaujeu [28]
Marchampt [29]
Perréon [30]
Saint-Étienne-des-Oullières [31]
Blacé [32]
Salles-Arbuissonnas-en-Beaujolais [33]
Vaux-en-Beaujolais [34]
Rivolet [35]
Montmelas-Saint-Sorlin [36]
Saint-Julien [37]
Denicé [38]

Villefranche-sur-Saône

Saône

BEAUJOLAIS

Bussières

Fontaines-sur-Saône

Rhône

47°784'N

Mi	0	3.11	6.21	9.32	12.43
Km	0	5	10	15	20

Département - - - - - - -
Body of Water
Commune / City ■
LAND FEATURE
MÂCON AOC
COTEAUX DU LYONNAIS AOC

N S E W

LYONNAIS
AOC [1]

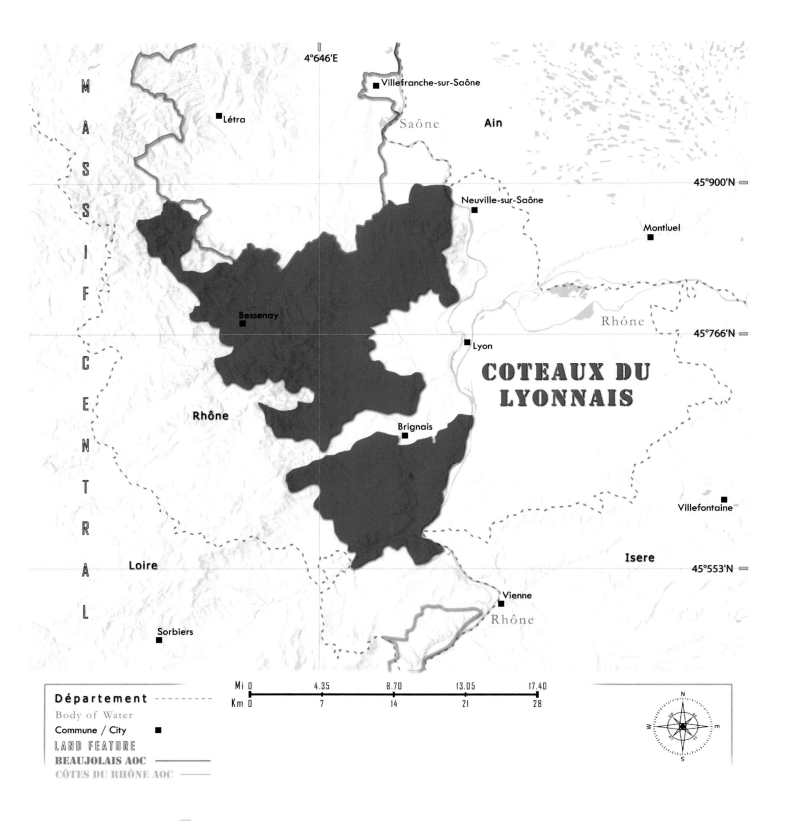

Département · · · · · · ·
Body of Water
Commune / City ■
LAND FEATURE
BEAUJOLAIS AOC ——
CÔTES DU RHÔNE AOC ——

France

RHÔNE
TOTAL AOC [31]

GENERIC AOC [1]
NORTHERN CÔTES DU RHÔNE (SEPTENTRIONAUX) [12]
SOUTHERN CÔTES DU RHÔNE (MÉRIDIONAUX) [18]

Geographic Designation of Côtes du Rhône-Villages AOC [22]

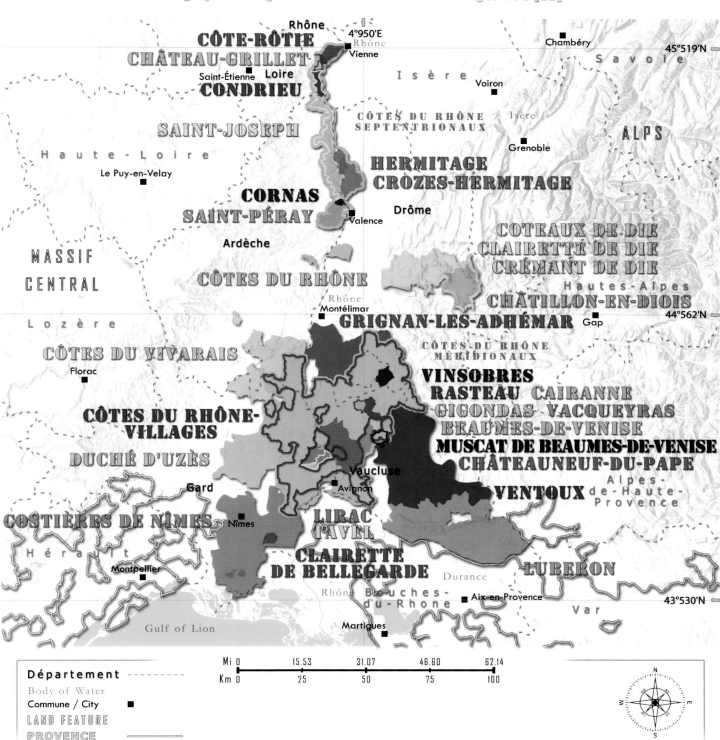

CÔTE-RÔTIE
CHÂTEAU-GRILLET
CONDRIEU
SAINT-JOSEPH
CORNAS
SAINT-PÉRAY
CÔTES DU RHÔNE
CÔTES DU VIVARAIS
CÔTES DU RHÔNE-VILLAGES
DUCHÉ D'UZÈS
COSTIÈRES DE NÎMES
LIRAC
TAVEL
CLAIRETTE DE BELLEGARDE

CÔTES DU RHÔNE SEPTENTRIONAUX
HERMITAGE
CROZES-HERMITAGE
COTEAUX DE DIE
CLAIRETTE DE DIE
CRÉMANT DE DIE
CHÂTILLON-EN-DIOIS
GRIGNAN-LES-ADHÉMAR
CÔTES DU RHÔNE MÉRIDIONAUX
VINSOBRES
RASTEAU CAIRANNE
GIGONDAS VACQUEYRAS
BEAUMES-DE-VENISE
MUSCAT DE BEAUMES-DE-VENISE
CHÂTEAUNEUF-DU-PAPE
VENTOUX
LUBERON

Rhône
Chambéry
Savoie
Vienne
Saint-Étienne
Loire
Isère
Voiron
Haute-Loire
Le Puy-en-Velay
Grenoble
ALPS
Drôme
Valence
Ardèche
MASSIF CENTRAL
Lozère
Rhône
Montélimar
Hautes-Alpes
Gap
Florac
Vaucluse
Avignon
Gard
Alpes-de-Haute-Provence
Nîmes
Hérault
Montpellier
Durance
Rhône
Bouches-du-Rhône
Aix-en-Provence
Var
Gulf of Lion
Martigues

45°519'N
4°950'E
44°562'N
43°530'N

| Mi 0 | 15.53 | 31.07 | 46.60 | 62.14 |
| Km 0 | 25 | 50 | 75 | 100 |

Département
- - - - - - -
Body of Water
Commune / City   ■
LAND FEATURE
PROVENCE ————
LANGUEDOC ————

Côtes du Rhône-Villages AOC

Geographic Designation [22]

Commune of Geographic Designation

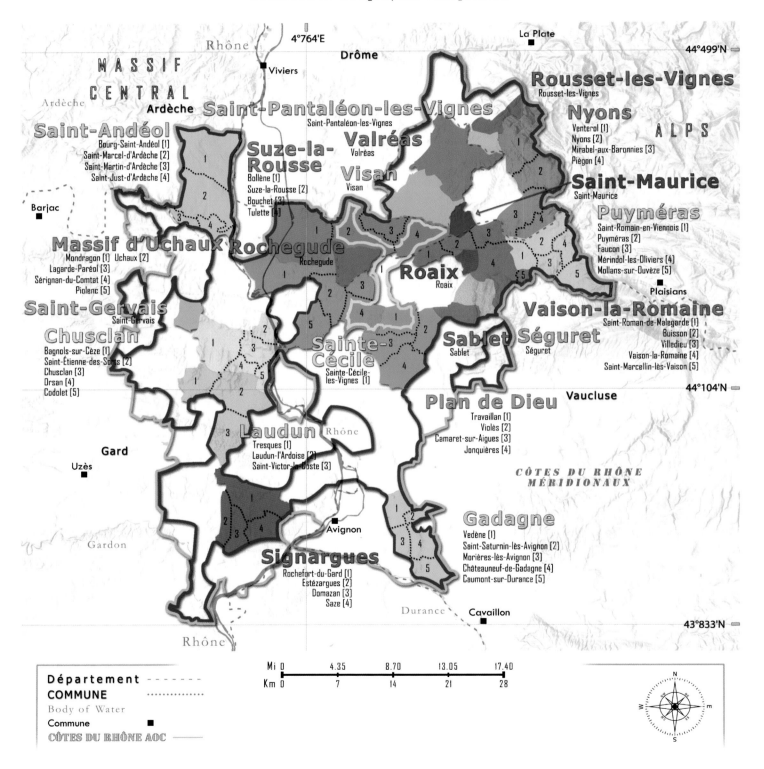

MASSIF CENTRAL

Ardèche

MASSIF d'Uchaux | Rochegude
Mondragon [1] Uchaux [2]
Lagarde-Paréol [3]
Sérignan-du-Comtat [4]
Piolenc [5]

Saint-Andéol
Bourg-Saint-Andéol [1]
Saint-Marcel-d'Ardèche [2]
Saint-Martin-d'Ardèche [3]
Saint-Just-d'Ardèche [4]

Saint-Pantaléon-les-Vignes
Saint-Pantaléon-les-Vignes

Suze-la-Rousse
Bollène [1]
Suze-la-Rousse [2]
Bouchet [3]
Tulette [4]

Valréas
Valréas

Visan
Visan

Rousset-les-Vignes
Rousset-les-Vignes

Nyons
Venterol [1]
Nyons [2]
Mirabel-aux-Baronnies [3]
Piégon [4]

Saint-Maurice
Saint-Maurice

Puyméras
Saint-Romain-en-Viennois [1]
Puyméras [2]
Faucon [3]
Mérindol-les-Oliviers [4]
Mollans-sur-Ouvèze [5]

Roaix
Roaix

Saint-Gervais
Saint-Gervais

Chusclan
Bagnols-sur-Cèze [1]
Saint-Étienne-des-Sorts [2]
Chusclan [3]
Orsan [4]
Codolet [5]

Sainte-Cécile
Sainte-Cécile-les-Vignes [1]

Sablet
Sablet

Séguret
Séguret

Vaison-la-Romaine
Saint-Roman-de-Malegarde [1]
Buisson [2]
Villedieu [3]
Vaison-la-Romaine [4]
Saint-Marcellin-lès-Vaison [5]

Plan de Dieu
Travaillan [1]
Violès [2]
Camaret-sur-Aigues [3]
Jonquières [4]

Laudun
Tresques [1]
Laudun-l'Ardoise [2]
Saint-Victor-la-Coste [3]

Signargues
Rochefort-du-Gard [1]
Estézargues [2]
Domazan [3]
Saze [4]

Gadagne
Vedène [1]
Saint-Saturnin-lès-Avignon [2]
Morières-lès-Avignon [3]
Châteauneuf-de-Gadagne [4]
Caumont-sur-Durance [5]

CÔTES DU RHÔNE MÉRIDIONAUX

Mi	0		4.35		8.70		13.05		17.40
Km	0		7		14		21		28

Département - - - - - -
COMMUNE ....
Body of Water
Commune ■
CÔTES DU RHÔNE AOC ——

Côte-Rôtie AOC
Total Vineyards [73]

SAINT-CYR-SUR-LE-RHÔNE [12]
AMPUIS [48]
TUPIN-ET-SEMONS [13]

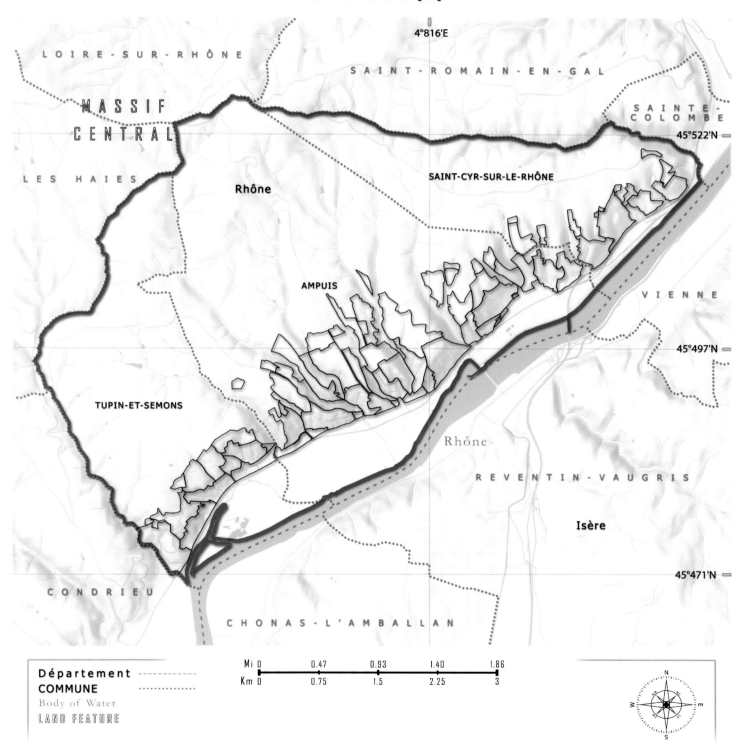

LOIRE-SUR-RHÔNE

SAINT-ROMAIN-EN-GAL

4°816'E

MASSIF CENTRAL

SAINTE-COLOMBE

45°522'N

LES HAIES

Rhône

SAINT-CYR-SUR-LE-RHÔNE

AMPUIS

VIENNE

45°497'N

TUPIN-ET-SEMONS

Rhône

REVENTIN-VAUGRIS

Isère

45°471'N

CONDRIEU

CHONAS-L'AMBALLAN

Département ------------
COMMUNE ··············
Body of Water
LAND FEATURE

| Mi 0 | 0.47 | 0.93 | 1.40 | 1.86 |
| Km 0 | 0.75 | 1.5 | 2.25 | 3 |

Côte-Rôtie vineyards
Saint-Cyr-sur-le-Rhône [12]

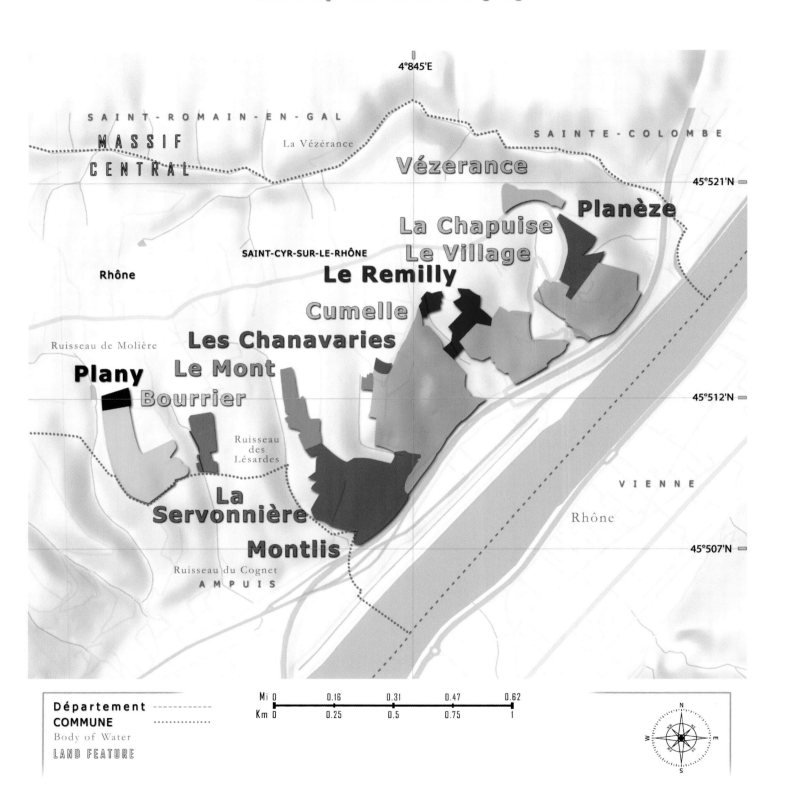

4°845'E

SAINT-ROMAIN-EN-GAL

MASSIF
CENTRAL

La Vézérance

SAINTE-COLOMBE

Vézerance

45°521'N

Planèze

La Chapuise
Le Village

SAINT-CYR-SUR-LE-RHÔNE

Rhône

Le Remilly

Cumelle

Les Chanavaries

Ruisseau de Molière

Le Mont

Plany

Bourrier

45°512'N

Ruisseau
des
Lésardes

VIENNE

Rhône

La
Servonnière

Montlis

45°507'N

Ruisseau du Cognet

AMPUIS

Département
COMMUNE
Body of Water
LAND FEATURE

| Mi 0 | 0.16 | 0.31 | 0.47 | 0.62 |
| Km 0 | 0.25 | 0.5 | 0.75 | 1 |

N
W   E
S

Côte-Rôtie vineyards
Ampuis [48]

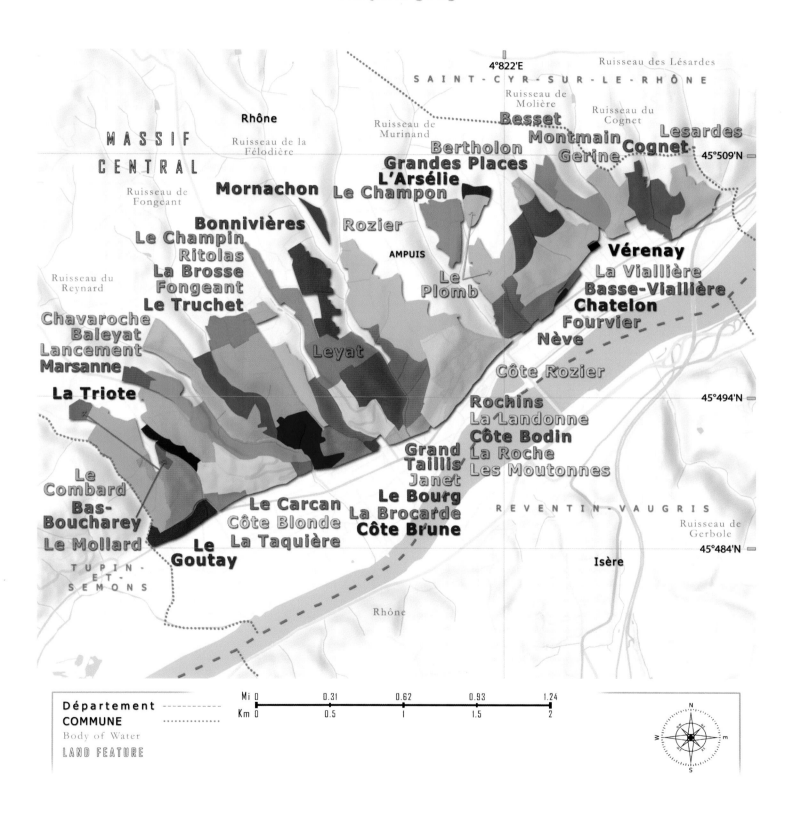

SAINT - CYR - SUR - LE - RHÔNE

4°822'E

Ruisseau des Lésardes

Ruisseau de Molière

Ruisseau du Cognet

Rhône

Ruisseau de la Félodière

Ruisseau de Murinand

Besset

Montmain

Lesardes

Bertholon

Gerine

Cognet

45°509'N

MASSIF

Grandes Places

CENTRAL

L'Arsélie

Ruisseau de Fongeant

Mornachon

Le Champon

Rozier

Bonnivières

AMPUIS

Vérenay

Le Champin

La Viallière

Ritolas

Ruisseau du Reynard

La Brosse

Le Plomb

Basse-Viallière

Fongeant

Chatelon

Le Truchet

Fourvier

Chavaroche

Nève

Baleyat

Leyat

Lancement

Côte Rozier

Marsanne

La Triote

Rochins

La Landonne

Côte Bodin

Le Combard

Grand Taillis

La Roche

Bas-Boucharey

Janet

Les Moutonnes

Le Mollard

Le Carcan

Le Bourg

REVENTIN - VAUGRIS

Côte Blonde

La Brocarde

Le Goutay

La Taquière

Côte Brune

Ruisseau de Gerbole

45°494'N

45°484'N

Isère

TUPIN - ET - SEMONS

Rhône

Mi 0   0.31   0.62   0.93   1.24

Km 0   0.5   1   1.5   2

Département ----------
COMMUNE ··············
Body of Water
LAND FEATURE

Côte-Rôtie vineyards
Tupin-et-Semons [13]

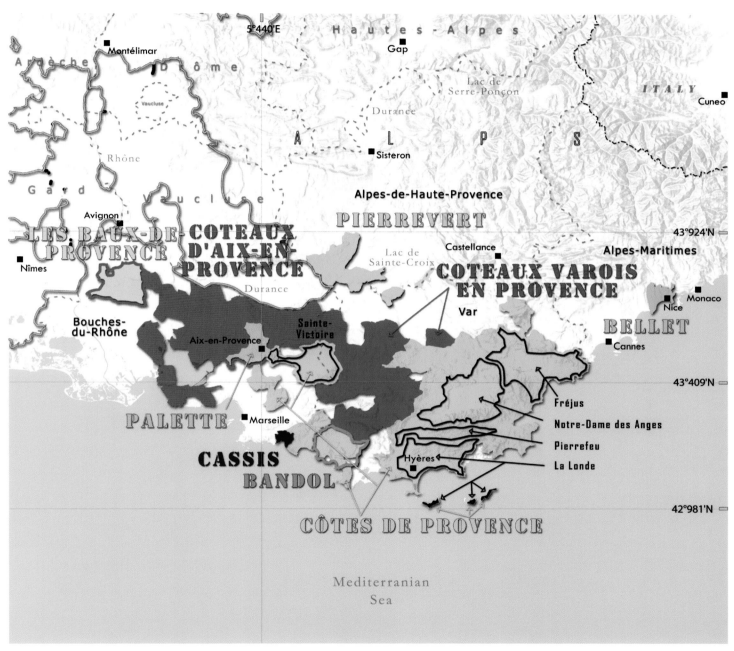

PROVENCE
AOC [9]
Subzone of Côtes de Provence AOC [5] ━━

LES BAUX-DE-PROVENCE

COTEAUX D'AIX-EN-PROVENCE

PIERREVERT

COTEAUX VAROIS EN PROVENCE

BELLET

PALETTE

CASSIS

BANDOL

CÔTES DE PROVENCE

Fréjus
Notre-Dame des Anges
Pierrefeu
La Londe

Montélimar
Gap
Cuneo
Sisteron
Avignon
Nîmes
Castellance
Nice
Monaco
Aix-en-Provence
Sainte-Victoire
Cannes
Marseille
Hyères

ITALY

Hautes-Alpes
Lac de Serre-Ponçon
Durance
Drôme
Vaucluse
Rhône
Gard
ALPS
Alpes-de-Haute-Provence
Alpes-Maritimes
Var
Bouches-du-Rhône
Durance
Lac de Sainte-Croix

Mediterranian Sea

5°440'E
43°924'N
43°409'N
42°981'N

Département
Body of Water
COUNTRY
Town / Commune ■
LAND FEATURE
RHÔNE

Mi 0   12.43   24.85   37.28   49.71
Km 0   20   40   60   80

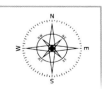

LANGUEDOC
TOTAL AOC [21]

GENERIC AOC [1]
OTHER AOC [20]

Geographical Designation of Languedoc AOC [11] ——
Subzone of Saint-Chinian [2] ——

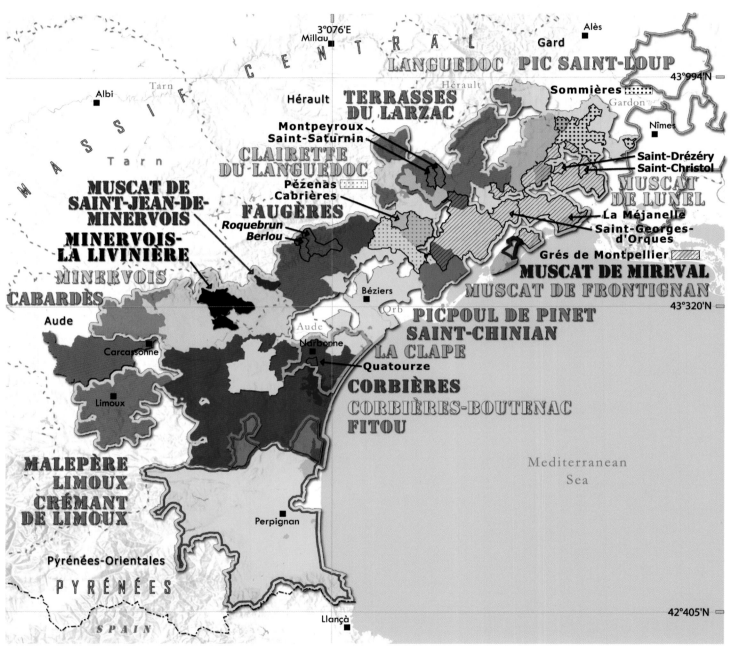

LANGUEDOC

PIC SAINT-LOUP

3°076'E
Millau

Gard
Alès

43°994'N

Tarn
Albi

Hérault

Sommières

Gardon

Héraut

Nîmes

Héraut

TERRASSES DU LARZAC

Tarn

Montpeyroux
Saint-Saturnin

Saint-Drézéry
Saint-Christol

CLAIRETTE DU-LANGUEDOC

Pézenas
Cabrières

MUSCAT DE LUNEL

MUSCAT DE SAINT-JEAN-DE-MINERVOIS

FAUGÈRES

Roquebrun
Berlou

La Méjanelle
Saint-Georges-d'Orques

MINERVOIS-LA LIVINIÈRE

Grés de Montpellier

MINERVOIS

MUSCAT DE MIREVAL

CABARDÈS

Béziers

MUSCAT DE FRONTIGNAN

Aude

Orb

Aude

PICPOUL DE PINET

43°320'N

Carcassonne

Narbonne

SAINT-CHINIAN

LA CLAPE

Quatourze

CORBIÈRES

Limoux

CORBIÈRES-BOUTENAC

FITOU

Mediterranean Sea

MALEPÈRE
LIMOUX
CRÉMANT DE LIMOUX

Perpignan

Pyrénées-Orientales

PYRÉNÉES

42°405'N

SPAIN

Llançà

Mi	0		12.43		24.85		37.28		49.71
Km	0		20		40		60		80

Département - - - - -
Body of Water
COUNTRY — · · — · · —
Commune / City ■
LAND FEATURE
RHÔNE ——
ROUSSILLON ——

France

ROUSSILLON

TOTAL AOC [9]

GENERIC AOC [1]
OTHER AOC [8]

Geographical Designation of Côtes du Roussillon-Villages [5] ——

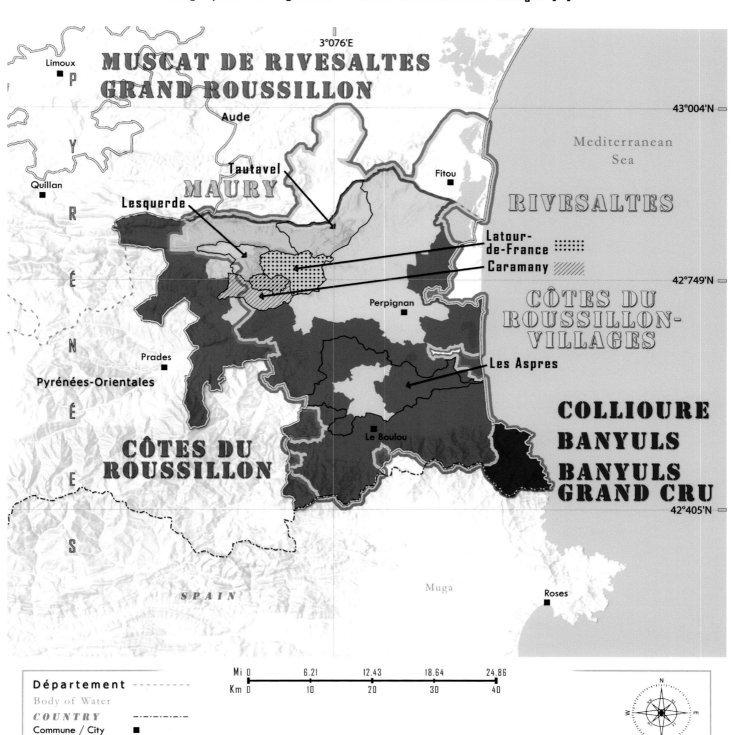

3°076'E

MUSCAT DE RIVESALTES
GRAND ROUSSILLON

Limoux

P

Aude

Quillan

Tautavel

MAURY

Lesquerde

Fitou

Mediterranean
Sea

43°004'N

RIVESALTES

Latour-
de-France

Caramany

42°749'N

Perpignan

CÔTES DU
ROUSSILLON-
VILLAGES

Prades

Pyrénées-Orientales

Les Aspres

COLLIOURE

BANYULS

Le Boulou

CÔTES DU
ROUSSILLON

BANYULS
GRAND CRU

42°405'N

S P A I N

Muga

Roses

Département

Body of Water

COUNTRY

Commune / City

LAND FEATURE

LANGUEDOC

Mi 0   6.21   12.43   18.64   24.86
Km 0   10   20   30   40

SOUTH WEST FRANCE
TOTAL AOC [32]

Subzone of Corrèze AOC [1] ——

Gaillac Premières Côtes AOC grape production ··········

Charente
Cognac
Charente
0°357'E
Charente-Maritime
Charente
Haute-Vienne
Ussel
Allier River
Puy-de-Dôme
Thiviers
Corrèze
Dordogne
Coteaux de la Vézère
45°323'N
Bay of Biscay
Gironde
Vézère
Dordogne
Dordogne
CORRÈZE
MASSIF CENTRAL
Cantal
Truyère
CÔTES DE BERGERAC
Isle
BERGERAC
MONTRAVEL
ROSETTE
HAUT-MONTRAVEL
Dordogne
Bordeaux
Aurillac
ENTRAYGUES-LE FEL
CÔTES DE MONTRAVEL
PÉCHARMANT
SAUSSIGNAC
MONBAZILLAC
Lozère
CÔTES DE DURAS
Garonne
Lot
Figeac
ESTAING
CÔTES DU MARMANDAIS
Lot-et-Garonne
Lot
CAHORS
Lot
MARCILLAC
Rodez
44°386'N
FLOC DE GASCOGNE
BUZET
Garonne
Agen
COTEAUX DU QUERCY
CÔTES DE MILLAU
Landes
BRULHOIS
Tarn-et-Garonne
Tarn
Albi
Aveyron
TURSAN
SAINT-SARDOS
Tarn
Adour
Gers
FRONTON
GAILLAC
Toulouse
Tarn
GAILLAC PREMIÈRES CÔTES
Bayonne
BÉARN
MADIRAN
Garonne
Hérault
IROULÉGUY
Ousse
PACHERENC-DU-VIC-BILH
Haute-Garonne
Pau
Gave d'Oloron
JURANÇON
Carcassonne
Pyrénées-Atlantiques
Hautes-Pyrénées
Ariege
Aude
43°009'N
SPAIN
Mediterranean Sea
Perpignan
P Y R É N É E S
ANDORRA
Pyrénées-Orientales

Mi 0   18.64   37.28   55.92   74.56
Km 0   30   60   90   120

Département --------
Body of Water
COUNTRY –·–·–·–
Town / Commune ■
LAND FEATURE
LANGUEDOC
BORDEAUX

BORDEAUX
TOTAL AOC [40]

GENERIC AOC [3]
OTHER AOC [37]

Subzone of Côtes de Bordeaux AOC [5] ——

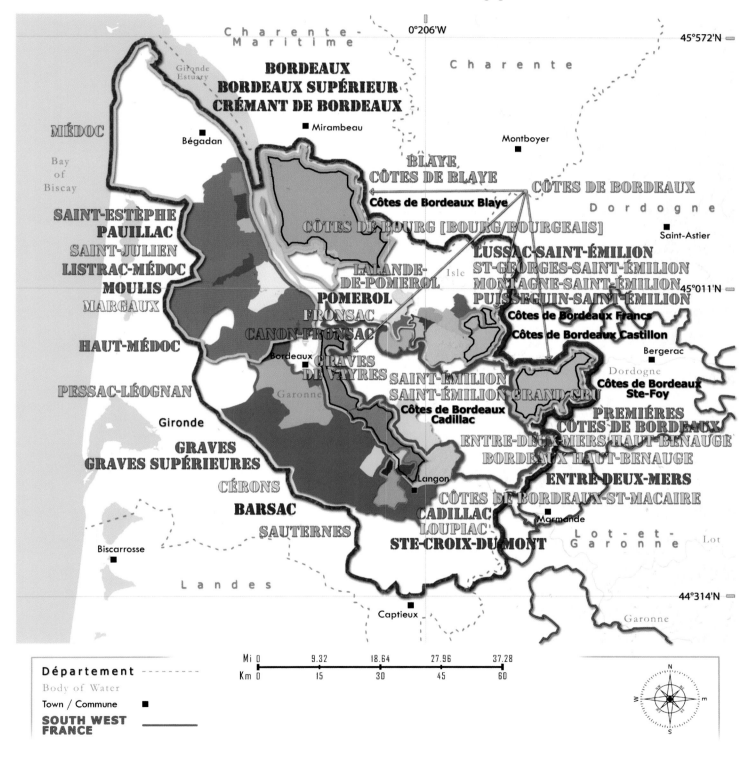

Département – – – – – –
Body of Water
Town / Commune ■
SOUTH WEST FRANCE ————

Mi 0   9.32   18.64   27.96   37.28
Km 0   15   30   45   60

Saint-Estèphe AOC
MÉDOC 1855 CLASSIFICATION (REVISED 1973)
TOTAL CHÂTEAUX [61]

2nd Growth [2] - 3rd Growth [1] - 4th Growth [1] - 5th Growth [1]

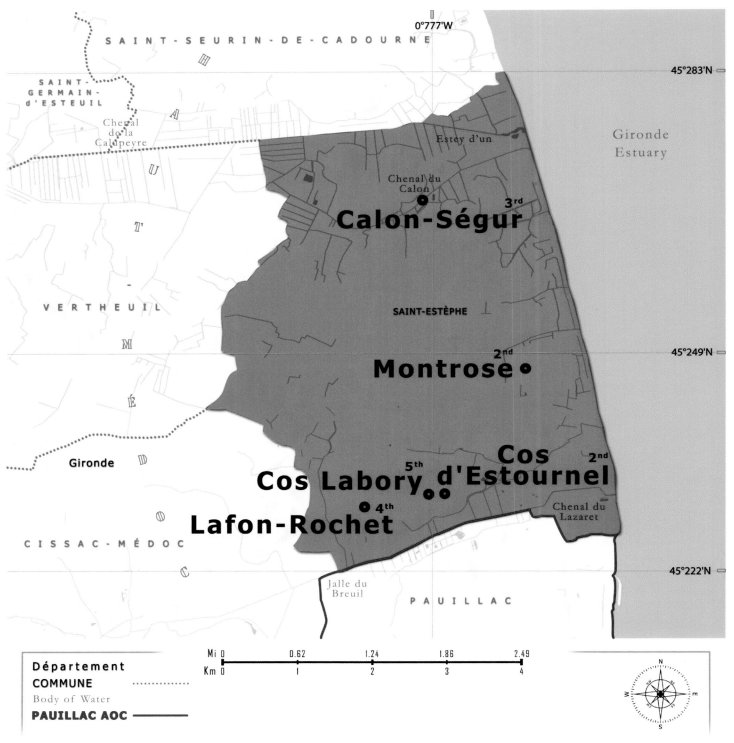

Pauillac AOC
MÉDOC 1855 CLASSIFICATION (REVISED 1973)
TOTAL CHÂTEAUX [61]

1st Growth [3] - 2nd Growth [2] - 4th Growth [1] - 5th Growth [12]

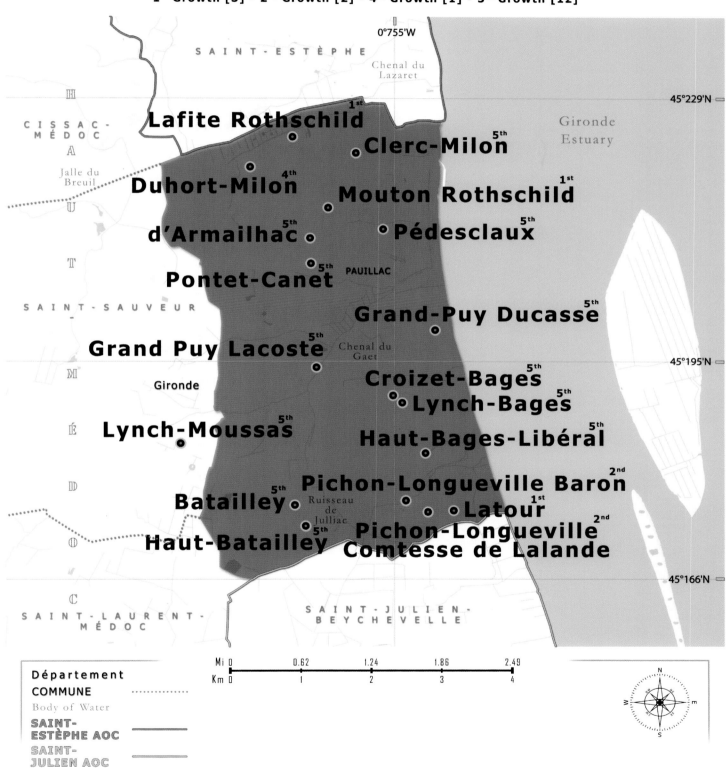

SAINT-ESTÈPHE

0°755'W

Chenal du Lazaret

45°229'N

CISSAC-MÉDOC

Gironde Estuary

Jalle du Breuil

Lafite Rothschild 1st

Clerc-Milon 5th

Duhort-Milon 4th

Mouton Rothschild 1st

d'Armailhac 5th

Pédesclaux 5th

Pontet-Canet 5th

PAUILLAC

SAINT-SAUVEUR

Grand-Puy Ducasse 5th

Grand Puy Lacoste 5th

Chenal du Gaet

45°195'N

Gironde

Croizet-Bages 5th

Lynch-Bages 5th

Lynch-Moussas 5th

Haut-Bages-Libéral 5th

Pichon-Longueville Baron 2nd

Batailley 5th

Ruisseau de Julliac

Latour 1st

Haut-Batailley 5th

Pichon-Longueville Comtesse de Lalande 2nd

45°166'N

SAINT-LAURENT-MÉDOC

SAINT-JULIEN-BEYCHEVELLE

Mi 0   0.62   1.24   1.86   2.49
Km 0   1   2   3   4

Département
COMMUNE ....
Body of Water
SAINT-ESTÈPHE AOC ———
SAINT-JULIEN AOC ———

Saint-Julien AOC
MÉDOC 1855 CLASSIFICATION (REVISED 1973)
TOTAL CHÂTEAUX [61]

2nd Growth [5] - 3rd Growth [2] - 4th Growth [4]

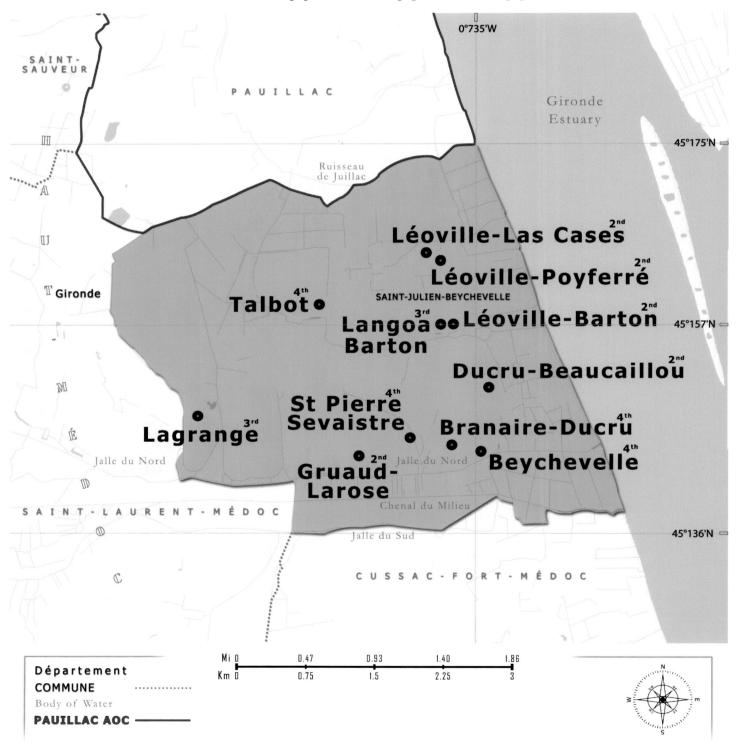

Léoville-Las Cases 2nd

Léoville-Poyferré 2nd

SAINT-JULIEN-BEYCHEVELLE

Talbot 4th

Langoa Barton 3rd

Léoville-Barton 2nd

Ducru-Beaucaillou 2nd

St Pierre Sevaistre 4th

Branaire-Ducru 4th

Lagrange 3rd

Gruaud-Larose 2nd

Beychevelle 4th

Département

COMMUNE ....

Body of Water

PAUILLAC AOC ————

| Mi 0 | 0.47 | 0.93 | 1.40 | 1.86 |
| Km 0 | 0.75 | 1.5 | 2.25 | 3 |

Margaux AOC

MÉDOC 1855 CLASSIFICATION (REVISED 1973)

TOTAL CHÂTEAUX [61]

1st Growth [1] - 2nd Growth [5] - 3rd Growth [10] - 4th Growth [3] - 5th Growth [2]

ARCINS

MOULIS-EN-MÉDOC

Estey de Tayac

0°668'W

45°063'N

Gironde Estuary

Ruisseau du Sable

SOUSSANS

La Louise

MARGAUX

Margaux 1st
Marquis d'Alesme-Becker 3rd
Malescot St-Exupéry 3rd
Durfort-Vivens 2nd
d'Issan 3rd
Palmer 3rd
Prieuré Lichine 4th
Desmirail 3rd
Boyd Cantenac 3rd

2nd Lascombes
3rd Ferriére
4th Marquis de Terme
2nd Rauzan Gassies
2nd Rauzan Ségla
3rd Cantenac-Brown
2nd Brane-Cantenac

CANTENAC

La Parise

3rd Kirwan
4th Pouget

HAUT-MÉDOC

Gironde

AVENSAN

LABARDE

Dauzac 5th

45°011'N

Le Moulinat

Du Tertre 5th

Giscours 3rd

MACAU

ARSAC

Ruisseau de Laurina

LUDON-MÉDOC

HAUT-MÉDOC

44°966'N

LE PIAN-MÉDOC

Mi 0 — 0.93 — 1.86 — 2.80 — 3.73
Km 0 — 1.5 — 3 — 4.5 — 6

Département
COMMUNE
Body of Water
MOULIS AOC
CÔTES DE BOURG AOC

Haut-Médoc AOC
Pessac-Léognan AOC
MÉDOC 1855 CLASSIFICATION (REVISED 1973)
TOTAL CHÂTEAUX [61]

1ST Growth [1] - 3rd Growth [1] - 4th Growth [1] - 5th Growth [3]

0°689'W

Charente

Lesparre-Médoc

Chevanceaux

45°283'N

Bay
of
Biscay

Charente-
Maritime

Donnezac

SAINT-ESTÈPHE AOC

PAUILLAC AOC

Belgrave5th

La Tour4th

Saint-Laurent-
Médoc

SAINT-JULIEN AOC

Carnet

Camensac5th

LISTRAC-MÉDOC AOC

MOULIS AOC

MARGAUX AOC

Isle

Bourg

Macau

Cantemerle5th

44°993'N

Ludon-Médoc

La Lagune3rd

Lacanau

Pomerol

Gironde

Dordogne

Libourne

Bordeaux

Haut-Brion1st

Pessac

Garonne

44°749'N

Lanton

Martillac

Arcachon Bay

Cérons

Cadillac

Mi 0	6.21	12.43	18.64	24.86
Km 0	10	20	30	40

Département - - - - -
Body of Water
City / Commune ■
GRAVES AOC ――――
MÉDOC AOC ――――
BORDEAUX AOC ――――

N

W E

S

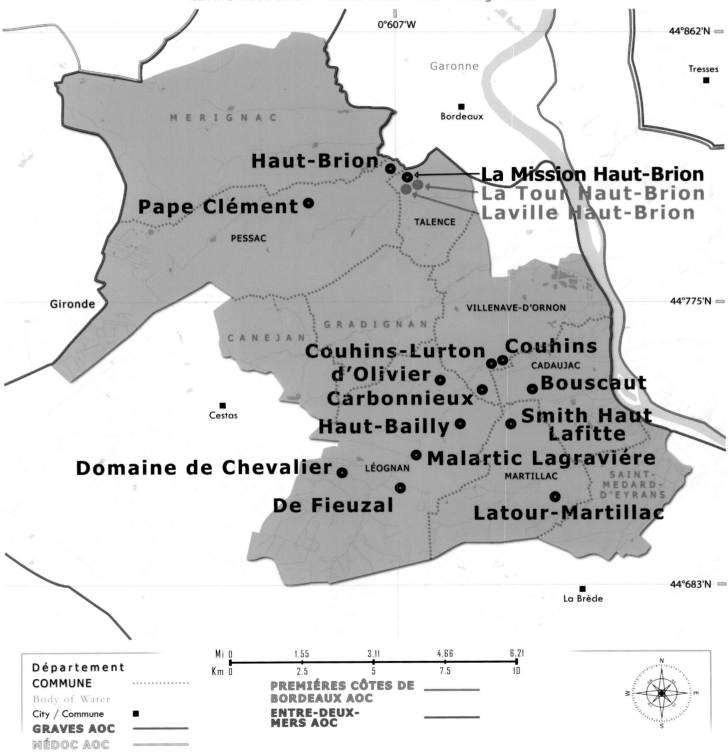

Pessac-Léognan AOC
GRAVES 1953 CLASSIFICATION (REVISED 1959)
TOTAL CHÂTEAUX [16]

In production [14]
Discontinued [2]
La Tour Haut-Brion - Red wine - Final vintage 2005
Laville Haut-Brion - White wine - Final vintage 2008

0°607'W
44°862'N

Garonne

Tresses

MERIGNAC

Bordeaux

Haut-Brion

La Mission Haut-Brion
La Tour Haut-Brion
Laville Haut-Brion

Pape Clément

TALENCE

PESSAC

Gironde

44°775'N

VILLENAVE-D'ORNON

GRADIGNAN

CANEJAN

Couhins-Lurton   **Couhins**

d'Olivier   CADAUJAC

Carbonnieux   **Bouscaut**

Cestas

Haut-Bailly   **Smith Haut Lafitte**

Domaine de Chevalier   **Malartic Lagraviére**

LÉOGNAN

MARTILLAC   SAINT-MEDARD-D'EYRANS

De Fieuzal

Latour-Martillac

44°683'N

La Brède

Mi 0 · 1.55 · 3.11 · 4.66 · 6.21
Km 0 · 2.5 · 5 · 7.5 · 10

Département
COMMUNE ···········
Body of Water
City / Commune ■
GRAVES AOC ──────
MÉDOC AOC ──────

PREMIÉRES CÔTES DE BORDEAUX AOC ──────
ENTRE-DEUX-MERS AOC ──────

N
W · E
S

Barsac AOC
Sauternes AOC
SAUTERNES 1855 CLASSIFICATION
TOTAL CHÂTEAUX [27]

Premier Cru Supérieur [1] '1ᵉʳS'
Premier Cru [11] '1ᵉʳ'
Deuxième Cru [15] '2ᵉᵐᵉ'

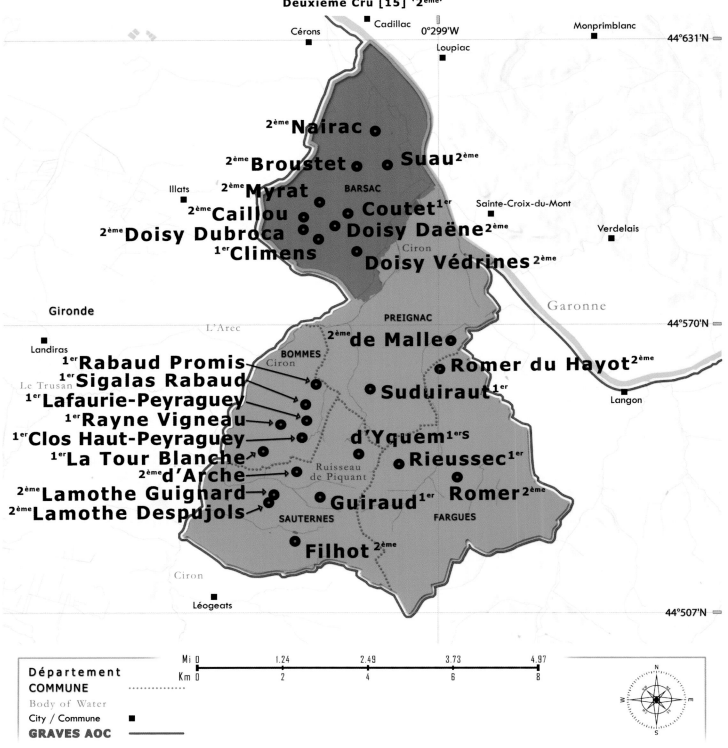

Cérons · Cadillac · 0°299'W · Monprimblanc · 44°631'N
Loupiac

2ᵉᵐᵉ Nairac

2ᵉᵐᵉ Broustet · Suau 2ᵉᵐᵉ

Illats · 2ᵉᵐᵉ Myrat · BARSAC

2ᵉᵐᵉ Caillou · Coutet 1ᵉʳ · Sainte-Croix-du-Mont

2ᵉᵐᵉ Doisy Dubroca · Doisy Daëne 2ᵉᵐᵉ · Verdelais

1ᵉʳ Climens · Ciron

Doisy Védrines 2ᵉᵐᵉ

Gironde · Garonne · 44°570'N

L'Arec · PREIGNAC

Landiras · 2ᵉᵐᵉ de Malle

1ᵉʳ Rabaud Promis · BOMMES · Ciron

1ᵉʳ Sigalas Rabaud · Romer du Hayot 2ᵉᵐᵉ

Le Trusan

1ᵉʳ Lafaurie-Peyraguey · Suduiraut 1ᵉʳ

1ᵉʳ Rayne Vigneau · Langon

1ᵉʳ Clos Haut-Peyraguey · d'Yquem 1ᵉʳS

1ᵉʳ La Tour Blanche · Ruisseau · Rieussec 1ᵉʳ
de Piquant

2ᵉᵐᵉ d'Arche

2ᵉᵐᵉ Lamothe Guignard · Guiraud 1ᵉʳ · Romer 2ᵉᵐᵉ

2ᵉᵐᵉ Lamothe Despujols · SAUTERNES · FARGUES

Filhot 2ᵉᵐᵉ

Ciron

Léogeats · 44°507'N

| Mi | 0 | 1.24 | 2.49 | 3.73 | 4.97 |
| Km | 0 | 2 | 4 | 6 | 8 |

Département
COMMUNE ···············
Body of Water
City / Commune ■
GRAVES AOC ———

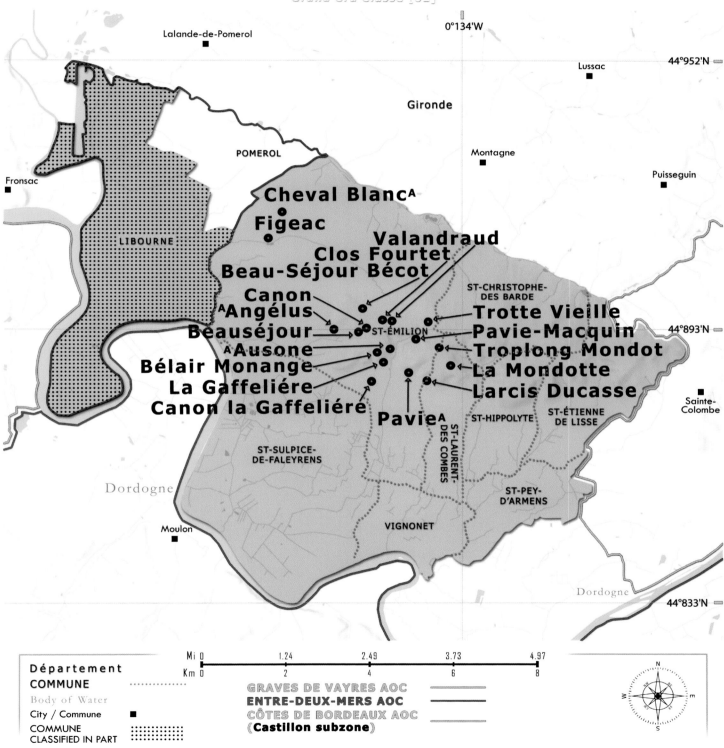

Saint-Émilion Grand Cru AOC

SAINT-ÉMILION 1955 CLASSIFICATION
AMENDED 1958. LATEST UPDATE 2012

TOTAL CHÂTEAUX [82]

Premier Grand Cru Classé A [4]
Premier Grand Cru Classé [14]
Grand Cru Classé [62]

Lalande-de-Pomerol

Lussac

44°952'N

Gironde

Montagne

POMEROL

Puisseguin

Fronsac

LIBOURNE

Cheval BlancA

Figeac

Valandraud

Clos Fourtet

Beau-Séjour Bécot

ST-CHRISTOPHE-
DES BARDE

Canon

A**Angélus**

Trotte Vieille

Beauséjour

ST-ÉMILION

Pavie-Macquin

44°893'N

A**Ausone**

Troplong Mondot

Bélair Monange

La Mondotte

La Gaffeliére

Larcis Ducasse

Canon la Gaffeliére

Sainte-
Colombe

PavieA

ST-HIPPOLYTE

ST-ÉTIENNE
DE LISSE

ST-LAURENT-
DES COMBES

ST-SULPICE-
DE-FALEYRENS

Dordogne

ST-PEY-
D'ARMENS

Moulon

VIGNONET

Dordogne

44°833'N

| Mi | 0 | | 1.24 | | 2.49 | | 3.73 | | 4.97 |
| Km | 0 | | | 2 | | 4 | | 6 | | 8 |

Département
COMMUNE
Body of Water
City / Commune ■
COMMUNE
CLASSIFIED IN PART

GRAVES DE VAYRES AOC
ENTRE-DEUX-MERS AOC
CÔTES DE BORDEAUX AOC
(Castillon subzone)

N
W E
S

LOIRE VALLEY
TOTAL AOC [53]

GENERIC AOC [2]
Sub-regions of Loire Valley - AOC [51]

English Channel

0°203'E

Seine

Paris

Troyes

Rennes

CRÉMANT DE LOIRE

Central Vineyards
(Upper Loire)
[9]

Sarthe

Touraine [13]

Loiret

47°901'N

Anjou-Saumur [17]

Loire

Auxerre

Loire-Atlantique

Maine-
et-
Loire

Loir-
et-
Cher

Cher

Pays Nantais
[7]

Nantes

Sancerre

47°325'N

Loire

Nièvre

Indre-
et-
Loire

Vendée

Deux-Sèvres

Indre

ROSÉ DE LOIRE

Loire

Vienne

Allier

Saône

46°347'N

Central France
[5]

Vichy

Bay of
Biscay

Puy-de-Dôme

Loire

Lyon

Cognac

Loire

45°438'N

MASSIF

Dordogne

Berberac

CENTRAL

Rhône

Bordeaux

Garonne

Cahors

Montélimar

Mi	0		31.7		62.14		93.21		124.27
Km	0		50		100		150		200

Département - - - - - - - -

Body of Water

Town / City ■

LAND FEATURE

N
W E
S

Pays Nantais
AOC [7]

Subzone

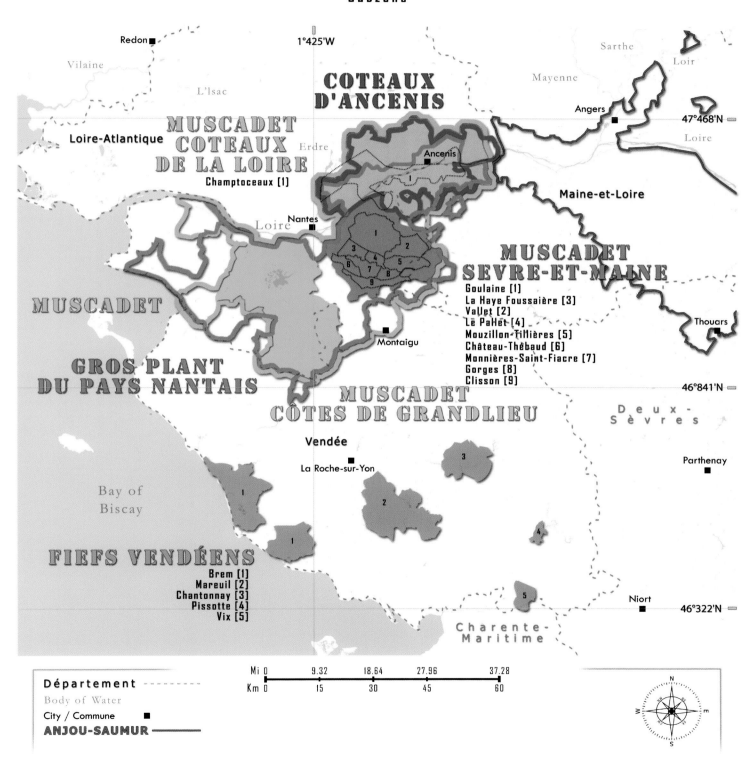

Redon

Vilaine

L'Isac

1°425'W

Sarthe

Loir

MUSCADET COTEAUX DE LA LOIRE

COTEAUX D'ANCENIS

Mayenne

Angers

47°468'N

Loire-Atlantique

Erdre

Ancenis

Loire

Champtoceaux [1]

Loire

Nantes

Maine-et-Loire

MUSCADET

MUSCADET SEVRE-ET-MAINE

Goulaine [1]
La Haye Foussaière [3]
Vallet [2]
Le Pallet [4]
Mouzillon-Tillières [5]
Château-Thébaud [6]
Monnières-Saint-Fiacre [7]
Gorges [8]
Clisson [9]

Thouars

GROS PLANT DU PAYS NANTAIS

Montaigu

MUSCADET CÔTES DE GRANDLIEU

46°841'N

Deux-Sèvres

Vendée

La Roche-sur-Yon

Parthenay

Bay of Biscay

FIEFS VENDÉENS

Brem [1]
Mareuil [2]
Chantonnay [3]
Pissotte [4]
Vix [5]

Niort

46°322'N

Charente-Maritime

Département - - - - - - -
Body of Water
City / Commune ■
ANJOU-SAUMUR ————

Mi 0   9.32   18.64   27.96   37.28
Km 0   15   30   45   60

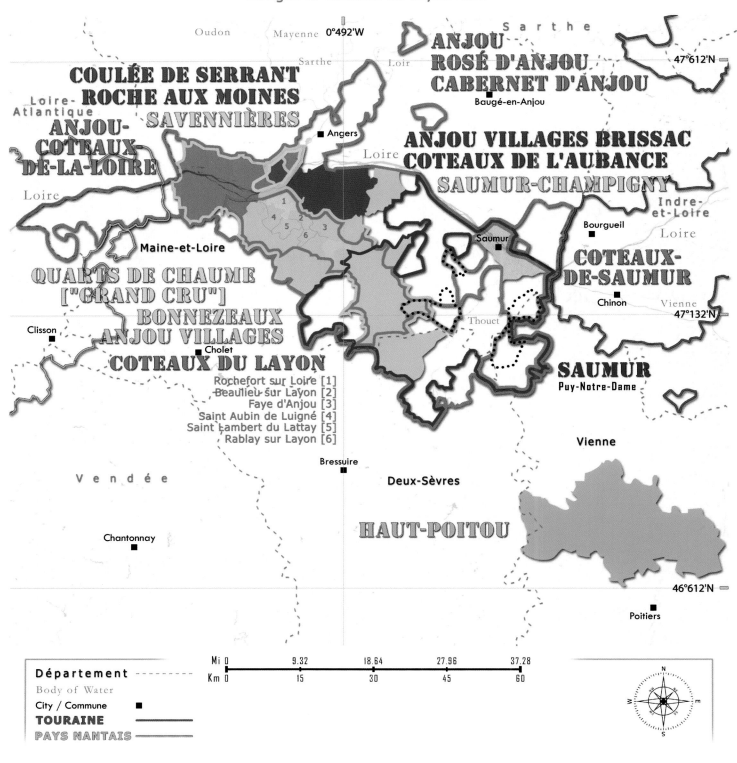

Anjou-Saumur
AOC [17]

Subzone of Saumur AOC ·····
Villages of Coteaux du Layon AOC ───

Oudon
Mayenne
0°492'W
Sarthe
47°612'N

COULÉE DE SERRANT
ROCHE AUX MOINES
SAVENNIÈRES

Loire-
Atlantique
ANJOU-
COTEAUX-
DE-LA-LOIRE

ANJOU
ROSÉ D'ANJOU
CABERNET D'ANJOU
Baugé-en-Anjou

Angers
Loire

ANJOU VILLAGES BRISSAC
COTEAUX DE L'AUBANCE
SAUMUR-CHAMPIGNY

Indre-
et-Loire
Loire

Loire

Bourgueil

Saumur

Maine-et-Loire

COTEAUX-
DE-SAUMUR

Chinon
Vienne
47°132'N

QUARTS DE CHAUME
["GRAND CRU"]
BONNEZEAUX
ANJOU VILLAGES
COTEAUX DU LAYON

Thouet

Clisson

Cholet

Rochefort sur Loire [1]
Beaulieu sur Layon [2]
Faye d'Anjou [3]
Saint Aubin de Luigné [4]
Saint Lambert du Lattay [5]
Rablay sur Layon [6]

SAUMUR
Puy-Notre-Dame

Vienne

Bressuire

Vendée

Deux-Sèvres

HAUT-POITOU

Chantonnay

46°612'N

Poitiers

	Mi 0	9.32	18.64	27.96	37.28
	Km 0	15	30	45	60

Département ---------
Body of Water
City / Commune ■
TOURAINE ──────
PAYS NANTAIS ──────

Touraine

AOC [13]

Subzone of Touraine AOC [5] ·····

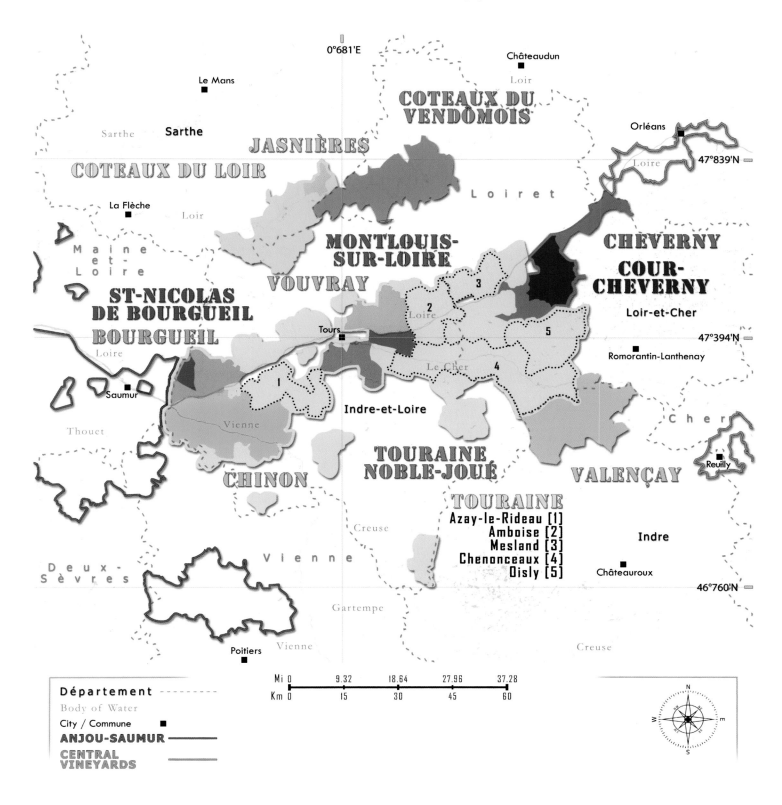

Châteaudun

Le Mans

Loir

COTEAUX DU VENDÔMOIS

Orléans

Sarthe   **Sarthe**

47°839'N

JASNIÈRES

Loire

COTEAUX DU LOIR

L o i r e t

La Flèche

Loir

M a i n e
e t -
L o i r e

**MONTLOUIS-
SUR-LOIRE**

CHEVERNY

VOUVRAY

**COUR-
CHEVERNY**

**ST-NICOLAS
DE BOURGUEIL**

3

Loir-et-Cher

BOURGUEIL

Loire

2

Tours

Loire

5

47°394'N

Romorantin-Lanthenay

Saumur

Le Cher

4

C h e r

Thouet

Vienne

1

Indre-et-Loire

Reuilly

CHINON

**TOURAINE
NOBLE-JOUÉ**

VALENÇAY

Indre

TOURAINE

Creuse

**Azay-le-Rideau [1]
Amboise [2]
Mesland [3]
Chenonceaux [4]
Oisly [5]**

Châteauroux

D e u x -
S è v r e s

V i e n n e

46°760'N

Gartempe

Poitiers

Vienne

Creuse

Mi 0	9.32	18.64	27.96	37.28
Km 0	15	30	45	60

Département ------

Body of Water

City / Commune ■

ANJOU-SAUMUR ——

**CENTRAL
VINEYARDS** ——

Central Vineyards (Upper Loire)
AOC [9]

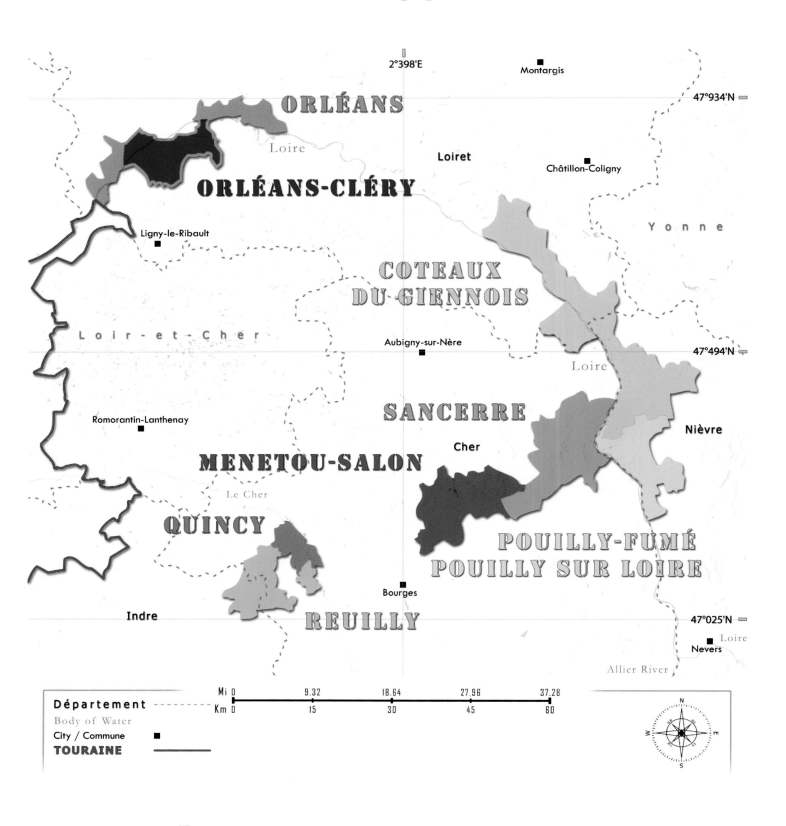

2°398'E

Montargis

47°934'N

ORLÉANS

Loire

Loiret

Châtillon-Coligny

ORLÉANS-CLÉRY

Y o n n e

Ligny-le-Ribault

COTEAUX
DU GIENNOIS

L o i r - e t - C h e r

Aubigny-sur-Nère

47°494'N

Loire

SANCERRE

Romorantin-Lanthenay

Nièvre

Cher

MENETOU-SALON

Le Cher

QUINCY

POUILLY-FUMÉ
POUILLY SUR LOIRE

Bourges

Indre

REUILLY

47°025'N

Loire

Nevers

Allier River

	Mi 0	9.32	18.64	27.96	37.28
	Km 0	15	30	45	60

Département ------
Body of Water
City / Commune ■
TOURAINE ▬▬▬

N
W   E
S

Central France

AOC [5]

Subzone of Côtes d'Auvergne AOC [5] ·····

Loire
Nevers   3°338'E
Le Cher
N i è v r e
Châteauroux
Cher
Indre
S a ô n e - e t - L o i r e
Saône
Allier River
Moulins
Loire
46°552'N

SAINT-POURÇAIN

CHÂTEAUMEILLANT
Allier
Montluçon
CÔTES ROANNAISES

Guéret
C r e u s e
Vichy
A i n
45°978'N

CÔTES D'AUVERGNE
Madargues [1]
Chateaugay [2]
Chanturgue [3]
Corent [4]
Boudes [5]

Haute-Vienne
Loire
Lyon
Puy-de-Dôme
Loire
Ussel
Allier River
Vienne
CÔTES DU FOREZ
45°438'N
5
Saint-Étienne
Isère

C o r r è z e
Rhône
Drôme
Dordogne   M A S S I F   C E N T R A L
C a n t a l
Saint-Flour
H a u t e - L o i r e
Ardèche
Aurillac
Lot
Valence
Beaune
Côte-d'Or
Chalon-sur-Saône
Mâcon

Mi 0 .... 15.53 .... 31.07 .... 46.60 .... 62.14
Km 0 .... 25 .... 50 .... 75 100

Département -------
Body of Water
City / Commune ■
LAND FEATURE
BOURGOGNE AOC ———
BEAUJOLAIS AOC ———

COTEAUX DU LYONNAIS AOC ———
CÔTES DU RHÔNE AOC ———
CORRÈZE AOC ———

N
W   E
S

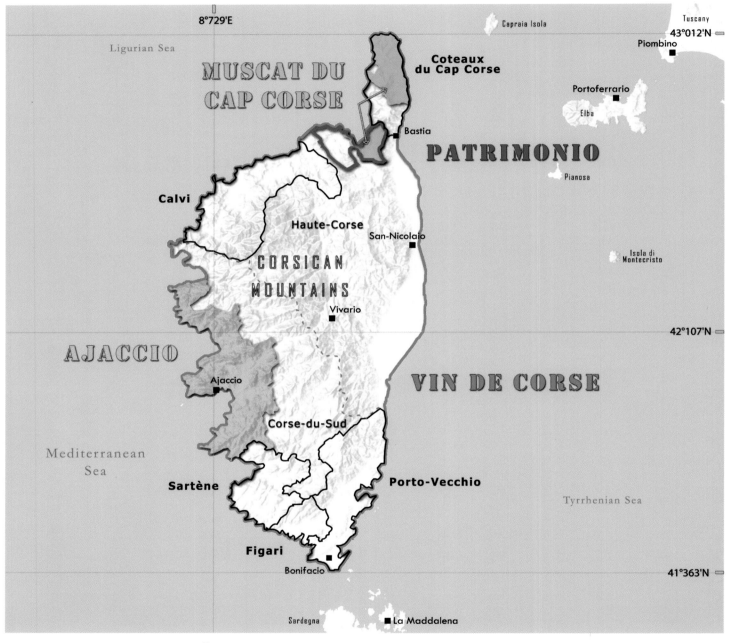

CORSE

TOTAL AOC [4]

GENERIC AOC [1]
OTHER AOC [3]

Subzone of Vin de Corse AOC [5] ——

Ligurian Sea

Capraia Isola

Tuscany

43°012'N

Piombino

8°729'E

MUSCAT DU
CAP CORSE

Coteaux
du Cap Corse

Portoferrario

Elba

Bastia

PATRIMONIO

Pianosa

Calvi

Haute-Corse

San-Nicolaio

CORSICAN
MOUNTAINS

Isola di
Montecristo

Vivario

42°107'N

AJACCIO

Ajaccio

VIN DE CORSE

Mediterranean
Sea

Corse-du-Sud

Porto-Vecchio

Tyrrhenian Sea

Sartène

Figari

Bonifacio

41°363'N

Sardegna

La Maddalena

| Mi 0 | 15.53 | 31.07 | 46.60 | 62.14 |
| Km 0 | 25 | 50 | 75 | 100 |

Département - - - - - - -
Body of Water
Commune / City ■
LAND FEATURE

CLASSIFICATION SYSTEM
DOCG [Denominazione di Origine Controllata e Garantita =
      Controlled and Guaranteed Designation of Origin]
DOC [Denominazione di Origine Controllata = Controlled Designation of Origin]
IGT [Indicazione Geografica Tipica = Indication of Geographical Typicality]
VINO D'ITALIA = VDT [Vino da Tavola = table wine]

20 Regions

76 DOCG

332 DOC

170 MGA vineyards of Barolo DOCG

66 MGA vineyards of Barbaresco DOCG

MGA = MENZIONI GEOGRAFICHE AGGIUNTIVE [Additional Geographical Definitions]

Shared DOCG, DOC and vineyards are counted only once in the total

ITALY

Valle d'Aosta [1 DOC]

DENOMINATION	RANK	EST.
VALLE D'AOSTA	DOC	1986

Piemonte [18 DOCG / 41 DOC]

DENOMINATION	RANK	EST.	DENOMINATION	RANK	EST.	DENOMINATION	RANK	EST.
ALBA	DOC	2010	COLLINE NOVARESI	DOC	1994	GRIGNOLINO DEL MONFERRATO CASALESE	DOC	1974
ALBUGNANO	DOC	1997	COLLINE SALUZZESI	DOC	1996	LANGHE	DOC	1994
ALTA LANGA	DOCG	2011	CORTESE DELL'ALTO MONFERRATO	DOC	1979	LESSONA	DOC	1976
ASTI	DOCG	1993	COSTE DELLA SESIA	DOC	1996	LOAZZOLO	DOC	1992
BARBARESCO	DOCG	1980	DOGLIANI	DOCG	2005	MALVASIA DI CASTELNUOVO DON BOSCO	DOC	1973
BARBERA D'ALBA	DOC	1970	DOLCETTO D'ACQUI	DOC	1972	MONFERRATO	DOC	1994
BARBERA D'ASTI	DOCG	2008	DOLCETTO D'ALBA	DOC	1974	NEBBIOLO D'ALBA	DOC	1970
BARBERA DEL MONFERRATO	DOC	1970	DOLCETTO D'ASTI	DOC	1974	NIZZA	DOCG	2014
BARBERA DEL MONFERRATO SUPERIORE	DOCG	2008	DOLCETTO DI DIANO D' ALBA	DOCG	2009	PIEMONTE	DOC	1994
BAROLO	DOCG	1980	DOLCETTO DI OVADA	DOC	1972	PINEROLESE	DOC	1996
BOCA	DOC	1969	DOLCETTO DI OVADA SUPERIORE	DOCG	2008	ROERO	DOCG	2004
BRACHETTO D'ACQUI (ACQUI)	DOCG	1996	ERBALUCE DI CALUSO (CALUSO)	DOCG	2010	RUBINO DI CANTAVENNA	DOC	1970
BRAMATERRA	DOC	1979	FARA	DOC	1968	RUCHÈ DI CASTAGNOLE MONFERRATO	DOCG	2010
CALOSSO	DOC	2011	FREISA D'ASTI	DOC	1972	SIZZANO	DOC	1969
CANAVESE	DOC	1996	FREISA DI CHIERI	DOC	1973	STREVI	DOC	2005
CAREMA	DOC	1967	GABIANO	DOC	1983	TERRE ALFIERI	DOCG	2020
CASORZO (MALVASIA DI CASORZO D'ASTI)	DOC	1968	GATTINARA	DOCG	1990	VALLI OSSOLANE	DOC	2009
CISTERNA D'ASTI	DOC	2002	GAVI (CORTESE DI GAVI)	DOCG	1998	VALSUSA	DOC	1997
COLLI TORTONESI	DOC	1973	GHEMME	DOCG	1997	VERDUNO PELAVERGA	DOC	1995
COLLINA TORINESE	DOC	1999	GRIGNOLINO D'ASTI	DOC	1973			

Liguria [8 DOC out of 1 shared]

DENOMINATION	RANK	EST.	DENOMINATION	RANK	EST.	DENOMINATION	RANK	EST.
CINQUE TERRE	DOC	1973	GOLFO DEL TIGULLIO-PORTOFINO (PORTOFINO)	DOC	1997	ROSSESE DI DOLCEACQUA	DOC	1972
COLLI DI LUNI [shared with Toscana]	DOC	1989	PORNASSIO (ORMEASCO DI PORNASSIO)	DOC	2003	VAL POLCA˝VERA	DOC	1999
COLLINE DI LEVANTO	DOC	1995	RIVIERA LIGURE DI PONENTE	DOC	1988			

Lombardia [5 DOCG] [21 DOC out of 3 shared]

DENOMINATION	RANK	EST.	DENOMINATION	RANK	EST.	DENOMINATION	RANK	EST.
BONARDA DELL'OLTREPÒ PAVESE	DOC	2010	GARDA COLLI MANTOVANI	DOC	1976	SAN MARTINO DELLA BATTAGLIA [shared with Veneto]	DOC	1970
BOTTICINO	DOC	1968	LAMBRUSCO MANTOVANO	DOC	1987	SANGUE DI GIUDA DELL'OLTREPÒ PAVESE	DOC	2010
BUTTAFUOCO DELL'OLTREPÒ PAVESE	DOC	2010	LUGANA [shared with Veneto]	DOC	1967	SCANZO (MOSCATO DI SCANZO)	DOCG	2009
CAPRIANO DEL COLLE	DOC	1980	OLTREPÒ PAVESE	DOC	1970	SFORZATO DI VALTELLINA	DOCG	2003
CASTEGGIO	DOC	2010	OLTREPÒ PAVESE METODO CLASSICO	DOCG	2007	TERRE DEL COLLEONI (COLLEONI)	DOC	2011
CELLATICA	DOC	1968	OLTREPÒ PAVESE PINOT GRIGIO	DOC	2010	VALCALEPIO	DOC	1976
CURTEFRANCA	DOC	1995	PINOT NERO DELL'OLTREPÒ PAVESE	DOC	2010	VALTELLINA ROSSO (ROSSO DI VALTELLINA)	DOC	1968
FRANCIACORTA	DOCG	1995	RIVIERA DEL GARDA BRESCIANO	DOC	1977	VALTELLINA SUPERIORE	DOCG	1998
GARDA [shared with Veneto]	DOC	1996	SAN COLOMBANO AL LAMBRO	DOC	1984			

Trentino-Alto Adige [9 DOCG out of 3 shared]

DENOMINATION	RANK	EST.	DENOMINATION	RANK	EST.	DENOMINATION	RANK	EST.
ALTO ADIGE (SÜDTIROL/SÜDTIROLER)	DOC	1975	LAGO DI CALDARO/CALDARO (KALTERERSEE/KALTERER)	DOC	1970	TRENTO	DOC	1993
CASTELLER	DOC	1974	TEROLDEGO ROTALIANO	DOC	1971	VALDADIGE (ETSCHTALER) [shared with Veneto]	DOC	1975
DELLE VENEZIE [shared with Veneto and Friuli-Venezia Giulia]	DOC	2017	TRENTINO	DOC	1971	VALDADIGE TERRADEIFORTI [shared with Veneto]	DOC	2006

Veneto [14 DOCG out of 1 shared] [29 DOC out of 8 shared]

DENOMINATION	RANK	EST.	DENOMINATION	RANK	EST.	DENOMINATION	RANK	EST.
AMARONE DELLA VALPOLICELLA	DOCG	2010	FRIULARO DI BAGNOLI (BAGNOLI FRIULARO)	DOCG	2011	RECIOTO DELLA VALPOLICELLA	DOCG	2010
ARCOLE	DOC	2000	GAMBELLARA	DOC	1970	RECIOTO DI GAMBELLARA	DOCG	2008
BAGNOLI DI SOPRA (BAGNOLI)	DOC	1995	GARDA [shared with Lombardia]	DOC	1996	RECIOTO DI SOAVE	DOCG	1998
BARDOLINO	DOC	1968	LESSINI DURELLO	DOC	2011	RIVIERA DEL BRENTA	DOC	2004
BARDOLINO SUPERIORE	DOCG	2001	LISON [shared with Friuli-Venezia Giulia]	DOCG	2010	SAN MARTINO DELLA BATTAGLIA [shared with Lombardia]	DOC	1970
BIANCO DI CUSTOZA (CUSTOZA)	DOC	1971	LISON-PRAMAGGIORE [shared with Friuli-Venezia Giulia]	DOC	1971	SOAVE	DOC	1968
BREGANZE	DOC	1969	LUGANA [shared with Lombardia]	DOC	1967	SOAVE SUPERIORE	DOCG	2002
COLLI ASOLANI (ASOLO PROSECCO)	DOCG	2009	MERLARA	DOC	2000	VALDADIGE (ETSCHTALER) [shared with Veneto]	DOC	1975
COLLI BERICI	DOC	1973	MONTELLO COLLI ASOLANI	DOC	1977	VALDADIGE TERRADEIFORTI [shared with Veneto]	DOC	2006
COLLI DI CONEGLIANO	DOCG	2011	MONTELLO ROSSO (MONTELLO)	DOC	2011	VALPOLICELLA	DOC	1968
COLLI EUGANEI	DOC	1969	MONTI LESSINI	DOC	1987	VALPOLICELLA RIPASSO	DOC	2010
COLLI EUGANEI FIOR D'ARANCIO	DOCG	2010	PIAVE (VINI DEL PIAVE)	DOC	1971	VENEZIA	DOC	2010
CONEGLIANO VALDOBBIADENE PROSECCO	DOCG	2009	PIAVE MALANOTTE (MALANOTTE DEL PIAVE)	DOCG	2010	VICENZA	DOC	2000
CORTI BENEDETTINE DEL PADOVANO	DOC	2004	PROSECCO [shared with Friuli-Venezia Giulia]	DOC	2009	VIGNETI DELLA SERENISSIMA	DOC	2011
DELLE VENEZIE [shared with Trentino-Alto Adige and Friuli-Venezia Giulia]	DOC	2017						

Friuli-Venezia Giulia [4 DOCG out of 1 shared] [12 DOC out of 3 shared]

Name	Type	Year	Name	Type	Year	Name	Type	Year
CARSO (CARSO-KAR)	DOC	1985	FRIULI AQUILEIA	DOC	1975	LISON [shared with Veneto]	DOCG	2010
COLLI ORIENTALI DEL FRIULI PICOLIT	DOCG	2006	FRIULI COLLI ORIENTALI	DOC	1970	LISON-PRAMAGGIORE [shared with Veneto]	DOC	1971
COLLIO GORIZIANO (COLLIO)	DOC	1968	FRIULI GRAVE	DOC	1970	PROSECCO [shared with Veneto]	DOC	2009
DELLE VENEZIE [shared with Veneto and Trentino-Alto Adige]	DOC	2017	FRIULI ISONZO (ISONZO DEL FRIULI)	DOC	1974	RAMANDOLO	DOCG	2001
FRIULI (FRIULI VENEZIA GIULIA)	DOC	2016	FRIULI LATISANA	DOC	1975	ROSAZZO	DOCG	2011
FRIULI ANNIA	DOC	1995						

Emilia-Romagna [2 DOCG / 19 DOC]

Name	Type	Year	Name	Type	Year	Name	Type	Year
BOSCO ELICEO	DOC	1989	COLLI D'IMOLA	DOC	1997	MODENA (DI MODENA)	DOC	2009
COLLI BOLOGNESI	DOC	1975	COLLI PIACENTINI	DOC	1967	ORTRUGO DEI COLLI PIACENTINI	DOC	2010
COLLI BOLOGNESI CLASSICO PIGNOLETTO	DOCG	2011	COLLI ROMAGNA CENTRALE	DOC	2001	PIGNOLETTO	DOC	2014
COLLI DI FAENZA	DOC	1997	GUTTURNIO	DOC	2010	REGGIANO	DOC	1971
COLLI DI PARMA	DOC	1982	LAMBRUSCO DI SORBARA	DOC	1970	RENO	DOC	1987
COLLI DI RIMINI	DOC	1996	LAMBRUSCO GRASPAROSSA DI CASTELVETRO	DOC	1970	ROMAGNA	DOC	2011
COLLI DI SCANDIANO E DI CANOSSA	DOC	1976	LAMBRUSCO SALAMINO DI SANTA CROCE	DOC	1970	ROMAGNA ALBANA	DOCG	1987

Toscana [11 DOCG] [41 DOC out of 1 shared]

Name	Type	Year	Name	Type	Year	Name	Type	Year
ANSONICA COSTA DELL'ARGENTARIO	DOC	1995	GRANCE SENESI	DOC	2010	SOVANA	DOC	1999
BARCO REALE DI CARMIGNANO	DOC	1975	MAREMMA TOSCANA	DOC	2011	SUVERETO	DOCG	2011
BIANCO DELL'EMPOLESE	DOC	1989	MONTECARLO	DOC	1969	TERRATICO DI BIBBONA	DOC	2006
BIANCO DI PITIGLIANO	DOC	1966	MONTECUCCO	DOC	1998	TERRE DI CASOLE	DOC	2007
BOLGHERI	DOC	1983	MONTECUCCO SANGIOVESE	DOCG	2011	TERRE DI PISA	DOC	2011
BOLGHERI SASSICAIA	DOC	2013	MONTEREGIO DI MASSA MARITTIMA	DOC	1994	VAL D'ARBIA	DOC	1985
BRUNELLO DI MONTALCINO	DOCG	1980	MONTESCUDAIO	DOC	1976	VAL D'ARNO DI SOPRA	DOC	2011
CANDIA DEI COLLI APUANI	DOC	1981	MORELLINO DI SCANSANO	DOCG	2006	VAL DI CORNIA	DOC	1989
CAPALBIO	DOC	1999	MOSCADELLO DI MONTALCINO	DOC	1984	VALDICHIANA TOSCANA	DOC	1972
CARMIGNANO	DOCG	1990	ORCIA	DOC	2000	VALDINIEVOLE	DOC	1976
CHIANTI	DOCG	1984	PARRINA	DOC	1971	VERNACCIA DI SAN GIMIGNANO	DOCG	1993
CHIANTI CLASSICO	DOCG	1984	POMINO	DOC	1983	VIN SANTO DEL CHIANTI	DOC	1997
COLLI DELL'ETRURIA CENTRALE	DOC	1990	ROSSO DELLA VAL DI CORNIA	DOCG	2011	VIN SANTO DEL CHIANTI CLASSICO	DOC	1995
COLLI DI LUNI [shared with Liguria]	DOC	1989	ROSSO DI MONTALCINO	DOC	1983	VIN SANTO DI CARMIGNANO	DOC	1975
COLLINE LUCCHESI	DOC	1968	ROSSO DI MONTEPULCIANO	DOC	1988	VIN SANTO DI MONTEPULCIANO	DOC	1996
CORTONA	DOC	1989	SAN GIMIGNANO	DOC	1996	VINO NOBILE DI MONTEPULCIANO	DOCG	1980
ELBA	DOC	1967	SAN TORPÈ	DOC	1980			
ELBA ALEATICO PASSITO (ALEATICO PASSITO DELL'ELBA)	DOCG	2011	SANT' ANTIMO	DOC	1996			

Marche [5 DOCG / 15 DOC]

Name	Type	Year	Name	Type	Year	Name	Type	Year
BIANCHELLO DEL METAURO	DOC	1969	I TERRENI DI SANSEVERINO	DOC	2004	SERRAPETRONA	DOC	2004
CASTELLI DI JESI VERDICCHIO RISERVA	DOCG	2009	LACRIMA DI MORRO D'ALBA	DOC	1985	TERRE DI OFFIDA	DOC	2001
COLLI MACERATESI	DOC	1975	OFFIDA	DOCG	2011	VERDICCHIO DEI CASTELLI DI JESI	DOC	1968
COLLI PESARESI	DOC	1972	PERGOLA	DOC	2005	VERDICCHIO DI MATELICA	DOC	1967
CÒNERO (CÒNERO RISERVA)	DOCG	2004	ROSSO CONERO	DOC	1968	VERDICCHIO DI MATELICA RISERVA	DOCG	2009
ESINO	DOC	1995	ROSSO PICENO	DOC	1968	VERNACCIA DI SERRAPETRONA	DOCG	2003
FALERIO	DOC	1975	SAN GINESIO	DOC	2007			

Umbria [2 DOCG] [13 DOC out of 1 shared]

Name	Type	Year	Name	Type	Year	Name	Type	Year
AMELIA	DOC	1989	COLLI PERUGINI	DOC	1981	ROSSO ORVIETANO	DOC	1998
ASSISI	DOC	1997	LAGO DI CORBARA	DOC	1998	SPOLETO	DOC	2011
COLLI ALTOTIBERINI	DOC	1980	MONTEFALCO	DOC	1979	TODI	DOC	2010
COLLI DEL TRASIMENO (TRASIMENO)	DOC	1972	MONTEFALCO SAGRANTINO	DOCG	1992	TORGIANO	DOC	1968
COLLI MARTANI	DOC	1988	ORVIETO [shared with Lazio]	DOC	1971	TORGIANO ROSSO RISERVA	DOCG	1990

Lazio [3 DOCG] [27 DOC out of 1 shared]

Name	Type	Year	Name	Type	Year	Name	Type	Year
ALEATICO DI GRADOLI	DOC	1972	CIRCEO	DOC	1996	MARINO	DOC	1970
APRILIA	DOC	1966	COLLI ALBANI	DOC	1970	MONTECOMPATRI-COLONNA	DOC	1973
ATINA	DOC	1999	COLLI DELLA SABINA	DOC	1996	NETTUNO	DOC	2003
BIANCO CAPENA	DOC	1975	COLLI ETRUSCHI VITERBESE (TUSCIA)	DOC	1996	ORVIETO [shared with Umbria]	DOC	1971
CANNELLINO DI FRASCATI	DOCG	2011	COLLI LANUVINI	DOC	1971	ROMA	DOC	2011
CASTELLI ROMANI	DOC	1996	CORI	DOC	1971	TARQUINIA	DOC	1996
CERVETERI	DOC	1974	EST! EST!! EST!!! DI MONTEFIASCONE	DOC	1966	TERRACINA (MOSCATO DI TERRACINA)	DOC	2007
CESANESE DEL PIGLIO (PIGLIO)	DOCG	2008	FRASCATI	DOC	1966	VELLETRI	DOC	1972
CESANESE DI AFFILE (AFFILE)	DOC	1973	FRASCATI SUPERIORE	DOCG	2011	VIGNANELLO	DOC	1992
CESANESE DI OLEVANO ROMANO (OLEVANO ROMANO)	DOC	1973	GENAZZANO	DOC	1992	ZAGAROLO	DOC	1973

Abruzzo [2 DOCG / 7 DOC]

Name	Class	Year	Name	Class	Year	Name	Class	Year
ABRUZZO	DOC	2010	MONTEPULCIANO D'ABRUZZO	DOC	1968	TERRE TOLLESI (TULLUM)	DOCG	2019
CERASUOLO D'ABRUZZO	DOC	2010	MONTEPULCIANO D'ABRUZZO COLLINE TERAMANE	DOCG	2003	TREBBIANO D'ABRUZZO	DOC	1972
CONTROGUERRA	DOC	1996	ORTONA	DOC	2011	VILLAMAGNA	DOC	2011

Molise [4 DOC]

Name	Class	Year	Name	Class	Year	Name	Class	Year
BIFERNO	DOC	1983	PENTRO DI ISERNIA	DOC	1983	TINTILIA DEL MOLISE	DOC	2011
MOLISE (DEL MOLISE)	DOC	1998						

Puglia [4 DOCG / 28 DOC]

Name	Class	Year	Name	Class	Year	Name	Class	Year
ALEATICO DI PUGLIA	DOC	1973	GALATINA	DOC	1997	ORTA NOVA	DOC	1984
ALEZIO	DOC	1983	GIOIA DEL COLLE	DOC	1987	OSTUNI (OSTUNI OTTAVIANELLO)	DOC	1972
BARLETTA	DOC	1977	GRAVINA	DOC	1983	PRIMITIVO DI MANDURIA	DOC	1974
BRINDISI	DOC	1979	LEVERANO	DOC	1979	PRIMITIVO DI MANDURIA DOLCE NATURALE	DOCG	2011
CACC'E MMITTE DI LUCERA	DOC	1975	LIZZANO	DOC	1998	ROSSO DI CERIGNOLA	DOC	1974
CASTEL DEL MONTE	DOC	1971	LOCOROTONDO	DOC	1969	SALICE SALENTINO	DOC	1976
CASTEL DEL MONTE BOMBINO NERO	DOCG	2011	MARTINA (MARTINA FRANCA)	DOC	1969	SAN SEVERO	DOC	1968
CASTEL DEL MONTE NERO DI TROIA RISERVA	DOCG	2011	MATINO	DOC	1971	SQUINZANO	DOC	1976
CASTEL DEL MONTE ROSSO RISERVA	DOCG	2011	MOSCATO DI TRANI	DOC	1975	TAVOLIERE DELLE PUGLIE (TAVOLIERE)	DOC	2011
COLLINE JONICHE TARANTINE	DOC	2008	NARDÒ	DOC	1987	TERRA D'OTRANTO	DOC	2011
COPERTINO	DOC	1976	NEGROAMARO DI TERRA D'OTRANTO	DOC	2011			

Campania [4 DOCG / 15 DOC]

Name	Class	Year	Name	Class	Year	Name	Class	Year
AGLIANICO DEL TABURNO	DOCG	2011	COSTA D'AMALFI	DOC	1995	IRPINIA	DOC	2005
AVERSA	DOC	1993	FALANGHINA DEL SANNIO	DOC	2011	ISCHIA	DOC	1966
CAMPI FLEGREI	DOC	1994	FALERNO DEL MASSICO	DOC	1989	PENISOLA SORRENTINA	DOC	1994
CAPRI	DOC	1977	FIANO DI AVELLINO	DOCG	2003	SANNIO	DOC	1997
CASAVECCHIA DI PONTELATONE	DOC	2011	GALLUCCIO	DOC	1997	TAURASI	DOCG	1993
CASTEL SAN LORENZO	DOC	1991	GRECO DI TUFO	DOCG	2003	VESUVIO	DOC	1983
CILENTO	DOC	1989						

Basilicata [1 DOCG / 4 DOC]

Name	Class	Year	Name	Class	Year	Name	Class	Year
AGLIANICO DEL VULTURE	DOC	1971	GROTTINO DI ROCCANOVA	DOC	2009	TERRE DELL'ALTA VAL D'AGRI	DOC	2003
AGLIANICO DEL VULTURE SUPERIORE	DOCG	2010	MATERA	DOC	2005			

Calabria [9 DOC]

Name	Class	Year	Name	Class	Year	Name	Class	Year
BIVONGI	DOC	1996	LAMEZIA	DOC	1978	SAVUTO	DOC	1975
CIRO`	DOC	1969	MELISSA	DOC	1979	SCAVIGNA	DOC	1994
GRECO DI BIANCO	DOC	1980	S. ANNA DI ISOLA CAPO RIZZUTO	DOC	1979	TERRE DI COSENZA	DOC	2011

Sicilia [1 DOCG / 23 DOC]

Name	Class	Year	Name	Class	Year	Name	Class	Year
ALCAMO	DOC	1972	FARO	DOC	1976	RIESI	DOC	2001
CERASUOLO DI VITTORIA	DOCG	2005	MALVASIA DELLE LIPARI	DOC	1973	SALAPARUTA	DOC	2006
CONTEA DI SCLAFANI	DOC	1996	MAMERTINO (MAMERTINO DI MILAZZO)	DOC	2004	SAMBUCA DI SICILIA	DOC	1995
CONTESSA ENTELLINA	DOC	1972	MARSALA	DOC	1969	SANTA MARGHERITA DI BELICE	DOC	1996
DELIA NIVOLELLI	DOC	1998	MENFI	DOC	1995	SCIACCA	DOC	1998
ELORO	DOC	1994	MONREALE	DOC	2000	SICILIA	DOC	2011
ERICE	DOC	2004	NOTO	DOC	1974	SIRACUSA	DOC	1973
ETNA	DOC	1968	PANTELLERIA (MOSCATO DI PANTELLERIA / PASSITO DI PANTELLERIA)	DOC	1971	VITTORIA	DOC	2005

Sardegna [1 DOCG / 17 DOC]

Name	Class	Year	Name	Class	Year	Name	Class	Year
ALGHERO	DOC	1995	GIRÒ DI CAGLIARI	DOC	1972	NASCO DI CAGLIARI	DOC	1972
ARBOREA	DOC	1987	MALVASIA DI BOSA	DOC	1972	NURAGUS DI CAGLIARI	DOC	1974
CAGLIARI	DOC	2011	MANDROLISAI	DOC	1981	SARDEGNA SEMIDANO	DOC	1995
CAMPIDANO DI TERRALBA (TERRALBA)	DOC	1975	MONICA DI SARDEGNA	DOC	1972	VERMENTINO DI GALLURA	DOCG	1996
CANNONAU DI SARDEGNA	DOC	1972	MOSCATO DI SARDEGNA	DOC	1979	VERMENTINO DI SARDEGNA	DOC	1988
CARIGNANO DEL SULCIS	DOC	1977	MOSCATO DI SORSO SENNORI	DOC	1972	VERNACCIA DI ORISTANO	DOC	1971

170 MGA vineyards of Barolo DOCG [Shared vineyards are counted only once in the total]

COMUNE / VINEYARD	SIZE	ALT [M]	VINEYARD	SIZE	ALT [M]	VINEYARD	SIZE	ALT [M]
Cherasco [1]								
MANTOETTO	2.76	345-360						
Verduno [11]								
BOSCATTO	27.96	250-370	MONVIGLIERO	25.51	220-310	ROCCHE DELL'OLMO	36.88	310-405
BRERI	53.94	220-250	NEIRANE	37.59	330-405	RODASCA	6.41	200-270
CAMPASSO	13.95	240-340	PISAPOLA	9.73	280-350	SAN LORENZO DI VERDUNO	32.46	210-260
MASSARA	50.31	230-370	RIVA ROCCA	13.55	270-340			
Roddi [1]								
BRICCO AMBROGIO	48.24	200-275						

Grinzane Cavour [8]

VINEYARD	SIZE	ALT [M]	VINEYARD	SIZE	ALT [M]	VINEYARD	SIZE	ALT [M]
BABLINO	2.68	230-265	CASTELLO	7.1	220-260	LA CORTE	7.87	210-290
BORZONE	7.08	200-245	GARRETTI	9	220-265	RAVIOLE	11.39	220-265
CANOVA	5.75	210-250	GUSTAVA	8.31	220-275			

La Morra [39 out of 3 shared]

VINEYARD	SIZE	ALT [M]	VINEYARD	SIZE	ALT [M]	VINEYARD	SIZE	ALT [M]
ANNUNZIATA	109.42	220-380	BRICCO SAN BIAGIO	28.84	220-290	RIVE	38.16	210-270
ARBORINA	10.81	250-320	BRUNATE [shared with Barolo]	28.34	230-405	ROCCHE DELL'ANNUNZIATA	29.92	240-385
ASCHERI	83.96	270-400	CAPALOT	34.94	295-440	ROCCHETTEVINO	34.98	280-440
BERRI	87.89	350-500	CASE NERE	10.21	300-370	ROERE DI SANTA MARIA	35.41	205-270
BETTOLOTTI	58.76	200-270	CASTAGNI	64.51	370-455	ROGGERI	21.31	240-340
BOIOLO	87.79	230-450	CEREQUIO [shared with Barolo]	24.12	290-400	RONCAGLIE	36.42	250-440
BRANDINI	87.14	400-445	CIOCCHINI	12.17	210-230	SAN GIACOMO	69.24	240-370
BRICCO CHIESA	13.75	210-290	CONCA	2.45	235-255	SANTA MARIA	70.77	210-330
BRICCO COGNI	43.91	250-330	FOSSATI [shared with Barolo]	33.78	340-480	SANT'ANNA	73.3	310-400
BRICCO LUCIANI	16.09	220-255	GALINA	8.74	260-310	SERRA DEI TURCHI	22.03	200-260
BRICCO MANESCOTTO	27.01	210-265	GATTERA	30.06	220-290	SERRADENARI	101.19	450-540
BRICCO MANZONI	11.98	210-230	GIACHINI	14.87	220-255	SILIO	41.56	230-350
BRICCO ROCCA	10.94	220-255	LA SERRA	17.79	370-450	TORRIGLIONE	7.62	250-285

Barolo [37 out of 5 shared]

VINEYARD	SIZE	ALT [M]	VINEYARD	SIZE	ALT [M]	VINEYARD	SIZE	ALT [M]
ALBARELLA	9.96	240-280	CEREQUIO [shared with La Morra]	24.12	290-400	RAVERA [shared with Novello]	130.41	300-480
BERGEISA	5.69	235-290	COSTE DI ROSE	16.83	250-310	RIVASSI	6.72	290-320
BOSCHETTI	23.87	300-360	COSTE DI VERGNE	10.52	420-480	RUÈ	8.49	280-320
BRICCO DELLE VIOLE	45.74	390-480	CROSIA	9.62	220-250	SAN LORENZO	2.13	300-310
BRICCO SAN GIOVANNI	3.84	370-400	DRUCÀ	5.03	320-370	SAN PIETRO	17.36	350-410
BRUNATE [shared with La Morra]	28.34	230-405	FOSSATI [shared with La Morra]	33.78	340-480	SAN PONZIO	17.54	380-410
BUSSIA [shared with Monforte d'Alba]	298.89	210-460	LA VOLTA	46.34	380-420	SARMASSA	33.74	240-300
CANNUBI	19.53	230-290	LE COSTE	6.01	290-320	TERLO	22.03	320-400
CANNUBI BOSCHIS	12.41	220-260	LISTE	12.45	290-370	VIGNANE	11.56	230-290
CANNUBI MUSCATEL	6.24	260-320	MONROBIOLO DI BUSSIA	6.09	240-270	ZOCCOLAIO	5.95	315-360
CANNUBI SAN LORENZO	2.38	300-315	PAIAGALLO	12.35	310-380	ZONCHETTA	12.28	230-280
CANNUBI VALLETTA	6.24	250-290	PREDA	20.68	230-300	ZUNCAI	7.81	240-300
CASTELLERO	13.07	220-270						

Novello [7 out of 1 shared]

VINEYARD	SIZE	ALT [M]	VINEYARD	SIZE	ALT [M]	VINEYARD	SIZE	ALT [M]
RAVERA [shared with Barolo]	130.41	300-480	CIOCCHINI-LOSCHETTO	50.1	350-460	PANEROLE	41.52	320-390
BERGERA-PEZZOLE	48.69	350-420	CORINI-PALLARETTA	105.88	380-460	SOTTOCASTELLO DI NOVELLO	59.73	340-420
CERVIANO-MERLI	65.17	350-450						

Monforte d'Alba [11 out of 2 shared]

VINEYARD	SIZE	ALT [M]	VINEYARD	SIZE	ALT [M]	VINEYARD	SIZE	ALT [M]
BRICCO SAN PIETRO	380.09	250-520	GRAMOLERE	41.4	320-470	RAVERA DI MONFORTE	36.63	320-430
BUSSIA [shared with Barolo]	298.89	210-460	LE COSTE DI MONFORTE	50.34	370-500	ROCCHE DI CASTIGLIONE [shared with Castiglione Falletto]	16.33	300-350
CASTELLETTO	128.52	250-520	MOSCONI	75.95	310-530	SAN GIOVANNI	68.48	260-440
GINESTRA	114.36	270-540	PERNO	190.96	220-450			

Castiglione Falletto [20 out of 1 shared]

VINEYARD	SIZE	ALT [M]	VINEYARD	SIZE	ALT [M]	VINEYARD	SIZE	ALT [M]
ROCCHE DI CASTIGLIONE [shared with Monforte d'Alba]	16.33	300-350	MARIONDINO	13.11	265-350	PUGNANE	4.97	240-260
ALTENASSO	4.27	220-240	MONPRIVATO	7.12	240-320	SCARRONE	20.55	220-340
BRICCO BOSCHIS	17.65	230-337	MONTANELLO	23.48	220-310	SOLANOTTO	2.86	220-270
BRICCO ROCCHE	1.46	350-365	PARUSSI	13.41	220-290	VALENTINO	11.68	260-325
BRUNELLA	5.01	280-320	PERNANNO	15.98	240-320	VIGNOLO	3.57	220-270
CODANA	9.66	230-270	PIANTÀ	6.27	220-275	VILLERO	22.07	230-350
FIASCO	8.3	225-280	PIRA	6.66	250-290			

Diano d'Alba [3 out of 1 shared]

VINEYARD	SIZE	ALT [M]	VINEYARD	SIZE	ALT [M]	VINEYARD	SIZE	ALT [M]
GALLARETTO	15.36	220-305	LA VIGNA	4.48	260-280	SORANO [shared with Serralunga d'Alba]	14.7	250-320

Serralunga d'Alba [39 out of 1 shared]

VINEYARD	SIZE	ALT [M]	VINEYARD	SIZE	ALT [M]	VINEYARD	SIZE	ALT [M]
ARIONE	5.72	340-430	COLOMBARO	3.56	300-395	MARGHERIA	8.1	240-335
BADARINA	21.02	340-440	COSTABELLA	8.29	215-300	MERIAME	17.14	230-360
BAUDANA	19.63	230-370	DAMIANO	15.98	250-380	ORNATO	6.7	300-395
BOSCARETO	53.15	285-435	FALLETTO	8.9	320-420	PARAFADA	7.92	260-370
BREA	10.99	300-370	FONTANAFREDDA	58.42	200-315	PRABON	3.84	240-310
BRICCO VOGHERA	7.15	370-405	FRANCIA	15.8	340-445	PRAPÒ	8.33	270-380
BRICCOLINA	17.93	280-385	GABUTTI	14.24	240-350	RIVETTE	8.42	320-390
BROGLIO	12.15	300-390	GIANETTO	22.4	240-380	SAN BERNARDO	4.44	330-390
CAPPALLOTTO	7.52	215-270	LAZZARITO	29.54	260-390	SAN ROCCO	6.43	280-320
CARPEGNA	7.12	215-290	LE TURNE	7.4	245-335	SERRA	10.28	350-390
CERRATI	12.96	260-395	LIRANO	12.77	320-390	SORANO [shared with Diano d'Alba]	14.7	250-320
CERRETTA	39.93	250-395	MANOCINO	5.55	340-430	TEODORO	23.58	230-350
COLLARETTO	14.37	265-340	MARENCIA	7.46	275-355	VIGNA RIONDA	10.24	260-360

66 MGA vineyards of Barbaresco DOCG [Shared vineyards are counted only once in the total]

COMUNE / VINEYARD	SIZE	ALT [M]	VINEYARD	SIZE	ALT [M]	VINEYARD	SIZE	ALT [M]
Alba [4 out of 3 shared]								
MERUZZANO [shared with reiso]	155.98	245-495	RIZZI [shared with Treiso]	69.9	180-300	ROCCHE MASSALUPO	60.71	200-300
MONTERSINO [shared with Treiso]	81.25	220-420						

Barbaresco [25]

Name			Name			Name		
ASILI	14.25	200-290	MONTESTEFANO	10.16	175-265	ROCCALINI	34.58	170-280
CÀ GROSSA	38.52	190-290	MUNCAGÖTA	9.65	250-315	RONCAGLIE	13.1	200-300
CARS	26.6	160-270	OVELLO	78.44	160-275	RONCAGLIETTE	21.69	175-305
CAVANNA	8.21	190-255	PAJÈ	7.82	210-260	RONCHI	18	190-290
COLE	3.76	210-270	PORA	22.48	170-255	SECONDINE	14.94	170-245
FASET	15.15	200-275	RABAJÀ	15.26	235-315	TRE STELLE	23.09	21-320
MARTINENGA	17.12	190-270	RABAJÀ BAS	1.81	265-285	TRIFOLERA	25.19	200-330
MONTARIBALDI	15.61	180-320	RIO SORDO	25.06	190-315	VICENZIANA	16.37	160-250
MONTEFICO	8.05	180-270						

Neive [20]

Name			Name			Name		
ALBESANI	72.68	160-270	COTTÀ	85.16	180-340	SAN CRISTOFORO	69.22	220-370
BALLURI	113.25	160-260	CURRÀ	22.68	200-320	SAN GIULIANO	18.09	230-270
BASARIN	66.57	210-370	FAUSONI	29.68	200-270	SERRABOELLA	54.64	220-315
BORDINI	73.64	210-280	GAIA PRINCIPE	75.18	170-290	SERRACAPELLI	142.5	210-305
BRIC MICCA	101.93	220-410	GALLINA	54.21	170-250	SERRAGRILLI	86.14	210-270
BRICCO DI NEIVE	155.63	250-450	MARCORINO	24.37	220-300	STARDERI	95.68	170-270
CANOVA	158.53	210-350	RIVETTI	79.53	210-290			

Treiso [20 out of 3 shared]

Name			Name			Name		
MERUZZANO [SHARED]	155.98	245-495	CASTELLIZZANO	18.24	240-380	NERVO	21.7	220-360
MONTERSINO [SHARED]	81.25	220-420	FERRERE	68.38	250-410	PAJORÈ	41.47	190-350
RIZZI [SHARED]	69.9	180-300	GARASSINO	17.42	180-260	ROMBONE	47.89	180-320
AUSARIO	46.23	220-370	GIACONE	90.88	230-460	SAN STUNET	36.87	280-420
BERNADOT	11.53	280-400	GIACOSA	31.48	300-410	VALEIRANO	20.29	220-310
BRICCO DI TREISO	30.87	310-410	MANZOLA	9.02	190-250	VALLEGRANDE	28.5	270-400
CASOT	18.26	230-360	MARCARINI	48.67	270-385			

REGIONS OF ITALY [20]

VALLE D'AOSTA

DOCG [0]
DOC [1]

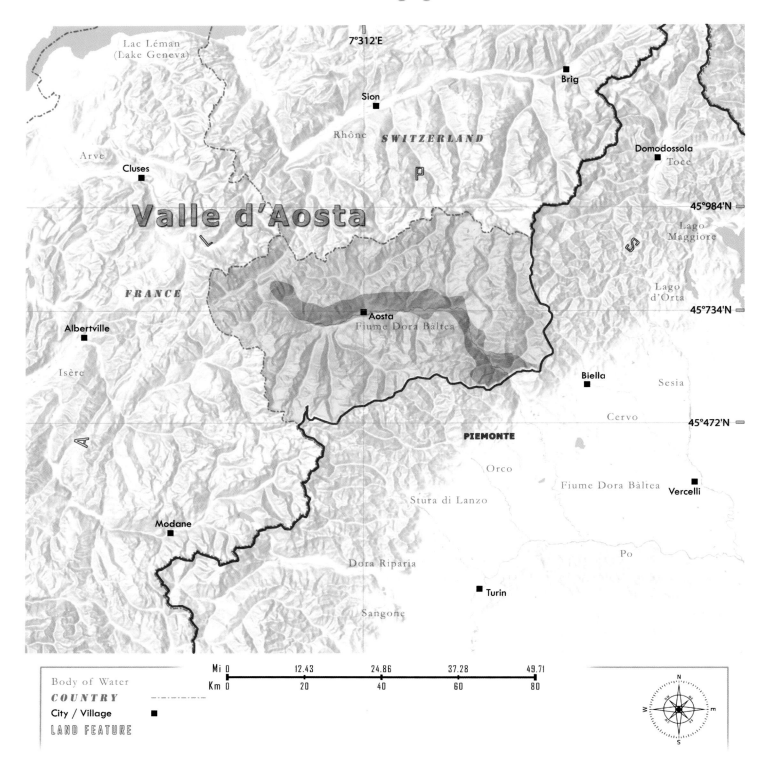

Lac Léman
(Lake Geneva)

7°312'E

Brig

Sion

Rhône

SWITZERLAND

Arve

Domodossola
Tocè

Cluses

P

45°984'N

Valle d'Aosta

Lago
Maggiore

L

S

FRANCE

Lago
d'Orta

Aosta
Fiume Dora Bàltea

45°734'N

Albertville

Isère

Biella

Sesia

Cervo

45°472'N

A

PIEMONTE

Orco

Fiume Dora Bàltea
Vercelli

Stura di Lanzo

Modane

Po

Dora Riparia

Turin

Sangone

| Mi | 0 | 12.43 | 24.86 | 37.28 | 49.71 |
| Km | 0 | 20 | 40 | 60 | 80 |

Body of Water

COUNTRY

City / Village

LAND FEATURE

N

W   E

S

Italy

PIEMONTE

PROVINCES OF PIEMONTE [8]

DOCG [18]
DOC [41]

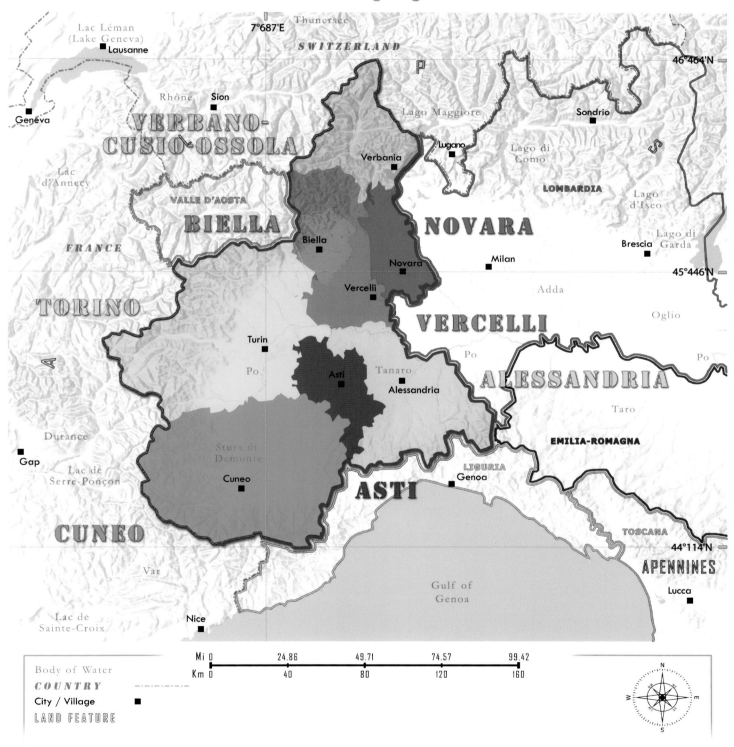

PIEMONTE

DOCG [18]
DOC [41]

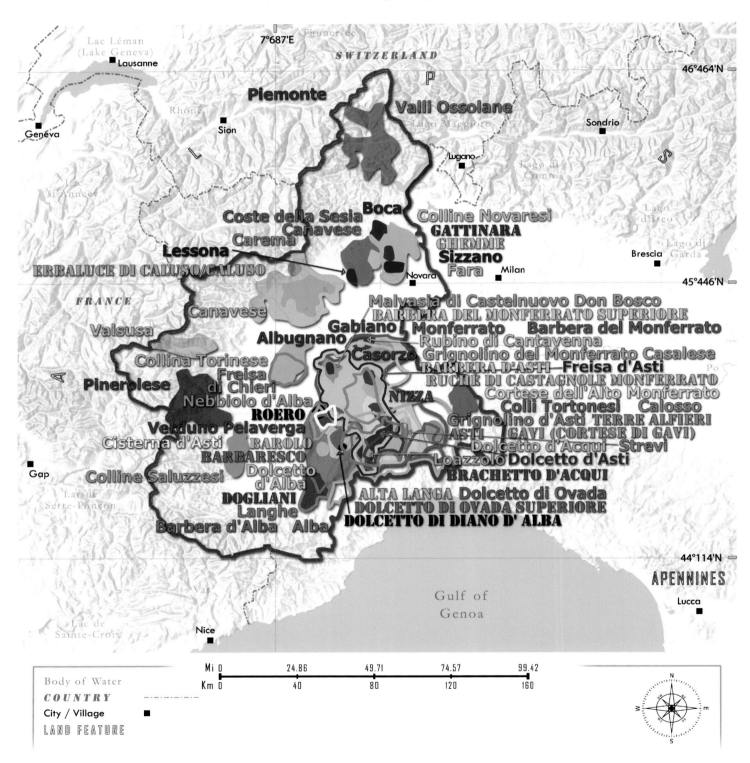

Italy

BARBARESCO DOCG
Total MGA (66) - 3 shared ┄┄┄┄┄►
(Menzioni Geografiche Aggiuntive 'vineyard')

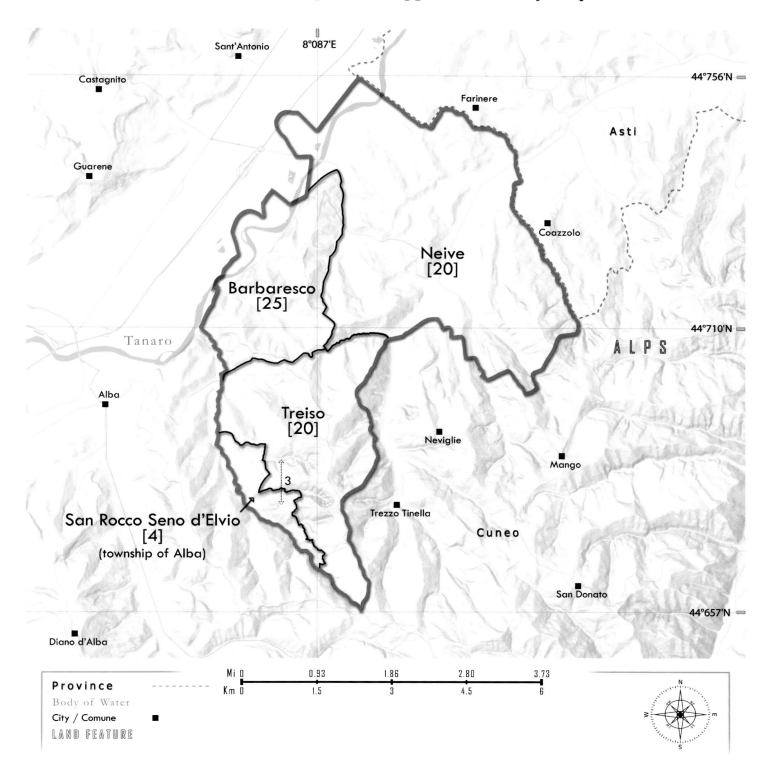

Sant'Antonio

Castagnito

8°087'E

44°756'N

Farinere

Asti

Guarene

Coazzolo

Neive
[20]

Barbaresco
[25]

Tanaro

44°710'N

A L P S

Alba

Treiso
[20]

Neviglie

Mango

3

San Rocco Seno d'Elvio
[4]

(township of Alba)

Trezzo Tinella

C u n e o

San Donato

44°657'N

Diano d'Alba

Province ┄┄┄┄┄┄┄┄

Body of Water

City / Comune ■

LAND FEATURE

| Mi | 0 | 0.93 | 1.86 | 2.80 | 3.73 |
| Km | 0 | 1.5 | 3 | 4.5 | 6 |

BARBARESCO

Total MGA (25)

(Menzioni Geografiche Aggiuntive 'vineyard')

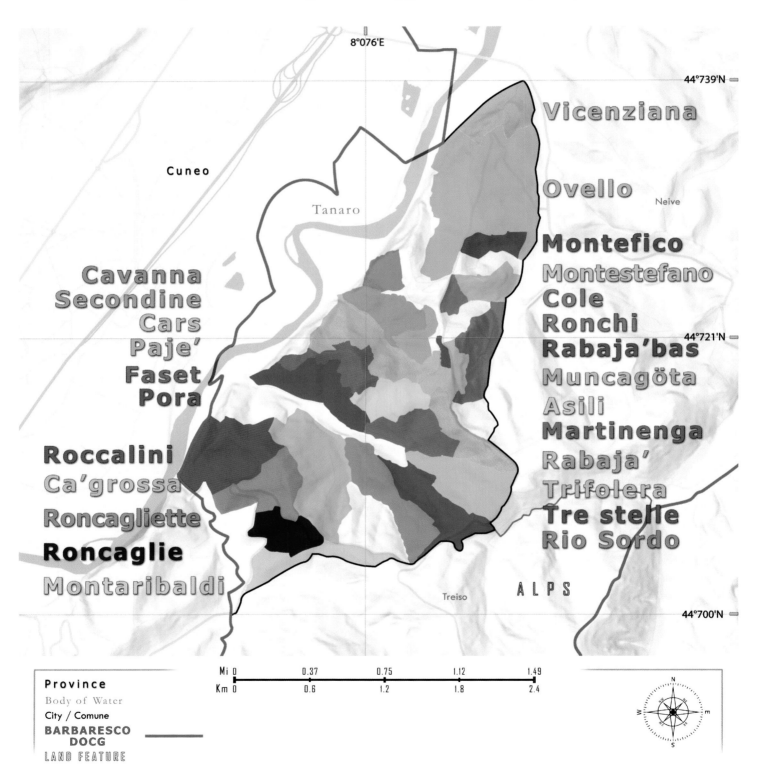

Vicenziana

Cuneo

Tanaro

Ovello

Neive

Montefico

Montestefano

Cole

Cavanna

Secondine

Cars

Paje'

Faset

Pora

Ronchi

Rabaja'bas

Muncagöta

Asili

Martinenga

Roccalini

Ca'grossa

Roncagliette

Roncaglie

Montaribaldi

Rabaja'

Trifolera

Tre stelle

Rio Sordo

Treiso

A L P S

8°076'E

44°739'N

44°721'N

44°700'N

| Mi 0 | 0.37 | 0.75 | 1.12 | 1.49 |
| Km 0 | 0.6 | 1.2 | 1.8 | 2.4 |

Province

Body of Water

City / Comune

BARBARESCO
DOCG

LAND FEATURE

NEVE

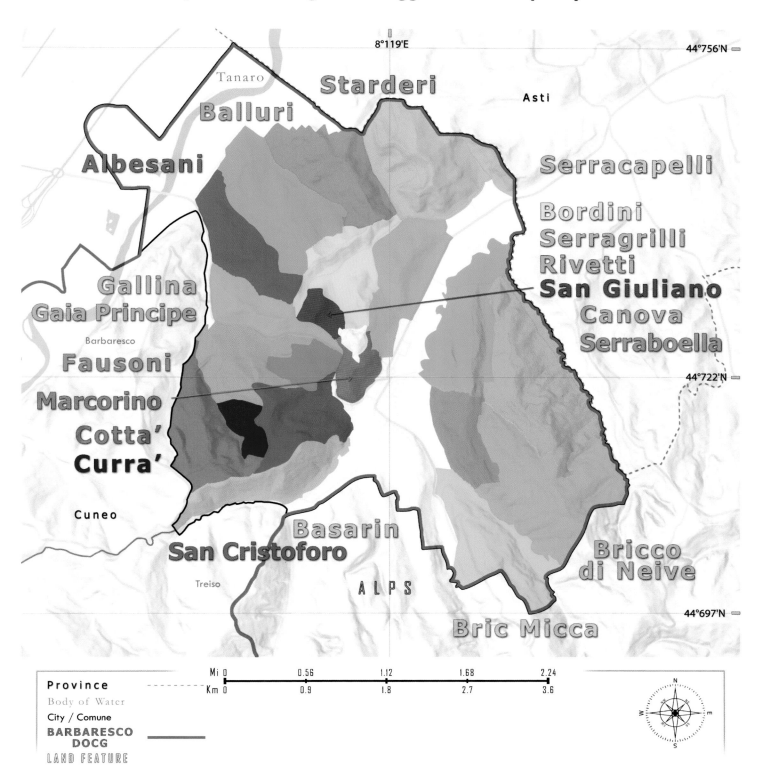

TREISO

Total MGA (20) - 3 shared

(Menzioni Geografiche Aggiuntive 'vineyard')

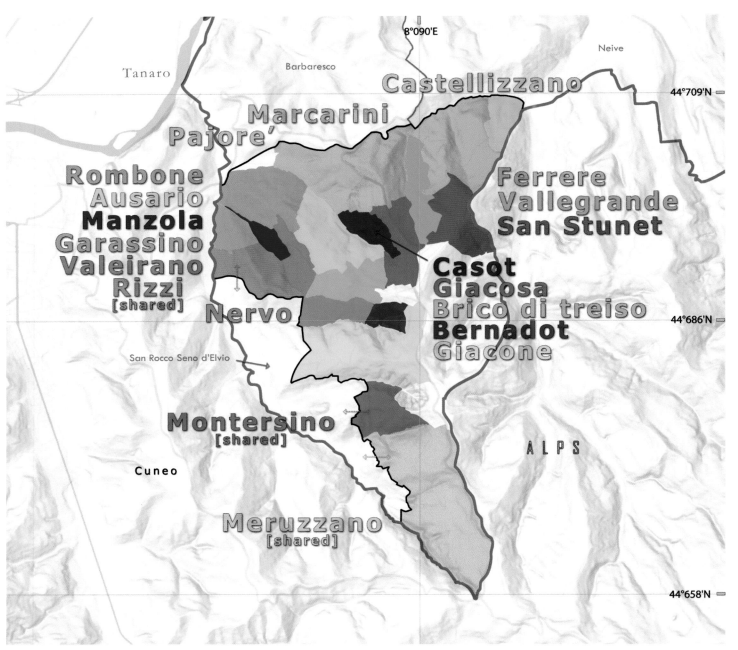

Tanaro

Barbaresco

Neive

Castellizzano

44°709'N

Marcarini

Pajore'

Rombone
Ausario
Manzola
Garassino
Valeirano
Rizzi
[shared]

Nervo

San Rocco Seno d'Elvio

Ferrere
Vallegrande
San Stunet

Casot
Giacosa
Brico di treiso
Bernadot
Giacone

44°686'N

ALPS

Montersino
[shared]

Cuneo

Meruzzano
[shared]

44°658'N

8°090'E

| Mi 0 | 0.56 | 1.12 | 1.68 | 2.24 |
| Km 0 | 0.9 | 1.8 | 2.7 | 3.6 |

Province
Body of Water
City / Comune
BARBARESCO
DOCG
LAND FEATURE

SAN ROCCO SENO D'ELVIO

Total MGA (4) - 3 shared

(Menzioni Geografiche Aggiuntive 'vineyard')

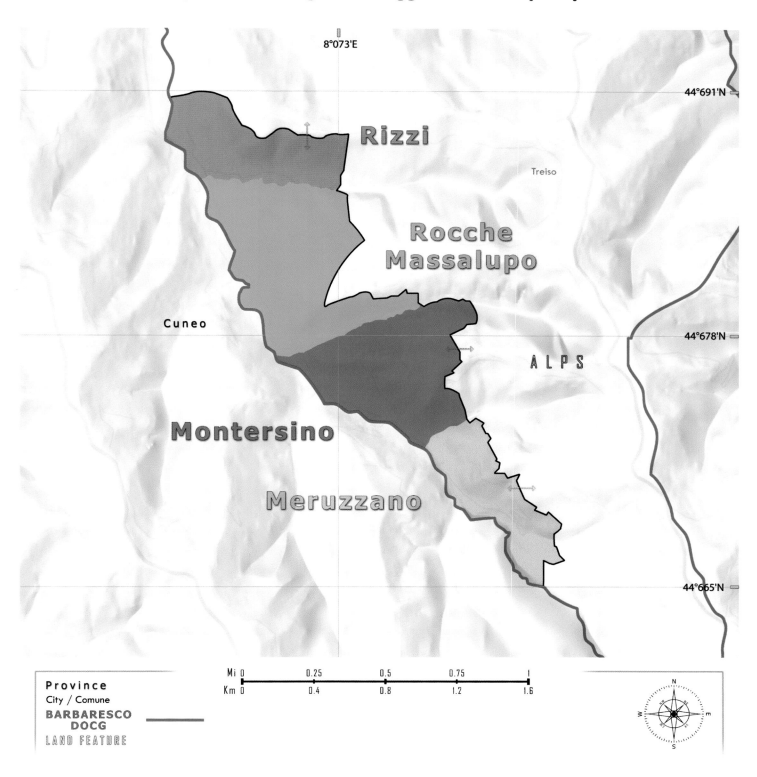

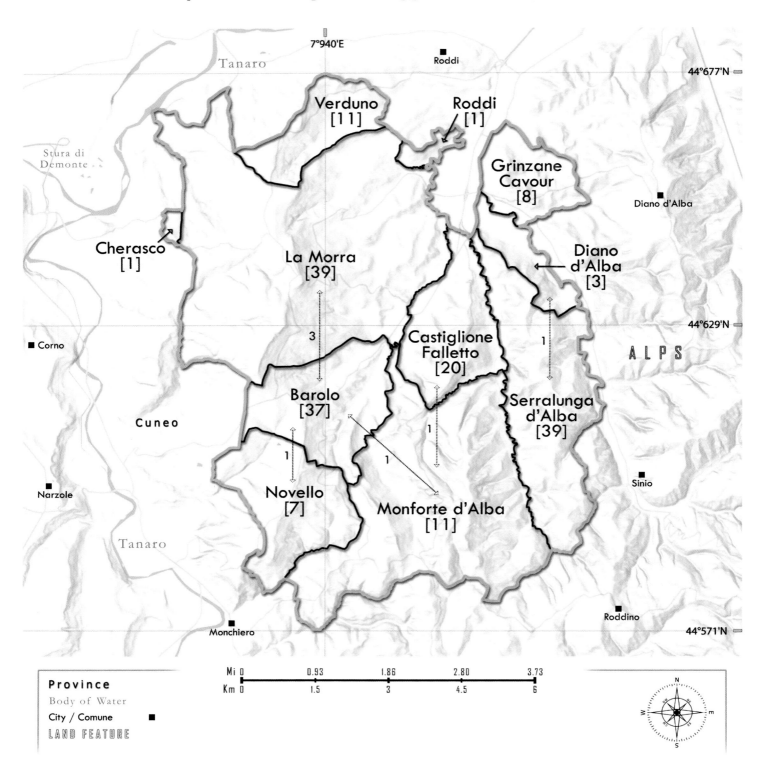

BAROLO DOCG
Total MGA (170) - 7 shared
(Menzioni Geografiche Aggiuntive 'vineyard')

Tanaro

7°940'E

Roddi

44°677'N

Verduno
[11]

Roddi
[1]

Stura di
Demonte

Grinzane
Cavour
[8]

Diano d'Alba

Cherasco
[1]

La Morra
[39]

Diano
d'Alba
[3]

Corno

3

44°629'N

Castiglione
Falletto
[20]

ALPS

1

Barolo
[37]

Serralunga
d'Alba
[39]

Cuneo

1

Novello
[7]

1

1

Sinio

Narzole

Monforte d'Alba
[11]

Tanaro

Roddino

Monchiero

44°571'N

Province

Body of Water

City / Comune ■

LAND FEATURE

| Mi 0 | 0.93 | 1.86 | 2.80 | 3.73 |
| Km 0 | 1.5 | 3 | 4.5 | 6 |

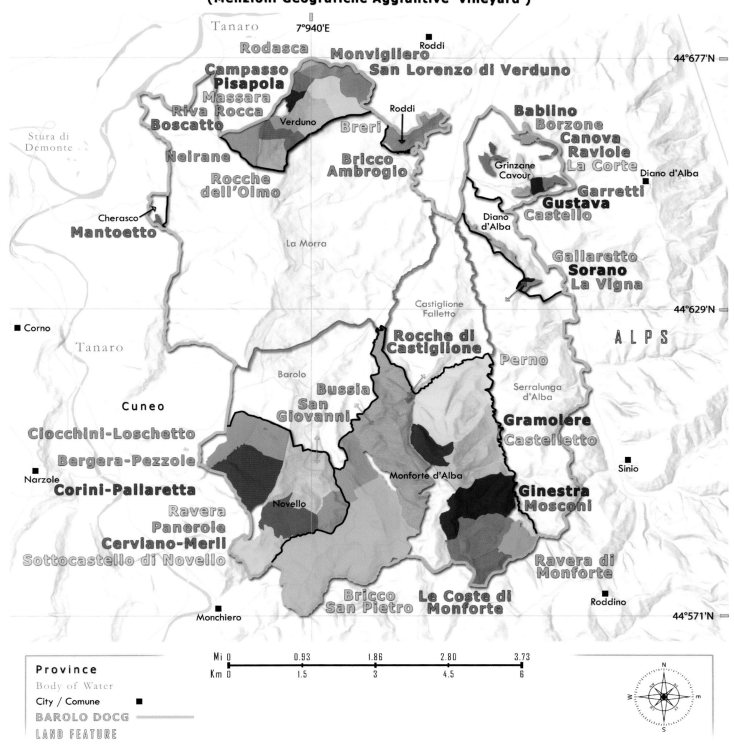

CHERASCO (1)
VERDUNO (11)
RODDI (1)
GRINZANE CAVOUR (8)
DIANO d'ALBA (3) - 1 shared
MONFORTE d'ALBA (11) - 2 shared
NOVELLO (7) - 1 shared
(Menzioni Geografiche Aggiuntive 'vineyard')

Tanaro
7°940'E
44°677'N

Rodasca
Monvigliero
Roddi
Campasso
San Lorenzo di Verduno
Pisapola
Massara
Babiino
Riva Rocca
Verduno
Borzone
Boscatto
Breri
Canova
Roddi
Raviole
Stura di
Demonte
La Corte
Neirane
Bricco
Grinzane
Ambrogio
Cavour
Diano d'Alba
Rocche
Garretti
dell'Olmo
Diano
Gustava
d'Alba
Castello
Cherasco
Mantoetto
La Morra
Gallaretto
Sorano
La Vigna
44°629'N
Corno
Castiglione
A L P S
Tanaro
Falletto
Rocche di
Castiglione
Barolo
Perno
Bussia
Serralunga
San
d'Alba
Giovanni
Cuneo
Gramolere
Ciocchini-Loschetto
Castelletto
Bergera-Pezzole
Sinio
Narzole
Ginestra
Corini-Pallaretta
Novello
Monforte d'Alba
Mosconi
Ravera
Panerole
Cerviano-Merli
Ravera di
Sottocastello di Novello
Monforte
Bricco
Le Coste di
Roddino
San Pietro
Monforte
Monchiero
44°571'N

Mi 0   0.93   1.86   2.80   3.73
Km 0   1.5   3   4.5   6

Province
Body of Water
City / Comune ■
BAROLO DOCG
LAND FEATURE

LA MORRA

Total MGA (39) - 3 shared
(Menzioni Geografiche Aggiuntive 'vineyard')

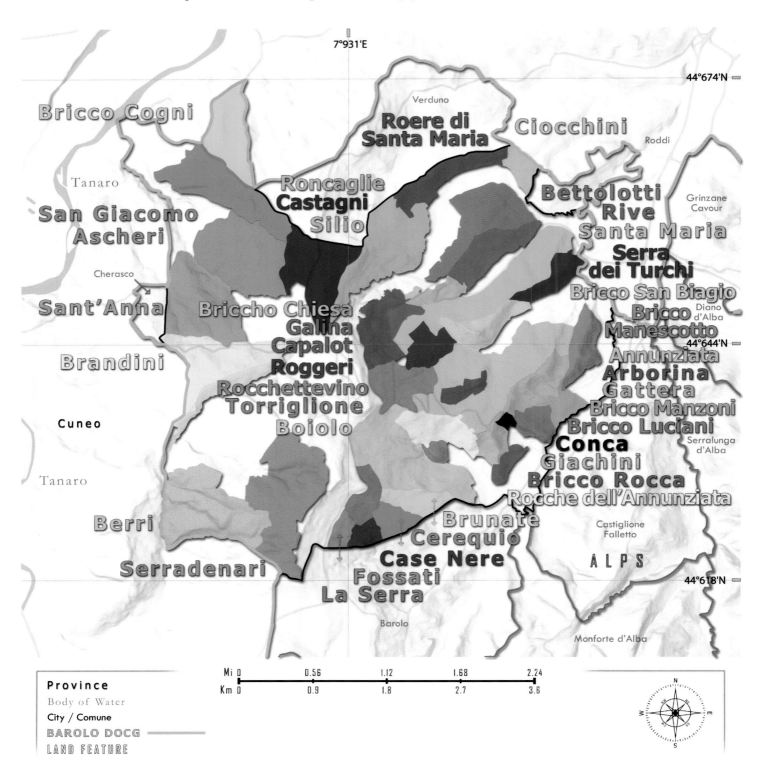

BAROLO
Total MGA (37) - 5 shared ┄┄┄┄┄┄>
(Menzioni Geografiche Aggiuntive 'vineyard')

CASTIGLIONE FALLETTO

Total MGA (20) - 1 shared
(Menzioni Geografiche Aggiuntive 'vineyard')

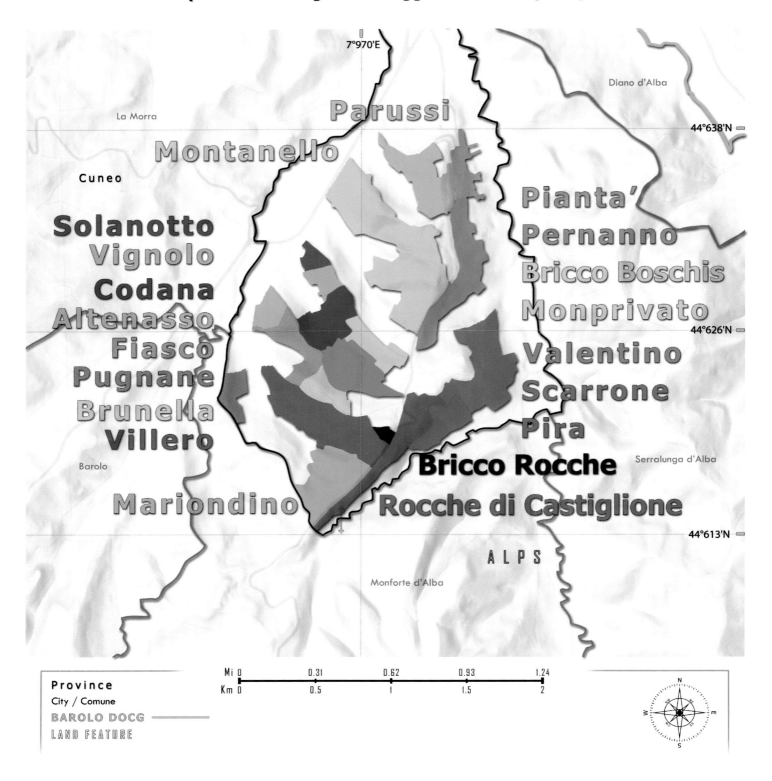

Diano d'Alba

44°638'N

7°970'E

La Morra

Parussi

Montanello

Cuneo

Pianta'

Pernanno

Solanotto

Bricco Boschis

Vignolo

Codana

Monprivato

Altenasso

44°626'N

Fiasco

Valentino

Pugnane

Scarrone

Brunella

Pira

Villero

Serralunga d'Alba

Barolo

Bricco Rocche

Mariondino

Rocche di Castiglione

44°613'N

ALPS

Monforte d'Alba

Province
City / Comune
BAROLO DOCG ——
LAND FEATURE

Mi 0   0.31   0.62   0.93   1.24
Km 0   0.5   1   1.5   2

SERRALUNGA D'ALBA
Total MGA (39) - 1 shared
(Menzioni Geografiche Aggiuntive 'vineyard')

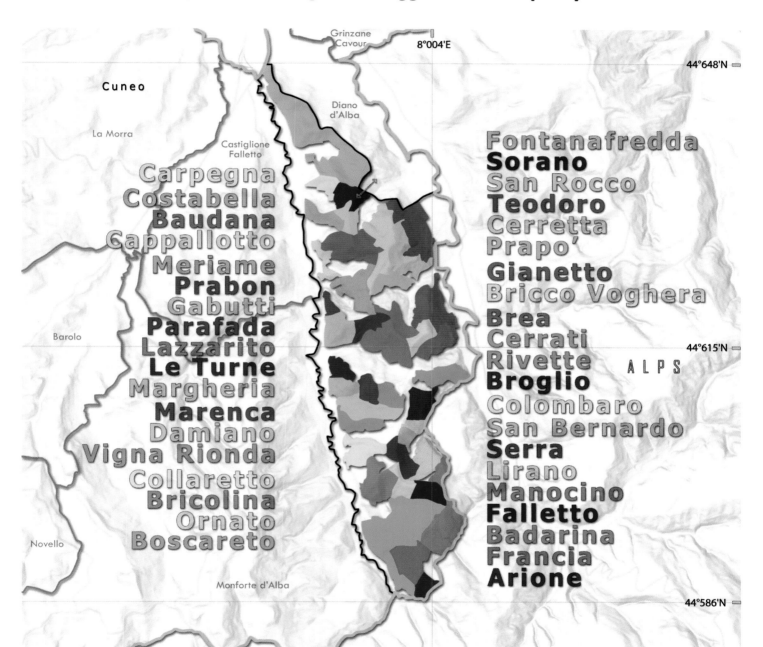

Cuneo

La Morra

Castiglione Falletto

Barolo

Novello

Monforte d'Alba

Diano d'Alba

Grinzane Cavour

8°004'E

44°648'N

44°615'N

44°586'N

ALPS

Carpegna
Costabella
Baudana
Cappallotto
Meriame
Prabon
Gabutti
Parafada
Lazzarito
Le Turne
Margheria
Marenca
Damiano
Vigna Rionda
Collaretto
Bricolina
Ornato
Boscareto

Fontanafredda
Sorano
San Rocco
Teodoro
Cerretta
Prapo'
Gianetto
Bricco Voghera
Brea
Cerrati
Rivette
Broglio
Colombaro
San Bernardo
Serra
Lirano
Manocino
Falletto
Badarina
Francia
Arione

Province
City / Comune
BAROLO DOCG ———
LAND FEATURE

| | Mi 0 | 0.56 | 1.12 | 1.68 | 2.24 |
| Km 0 | | 0.9 | 1.8 | 2.7 | 3.6 |

LOMBARDIA
DOCG [5]
DOC [21] - 3 SHARED

Lake Lucerne
Altdorf
Davos
10°039'E

SWITZERLAND

TRENTINO-ALTO ADIGE

46°601'N

Bolzano

A L P S

Bellinzona

VALTELLINA SUPERIORE
SFORZATO DI VALTELLINA
Valtellina Rosso

Lago Maggiore
Lago di Lugano
Lago di Como

Trento

Piave

MOSCATO DI SCANZO

Terre del Colleoni

Botticino

Riviera del Garda Bresciano

Lago d'Iseo

Lago di Garda

VENETO

Treviso

Valcalepio

FRANCIACORTA

Curtefranca

(SHARED)

Garda

PIEMONTE

Novara

Ticino

Milan

Cellatica

San Martino della Battaglia (SHARED)

45°542'N

Sesia

Capriano del Colle

Lugana (SHARED)

Venice

Gulf of Venice

San Colombano al Lambro

Sangue di Giuda dell'Oltrepò Pavese

Po

Piacenza

Garda Colli Mantovani

Lambrusco Mantovano

Po

Buttafuoco dell'Oltrepò Pavese

Casteggio
Oltrepò Pavese
OLTREPÒ PAVESE METODO CLASSICO
Pinot Nero dell'Oltrepò Pavese
Oltrepò Pavese Pinot Grigio
Bonarda dell'Oltrepò Pavese

44°681'N

Adriatic Sea

Genoa

LIGURIA

EMILIA-ROMAGNA

Ravenna

Gulf of Genoa

A P E N N I N E S

La Spezia

TOSCANA

Mi 0	24.86	49.71	74.57	99.42
Km 0	40	80	120	160

Body of Water
COUNTRY
City / Village
LAND FEATURE

TRENTINO-ALTO ADIGE
DOCG [0]
DOC [9] - 3 SHARED

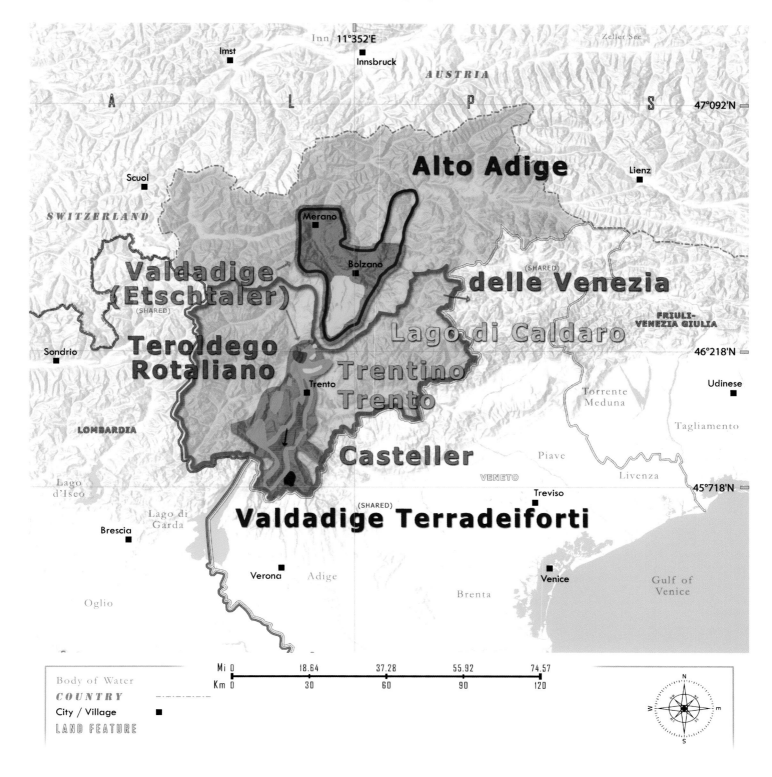

Alto Adige

delle Venezia
(SHARED)

Valdadige
(Etschtaler)
(SHARED)

Teroldego
Rotaliano

Lago di Caldaro

Trentino
Trento

Casteller

Valdadige Terradeiforti
(SHARED)

Merano
Bolzano
Trento

Innsbruck
Imst
Scuol
Sondrio
Brescia
Verona
Venice
Treviso
Udinese
Lienz

AUSTRIA
SWITZERLAND
LOMBARDIA
VENETO
FRIULI-VENEZIA GIULIA

A   L   P   S

Inn 11°352'E
47°092'N
46°218'N
45°718'N

Zeller See
Lago d'Iseo
Lago di Garda
Adige
Brenta
Piave
Livenza
Torrente Meduna
Tagliamento
Oglio
Gulf of Venice

| Mi 0 | 18.64 | 37.28 | 55.92 | 74.57 |
| Km 0 | 30 | 60 | 90 | 120 |

Body of Water
COUNTRY
City / Village
LAND FEATURE

VENETO
DOCG [14] - 1 SHARED
DOC [29] - 8 SHARED

AUSTRIA

SWITZERLAND

TRENTINO-ALTO ADIGE

Lienz

AUSTRIA

Delle Venezie (SHARED)

12°313'E

46°679'N

Villach

Vigneti della Serenissima

Bolzano

(SHARED) Prosecco

FRIULI-VENEZIA GIULIA

SLOVENIA

RECIOTO DI SOAVE
SOAVE SUPERIORE
Soave

Sondrio

LOMBARDIA
(SHARED)

Trento

Piave

Tagliamento

Montello Colli Asolani
MONTELLO ROSSO/MONTELLO
COLLI ASOLANI (ASOLO PROSECCO)

Venezia

Monti Lessini
Lessini Durello

COLLI DI CONEGLIANO

Valdadige Terradeiforti
(SHARED) Valdadige (Etschtaler)
BARDOLINO SUPERIORE
Bardolino (SHARED) Garda

CONEGLIANO VALDOBBIADENE
PROSECCO

Breganze

Trieste

45°771'N

Vicenza

(SHARED)

Bergamo

AMARONE DELLA
VALPOLICELLA
RECIOTO DELLA
VALPOLICELLA
Valpolicella Ripasso
Valpolicella Lugana
(SHARED)
San Martino della
Battaglia (SHARED)
Bianco di Custoza

Colli Berici

LISON
Lison-Pramaggiore

(SHARED)

PIAVE MALANOTTE
Piave

CROATIA

Merlara

Venice

Arcole

Riviera del Brenta

Corti Benedettine del Padovano

Gulf of
Venice

Po

Po

RECIOTO DI GAMBELLARA
Gambellara

Parma

FRIULARO DI BAGNOLI
Bagnoli di Sopra/Bagnoli

44°798'N

COLLI EUGANEI FIOR D'ARANCIO
Colli Euganei

EMILIA-ROMAGNA

Ravenna

Adriatic
Sea

APENNINES

LIGURIA

TOSCANA

| Mi 0 | 24.86 | 49.71 | 74.57 | 99.42 |
| Km 0 | 40 | 80 | 120 | 160 |

Body of Water
COUNTRY
City / Village ■
LAND FEATURE

FRIULI-VENEZIA GIULIA
DOCG [4] - 1 SHARED
DOC [12] - 3 SHARED

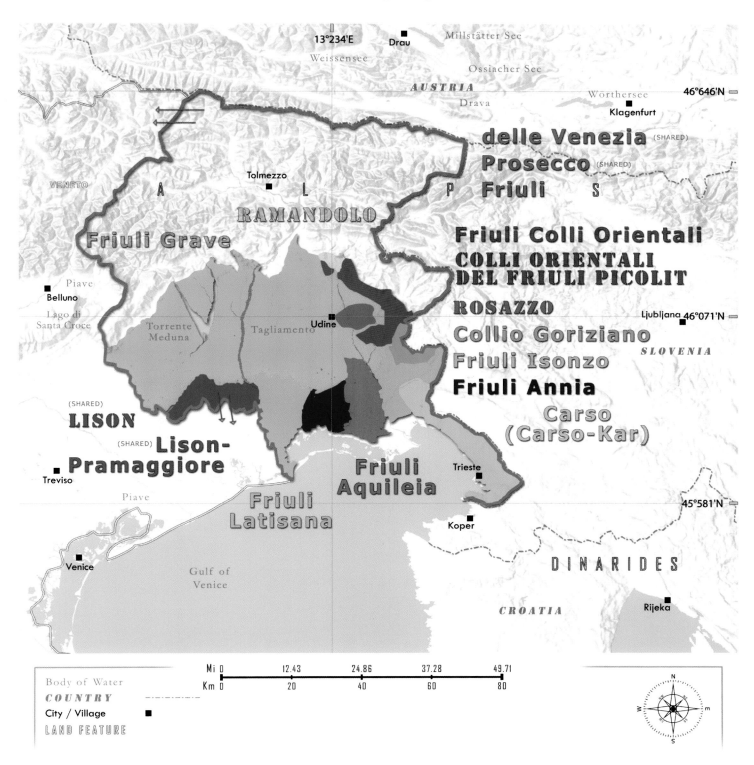

13°234'E
Drau
Millstätter See
Weissensee
Ossiacher See
AUSTRIA
46°646'N
Drava
Wörthersee
Klagenfurt

delle Venezia (SHARED)
Prosecco (SHARED)
Friuli

VENETO
Tolmezzo
A L P S

RAMANDOLO

Friuli Grave

Friuli Colli Orientali
COLLI ORIENTALI
DEL FRIULI PICOLIT

Piave
Belluno

ROSAZZO
Ljubljana 46°071'N

Lago di
Santa Croce
Torrente
Meduna
Tagliamento
Udine

Collio Goriziano
Friuli Isonzo

SLOVENIA

Friuli Annia

(SHARED)
LISON

Carso
(Carso-Kar)

(SHARED) **Lison-**
Pramaggiore

Treviso

Friuli
Aquileia

Trieste

Friuli
Latisana

Piave

45°581'N

Koper

Venice

Gulf of
Venice

D I N A R I D E S

CROATIA
Rijeka

Body of Water
COUNTRY
City / Village
LAND FEATURE

Mi 0   12.43   24.86   37.28   49.71
Km 0   20   40   60   80

N
W   E
S

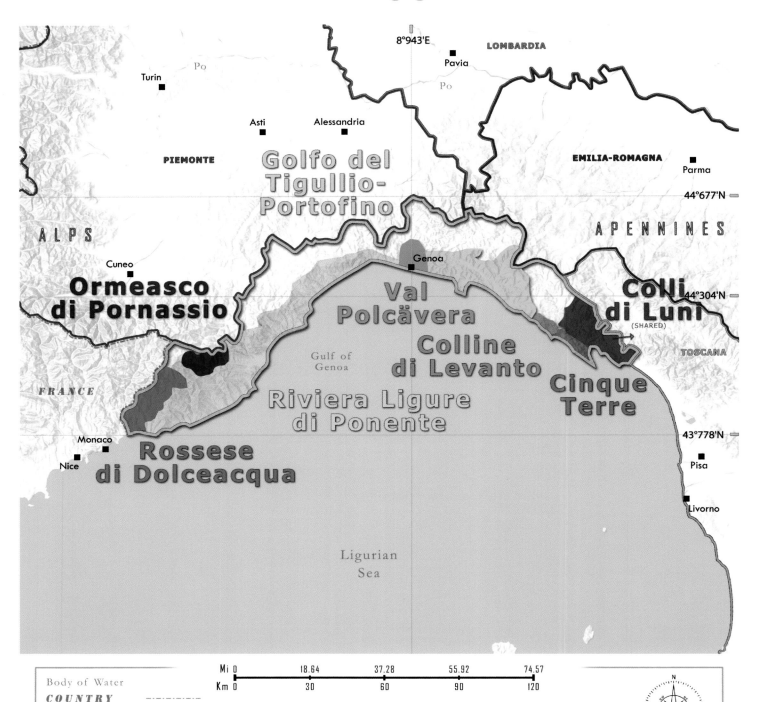

LIGURIA

DOCG [0]
DOC [8] - 1 SHARED

8°943'E

LOMBARDIA

Po

Turin

Po

Pavia

Asti   Alessandria

PIEMONTE

Golfo del Tigullio-Portofino

EMILIA-ROMAGNA

Parma

44°677'N

A P E N N I N E S

ALPS

Cuneo

Genoa

44°304'N

Ormeasco di Pornassio

Val Polcävera

Colli di Luni
(SHARED)

Gulf of Genoa

Colline di Levanto

TOSCANA

FRANCE

Riviera Ligure di Ponente

Cinque Terre

Monaco

43°778'N

Nice

Rossese di Dolceacqua

Pisa

Livorno

Ligurian Sea

Mi 0	18.64	37.28	55.92	74.57
Km 0	30	60	90	120

Body of Water

COUNTRY

City / Village

LAND FEATURE

EMILIA-ROMAGNA

DOCG [2]
DOC [19]

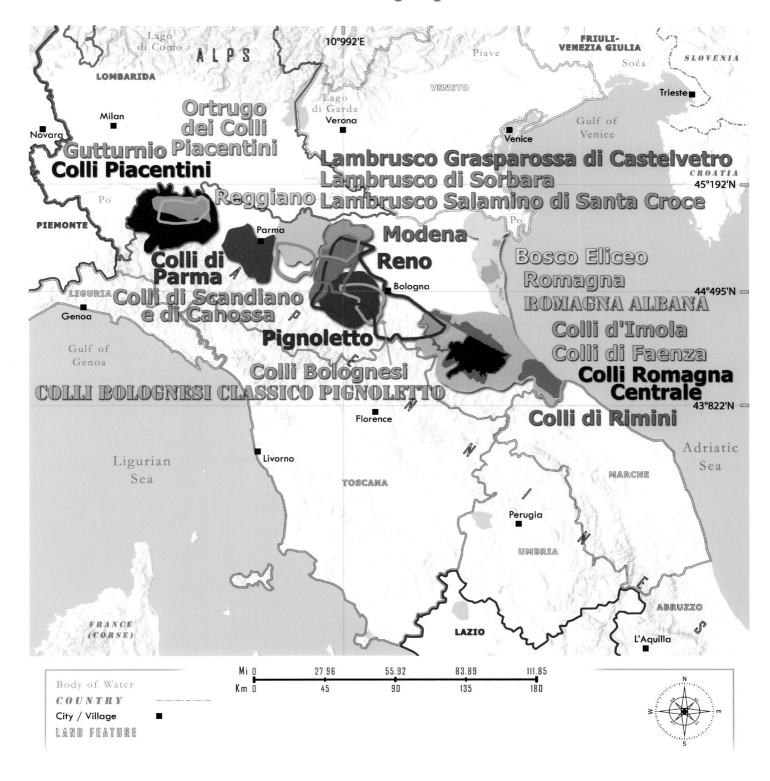

Ortrugo
dei Colli
Piacentini

Gutturnio

Colli Piacentini

Reggiano

Lambrusco Grasparossa di Castelvetro
Lambrusco di Sorbara
Lambrusco Salamino di Santa Croce

Modena
Reno

Bosco Eliceo
Romagna
ROMAGNA ALBANA

Colli di Parma

Colli di Scandiano
e di Canossa

Pignoletto

Colli d'Imola
Colli di Faenza

Colli Romagna Centrale

Colli Bolognesi

COLLI BOLOGNESI CLASSICO PIGNOLETTO

Colli di Rimini

	Mi 0	27.96	55.92	83.89	111.85
	Km 0	45	90	135	180

Body of Water
COUNTRY
City / Village ■
LAND FEATURE

TOSCANA
DOCG [11]
DOC [41] - 1 SHARED

LIGURIA

A

P

E

EMILIA-ROMAGNA

Bologna
11°255'E

Imola

Adriatic
Sea

44°210'N

Colli di Luni
(SHARED)

Candia
dei Colli Apuani

Massa

Vin Santo di Carmignano
Barco Reale di Carmignano
Valdinievole
CARMIGNANO

CHIANTI
Vin Santo del Chianti
Colli dell'Etruria Centrale

Marecchia

Colline Lucchesi

Montecarlo

San Torpè
Terre di Pisa

Terratico di Bibbona

Arno

Livorno

Florence

Pomino
Bianco dell'Empolese

CHIANTI CLASSICO
Vin Santo del Chianti Classico

MARCHE

VERNACCIA DI SAN GIMIGNANO
San Gimignano

Jesi

Arezzo

Val d'Arno di Sopra

Terre di
Casole

Siena

Valdichiana Toscana
Cortona

43°305'N

Montescudaio

Bolgheri
Bolgheri Sassicaia

SUVERETO

ROSSO DELLA VAL DI CORNIA
Val di Cornia

ELBA ALEATICO PASSITO
Elba

Bastia

Grance
Senesi

Val d'Arbia

Rosso di Montepulciano
Vin Santo di Montepulciano

VINO NOBILE DI MONTEPULCIANO

Orcia

UMBRIA

BRUNELLO DI MONTALCINO
Rosso di Montalcino
Moscadello di Montalcino
Sovana Sant' Antimo

Grosseto

Monteregio di Massa Marittima

MORELLINO DI SCANSANO
Parrina
Capalbio

Ansonica Costa dell'Argentario
Maremma Toscana

FRANCE
(CORSE)

MONTECUCCO SANGIOVESE
Montecucco

Terni

Bianco di
Pitigliano

42°365'N

Tyrrhenian
sea

LAZIO

Rome

	Mi 0	24.86	49.71	74.57	99.42
	Km 0	40	80	120	160

Body of Water
COUNTRY
City / Village ■
LAND FEATURE

N
W E
S

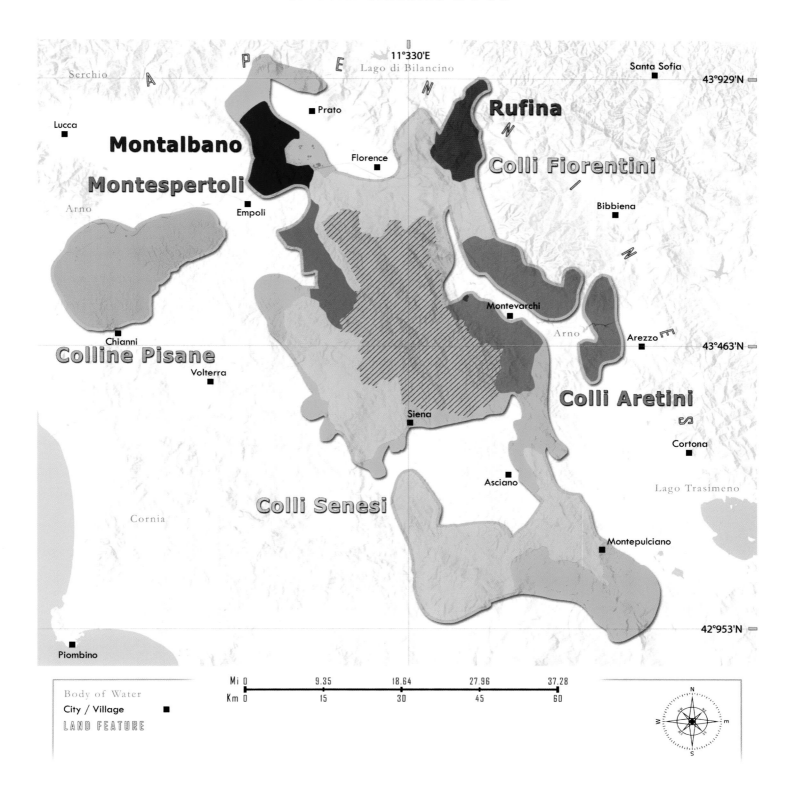

CHIANTI DOCG
7 Subzones
Chianti Classico DOCG //////

Serchio

Lago di Bilancino

Santa Sofia

43°929'N

Lucca

Prato

Rufina

Montalbano

Florence

Colli Fiorentini

Montespertoli

Arno

Empoli

Bibbiena

Chianni

Montevarchi

Arno

Arezzo

43°463'N

Colline Pisane

Volterra

Colli Aretini

Cortona

Siena

Lago Trasimeno

Asciano

Colli Senesi

Cornia

Montepulciano

42°953'N

Piombino

| Mi 0 | 9.35 | 18.64 | 27.96 | 37.28 |
| Km 0 | 15 | 30 | 45 | 60 |

Body of Water

City / Village ■

LAND FEATURE

11°330'E

CHIANTI CLASSICO DOCG
(11 Subzones)

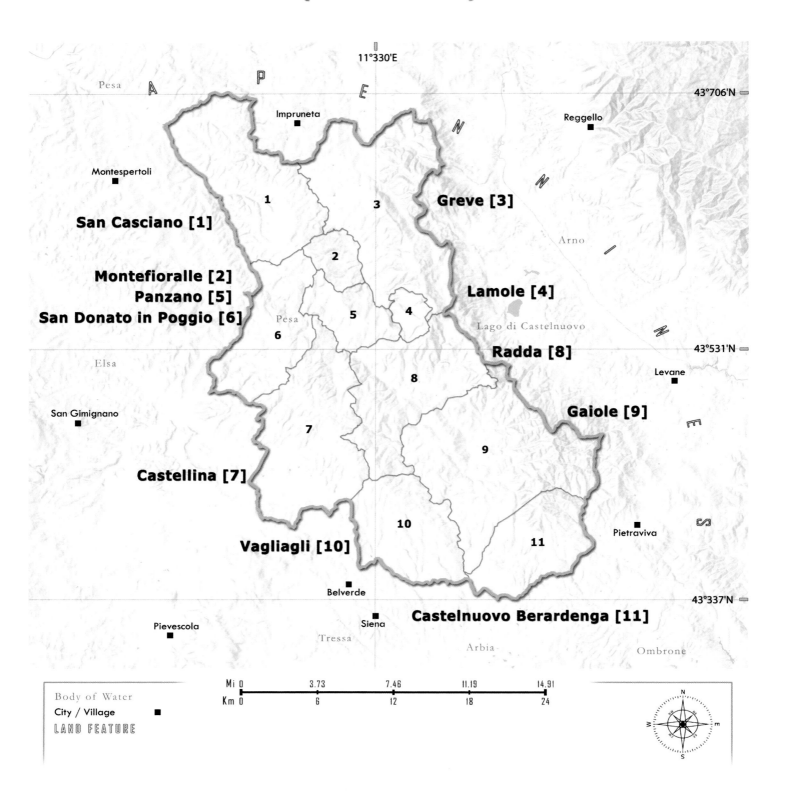

San Casciano [1]

Montefioralle [2]
Panzano [5]
San Donato in Poggio [6]

Greve [3]

Lamole [4]

Radda [8]

Gaiole [9]

Castellina [7]

Vagliagli [10]

Castelnuovo Berardenga [11]

Body of Water
City / Village ■
LAND FEATURE

Mi 0   3.73   7.46   11.19   14.91
Km 0   6   12   18   24

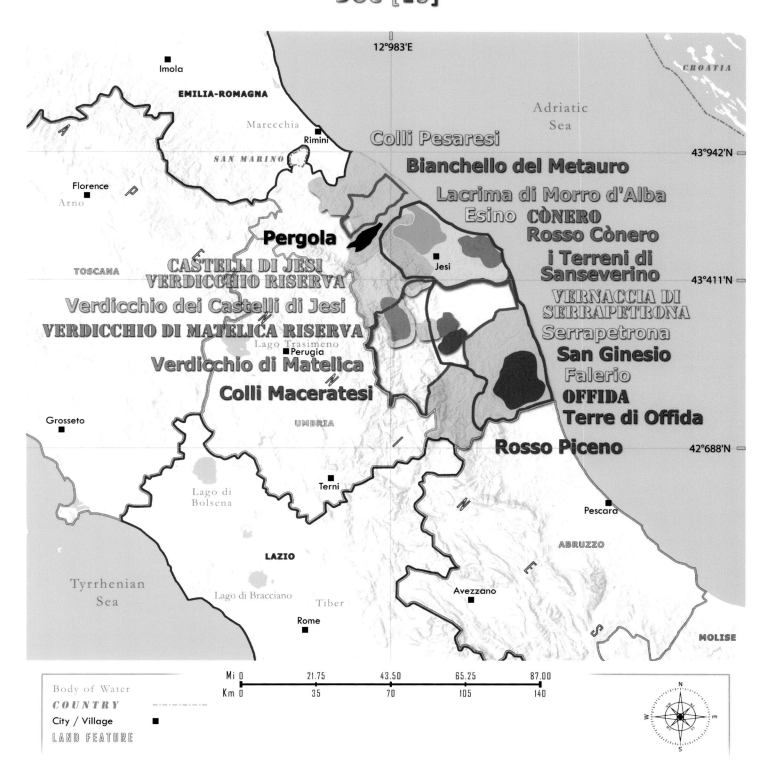

MARCHE
DOCG [5]
DOC [15]

EMILIA-ROMAGNA

Imola

CROATIA

Adriatic
Sea

Marecchia

Rimini

Colli Pesaresi

SAN MARINO

43°942'N

Florence

Arno

Bianchello del Metauro

Lacrima di Morro d'Alba

Esino **CÒNERO**

Rosso Cònero

Pergola

i Terreni di
Sanseverino

TOSCANA

CASTELLI DI JESI
VERDICCHIO RISERVA

Jesi

43°411'N

Verdicchio dei Castelli di Jesi

VERNACCIA DI
SERRAPETRONA

VERDICCHIO DI MATELICA RISERVA

Lago Trasimeno

Perugia

Serrapetrona

Verdicchio di Matelica

San Ginesio

Falerio

Colli Maceratesi

OFFIDA

Terre di Offida

Grosseto

UMBRIA

Rosso Piceno

42°688'N

Lago di
Bolsena

Terni

LAZIO

Pescara

ABRUZZO

Tyrrhenian
Sea

Lago di Bracciano

Tiber

Avezzano

Rome

MOLISE

Body of Water
COUNTRY
City / Village ■
LAND FEATURE

Mi 0   21.75   43.50   65.25   87.00
Km 0   35   70   105   140

UMBRIA
DOCG [2]
DOC [13] - 1 SHARED

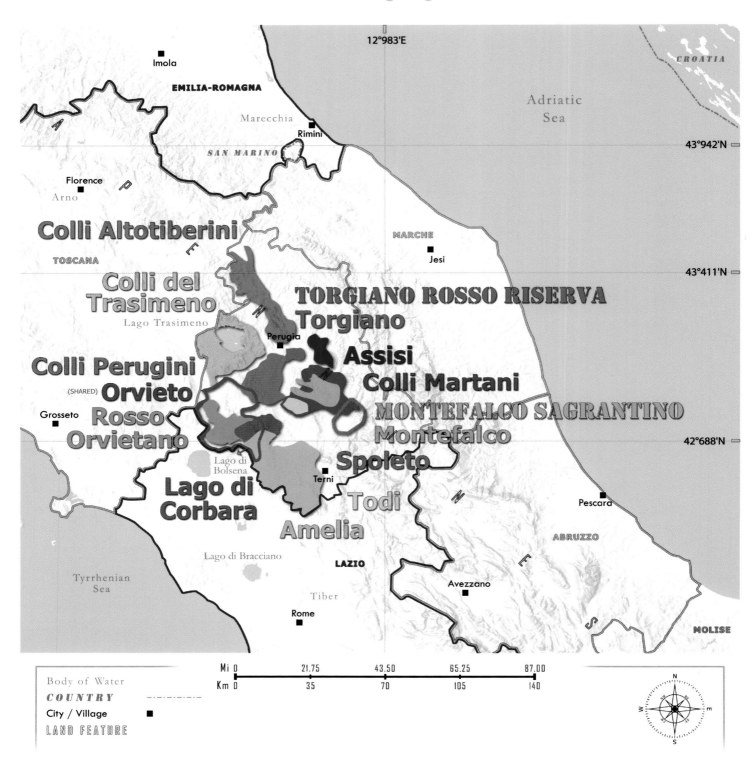

12°983'E

CROATIA

EMILIA-ROMAGNA

Imola

Adriatic
Sea

Marecchia

Rimini

43°942'N

SAN MARINO

Florence

Arno

MARCHE

Colli Altotiberini

Jesi

TOSCANA

43°411'N

Colli del
Trasimeno

TORGIANO ROSSO RISERVA

Lago Trasimeno

Torgiano

Perugia

Assisi

Colli Perugini

Colli Martani

(SHARED)

Orvieto

MONTEFALCO SAGRANTINO

Grosseto

Rosso
Orvietano

Montefalco

42°688'N

Spoleto

Lago di
Bolsena

Terni

Lago di
Corbara

Todi

Pescara

Amelia

ABRUZZO

Lago di Bracciano

LAZIO

Tyrrhenian
Sea

Tiber

Avezzano

Rome

MOLISE

| Mi 0 | 21.75 | 43.50 | 65.25 | 87.00 |
| Km 0 | 35 | 70 | 105 | 140 |

Body of Water

COUNTRY

City / Village

LAND FEATURE

LAZIO
DOCG [3]
DOC [27] - 1 SHARED

Siena

12°496'E

Macerata

Perugia

Adriatic Sea

TOSCANA

UMBRIA

MARCHE

42°837'N

Grosseto

Colli Etruschi Viterbese

Aleatico di Gradoli

Est! Est!! Est!!! di Montefiascone

Orvieto
(SHARED)

Terni

Pescara

Vignanello

L'Aquila

ABRUZZO

Tarquinia

Colli della Sabina

Cerveteri

Roma

Bianco Capena

Frascati

Genazzano

Cesanese di Affile

CANNELLINO DI FRASCATI

Cesanese di

FRASCATI SUPERIORE

Rome

Olevano Romano

41°767'N

Montecompatri-Colonna Zagarolo

Tiber

CESANESE DEL PIGLIO

MOLISE

Marino Castelli Romani

Campobasso

Colli Lanuvini Colli Albani

Atina

Velletri

Cori

Aprilia

Nettuno

Circeo

Volturno

41°225'N

Terracina

(Moscato di Terracina)

CAMPANIA

Naples

Tyrrhenian
Sea

Body of Water

City / Village ■

LAND FEATURE

| Mi 0 | 21.75 | 43.50 | 65.25 | 87.00 |
| Km 0 | 35 | 70 | 105 | 140 |

ABRUZZO
DOCG [2]
DOC [7]

Macerata

MARCHE

UMBRIA

Terni

Controguerra

COLLINE TERAMANE
MONTEPULCIANO D'ABRUZZO

42°896'N

Teramo

Adriatic
Sea

Villamagna
Ortona

Pescara

42°352'N

TERRE TOLLESI
(TULLUM)

Tiber

LAZIO

Avezzano

Rome

MOLISE

Fortore

41°685'N

Abruzzo
Cerasuolo d'Abruzzo
Trebbiano d'Abruzzo
Montepulciano d'Abruzzo

Frosinone

PUGLIA

Foggia

Tyrrhenian
Sea

CAMPANIA

Mondragone

Benevento

BASILICATA

| Mi 0 | 21.75 | 43.50 | 65.25 | 87.00 |
| Km 0 | 35 | 70 | 105 | 140 |

Body of Water

City / Village ■

LAND FEATURE

MOLISE

DOCG [0]
DOC [4]

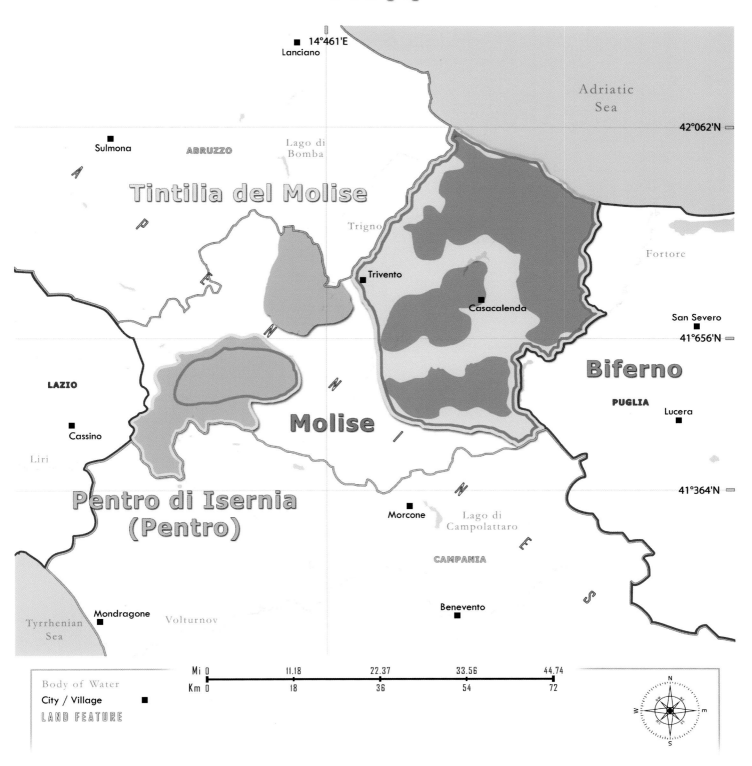

14°461'E
Lanciano

Adriatic
Sea

42°062'N

Sulmona

ABRUZZO

Lago di
Bomba

Tintilia del Molise

Trigno

Fortore

Trivento

Casacalenda

San Severo

41°656'N

LAZIO

Biferno

PUGLIA

Lucera

Cassino

Molise

Liri

41°364'N

Pentro di Isernia
(Pentro)

Morcone

Lago di
Campolattaro

CAMPANIA

Benevento

Tyrrhenian
Sea

Mondragone

Volturnov

| Mi | 0 | 11.18 | 22.37 | 33.56 | 44.74 |
| Km | 0 | 18 | 36 | 54 | 72 |

Body of Water
City / Village ■
LAND FEATURE

PUGLIA
DOCG [4]
DOC [28]

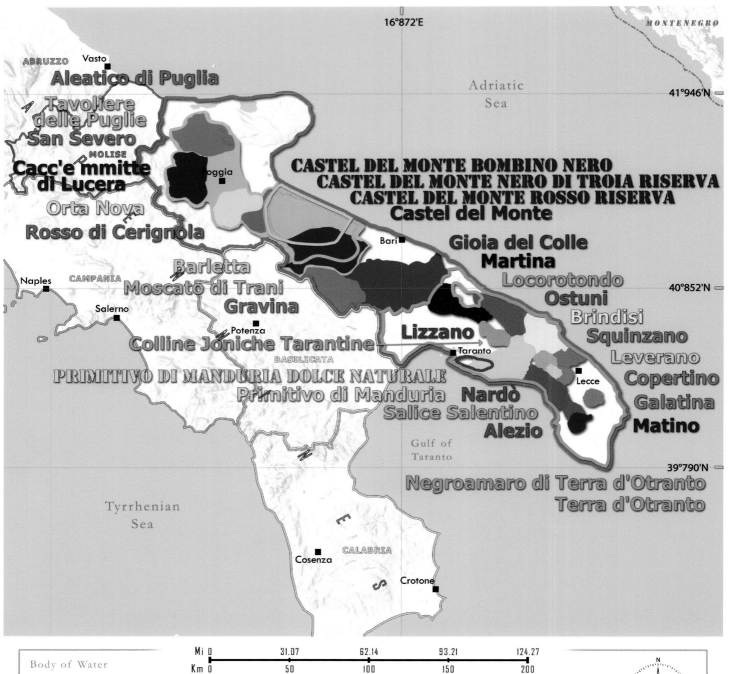

Aleatico di Puglia

Tavoliere delle Puglie

San Severo

Cacc'e mmitte di Lucera

Orta Nova

Rosso di Cerignola

CASTEL DEL MONTE BOMBINO NERO
CASTEL DEL MONTE NERO DI TROIA RISERVA
CASTEL DEL MONTE ROSSO RISERVA
Castel del Monte

Gioia del Colle
Martina

Barletta
Moscato di Trani
Gravina

Locorotondo
Ostuni
Brindisi
Squinzano
Leverano

Colline Joniche Tarantine

Lizzano

PRIMITIVO DI MANDURIA DOLCE NATURALE

Primitivo di Manduria

Nardò
Salice Salentino
Alezio

Copertino
Galatina
Matino

Negroamaro di Terra d'Otranto
Terra d'Otranto

ABRUZZO

Vasto

MOLISE

Foggia

Bari

Naples

CAMPANIA

Salerno

Potenza

BASILICATA

Taranto

Lecce

Adriatic Sea

MONTENEGRO

Gulf of Taranto

Tyrrhenian Sea

CALABRIA

Cosenza

Crotone

16°872'E

41°946'N

40°852'N

39°790'N

| Mi 0 | 31.07 | 62.14 | 93.21 | 124.27 |
| Km 0 | 50 | 100 | 150 | 200 |

Body of Water
COUNTRY
City / Village
LAND FEATURE

CAMPANIA

DOCG [4]
DOC [15]

ABRUZZO

Avezzano

Vasto

14°767'E

Adriatic Sea

Vieste

LAZIO

Frosinone

MOLISE

Fortore

Falanghina del Sannio
Sannio

PUGLIA

Foggia

41°506'N

Galluccio
Falerno del Massico

AGLIANICO DEL TABURNO
TAURASI

Barletta

Casavecchia di Pontelatone

Volturno

FIANO DI AVELLINO
GRECO DI TUFO

Aversa

Campi Flegrei

Naples

Vesuvio

Irpinia

40°852'N

Ischia

Penisola Sorrentina

Salerno

Capri

Costa d'Amalfi

Potenza

BASILICATA

Matera

Cilento

Castel San Lorenzo

Tyrrhenian Sea

39°993'N

Castrovillari

CALABRIA

Gulf of Taranto

Body of Water

City / Village ■

LAND FEATURE

Mi	0	21.75	43.50	65.25	87.00
Km	0	35	70	105	140

BASILICATA
DOCG [1]
DOC [4]

MOLISE

Foggia

15°805'E

Adriatic
Sea

Barletta

AGLIANICO DEL VULTURE SUPERIORE

41°140'N

CAMPANIA

Aglianico del Vulture

Monopoli

PUGLIA

Salerno

Sele

Potenza

Matera

Agropoli

Agri

40°465'N

Taranto

Terre dell'Alta Val d'Agri

Grottino di Roccanova

Gulf of Taranto

39°902'N

Castrovillari

Tyrrhenian Sea

CALABRIA

Cosenza

Mi	0	21.75	43.50	65.25	87.00
Km	0	35	70	105	140

Body of Water
City / Village ■
LAND FEATURE

CALABRIA

DOCG [0]
DOC [9]

CAMPANIA

BASILICATA

Scario

Tyrrhenian
Sea

Calabro

Savuto
Scavigna
Lamezia

Vibo Valentia

Bivongi

Greco di Bianco

SICILIA

Catania

Taranto

PUGLIA

Lecce

Adriatic
Sea

Gulf of
Taranto

40°137'N

Terre di Cosenza

Cirò

Melissa

Crotone

38°909'N

S. Anna di Isola
Capo Rizzuto

37°920'N

Ionian
Sea

16°587'E

| Mi 0 | 24.85 | 49.71 | 74.56 | 99.42 |
| Km 0 | 40 | 80 | 120 | 160 |

Body of Water
City / Village ■
LAND FEATURE

SICILIA

DOCG [1]
DOC [23]

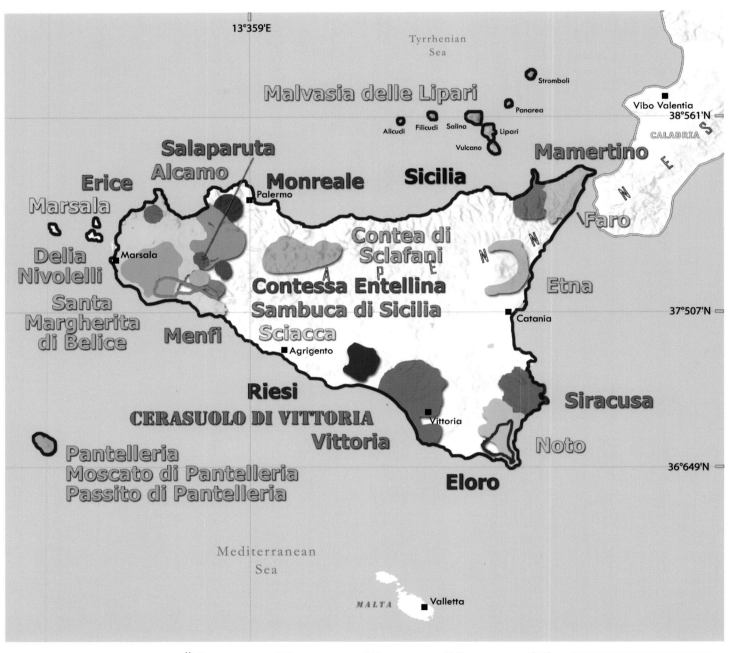

13°359'E

Tyrrhenian
Sea

Malvasia delle Lipari

Stromboli

Panarea

Vibo Valentia

38°561'N

CALABRIA

Alicudi   Filicudi   Salina   Lipari

Vulcano

Salaparuta

Alcamo

Erice

Marsala

Monreale

Palermo

Sicilia

Mamertino

Faro

Contea di
Sclafani

Delia
Nivolelli

Marsala

Contessa Entellina

Sambuca di Sicilia

Etna

Santa
Margherita
di Belice

Menfi

Sciacca

Catania

37°507'N

Agrigento

Riesi

Siracusa

CERASUOLO DI VITTORIA

Vittoria

Noto

Vittoria

36°649'N

Pantelleria
Moscato di Pantelleria
Passito di Pantelleria

Eloro

Mediterranean
Sea

MALTA   Valletta

| Mi 0 | 31.07 | 62.14 | 93.21 | 124.27 |
| Km 0 | 50 | 100 | 150 | 200 |

SARDEGNA

DOCG [1]
DOC [17]

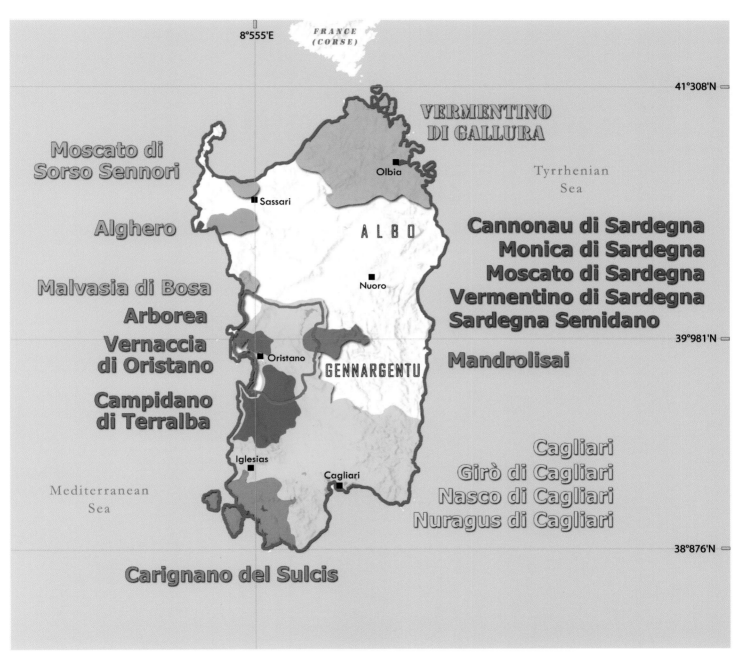

FRANCE
(CORSE)

8°555'E

41°308'N

VERMENTINO
DI GALLURA

Moscato di
Sorso Sennori

Olbia

Tyrrhenian
Sea

Sassari

ALBO

Alghero

Cannonau di Sardegna
Monica di Sardegna
Moscato di Sardegna
Vermentino di Sardegna
Sardegna Semidano

Malvasia di Bosa
Nuoro

Arborea

Vernaccia
di Oristano

39°981'N

Oristano

GENNARGENTU

Mandrolisai

Campidano
di Terralba

Cagliari
Girò di Cagliari
Nasco di Cagliari
Nuragus di Cagliari

Iglesias

Cagliari

Mediterranean
Sea

38°876'N

Carignano del Sulcis

Body of Water

City / Village ■

LAND FEATURE

| Mi 0 | 27.96 | 55.92 | 83.89 | 111.85 |
| Km 0 | 45 | 90 | 135 | 180 |

CLASSIFICATION SYSTEM
DOCa [Denominacion de Origen Calificada = Controlled Designation of Origin]
DO [Denominacion de Origen = Designation of Origin]
VCIG [Vinos de Calidad con Indicación Geográfica]
IGP [Indicación Geográfica Protegida = Protected Geographical Indication
    = Vino de la Tierra]
VINO DE ESPAÑA = VdM [Vino de Mesa = table wine]

17 Regions

2 DOCa (DOQ in Catalan)

69 DO

24 Vino de Pago

S P A I N

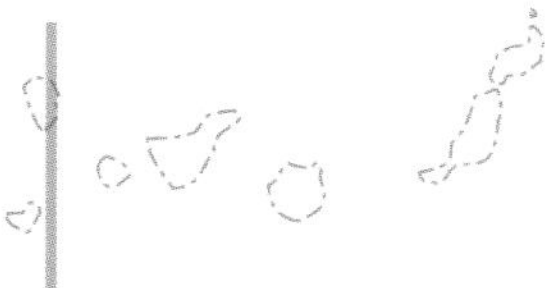

1 7   R E G I O N S   /   2   D O C a   (D O Q)   /   6 9   D O

REGION / DENOMINACION	RANK	EST.	DENOMINACION	RANK	EST.	DENOMINACION	RANK	EST.
Galicia [5 DO]								
MONTERREI	DO	1996	RIBEIRA SACRA	DO	1996	VALDEORRAS	DO	1945
RÍAS BAIXAS	DO	1988	RIBEIRO	DO	1932			
Castilla y León [9 DO]								
ARLANZA	DO	2007	CIGALES	DO	1991	TIERRA DE LEÓN	DO	2007
ARRIBES	DO	2007	RIBERA DEL DUERO	DO	1982	TIERRA DEL VINO DE ZAMORA	DO	2007
BIERZO	DO	1989	RUEDA	DO	1980	TORO	DO	1987
Asturias [1 DO]			CANGAS	DO	2018			
Basque Country / País Vasco [3 DO and 1 DOCa shared]								
ARABAKO TXAKOLINA / CHACOLÍ DE ÁLAVA	DO	2001	BIZKAIKO TXAKOLINA / CHACOLÍ DE BIZKAIA	DO	1994	GETARIAKO TXAKOLINA / CHACOLÍ DE GUETARIA	DO	1994
RIOJA [shared with La Rioja and Navarra]	DOCa	1991	RIOJA [shared with País Vasco and Navarra]	DOCa	1991			
La Rioja [1 DOCa shared]								
Navarra [1 DO and 1 DOCa shared]								
NAVARRA	DO	1933	RIOJA [shared with La Rioja and País Vasco]	DOCa	1991			
Aragón [4 DO]								
CALATAYUD	DO	1989	CARIÑENA	DO	1932	SOMONTANO	DO	1984
CAMPO DE BORJA	DO	1980						
Catalonia / Catalunya [1 DOQ and 10 DO]								
ALELLA	DO	1953	EMPORDÀ	DO	1975	PRIORAT	DOQ	2000
CATALUNYA	DO	1999	MONTSANT	DO	2001	TARRAGONA	DO	1947
CONCA DE BARBERÀ	DO	1985	PENEDÈS	DO	1960	TERRA ALTA	DO	1972
COSTERS DEL SEGRE	DO	1988	PLA DE BAGES	DO	1995			
Valencia [3 DO]								
ALICANTE	DO	1957	UTIEL-REQUENA	DO	1957	VALENCIA	DO	1957
Murcia [3 DO out of 1 shared]								
BULLAS	DO	1994	JUMILLA [shared with Castilla-La Mancha]	DO	1966	YECLA	DO	1975
Castilla-La Mancha [9 DO out of 1 shared]								
ALMANSA	DO	1966	MANCHUELA	DO	2000	RIBERA DEL JÚCAR	DO	2003
JUMILLA [shared with Murcia]	DO	1966	MÉNTRIDA	DO	1976	UCLÉS	DO	2005
LA MANCHA	DO	1976	MONDÉJAR	DO	1997	VALDEPEÑAS	DO	1932
Madrid [1 DO]			VINOS DE MADRID	DO	1990			
Extremadura [1 DO]			RIBERA DEL GUADIANA	DO	1999			
Andalucia [6 DO]								
CONDADO DE HUELVA	DO	1963	MÁLAGA	DO	1935	MONTILLA-MORILES	DO	1945
JEREZ-XÉRÈS-SHERRY	DO	1933	MANZANILLA SANLÚCAR DE BARRAMEDA	DO	1933	SIERRAS DE MÁLAGA	DO	2001
Balearic Islands [2 DO]								
BINISSALEM	DO	1991	PLA I LLEVANT	DO	1999			
Canary Islands [11 DO]								
ABONA	DO	1995	LA ISLAS CANARIAS	DO	2012	VALLE DE GÜÍMAR	DO	1995
EL HIERRO	DO	1994	LA PALMA	DO	1994	VALLE DE LA OROTAVA	DO	1995
GRAN CANARIA	DO	2005	LANZAROTE	DO	1993	YCODEN-DAUTE-ISORA	DO	1994
LA GOMERA	DO	2003	TACORONTE-ACENTEJO	DO	1992			
Cantabria [no denominacion]								
Multi-region Denominacion								
CAVA [La Rioja, País Vasco, Navarra, Catalonia, Valencia, Extremadura]	DO	1986						

2 4   V I N O   D E   P A G O

REGION / VINO DE PAGO	SINCE	VINO DE PAGO	SINCE	VINO DE PAGO	SINCE
Aragón [1]					
AYLÉS	2011				
Castilla-La Mancha [12]					
CAMPO DE LA GUARDIA	2009	EL VICARIO	2019	LOS CERRILLOS	2019
CASA DEL BLANCO	2010	FINCA ÉLEZ	2003	PAGO CALZADILLA	2011
DEHESA DEL CARRIZAL	2006	GUIJOSO	2005	PAGO FLORENTINO	2009
DOMINIO DE VALDEPUSA	2003	LA JARABA	2019	VALLEGARCÍA	2019
Castilla y León [3]					
ABADÍA RETUERTA	2022	DEHESA PEÑALBA	2022	URUEÑA	2021
Navarra [4]					
ARÍNZANO	2007	BOLANDIN	2022	OTAZU	2009
PRADO DE IRACHE	2008				
Valencia [4]					
CHOZAS CARRASCAL	2020	EL TERRERAZO	2010	LOS BALAGUESES	2011
VERA DE ESTENAS	2019				

REGIONS OF SPAIN [17]

Mi 0   93.21   186.41   279.62   372.82

Km 0   150   300   450   600

Body of Water

COUNTRY

City ■

LAND FEATURE

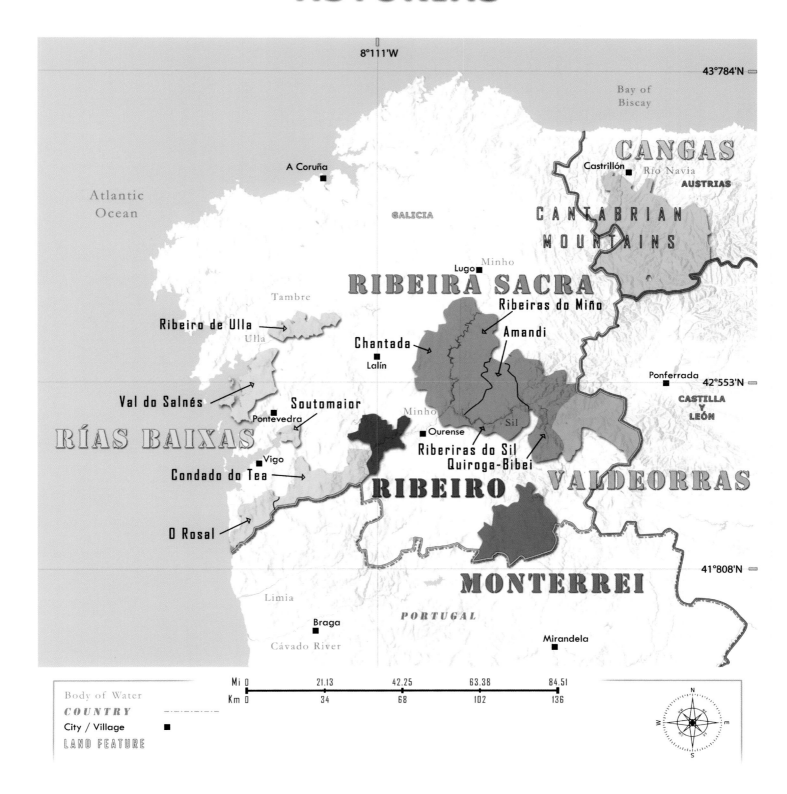

GALICIA DO [5]

Sub-region of Rías Baixas DO [5]
Sub-region of Ribeira Sacra DO [5]

ASTURIAS DO [1]

8°111'W

43°784'N

Bay of
Biscay

A Coruña

Atlantic
Ocean

GALICIA

CANGAS

Castrillón · Río Navia

AUSTRIAS

CANTABRIAN
MOUNTAINS

Minho

Lugo

RIBEIRA SACRA

Ribeiras do Miño

Tambre

Ribeiro de Ulla

Chantada

Amandi

Ulla

Lalín

Ponferrada

42°553'N

Val do Salnés

Soutomaior

CASTILLA
Y
LEÓN

Pontevedra

Minho

RÍAS BAIXAS

Ourense

Sil

Vigo

Riberiras do Sil
Quiroga-Bibei

Condado do Tea

RIBEIRO

VALDEORRAS

O Rosal

41°808'N

MONTERREI

Limia

PORTUGAL

Braga

Mirandela

Cávado River

| Mi 0 | 21.13 | 42.25 | 63.38 | 84.51 |
| Km 0 | 34 | 68 | 102 | 136 |

Body of Water
COUNTRY
City / Village ■
LAND FEATURE

N
W E
S

CASTILLA Y LEÓN

DO [9]
Vino de Pago [3]

Abadía Retuerta [1]
Dehesa Peñalba [2]
Urueña [3]

Body of Water
COUNTRY
City / Village
LAND FEATURE

Mi 0   31.07   62.14   93.21   124.27
Km 0   50   100   150   200

LA RIOJA

DOCa (DOQ) [1] - shared

Sub-region of Rioja DOCa [3] ——

Rioja Alta located entirely in La Rioja
Rioja Alavesa located entirely in País Vasco
Rioja Oriental overlapping with Navarra

CANTABRIAN MOUNTAINS

PYRÉNÉES

2°444'W

Vitoria-Gasteiz

Ebro

Bayas

PAÍS VASCO

Zadorra

Pamplona

Ayuda

Rioja Alavesa

42°662'N

NAVARRA

Miranda de Ebro

Haro

Tirón

Oja

Ebro

Logroño

Ega

Zidacos

Arga

RIOJA

Briviesca

Najerilla

Iregua

Belorado

Leza

42°370'N

Rioja Alta

Calahorra

Caparroso

LA RIOJA

Aragón

I B E R I A N

Cidacos

Rioja Oriental

Ebro

Tudela

S Y S T E M

41°965'N

CASTILLA Y LEÓN

Ágreda

Duero

ARAGÓN

Soria

Mi	0	11.18	22.37	33.55	44.74
Km	0	18	36	54	72

Body of Water
City / Village ■
LAND FEATURE

Spain

www.thewineregionatlas.com
by Istvan Barczikay

PAÍS VASCO DO [4] (1 shared)

Vino de Pago [4] NAVARRA DO [2] (1 shared)
Sub-region of Navarra DO [5] ———

Vino de Pago [1] ARAGÓN DO [4]

BIZKAIKO TXAKOLINA

ARABAKO TXAKOLINA 1°740'W

GETARIAKO TXAKOLINA

43°448'N

Bay of Biscay

CANTABRIA

Bilbao

Eibar

Pau

FRANCE

Prado de Irache [1]
Pago de Arínzano [2]
Pago de Otazu [3]
Bolandin [4]

CANTABRIAN MOUNTAINS

PAÍS VASCO

NAVARRA

NAVARRA

Pamplona

RIOJA
Alavesa subregion (entirely)

Ebro

Logroño

RIOJA
Oriental subregion (overlapping)

LA RIOJA

3
1 2
2
1
3
4

Tierra de Estella [1]
Valdizarbe [2]
Baja Montaña [3]
Ribera Alta [4]
Ribera Baja [5]

Burgos

CASTILLA Y LEÓN

Aranda de Duero

Soria

Tudela
5
4

Huesca

CAMPO
DE BORJA
SOMONTANO

Cinca

41°910'N

Lleida

Segre

Zaragoza

Ebro

ARAGÓN

CATALONIA

Aylés

Tarragona

CARIÑENA
CALATAYUD

Ebro

Segovia

SISTEMA CENTRAL

CASTILLA-LA MANCHA

MADRID

Madrid

Teruel

Mediterranean
Sea

Tagus

VALENCIA

39°847'N

| | Mi 0 | 35.42 | 70.84 | 106.25 | 141.67 |
| | Km 0 | 57 | 114 | 171 | 228 |

Body of Water
COUNTRY
City / Village ■
LAND FEATURE

CATALONIA
DOCa (DOQ) [1]
DO [10]

FRANCE

42°860'N

Agly

ANDORRA

Perpignan

Tét

P Y R É N É E S

Tech

COSTERS
DEL
SEGRE

Segre

CATALONIA

El Fluvià

Berga

EMPORDÀ

Monzón

El Llobregat

PLA DE BAGES

ARAGÓN

Ter Girona

Cinca

Alcanadre

Lleida

Segre

MONTSANT·
PRIORAT

Mataró

ALELLA

Ebro

El Llobregat

Barcelona

41°385'N

Alcañiz

PENEDÈS

Tarragona

CONCA DE BARBERÀ

TERRA
ALTA

CATALONIA

TARRAGONA

Ebro Tortosa

Mediterranean
Sea

40°524'N

VALENCIA

Benicarló

1°235'E

| Mi 0 | 24.86 | 49.71 | 74.56 | 99.42 |
| Km 0 | 40 | 80 | 120 | 160 |

Body of Water
COUNTRY
City / Village ■
LAND FEATURE

PRIORAT DOCa (DOQ)

Villages of Priorat DOCa (DOQ) [12]

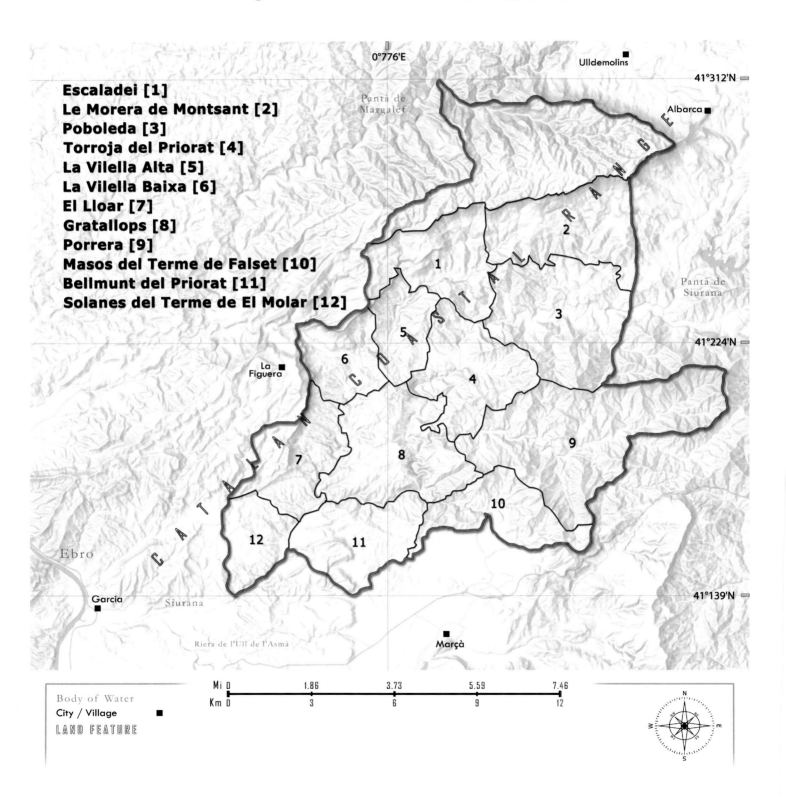

Escaladei [1]
Le Morera de Montsant [2]
Poboleda [3]
Torroja del Priorat [4]
La Vilella Alta [5]
La Vilella Baixa [6]
El Lloar [7]
Gratallops [8]
Porrera [9]
Masos del Terme de Falset [10]
Bellmunt del Priorat [11]
Solanes del Terme de El Molar [12]

Body of Water
City / Village ■
LAND FEATURE

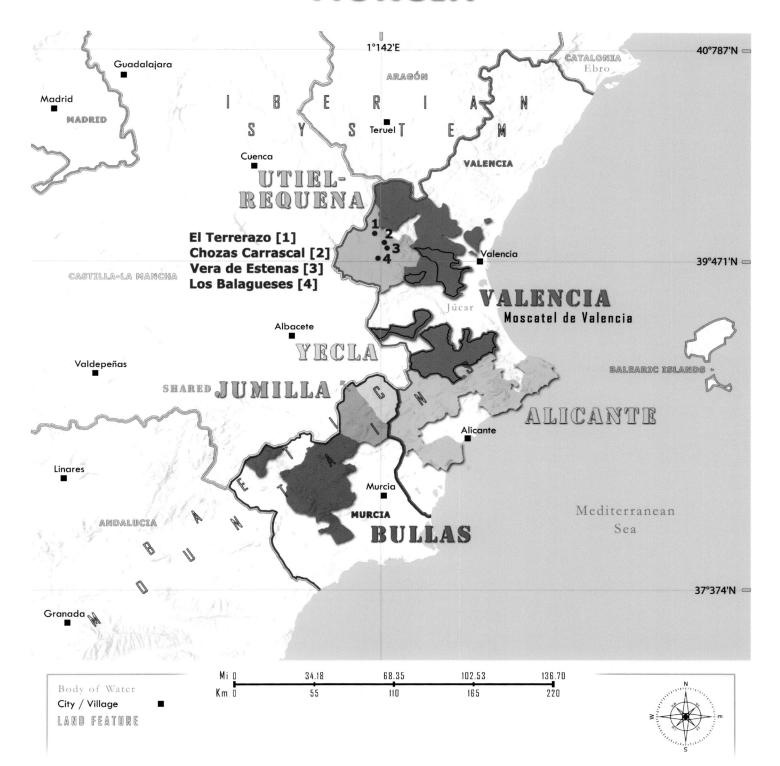

Vino de Pago [4] VALENCIA DO [3]

Sub-region of Valencia DO [1] ——

MURCIA DO [3] (1 shared)

El Terrerazo [1]
Chozas Carrascal [2]
Vera de Estenas [3]
Los Balagueses [4]

UTIEL-REQUENA

VALENCIA

Moscatel de Valencia

YECLA

SHARED JUMILLA

ALICANTE

BULLAS

MURCIA

1°142'E

40°787'N

39°471'N

37°374'N

Guadalajara

Madrid

MADRID

ARAGÓN

Teruel

CATALONIA
Ebro

IBERIAN SYSTEM

Cuenca

VALENCIA

Valencia

CASTILLA-LA MANCHA

Júcar

Albacete

Valdepeñas

BALEARIC ISLANDS

Linares

Alicante

ANDALUCIA

Murcia

Mediterranean Sea

Granada

Body of Water
City / Village
LAND FEATURE

| Mi 0 | 34.18 | 68.35 | 102.53 | 136.70 |
| Km 0 | 55 | 110 | 165 | 220 |

CASTILLA-LA MANCHA
Vino de Pago [12] DO [9] (1 shared)
MADRID DO [1]
EXTREMADURA DO [1]

GALICIA

Braganca

Tera

Valladolid
CASTILLA Y LEÓN
Duero

3°705'W

Aranda de Duero

LA RIOJA

NAVARRA

Zaragoza

Ebro

41°325'N

ARAGÓN

Calatayud

Douro

Portugal

Tormes

Salamanca

VINOS DE
MADRID

MÉNTRIDA

MADRID
Madrid

MONDÉJAR

UCLÉS

Cuenca

MANCHUELA

1

SISTEMA CENTRAL

Plasencia

Tajo

3

Toledo

2

RIBERA DEL JÚCAR

CASTILLA-
LA MANCHA

EXTREMADURA

4 • 5

12

VALENCIA

39°672'N

Valencia

Tejo

Mérida

Guadiana

Tomelloso

6

7

8

9

10

11

Albacete

Evora

LA
MANCHA

VALDEPEÑAS

JUMILLA
SHARED

ALMANSA

38°026'N

MURCIA

Guadiana

RIBERA DEL
GUADIANA

Córdoba

ANDALUCIA

Cartagena

Huelva

Seville

Granada

Mediterranean
Sea

Atlantic Ocean

Pago Calzadilla [1]   **El Vicario [7]**
Campo de la Guardia [2] **Casa del Blanco [8]**
Dominio de Valdepusa [3] **Los Cerrillos [9]**
Dehesa del Carrizal [4] Granada **Guijoso [10]**
Vallegarcía [5] **Finca Élez [11]**
Pago Florentino [6] **La Jaraba [12]**

| Mi 0 | 46.60 | 93.21 | 139.81 | 186.41 |
| Km 0 | 75 | 150 | 225 | 300 |

Body of Water
COUNTRY
City / Village
LAND FEATURE

ANDALUCIA
DO [6]
Sub-region of Málaga DO and Sierras de Málaga DO [5]

CASTILLA-LA MANCHA

Guadiana

Mérida

Valdepeñas

38°729'N

EXTREMADURA

Evora

MONTILLA-MORILES

MURCIA

PORTUGAL

Guadiana

CONDADO
DE HUELVA

ANDALUCIA

Jaén

Lucena

MÁLAGA
SIERRAS DE MÁLAGA

Odiel

Tinto

Seville

Huelva

Guadalquivir

1

Granada

37°019'N

MANZANILLA
SANLÚCAR DE
BARRAMEDA

JEREZ-
XÉRÈS-
SHERRY

Jerez
de la
Frontera

4

3

2

Almería

Málaga

5

Cádiz

Norte [1]
Axarquía [2]
Montes de Málaga [3]
Serranía de Ronda [4]
Manilva [5]

GIBRALTAR

36°009'N

Mediterranean
Sea

Tangier

Atlantic
Ocean

Melilla

A T L A S

MOROCCO

ALGERIA

Mi 0	40.39	80.78	121.17	161.57
Km 0	65	130	195	260

Body of Water
COUNTRY
City / Village
LAND FEATURE

Spain

www.thewineregionatlas.com
by Istvan Barczikay

Spain

167

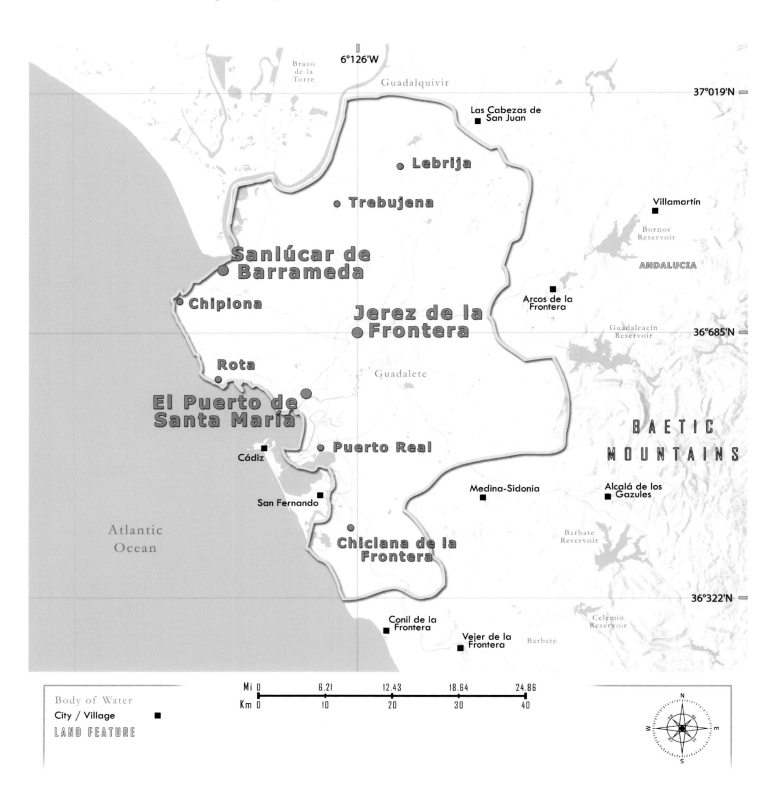

JEREZ-XÉRÈS-SHERRY DO
Municipality of Jerez-Xérès-Sherry DO [9]

Brazo
de la
Torre

6°126'W

Guadalquivir

37°019'N

Las Cabezas de
San Juan

Lebrija

Trebujena

Villamartín

Bornos
Reservoir

ANDALUCIA

Sanlúcar de
Barrameda

Chipiona

Jerez de la
Frontera

Arcos de la
Frontera

Guadalacín
Reservoir

36°685'N

Rota

Guadalete

El Puerto de
Santa María

BAETIC

MOUNTAINS

Cádiz

Puerto Real

San Fernando

Medina-Sidonia

Alcalá de los
Gazules

Atlantic
Ocean

Chiclana de la
Frontera

Barbate
Reservoir

36°322'N

Conil de la
Frontera

Celemín
Reservoir

Vejer de la
Frontera

Barbate

Mi 0   6.21   12.43   18.64   24.86
Km 0   10   20   30   40

Body of Water
City / Village   ■
LAND FEATURE

N
W   E
S

JEREZ-XÉRÈS-SHERRY DO

IMPORTANT PAGOS OF JEREZ-XÉRÈS-SHERRY DO [48]
(vineyards)
Albariza soil
Barros and Arenas soil

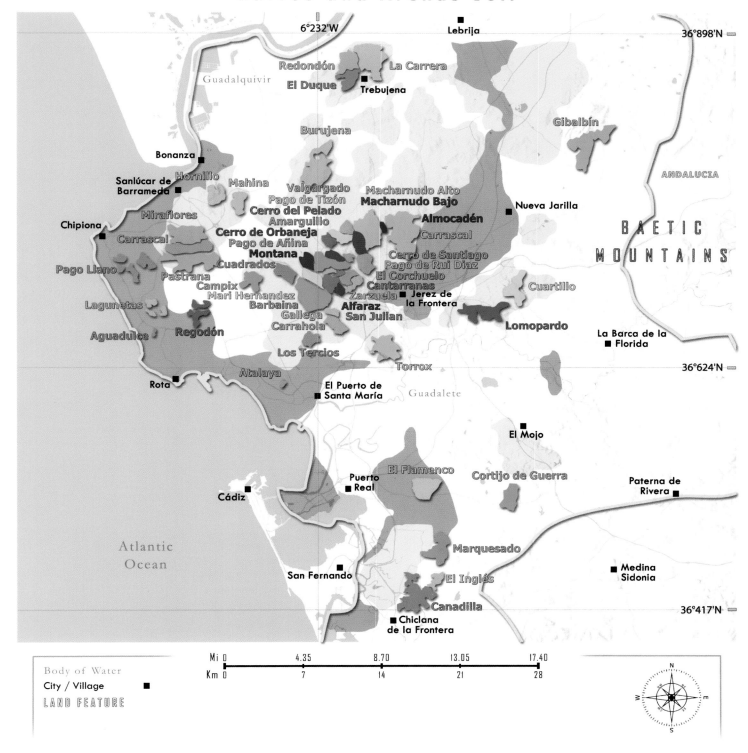

Lebrija

6°232'W

36°898'N

Redondón   La Carrera

Guadalquivir

El Duque

Trebujena

Gibalbín

Burujena

ANDALUCIA

Bonanza

Hornillo

Sanlúcar de Barrameda

Mahina

Vaigargado

Macharnudo Alto

Pago de Tizón

Macharnudo Bajo

Nueva Jarilla

Miraflores

Cerro del Pelado

Amarguillo

Almocadén

BAETIC

Chipiona

Cerro de Orbaneja

Carrascal

MOUNTAINS

Carrascal

Pago de Añina

Cerro de Santiago

Pago Llano

Montana

Pago de Rui Diaz

Cuadrados

El Corchuelo

Cuartillo

Pastrana

Cantarranas

Campix

Zarzuela   Jerez de la Frontera

Mari Hernandez

La Barca de la Florida

Lagunetas

Barbaina

Alfaraz

Gallega

San Julian

Aguadulce

Carrahola

Lomopardo

Regodón

36°624'N

Los Tercios

Atalaya

Torrox

Rota

El Puerto de Santa María

Guadalete

El Mojo

El Flamenco

Cortijo de Guerra

Paterna de Rivera

Puerto Real

Cádiz

Medina Sidonia

Atlantic Ocean

Marquesado

San Fernando

El Inglés

Canadilla

36°417'N

Chiclana de la Frontera

Body of Water

City / Village ■

LAND FEATURE

Mi 0   4.35   8.70   13.05   17.40

Km 0   7   14   21   28

BALEARIC ISLANDS
DO [2]

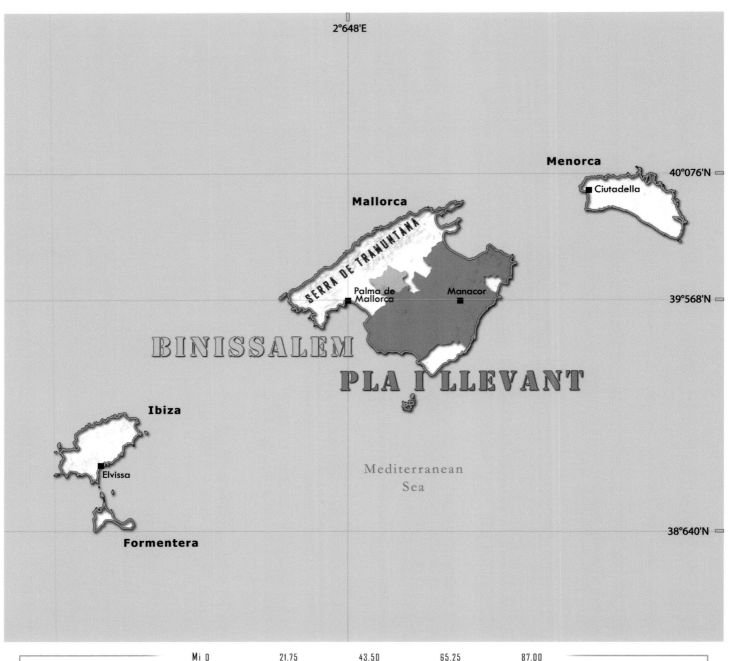

2°648'E

Menorca

40°076'N

■ Ciutadella

Mallorca

SERRA DE TRAMUNTANA

Palma de Mallorca ■

Manacor ■

39°568'N

BINISSALEM

PLA I LLEVANT

Ibiza

Elvissa ■

Mediterranean Sea

38°640'N

Formentera

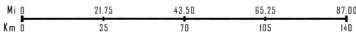

| Mi 0 | 21.75 | 43.50 | 65.25 | 87.00 |
| Km 0 | 35 | 70 | 105 | 140 |

CANARY ISLANDS

DO [11]

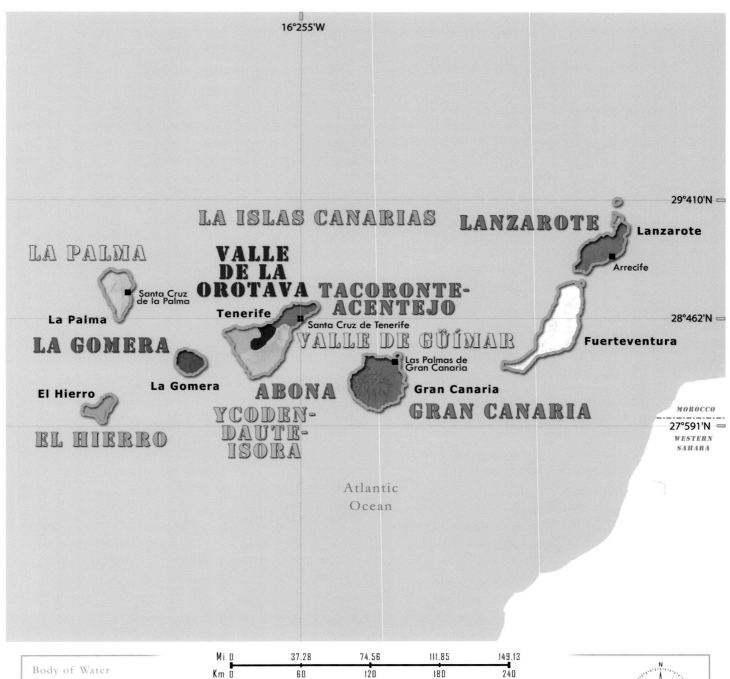

16°255'W

29°410'N

LA ISLAS CANARIAS

LANZAROTE

Lanzarote

LA PALMA

VALLE DE LA OROTAVA

TACORONTE-ACENTEJO

Arrecife

Santa Cruz de la Palma

Tenerife

28°462'N

La Palma

Santa Cruz de Tenerife

VALLE DE GÜÍMAR

Fuerteventura

LA GOMERA

Las Palmas de Gran Canaria

El Hierro

La Gomera

ABONA

Gran Canaria

MOROCCO

YCODEN-DAUTE-ISORA

GRAN CANARIA

27°591'N

EL HIERRO

WESTERN SAHARA

Atlantic Ocean

Body of Water
COUNTRY
City / Village
LAND FEATURE

| Mi 0 | 37.28 | 74.56 | 111.85 | 149.13 |
| Km 0 | 60 | 120 | 180 | 240 |

CAVA DO

CLASSIFIED CAVA DO AREA

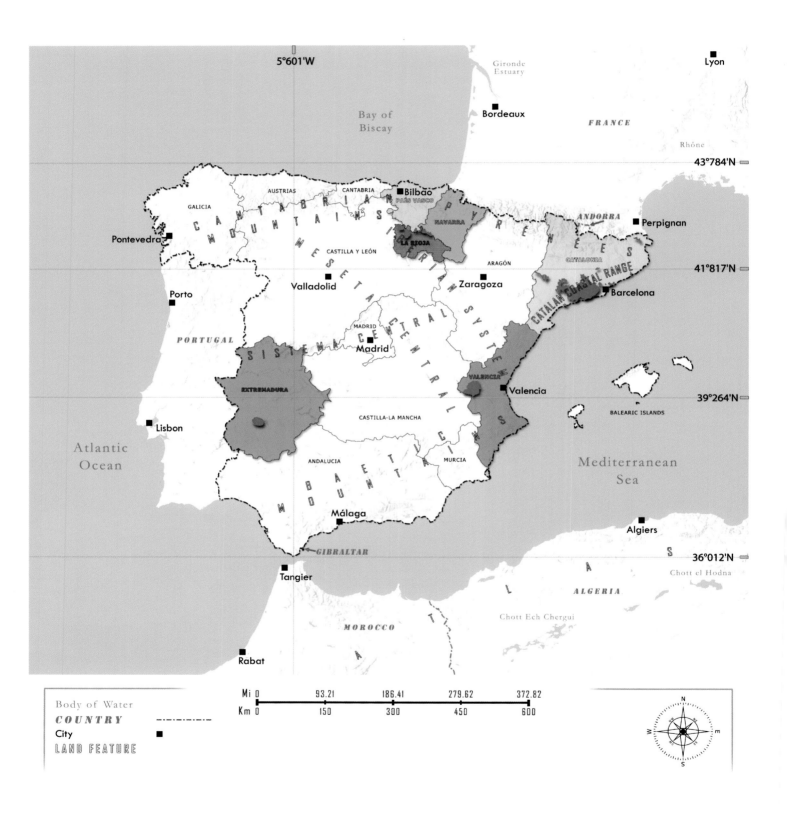

5°601'W

Lyon

Gironde
Estuary

Bay of
Biscay

Bordeaux

FRANCE

Rhône

43°784'N

AUSTRIAS   CANTABRIA

Bilbao

GALICIA   PAÍS VASCO

CANTABRIAN

NAVARRA

ANDORRA

Perpignan

Pontevedra

MOUNTAINS

LA RIOJA

PYRENEES

CATALONIA

MESETA

CASTILLA Y LEÓN

ARAGÓN

CATALAN COASTAL RANGE

41°817'N

Porto

Valladolid

Zaragoza

Barcelona

PORTUGAL

MADRID

SISTEMA

CENTRAL

SYSTEM

Madrid

IBERIAN

VALENCIA

EXTREMADURA

Valencia

39°264'N

BALEARIC ISLANDS

Lisbon

CASTILLA-LA MANCHA

Atlantic
Ocean

ANDALUCIA

MURCIA

Mediterranean
Sea

BAETIC

MOUNTAINS

Málaga

Algiers

GIBRALTAR

S

36°012'N

Tangier

A

Chott el Hodna

L

ALGERIA

Chott Ech Chergui

T

MOROCCO

A

Rabat

Mi	0	93.21	186.41	279.62	372.82
Km	0	150	300	450	600

Body of Water
COUNTRY   ———·———
City   ■
LAND FEATURE

14 Regions

31 DOC

PORTUGAL

1 4 R E G I O N S

MINHO	TERRAS DO DÃO	TEJO	TERRAS MADEIRENSES
TRANSMONTANO	BEIRA ATLÂNTICO	PENÍNSULA DE SETÚBAL	AÇORES
DURIENSE	LISBOA	ALENTEJANO	
TERRAS DE CISTER	TERRAS DE BEIRA	ALGARVE	

3 1 D O C

R E G I O N / DENOMINAÇÃO	SINCE
M i n h o [1]	
VINHO VERDE	1999
T r a n s m o n t a n o [1]	
TRÁS-OS-MONTES	2006
D u r i e n s e [2]	
DOURO	1998
PORTO [Licoroso (fortified)]	1986 [1756]
T e r r a s d e C i s t e r [1]	
TÁVORA-VAROSA	1990
B e i r a A t l â n t i c o [1]	
BAIRRADA	1991
T e r r a s d a B e i r a [1]	
BEIRA INTERIOR	2005
L i s b o a [9]	
ALENQUER	
ARRUDA	
BUCELAS	
CARCAVELOS [Licoroso (fortified)]	1994
COLARES	1994
ENCOSTAS D'AIRE	2005
LOURINHÃ [Aguardente (brandy)]	
ÓBIDOS	2006
TORRES VEDRAS	
T e r r a s d o D ã o [2]	
DÃO	1990
LAFÕES	1990
T e j o [1]	
DO TEJO	2003
P e n í n s u l a d e S e t ú b a l [2]	
PALMELA	
SETÚBAL [Licoroso (fortified)]	
A l e n t e j a n o [1]	
ALENTEJO	2003
A l g a r v e [4]	
LAGOA	1990
LAGOS	1990
PORTIMÃO	1990
TAVIRA	1990
A ç o r e s [3]	
BISCOITOS	1994
GRACIOSA	1994
PICO	1994
T e r r a s M a d e i r e n s e s [2]	
MADEIRA [Licoroso (fortified)]	
MADEIRENSE	1999

REGIONS OF PORTUGAL [14]

AÇORES

Page 178

Graciosa
Terceira
Madalena Pico

8°626'W

Minho

CANTABRIAN
MOUNTAINS

42°144'N

TRANSMONTANO

Bragança

Limia

Braga

TRÁS-OS-MONTES

Valladolid

Cávado

Duero

MINHO

Porto

Douro

41°157'N

DURIENSE

Salamanca

BEIRA ATLÂNTICO

TERRAS DO DÃO

Viseu

TERRAS
DE CISTER

Madrid

Mondego

SISTEMA CENTRAL

Coimbra

TERRAS DE BEIRA

Toledo

LISBOA

ESTRELA MOUNTAINS

Tajo

TEJO

Tejo

Atlantic
Ocean

Guadiana

Mérida

38°718'N

Lisbon Setúbal

Evora

ALENTEJANO

PENÍNSULA
DE SETÚBAL

Córdoba

Porto Santo

Madeira

ALGARVE

Guadalquivir

SPAIN

Seville

Funchal

Page 177

Huelva

BAETIC

Faro

MOUNTAINS

36°961'N

TERRAS MADEIRENSES

Málaga

Mediterranean
Sea

Body of Water
COUNTRY
City
LAND FEATURE

Mi 0   49.71   99.42   149.13   198.84
Km 0   80   160   240   320

N

W   E

S

DOCs OF PORTUGAL [31]

MAINLAND [26]
ISLANDS [5]

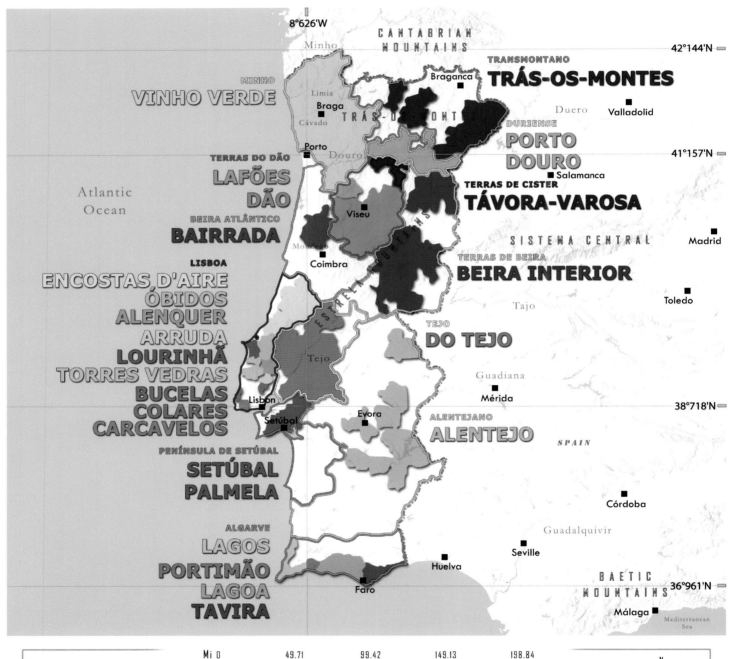

CANTABRIAN MOUNTAINS

8°626'W

42°144'N

Minho

TRANSMONTANO
TRÁS-OS-MONTES

Bragança

MINHO
VINHO VERDE

Limia

Braga

Cávado

TRÁS-O--ONT

Duero

Valladolid

DURIENSE
PORTO
DOURO

Porto

Douro

41°157'N

Salamanca

TERRAS DO DÃO
LAFÕES
DÃO

TERRAS DE CISTER
TÁVORA-VAROSA

Atlantic
Ocean

Viseu

BEIRA ATLÂNTICO
BAIRRADA

SISTEMA CENTRAL

Madrid

Mondego

TERRAS DE BEIRA
BEIRA INTERIOR

LISBOA
ENCOSTAS D'AIRE
ÓBIDOS
ALENQUER
ARRUDA
LOURINHÃ
TORRES VEDRAS
BUCELAS
COLARES
CARCAVELOS

Coimbra

Toledo

Tajo

TEJO
DO TEJO

Tejo

Guadiana

Mérida

Lisbon

Setúbal

Évora

ALENTEJANO
ALENTEJO

SPAIN

PENÍNSULA DE SETÚBAL
SETÚBAL
PALMELA

38°718'N

Córdoba

ALGARVE
LAGOS
PORTIMÃO
LAGOA
TAVIRA

Guadalquivir

Huelva

Seville

BAETIC
MOUNTAINS

36°961'N

Faro

Málaga

Mediterranean
Sea

Mi 0	49.71	99.42	149.13	198.84
Km 0	80	160	240	320

Body of Water
COUNTRY — · — · —
City ■
LAND FEATURE

TERRAS MADEIRENSES
DOC [2]

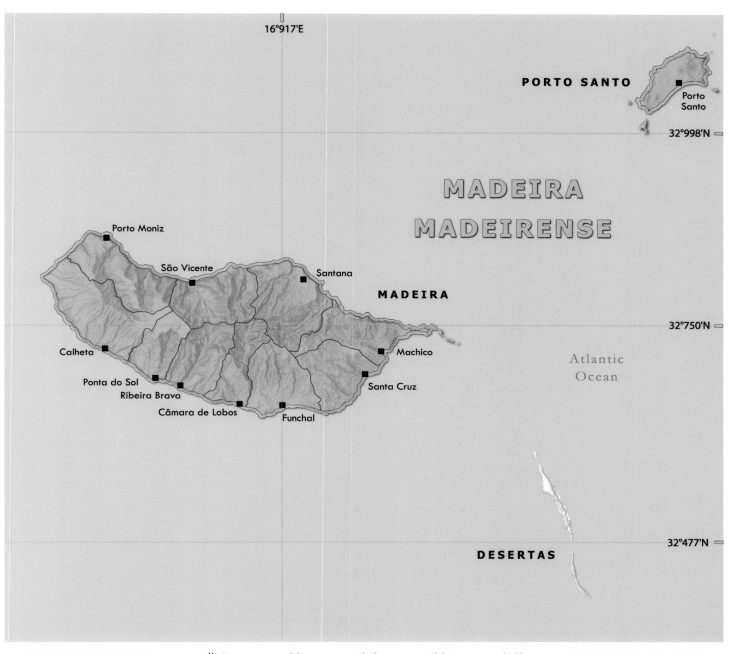

16°917'E

PORTO SANTO

Porto Santo

32°998'N

MADEIRA
MADEIRENSE

Porto Moniz

São Vicente

Santana

MADEIRA

32°750'N

Calheta

Machico

Atlantic
Ocean

Ponta do Sol
Ribeira Brava

Santa Cruz

Câmara de Lobos

Funchal

32°477'N

DESERTAS

Body of Water

City / Village ■

| Mi 0 | 6.21 | 12.43 | 18.64 | 24.85 |
| Km 0 | 10 | 20 | 30 | 40 |

AÇORES
DOC [3]

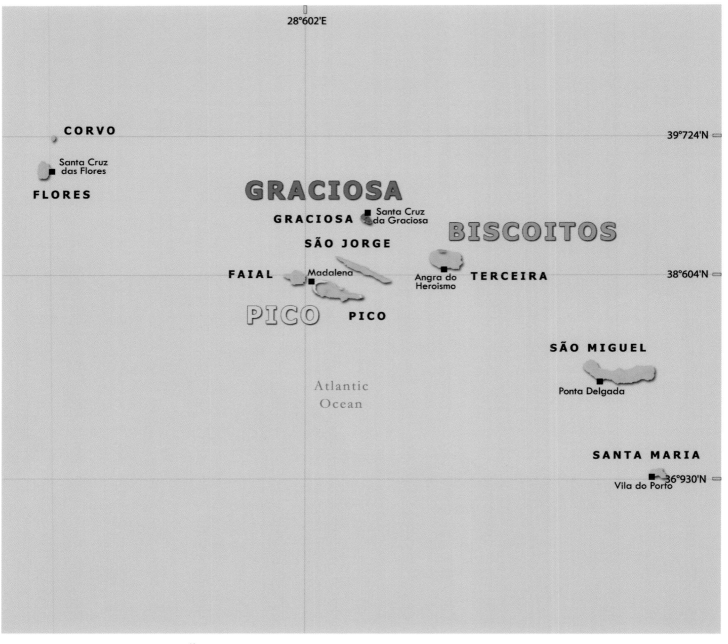

28°602'E

CORVO

Santa Cruz
das Flores
FLORES

GRACIOSA

GRACIOSA   Santa Cruz
da Graciosa

SÃO JORGE

BISCOITOS

FAIAL   Madalena

Angra do
Heroismo   TERCEIRA

39°724'N

38°604'N

PICO   PICO

SÃO MIGUEL

Atlantic
Ocean

Ponta Delgada

SANTA MARIA

Vila do Porto   36°930'N

Body of Water

City / Village   ■

Mi	0	43.50	87.00	130.50	174.00
Km	0	70	140	210	280

CLASSIFICATION SYSTEM

QUALITÄTSWEIN [2 categories]

I. Prädikatswein

II. Qualitätswein bestimmter Anbaugebiete

Low ↑
Ripeness/
sweetness
High ↓

- Kabinett
- Spätlese
- Auslese
- Beerenauslese
- Eiswein
- Trockenbeerenauslese

- Landwein
- Deutscher Wein

13 Anbaugebieten

41 Bereichen

164 Grosslagen [list only]

GERMANY

VINEYARD CATEGORIZATION [large to small]
- Anbaugebiete [wine region]
- Bereiche [subdivision or district]
- Grosslage [large site]
- Einzellage [individual vineyard site] [top to basic]
  a) Grosse Lage
  b) Erste Lage
  c) Ortswein
  d) Gutswein

418 Grosse Lagen [list only]

330 Erste Lagen [list only]

ANBAUGEBIETE / BEREICHE	GROSSLAGE				
Ahr [1] [1]					
WALPORZHEIM-AHRTAL	Klosterberg				
Mosel [6] [19]					
BURG COCHEM	Goldbäumchen	Grafschaft	Rosenhang	Schwarze Katz	Weinhex
BERNKASTEL	Badstube	Michelsberg	Nacktarsch	Römerlay	St. Michael
	Kurfürstlay	Münzlay	Propstberg	Schwarzlay	Vom heissen Stein
RUWERTAL	none				
SAAR	Scharzberg				
OBERMOSEL	Gipfel	Königsberg			
MOSELTOR	Schloss Bübingen				
Mittelrhein [2] [10]					
SIEBENGEBIRGE	Petersberg				
LORELEY	Burg Hammerstein	Burg Rheinfels	Herrenberg	Loreleyfelsen	Schloss Schönburg
	Burg Reichenstein	Gedeonseck	Lahntal	Marksburg	Schloss Stahleck
Rheingau [1] [10]					
JOHANNISBERG	Burgweg	Deutelsberg	Gotteshal	Honigberg	Steil
	Daubhaus	Erntebringer	Heiligenstock	Mehrhölzchen	Steinmächer
Nahe [1] [7]					
NAHETAL	Burgweg	Paradiesgarten	Rosengarten	Schlosskapelle	Sonnenborn
	Kronenberg	Pfarrgarten			
Rheinhessen [3] [24]					
NIERSTEIN	Auflangen	Gutes Domtal	Petersberg	Rheinblick	Spiegelberg
	Domherr	Krötenbrunnen	Rehbach	Sankt Alban	Vögelsgärten
	Güldenmorgen				
BINGEN	Abtey	Kaiserpfalz	Kurfürstenstück	Rheingrafenstein	Sankt Rochuskapelle
	Adelberg				
WONNEGAU	Bergkloster	Domblick	Liebfrauenmorgen	Pilgerpfad	Sybillenstein
	Burg Rodenstein	Gotteshilfe			
Pfalz [2] [25]					
MITTELHAARDT-DEUTSCHE WEINSTRASSE	Höllenpfad	Kobnert	Pfaffengrund	Schenkenböhl	Honigsäckel
	Schwarzerde	Hofstück	Rebstöckel	Rosenbühl	Schnepfenflug vom Zellertal
	Feuerberg	Mariengarten	Hochmess	Meerspinne	Schnepfenflug an der Weinstraße
	Grafenstück				
SÜDLICHE WEINSTRASSE	Bischofskreuz	Mandelhöhe	Kloster Liebfrauenberg	Schloss Ludwigshöhe	Herrlich
	Königsgarten	Trappenberg	Guttenberg	Ordensgut	
Hessische Bergstrasse [2] [3]					
UMSTADT	none				
STARKENBURG	Rott	Schlossberg	Wolfsmagen		
Baden [9] [17]					
TAUBERFRANKEN	Tauberklinge				
BADISCHE-BERGSTRASSE	Rittersberg				
KRAICHGAU	Hohenberg	Mannaberg	Stiftsberg		
ORTENAU	Fürsteneck	Schloss Rodeck			
BREISGAU	Burg Lichteneck	Burg Zähringen	Schutter-Lindenberg		
KAISERSTUHL	Vulkanfelsen				
TUNIBERG	Attilafelsen				
MARKGRÄFLERLAND	Burg Neuenfels	Lorettoberg	Vogtei Rötteln		
BODENSEE	Sonnenufer				
Württemberg [6] [17]					
KOCHER-JAGST-TAUBER	Kocherberg	Tauberberg			
WÜRTTEMBERGISCHES UNTERLAND	Heuchelberg	Lindelberg	Schalkstein	Staufenberg	Wunnenstein
	Kirchenweinberg	Salzberg	Schozachtal	Stromberg	
REMSTAL-STUTTGART	Hohenneuffen	Kopf	Sonnenbühl	Wartbühl	Weinsteige
OBERER NECKAR	none				
WÜRTTEMBERGISCHER BODENSEE	none				
BAYERISCHER BODENSEE	Lindauer Seegarten				
Franken [3][23]					
MAINVIERECK	Heiligenthal	Ewig Leben	Honigberg	Markgraf Babenberg	Rosstal
MAINDREIECK	Burg	Reuschberg	Kirchberg	Ölspiel	Teufelstor
	Engelsberg	Hofrat	Marienberg	Ravensburg	
STEIGERWALD	Burgberg	Herrenberg	Schild	Schlossstück	Zabelstein
	Burgweg	Kapellenberg	Schlossberg	Steige	
Sachsen [2] [4]					
ELSTERTAL	none				
MEISSEN	Elbhänge	Lössnitz	Schlossweinberg	Spaargebirge	
Saale-Unstrut [3] [4]					
MANSFELDER SEEN	Kelterberg				
SCHLOSS NEUENBURG	Blütengrund	Göttersitz	Schweigenberg		
THÜRINGEN	none				

418 GROSSE LAGEN / 330 ERSTE LAGEN

AHR / 18 Grosse Lagen

DORF	EINZELLAGE	DORF	EINZELLAGE	DORF	EINZELLAGE	DORF	EINZELLAGE
Ahrweiler	DAUBHAUS	Bad Neuenahr	SCHIEFERLAY	Heimersheim	LANDSKRONE	Walporzheim	ALTE LAY
Ahrweiler	ROSENTHAL	Bad Neuenahr	SONNENBERG	Marienthal	TROTZENBERG	Walporzheim	DOMLAY
Ahrweiler	SILBERBERG	Dernau	HARDTBERG	Mayschoß	MÖNCHBERG	Walporzheim	GÄRKAMMER
Altenahr	ECK	Dernau	PFARRWINGERT	Rech	HERRENBERG	Walporzheim	KRÄUTERBERG
Bad Neuenahr	KIRCHTÜRMCHEN	Heimersheim	BURGGARTEN				

MOSEL-SAAR-RUWER / 78 Grosse Lagen
M = Mosel / S = Saar / R = Ruwer

	DORF	EINZELLAGE		DORF	EINZELLAGE		DORF	EINZELLAGE
S	Ayl	KUPP	R	Kasel	NIES'CHEN	S	Serrig	SCHLOSS SAARSTEIN
S	Ayl	KUPP NEUENBERG	M	Kesten	PAULINSHOFBERG	S	Serrig	WÜRTZBERG
S	Ayl	KUPP UNTERSTENBERG	M	Kinheim	ROSENBERG	R	Trier	AUGENSCHEINER
S	Ayl	LAMBERTSKIRCH	M	Leiwen	LAURENTIUSLAY	R	Trier	KARTHÄUSERHOFBERG
S	Ayl	SCHONFELS	M	Lieser	NIEDERBERG HELDEN	M	Trittenheim	APOTHEKE
M	Bernkastel-Kues	BADSTUBE	M	Lösnich	FÖRSTERLAY	M	Trittenheim	FELSENKOPF
M	Bernkastel-Kues	DOCTOR	M	Mehring	LAYET	M	Trittenheim	LEITERCHEN
M	Bernkastel-Kues	GRABEN	R	Mertesdorf	ABTSBERG	M	Ürzig	WÜRZGARTEN
M	Bernkastel-Kues	JOHANNISBRÜNNCHEN	R	Mertesdorf	BRUDERBERG	S	Wawern	GOLDBERG
M	Bernkastel-Kues	LAY	R	Mertesdorf	HERRENBERG	S	Wawern	HERRENBERGER
M	Brauneberg	JUFFER	M	Monzel	KÄTZCHEN	S	Wawern	RITTERPFAD
M	Brauneberg	JUFFER SONNENUHR	S	Oberemmel	HÜTTE	M	Wehlen	SONNENUHR
M	Brauneberg	JUFFER SONNENUHR IM FALKENBERG	S	Ockfen	BOCKSTEIN	S	Wiltingen	BRAUNE KUPP
M	Dhron	HÄS'CHEN	M	Piesport	DOMHERR	S	Wiltingen	BRAUNFELS
M	Dhron	HOFBERG	M	Piesport	GOLDTRÖPFCHEN	S	Wiltingen	GOTTESFUSS
M	Erden	PRÄLAT	M	Piesport	GRAFENBERG	S	Wiltingen	HÖLLE
M	Erden	TREPPCHEN	M	Piesport	KREUZWINGERT	S	Wiltingen	KUPP
S	Filzen	PULCHEN	M	Piesport	SCHUBERTSLAY	S	Wiltingen	SCHARZHOFBERGER
M	Graach	DOMPROBST	M	Pünderich	MARIENBURG	S	Wiltingen	SCHARZHOFBERGER PERGENTSKNOPP
M	Graach	HIMMELREICH	M	Pünderich	NONNENGARTEN	S	Wiltingen	VOLZ
M	Graach	JOSEPHSHÖFER	S	Saarburg	AUF DER RAUSCH	M	Winningen	RÖTTGEN
M	Hatzenport	KIRCHBERG	S	Saarburg	KUPP	M	Winningen	UHLEN BLAUFÜSSER LAY
M	Hatzenport	STOLZENBERG	S	Saarburg	RAUSCH	M	Winningen	UHLEN LAUBACH
S	Kanzem	ALTENBERG	S	Schoden	FEILS	M	Winningen	UHLEN ROTH LAY
S	Kanzem	HÖRECKER	S	Serrig	HERRENBERG	M	Wintrich	OHLIGSBERG
R	Kasel	KEHRNAGEL	S	Serrig	SCHLOSS SAARFELSER SCHLOSSBERG	M	Zeltingen	SONNENUHR

MITTELRHEIN / 11 Grosse Lagen / 10 Erste Lagen

LAGE	DORF	EINZELLAGEN	LAGE	DORF	EINZELLAGE	LAGE	DORF	EINZELLAGE
Erste	Bacharach	HAHN	Grosse	Boppard	AN DER RABENLEI	Grosse	Engehöll	BERNSTEIN - AM LAUERBAUM
Grosse	Bacharach	IM HAHN	Grosse	Boppard	FÄSSERLAY	Erste	Oberdiebach	AM SCHLOSSBERG
Erste	Bacharach	INSEL HEYLES'EN WERTH	Grosse	Boppard	FEUERLAY	Erste	Oberdiebach	FÜRSTENBERG
Erste	Bacharach	KLOSTER FÜRSTENTAL	Erste	Boppard	MANDELSTEIN	Erste	Oberdiebach	SCHLOSS FÜRSTENBERG
Grosse	Bacharach	POSTEN	Grosse	Boppard	OHLENBERG	Erste	Oberwesel	GOLDEMUND
Grosse	Bacharach	ST. JOST	Grosse	Boppard, Spay	ENGELSTEIN	Erste	Oberwesel	IN DER RHEINHELL
Grosse	Bacharach	WOLFSHÖHLE	Erste	Engehöll	BERNSTEIN	Grosse	Oberwesel	ÖLSBERG

RHEINGAU / 51 Grosse Lagen / 55 Erste Lagen
W = West / C = Central / E = East

	LAGE	DORF	EINZELLAGE		LAGE	DORF	EINZELLAGE		LAGE	DORF	EINZELLAGE
C	Erste	Assmannshausen	FRANKENTHAL	C	Grosse	Geisenheim	MÄUERCHEN	C	Grosse	Hattenheim	STEINBERG GOLDENER BECHER
C	Erste	Assmannshausen	HINTERKIRCH	C	Erste	Geisenheim	MÖNCHSPFAD	C	Erste	Hattenheim	STEINBERG ZEHNSTÜCK
C	Grosse	Assmannshausen	HÖLLENBERG	C	Grosse	Geisenheim	ROTHENBERG	C	Grosse	Hattenheim	WISSELBRUNNEN
C	Erste	Eltville	LANGENSTÜCK	C	Erste	Geisenheim	SCHLOSSGARTEN	E	Erste	Hochheim	DOMDECHANEY
C	Erste	Eltville	RHEINBERG	C	Erste	Hallgarten	FRÜHERBERG	E	Grosse	Hochheim	DOMPRÄSENZ
C	Erste	Eltville	SONNENBERG	C	Erste	Hallgarten	HENDELBERG	E	Erste	Hochheim	HERRNBERG
C	Erste	Eltville	TAUBENBERG	C	Grosse	Hallgarten	JUNGFER	E	Grosse	Hochheim	HÖLLE
C	Grosse	Erbach	HOHENRAIN	C	Grosse	Hallgarten	SCHÖNHELL	E	Erste	Hochheim	KIRCHENSTÜCK
C	Grosse	Erbach	MARCOBRUNN	C	Erste	Hallgarten	WÜRZGARTEN	E	Grosse	Hochheim	KIRCHENSTÜCK IM STEIN
C	Erste	Erbach	MICHELMARK	C	Erste	Hattenheim	ENGELMANNSBERG	E	Grosse	Hochheim	KÖNIGIN VIKTORIABERG
C	Grosse	Erbach	SIEGELSBERG	C	Grosse	Hattenheim	HASSEL	E	Grosse	Hochheim	REICHESTAL
C	Erste	Erbach	STEINMORGEN	C	Erste	Hattenheim	MANNBERG	E	Erste	Hochheim	STEIN
E	Erste	Frauenstein	HERRNBERG	C	Grosse	Hattenheim	NUSSBRUNNEN	E	Erste	Hochheim	STIELWEG
C	Erste	Geisenheim	FUCHSBERG	C	Erste	Hattenheim	SCHLOSS REICHARTSHAUSEN	C	Erste	Johannisberg	AUF DER HÖLL
C	Grosse	Geisenheim	KLÄUSERWEG	C	Erste	Hattenheim	SCHÜTZENHAUS	C	Grosse	Johannisberg	HÖLLE

C	Grosse	Johannisberg	KLAUS	C	Erste	Oestrich-Winkel	DACHSBERG	C	Erste	Rüdesheim	HINTERHAUS
C	Grosse	Johannisberg	MITTELHÖLLE	C	Grosse	Oestrich-Winkel	DOOSBERG	C	Grosse	Rüdesheim	KIRCHENPFAD
C	Grosse	Johannisberg	SCHLOSS JOHANNISBERG	C	Erste	Oestrich-Winkel	EDELMANN	C	Erste	Rüdesheim	KLOSTERLAY
C	Erste	Johannisberg	SCHWARZENSTEIN	C	Grosse	Oestrich-Winkel	JESUITENGARTEN	C	Erste	Rüdesheim	MADGALENENKREUZ
C	Grosse	Kiedrich	GRÄFENBERG	C	Erste	Oestrich-Winkel	KLOSTERBERG	C	Erste	Rüdesheim	RAMSTEIN
C	Erste	Kiedrich	KLOSTERBERG	C	Grosse	Oestrich-Winkel	LENCHEN	C	Grosse	Rüdesheim	ROSENGARTEN
C	Erste	Kiedrich	SANDGRUB	C	Grosse	Oestrich-Winkel	ROSENGARTEN	C	Erste	Rüdesheim	SCHIRM
C	Erste	Kiedrich	TURMBERG	C	Grosse	Oestrich-Winkel	ST. NIKOLAUS	C	Grosse	Rüdesheim	UNTERER BISCHOFSBERG
C	Erste	Kiedrich	WASSEROS	C	Erste	Rauenthal	BAIKEN	C	Grosse	Schloss Vollrads	GREIFENBERG
E	Grosse	Kostheim	WEIß ERD	C	Grosse	Rauenthal	BAIKENKOPF	C	Grosse	Schloss Vollrads	SCHLOSSBERG
W	Erste	Lorch	BODENTAL-STEINBERG	C	Erste	Rauenthal	GEHRN	C	Erste	Walluf	OBERBERG
W	Grosse	Lorch	KAPELLENBERG	C	Grosse	Rauenthal	GEHRN KESSELRING	C	Grosse	Walluf	WALKENBERG
W	Erste	Lorch	KRONE	C	Grosse	Rauenthal	IM ROTHENBERG	E	Erste	Wicker	HERRNBERG
W	Erste	Lorch	PFAFFENWIES	C	Erste	Rauenthal	ROTHENBERG	E	Erste	Wicker	MÖNCHSGEWANN
W	Grosse	Lorch	PFAFFENWIES RÖDER	C	Grosse	Rüdesheim	BERG KAISERSTEINFELS	E	Erste	Wicker	NONNBERG
W	Erste	Lorch	SCHLOSSBERG	C	Grosse	Rüdesheim	BERG ROSENECK	E	Grosse	Wicker	NONNBERG FUSSHOL
W	Grosse	Lorchhausen	SELIGMACHER	C	Grosse	Rüdesheim	BERG ROTTLAND	E	Grosse	Wicker	NONNBERG VIER MORGEN
C	Grosse	Martinsthal	LANGENBERG	C	Grosse	Rüdesheim	BERG SCHLOSSBERG	E	Erste	Wicker	STEIN
C	Grosse	Martinsthal	RÖDCHEN	C	Erste	Rüdesheim	BISCHOFSBERG	E	Erste	Wiesbaden	NEROBERG
C	Grosse	Martinsthal	SCHLENZENBERG	C	Erste	Rüdesheim	DRACHENSTEIN	C	Grosse	Winkel	HASENSPRUNG
C	Erste	Martinsthal	WILDSAU								

N A H E / 3 0 G r o s s e L a g e n / 1 9 E r s t e L a g e n

LAGE	DORF	EINZELLAGE	LAGE	DORF	EINZELLAGE	LAGE	DORF	EINZELLAGE
Grosse	Altenbamberg	ROTENBERG	Erste	Monzingen	NIEDERBERG	Grosse	Oberhausen	LEISTENBERG
Grosse	Bad Kreuznach	IM KAHLENBERG	Grosse	Münster-Sarmsheim	DAUTENPFLÄNZER	Erste	Roxheim	BERG
Erste	Bad Kreuznach	KAHLENBERG	Grosse	Münster-Sarmsheim	IM LANGENBERG	Erste	Roxheim	HÖLLENPFAD
Grosse	Bad Kreuznach	KRÖTENPFUHL	Grosse	Münster-Sarmsheim	IM PITTERSBERG	Grosse	Roxheim	IM MÜHLBERG
Grosse	Bockenau	FELSENECK	Erste	Münster-Sarmsheim	KAPELLENBERG	Erste	Rümmelsheim	JOHANNISBERG
Grosse	Bockenau	STROMBERG	Erste	Münster-Sarmsheim	PITTERSBERG	Erste	Rümmelsheim	STEINKÖPFCHEN
Erste	Burg Layen	HÖLLE	Erste	Münster-Sarmsheim	RHEINBERG	Grosse	Schloßböckelheim	FELSENBERG
Erste	Burg Layen	SCHLOSSBERG	Grosse	Niederhausen	FELSENSTEYER	Grosse	Schloßböckelheim	KUPFERGRUBE
Erste	Dalberg	RITTERHÖLLE	Grosse	Niederhausen	HERMANNSBERG	Erste	Sommerloch	STEINROSSEL
Grosse	Dorsheim	BURGBERG	Grosse	Niederhausen	HERMANNSHÖHLE	Grosse	Traisen	BASTEI
Grosse	Dorsheim	GOLDLOCH	Grosse	Niederhausen	KLAMM	Grosse	Traisen	MÜHLBERG
Grosse	Dorsheim	PITTERMÄNNCHEN	Grosse	Niederhausen	STEINBERG	Erste	Traisen	ROTENFELS
Erste	Laubenheim	KARTHÄUSER	Grosse	Norheim	DELLCHEN	Grosse	Traisen	STEINBERG
Erste	Laubenheim	KRONE	Erste	Norheim	IN DER KIRSCHHECK	Grosse	Wallhausen	FELSENECK
Grosse	Monzingen	AUF DER LEY	Grosse	Norheim	KIRSCHHECK	Grosse	Wallhausen	JOHANNISBERG
Grosse	Monzingen	FRÜHLINGS-PLÄTZCHEN	Grosse	Oberhausen	BRÜCKE	Erste	Weiler	ABSTEI RUPERTSBERG
Grosse	Monzingen	HALENBERG						

R H E I N H E S S E N / 3 8 G r o s s e L a g e n / 2 5 E r s t e L a g e n

LAGE	DORF	EINZELLAGE	LAGE	DORF	EINZELLAGE	LAGE	DORF	EINZELLAGE
Erste	Alsheim	ALSHEIM	Erste	Gundersheim	GUNDERSHEIM	Grosse	Nierstein	KRANZBERG
Erste	Appenheim	APPENHEIM	Erste	Gundheim	GUNDHEIM	Erste	Nierstein	NIERSTEIN
Grosse	Appenheim	HUNDERTGULDEN	Erste	Guntersblum	GUNTERSBLUM	Grosse	Nierstein	ÖLBERG
Erste	Bingen	BINGEN	Erste	Hohen-Sülzen	HOHEN-SÜLZEN	Grosse	Nierstein	ORBEL
Grosse	Bingen	KIRCHBERG	Grosse	Hohen-Sülzen	KIRCHENSTÜCK	Grosse	Nierstein	PATERBERG
Grosse	Bingen	SCHARLACHBERG	Grosse	Ingelheim	HORN	Grosse	Nierstein	PETTENTHAL
Erste	Bodenheim	BODENHEIM	Grosse	Ingelheim	PARES	Grosse	Nierstein	ZEHNMORGEN
Grosse	Bodenheim	BURGWEG	Grosse	Ingelheim	SCHLOSS WESTERHAUS	Erste	Ober-Ingelheim	OBER-INGELHEIM
Erste	Dalsheim	DALSHEIM	Grosse	Ingelheim	SONNENBERG	Grosse	Oppenheim	HERRENBERG
Erste	Dienheim	DIENHEIM	Erste	Ludwigshöhe	LUDWIGSHÖHE	Grosse	Oppenheim	KREUZ
Grosse	Dienheim	FALKENBERG	Erste	Mölsheim	MÖLSHEIM	Erste	Oppenheim	OPPENHEIM
Grosse	Dienheim	TAFELSTEIN	Grosse	Mölsheim	ZELLERWEG AM SCHWARZEN HERRGOTT	Grosse	Oppenheim	SACKTRÄGER
Erste	Dittelsheim	DITTELSHEIM	Erste	Monsheim	MONSHEIM	Grosse	Siefersheim	HEERKRETZ
Grosse	Dittelsheim	GEIERSBERG	Erste	Nackenheim	NACKENHEIM	Grosse	Siefersheim	HÖLLBERG
Grosse	Dittelsheim	KLOPPBERG	Grosse	Nackenheim	ROTHENBERG	Erste	Siefersheim	SIEFERSHEIM
Grosse	Dittelsheim	LECKERBERG	Erste	Neu-Bamberg	NEU-BAMBERG	Grosse	Westhofen	AULERDE
Erste	Dorn-Dürkheim	DORN-DÜRKHEIM	Grosse	Nieder-Flörsheim	FRAUENBERG	Grosse	Westhofen	BRUNNENHÄUSCHEN
Grosse	Flörsheim-Dalsheim	BÜRGEL	Erste	Nieder-Flörsheim	NIEDER-FLÖRSHEIM	Grosse	Westhofen	KIRCHSPIEL
Grosse	Flörsheim-Dalsheim	OBERER HUBACKER	Grosse	Nierstein	BRUDERSBERG	Grosse	Westhofen	MORSTEIN
Erste	Fürfeld	FÜRFELD	Grosse	Nierstein	GLÖCK	Erste	Westhofen	WESTHOFEN
Erste	Gau-Algesheim	GAU-ALGESHEIM	Grosse	Nierstein	HIPPING	Grosse	Worms	LIEBFRAUENSTIFT-KIRCHENSTÜCK

PFALZ / 57 Grosse Lagen / 79 Erste Lagen

LAGE	DORF	EINZELLAGE	LAGE	DORF	EINZELLAGE	LAGE	DORF	EINZELLAGE
Erste	Albersweiler	LATT	Erste	Freinsheim	SCHWARZES KREUZ	Erste	Neustadt	MÖNCHGARTEN
Erste	Arzheim	ROSENBERG	Erste	Gimmeldingen	BIENGARTEN	Grosse	Neustadt	VOGELSANG
Erste	Bad Dürkheim	ABTSFRONHOF	Erste	Gimmeldingen	KAPELLENBERG	Erste	Ranschbach	AM FÜRSTENWEG
Erste	Bad Dürkheim	FUCHSMANTEL	Erste	Gimmeldingen	MANDELGARTEN	Erste	Ranschbach	SELIGMACHER
Erste	Bad Dürkheim	HOCHBENN	Grosse	Gimmeldingen	MEERSPINNE-IM MANDELGARTEN	Erste	Rechtenbach	HERRENWINGERT
Grosse	Bad Dürkheim	MICHELSBERG	Erste	Gimmeldingen	SCHLÖSSEL	Grosse	Ruppertsberg	GAISBÖHL
Erste	Bad Dürkheim	RITTERGARTEN	Erste	Gleisweiler	HÖLLE	Erste	Ruppertsberg	HOHEBURG
Erste	Bad Dürkheim	SPIELBERG	Grosse	Gleisweiler	HÖLLE - UNTERER FAULENBERG	Erste	Ruppertsberg	LINSENBUSCH
Erste	Birkweiler	AM DACHSBERG	Erste	Gleisweiler	IM OBEREN LETTEN	Erste	Ruppertsberg	NUßBIEN
Grosse	Birkweiler	KASTANIENBUSCH	Erste	Godramstein	AFFOLTER	Erste	Ruppertsberg	REITERPFAD
Grosse	Birkweiler	KASTANIENBUSCH-KÖPPEL	Erste	Godramstein	STAHLBÜHL	Grosse	Ruppertsberg	REITERPFAD-AN DEN ACHTMORGEN
Grosse	Birkweiler	MANDELBERG	Erste	Großkarlbach	BURGWEG	Grosse	Ruppertsberg	REITERPFAD-HOFSTÜCK
Erste	Birkweiler	ROSENBERG	Grosse	Großkarlbach	IM GROSSEN GARTEN	Grosse	Ruppertsberg	REITERPFAD-IN DER HOHL
Erste	Böchingen	ROSENKRANZ	Erste	Haardt	BÜRGERGARTEN	Erste	Ruppertsberg	SPIEß
Grosse	Böchingen	ROSENKRANZ-IM UNTERN KREUZ	Grosse	Haardt	BÜRGERGARTEN IM BREUMEL	Erste	Schweigen	ENGGASSE
Grosse	Böchingen	ROSENKRANZ-ZINKELERDE	Erste	Haardt	HERRENLETTEN	Erste	Schweigen	FINSTERGASSE
Erste	Burrweiler	ALTENFORST	Erste	Haardt	HERZOG	Grosse	Schweigen	GÜLDENWINGERT
Grosse	Burrweiler	AUF DER HOHL	Erste	Haardt	MANDELRING	Grosse	Schweigen	HEYDENREICH
Grosse	Burrweiler	IM GOLDENEN JOST	Grosse	Ilbesheim	KALMIT	Grosse	Schweigen	KAMMERBERG
Grosse	Burrweiler	SCHÄWER	Grosse	Ilbesheim	KIRCHBERG	Grosse	Schweigen	KOSTERT
Erste	Burrweiler	SCHLOSSGARTEN	Erste	Ilbesheim	WESTERBERG	Grosse	Schweigen	RÄDLING
Grosse	Deidesheim	GRAINHÜBEL	Erste	Kallstadt	ANNABERG	Grosse	Schweigen	SANKT PAUL
Erste	Deidesheim	HERRGOTTSACKER	Erste	Kallstadt	KREIDKELLER	Grosse	Schweigen	SONNENBERG
Grosse	Deidesheim	HOHENMORGEN	Grosse	Kallstadt	SAUMAGEN	Erste	Schweigen	STEINWINGERT
Grosse	Deidesheim	KALKOFEN	Erste	Kallstadt	STEINACKER	Erste	Schweigen	WORMBERG
Erste	Deidesheim	KIESELBERG	Erste	Kirrweiler	MANDELBERG	Erste	Schweigen-Rechtenbach	PFARRWINGERT
Erste	Deidesheim	KIESELBERG-KEHR	Grosse	Kirrweiler	MANDELBERG AM SPEYRER WEG	Grosse	Siebeldingen	IM SONNENSCHEIN
Grosse	Deidesheim	LANGENMORGEN	Grosse	Königsbach	IDIG	Erste	Siebeldingen	IM SONNENSCHEIN O.T.
Erste	Deidesheim	LEINHÖHLE	Erste	Königsbach	ÖLBERG	Grosse	Siebeldingen	IM SONNENSCHEIN-GANZ HORN
Erste	Deidesheim	MÄUSHÖHLE	Grosse	Königsbach	ÖLBERG-HART	Erste	Siebeldingen	ROSENBERG
Erste	Deidesheim	PARADIESGARTEN	Erste	Landau	AM MÜTTERLE	Grosse	Ungstein	HERRENBERG
Grosse	Dirmstein	MANDELPFAD	Erste	Landau	KALKGRUBE	Erste	Ungstein	NUßRIEGEL
Grosse	Duttweiler	KALKBERG	Erste	Landau	KLINGENWINGERT	Grosse	Ungstein	WEILBERG
Erste	Duttweiler	KREUZBERG	Grosse	Landau	MÜNZBERG	Erste	Wachenheim	ALTENBURG
Erste	Duttweiler	MANDELBERG	Erste	Landau	MÜNZBERG LAMBERTSRÜCK	Erste	Wachenheim	BÖHLIG
Erste	Flemlingen	HERRENBUCKEL	Erste	Landau	OCHSENLOCH	Erste	Wachenheim	GERÜMPEL
Erste	Forst	ELSTER	Erste	Landau	SCHNECKENBERG	Erste	Wachenheim	GOLDBÄCHEL
Grosse	Forst	FREUNDSTÜCK	Erste	Laumersheim	KAPELLENBERG	Erste	Wachenheim	LUGINSLAND
Grosse	Forst	JESUITENGARTEN	Grosse	Laumersheim	KIRSCHGARTEN	Grosse	Wachenheim	ODINSTAL
Grosse	Forst	KIRCHENSTÜCK	Grosse	Laumersheim	STEINBUCKEL	Erste	Wachenheim	RECHBÄCHEL
Erste	Forst	MUSENHANG	Erste	Leinsweiler	AM HEILIGEN BÄUMEL	Erste	Wachenheim	SCHLOSSBERG
Grosse	Forst	PECHSTEIN	Grosse	Leinsweiler	SONNENBERG	Grosse	Weyher	MICHELSBERG
Erste	Forst	STIFT	Grosse	Leistadt	FELSENBERG	Grosse	Zell	PHILIPPSBRUNNEN
Grosse	Forst	UNGEHEUER	Erste	Leistadt	KALKOFEN	Grosse	Zellertal	KREUZBERG
Erste	Forst	UNGEHEUER-ZIEGLER	Erste	Mußbach	ESELSHAUT	Grosse	Zellertal	SCHWARZER HERRGOTT
Erste	Frankweiler	BIENGARTEN						

HESSISCHE BERGSTRASSE / 1 Grosse Lage / 4 Erste Lagen

LAGE	DORF	EINZELLAGE	LAGE	DORF	EINZELLAGE	LAGE	DORF	EINZELLAGE
Erste	Bensheim	KALKGASSE	Grosse	Heppenheim	IM LANDBERG	Erste	Schönberg	HERRNWINGERT
Erste	Heppenheim	CENTGERICHT	Erste	Heppenheim	STEINKOPF			

BADEN / 52 Grosse Lagen / 40 Erste Lagen

T = Taubertal / BB = Badische Bergstrasse / K = Kraichgau / O = Ortenau / BR = Breisgau / K = Kaiserstuhl / M = Markgräflerland / BO = Bodensee

	LAGE	DORF	EINZELLAGE		LAGE	DORF	EINZELLAGE		LAGE	DORF	EINZELLAGE
KA	Grosse	Achkarren	SCHLOSSBERG	KA	Erste	Bickensohl	STEINFELSEN	KA	Erste	Burkheim	FEUERBERG
M	Erste	Ballrechten-Dottingen	ALTENBERG	BO	Erste	Birnau	KIRCHHALDE	KA	Grosse	Burkheim	FEUERBERG HASLEN
O	Erste	Berghaupten	SCHÜTZENBERG	KA	Grosse	Blanken hornsberg	DOKTORGARTEN	KA	Grosse	Burkheim	FEUERBERG KESSELBERG
O	Grosse	Berghaupten	SCHÜTZENBERG ZUM HIMMELREICH	BR	Grosse	Bombach	SOMMERHALDE	KA	Erste	Burkheim	SCHLOSSGARTEN
BO	Erste	Bermatingen	LEOPOLDSBERG	KA	Erste	Breisach	ECKARTSBERG	KA	Grosse	Burkheim	SCHLOSSGARTEN VILLINGER
BO	Grosse	Bermatingen	LEOPOLDSBERG BUCHBERG	M	Erste	Britzingen	MUGGARDTER BERG	O	Erste	Durbach	PLAUELRAIN

LAGE	DORF	EINZELLAGE	LAGE	DORF	EINZELLAGE	LAGE	DORF	EINZELLAGE
O	Grosse	Durbach	PLAUELRAIN AM BÜHL	BR	Erste	Köndringen	ALTE BURG	KA	Erste	Oberbergen	PULVERBUCK
O	Grosse	Durbach	PLAUELRAIN STOLLENBERG	BR	Grosse	Lahr	HERRENTISCH	KR	Erste	Oberöwisheim	KIRCHBERG
O	Erste	Durbach	SCHLOSS STAUFENBERG	BR	Grosse	Lahr	KIRCHGASSE	KA	Grosse	Oberrotweil	EICHBERG
O	Grosse	Durbach	SCHLOSS STAUFENBERG SOPHIENBERG	BR	Erste	Lahr	KRONENBÜHL	KA	Grosse	Oberrotweil	HENKENBERG
KR	Grosse	Eichelberg	KAPELLENBERG	BR	Grosse	Lahr	KRONENBÜHL GOTTSACKER	KA	Grosse	Oberrotweil	KIRCHBERG
KR	Erste	Eichelberg	KAPELLENBERG GÖTZEN	O	Erste	Lauf	GUT ALSENHOF	KR	Grosse	Odenheim	KÖNIGSBECHER
KR	Grosse	Eichelberg	WIGOLDESBERG	M	Grosse	Laufen	WINGERTE	KR	Erste	Rauenberg	BURGGRAF
BR	Erste	Freiburg	JESUITENSCHLOSS	BB	Erste	Leimen	HERRENBERG	T	Erste	Reicholzheim	FIRST
BR	Erste	Freiburg	KAMMER	BB	Grosse	Leimen	HERRENBERG LANGE WINGERT	T	Grosse	Reicholzheim	OBERER FIRST
BR	Grosse	Freiburg	SCHLOSSBERG	BB	Grosse	Leimen	HERRENBERG OBERKLAMM	KA	Erste	Sasbach	LIMBURG
BR	Erste	Freiburg	SCHLOSSBERG JÄGERHÄUSLEWEG	BB	Grosse	Leimen	HERRENBERG SPERMEN	M	Erste	Schliengen	ROGGENBACH
BR	Grosse	Hecklingen	SCHLOSSBERG	BR	Grosse	Malterdingen	BIENENBERG	M	Grosse	Schliengen	SONNENSTÜCK
BB	Erste	Heidelberg	HERRENBERG	BR	Grosse	Malterdingen	BIENENBERG WILDENSTEIN	KR	Grosse	Sulzfeld	DICKER FRANZ
KR	Grosse	Hilsbach	EICHELBERG	M	Grosse	Mauchen	FRAUENBERG	KR	Grosse	Sulzfeld	HUSARENKAPPE
KA	Erste	Ihringen	FOHRENBERG	M	Erste	Mauchen	SONNENSTÜCK	KR	Erste	Sulzfeld	LERCHENBERG
KA	Grosse	Ihringen	VORDERER WINKLERBERG	BO	Grosse	Meersburg	CHORHERRN HALDE	KR	Grosse	Sulzfeld	LÖCHLE
KA	Grosse	Ihringen	WINKLEN	KR	Erste	Neuenbürg	SILBERBERG	KR	Erste	Tiefenbach	HAßAPFEL
KA	Erste	Ihringen	WINKLERBERG	O	Grosse	Neuweier	GOLDENES LOCH	KR	Grosse	Tiefenbach	HEINBERG
KA	Grosse	Ihringen	WINKLERBERG "FOHRENBERG"	O	Erste	Neuweier	HEILIGENSTEIN	KR	Grosse	Tiefenbach	SCHELLENBRUNNEN
KA	Grosse	Ihringen	WINKLERBERG HINTER WINKLEN	O	Erste	Neuweier	MAUERBERG	KR	Grosse	Tiefenbach	SPIEGELBERG
KA	Grosse	Ihringen	WINKLERBERG WANNE	O	Grosse	Neuweier	MAUERBERG "MAUERWEIN"	KR	Grosse	Tiefenbach	WORMSBERG
KA	Grosse	Ihringen	WINKLERBERG WINKLERFELD	O	Erste	Neuweier	SCHLOSSBERG	O	Erste	Umwegen	STICH DEN BUBEN
KA	Erste	Jechtingen	EICHERT	KA	Erste	Oberbergen	BASSGEIGE	O	Erste	Zell-Weierbach	ABTSBERG
KA	Grosse	Jechtingen	ENSELBERG	KA	Grosse	Oberbergen	BASSGEIGE KÄHNER	O	Grosse	Zell-Weierbach	NEUGESETZ
KA	Erste	Jechtingen	STEINGRUBE	KA	Grosse	Oberbergen	BASSGEIGE LEH				

WÜRTTEMBERG / 48 Grosse Lagen / 37 Erste Lagen

LAGE	DORF	EINZELLAGE	LAGE	DORF	EINZELLAGE	LAGE	DORF	EINZELLAGE
Erste	Beinstein	GROSSMULDE	Grosse	Heilbronn	STAHLBÜHL	Erste	Schorndorf	GRAFENBERG
Grosse	Besigheim	NIEDERNBERG	Erste	Heilbronn	STIFTSBERG	Erste	Schozach	ROTER BERG
Erste	Besigheim	WURMBERG	Grosse	Heilbronn	STIFTSBERG KLINGE	Grosse	Schozach	ROTER BERG
Erste	Beutelsbach	ALTENBERG	Erste	Heilbronn	WARTBERG	Grosse	Schwaigern	RUTHE
Grosse	Beutelsbach	BURGHALDE	Grosse	Heilbronn	WARTBERG SONNENSTRAHL	Grosse	Stetten	BERGE
Grosse	Bönnigheim	SCHLIPSHÄLDE	Grosse	Hohenbeilstein	SCHLOSSWENGERT	Erste	Stetten	BROTWASSER
Erste	Bönnigheim	SONNENBERG	Erste	Hohenhaslach	KIRCHBERG	Grosse	Stetten	BROTWASSER STEINGRUBE
Grosse	Bönnigheim	STEINGRÜBEN	Grosse	Kleinbottwar	GÖTZENBERG	Erste	Stetten	HÄDER
Erste	Burg Wildeck	BURG WILDECK	Erste	Kleinbottwar	LICHTENBERG	Erste	Stetten	LINDHÄLDER
Grosse	Burg Wildeck	BURG WILDECK HERRSCHAFTSBERG	Grosse	Kleinbottwar	OBERER BERG	Grosse	Stetten	MÖNCHBERG "BERGE"
Grosse	Cleebronn	MICHAELSBERG	Grosse	Kleinbottwar	SÜSSMUND	Grosse	Stetten	MÖNCHBERG GEHRNHALDE
Erste	Dürrenzimmern	MÖNCHSBERG	Erste	Maulbronn	EILFINGERBERG	Grosse	Stetten	MÖNCHBERG ÖDE HALDE
Erste	Endersbach	HINTERE KLINGE	Grosse	Maulbronn	EILFINGERBERG KLOSTERSTÜCK	Grosse	Stetten	MÖNCHBERG SCHALKSBERG
Erste	Endersbach	WETZSTEIN	Grosse	Mundelsheim	KÄSBERG	Grosse	Stetten	PULVERMÄCHER
Erste	Fellbach	GOLDBERG	Erste	Mundelsheim	KÄSBERG	Erste	Strümpfelbach	ALTENBERG
Grosse	Fellbach	LÄMMLER	Grosse	Neckarsulm	SCHEUERBERG ORTHGANG	Erste	Strümpfelbach	NONNENBERG
Erste	Flein	ESELSBERG	Grosse	Neckarsulm	SCHEUERBERG STEINKREUZ	Grosse	Uhlbach	GÖTZENBERG
Erste	Geradstetten	LICHTENBERG	Grosse	Neipperg	SCHLOSSBERG	Erste	Untertürkheim	ALTENBERG
Erste	Güglingen	KAISERBERG	Grosse	Oberstenfeld	FORSTBERG	Grosse	Untertürkheim	GIPS
Erste	Gündelbach	STEINBACHHOF	Grosse	Pfaffenhofen	GAIßBERG	Grosse	Untertürkheim	GIPS MARIENGLAS
Grosse	Gundelsheim	HIMMELREICH	Erste	Pfaffenhofen	HOHENBERG	Grosse	Untertürkheim	HERZOGENBERG
Erste	Gundelsheim	HOHENECK	Grosse	Pfaffenhofen	MÜHLBERG	Grosse	Untertürkheim	MÖNCHBERG
Erste	Gundelsheim	WOLKENSTEIN	Grosse	Pfaffenhofen	SPITZENBERG	Erste	Verrenberg	GOLDBERG
Erste	Hanweiler	BERG	Grosse	Pfaffenhofen	STEINGRUBE	Grosse	Verrenberg	VERRENBERG
Erste	Hanweiler	MAIEN	Erste	Rotenberg	SCHLOSSBERG	Erste	Weinsberg	RANZENBERG
Grosse	Hebsack	BERG	Grosse	Schnait	ALTENBERG	Grosse	Weinsberg	SCHEMELSBERG
Erste	Hebsack	LICHTENBERG	Grosse	Schnait	BURGHALDE	Erste	Weinsberg	WANNE
Grosse	Hebsack	LINNENBRUNNEN	Erste	Schnait	SONNENBERG	Grosse	Winterbach	HUNGERBERG

FRANKEN / 23 Grosse Lagen / 50 Erste Lagen

LAGE	DORF	EINZELLAGE	LAGE	DORF	EINZELLAGE	LAGE	DORF	EINZELLAGE
Erste	Abtswind	ALTENBERG	Erste	Castell	HOHNART	Erste	Dettelbach	BERG-RONDELL
Erste	Bürgstadt	BERG	Erste	Castell	KIRCHBERG	Erste	Dettelbach	SONNENLEITE
Grosse	Bürgstadt	CENTGRAFENBERG	Erste	Castell	KUGELSPIEL	Erste	Eibelstadt	KAPELLENBERG
Grosse	Bürgstadt	HUNDSRÜCK	Erste	Castell	REITSTEIG	Grosse	Escherndorf	AM LUMPEN 1655
Erste	Bürgstadt	MAINHÖLLE	Grosse	Castell	SCHLOSSBERG	Erste	Escherndorf	FÜRSTENBERG
Erste	Castell	BAUSCH	Erste	Castell	TRAUTBERG	Erste	Escherndorf	LUMP

Erste	Frickenhausen	KAPELLENBERG	Grosse	Randersacker	PFÜLBEN	Erste	Sulzfeld	SONNENBERG
Grosse	Frickenhausen	MÖNCHSHOF	Erste	Randersacker	SONNENSTUHL	Erste	Thüngersheim	JOHANNISBERG
Grosse	Großheubach	BISCHOFSBERG	Erste	Randersacker	TEUFELSKELLER	Grosse	Thüngersheim	ROTHLAUF
Erste	Handthal	STOLLBERG	Erste	Retzbach	BENEDIKTUSBERG	Erste	Thüngersheim	SCHARLACHBERG
Grosse	Homburg	FÜRSTLICHER KALLMUTH	Erste	Retzstadt	DER SCHÄFER	Erste	Trautlestal	TRAUTLESTAL
Erste	Hörstein	ABTSBERG	Grosse	Retzstadt	HIMMELSPFAD	Erste	Veitshöchheim	SONNENSCHEIN
Grosse	Iphofen	JULIUS-ECHTER-BERG	Erste	Retzstadt	LANGENBERG	Erste	Vögelein	KREUZBERG
Erste	Iphofen	KALB	Grosse	Rödelsee	HOHELEITE	Grosse	Volkach	KARTHÄUSER
Grosse	Iphofen	KAMMER	Erste	Rödelsee	KÜCHENMEISTER	Grosse	Volkach	RATSHERR
Erste	Iphofen	KRONSBERG	Erste	Rödelsee	SCHWANLEITE	Erste	Volkach	VOGELSBURGER PFORTE
Erste	Iphofen	MÖNCHSHÜTTE	Erste	Sommerach	KATZENKOPF	Erste	Würzburg	ABTSLEITE
Grosse	Klingenberg	SCHLOSSBERG	Grosse	Sommerhausen	ALTENBERG 1172	Erste	Würzburg	FESTUNGSBLICK
Erste	Lengfurt	OBERROT	Erste	Sommerhausen	REIFENSTEIN	Erste	Würzburg	INNERE LEISTE
Grosse	Michelbach	APOSTOLGARTEN	Erste	Sommerhausen	STEINBACH	Erste	Würzburg	PFAFFENBERG
Erste	Michelbach	STEINBERG	Erste	Stetten	ROSSTHALBERG	Erste	Würzburg	SCHLOSSBERG
Erste	Nordheim	VÖGELEIN	Grosse	Stetten	STEIN	Erste	Würzburg	STEIN
Grosse	Randersacker	HOHENROTH	Erste	Sulzfeld	BERG I	Grosse	Würzburg	STEIN-BERG
Erste	Randersacker	LÄMMERBERG	Grosse	Sulzfeld	MAUSTAL	Grosse	Würzburg	STEIN-HARFE
Erste	Randersacker	MARSBERG						

S A C H S E N / 5 G r o s s e L a g e n / 3 E r s t e L a g e n

LAGE	DORF	EINZELLAGE	LAGE	DORF	EINZELLAGE	LAGE	DORF	EINZELLAGE
Grosse	Diesbar-Seusslitz	SCHLOSS PROSCHWITZ	Grosse	Pillnitz	KÖNIGLICHER WEINBERG	Erste	Sieglitz	KLOSTER HEILIG KREUZ
Erste	Jesseritz	KLOSTER HEILIG KREUZ	Grosse	Proschwitz	SCHLOSS PROSCHWITZ	Grosse	Zadel	SCHLOSS PROSCHWITZ
Erste	Mischwitz	KLOSTER HEILIG KREUZ	Grosse	Rottewitz	SCHLOSS PROSCHWITZ			

S A A L E U N S T R U T / 3 G r o s s e L a g e n / 3 E r s t e L a g e n

LAGE	DORF	EINZELLAGE	LAGE	DORF	EINZELLAGE	LAGE	DORF	EINZELLAGE
Grosse	Freyburg	EDELACKER	Grosse	Karsdorf	HOHE GRÄTE	Grosse	Naumburg	STEINMEISTER
Erste	Freyburg	MÜHLBERG	Erste	Naumburg	SONNECK	Erste	Weischütz	NÜSSENBERG

REGIONS OF GERMANY [13]

NETHERLKANDS
De Lek
Waal
Breda
Meuse
Rhine
Dortmund
8°402'E
Hanover
Elbe
51°781'N

BELGIUM
Namur
Bonn
AHR
Koblenz
Rhine
MOSEL
Trier
LUXEMBOURG
Meuse

SAALE-UNSTRUT
Halle
Leipzig
SACHSEN
Elbe
Dresden

MITTELRHEIN
RHEINGAU
RHEINHESSEN
Main
Würzburg
Main

HESSISCHE-BERGSTRASSE
Prague
Vltava
Pilsen
CZECH REPUBLIC

NAHE
PFALZ
FRANKEN
Nuremberg
Regnitz

Moselle
Nancy
Rhine
Karlsruhe
Strasbourg
Stuttgart
WÜRTTEMBERG
Danube
Isar
Danube

FRANCE
VOSGES MOUNTAINS
BLACK FOREST
BADEN
Lech
Iller
Ammersee
Munich
Inn
Starnberger See
Chiemsee
Salzburg

Dijon
Le Doubs
Basel
SWITZERLAND
Bodensee
47°559'N
AUSTRIA

Saône
Lake Neuchâtel
LIECHTENSTEIN
Innsbruck
A   L   P   S

50°466'N

49°007'N

Body of Water
COUNTRY
City
LAND FEATURE

Mi 0   46.60   93.21   139.81   186.41
Km 0   75   150   225   300

N
W   E
S

AHR

BEREICHE [1] ----------

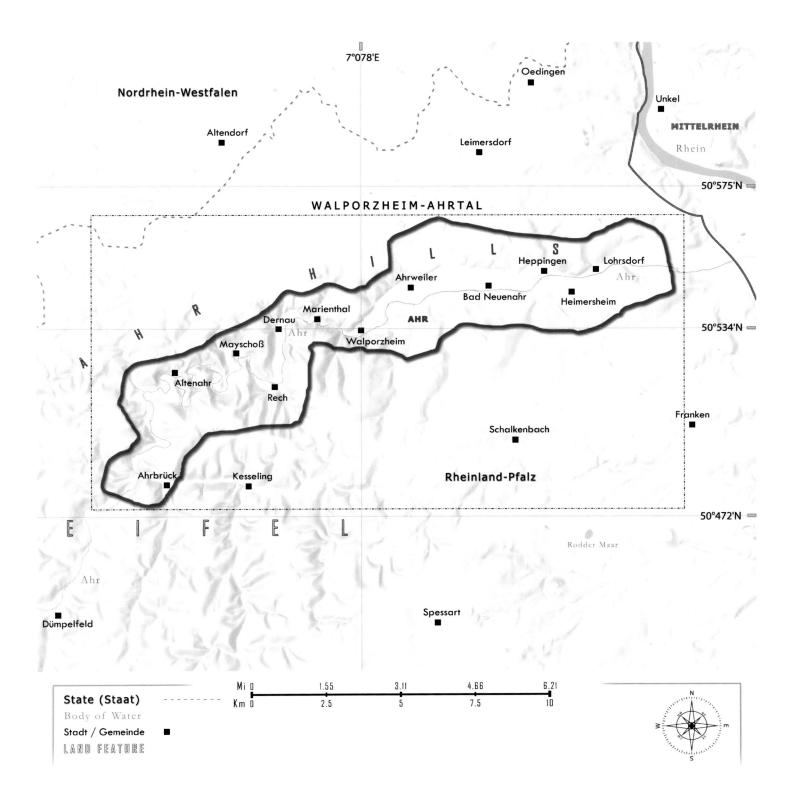

Nordrhein-Westfalen

7°078'E

Oedingen

Unkel

MITTELRHEIN

Altendorf

Leimersdorf

Rhein

50°575'N

WALPORZHEIM-AHRTAL

H

I

L

L

S

Heppingen

Lohrsdorf

H

Ahrweiler

Ahr

R

Marienthal

Bad Neuenahr

Heimersheim

Dernau

AHR

50°534'N

H

Ahr

Mayschoß

Walporzheim

A

Altenahr

Rech

Franken

Schalkenbach

Ahrbrück

Kesseling

Rheinland-Pfalz

50°472'N

E

I

F

E

L

Rodder Maar

Ahr

Spessart

Dümpelfeld

State (Staat) - - - - -

Mi 0   1.55   3.11   4.66   6.21

Body of Water

Km 0   2.5   5   7.5   10

Stadt / Gemeinde ■

LAND FEATURE

MITTELRHEIN
BEREICHE [2]

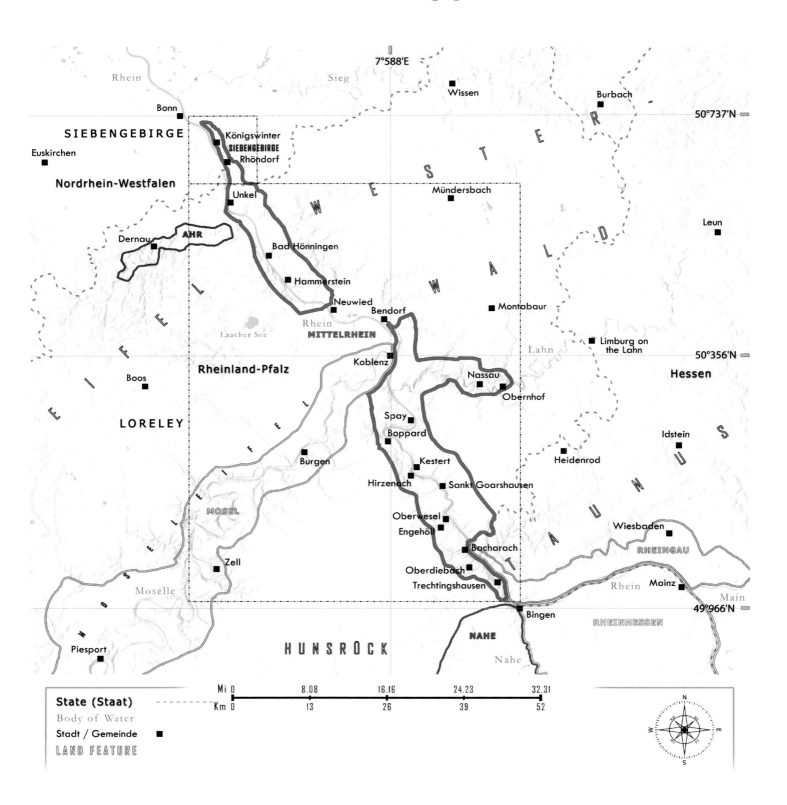

7°588'E

Rhein

Sieg

Wissen

Burbach

Bonn

50°737'N

SIEBENGEBIRGE

Euskirchen

SIEBENGEBIRGE

Königswinter

Rhöndorf

Nordrhein-Westfalen

Unkel

Mündersbach

Leun

AHR

Dernau

Bad Hönningen

W E S T E R W A L D

Hammerstein

Montabaur

Neuwied

Bendorf

Rhein

Laacher See

MITTELRHEIN

Limburg on
the Lahn

50°356'N

Koblenz

Lahn

Boos

Rheinland-Pfalz

Nassau

Hessen

Obernhof

LORELEY

Spay

Idstein

Boppard

Burgen

Kestert

Heidenrod

Hirzenach

Sankt Goarshausen

MOSEL

Oberwesel

Engehöll

Wiesbaden

RHEINGAU

Bacharach

Zell

Oberdiebach

Trechtingshausen

Rhein

Mainz

Main

Moselle

49°966'N

Bingen

RHEINHESSEN

Piesport

HUNSRÜCK

NAHE

Nahe

| Mi 0 | 8.08 | 16.16 | 24.23 | 32.31 |
| Km 0 | 13 | 26 | 39 | 52 |

State (Staat)

Body of Water

Stadt / Gemeinde

LAND FEATURE

N

W   E

S

m

MOSEL
BEREICHE [6]

Nordrhein-Westfalen

7°062'E

Laacher See

Neuwied

Rhein

BELGIUM

Adenau

Mendig

MITTELRHEIN

50°379'N

St Vith

Winningen

Koblenz

Lahn

Kelberg

BURG COCHEM

Lehmen

Moselle

Prüm

Burgen

Boppard

Rheinland-Pfalz

Cochem

Treis-Karden

Rhein

E I F E L

Bruttig-Fankel

Bremm

Oberwesel

Hessen

Moselle

Zell

MOSEL

Enkirch

RHEINGAU

Wittlich

Bitburg

Bernkastel-Kues

Traben-Trarbach

49°919'N

NAHE

Piesport

Brauneberg

BERNKASTEL

Bad Kreuznach

Diekirch

Nahe

LUXEMBOURG

Monzingen

Leiwen

RHEINHESSEN

Mertesdorf

Kirn

Trier

Ruwer

OBERMOSEL

Oberemmel

RUWERTAL

Wiltingen

Saar

Luxembourg

Baumholder

Saarburg

Serrig

SAAR

MOSELTOR

Bostalsee

Perl

Saarland

49°464'N

Merzig

Kaiserslautern

Moselle

Saar

Thionville

FRANCE

	Mi 0	9.32	18.64	27.96	37.28
State (Staat)	Km 0	15	30	45	60

Body of Water

COUNTRY

Stadt / Gemeinde ■

LAND FEATURE

RHEINGAU

BEREICHE [1]

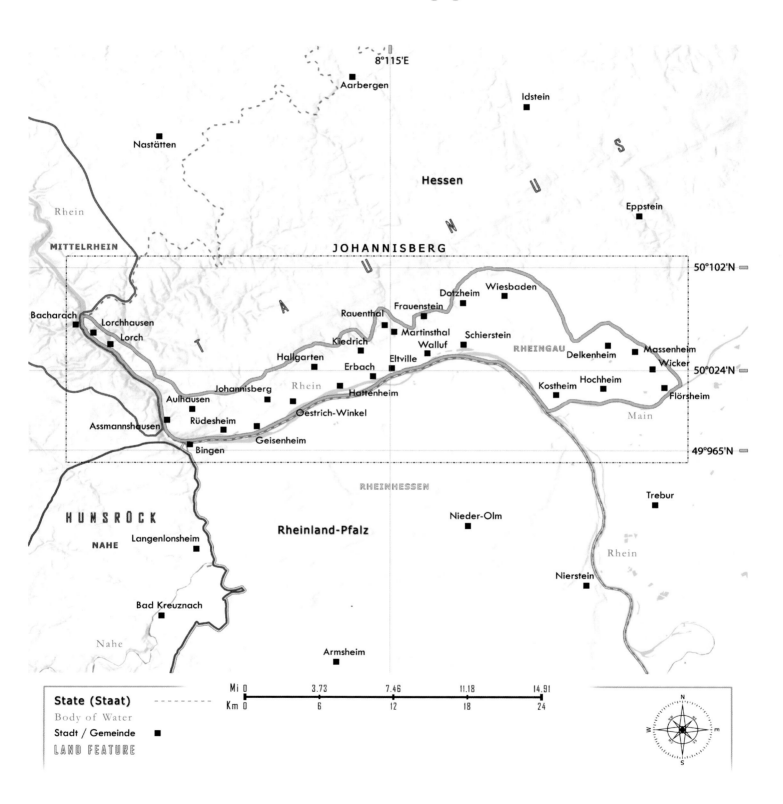

8°115'E

Aarbergen

Idstein

Nastätten

Hessen

Eppstein

Rhein

MITTELRHEIN

JOHANNISBERG

50°102'N

Wiesbaden

Dotzheim

Frauenstein

Rauenthal

Bacharach

Lorchhausen

Martinsthal

Schierstein

Lorch

Kiedrich

Walluf

RHEINGAU

Delkenheim

Massenheim

Wicker

Hallgarten

Eltville

50°024'N

Erbach

Hochheim

Johannisberg

Rhein

Kostheim

Aulhausen

Hattenheim

Flörsheim

Oestrich-Winkel

Rüdesheim

Main

Assmannshausen

Geisenheim

Bingen

49°965'N

RHEINHESSEN

HUNSRÜCK

Trebur

NAHE

Langenlonsheim

Nieder-Olm

Rheinland-Pfalz

Rhein

Nierstein

Bad Kreuznach

Nahe

Armsheim

| Mi 0 | 3.73 | 7.46 | 11.18 | 14.91 |
| Km 0 | 6 | 12 | 18 | 24 |

State (Staat) - - - - -

Body of Water

Stadt / Gemeinde ■

LAND FEATURE

N

W   E

S

NAHE

BEREICHE [1]

Külz

7°726'E
Rheinböllen

MITTELRHEIN   Hessen

RHEINGAU

NAHETAL   Geisenheim

49°971'N

Weiler   Bingen

Münster-Sarmsheim

Rümmelsheim

Schweppenhausen   Nahe

Laubenheim

Guldenbach

Gemünden   Windesheim   RHEINHESSEN

Grafenbach

Wallhausen

Winterbach   Sommerloch   NAHE   Vendersheim

Rheinland-Pfalz   Roxheim   Planig

Ellerbach   Weinsheim   Bad Kreuznach

Bockenau

49°815'N

Norheim

Steinhardt   Schlossböckelheim

Monzingen   Nahe   Niederhausen   Applebach   Flonheim

Kirn   Merxheim   Sobernheim   Oberhausen

Nahe   Altenbamberg

Alsenz

Odernheim

Glan
Rehborn

Alsenz

Unkenbach

Moschelbach

Cölln

Odenbach

49°654'N

Lauterecken   NORDPFÄLZER BERGLAND   PFALZ

Glan   Alsenz   Bolanden

Rockenhausen

| | Mi 0 | 3.11 | 6.21 | 9.32 | 12.43 |
| State (Staat) | Km 0 | 5 | 10 | 15 | 20 |

State (Staat)   - - - - - - - -

Body of Water

Stadt / Gemeinde   ■

LAND FEATURE

RHEINHESSEN
BEREICHE [3]

T A U N U S
8°212'E
Nordenstadt
Kelsterbach
Lorch
MITTELRHEIN
50°035'N
RHEINGAU
Eltville
Hochheim
Oestrich-Winkel
Mainz
Rhein
Ingelheim
Hessen
Bingen
Waldalgesheim
Gau-Algesheim
Rhein
BINGEN
Appenheim
Bodenheim
Trebur
Nahe
Nieder-Olm
Nackenheim
NIERSTEIN
Engelstadt
Weiterstadt
Rheinland-Pfalz
RHEINHESSEN
Sprendlingen
Nierstein
Bad
Hahnheim
Oppenheim
Kreuznach
Wörrstadt
Dienheim
49°833'N
Nahe
Wöllstein
Ludwigshöhe
Pfungstadt
Armsheim
Neu-Bamberg
Flonheim
Guntersblum
Fürfeld
Dorn-Dürkheim
NAHE
Alsheim
Alzey
Dittelsheim
Alsenz
Offenheim
Westhofen
Osthofen
N O R D P F Ä L Z E R
Gundersheim
Biblis
Bolanden
Gundheim
B E R G L A N D
Flörsheim-Dalsheim
Lorsch
Mölsheim
Monsheim
HESSISCHE
Worms
BERGSTRASSE
Hohen-Sülzen
Rhein
BADEN
PFALZ
49°584'N
Winnweiler
WONNEGAU
Eisenberg
Baden-
Württemberg

| Mi 0 | 4.35 | 8.70 | 13.05 | 17.40 |
| Km 0 | 7 | 14 | 21 | 28 |

State (Staat) - - - - - - -
Body of Water
Stadt / Gemeinde ■
LAND FEATURE

PFALZ

BEREICHE [2]

NAHE

8°197'E

Westhofen

49°688'N

RHEINHESSEN

Zellertal

Worms

HESSISCHE
BERGSTRASSE

Heppenheim

Rockenhausen

Hessen

NORDPFÄLZER
BERGLAND

Rüssingen

Mertesheim

Dirmstein

Laumersheim

Rhein

Großkarlbach

MITTELHAARDT-
DEUTSCHE
WEINSTRAßE

Leistadt

Freinsheim

Kallstadt

Mannheim

Ungstein

Kaiserslautern

Bad Dürkheim

Neckar

Wachenheim

Forst

Deidesheim

Ruppertsberg

49°399'N

Königsbach

Rheinland-Pfalz

Gimmeldingen

Mußbach

Haardt

Neustadt

BADEN

PFALZ

Hockenheim

Kirrweiler

Duttweiler

Leimen

Römerberg

Weyher

SÜDLICHE
WEINSTRAßE

Burrweiler

Flemlingen

Zeiskam

Gleisweiler

Böchingen

Frankweiler

Albersweiler

Godramstein

Siebeldingen

Bellheim

Birkweiler

Landau

Ranschbach

Rhein

Leinsweiler

Ilbesheim

Baden-Württemberg

Klingenmünster

Kandel

49°083'N

Dörrenbach

WÜRTTEMBERG

Rechtenbach
Schweigen

Wissembourg

Karlsruhe

FRANCE

Lembach

| Mi | 0 | 6.21 | 12.43 | 18.64 | 24.86 |
| Km | 0 | 10 | 20 | 30 | 40 |

State (Staat)

Body of Water

COUNTRY

Stadt / Gemeinde

LAND FEATURE

N

W — m

S

HESSISCHE BERGSTRASSE

BEREICHE [2]

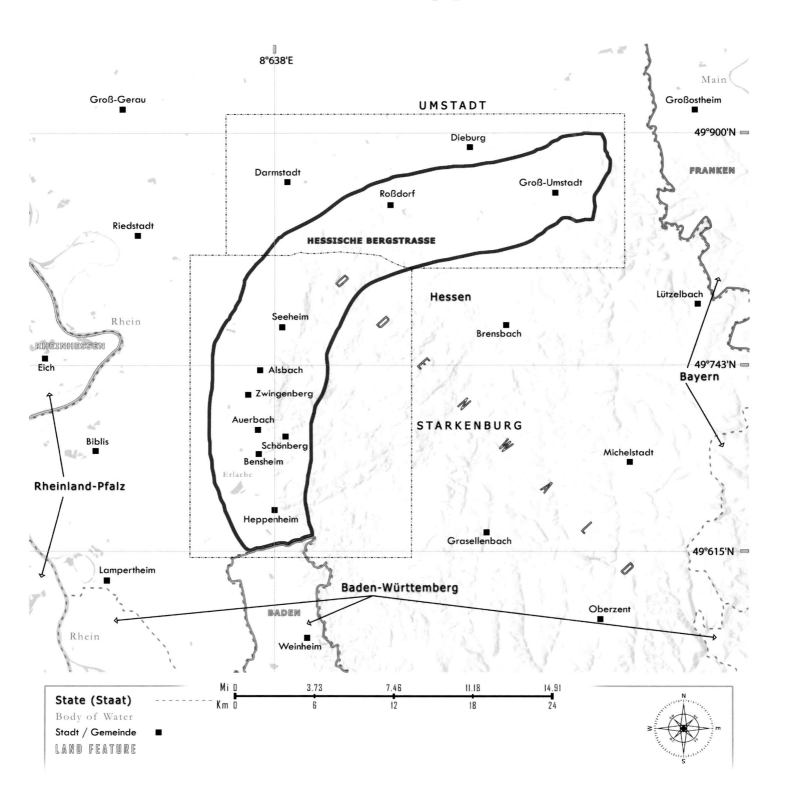

8°638'E

Groß-Gerau

UMSTADT

Dieburg

49°900'N

Großostheim

FRANKEN

Darmstadt

Roßdorf

Groß-Umstadt

Riedstadt

HESSISCHE BERGSTRASSE

Rhein

Hessen

Lützelbach

RHEINHESSEN

Seeheim

Brensbach

Eich

49°743'N

Bayern

Alsbach

Zwingenberg

STARKENBURG

Rheinland-Pfalz

Auerbach

Schönberg

Bensheim

Michelstadt

Biblis

Erlache

Heppenheim

Grasellenbach

49°615'N

Lampertheim

Baden-Württemberg

Oberzent

BADEN

Rhein

Weinheim

	Mi 0	3.73	7.46	11.18	14.91
	Km 0	6	12	18	24

State (Staat) - - - - -

Body of Water

Stadt / Gemeinde ■

LAND FEATURE

FRANKEN
BEREICHE [3] ----

Thüringen

Kalbach 9°953'E

Münnerstadt

Coburg

Hessen   MAINVIERECK   MAINDREIECK   STEIGERWALD   50°177'N

Hanau

Michelbach   Sulzthal

Hörstein   Höllrich   Schweinfurt   Unfinden   Main

Main   FRANKEN   Donnersdorf   Eltmann

Aschaffenburg   Stetten   Bamberg

Großwallstadt   Retzstadt   Volkach   Handthal

Thüngersheim   Escherndorf   Nordheim

Veitshöchheim   Dettelbach   Sommerach

Klingenberg   Lengfurt   Main   Würzburg   Abtswind   49°792'N

HESSISCHE   Homburg   Randersacker   Rödelsee

BERGSTRASSE   Großheubach   Eibelstadt   Castell

Michelstadt   Bürgstadt   Sommerhausen   Iphofen

Frickenhausen   Bayern

Regnitz

BADEN

Buchen   Ergersheim   Fürth

Baden-Württemberg

Rothenburg   49°365'N

Ansbach

WÜRTTEMBERG

Heilbronn   Crailsheim

Neckar

| Mi 0 | | 12.43 | | 24.86 | | 37.28 | | 49.71 |
| Km 0 | | 20 | | 40 | | 60 | | 80 |

State (Staat) - - - - -
Body of Water
Stadt / Gemeinde ■
LAND FEATURE

BADEN

BEREICHE [9]

LUXEMBOURG · Moselle
MOSEL
Trier
HUNSROCK
Rheinland-Pfalz
NORDPFÄLZER BERGLAND
Saarland
Saarbrücken
NAHE
RHEINHESSEN
Westhofen
Rhein
BADISCHE BERGSTRASSE
HAARDT
PFALZ
Landau
FRANCE
BADEN
Karlsruhe
Sarrebourg
Rhein
Steinbach
Neuweier
Lauf
Strasbourg
Durbach
Zell-Weierbach
Berghaupten
Lahr
VOSGES MOUNTAINS
KAISERSTUHL
Hecklingen
Sasbach
Malterdingen
Oberrotweil
Köndringen
Colmar · Ihringen
Jechtingen
Breisach
TUNIBERG
Opfingen
Freiburg
Ballrechten-Dottingen
Laufen
Britzingen
Mulhouse
Mauchen
MARKGRÄFLERLAND
Schliengen
Belfort
Le Doubs
Rhein
Basel
JURA MOUNTAINS
Aare
Darmstadt
8°161'E
Hessen
HESSISCHE BERGSTRASSE
ODENWALD
SPESSART
Main
Würzburg
FRANKEN
Reicholzheim
Impfingen
Dittwar
TAUBERFRANKEN
Unterschüpf
Heidelberg
Neckar
Buchen
Krautheim
Leimen
Mosbach
Rauenberg
Hilsbach
Eichelberg
Odenheim
Tiefenbach
Heilbronn
Oberöwisheim
Obergrombach
KRAICHGAU
Crailsheim
Stuttgart
48°765'N
ORTENAU
Neckar
SCHWARZWALD
Baden-Württemberg
Baden-Baden
SCHWÄBISCHE ALB
WÜRTTEMBERG
Bayern
Ulm
Danube
BREISGAU
Albstadt
Iller
Danube
Memmingen
BODENSEE
Birnau
Bermatingen
Meersburg
Rhein
Bodensee
Bregenz
AUSTRIA
SWITZERLAND
Limmat
Zürich
Reuss
A · L · P · S

				State (Staat)

State (Staat) --------
Body of Water
COUNTRY — —
Stadt / Gemeinde ■
LAND FEATURE

Mi 0	21.13	42.25	63.38	84.51
Km 0	34	68	102	136

WÜRTTEMBERG
BEREICHE [6]

Darmstadt
Hessen
Hessische Bergstrasse
9°290'E
Main
Würzburg
49°844'N

NAHE
RHEINHESSEN
Rheinland-Pfalz
Westhofen
Rhein
SPESSART
FRANKEN
Regnitz

NORDPFÄLZER BERGLAND
Heidelberg
Neckar
Impfingen
Fürth
Markelsheim
Laudenbach
KOCHER- JAGST-TAUBER

Saarland
PFALZ
Landau
Dörzbach
Ingelfingen
Gundelsheim
Künzelsau
Crailsheim

HAARDT
Karlsruhe
Neckarsulm
Heilbronn
Neipperg
Bönnigheim
WÜRTTEMBERGISCHES UNTERLAND

Gündelbach
BADEN
Besigheim
Mundelsheim
Hanweiler
REMSTAL-STUTTGART

FRANCE
Fellbach
Stuttgart
Schorndorf
48°765'N
Uhlbach

Rhein
Neckar
Neuffen
SCHWÄBISCHE ALB
Bayern

Strasbourg
Tübingen
WÜRTTEMBERG
Durbach
Rottenburg
Ulm
Danube

OBERER NECKAR
Reutlingen
Augsburg

VOSGES MOUNTAINS
SCHWARZWALD
Albstadt
Iller
Lech

Colmar
Baden-Württemberg
Danube
Starnberger See

Freiburg
Memmingen
Ammersee

WÜRTTEMBERGISCHER BODENSEE

Rhein
Meersburg
Ravensburg

Basel
Nonnenhorn
Lindau
BAYERISCHER BODENSEE
47°640'N

JURA MOUNTAINS
SWITZERLAND
Limmat
Bregenz
Bodensee
AUSTRIA
A L P S

Zürich
Aare
Reuss

| | Mi 0 | 21.13 | 42.25 | 63.38 | 84.51 |
| State (Staat) | Km 0 | 34 | 68 | 102 | 136 |

Body of Water
COUNTRY
Stadt / Gemeinde ■
LAND FEATURE

SAALE-UNSTRUT
BEREICHE [3]

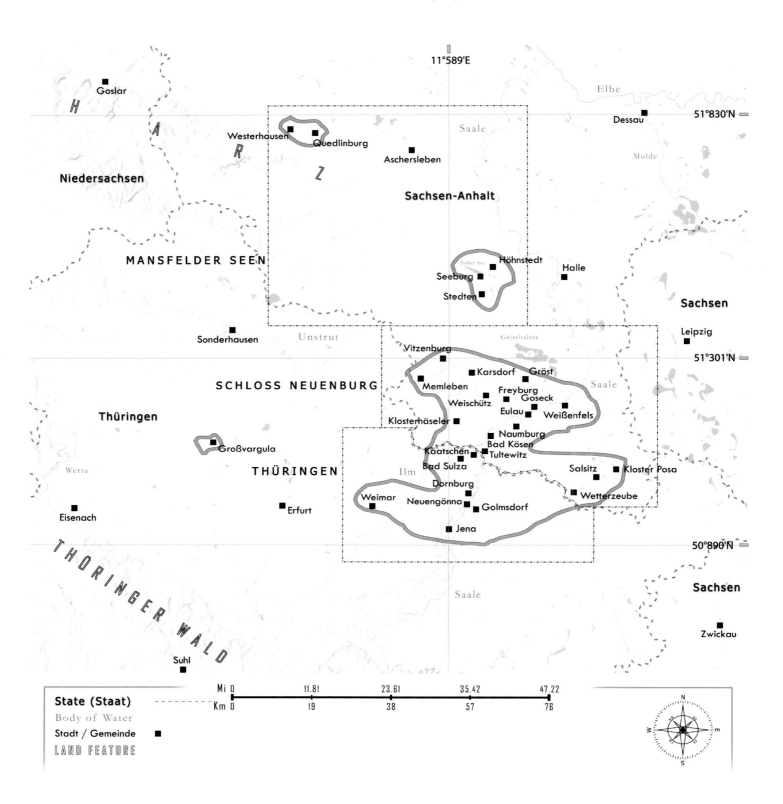

Goslar

H

A

R

Z

Niedersachsen

Westerhausen Quedlinburg

Aschersleben

Saale

Elbe

Dessau 51°830'N

Mulde

Sachsen-Anhalt

MANSFELDER SEEN

Süßer See Höhnstedt

Seeburg Halle

Stedten

Sachsen

Sonderhausen

Unstrut

Vitzenburg

Geiseltalsee

Leipzig

51°301'N

SCHLOSS NEUENBURG

Karsdorf Gröst

Memleben Freyburg

Weischütz Goseck

Eulau Saale

Klosterhäseler Weißenfels

Thüringen

Naumburg

Großvargula

Bad Kösen

Kaatschen Tultewitz

THÜRINGEN

Bad Sulza Salsitz Kloster Posa

Ilm

Werra

Dornburg Wetterzeube

Weimar Neuengönna Golmsdorf

Eisenach

Erfurt

Jena 50°890'N

Saale

Sachsen

Zwickau

T H Ü R I N G E R   W A L D

Suhl

11°589'E

Mi	0	11.81	23.61	35.42	47.22
Km	0	19	38	57	76

State (Staat) — — —
Body of Water
Stadt / Gemeinde ■
LAND FEATURE

N
W E
S

SACHSEN
BEREICHE [2]

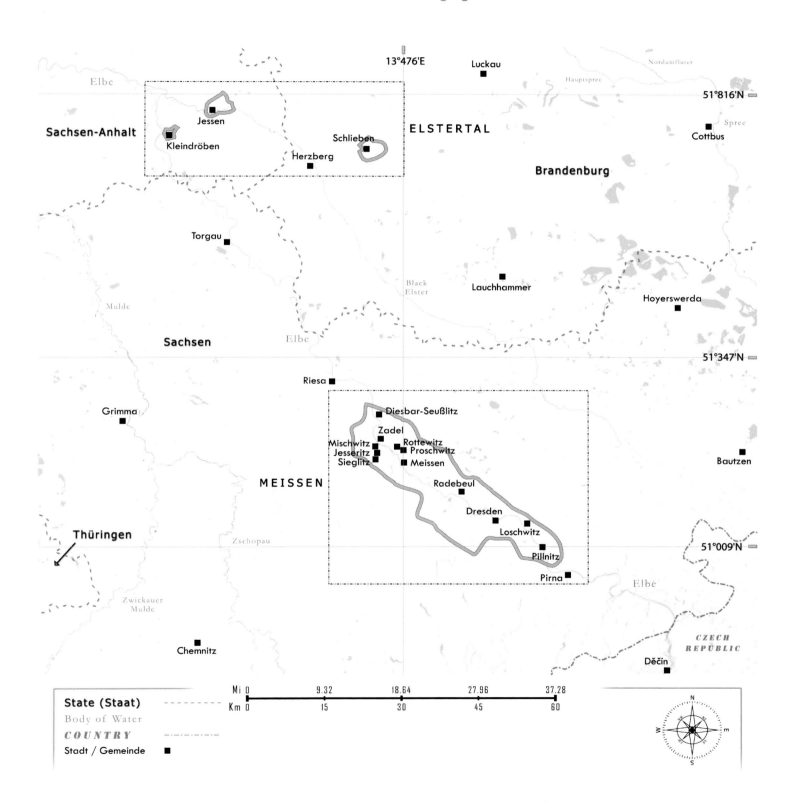

13°476'E

Luckau

Nordumfluter

51°816'N

Elbe

Sachsen-Anhalt

Jessen

Kleindröben

Herzberg

Schlieben

ELSTERTAL

Brandenburg

Hauptspree

Spree

Cottbus

Torgau

Black
Elster

Lauchhammer

Hoyerswerda

Mulde

Sachsen

Elbe

51°347'N

Riesa

Grimma

Diesbar-Seußlitz

Zadel

Mischwitz
Jesseritz
Sieglitz

Rottewitz
Proschwitz

Meissen

MEISSEN

Radebeul

Bautzen

Dresden

Loschwitz

Thüringen

Zschopau

Pillnitz

Pirna

Elbe

51°009'N

Zwickauer
Mulde

CZECH
REPUBLIC

Chemnitz

Děčín

Mi	0		9.32		18.64		27.96		37.28
Km	0		15		30		45		60

State (Staat)
Body of Water
COUNTRY
Stadt / Gemeinde

N
NE
NW
W   E
SW   SE
S

CLASSIFICATION SYSTEM
DAC [Disctrictus Austriae Controllatus. Modeled after the French AOC.]

9 Regions

17 DAC

95 Erste Lagen (1^{ÖTW}) [list only]
ÖTW - Österreichische Traditionsweingüter
Kamptal / Kremstal / Traisental / Wagram / Wien / Carnuntum

AUSTRIA

9 REGIONS

NIEDERÖSTERREICH	BURGENLAND	OBERÖSTERREICH	VORARLBERG	TIROL
WIEN	STEIERMARK	SALZBURG	KÄRNTEN	

17 DAC

REGION / DAC	EST.	DAC	EST.	DAC	EST.	DAC	EST.	DAC	EST.
Niederösterreich [7]									
WACHAU	2020	KAMPTAL	2008	WAGRAM	2021	WEINVIERTEL	2002	CARNUNTUM	2019
KREMSTAL	2007	TRAISENTAL	2006						
Wien [1]									
WIENER GEMISCHTER SATZ									
Burgenland [6]									
NEUSIEDLERSEE	2011	LEITHABERG	2008	MITTELBURGENLAND	2005	EISENBERG	2009	ROSALIA	2017
RUSTER AUSBRUCH	2020								
Steiermark [3]									
VULKANLAND STEIERMARK	2018	SÜDSTEIERMARK		WESTSTEIERMARK	2018				

95 ERSTE LAGEN (1 ÖTW)

DORF	RIED	DORF	RIED	DORF	RIED	DORF	RIED
DAC Kamptal [20]							
Engabrunn	STEIN	Langenlois	DECHANT	Langenlois	SEEBERG	Strass	OFFENBERG
Kammern	GAISBERG	Langenlois	KÄFERBERG	Langenlois	SPIEGEL	Strass	WECHSELBERG SPIEGEL
Kammern	GRUB	Langenlois	KITTMANNSBERG	Langenlois	STEINHAUS	Zöbing	GAISBERG
Kammern	LAMM	Langenlois	LOISERBERG	Langenlois	STEINMASSL	Zöbing	HEILIGENSTEIN
Kammern	RENNER	Langenlois	SCHENKENBICHL	Strass	GAISBERG	Zöbing	KOGELBERG
DAC Kremstal [36]							
Angern	GAISBERG	Hollenburg	GOLDBERG	Oberfucha	STEINLEITHN	Senftenberg	KIRCHENBERG
Furth	GOTTSCHELLE	Krems	FRECHAU	Palt	STEINBÜHEL	Senftenberg	PELLINGEN
Furth	OBERFELD	Krems	GEBLING	Rehberg	GOLDBERG	Senftenberg	PFENINGBERG
Furth	SILBERBICHL	Krems	LINDBERG	Rehberg	ZWETL	Stein	GAISBERG
Gedersdorf	MOOSBURGERIN	Krems	MARTHAL	Rohrendorf	BREITER RAIN	Stein	GRILLENPARZ
Gedersdorf	SPIEGEL	Krems	THURNERBERG	Rohrendorf	GEBLING	Stein	KÖGL
Gedersdorf	STEINGRABEN	Krems	WACHTBERG	Rohrendorf	SCHNABEL	Stein	PFAFFENBERG
Gedersdorf	VORDERNBERG	Krems	WEINZIERLBERG	Senftenberg	EHRENFELS	Stein	SCHRECK
Gedersdorf	WIELAND	Oberfucha	KIRCHENSTEIG	Senftenberg	HOCHÄCKER	Stratzing	SUNOGELN
DAC Traisental [6]							
Getzersdorf	BERG	Inzersdorf	ROTHENBART	Neusiedl	HOCHSCHOPF	Reichersdorf	ALTE SETZEN
Inzersdorf	PLETZENGRABEN	Inzersdorf	ZWIRCH				
DAC Wagram [12]							
Fels am Wagram	BRUNNTHAL	Feuersbrunn	SPIEGEL	Grossweikersdorf	GEORGENBERG	Oberstockstall	SCHLOSSBERG
Fels am Wagram	SCHEIBEN	Grossriedenthal	EISENHUT	Grossweikersdorf	HOHENBERG	Ruppersthal	MORDTHAL
Feuersbrunn	ROSENBERG	Grossriedenthal	GOLDBERG	Mitterstockstall	SCHLOSSBERG	Ruppersthal	STEINBERG
DAC Wien [12]							
Bisamberg	FALKENBERG	Grinzing	SEIDENHAUS	Maurerberg	SÄTZEN	Nussberg	PREUSSEN
Bisamberg	WIESTHALEN	Grinzing	STEINBERG	Nussberg	GOLLIN	Nussberg	ROSENGARTEL
Grinzing	SCHENKENBERG	Maurerberg	HIMMEL	Nussberg	LANGTEUFEL	Nussberg	ULM
DAC Carnuntum [9]							
Göttlesbrunn	HAIDACKER	Göttlesbrunn	STUHLWERKER	Höflein	BÄRNREISER	Höflein	STEINÄCKER
Göttlesbrunn	ROSENBERG	Höflein	AUBÜHL	Höflein	KIRCHWEINGARTEN	Prellenkirchen	SPITZERBERG
Göttlesbrunn	SCHÜTTENBERG						

REGIONS OF AUSTRIA [9]

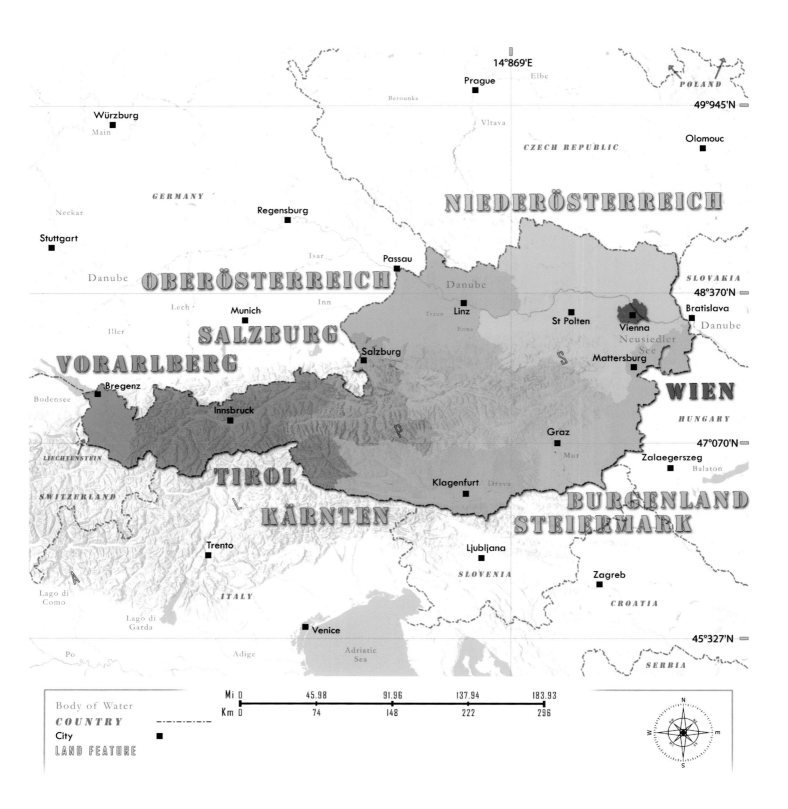

14°869'E

Prague

Elbe

POLAND

49°945'N

Würzburg

Main

Berounka

Vltava

CZECH REPUBLIC

Olomouc

GERMANY

Regensburg

NIEDERÖSTERREICH

Neckar

Stuttgart

Isar

Passau

Danube

SLOVAKIA

48°370'N

Danube

OBERÖSTERREICH

Inn

Linz

St Polten

Bratislava

Lech

Munich

Traun

Vienna

Danube

SALZBURG

Iller

Salzburg

Enns

Neusiedler See

Mattersburg

VORARLBERG

Bodensee

Bregenz

WIEN

Innsbruck

HUNGARY

P

LIECHTENSTEIN

S

Graz

47°070'N

SWITZERLAND

Mur

Zalaegerszeg

Balaton

TIROL

L

KÄRNTEN

Klagenfurt

Drava

BURGENLAND

STEIERMARK

A

Trento

Ljubljana

Lago di Como

ITALY

SLOVENIA

Zagreb

Lago di Garda

Venice

CROATIA

45°327'N

Po

Adige

Adriatic Sea

SERBIA

| | Mi 0 | 45.98 | 91.96 | 137.94 | 183.93 |
| Body of Water | Km 0 | 74 | 148 | 222 | 296 |

COUNTRY

City

LAND FEATURE

N

W   E

S

NIEDERÖSTERREICH
DAC [7] Unclassified [1]
WIEN
DAC [1] ⣿⣿⣿

15°741'E

CZECH REPUBLIC

48°956'N

Budweis

NIEDERÖSTERREICH

Gmünd

Znojmo

DAC WEINVIERTEL

Geras

Retz

Pulkau

Breclav

Morava

Falkenstein

Haugsdorf

Laa an der Thaya

Herrnbaumgarten

Thaya

DAC KAMPTAL

DAC KREMSTAL

DAC WACHAU

Horn

Röschitz

Mailberg

Poysdorf

Ziersdorf

Hollabrunn

Zistersdorf

Großriedenthal

Großweikersdorf

Mistelbach

SLOVAKIA

Kamp

Gösing

Kirchberg

Hohenruppersdorf

Malacky

Krems

Fels

Leobendorf

Wolkersdorf

OBERÖSTERREICH

next page

Nußdorf

Traismauer

Reichersdorf

Inzersdorf

Tulln

Danube

Klosterneuburg

Gänserndorf

Mannersdorf

Danube

Herzogenburg

48°309'N

Pielach

DAC WAGRAM

St Pölten

Neulengbach

Vienna

DAC WIENER GEMISCHTER SATZ

Enns

Danube

Amstetten

Ybbs

DAC TRAISENTAL

Traisen

Mödling

Himberg

Prellenkirchen

Bratislava

Steyr

Steyr

Warth

S

Gumpoldskirchen

Pfaffstätten

Baden

Sooß

Bad Vöslau

Traiskirchen

Tattendorf

Göttlesbrunn

Sommerein

Höflein

Leitha

Neusiedler See

Gutenstein

P

Eisenstadt

DAC CARNUNTUM

Wiener Neustadt

BURGENLAND

L

THERMENREGION

Ternitz

Sopron

Enns

Aspang-Markt

HUNGARY

A

Beled

STEIERMARK

Kapfenberg

Mur

47°422'N

| Mi 0 | 14.91 | 29.83 | 44.74 | 59.65 |
| Km 0 | 24 | 48 | 72 | 96 |

Body of Water

COUNTRY

Stadt / Gemeinde ■

LAND FEATURE

N

W m

S

KAMPTAL DAC
KREMSTAL DAC
WACHAU DAC

Austria / Niederösterreich

BURGENLAND
DAC [6]
STEIERMARK
DAC [3]

Krems

16°031'E

SLOVAKIA

Danube

Linz

St Pölten

48°207'N

Amstetten

Traisen

WIEN

NIEDERÖSTERREICH

Vienna

Danube

Enns

Traun

Ybbs

NEUSIEDLERSEE

Parndorf

Jois

Neusiedl

OBERÖSTERREICH

RUSTER AUSBRUCH

Purbach

Gols

Attersee

Traunsee

Steyr

LEITHABERG

Eisenstadt

Frauenkirchen

Großhöflein

Ilmitz

Andau

ROSALIA

Sigleß

Bad Ischl

Mattersburg

Pöttelsdorf

Pamhagen

Ternitz

Sopron

Neusiedler See

Liezen

MITTELBURGENLAND

Neckenmarkt

Deutschkreutz

Horitschon

Enns

Kapfenberg

Friedberg

Oberpullendorf

47°444'N

Leoben

Lutzmannsburg

STEIERMARK

Mur

Lockenhaus

Birkfeld

Pinkafeld

VULKANLAND

Frohnleiten

Hartberg

Oberwart

Rechnitz

BURGENLAND

STEIERMARK

Weiz

Bad

Waltersdorf

Stegersbach

Eisenberg

SALZBURG

Gratkorn

Deutsch Schützen

Gleisdorf

Bad Blumau

Eberau

Graz

Fürstenfeld

Güssing

EISENBERG

Voitsberg

Kirchberg

Riegersburg

Heiligenbrunn

Ligist

Zalaegerszeg

WESTSTEIERMARK

St Stefan

Feldbach

Jennersdorf

Stainz

St Stefan

Kapfenstein

Mur

Wildon

Straden

St Anna

KÄRNTEN

Deutschlandsberg

Leibnitz

St Peter

Klöch

HUNGARY

Kitzeck

Bad Schwanberg

Gamlitz

Ehrenhausen

Kis-Balaton

Wörthersee

Eibiswald

Klagenfurt

Leutschach

Nagykanizsa

Villach

46°579'N

Drava

SÜDSTEIERMARK

ITALY

SLOVENIA

Mur

CROATIA

Celje

Varazdin

Mi 0	19.26	38.53	57.79	77.05
Km 0	31	62	93	124

Body of Water

COUNTRY

Stadt / Gemeinde ■

LAND FEATURE

Austria

www.thewineregionatlas.com
by Istvan Barczikay

Austria

CLASSIFICATION SYSTEM
OEM [Oltalom alatt álló Eredetmegjelölés (Hungarian term for PDO wines)]
OFJ [Oltalom alatt álló Földrajzi Jelzés (Hungarian term for PGI wines)]

6 OFJ

32 OEM

27 Villages of Tokaj OEM

415 Vineyards of Tokaj OEM

6 OFJ

FELSŐ-MAGYARORSZÁG	ZEMPLÉN	DUNA-TISZA-KÖZE
DUNÁNTÚL	BALATON	BALATONMELLÉKI

32 OEM

Felső-Magyarország [4]

BÜKK	EGER	DEBRŐI HÁRSLEVELŰ [WITHIN EGER]	MÁTRA

Zemplén [1]

TOKAJ

Duna-Tisza-köze [7]

KUNSÁG	IZSÁKI ARANY SÁRFEHÉR [WITHIN KUNSÁG]	MONOR [WITHIN KUNSÁG]	SOLTVADKERTI EZERJÓ [WITHIN KUNSÁG]
CSONGRÁD	HAJÓS-BAJA	DUNA	

Balaton [10]

BADACSONY	BALATON-FELVIDÉK	SOMLÓ	KÁLI
BALATONFÜRED-CSOPAK	BALATONBOGLÁR	NAGY-SOMLÓ	ZALA
TIHANY [WITHIN BALATONFÜRED-CSOPAK]	CSOPAK		

Dunántúl [10]

ETYEK-BUDA	PANNON	SOPRON	TOLNA
MÓR	PANNONHALMA	SZEKSZÁRD	VILLÁNY
NESZMÉLY	PÉCS		

27 VILLAGES OF TOKAJ OEM

ABAÚJSZÁNTÓ	ERDŐBÉNYE	MÁD	RÁTKA	SZEGI	TÁLLYA
BEKECS	ERDŐHORVÁTI	MAKKOSHOTYKA	SÁRAZSADÁNY	SZEGILONG	TOKAJ
BODROGKERESZTÚR	GOLOP	MEZŐZOMBOR	SÁROSPATAK	SZERENCS	TOLCSVA
BODROGKISFALUD	HERCEGKÚT	MONOK	SÁTORALJAÚJHELY	TARCAL	VÁMOSÚJFALU
BODROGOLASZI	LEGYESBÉNYE	OLASZLISZKA			

415 VINEYARDS OF TOKAJ OEM   [Shared vineyards are counted only once in the total]

Abaújszántó [12]

AGYAG	GALAGONYÁS	KRAKKÓ	PENDICS	SULYOM [DÉLREFEKVŐ-SULYOM, KELETI-SULYOM, TRUSKÓCZKI-SZŐLŐ]
BEA [ALSÓ-BEA, FELSŐ-BEA]	GELENCÉR	MARGITA	SÁTOR	VIGYORGÓ
BOGÁR	KASSAVÁROS			

Bekecs [1]

NAGY-HEGY [KOZÉR, KUTYAFOGÓ, NAPOS, PALOTA]

Bodrogkeresztúr [16 out of 2 shared]

ARANY-SAJGÓ	HEGYFAROK	KASTÉLY-TÁBLA	LAPIS [HALAS, LAPIS-TETŐ] [shared with Bodrogkisfalud]	MESSZELÁTÓ
BENDECZ	HENYE	KIS-HENYE	LÉHELY	SAJGÓ [shared with Mád]
CSADÓ	KAKAS	KŐVÁGÓ	MEDVE	SZEPSY
DERESZLA				

Bodrogkisfalud [8 out of 1 shared]

BARAKONYI	CSIRKE-MÁJ	GŐBÖLY	LAPIS [LAPIS-TETŐ] [shared with Bodrogkeresztúr]	VÁRHEGY [HÚZA-DŰLŐ]
CIGÁNY	FARKAS-DŰLŐ	KISVÁR		

Bodrogolaszi [5]

BIALKA	KUTYA-HEGY	MAGOS-HEGY	PAJZOS	SOMOS

Erdőbénye [40 out of 2 shared]

ACÉL	DISZNÓDÉLŐ	KAPOSI	MOGYORÓSOK	PARLAG
BAKSA	ERESZTVÉNY	KIS-MESSZELÁTÓ	MONDOHA	PERESEK
BARNA-MÁJ	FEHÉR-KÚT	LEPÉNY	MULATÓ	PINCESZER
BECSK	FERENC DIÁK	LIGET	NAGY-BAJÓKA	RAFAJ
BENCSIK	GÖRBE	LŐCSE	OMLÁS	SÁROS [HERCZEG]
BUDAHÁZI	GYŐR MESTER [BRADA]	MÉSZÁRKA	ÖSZTVÉR	SZÁR-HEGY
DANSZÁLLÁS	HARSAD	MESZES [shared with Olaszliszka]	PALÁNKOS	SZEMSZÚRÓ
DIÓ-KÚT [BARKÓCZI]	HATÁRI [NÉGYSZÖGŰ] [shared with Olaszliszka]	MESSZELÁTÓ	PALÁSTI	SZENYES

Erdőhorváti [7]

AGÁROS [HARAGOS, HATÁRSZÚG, KALAP]	KŐCSERE	MELEG-MÁLY	RIGÓSKA [CSILLAGDOMB]	VÉG-HEGY [BÁRÓ KÚTJA, GÖNDÖRKE]
FÖVENYES-OLDAL	MÁK-HEGY			

Golop [1]

SOMOS [GAZSÓ, KAKAS, MALOM-ZUG, PANKA]

Hercegkút [7 out of 3 shared]

GOMBOS-HEGY [shared with Sárospatak]	KERESZT-DŰLŐ	MAKRA [shared with Makkoshotyka]	POGÁNY-KÚT	TEICHI-SZŐLŐK
HOSSZÚ-HEGY [shared with Sárospatak]	KŐPOROS			

Legyesbénye [3]

FÚLÓ-HEGY [BARNA, CSEREPES, HEGYMEGE, KUTYAFOGÓ]	HASZNOS	NAGY-MAJOS

Mád [27 out of 3 shared]

BACSKAI	HOLD-VÖLGY [shared with Rátka]	KŐVÁGÓ	RÉPÁS	SZILVÁS
BETSEK	HOSSZÚ-KÖTELEK	KÖZÉP-HEGY [shared with Rátka]	SAJGÓ [shared with Bodrogkeresztúr]	ÚRÁGYA
BIRSALMÁS	JUHAROS	NYULÁSZÓ	SARKAD	URBÁN
BOMBOLY	KAKAS	ŐSZ-HEGY	SUBA	VERESEK
DANCKA	KIRÁLY	PERCZE	SZENT TAMÁS	VILMÁNY
HINTÓS	KIS-HEGYEK			

Makkoshotyka [3 out of 1 shared]

KIS-SZŐLŐK	KUTYA-HEGY	MAKRA [shared with Hercegkút]

Mezőzombor [17]

BORKÚT	HARCSA	KAPI	LAJOSOK	SZEMERE
DORGÓ	HARCSA-TETŐ	KOSZORÚ	MAKKOS	VIRGINÁS
GALAMBOS	HEGYMEGI	KŐPOROS	SÓS	ZOMBORKA
HANGÁCS	ILLÉSHÁZY			

Monok [5]

LETE [ALSÓ-LETE, FELSŐ-LETE]	MEGGYES	SZŐLŐSHEGY	TÁNCOS	ZSEBRIK

Olaszliszka [30 out of 3 shared]

BANDUSZ	GINTER	KOMORÓC	NARANCSI	SAJGÓ
BUDAHÁZI	GYÖRGYIKE	KULCSÁR	Ó-MOGYORÓS	SUJTÓ
CSONTOS [PÁPA, ZSEDÉNYI]	HALASI	KUPAK	ÖREG-DIÓS	SZENT MIHÁLY
DEZSŐ	HARASZT	LÓKÖTŐ	PALANDOR	ÚJ-DIÓS
DONGÓ	HATÁRI [CSUKA, NÉGYSZÖGŰ, TOPLEC] [shared with Erdőbénye]	MAGITA	RAKOTTYÁS	ÚJ-MOGYORÓS
GELLÉRT	KÁSÁS	MESZES [CSÁKI, KÜLSŐ-MESZES, VAY] [shared with Erdőbénye]	RÁNY [ÖREG-BUCKLER, ÚJ-BUCKLER] [shared with Tolcsva and Vámosújfalu]	VERES BÁLINT

Rátka [11 out of 2 shared]

GYEPFÖLD	ISTEN-HEGY [ISTEN-HEGY ALJA]	KOLDU	MEGGYES	SARKAD
HERCEG	KERÉK-TÖLGYES	KÖZÉP-HEGY [shared with Mád]	PADI-HEGY	ÚJ-HEGY
HOLD-VÖLGY [shared with Mád]				

Sárazsadány [7 out of 1 shared]

BARKÓCZI	ELŐHEGY [ROHÁLY]	SZÁR-HEGY [shared with Tolcsva]	TEMPLOMŐRZÉS	ZSADÁNYI
DOBRA	RUDNOK			

Sárospatak [19 out of 2 shared]

ALSÓ-GÁT	FELSŐ-GÁT	HOSSZÚ-HEGY [shared with Hercegkút]	MANDULÁS	SZEMINCE
CIRKÁLÓ	FÜRDŐS	KÁCSÁRD	MEGYER	TEHÉNTÁNC
CIRÓKA	GOMBOS-HEGY [shared with Hercegkút]	KIRÁLY-HEGY	SOMLYÓD	VÉRMÁNY
DARNÓ	GYAKA-LYUK	KÚTPATKA	SZEGFŰ	

Sátoraljaújhely [21]

ALSÓ-ESZTÁVA	FEKETE-HEGY	KIS-BOGLYOSKA	MELEG-OLDAL	SZÁR-HEGY
BÁNYI-HEGY	FELSŐ-ESZTÁVA	KIS-KÖVES-HEGY	NAGY-BOGLYOSKA	SZEMSZÚRÓ
BÓDA	GALAMBOS	KÖVES-HEGY	OREMUS	TOMPA-KŐ
CEPRE	HOSSZÚ-FÖLDEK	MELEG-FÖLD	SÁTOR-HEGY	VIÓKA
DÖRZSIKE				

Szegi [8]

GÖRBE	HOSSZÚ-MÁLY	MURÁNY	POKLOS [ALMÁSI, CSÁKI]	SOMOS
HAMASBERG	KASSI	NAGYKA		

Szegilong [4]

GYERTYÁNOS	HATALOS	HOSSZÚ-MÁJ	PÉCSI-OLDAL

Szerencs [25]

ARANKA-TETŐ	CSERFÁS	ELŐ-HEGY	KÁCSA	RÁCZ-DŰLŐ
BÁBA-VÖLGY	CSERŐCZI	GÁRDONY	KERTÉSZ	SZEMERE
BÁRÁNY	CSICSIRI [SZILVÁS]	GERENDÁS	KŐPOROS	TÓKUS-TETŐ
BERKECZ	CSICSIRI ALJA	GYŐRI [GYŐRI-TETŐ]	KÖVES-HEGY	VIDA
CSEMEGE-TÁBLA	DŐRI	HEGYFARK	PIROSKA	ZOMBORKA

Tarcal [47]

AGYAG	ELŐHEGY	LESTÁR	PENGŐ	SZIL-VÖLGY
ALSÓ-REMETE	FARKAS	LÓNYAI	PERŐCZ	TERÉZIA
BAJUSZ	FEKETE-HEGY	MANDULÁS	PÉTER DEÁK	THURZÓ
BAKONYI	FORRÁS	MELEG-MÁJ	REMETÉK	UGAR
BAKSÓ	GÖRBE-BAKSÓ	MESTER-VÖLGY	REMETÉK ALJA	VÁTI
BARÁT	KASSAI	MÉZES-MÁLY	SILLER-OLDAL	VERES-MOGYORÓS
BIGE	KEPÉSEK	MOGYORÓS	SÓHAJÓ	VINNAI
CZEKE	KIRÁLY-GÁT	NAGY-KÖVESD	SZARVAS	ZAFÍR
DEÁK	KÖVESD [VIGYORGÓ]	NYULAS	SZENTKERESZT	ZÁPOROS
DOBAI	LANTOS			

Tállya [44]

BÁNYÁSZ	DUKÁT	KEREK-DOMB	NAGY-ROHOS	REMETE
BÁRTFAI	GALUSKA	KEREK-DOMB ALJA	NYERGESEK	SAS ALJA
BÁTORI	GALYAGOS	KÉT ÚT KÖZI [ÖTVENHOLD, MELEG-OLDAL]	NYÍRJES	SIPOS
BOHOMÁJ	GOMBOSKA	KIS-ROHOS	ŐSZ-HEGY	SOMSZÖG
BOJTÁK	GÖRBE	KOLDU	ÖKÖRTÁNC	TEKENŐ
CSATORNA	HALASTÓ	KŐVÁGÓ	PALÁNTA	TÖKÖS-MÁJ
CSONKA-TETŐ	HASZNOS [KASSAI HASZNOS, KIS-HASZNOS, NAGY-HASZNOS]	KÖVES-HEGY	PALOTA	TÚRÓSKA
DONGÓ	HETÉNY	MEGGYESEK	PATÓCS	VÁROLDAL
DORGÓ	JÓNAP	MULATÓ	PIPISKE	

Tokaj [23]

ARANYOS	DONÁTH	LENCSÉS [VECSEY]	PÉCSI	SZERELMI
BARTUS	GARAI	MALOMFELI	PINKÓCZI	SZIRMAI
BINÉT	HÉTSZŐLŐ	MELEG-OLDAL	RÁKÓCZI	TELEKI [TAJPÓ]
DESSEWFFY	IZDENCZI	NAGY-SZŐLŐ	SZARKA	VEREBES
DOBÓ	KIS-GARAI	PALOTA		

Tolcsva [35 out of 2 shared]

ANTALKA	BOSZORKÁNY	HENDERKE	NAGY-KŐ	RÉZLÓ
ARANY-PATKÓ	CIRÓKA	KINCSEM [KINCSEM ALJA]	NYAKVÁGÓ	SERÉDI [GALUSKA, PETRUSKA]
BÁNYA	CSETŐ	KOPASZKA	PÉNZÁSÓ	SOM
BARTALOS	ELŐHEGY	KÚTPATKA	PETRÁCS	SZÁR-HEGY [shared with Sárazsadány]
BELLŐ	GALAGONYÁS	MALOMHEGY	PETŐ	SZENTVÉR
BIKOLDAL	GILÁNYI [ÖKRÖS, PALOTA, VIDLÁM]	MULATÓ	RADOSKA [AKASZTÓDOMB]	TÉRHEGY
BOGLYOS [BÁBAKÚTA]	GYOPÁROS [BANGÓ]	MANDULÁS	RÁNY [shared with Olaszliszka and Vámosújfalu]	VÁRHEGY

Vámosújfalu [1 shared]

RÁNY [shared with Olaszliszka and Tolcsva]

HUNGARY
OFJ [6]

HUNGARY (EAST)
OEM [12]

Prievidza

Košice

20°376'E

48°621'N

UKRAINE

Latorica

SLOVAKIA

FELSŐ-MAGYARORSZÁG

Mukachevo

Levice

Hornád

Sárospatak

Váh

Hron

DEBRŐI

EGER

Bodrog

Tokaj

TOKAJ

Tisza

HÁRSLEVELŰ

Miskolc

MÁTRA

ZEMPLÉN

Mátészalka

Gyöngyös

Eger

BÜKK

Somcş

Danube

DUNÁNTÚL
(transdanubia)

Tisza-tó

Tisza

Budapest

Debrecen

DUNA-TISZA KÖZI

MONOR

Velencei-tó

Szolnok

Tisza

47°185'N

BALATONMELLÉKI

ROMANIA

Székesfehérvár

IZSÁKI ARANY

Crişul Repede

BALATON

Balaton

SÁRFEHÉR

Oradea

DUNA

Kecskemét

KUNSÁG

Körös

Izsák

Paks

CSONGRÁD

Crişul Alb

SOLTVADKERT

EZERJÓ

Kiskunhalas

Baja

Szeged

Arad

Pécs

Danube

Mureş

Villány

SERBIA

Tisza

45°870'N

HAJÓS-BAJA

CROATIA

Kikinda

| Mi 0 | 26.10 | 52.20 | 78.29 | 104.39 |
| Km 0 | 42 | 84 | 126 | 168 |

Body of Water

COUNTRY

City

LAND FEATURE

HUNGARY (WEST)
OEM [20]

TOKAJ
Village/town (település) [27] ■
Vineyard (dűlő) [415]
Shared vineyards are counted only once in the total

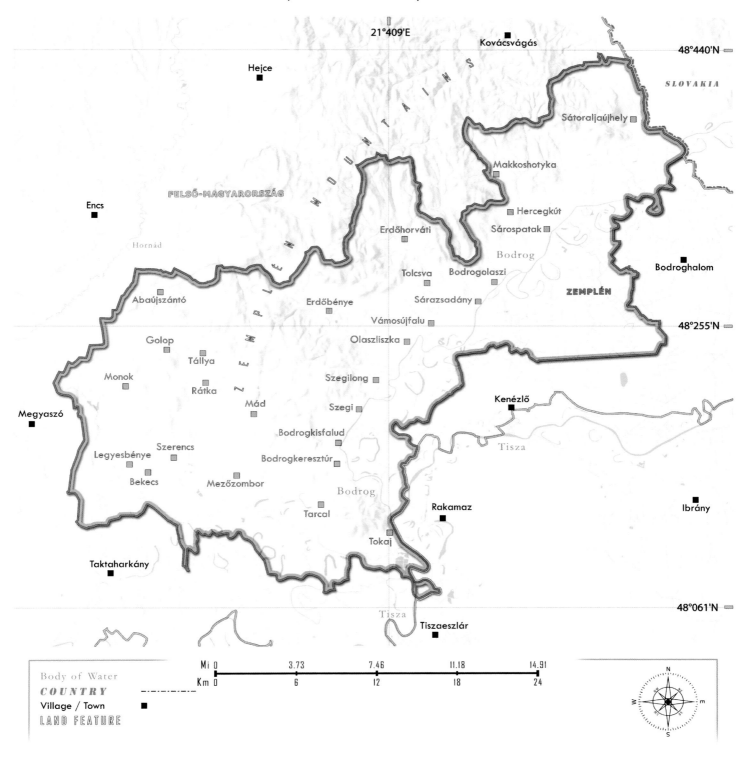

ABAÚJSZÁNTÓ [12] Vineyard (dűlő)
GOLOP [1] MONOK [5]
LEGYESBÉNYE [3] BEKECS [1]

The numbered areas are sub-vinyards (aldűlő)

INÁNCS

21°140'E

ABAÚJSZÁNTÓ

Bogár

Sátor

48°274'N

PERE

Vigyorgó

Bea

Alsó-Bea [1]
Felső-Bea [2]

CSOBÁD

Hornád

Pendics

Krakkó

3

2

1

2

FELSŐDOBSZA

Sulyom

Agyag
Margita

Truskóczki-szőlő [1]
Délrefekvő-Sulyom [2]
Keleti-Sulyom [3]

Kassaváros
Galagonyás

Gelencér

ZEMPLÉN

HERNÁDKÉRCS

Szerencs-patak

GOLOP

Somos

TÁLLYA

Malom-zug [1]
Kakas [2]
Gazsó [3]
Panka [4]

2

1

1

NAGYKINIZS

Szőlőshegy

3

4

SZENTISTVÁNBAKSA

48°211'N

ZEMPLÉN

MONOK

RÁTKA

FELSŐ-MAGYARORSZÁG

Zsebrik

Szerencs-patak

MÁD

Meggyes

Gilip-patak

MEGYASZÓ

Táncos

Lete

Felső-Lete [1]
Alsó-Lete [2]

1

2

1

Nagy-hegy

Hasznos

Kutyafogó [1]
Kozér [2]
Napos [3]
Palota [4]

Fúló-hegy

2

4

Hegymege [1]
Cserepes [2]
Barna [3]
Kutyafogó [4]

3

SZERENCS

4

1

Mádi-patak

2

3

MEZŐZOMBOR

Nagy-Majos

LEGYESBÉNYE

BEKECS

48°151'N

| Mi 0 | | 1.24 | | 2.49 | | 3.73 | | 4.97 |
| Km 0 | | 2 | | 4 | | 6 | | 8 |

Település
Body of Water
LAND FEATURE

N

W
E
S

TÁLLYA

Vineyard (dűlő) [44]

The numbered areas are sub-vinyards (aldűlő)

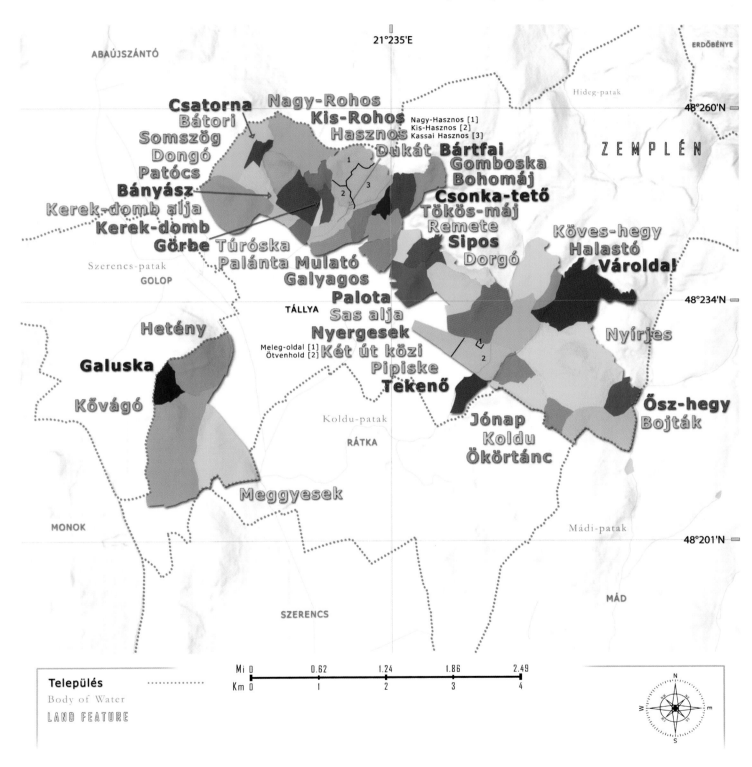

ABAÚJSZÁNTÓ

21°235'E

ERDŐBÉNYE

Hideg-patak

48°260'N

Csatorna Nagy-Rohos
Bátori **Kis-Rohos** Nagy-Hasznos [1]
Somszög Hasznos Kis-Hasznos [2]
Kassai Hasznos [3]
Dongó Dukát **Bártfai**
Patócs Gomboska
Bányász Bohomáj
Kerek-domb alja **Csonka-tető**
Kerek-domb Tökös-máj
Görbe Túróska Remete
Palánta Mulató **Sipos**
Galyagos Dorgó

Z E M P L É N

Köves-hegy
Halastó
Város

Szerencs-patak
GOLOP

Palota
TÁLLYA Sas alja

48°234'N

Nyergesek
Hetény Meleg-oldal [1] **Két út közi**
Ötvenhold [2] Pipiske
Galuska **Tekenő**

Nyírjes

Ősz-hegy
Kővágó Bojták

Koldu-patak
RÁTKA **Jónap**
Koldu
Ökörtánc

MONOK Meggyesek Mádi-patak

48°201'N

MÁD

SZERENCS

Mi 0	0.62	1.24	1.86	2.49
Km 0	1	2	3	4

Település ·············
Body of Water
LAND FEATURE

SZERENCS
Vineyard (dűlő) [25]

The numbered areas are sub-vinyards (aldűlő)

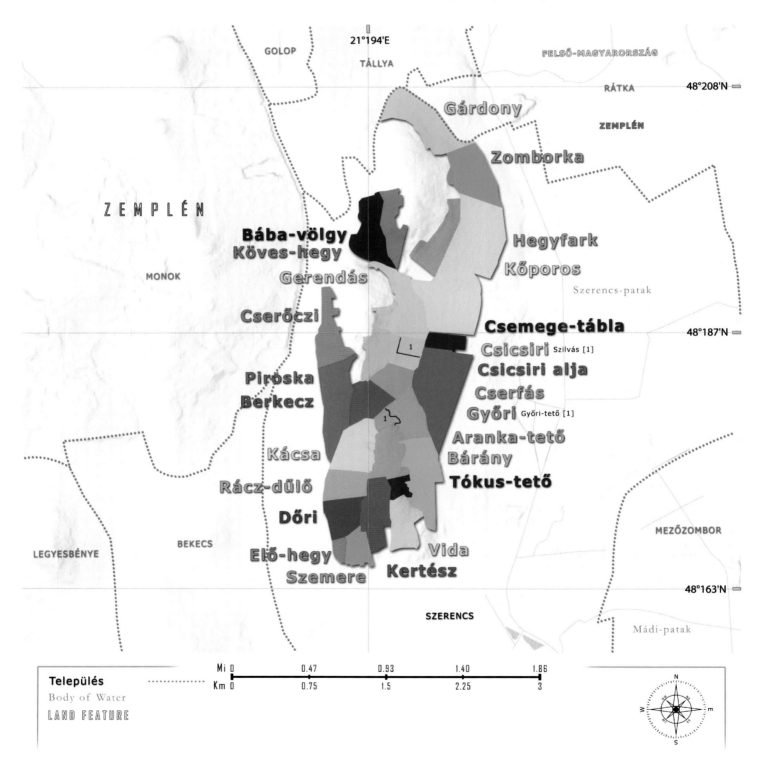

RÁTKA

Vineyard (dűlő) [11] [2 shared]

MEZŐZOMBOR

Vineyard (dűlő) [17]

The numbered areas are sub-vinyards (aldűlő)

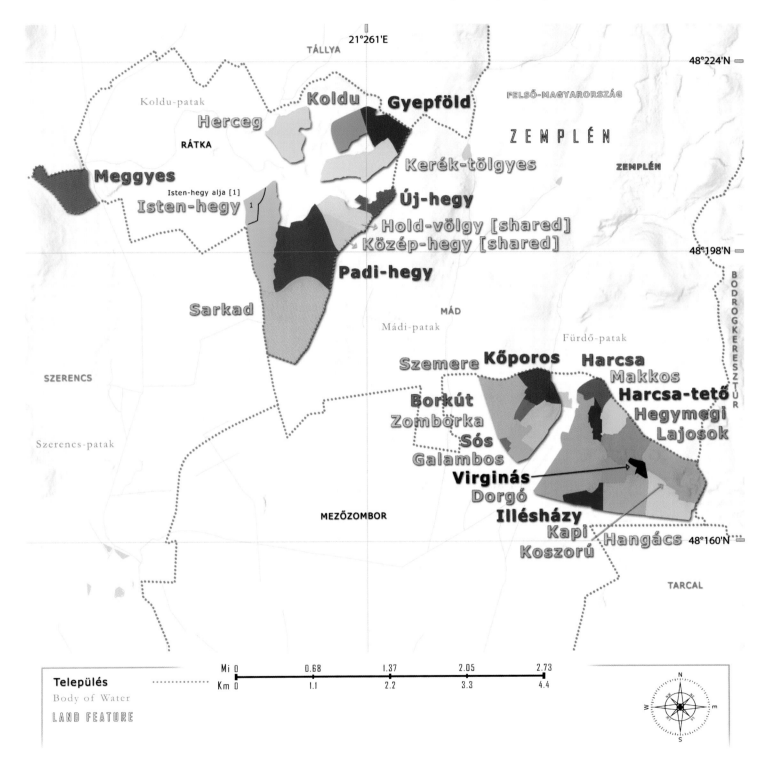

TÁLLYA

21°261'E

48°224'N

FELSŐ-MAGYARORSZÁG

Koldu-patak

Koldu

Gyepföld

Z E M P L É N

Herceg

RÁTKA

Kerék-tölgyes

ZEMPLÉN

Meggyes

Isten-hegy alja [1]

Új-hegy

Isten-hegy

1

Hold-völgy [shared]

Közép-hegy [shared]

48°198'N

Padi-hegy

BODROGKERESZTÚR

Sarkad

MÁD

Mádi-patak

SZERENCS

Fürdő-patak

Szemere **Kőporos** **Harcsa**

Szerencs-patak

Borkút

Makkos

Harcsa-tető

Zombörka

Hegymegi

Sós

Lajosok

Galambos

Virginás

Dorgó

MEZŐZOMBOR

Illésházy

Kapi

Koszorú

Hangács 48°160'N

TARCAL

Település

Mi 0   0.68   1.37   2.05   2.73

Body of Water

Km 0   1.1   2.2   3.3   4.4

LAND FEATURE

N

W   E

S

MÁD

Vineyard (dűlő) [27] [3 shared]

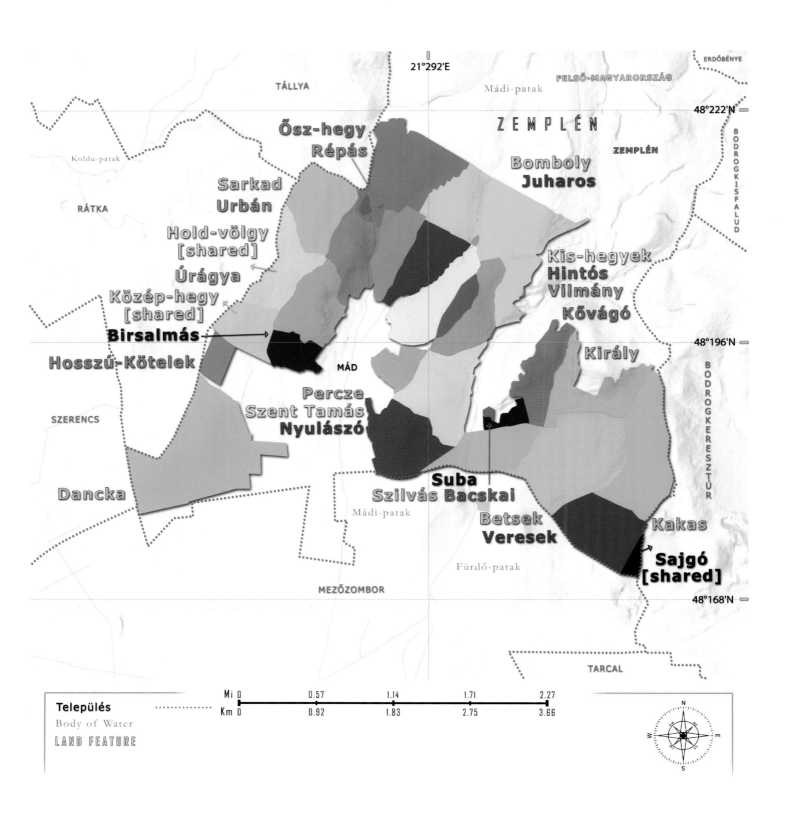

TÁLLYA

21°292'E

Mádi-patak

FELSŐ-MAGYARORSZÁG

ERDŐBÉNYE

48°222'N

Z E M P L É N

ZEMPLÉN

BODROGKISFALUD

Koldu-patak

Ősz-hegy
Répás

Bomboly
Juharos

RÁTKA

Sarkad
Urbán

Hold-völgy
[shared]

Kis-hegyek
Hintós
Vilmány
Kővágó

Úrágya

Közép-hegy
[shared]

MÁD

BODROGKERESZTÚR

Birsalmás

48°196'N

Hosszú-Kötelek

Király

SZERENCS

Percze
Szent Tamás
Nyulászó

Dancka

Suba
Szilvás Bacskai

Kakas

Mádi-patak

Betsek
Veresek

Sajgó
[shared]

Fürdő-patak

48°168'N

MEZŐZOMBOR

TARCAL

	Mi 0	0.57	1.14	1.71	2.27
Település	Km 0	0.92	1.83	2.75	3.66

Body of Water

LAND FEATURE

TARCAL

Vineyard (dűlő) [47]

The numbered areas are sub-vinyards (aldűlő)

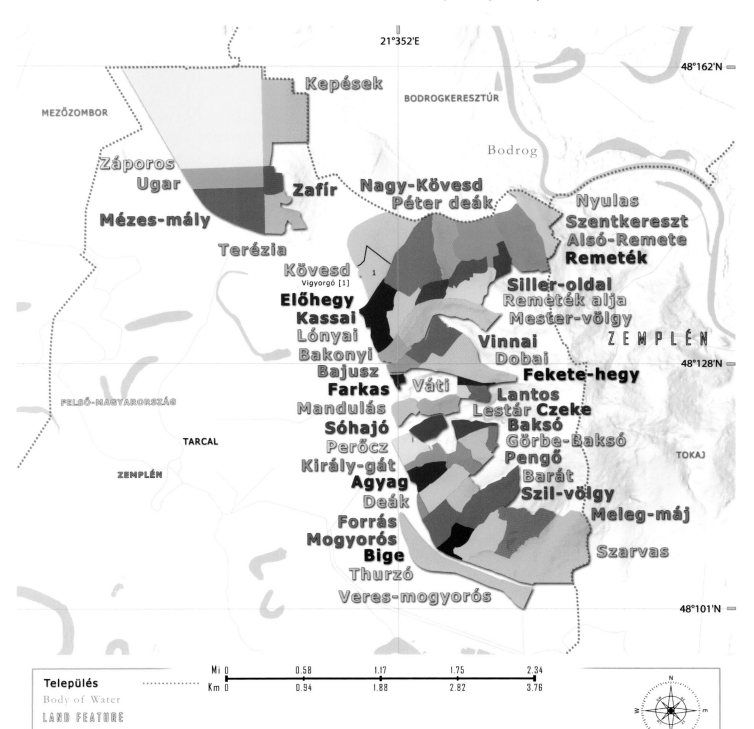

Mi scale: 0, 0.58, 1.17, 1.75, 2.34
Km scale: 0, 0.94, 1.88, 2.82, 3.76

Település
Body of Water
LAND FEATURE

TOKAJ (Település)
Vineyard (dűlő) [23]

The numbered areas are sub-vinyards (aldűlő)

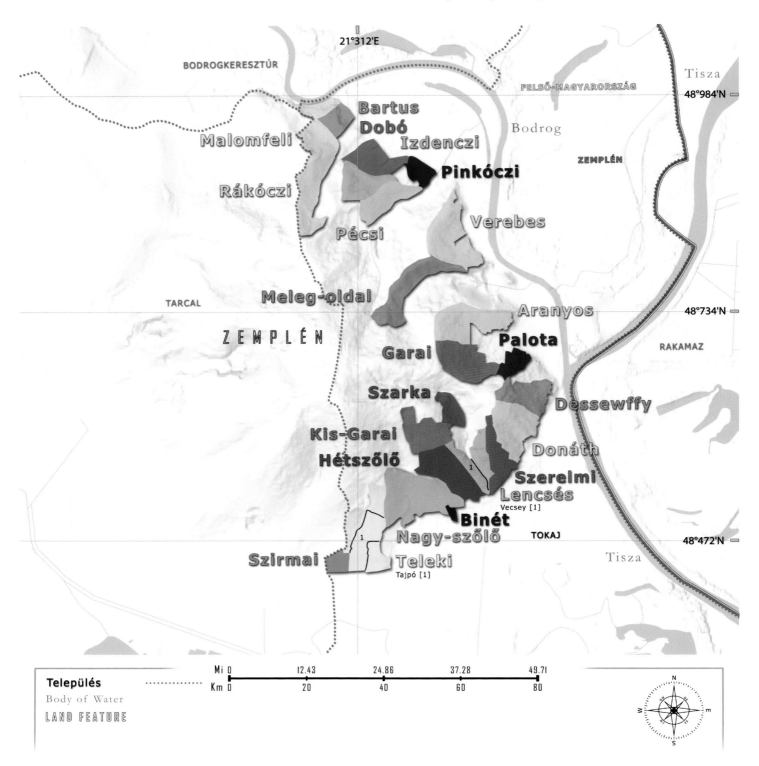

BODROGKERESZTÚR Vineyard (dűlő) [16]
[2 shared]
BODROGKISFALUD [8] [1 shared]
SZEGI [8] SZEGILONG [4]

The numbered areas are sub-vinyards (aldűlő)

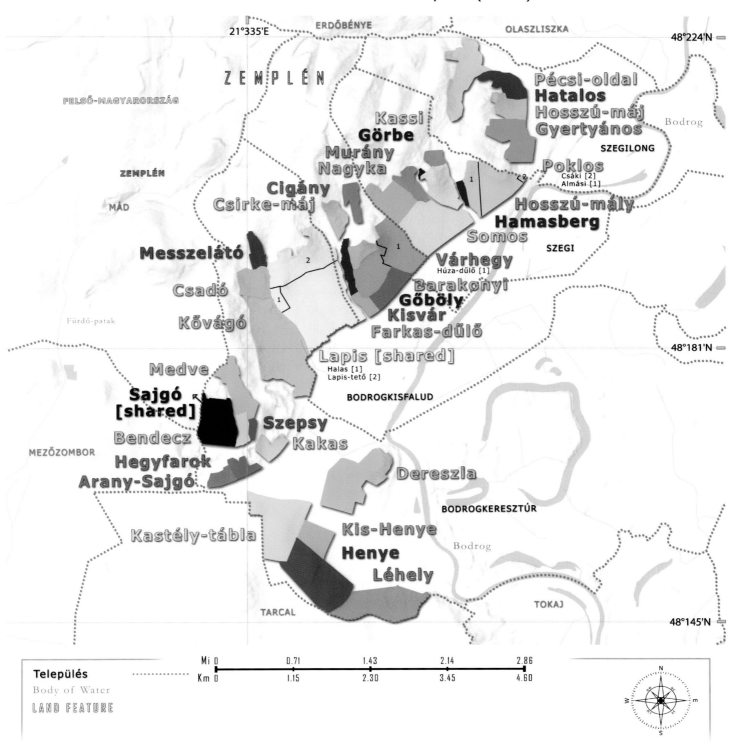

ERDŐBÉNYE
21°335'E
OLASZLISZKA
48°224'N

Z E M P L É N

FELSŐ-MAGYARORSZÁG

Pécsi-oldal
Hatalos
Hosszú-máj
Gyertyános
Bodrog

ZEMPLÉN

MÁD

Kassi
Görbe
Murány
Nagyka

SZEGILONG

Poklos
Csáki [2]
Almási [1]

Cigány
Csirke-máj

Hosszú-mály
Hamasberg
Somos
SZEGI

Messzelátó

Csadó

Kővágó

Fürdő-patak

2

1

Várhegy
Húza-dűlő [1]
Barakonyi
Gőböly
Kisvár
Farkas-dűlő

1

Lapis [shared]
Halas [1]
Lapis-tető [2]

Medve

BODROGKISFALUD

Sajgó
[shared]

Szepsy
Kakas

Bendecz
Hegyfarok
Arany-Sajgó

MEZŐZOMBOR

Dereszla

BODROGKERESZTÚR

Kastély-tábla

Kis-Henye
Henye
Léhely

Bodrog

48°181'N

TARCAL

TOKAJ

48°145'N

Mi 0   0.71   1.43   2.14   2.86
Km 0   1.15   2.30   3.45   4.60

Település
Body of Water
LAND FEATURE

N
W   E
S

OLASZLISZKA   VÁMOSÚJFALU

Vineyard (dűlő) [30] [3 shared]   Vineyard (dűlő) [1] [shared]

The numbered areas are sub-vinyards (aldűlő)

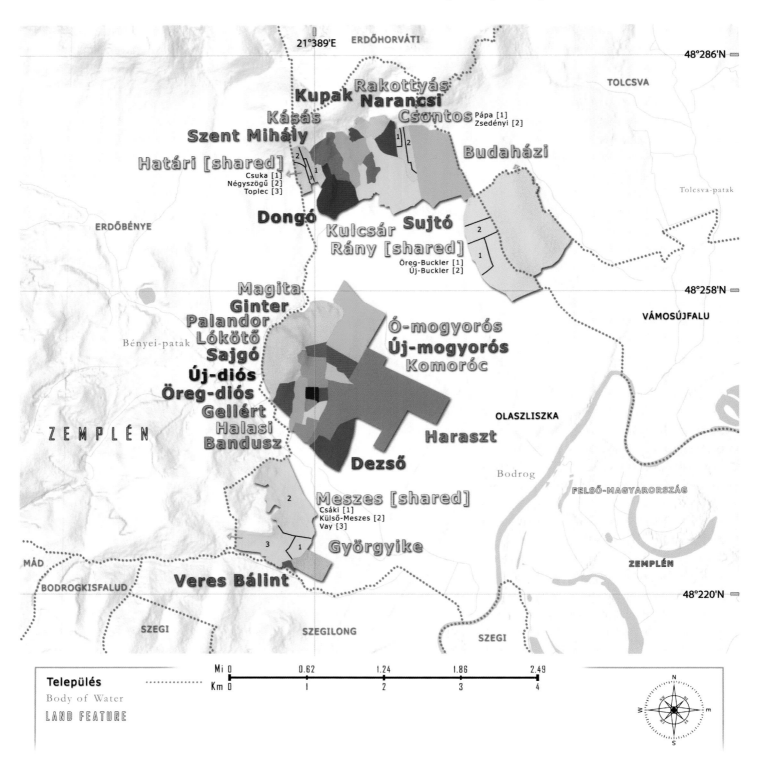

21°389'E   ERDŐHORVÁTI   48°286'N   TOLCSVA

Kupak   Rakottyás
Narancsi
Kásás   Csontos   Pápa [1]
Szent Mihály   Zsedényi [2]
Határi [shared]   Budaházi
Csuka [1]   Tolcsva-patak
Négyszögű [2]
Toplec [3]
ERDŐBÉNYE   Dongó   Sujtó
Kulcsár   2
Rány [shared]   1
Öreg-Buckler [1]
Új-Buckler [2]

Magita   48°258'N   VÁMOSÚJFALU
Ginter
Palandor   Ó-mogyorós
Bényei-patak   Lókötő   Új-mogyorós
Sajgó   Komoróc
Új-diós
Öreg-diós   OLASZLISZKA
Gellért
ZEMPLÉN   Halasi   Haraszt
Bandusz
Dezső   Bodrog   FELSŐ-MAGYARORSZÁG

2   Meszes [shared]
Csáki [1]
Külső-Meszes [2]   ZEMPLÉN
3   1   Vay [3]
Györgyike
MÁD   48°220'N
BODROGKISFALUD   Veres Bálint

SZEGI   SZEGILONG   SZEGI

Mi 0   0.62   1.24   1.86   2.49
Km 0   1   2   3   4

Település
Body of Water
LAND FEATURE

N
W   E
S

ERDŐBÉNYE

Vineyard (dűlő) [40] [2 shared]

The numbered areas are sub-vinyards (aldűlő)

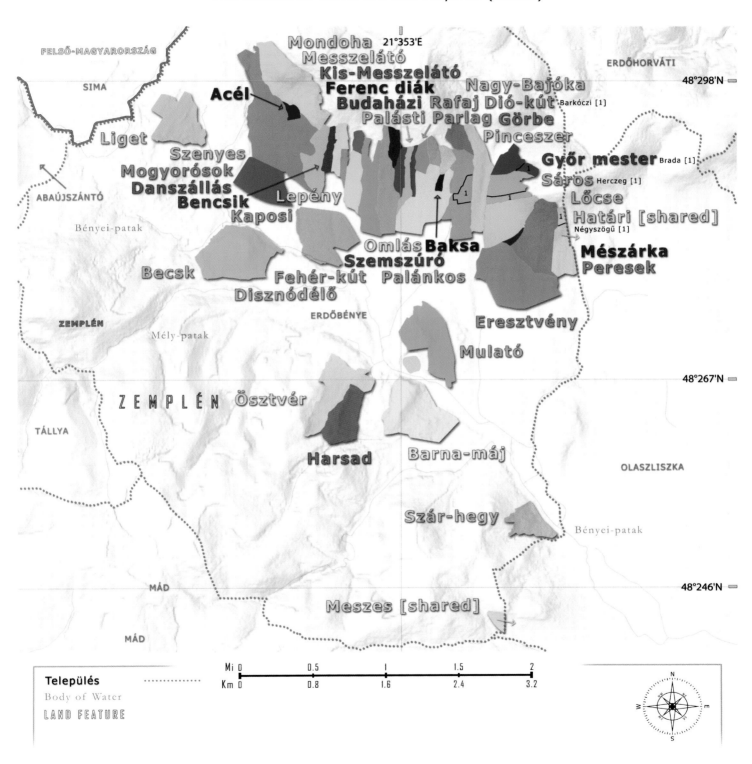

FELSŐ-MAGYARORSZÁG

SIMA

ERDŐHORVÁTI

48°298'N

Mondoha 21°353'E
Messzelátó
Kis-Messzelátó
Ferenc diák   Nagy-Bajóka
Acél   **Budaházi** Rafaj Dió-kút   Barkóczi [1]
Palásti Parlag Görbe
Liget   Pinceszer
   Győr mester Brada [1]
Szenyes
Mogyorósok   **Sáros** Herczeg [1]
Danszállás   **Lőcse**
Bencsik Lepény   Határi [shared]
Kaposi   Négyszögű [1]

ABAÚJSZÁNTÓ

Bényei-patak

Omlás **Baksa**   **Mészárka**
Szemszúró   **Peresek**
Becsk   Fehér-kút Palánkos
Disznódélő

ZEMPLÉN   ERDŐBÉNYE

Mély-patak   **Eresztvény**

Mulató

48°267'N

Z E M P L É N   Ösztvér

TÁLLYA

Harsad   Barna-máj

OLASZLISZKA

Szár-hegy   Bényei-patak

48°246'N

MÁD

Meszes [shared]

MÁD

	Mi 0	0.5	1	1.5	2
	Km 0	0.8	1.6	2.4	3.2

Település ············
Body of Water
LAND FEATURE

TOLCSVA
Vineyard (dűlő) [35] [2 shared]

The numbered areas are sub-vinyards (aldűlő)

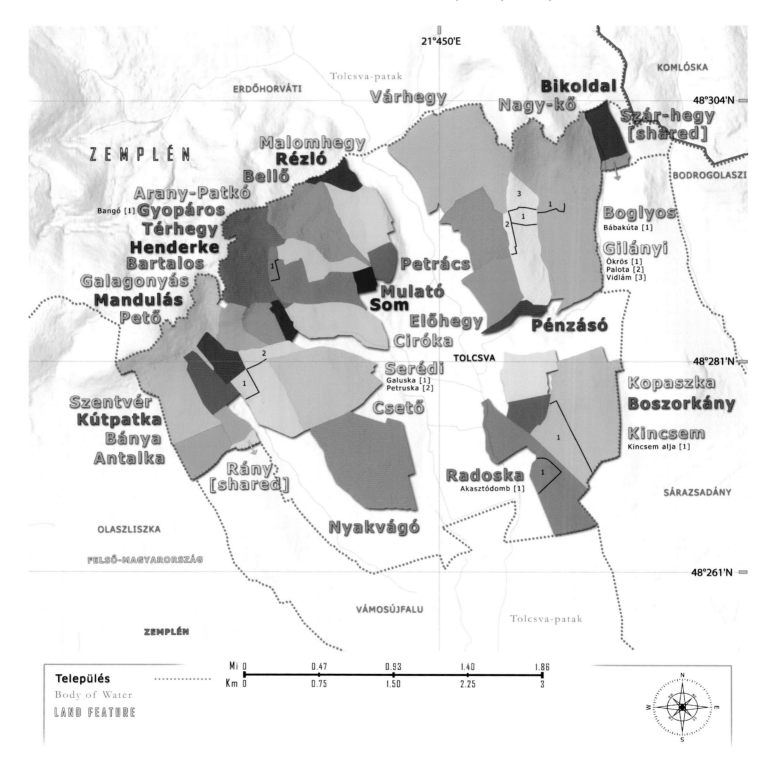

ERDŐHORVÁTI
SÁRAZSADÁNY
BODROGOLASZI

Vineyard (dűlő) [7]

[7] [1 shared]

[5]

The numbered areas are sub-vinyards (aldűlő)

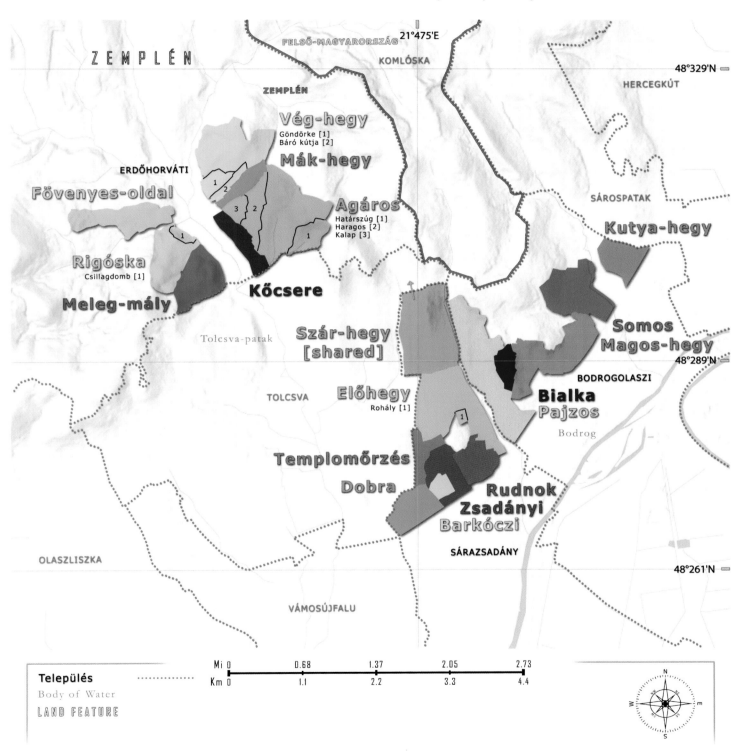

ZEMPLÉN

FELSŐ-MAGYARORSZÁG   21°475'E

KOMLÓSKA

48°329'N

HERCEGKÚT

ZEMPLÉN

ERDŐHORVÁTI

SÁROSPATAK

Vég-hegy
Göndörke [1]
Báró kútja [2]

Mák-hegy

Fövenyes-oldal

Kutya-hegy

Agáros
Határszúg [1]
Haragos [2]
Kalap [3]

Rigóska
Csillagdomb [1]

Kőcsere

Somos
Magos-hegy

Meleg-mály

Tolcsva-patak

Szár-hegy
[shared]

48°289'N

BODROGOLASZI

TOLCSVA

Előhegy
Rohály [1]

Bialka
Pajzos

Bodrog

Templomőrzés

Dobra

Rudnok
Zsadányi
Barkóczi

OLASZLISZKA

SÁRAZSADÁNY

48°261'N

VÁMOSÚJFALU

Mi 0   0.68   1.37   2.05   2.73
Km 0   1.1   2.2   3.3   4.4

Település
Body of Water
LAND FEATURE

N
W   m
S

SÁROSPATAK Vineyard (dűlő) [19] [2 shared]
HERCEGKÚT [7] [3 shared]
MAKKOSHOTYKA [3] [1 shared]

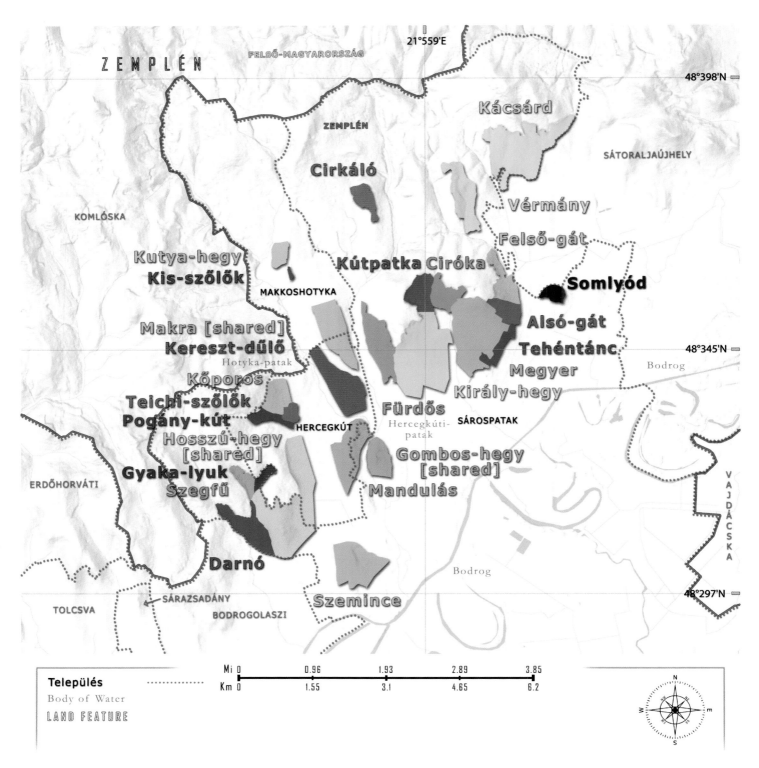

ZEMPLÉN

FELSŐ-MAGYARORSZÁG

21°559'E

48°398'N

ZEMPLÉN

Kácsárd

SÁTORALJAÚJHELY

KOMLÓSKA

Cirkáló

Vérmány

Felső-gát

Kutya-hegy
Kis-szőlők

MAKKOSHOTYKA

Kútpatka Ciróka

Somlyód

Makra [shared]
Kereszt-dűlő

Hotyka-patak

Alsó-gát

Tehéntánc

48°345'N

Bodrog

Kőporos

Megyer

Király-hegy

Teichi-szőlők
Pogány-kút

HERCEGKÚT

Fürdős

Hercegkúti-
patak

SÁROSPATAK

Hosszú-hegy
[shared]
Gyaka-lyuk
Szegfű

Gombos-hegy
[shared]

Mandulás

VAJDÁCSKA

ERDŐHORVÁTI

Darnó

Bodrog

48°297'N

TOLCSVA

SÁRAZSADÁNY

BODROGOLASZI

Szemince

Mi 0	0.96	1.93	2.89	3.85
Km 0	1.55	3.1	4.65	6.2

Település
Body of Water
LAND FEATURE

N
W E
S

SÁTORALJAÚJHELY

Vineyard (dűlő) [21]

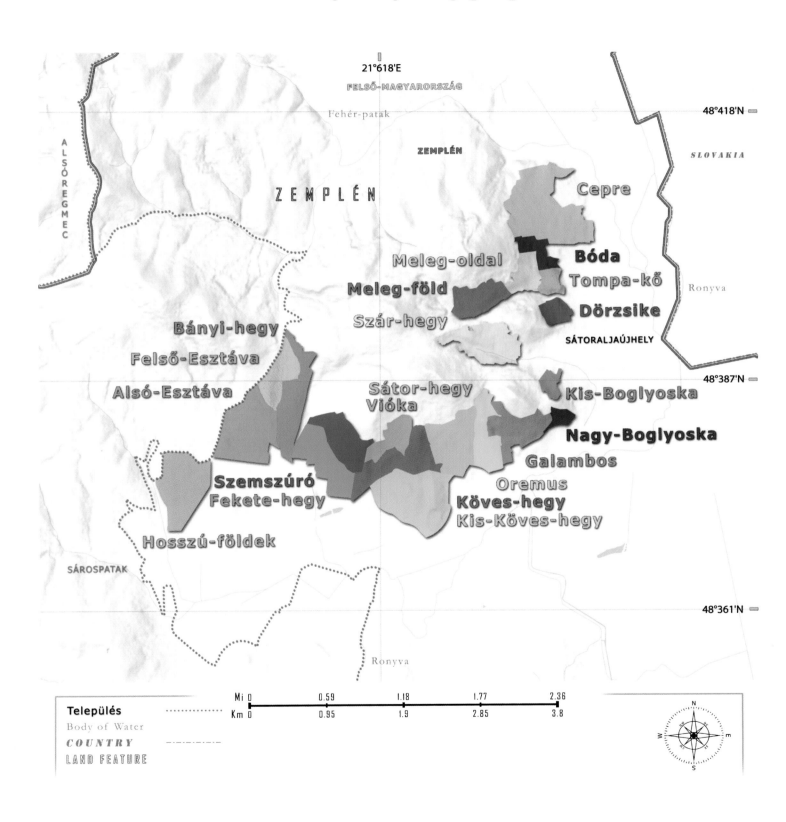

CLASSIFICATION SYSTEM
AOC [Appellation d'Origine Contrôlée = Controlled Designation of Origin]

6 Regions

26 Canton

62 AOC

27 AOC cantonale
13 AOC regionale
22 AOC locale [list only]

SWITZERLAND

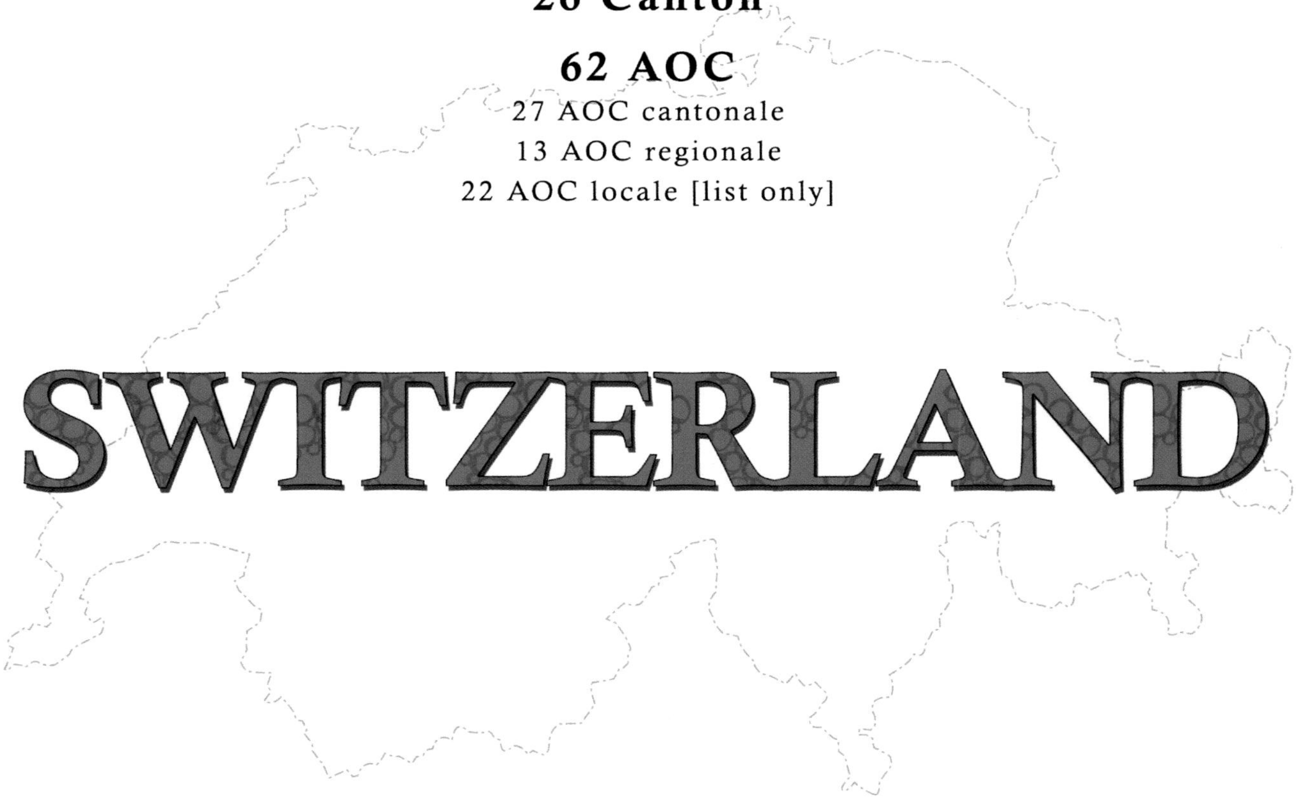

6 REGIONS

GENEVA	VALAIS	THREE LAKES
VAUD	TICINO	GERMAN SWISS

26 CANTONS

Geneva [1]   Vaud [1]   Valais [1]   Ticino [1]

GENEVA	VAUD	VALAIS	TICINO

Three Lakes [4]

NEUCHÂTEL	JURA	BERN	FRIBOURG

German Swiss [18]

AARGAU	BASEL-LANDSCHAFT	GRAUBÜNDEN	OBWALDEN	SOLOTHURN	URI
APPENZEL AUSSERHODEN	BASEL-STADT	LUZERN	SCHAFFHAUSEN	ST. GALLEN	ZUG
APPENZELL INNERHODEN	GLARUS	NIDWALDEN	SCHWYZ	THURGAU	ZÜRICH

62 AOC

AOC cantonale [27]

AARGAU	GENEVA	NEUCHÂTEL	SOLOTHURN	ROSSO DEL TICINO	VALAIS
APPENZEL AUSSERHODEN	GLARUS	NIDWALDEN	ST. GALLEN	BIANCO DEL TICINO	VAUD
BASEL-LANDSCHAFT	GRAUBÜNDEN	OBWALDEN	THURGAU	ROSATO DEL TICINO	ZUG
BASEL-STADT	JURA	SCHAFFHAUSEN	TICINO	URI	ZÜRICH
BERN	LUZERN	SCHWYZ			

AOC regionale [13]

BIELERSEE	CHABLAIS	CÔTES-DE- L'ORBE	DÉZALEY-MARSENS	LAVAUX	VULLY [shared with Vaud and Three Lakes]
BONVILLARS	CHEYRES	DÉZALEY	LA CÔTE	THUNERSEE	ZÜRICHSEE
CALAMIN					

AOC locale [22] [all within AOC Geneva (cantonale)]

CHÂTEAU DE CHOULLY	COTEAU DE BOURDIGNY	COTEAU DE DARDAGNY	COTEAU DE PEISSY	CÔTES DU RUSSIN	LA FEUILLEE
CHÂTEAU DE COLLEX	COTEAU DE CHEVRENS	COTEAU DE GENTHOD	COTEAU DE PENEY	DOMAINE DE L'ABBAYE	MANDEMENT DE JUSSY
CHÂTEAU DU CREST	COTEAU DE CHOULEX	COTEAU DE LA VIGNE BLANCHE	COTEAU DES BAILLETS	GRAND CARRAZ	ROUGEMONT
COTEAU DE BOSSY	COTEAU DE CHOULLY	COTEAU DE LULLY	COTES DE LANDECY		

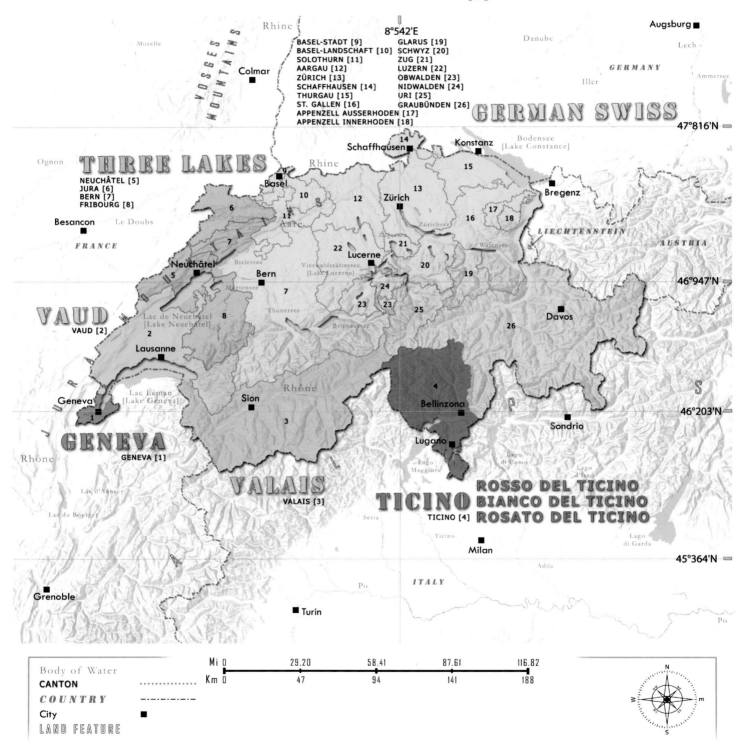

REGIONS OF SWITZERLAND [6]
CANTONS OF SWITZERLAND [26]
TOTAL AOC cantonale [27]
Each canton is AOC except no.8 and no.18 [24]
Ticino has additional AOCs [3]

BASEL-STADT [9]
BASEL-LANDSCHAFT [10]
SOLOTHURN [11]
AARGAU [12]
ZÜRICH [13]
SCHAFFHAUSEN [14]
THURGAU [15]
ST. GALLEN [16]
APPENZELL AUSSERHODEN [17]
APPENZELL INNERHODEN [18]

GLARUS [19]
SCHWYZ [20]
ZUG [21]
LUZERN [22]
OBWALDEN [23]
NIDWALDEN [24]
URI [25]
GRAUBÜNDEN [26]

GERMAN SWISS

THREE LAKES
NEUCHÂTEL [5]
JURA [6]
BERN [7]
FRIBOURG [8]

VAUD
VAUD [2]

GENEVA
GENEVA [1]

VALAIS
VALAIS [3]

TICINO
TICINO [4]

ROSSO DEL TICINO
BIANCO DEL TICINO
ROSATO DEL TICINO

Body of Water
CANTON ....
COUNTRY — · — · — ·
City ■
LAND FEATURE

| Mi | 0 | 29.20 | 58.41 | 87.61 | 116.82 |
| Km | 0 | 47 | 94 | 141 | 188 |

SWITZERLAND
AOC regionale [13]
AOC locale [22]
All AOC locale are located in the AOC Geneve.

7°014'E

Montbéliard

Rhine

BASEL-STADT

THURGAU →

Ognon

Le Doubs

JURA

BASEL-LANDSCHAFT

Aarau

Reuss

ZÜRICH

Zürich

47°387'N

Besancon

FRANCE

THREE LAKES

BERN

SOLOTHURN

AARGAU

ZÜRICHSEE

Zürichsee

ZUG

Aare

LUZERN

Lucerne

Zugersee

SCHWYZ

BIELERSEE

Biel

Bielersee

GERMAN SWISS

Vierwaldstätter-see
[Lake Lucerne]

NEUCHÂTEL

Lac de Neuchâtel
[Lake Neuchâtel]

Neuchâtel

Murtensee

NIDWALDEN

Bevaix

VULLY [SHARED]

BERN

Altdorf

BONVILLARS

Lully

CHEYRES

Aare

Thun

OBWALDEN

URI

46°757'N

CÔTES-DE-L'ORBE

Orbe

VAUD

VAUD

FRIBOURG

Thunersee

Brienzersee

GRAUBÜNDEN

LAVAUX

THUNERSEE

LA CÔTE

Lausanne

TICINO
TICINO

Nyon

Montreux

Lac Léman
[Lake Geneva]

Yvorne

Varen

Brig

CALAMIN

Bex

CHABLAIS

Geneva

DÉZALEY

Rhône

GENEVA

DÉZALEY-MARSENS

Sion

VALAIS

Rhône

GENEVA

Cluses

Tzoumaz

VALAIS

Arve

Toce

Lago
Maggiore

Annecy

Lac d'Annecy

ITALY

Varese

Lago
d'Orta

45°896'N

Aosta

| Mi 0 | 15.53 | 31.07 | 46.60 | 62.14 |
| Km 0 | 25 | 50 | 75 | 100 |

Body of Water

CANTON ....

COUNTRY — ∙ — ∙ —

City ■

LAND FEATURE

CLASSIFICATION SYSTEM
OPAP [Onomasia Proelefsis Anoteras Poiotitos = Designation of Origin of Superior Qualtiy]
OPE [Onomasia Proelefsis Eleghomeni = Controlled Apellation of Origin]
Dry wines categorized as OPAP, and sweet wines as OPE.

9 Regions

21 OPAP

12 OPE

GREECE

9 REGIONS

THRACE	EPIRUS	CENTRAL GREECE	IONIAN ISLANDS	CRETE
MACEDONIA	THESSALY	PELOPONNESE	AEGEAN ISLANDS	

21 OPAP / 12 OPE

REGION / APPELLATION	RANK	EST.	APPELLATION	RANK	EST.	APPELLATION	RANK	EST.
Macedonia [4 OPAP]								
AMYNTEO	OPAP	1972	NAOUSSA	OPAP	1971	SLOPES OF MELITON	OPAP	1982
GOUMENISSA	OPAP	1979						
Epirus [1 OPAP]								
ZITSA	OPAP	1972						
Thessaly [3 OPAP]								
ANCHIALOS	OPAP	1971	MESSENIKOLA	OPAP	1994	RAPSANI	OPAP	1971
Peloponnese [3 OPAP] [4 OPE]								
PATRAS	OPAP	1972	MAVRODAPHNE OF PATRAS	OPE	1971	MUSCAT OF PATRAS	OPE	1971
NEMEA	OPAP	1971	MONEMVASSIA MALVASIA	OPE	2009	MUSCAT OF RIO PATRAS	OPE	1971
MANTINIA	OPAP	1971						
Ionian Islands [1 OPAP] [2 OPE]								
ROBOLA OF CEPHALONIA	OPAP	1971	MAVRODAPHNE OF CEPHALONIA	OPE	1971	MUSCAT OF CEPHALONIA	OPE	1971
Aegean Islands [4 OPAP] [4 OPE]								
LEMNOS	OPAP	1971	MALVASIA PAROS	OPE	1981	MUSCAT OF RHODES	OPE	1971
PAROS	OPAP	1981	MUSCAT OF LEMNOS	OPE	1971	SAMOS	OPE	1970
SANTORINI	OPAP	1971						
RHODES	OPAP	1971						
Crete [5 OPAP] [2 OPE]								
ARCHANES	OPAP		PEZA	OPAP	1971	MALVASIA CANDIA	OPE	2011
CANDIA	OPAP	2011	SITIA	OPAP	1971	MALVASIA SITIA	OPE	1971
DAFNES	OPAP	1971						
Thrace [no appellation]								
Central Greece [no appellation]								

REGIONS OF GREECE [9]

Split

BOSNIA & HERZEGOVINA

SERBIA

Nis

23°528'E

Varna

CROATIA

MONTENEGRO

KOSOVO

Sofia

B A L K A N

Burgas

Podgorica

Skopje

BULGARIA

Black Sea

Adriatic Sea

MACEDONIA

41°747'N

NORTH MACEDONIA

RHODOPE

THRACE

Tirana

Komotini

Istanbul

Bari

ALBANIA

Thessaloniki

Sea of Marmara

ITALY

Gulf of Taranto

Corfu

THESSALY

39°540'N

EPIRUS

Ioannina

Larissa

Aegean Sea

IONIAN ISLANDS

Catanzaro

Lamia

TURKEY

CENTRAL GREECE

Patra

Izmir

Athens

37°812'N

Ionian Sea

Denizli

T A U R U S

PELOPONNESE

Rhodes

Sea of Crete

AEGEAN ISLANDS

Heraklion

CRETE

34°812'N

Mediterranean Sea

Mi	0	87	174	261	348
Km	0	140	280	420	560

Body of Water

COUNTRY

City

LAND FEATURE

Greece

GREECE [MAINLAND]
OPAP [11]
OPE [4]

NORTH MACEDONIA

Elbasan

Bitola

Serres

Xanthi THRACE

MACEDONIA

GOUMENISSA

Adriatic Sea

22°128'E

Thessaloniki

40°572'N

Vlorë

AMYNTEO

Veroia NAOUSSA

ALBANIA

SLOPES OF MELITON

Corfu

Ioannina

ZITSA

RAPSANI

Larissa

THESSALY

MESSENIKOLA

EPIRUS

ANCHIALOS

Aegean Sea

Preveza

Lamia

38°833'N

IONIAN ISLANDS

CENTRAL GREECE

Mavrodaphne of Patras

AEGEAN ISLANDS

Muscat of Rio Patras

Patra

Muscat of Patras

Athens

Ionian Sea

PATRAS

NEMEA

Argos

MANTINIA

PELOPONNESE

Myrtoan Sea

36°889'N

Kalamata

Monemvasia

Monemvasia Malvasia

| Mi 0 | 42.87 | 85.75 | 128.62 | 171.49 |
| Km 0 | 69 | 138 | 207 | 276 |

Body of Water

COUNTRY

City / Village

LAND FEATURE

GREECE [ISLANDS]
OPAP [10]
OPE [8]

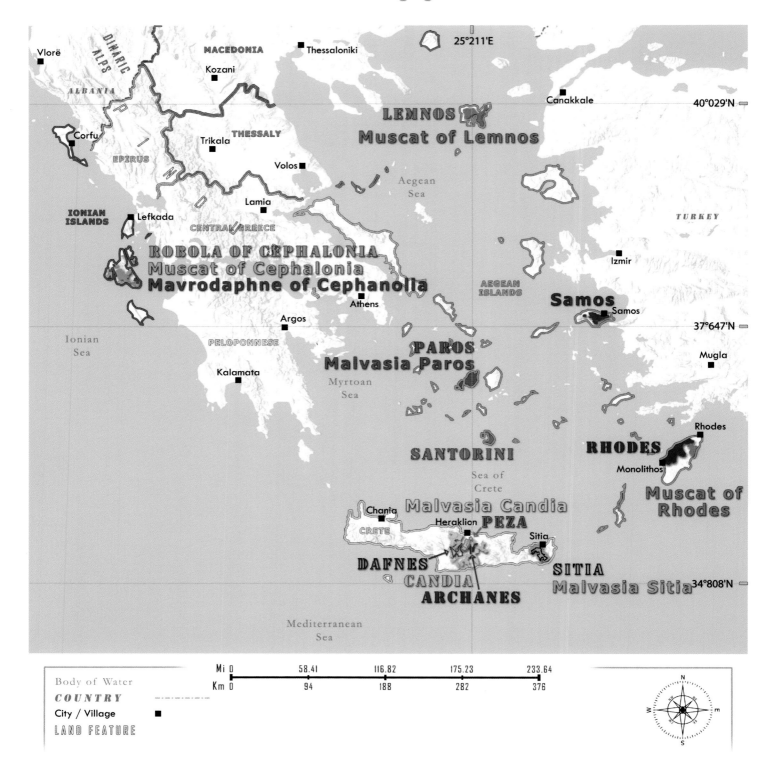

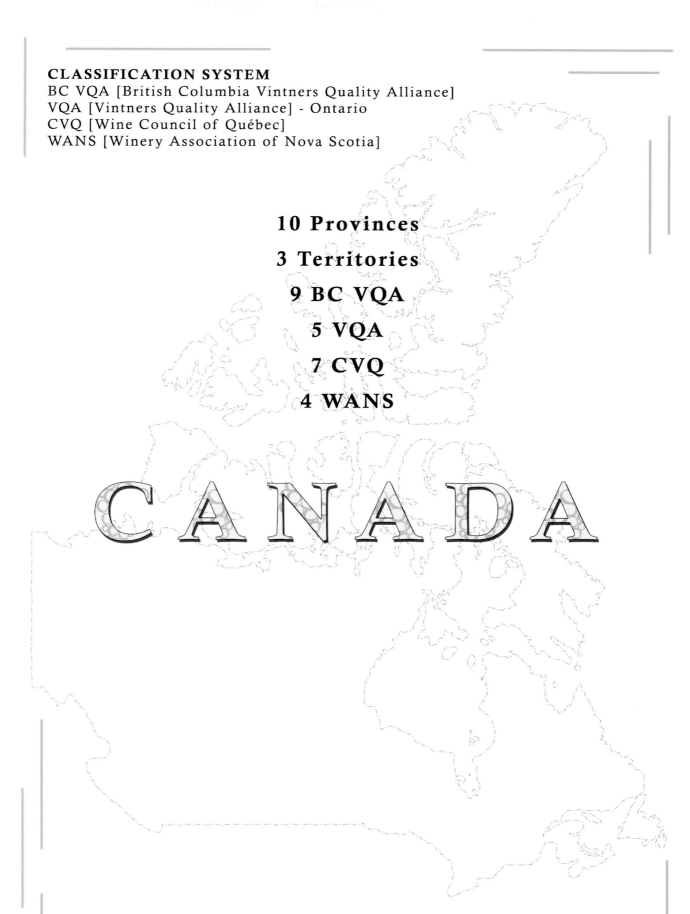

CLASSIFICATION SYSTEM
BC VQA [British Columbia Vintners Quality Alliance]
VQA [Vintners Quality Alliance] - Ontario
CVQ [Wine Council of Québec]
WANS [Winery Association of Nova Scotia]

10 Provinces

3 Territories

9 BC VQA

5 VQA

7 CVQ

4 WANS

CANADA

10 PROVINCES

BRITISH COLUMBIA	SASKATCHEWAN	ONTARIO	NEWFOUNDLAND AND LABRADOR	NEW BRUNSWICK
ALBERTA	MANITOBA	QUEBEC	PRINCE EDWARD ISLAND	NOVA SCOTIA

3 TERRITORIES

YUKON	NORTHWEST TERRITORIES	NUNAVUT

25 REGIONS

PROVINCE / REGION	SUB-REGION
British Columbia [9 BC VQA]	
VANCOUVER ISLAND	
GULF ISLANDS	
FRASER VALLEY	
SIMILKAMEEN VALLEY	
OKANAGAN VALLEY	Golden Mile Bench, Okanagan Falls, Naramata Bench, Skaha Bench
KOOTENAYS	
LILLOOET	
SHUSWAP	
THOMPSON VALLEY	
Ontario [5 VQA]	
LAKE ERIE NORTH SHORE	South Islands (contains 9 islands, including Pelee Island)
NIAGARA PENINSULA	Vinemount Ridge, Creek Shores, Lincoln Lakeshore
NIAGARA-ON-THE-LAKE [within Niagara Peninsula]	Niagara River, Niagara Lakeshore, Four Mile Creek, St. David's Bench
NIAGARA ESCARPMENT [within Niagara Peninsula]	Short Hills Bench, Beamsville Bench, Twenty Mile Bench
PRINCE EDWARD COUNTY	
Québec [7 CVQ]	
DEUX-MONTAGNES	
RICHELIEU RIVER VALLEY	
APPALACHIAN FOOTHILLS	
MONTEREGIAN HILLS	
APPALACHIAN PLATEAU	
LAKE SAINT-PIERRE	
QUEBEC AND THE BANKS OF THE ST. LAWRENCE RIVER	
Nova Scotia [5 WANS]	
CAPE BRETON ISLAND	
NORTHUMBERLAND SHORE	
ANNAPOLIS VALLEY	
SOUTH SHORE	

Canada

PROVINCES OF CANADA [10]

TERRITORIES OF CANADA [3]

123°119'W

82°189'N

Arctic
Ocean

GREENLAND
[DENMARK]

74°564'N

Baffin
Bay

Beaufort
Sea

Utqiagvik

Inuvik

UNITED STATES
OF AMERICA

Great Bear
Lake

NUNAVUT

Davis
Strait

Nuuk

62°972'N

NORTHWEST
TERRITORIES

YUKON

Great
Slave
Lake

MANITOBA

QUÉBEC

Labrador
Sea

Anchorage

Akulivik

NEWFOUNDLAND
AND LABRADOR

Juneau

Gulf of
Alaska

Lake Athabasca

Hudson
Bay

Atlantic
Ocean

BRITISH
COLUMBIA

Edmonton

Lake Winnipeg

PRINCE
EDWARD
ISLAND

ALBERTA

Vancouver

Winnipeg

Wawa

SASKATCHEWAN

Seattle

Lake Superior

Lake Huron

Georgian Bay

NEW BRUNSWICK

Pacific
Ocean

ONTARIO

Lake Michigan

Montreal

Lake
Ontario

NOVA SCOTIA

41°631'N

Toronto

San Francisco

UNITED STATES OF AMERICA

Chicago

Lake Erie

New York

Body of Water

COUNTRY

City / Town

LAND FEATURE

| Mi 0 | | 777 | | 1553 | | 2330 | | 3107 |
| Km 0 | | 1250 | | 2500 | | 3750 | | 5000 |

BRITISH COLUMBIA
BC VQA [9]
SUB-REGION OF OKANAGAN VALLEY [4]

Naramata Bench [a]
Skaha Bench [b]
Okanagan Falls [c]
Golden Mile Bench [d]

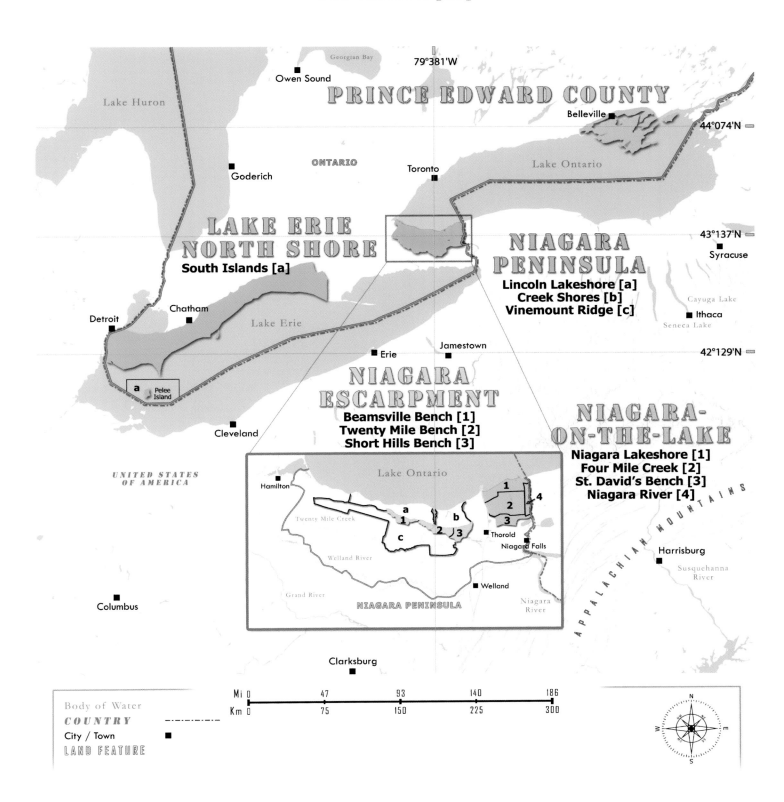

ONTARIO
VQA [5]
SUB-REGION [11]

PRINCE EDWARD COUNTY

79°381'W

Owen Sound

Lake Huron

Georgian Bay

Belleville

44°074'N

ONTARIO

Goderich

Toronto

Lake Ontario

43°137'N

Syracuse

LAKE ERIE NORTH SHORE

South Islands [a]

NIAGARA PENINSULA

Lincoln Lakeshore [a]
Creek Shores [b]
Vinemount Ridge [c]

Cayuga Lake

Ithaca

Seneca Lake

Chatham

Lake Erie

Detroit

Jamestown

Erie

42°129'N

NIAGARA ESCARPMENT

Beamsville Bench [1]
Twenty Mile Bench [2]
Short Hills Bench [3]

NIAGARA-ON-THE-LAKE

Niagara Lakeshore [1]
Four Mile Creek [2]
St. David's Bench [3]
Niagara River [4]

a
Pelee Island

Cleveland

UNITED STATES OF AMERICA

Columbus

Hamilton

Lake Ontario

Twenty Mile Creek

a
1

2

b

4

1

2

3

c

3

Thorold

Niagara Falls

Welland River

APPALACHIAN MOUNTAINS

Harrisburg

Susquehanna River

Grand River

Welland

NIAGARA PENINSULA

Niagara River

Clarksburg

Body of Water

COUNTRY

City / Town

LAND FEATURE

Mi 0   47   93   140   186
Km 0   75   150   225   300

N

W   E

S

QUÉBEC
CVQ [7]

73°563'W

47°525'N

La Tuque

St Lawrence River

QUÉBEC AND THE BANKS OF THE ST. LAWRENCE RIVER

Mont-Laurier

Québec City

LAKE SAINT-PIERRE

QUEBEC

Chaudière River

RICHELIEU RIVER VALLEY

Lac Saint-Pierre

Trois-Rivières

MONTEREGIAN HILLS

46°014'N

DEUX-MONTAGNES

APPALACHIAN PLATEAU

Rivière Saint-François

Ottawa River

Montréal

Sherbrooke

Ottawa

ONTARIO

Cornwall

St Lawrence River

APPALACHIAN FOOTHILLS

Plattsburgh

Lake Champlain

44°590'N

Augusta

Montpelier

Watertown

UNITED STATES OF AMERICA

APPALACHIAN MOUNTAINS

Gulf of Maine

Atlantic Ocean

Concord

Mi	0	39	77	116	154
Km	0	62	124	186	248

Body of Water

COUNTRY

City / Town

LAND FEATURE

N

W   E

S

NOVA SCOTIA

WINE ASSOCIATION OF NOVA SCOTIA [4]

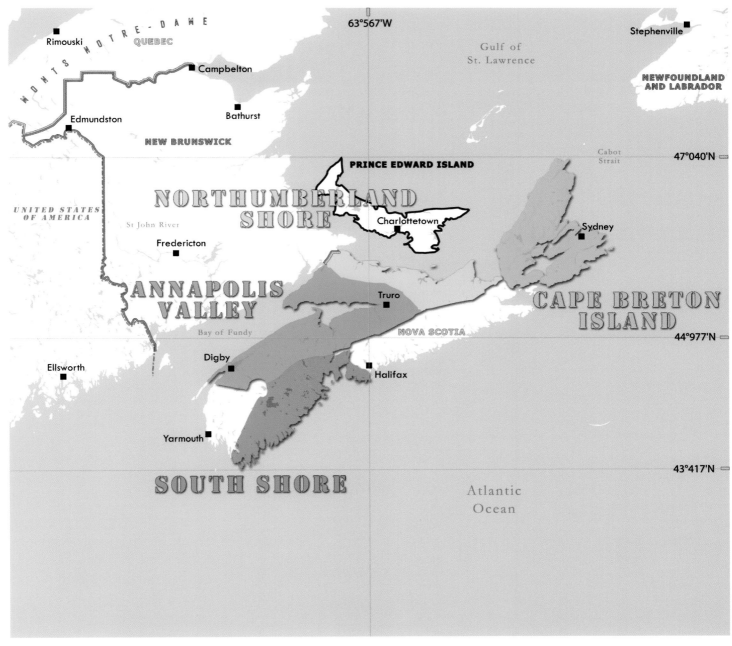

Rimouski

QUEBEC

MONTS NOTRE-DAME

Campbelton

Edmundston

Bathurst

NEW BRUNSWICK

St John River

Fredericton

UNITED STATES
OF AMERICA

NORTHUMBERLAND SHORE

PRINCE EDWARD ISLAND

Charlottetown

Gulf of
St. Lawrence

Stephenville

NEWFOUNDLAND
AND LABRADOR

Cabot
Strait

47°040'N

Sydney

ANNAPOLIS VALLEY

Truro

CAPE BRETON ISLAND

NOVA SCOTIA

Bay of Fundy

44°977'N

Ellsworth

Digby

Halifax

Yarmouth

SOUTH SHORE

43°417'N

Atlantic
Ocean

63°567'W

Body of Water
COUNTRY
City / Town
LAND FEATURE

| Mi 0 | 61 | 122 | 183 | 244 |
| Km 0 | 98 | 196 | 294 | 392 |

CLASSIFICATION SYSTEM
AVA [American Viticultural Area]

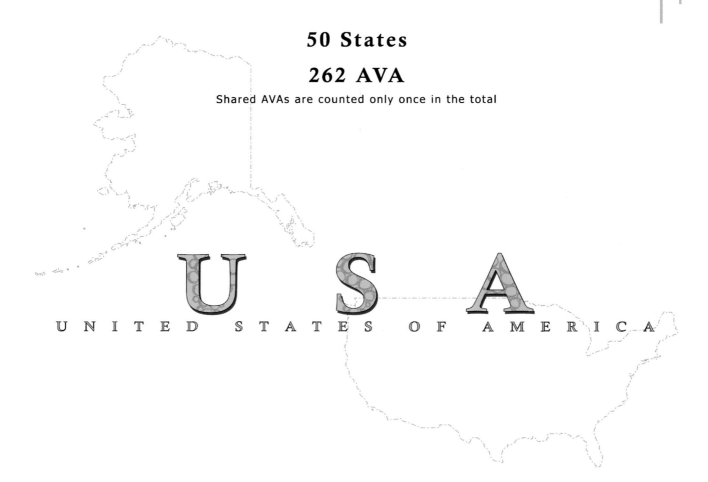

50 States

262 AVA

Shared AVAs are counted only once in the total

U S A

UNITED STATES OF AMERICA

STATE / AVA	EST.	AVA	EST.	AVA	EST.	AVA	EST.
Arizona [3]							
SONOITA	1984	VERDE VALLEY	2021	WILLCOX	2016		
Arkansas [3 out of 1 shared]							
ALTUS	1984	ARKANSAS MOUNTAIN	1986	OZARK MOUNTAIN [shared with Missouri and Oklahoma]	1986		
California [143]							
ADELAIDA DISTRICT	2014	DOS RIOS	1983	MONTEREY	1984	SAN LUIS OBISPO COAST	2022
ALEXANDER VALLEY	1984	DRY CREEK VALLEY	2005	MOON MOUNTAIN DISTRICT SONOMA COUNTY	2013	SAN MIGUEL DISTRICT	2014
ALISOS CANYON	2020	DUNNIGAN HILLS	1993	MT. HARLAN	1990	SAN PASQUAL VALLEY	1981
ALTA MESA	2006	EAGLE PEAK MENDOCINO COUNTY	2014	MT. VEEDER	1990	SAN YSIDRO DISTRICT	1990
ANDERSON VALLEY	1983	EDNA VALLEY	1982	NAPA VALLEY	1981	SANTA CLARA VALLEY	1989
ANTELOPE VALLEY OF THE CALIFORNIA HIGH DESERT	2011	EL DORADO	1983	NORTH COAST	1983	SANTA CRUZ MOUNTAINS	1981
ARROYO GRANDE VALLEY	1990	EL POMAR DISTRICT	2014	NORTH YUBA	1985	SANTA LUCIA HIGHLANDS	1992
ARROYO SECO	1983	FAIR PLAY	2001	NORTHERN SONOMA	1985	SANTA MARGARITA RANCH	2014
ATLAS PEAK	1992	FIDDLETOWN	1983	OAK KNOLL DISTRICT OF NAPA VALLEY	2004	SANTA MARIA VALLEY	1981
BALLARD CANYON	2013	FORT ROSS-SEAVIEW	2011	OAKVILLE	1993	SANTA YNEZ VALLEY	1983
BEN LOMOND MOUTAIN	1987	FOUNTAINGROVE DISTRICT	2015	PACHECO PASS	1984	SEIAD VALLEY	1994
BENMORE VALLEY	1991	GREEN VALLEY OF RUSSIAN RIVER VALLEY	1983	PAICINES	1982	SIERRA FOOTHILLS	1987
BENNETT VALLEY	2003	GUENOC VALLEY	1994	PALOS VERDES PENINSULA	2021	SIERRA PELONA	2010
BIG VALLEY DISTRICT-LAKE COUNTY	2013	HAMES VALLEY	1994	PASO ROBLES	1983	SLOUGHHOUSE	2006
BORDEN RANCH	2006	HAPPY CANYON OF SANTA BARBARA	2009	PASO ROBLES ESTRELLA DISTRICT	2014	SOLANO COUNTY GREEN VALLEY	1982
CALIFORNIA SHENANDOAH VALLEY	1982	HIGH VALLEY	2005	PASO ROBLES GENESEO DISTRICT	2014	SONOMA COAST	1987
CALISTOGA	2009	HOWELL MOUNTAIN	1983	PASO ROBLES HIGHLANDS DISTRICT	2014	SONOMA MOUNTAIN	1985
CAPAY VALLEY	2002	INWOOD VALLEY	2012	PASO ROBLES WILLOW CREEK DISTRICT	2014	SONOMA VALLEY	1981
CARMEL VALLEY	1982	JAHANT	2006	PETALUMA GAP	2017	SOUTH COAST	1985
CARNEROS (LOS CARNEROS)	1983	KELSEY BENCH-LAKE COUNTY	2013	PINE MOUNTAIN-CLOVERDALE PEAK	2011	SPRING MOUNTAIN DISTRICT	1993
CENTRAL COAST	1985	KNIGHTS VALLEY	1983	POTTER VALLEY	1983	SQUAW VALLEY-MIRAMONTE	2015
CHALK HILL	1983	LAMORINDA	2016	RAMONA VALLEY	2005	ST. HELENA	1995
CHALONE	1982	LEONA VALLEY	2008	RED HILLS LAKE COUNTY	2004	STA. RITA HILLS	2001
CHILES VALLEY	1999	LIME KILN VALLEY	1982	REDWOOD VALLEY	1996	STAGS LEAP DISTRICT	1989
CIENEGA VALLEY	1982	LIVERMORE VALLEY	1982	RIVER JUNCTION	2001	SUISUN VALLEY	1982
CLARKSBURG	1984	LODI	1986	ROCKPILE	2002	TEHACHAPI MOUNTAINS	2020
CLEAR LAKE	1984	LOS OLIVOS DISTRICT	2016	RUSSIAN RIVER VALLEY	1983	TEMECULA VALLEY	1984
CLEMENTS HILLS	2006	MADERA	1984	RUTHERFORD	1993	TEMPLETON GAP DISTRICT	2014
COLE RANCH	1983	MALIBU COAST	2014	SADDLE ROCK-MALIBU	2006	TRACY HILLS	2006
COOMBSVILLE	2011	MALIBU-NEWTON CANYON	1996	SALADO CREEK	2004	TRINITY LAKES	2005
COSUMNES RIVER	2006	MANTON VALLEY	2014	SAN ANTONIO VALLEY	2006	WILD HORSE VALLEY	1988
COVELO	2006	McDOWELL VALLEY	1981	SAN BENITO	1987	WILLOW CREEK	1983
CRESTON DISTRICT	2014	MENDOCINO	1984	SAN BERNABE	2004	YORK MOUNTAIN	1983
CUCAMONGA VALLEY	1995	MENDOCINO RIDGE	1997	SAN FRANCISCO BAY	1999	YORKVILLE HIGHLANDS	1998
DIABLO GRANDE	1998	MERRITT ISLAND	1987	SAN JUAN CREEK	2014	YOUNTVILLE	1998
DIAMOND MOUNTAIN DISTRICT	2001	MOKELUMNE RIVER	2006	SAN LUCAS	1987		
Colorado [2]							
GRAND VALLEY	1991	WEST ELKS	2001				
Connecticut [3 out of 1 shared]							
EASTERN CONNECTICUT HIGHLANDS	2019	SOUTHEASTERN NEW ENGLAND [shared with Rhode Island and Massachusetts]	1984			WESTERN CONNECTICUT HIGHLANDS	1988
Georgia [2 out of 1 shared]							
DAHLONEGA PLATEAU	2018	UPPER HIWASSEE HIGHLANDS [shared with North Carolina]	2014				
Hawaii [1]		**Idaho [3 out of 2 shared]**					
ULUPALAKUA [not mapped]	2021	EAGLE FOOTHILLS	2015	LEWIS-CLARK VALLEY [shared with Washington]	2016	SNAKE RIVER VALLEY [shared with Oregon]	2007
Illinois [2 out of 1 shared]				**Indiana [2 out of 1 shared]**			
UPPER MISSISSIPPI RIVER VALLEY [shared with Iowa, Minnesota and Wisconsin]	2009	SHAWNEE HILLS	2006	INDIANA UPLANDS	2013	OHIO RIVER VALLEY [shared with Kentucky, Ohio and West Virginia]	1983
Iowa [2 shared]				**Kentucky [1 shared]**			
LOESS HILLS DISTRICT [shared with Missouri]	2016	UPPER MISSISSIPPI RIVER VALLEY [shared with Illinois, Minnesota and Wisconsin]	2009	OHIO RIVER VALLEY [shared with Indiana, Ohio and West Virginia]	1983		
Maryland [3 out of 1 shared]							
CATOCTIN	1983	CUMBERLAND VALLEY [shared with Pennsylvania]	1985	LINGANORE	1983		
Massachusetts [2 out of 1 shared]							
MARTHA'S VINEYARD	1985	SOUTHEASTERN NEW ENGLAND [shared with Connecticut and Rhode Island]	1984				

Michigan [5]

FENNVILLE	1981	LEELANAU PENINSULA	1982	OLD MISSION PENINSULA	1987	TIP OF THE MITT	2016
LAKE MICHIGAN SHORE	1983						

Minnesota [2 out of 1 shared] Mississippi [1]

ALEXANDRIA LAKES	2005	UPPER MISSISSIPPI RIVER VALLEY [shared with Illinois, Iowa and Wisconsin]	2009	MISSISSIPPI DELTA	1984

Missouri [5 out of 2 shared]

AUGUSTA	1980	LOESS HILLS DISTRICT [shared with Iowa]	2016	OZARK HIGHLANDS	1987	OZARK MOUNTAIN [shared with Arkansas and Oklahoma]	1986
HERMANN	1983						

New Jersey [4 out of 1 shared]

CAPE MAY PENINSULA	2018	CENTRAL DELAWARE VALLEY [shared with Pennsylvania]	1984	OUTER COASTAL PLAIN	2007	WARREN HILLS	1988

New Mexico [3 out of 1 shared]

MESILLA VALLEY [shared with Texas]	1985	MIDDLE RIO GRANDE VALLEY	1988	MIMBRES VALLEY	1985

New York [11 out of 1 shared]

CAYUGA LAKE	1988	HUDSON RIVER REGION	1982	NIAGARA ESCARPMENT	2005	THE HAMPTONS, Long Island	1985
CHAMPLAIN VALLEY OF NEW YORK	2016	LAKE ERIE [shared with Pennsylvania and Ohio]	1983	NORTH FORK OF LONG ISLAND	1986	UPPER HUDSON	2019
FINGER LAKES	1982	LONG ISLAND	2001	SENECA LAKE	1988		

North Carolina [6 out of 2 shared]

APPALACHIAN HIGH COUNTRY [shared with Tennessee and Virginia]	2016	HAW RIVER VALLEY	2009	UPPER HIWASSEE HIGHLANDS [shared with Georgia]	2014	YADKIN VALLEY	2002
CREST OF THE BLUE RIDGE HENDERSON COUNTY	2019	SWAN CREEK	2008				

Ohio [5 out of 2 shared]

GRAND RIVER VALLEY	1983	LAKE ERIE [shared with New York and Pennsylvania]	1983	LORAMIE CREEK	1982	OHIO RIVER VALLEY [shared with Indiana, Kentucky and West Virginia]	1983
ISLE ST. GEORGE	1982						

Oklahoma [1 shared]

OZARK MOUNTAIN [shared with Arkansas and Missouri]	1986

Oregon [23 out of 4 shared]

APPLEGATE VALLEY	2000	EOLA-AMITY HILLS	2006	RIBBON RIDGE	2005	UMPQUA VALLEY	1984
CHEHALEM MOUNTAINS	2006	LAURELWOOD DISTRICT	2020	ROGUE VALLEY	1991	VAN DUZER CORRIDOR	2019
COLUMBIA GORGE [shared with Washington]	2004	LOWER LONG TOM	2021	SNAKE RIVER VALLEY [shared with Idaho]	2007	WALLA WALLA VALLEY [shared with Washington]	1984
COLUMBIA VALLEY [shared with Washington]	1984	McMINNVILLE	2005	SOUTHERN OREGON	2004	WILLAMETTE VALLEY	1983
DUNDEE HILLS	2004	MT. PISGAH POLK COUNTY OREGON	2022	THE ROCKS DISTRICT OF MILTON-FREEWATER	2015	YAMHILL-CARLTON	2004
ELKTON OREGON	2013	RED HILL DOUGLAS COUNTY	2005	TUALATIN HILLS	2020		

Pennsylvania [5 out of 3 shared]

CENTRAL DELAWARE VALLEY [shared with New Jersey]	1984	LANCASTER VALLEY	1982	LAKE ERIE [shared with New York and Ohio]	1983	LEHIGH VALLEY	2008
CUMBERLAND VALLEY [shared with Maryland]	1985						

Rhode Island [1 shared] Tennessee [1 shared]

SOUTHEASTERN NEW ENGLAND [shared with Connecticut and Massachusetts]	1984	APPALACHIAN HIGH COUNTRY [shared with North Carolina and Virginia]	2016

Texas [8 out of 1 shared]

BELL MOUNTAIN	1986	FREDERICKSBURG in the Texas Hill Country	1988	TEXAS DAVIS MOUNTAINS	1998	TEXAS HILL COUNTY	1991
ESCONDIDO VALLEY	1992	MESILLA VALLEY [shared with New Mexico]	1985	TEXAS HIGH PLAINS	1993	TEXOMA	2005

Virginia [9 out of 1 shared]

APPALACHIAN HIGH COUNTRY [shared with North Carolina and Tennessee]	2016	NORTH FORK OF ROANOKE	1983	ROCKY KNOB	1983	VIRGINIA'S EASTERN SHORE	1991
MIDDLEBURG VIRGINIA	2012	NORTHERN NECK GEORGE WASHINGTON BIRTHPLACE	1987	SHENANDOAH VALLEY [shared with West Virginia]	1982	VIRGINIA PENINSULA	2021
MONTICELLO	1984						

Washington [19 out of 4 shared]

ANCIENT LAKES OF COLUMBIA VALLEY	2012	HORSE HEAVEN HILLS	2005	RATTLESNAKE HILLS	2006	WAHLUKE SLOPE	2006
CANDY MOUNTAIN	2020	LAKE CHELAN	2009	RED MOUNTAIN	2001	WALLA WALLA VALLEY [shared with Oregon]	1984
COLUMBIA GORGE [shared with Oregon]	2004	LEWIS-CLARK VALLEY [shared with Idaho]	2016	ROYAL SLOPE	2020	WHITE BLUFFS	2021
COLUMBIA VALLEY [shared with Oregon]	1984	NACHES HEIGHTS	2011	SNIPES MOUNTAIN	2009	YAKIMA VALLEY	1983
GOOSE GAP	2021	PUGET SOUND	1995	THE BURN OF COLUMBIA VALLEY	2021		

West Virginia [3 out of 2 shared]

KANAWHA RIVER VALLEY	1986	OHIO RIVER VALLEY [shared with Indiana, Kentucky and Ohio]	1983	SHENANDOAH VALLEY [shared with Virginia]	1982

Wisconsin [3 out of 1 shared]

LAKE WISCONSIN	1994	UPPER MISSISSIPPI RIVER VALLEY [shared with Illinois, Minnesota and Iowa]	2009	WISCONSIN LEDGE	2012

STATES OF USA [50]

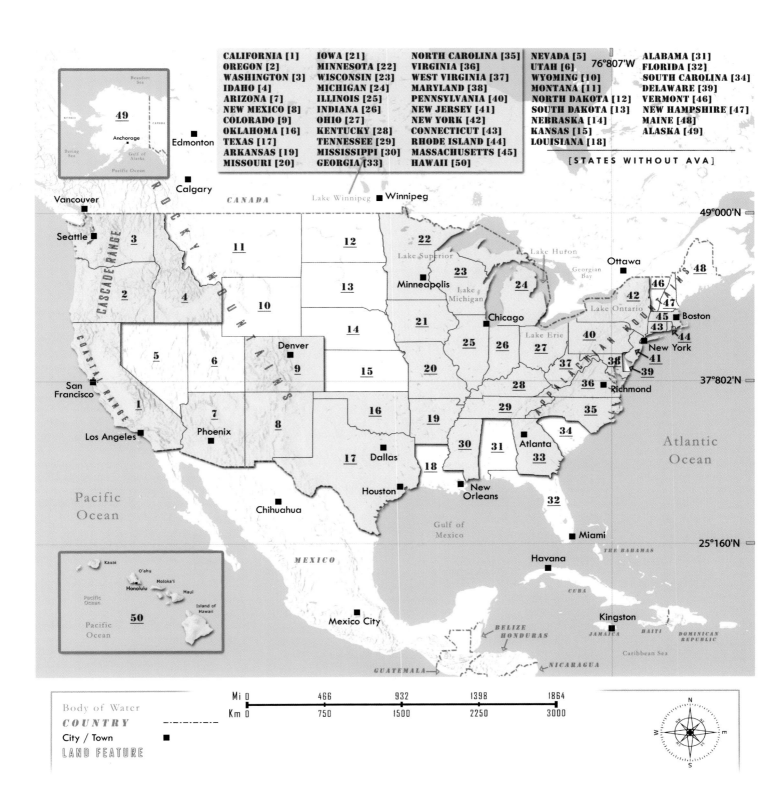

CALIFORNIA [1]	IOWA [21]	NORTH CAROLINA [35]	NEVADA [5]	ALABAMA [31]
OREGON [2]	MINNESOTA [22]	VIRGINIA [36]	UTAH [6]	FLORIDA [32]
WASHINGTON [3]	WISCONSIN [23]	WEST VIRGINIA [37]	WYOMING [10]	SOUTH CAROLINA [34]
IDAHO [4]	MICHIGAN [24]	MARYLAND [38]	MONTANA [11]	DELAWARE [39]
ARIZONA [7]	ILLINOIS [25]	PENNSYLVANIA [40]	NORTH DAKOTA [12]	VERMONT [46]
NEW MEXICO [8]	INDIANA [26]	NEW JERSEY [41]	SOUTH DAKOTA [13]	NEW HAMPSHIRE [47]
COLORADO [9]	OHIO [27]	NEW YORK [42]	NEBRASKA [14]	MAINE [48]
OKLAHOMA [16]	KENTUCKY [28]	CONNECTICUT [43]	KANSAS [15]	ALASKA [49]
TEXAS [17]	TENNESSEE [29]	RHODE ISLAND [44]	LOUISIANA [18]	
ARKANSAS [19]	MISSISSIPPI [30]	MASSACHUSETTS [45]		
MISSOURI [20]	GEORGIA [33]	HAWAII [50]		

76°807'W

[STATES WITHOUT AVA]

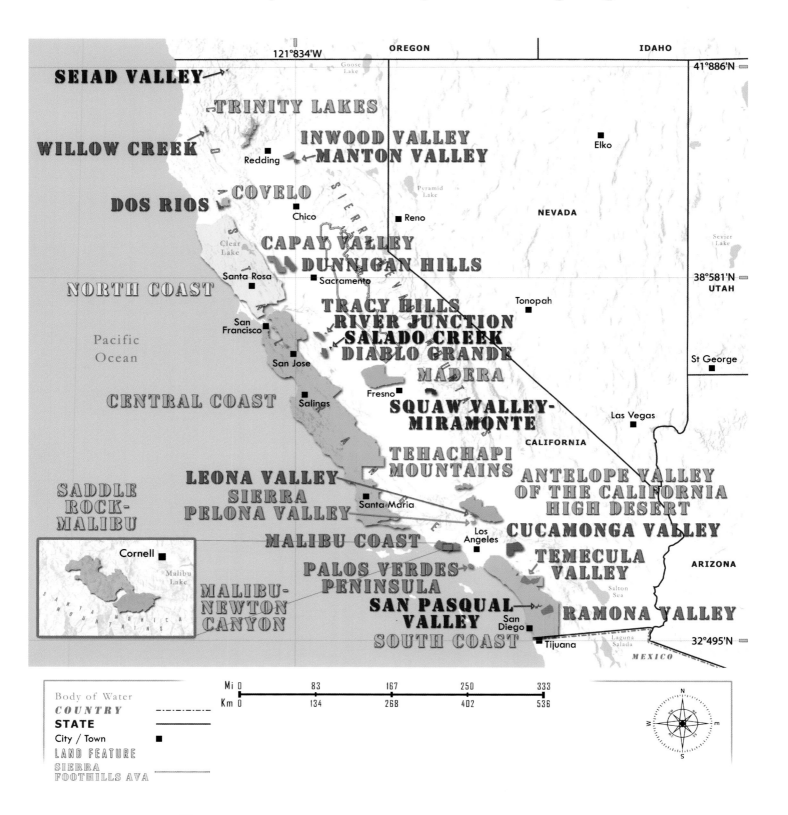

CALIFORNIA
TOTAL AVA [143]
NORTH, CENTRAL, SOUTH [30]

SEIAD VALLEY

TRINITY LAKES

WILLOW CREEK

INWOOD VALLEY
MANTON VALLEY

COVELO

DOS RIOS

CAPAY VALLEY
DUNNIGAN HILLS

NORTH COAST

TRACY HILLS
RIVER JUNCTION
SALADO CREEK
DIABLO GRANDE
MADERA

CENTRAL COAST

SQUAW VALLEY-
MIRAMONTE

SADDLE
ROCK-
MALIBU

TEHACHAPI
MOUNTAINS

ANTELOPE VALLEY
OF THE CALIFORNIA
HIGH DESERT

LEONA VALLEY
SIERRA
PELONA VALLEY

CUCAMONGA VALLEY

MALIBU COAST

TEMECULA
VALLEY

PALOS VERDES
PENINSULA

MALIBU-
NEWTON
CANYON

SAN PASQUAL
VALLEY

RAMONA VALLEY

SOUTH COAST

OREGON

IDAHO

Redding

Elko

Chico

Reno

NEVADA

Clear
Lake

Santa Rosa

Sacramento

Tonopah

UTAH

San
Francisco

San Jose

St George

Salinas

Fresno

Las Vegas

CALIFORNIA

Santa Maria

Los
Angeles

ARIZONA

San
Diego

Tijuana

MEXICO

Pacific
Ocean

Goose
Lake

Pyramid
Lake

Sevier
Lake

Salton
Sea

Laguna
Salada

121°834'W

41°886'N

38°581'N

32°495'N

Cornell

Malibu
Lake

SANTA MONICA MOUNTAINS

USA

Body of Water
COUNTRY
STATE
City / Town
LAND FEATURE
SIERRA
FOOTHILLS AVA

Mi 0   83   167   250   333
Km 0   134   268   402   536

NORTH OF THE NORTH COAST AVA [17]

MENDOCINO COUNTY AND LAKE COUNTY

Pine Mountain-Cloverdale Peak AVA is shared with Sonoma county

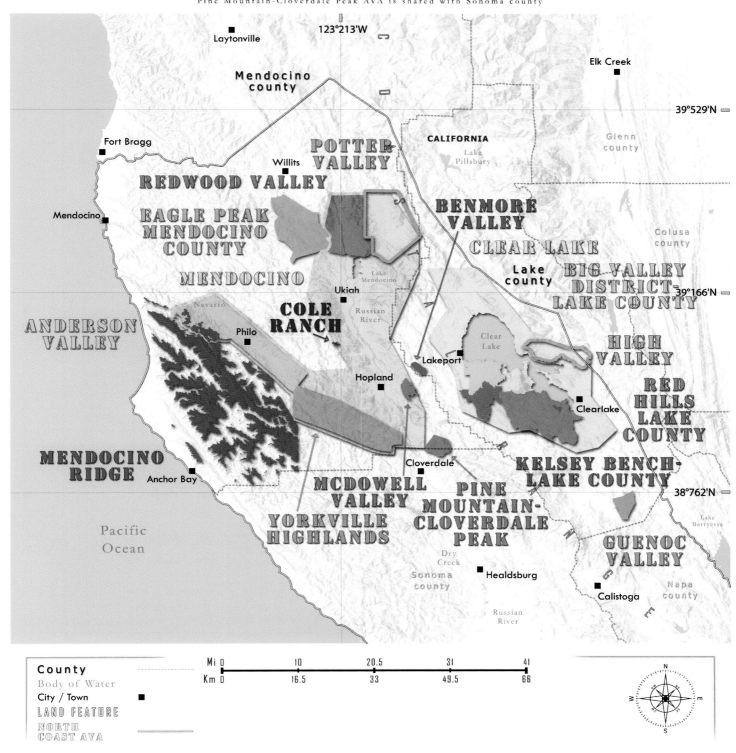

Laytonville

123°213'W

Elk Creek

Mendocino county

CALIFORNIA

39°529'N

Fort Bragg

Lake Pillsbury

Glenn county

POTTER VALLEY

Willits

BENMORE VALLEY

REDWOOD VALLEY

Mendocino

EAGLE PEAK MENDOCINO COUNTY

CLEAR LAKE

Colusa county

BIG VALLEY DISTRICT LAKE COUNTY

MENDOCINO

Lake Mendocino

Lake county

Ukiah

39°166'N

Navarro

ANDERSON VALLEY

COLE RANCH

Russian River

Philo

Clear Lake

HIGH VALLEY

Lakeport

RED HILLS LAKE COUNTY

Hopland

Clearlake

MENDOCINO RIDGE

Anchor Bay

KELSEY BENCH-LAKE COUNTY

Cloverdale

38°762'N

Pacific Ocean

MCDOWELL VALLEY

PINE MOUNTAIN-CLOVERDALE PEAK

Lake Berryessa

YORKVILLE HIGHLANDS

GUENOC VALLEY

Dry Creek

Sonoma county

Healdsburg

Napa county

Calistoga

Russian River

County

Body of Water

City / Town ■

LAND FEATURE

NORTH COAST AVA

Mi 0	10	20.5	31	41
Km 0	16.5	33	49.5	66

CALIFORNIA
TOTAL AVA [143]
SOUTH OF THE NORTH COAST AVA [19]
NAPA COUNTY AND SOLANO COUNTY
Los Carneros AVA is shared with Sonoma county

122°392'W

Cobb

Knoxville

Yolo County

38°755'N

NAPA VALLEY

Napa county

HOWELL MOUNTAIN

Madison

ROCKY RIDGE

CALISTOGA

Pope Valley

CHILES MOUNTAIN

Healdsburg

DIAMOND MOUNTAIN DISTRICT

Napa River

Lake Berryessa

Russian River

ST. HELENA

St Helena

SPRING MOUNTAIN DISTRICT

Lake Hennessey

38°780'N

RUTHERFORD

Dixon

Sonoma county

Santa Rosa

OAKVILLE

ATLAS PEAK

YOUNTVILLE

Solano county

STAGS LEAP DISTRICT

OAK KNOLL DISTRICT OF NAPA VALLEY

Lake Curry

COMBSVILLE

MT. VEEDER

Napa

WILD HORSE VALLEY

LOS CARNEROS

Napa River

SUISUN VALLEY

CALIFORNIA

Petaluma

SOLANO COUNTY GREEN VALLEY

38°192'N

Tomales Bay

Grizzly Bay

Novato

Vallejo

San Pablo Bay

| Mi 0 | 6.5 | 12.9 | 19.4 | 25.8 |
| Km 0 | 10.4 | 20.8 | 31.2 | 41.6 |

County ....

Body of Water

City / Town ■

LAND FEATURE

NORTH COAST AVA

USA

CALIFORNIA
TOTAL AVA [143]

SOUTH OF THE NORTH COAST AVA [18]
SONOMA COUNTY AND MARIN COUNTY
Pine Mountain-Cloverdale Peak AVA is shared with Mendocino county
Los Carneros AVA is shared with Napa county

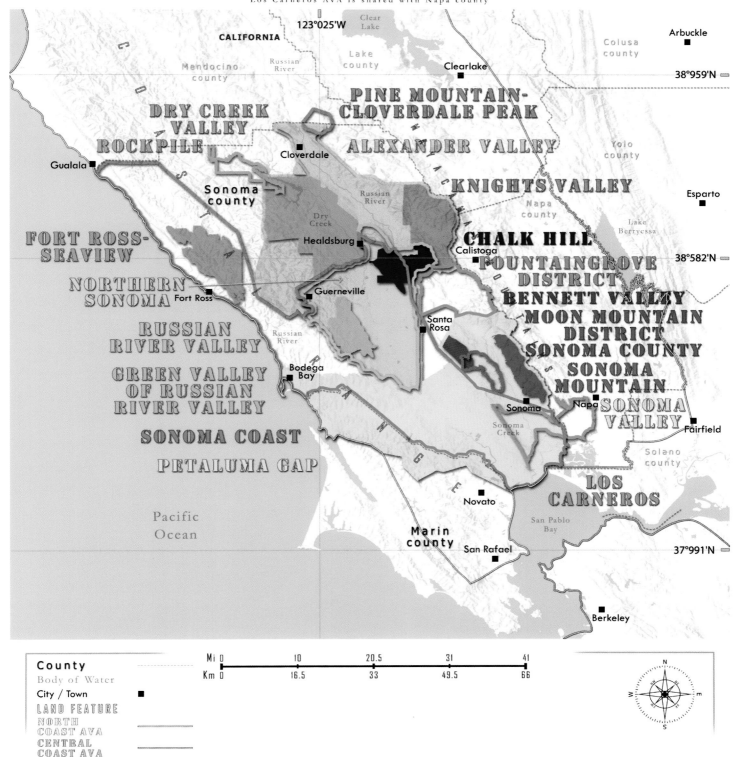

123°025'W
CALIFORNIA
Arbuckle
Colusa county
Clear Lake
Mendocino county
Russian River
Lake county
Clearlake
38°959'N

PINE MOUNTAIN-CLOVERDALE PEAK

DRY CREEK VALLEY
ROCKPILE

Gualala

Sonoma county

Cloverdale

ALEXANDER VALLEY

Russian River

Yolo county

Esparto

KNIGHTS VALLEY

Napa county

Lake Berryessa

Dry Creek

FORT ROSS-SEAVIEW

Healdsburg

CHALK HILL

Calistoga

38°582'N

NORTHERN SONOMA

Fort Ross

Guerneville

FOUNTAINGROVE DISTRICT
BENNETT VALLEY
MOON MOUNTAIN DISTRICT
SONOMA COUNTY
SONOMA MOUNTAIN

RUSSIAN RIVER VALLEY

Santa Rosa

Russian River

GREEN VALLEY OF RUSSIAN RIVER VALLEY

Bodega Bay

SONOMA VALLEY

Sonoma

Napa

Fairfield

SONOMA COAST
PETALUMA GAP

Sonoma Creek

Solano county

LOS CARNEROS

Novato

San Pablo Bay

Pacific Ocean

Marin county

San Rafael

37°991'N

Berkeley

Mi 0   10   20.5   31   41
Km 0   16.5   33   49.5   66

N
W — E
S

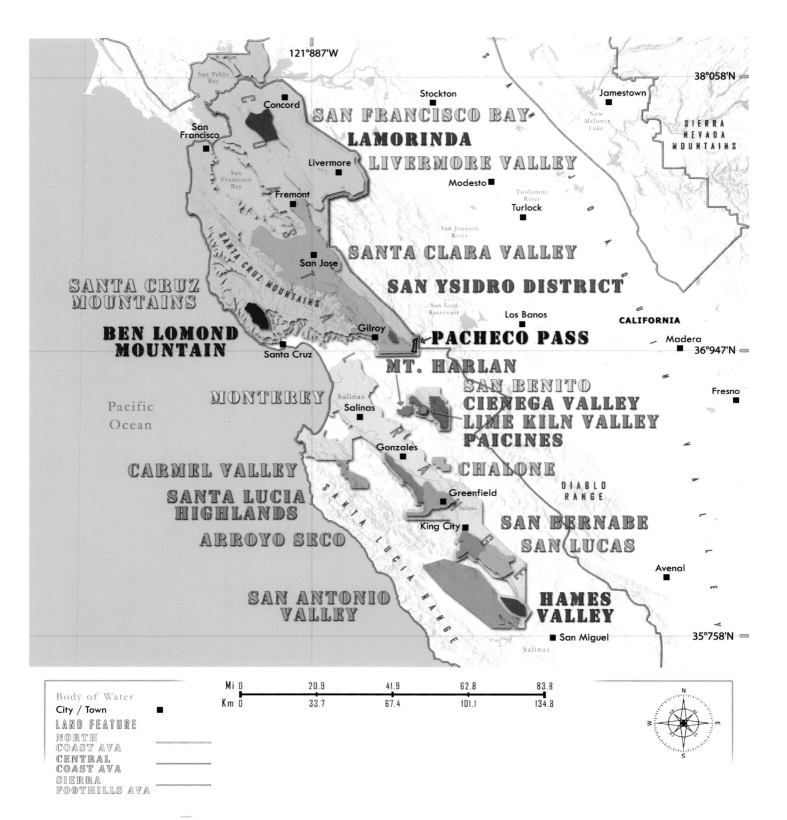

121°887'W

38°058'N

SIERRA
NEVADA
MOUNTAINS

San Pablo Bay

Stockton

Jamestown

New Melones Lake

Concord

San Francisco

SAN FRANCISCO BAY

LAMORINDA

Livermore

LIVERMORE VALLEY

Modesto

Tuolumne River

San Francisco Bay

Fremont

Turlock

San Joaquin River

SANTA CLARA VALLEY

San Jose

SAN YSIDRO DISTRICT

SANTA CRUZ
MOUNTAINS

San Luis Reservoir

Los Banos

CALIFORNIA

Madera

BEN LOMOND
MOUNTAIN

Gilroy

PACHECO PASS

36°947'N

Santa Cruz

MT. HARLAN

Pacific
Ocean

MONTEREY

Salinas

SAN BENITO
CIENEGA VALLEY
LIME KILN VALLEY
PAICINES

Fresno

Salinas

Gonzales

CHALONE

DIABLO
RANGE

CARMEL VALLEY

SANTA LUCIA
HIGHLANDS

Greenfield

Salinas

SAN BERNABE

ARROYO SECO

King City

SAN LUCAS

Avenal

SAN ANTONIO
VALLEY

HAMES
VALLEY

SANTA LUCIA RANGE

San Miguel

35°758'N

Salinas

Mi 0   20.9   41.9   62.8   83.8
Km 0   33.7   67.4   101.1   134.8

USA

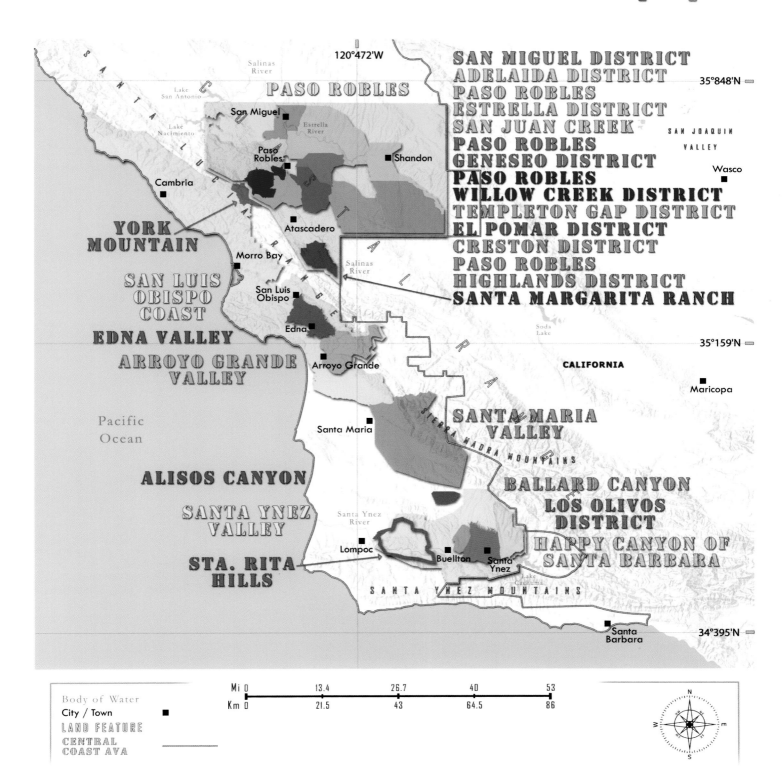

CALIFORNIA
TOTAL AVA [143]
SOUTH OF THE CENTRAL COAST AVA [23]

120°472'W

Salinas River

Lake San Antonio

Lake Nacimiento

PASO ROBLES

San Miguel

Estrella River

Paso Robles

Shandon

35°848'N

SAN MIGUEL DISTRICT
ADELAIDA DISTRICT
PASO ROBLES
ESTRELLA DISTRICT
SAN JUAN CREEK
PASO ROBLES
GENESEO DISTRICT
PASO ROBLES
WILLOW CREEK DISTRICT
TEMPLETON GAP DISTRICT
EL POMAR DISTRICT
CRESTON DISTRICT
PASO ROBLES
HIGHLANDS DISTRICT
SANTA MARGARITA RANCH

SAN JOAQUIN VALLEY

Wasco

Cambria

YORK MOUNTAIN

Atascadero

Salinas River

SAN LUIS OBISPO COAST

Morro Bay

San Luis Obispo

EDNA VALLEY

Edna

Soda Lake

35°159'N

CALIFORNIA

ARROYO GRANDE VALLEY

Arroyo Grande

Pacific Ocean

Maricopa

ALISOS CANYON

Santa Maria

SANTA MARIA VALLEY

SIERRA MADRE MOUNTAINS

SANTA YNEZ VALLEY

Santa Ynez River

BALLARD CANYON
LOS OLIVOS DISTRICT

STA. RITA HILLS

Lompoc

Buellton

Santa Ynez

HAPPY CANYON OF SANTA BARBARA

Lake Cachuma

SANTA YNEZ MOUNTAINS

34°395'N

Santa Barbara

Mi 0   13.4   26.7   40   53
Km 0   21.5   43   64.5   86

Body of Water
City / Town ■
LAND FEATURE
CENTRAL COAST AVA ⎯⎯⎯

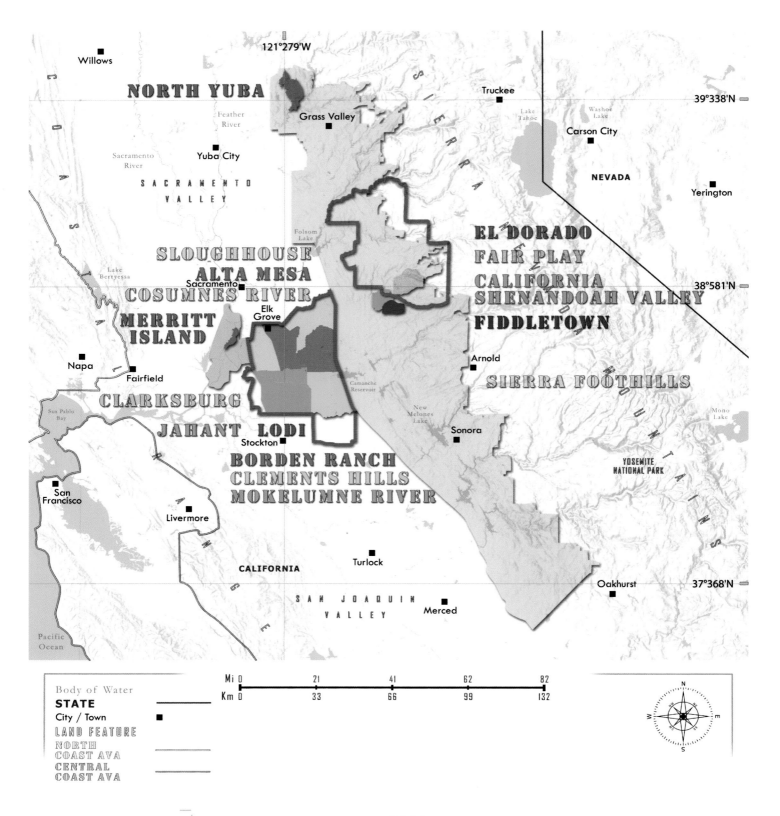

121°279'W

NORTH YUBA

39°338'N

Willows

Truckee

Grass Valley

Lake Tahoe

Washoe Lake

Carson City

Feather River

Yuba City

Sacramento River

NEVADA

Yerington

SACRAMENTO VALLEY

Folsom Lake

SLOUGHHOUSE

EL DORADO

FAIR PLAY

ALTA MESA

CALIFORNIA

COSUMNES RIVER

SHENANDOAH VALLEY

38°581'N

Lake Berryessa

Sacramento

Elk Grove

FIDDLETOWN

MERRITT ISLAND

Napa

Arnold

Fairfield

Camanche Reservoir

SIERRA FOOTHILLS

CLARKSBURG

New Melones Lake

Mono Lake

San Pablo Bay

JAHANT LODI

Stockton

Sonora

BORDEN RANCH

YOSEMITE NATIONAL PARK

San Francisco

CLEMENTS HILLS

MOKELUMNE RIVER

Livermore

CALIFORNIA

Turlock

Oakhurst

37°368'N

SAN JOAQUIN VALLEY

Merced

Pacific Ocean

Mi 0   21   41   62   82
Km 0   33   66   99   132

N

W   E

S

OREGON [23]
IDAHO [3]

123°086'W

WASHINGTON

Yakima

Kennewick

Columbia River

Portland

[SHARED]
LEWIS-CLARK
VALLEY

[SHARED]
WALLA WALLA VALLEY
THE ROCKS DISTRICT OF
MILTON-FREEWATER

45°326'N

MONTANA

COLUMBIA
GORGE
[SHARED]
WILLAMETTE
VALLEY

Salem

COLUMBIA
VALLEY
[SHARED]
SNAKE RIVER
VALLEY
[SHARED]

IDAHO

LOWER LONG TOM

Eugene   Bend   OREGON

EAGLE
FOOTHILLS

Boise

43°614'N

ELKTON OREGON

RED HILL DOUGLAS COUNTY

UMPQUA VALLEY

SOUTHERN
OREGON

Medford

APPLEGATE
VALLEY

Snake
River

Twin Falls

ROGUE
VALLEY

Columbia
River

Forest Grove

Yamhill

McMinnville

Willamette
River

TUALATIN HILLS
YAMHILL-CARLTON
LAURELWOOD DISTRICT
CHEHALEM MOUNTAINS
RIBBON RIDGE
DUNDEE HILLS
MCMINNVILLE
VAN DUZER CORRIDOR
EOLA-AMITY HILLS
MT. PISGAH
POLK COUNTY OREGON

UTAH

Arthur   NEVADA

39°728'N

Redding

CALIFORNIA

Chico

Reno

Mi 0   60   121   181   241
Km 0   97   194   291   388

Body of Water
STATE
City / Town
LAND FEATURE

AVA [15]

Columbia Valley AVA, Columbia Gorge AVA, Walla Walla Valley AVA and
Lewis-Clark Valley AVA are counted on page ....

WASHINGTON [19]

4 SHARED AVA

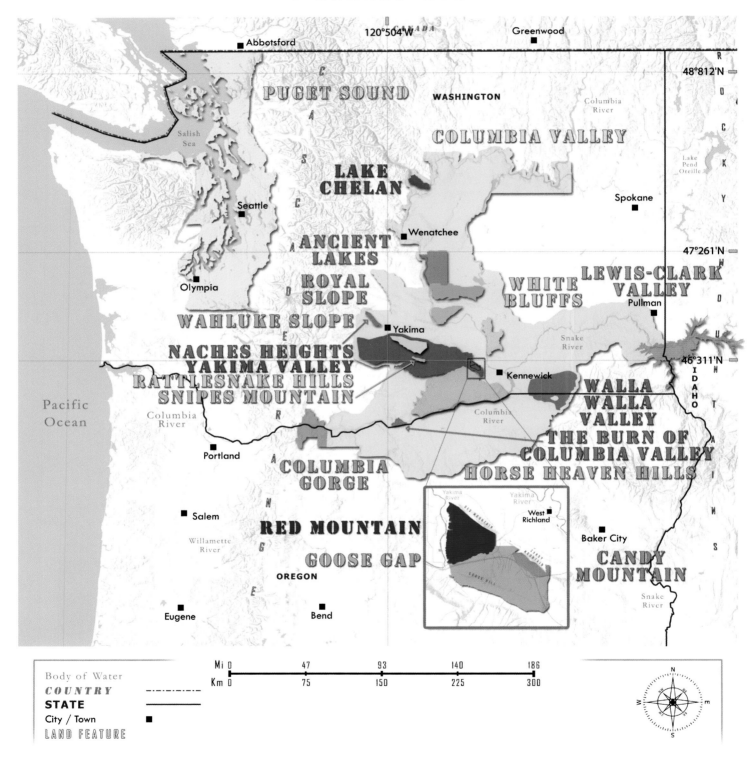

PUGET SOUND

WASHINGTON

COLUMBIA VALLEY

LAKE CHELAN

ANCIENT LAKES

ROYAL SLOPE

WAHLUKE SLOPE

NACHES HEIGHTS

YAKIMA VALLEY

RATTLESNAKE HILLS

SNIPES MOUNTAIN

WHITE BLUFFS

LEWIS-CLARK VALLEY

COLUMBIA GORGE

RED MOUNTAIN

GOOSE GAP

WALLA WALLA VALLEY

THE BURN OF COLUMBIA VALLEY

HORSE HEAVEN HILLS

CANDY MOUNTAIN

OREGON

Pacific Ocean

Salish Sea

Columbia River

Willamette River

Snake River

Lake Pend Oreille

IDAHO

MONTANA

ROCKY

CANADA

120°504'W

48°812'N

47°261'N

46°311'N

Abbotsford
Greenwood
Seattle
Olympia
Wenatchee
Spokane
Yakima
Pullman
Kennewick
Portland
Salem
Baker City
Eugene
Bend
West Richland

Yakima River

RED MOUNTAIN

CANDY MOUNTAIN

GOOSE HILL

Body of Water
COUNTRY
STATE
City / Town
LAND FEATURE

| Mi | 0 | 47 | 93 | 140 | 186 |
| Km | 0 | 75 | 150 | 225 | 300 |

ARIZONA [3] COLORADO [2] NEW MEXICO [3] TEXAS [8]

1 SHARED AVA

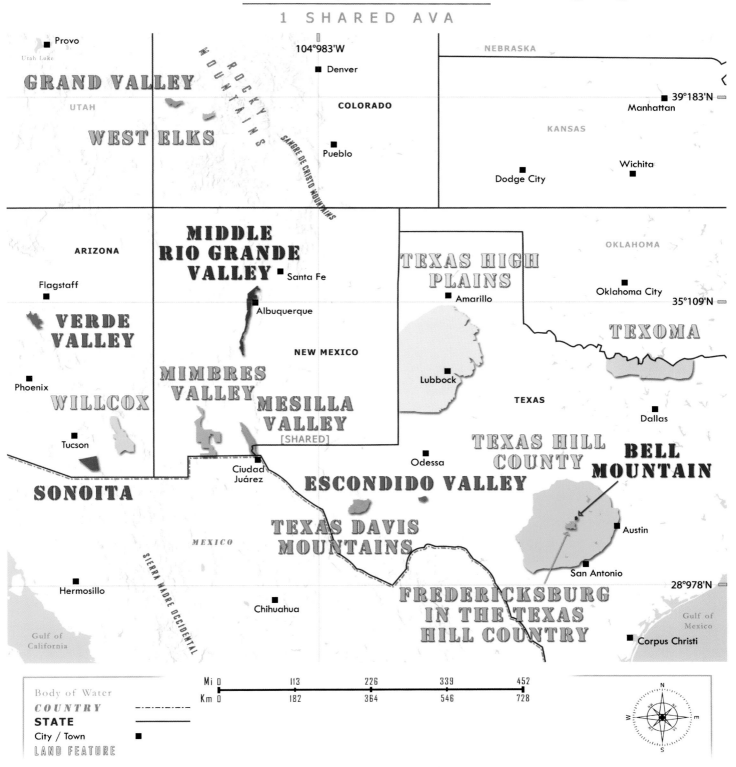

Provo

Utah Lake

GRAND VALLEY

UTAH

WEST ELKS

ROCKY MOUNTAINS

104°983'W

Denver

COLORADO

NEBRASKA

39°183'N
Manhattan

KANSAS

Pueblo

SANGRE DE CRISTO MOUNTAINS

Dodge City

Wichita

ARIZONA

MIDDLE RIO GRANDE VALLEY

Santa Fe

Flagstaff

VERDE VALLEY

Albuquerque

NEW MEXICO

Phoenix

MIMBRES VALLEY

WILLCOX

MESILLA VALLEY
[SHARED]

Tucson

TEXAS HIGH PLAINS

Amarillo

OKLAHOMA

Oklahoma City

35°109'N

TEXOMA

Lubbock

TEXAS

Dallas

Odessa

SONOITA

Ciudad Juárez

ESCONDIDO VALLEY

TEXAS HILL COUNTY

BELL MOUNTAIN

MEXICO

TEXAS DAVIS MOUNTAINS

Austin

San Antonio

28°978'N

Hermosillo

Chihuahua

FREDERICKSBURG IN THE TEXAS HILL COUNTRY

SIERRA MADRE OCCIDENTAL

Gulf of California

Gulf of Mexico

Corpus Christi

| Mi 0 | 113 | 226 | 339 | 452 |
| Km 0 | 182 | 364 | 546 | 728 |

Body of Water
COUNTRY
STATE
City / Town
LAND FEATURE

N
W E
S

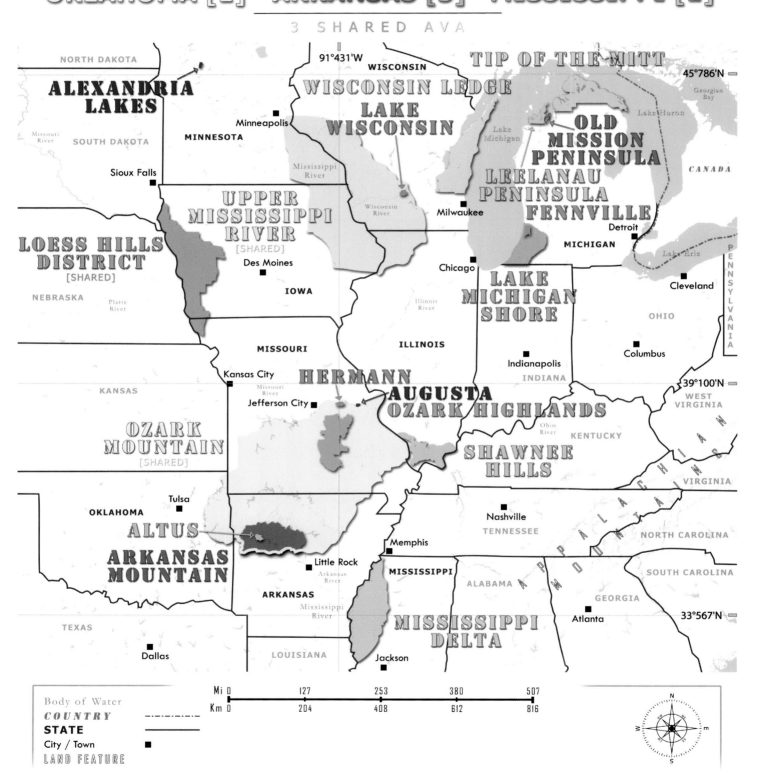

AVA [18]

MINNESOTA [2]   WISCONSIN [3]   MICHIGAN [5]
IOWA [2]   ILLINOIS [2]   MISSOURI [5]
OKLAHOMA [1]   ARKANSAS [3]   MISSISSIPPI [1]

3 SHARED AVA

NORTH DAKOTA

91°431'W

WISCONSIN

TIP OF THE MITT

45°786'N

ALEXANDRIA LAKES

WISCONSIN LEDGE

Georgian Bay

Lake Huron

MINNESOTA

Minneapolis

LAKE WISCONSIN

Lake Michigan

OLD MISSION PENINSULA

SOUTH DAKOTA

Missouri River

CANADA

Sioux Falls

Mississippi River

LEELANAU PENINSULA FENNVILLE

UPPER MISSISSIPPI RIVER
[SHARED]

Wisconsin River

Milwaukee

Detroit

LOESS HILLS DISTRICT
[SHARED]

Des Moines

MICHIGAN

NEBRASKA

Platte River

IOWA

Chicago

LAKE MICHIGAN SHORE

Lake Erie

Cleveland

PENNSYLVANIA

Illinois River

OHIO

MISSOURI

ILLINOIS

Columbus

Kansas City

HERMANN

Indianapolis

INDIANA

39°100'N

KANSAS

Missouri River

AUGUSTA

WEST VIRGINIA

Jefferson City

OZARK HIGHLANDS

OZARK MOUNTAIN
[SHARED]

KENTUCKY

Ohio River

SHAWNEE HILLS

VIRGINIA

Tulsa

OKLAHOMA

Nashville

APPALACHIANS

NORTH CAROLINA

ALTUS

TENNESSEE

Memphis

ARKANSAS MOUNTAIN

Little Rock

Arkansas River

MISSISSIPPI

SOUTH CAROLINA

ARKANSAS

Mississippi River

ALABAMA

GEORGIA

Atlanta

33°567'N

TEXAS

MISSISSIPPI DELTA

LOUISIANA

Jackson

Dallas

Body of Water
COUNTRY -·-·-·-
STATE ———
City / Town ■
LAND FEATURE

| Mi 0 | 127 | 253 | 380 | 507 |
| Km 0 | 204 | 408 | 612 | 816 |

N
W — E
S

AVA [22]

INDIANA [2]   OHIO [5]   WEST VIRGINIA [3]
KENTUCKY [1]   VIRGINIA [9]   TENNESSEE [1]
NORTH CAROLINA [6]   GEORGIA [2]

4 SHARED AVA

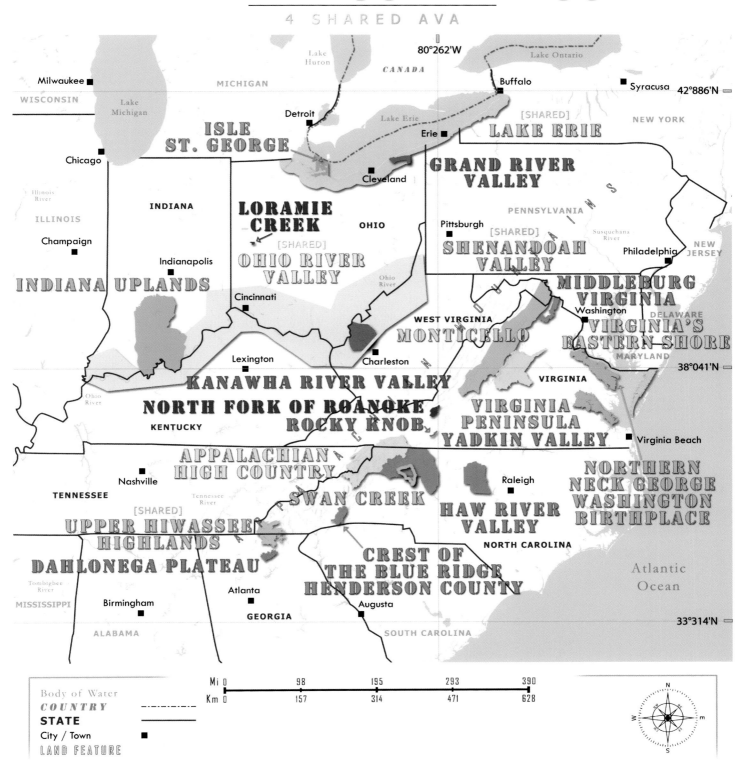

USA

NEW YORK [11]   MASSACHUSETTS [2]
RHODE ISLAND [1]   CONNECTICUT [3]
NEW JERSEY [4] PENNSYLVANIA [5] MARYLAND [3]

4 SHARED AVA

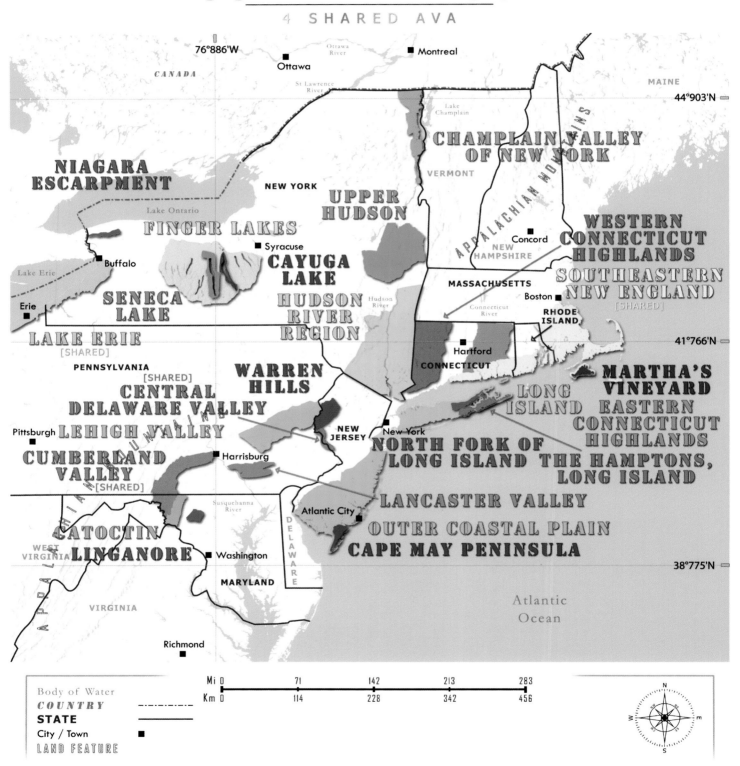

CLASSIFICATION SYSTEM
DO [Denomination of Origin]
3 Area denominations: Costa, Entre Cordilleras, Andes

35 DO
6 Regions
17 Sub-Regions
8 Zones
4 Areas

CHILE

REGION / SUB-REGION	ZONE	AREA
A t a c a m a [2]		
COPIAPÓ VALLEY		
HUASCO VALLEY		
C o q u i m b o [3]		
ELQUI VALLEY		
LIMARÍ VALLEY		
CHOAPA VALLEY		
A c o n c a g u a [3]		
ACONCAGUA VALLEY		
CASABLANCA VALLEY		
SAN ANTONIO VALLEY	Leyda Valley	Lo Abarca DO [Costa]
C e n t r a l V a l l e y [4]		
MAIPO VALLEY		
RAPEL VALLEY	Cachapoal Valley Colchagua Valley	Apalta DO [Entre Cordilleras] [within Colchagua Valley] Los Lingues DO [Andes] [within Colchagua Valley]
CURICÓ VALLEY	Lontué Valley Teno Valley	Licantén DO [Costa] [within Teno Valley]
MAULE VALLEY	Claro Valley Loncomilla Valley Tutuvén Valley	
S u r [3]		
ITATA VALLEY		
BÍO BÍO VALLEY		
MALLECO VALLEY		
A u s t r a l [2]		
CAUTÍN VALLEY		
OSORNO VALLEY		

Chile

REGIONS OF CHILE [6]
SUB-REGION [17]
Zone [8]

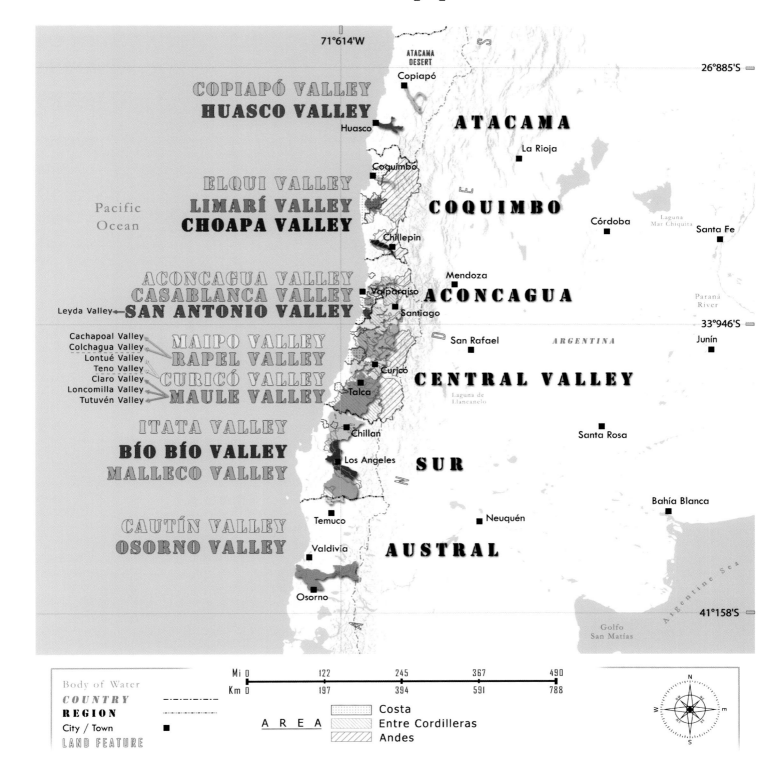

REGIONS OF CHILE [6]
SUB-REGION [17]
Zone [8]

71°614'W

ATACAMA DESERT

26°885'S

COPIAPÓ VALLEY
HUASCO VALLEY

Copiapó

ATACAMA

Huasco

La Rioja

Coquimbo

ELQUI VALLEY
LIMARÍ VALLEY
CHOAPA VALLEY

Pacific
Ocean

COQUIMBO

Córdoba

Laguna
Mar Chiquita

Santa Fe

Chillepin

ACONCAGUA VALLEY
CASABLANCA VALLEY
SAN ANTONIO VALLEY

Leyda Valley

Valparaíso

Mendoza

ACONCAGUA

Paraná
River

Santiago

33°946'S

Cachapoal Valley
Colchagua Valley
Lontué Valley
Teno Valley
Claro Valley
Loncomilla Valley
Tutuvén Valley

MAIPO VALLEY
RAPEL VALLEY
CURICÓ VALLEY
MAULE VALLEY

San Rafael

ARGENTINA

Junín

Curicó

Talca

CENTRAL VALLEY

Laguna de
Llancanelo

ITATA VALLEY
BÍO BÍO VALLEY
MALLECO VALLEY

Chillán

Santa Rosa

Los Angeles

SUR

Bahía Blanca

CAUTÍN VALLEY
OSORNO VALLEY

Temuco

Neuquén

Valdivia

AUSTRAL

Argentine Sea

Osorno

41°158'S

Golfo
San Matías

Body of Water
COUNTRY
REGION
City / Town
LAND FEATURE

Mi 0   122   245   367   490
Km 0   197   394   591   788

A R E A
Costa
Entre Cordilleras
Andes

CLASSIFICATION SYSTEM

DOC [Denominación de Origen Controlada = Controlled Designation of Origin]
- it identifies an IG unique to their place

IG [Indicación Geográfica = Geographical Indication]
- it identifies a product from region, village, or geographical entity

IP [Indicación de Procedencia = Indication of Provenance]
- used for table or regional wines

103 TOTAL IG

5 Regions out of 2 IG

14 Provinces out of 11 IG

2 DOC

64 Departments

24 Districts

Not every region and province are recognized as IG.

ARGENTINA

REGION / PROVINCE	DEPARTMENT	DISTRICT	ELEVATION
The North [not an IG] [15]			
JUJUY	Quebrada de Humahuaca		1,250-3329m
SALTA	Cachi Cafayate - Valle de Cafayate Molinos San Carlos		1,280-3,110m
TUCUMÁN	Tafí		1,675-2,230m
CATAMARCA	Belén Pomán Santa María Tinogasta		750-2,300m
SALTA, TUCUMÁN, CATAMARCA	Valles Calchaquíes - Valle Calchaquí		
Cuyo [70]			
LA RIOJA ARGENTINA	Arauco Castro Barros Chilecito Famatina Felipe Varela General Lamadrid San Blas de los Sauces Sanagasta Valles del Famatina Vinchina	Valle de Chañarmuyo [within Famatina]	770-1,850m
SAN JUAN	25 de Mayo 9 de Julio Albardón Angaco Calingasta - Valle de Calingasta Caucete Chimbas Iglesia Jáchal Pocito Rawson Rivadavia San Martín Santa Lucía Sarmiento Ullum Valle del Tulum Valle Fértil Zonda	Barreal [within Calingasta] Pozo de los Algarrobos [within Caucete] Valle de Zonda [within Zonda] Valle del Pedernal [within Sarmiento]	580-2,000m
MENDOZA 1. Primera Zone [not an IG] 2. North [not an IG] 3. East [not an IG] 4. Valle de Uco 5. South [not an IG]	1.1. Luján de Cuyo DOC 1.2. Maipú 1.3. Godoy Cruz 2.1. Guaymallén 2.2. Las Heras 2.3. Lavalle - Desierto de Lavalle 3.1. Rivadavia 3.2. Junín 3.3. San Martín 3.4. Santa Rosa 3.5. La Paz 4.1. Tupungato - Valle de Tupungato 4.2. Tunuyán 4.3. San Carlos 5.1. San Rafael DOC 5.2. General Alvear	1.1.1. Agrelo 1.1.2. Las Compuertas 1.2.1. Barrancas 1.2.2. Lunlunta 1.2.3. El Paraíso 1.2.4. Russel 2.2.1. Canota - Valle de Canota 3.1.1. Distrito Medrano [within Rivadavia and Junín] 4.2.1. San Pablo 4.2.2. Los Chacayes 4.2.3. Vista Flores 4.3.1. La Consulta 4.3.2. Paraje Altamira 4.3.3. Pampa el Cepillo	430-1600m
SAN LUIS			
Center [not an IG] [5]			
CÓRDOBA ARGENTINA	Colón Cruz del Eje San Javier	Colonia Caroya [within Colón]	
Patagonia [11]			
LA PAMPA [not an IG]			300-370m
NEUQUÉN	Añelo Confluencia		270-425m
RÍO NEGRO	Avellaneda General Conesa General Roca Pichimahuida	Alto Valle de Río Negro [within General Roca]	4-370m
CHUBUT [not an IG]		Trevelin [within the Futaleufú departement]	10-670m
Atlantic Region [not an IG] [2]			
BUENOS AIRES [not an IG]		Chapadmalal Villa Ventana	25-500m

REGIONS OF ARGENTINA [5]
PROVINCE [14]

The territories marked with # are not recognized as Geographical Indication [IG].

#THE NORTH
JUJUY
SALTA
CATAMARCA
TUCUMÁN

CUYO
LA RIOJA ARGENTINA
SAN JUAN
MENDOZA
SAN LUIS

PATAGONIA
NEUQUÉN
#LA PAMPA
RÍO NEGRO
#CHUBUT

#CENTER
CÓRDOBA ARGENTINA

#ATLANTIC REGION
#BUENOS AIRES

	Mi 0	199	398	597	795
	Km 0	320	640	960	1280

Body of Water
COUNTRY
REGION
City / Town
LAND FEATURE

THE NORTH
DEPARTMENT [11]

Jujuy [1 (multi-department)] - Salta [4] - Tucumán [1] - Catamarca [4]
Multi-Province [1 (shared with Salta-Catamarca-Tucumán)]

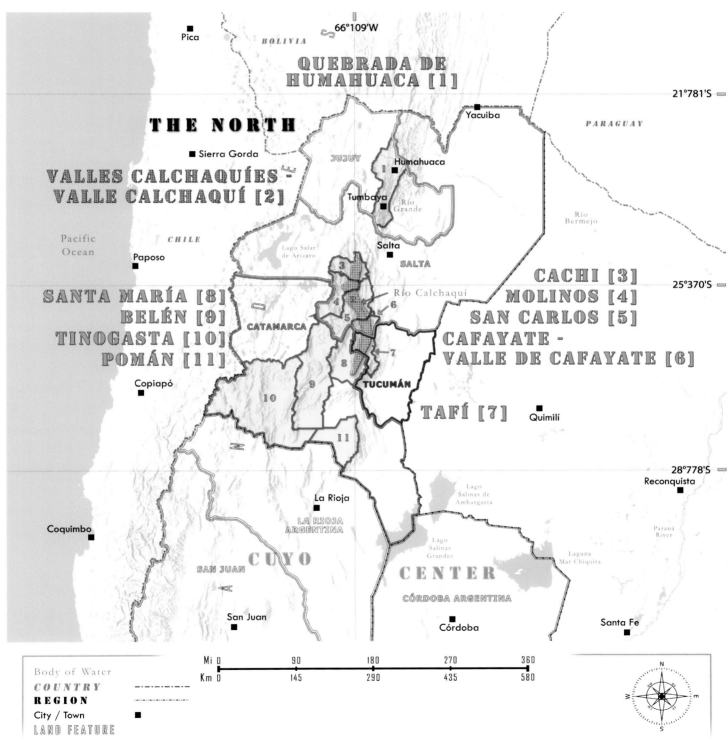

LA RIOJA ARGENTINA & SAN JUAN

DEPARTMENT [29]
District [5]

La Rioja Argentina [9 department - 1 multi-department ███████ - 1 district]
San Juan [18 department - 1 multi-department ░░░░░░ - 4 district]

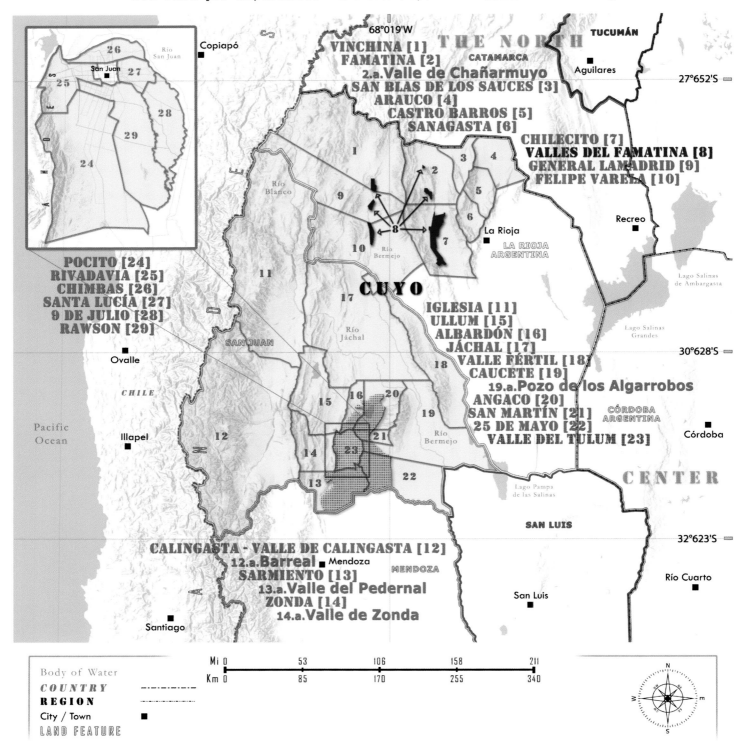

VINCHINA [1]
FAMATINA [2]
  2.a.Valle de Chañarmuyo
SAN BLAS DE LOS SAUCES [3]
ARAUCO [4]
CASTRO BARROS [5]
SANAGASTA [6]

CHILECITO [7]
VALLES DEL FAMATINA [8]
GENERAL LAMADRID [9]
FELIPE VARELA [10]

POCITO [24]
RIVADAVIA [25]
CHIMBAS [26]
SANTA LUCÍA [27]
9 DE JULIO [28]
RAWSON [29]

CUYO

IGLESIA [11]
ULLUM [15]
ALBARDÓN [16]
JÁCHAL [17]
VALLE FÉRTIL [18]
CAUCETE [19]
  19.a.Pozo de los Algarrobos
ANGACO [20]
SAN MARTÍN [21]
25 DE MAYO [22]
VALLE DEL TULUM [23]

CALINGASTA - VALLE DE CALINGASTA [12]
  12.a.Barreal
SARMIENTO [13]
  13.a.Valle del Pedernal
ZONDA [14]
  14.a.Valle de Zonda

THE NORTH
TUCUMÁN
CATAMARCA
CÓRDOBA ARGENTINA
CENTER
SAN LUIS
MENDOZA
CHILE
Pacific Ocean

Body of Water
COUNTRY
REGION
City / Town
LAND FEATURE

| Mi 0 | 53 | 106 | 158 | 211 |
| Km 0 | 85 | 170 | 255 | 340 |

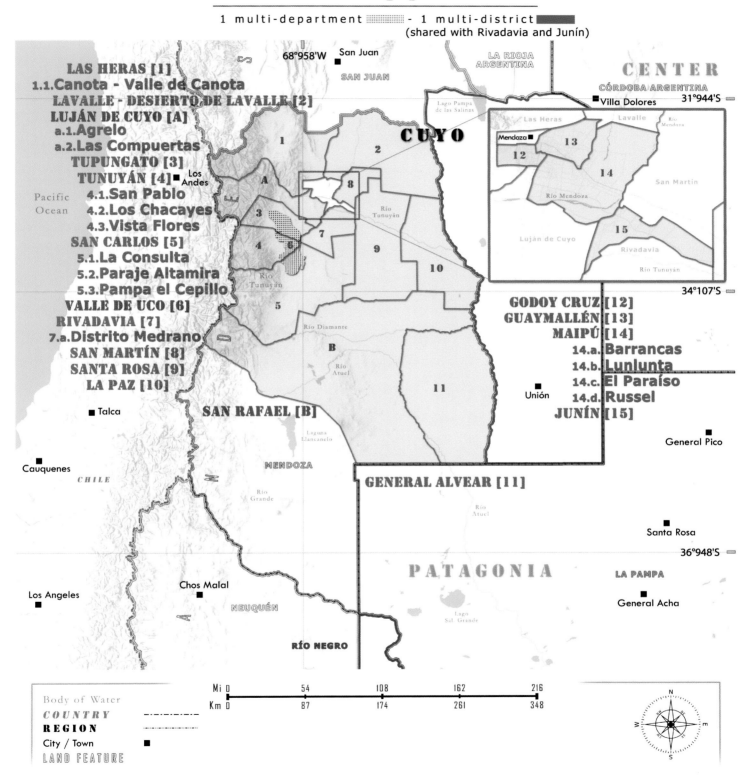

MENDOZA
DEPARTMENT [15]
District [14]
DOC [2]

1 multi-department ▒▒▒▒ - 1 multi-district ▬▬
(shared with Rivadavia and Junín)

LAS HERAS [1]
1.1.**Canota - Valle de Canota**
LAVALLE - DESIERTO DE LAVALLE [2]
LUJÁN DE CUYO [A]
a.1.**Agrelo**
a.2.**Las Compuertas**
TUPUNGATO [3]
TUNUYÁN [4]
4.1.**San Pablo**
4.2.**Los Chacayes**
4.3.**Vista Flores**
SAN CARLOS [5]
5.1.**La Consulta**
5.2.**Paraje Altamira**
5.3.**Pampa el Cepillo**
VALLE DE UCO [6]
RIVADAVIA [7]
7.a.**Distrito Medrano**
SAN MARTÍN [8]
SANTA ROSA [9]
LA PAZ [10]

GODOY CRUZ [12]
GUAYMALLÉN [13]
MAIPÚ [14]
14.a. **Barrancas**
14.b. **Lunlunta**
14.c. **El Paraíso**
14.d. **Russel**
JUNÍN [15]

SAN RAFAEL [B]

GENERAL ALVEAR [11]

Pacific Ocean

CENTER
CÓRDOBA ARGENTINA

CUYO

LA RIOJA ARGENTINA

SAN JUAN

PATAGONIA

LA PAMPA

CHILE

MENDOZA

NEUQUÉN

RÍO NEGRO

68°958'W
31°944'S
34°107'S
36°948'S

Body of Water
COUNTRY
REGION
City / Town
LAND FEATURE

Mi 0   54   108   162   216
Km 0   87   174   261   348

CENTER, PATAGONIA & ATLANTIC
DEPARTMENT [9]
District [5]

Córdoba Argentina [3 department - 1 district]
Neuquén [2 department] - Río Negro [4 department, 1 district] - Chubut [1 district]
Buenos Aires [2 district]

La Serena

67°730'W

CATAMARCA

Reconquista

Río Uruguay

BRAZIL

30°130'S

LA RIOJA ARGENTINA

SAN JUAN

1

2

3 · Córdoba

CRUZ DEL EJE [1]
COLÓN [2]
2.a.Colonia Caroya
SAN JAVIER [3]

CENTER
CÓRDOBA ARGENTINA

Río Paraná

URUGUAY

Valparaíso

CUYO

SAN LUIS

Río Cuarto

Pacific Ocean

MENDOZA

Montevideo

Curicó

Buenos Aires

Laguna Llancanelo

CHILE

ATLANTIC REGION

BUENOS AIRES

Concepción

Santa Rosa

Villa Ventana
Chapadmalal

LA PAMPA

37°699'S

AÑELO [4]
CONFLUENCIA [5]

4

5

6

Río Colorado

Bahía Blanca

Argentine Sea

Valdivia

7

8

NEUQUÉN

GENERAL ROCA [6]
6.a.Alto Valle de Río Negro
AVELLANEDA [7]
PICHIMAHUIDA [8]
GENERAL CONESA [9]

9

PATAGONIA

Los Menucos

RÍO NEGRO

Trevelin

Rawson

Atlantic Ocean

43°522'S

Río Pico

CHUBUT

Argentine Sea

Coyhaique

Lago Musters

| Mi | 0 | 127 | 255 | 382 | 509 |
| Km | 0 | 205 | 410 | 615 | 820 |

Body of Water
COUNTRY
REGION
City / Town
LAND FEATURE

CLASSIFICATION SYSTEM

WO [Wine of Origin. Administered by the WSB (Wine and Spirit Board)]

    Categories (established by WO in 1973):
- Geographical Unit
- Region
- District
- Ward
- Estate

6 Geographical Units

5 Regions

30 Districts

97 Wards

SOUTH AFRICA

GEOGRAPHICAL UNIT / REGION	DISTRICT	WARD	
Western Cape [5] [25] [87]			
OLIFANTS RIVER	CITRUSDAL MOUNTAIN	PIEKENIERSKLOOF	
OLIFANTS RIVER	CITRUSDAL VALLEY		
OLIFANTS RIVER	-	SPRUITDRIFT	
		VREDENDAL	
COASTAL REGION [Cape Coast]	CAPE TOWN	CONSTANTIA	HOUT BAY
		DURBANVILLE	PHILADELPHIA
COASTAL REGION [Cape Coast]	DARLING	GROENEKLOOF	
COASTAL REGION [Cape Coast]	FRANSCHHOEK VALLEY		
COASTAL REGION [Cape Coast]	LUTZVILLE VALLEY	KOEKENAAP	
COASTAL REGION [Cape Coast]	PAARL	AGTER-PAARL	
		SIMONSBERG-PAARL	
		VOOR-PAARDEBERG	
COASTAL REGION [Cape Coast]	STELLENBOSCH	BANGHOEK	PAPEGAAIBERG
		BOTTELARY	POLKADRAAI HILLS
		DEVON VALLEY	SIMONSBERG-STELLENBOSCH
		JONKERSHOEK VALLEY	VLOTTENBURG
COASTAL REGION [Cape Coast]	SWARTLAND	MALMESBURY	PORSELEINBERG
		PAARDEBERG	RIEBEEKBERG
		PAARDEBERG SOUTH	RIEBEEKSRIVIER
		PIKET-BO-BERG	ST HELENA BAY
COASTAL REGION [Cape Coast]	TULBAGH		
COASTAL REGION [Cape Coast]	WELLINGTON	BLOUVLEI	LIMIETBERG
		BOVLEI	MID-BERG RIVER
		GROENBERG	
COASTAL REGION [Cape Coast]	-	BAMBOES BAY	
		LAMBERTS BAY	
CAPE SOUTH COAST [Cape Coast]	CAPE AGULHAS	ELIM	
CAPE SOUTH COAST [Cape Coast]	ELGIN		
CAPE SOUTH COAST [Cape Coast]	LOWER DUIVENHOKS RIVER		
CAPE SOUTH COAST [Cape Coast]	OVERBERG	ELANDSKLOOF	KLEIN RIVER
		GREYTON	THEEWATER
CAPE SOUTH COAST [Cape Coast]	PLETTENBERG BAY		
CAPE SOUTH COAST [Cape Coast]	SWELLENDAM	BUFFELJAGS	
		MALGAS	
		STORMSVLEI	
CAPE SOUTH COAST [Cape Coast]	WALKER BAY	BOT RIVER	SUNDAY'S GLEN
		HEMEL-EN-AARDE RIDGE	SPRINGFONTEIN RIM
		HEMEL-EN-AARDE VALLEY	STANFORD FOOTHILLS
		UPPER HEMEL-EN-AARDE VALLEY	
CAPE SOUTH COAST [Cape Coast]	-	HERBERTSDALE	
		NAPIER	
		STILL BAY EAST	
BREEDE RIVER VALLEY	BREEDEKLOOF	GOUDINI	
		SLANGHOEK	
BREEDE RIVER VALLEY	ROBERTSON	AGTERKLIPHOOGTE	GOUDMYN
		ASHTON	HOOPSRIVIER
		BOESMANSRIVIER	KLAASVOOGDS
		BONNIEVALE	LE CHASSEUR
		EILANDIA	MCGREGOR
		GOEDEMOED	VINKRIVIER
		GOREE	ZANDRIVIER
BREEDE RIVER VALLEY	WORCESTER	HEX RIVER VALLEY	SCHERPENHEUVEL
		NUY	STETTYN
KLEIN KAROO	CALITZDORP	GROENFONTEIN	
KLEIN KAROO	LANGEBERG-GARCIA		
KLEIN KAROO	-	CANGO VALLEY	TRADOUW
		KOO PLATEAU	TRADOUW HIGHLANDS
		MONTAGU	UPPER LANGKLOOF
		OUTENIQUA	
-	CERES PLATEAU	CERES	
	PRINCE ALBERT	KWEEKVALLEI	
		PRINCE ALBERT VALLEY	
		SWARTBERG	
-	-	CEDERBERG	
		LEIPOLDTVILLE-SANDVELD	
Northern Cape [0] [3] [8]			
-	DOUGLAS		
-	SUTHERLAND-KAROO		
-	CENTRAL ORANGE RIVER	GROBLERSHOOP	KEIMOES
		GROOTDRINK	UPINGTON
		KAKAMAS	
-	-	HARTSWATER	
		NIEUWOUDTVILLE	
		PRIESKA	
Eastern Cape [0] [0] [1]			
-	-	ST FRANCIS BAY	
Kwazulu-Natal [0] [2] [0]			
-	CENTRAL DRAKENSBERG		
-	LIONS RIVER		
Limpopo [0] [0] [0]			
Free State [0] [0] [1]			
		RIETRIVIER FS	

GEOGRAPHICAL UNITS OF SOUTH AFRICA [6]
Region [5] Sub-region ▨▨▨▨

All regions of South Africa are located within the Western Cape Geographical Unit.

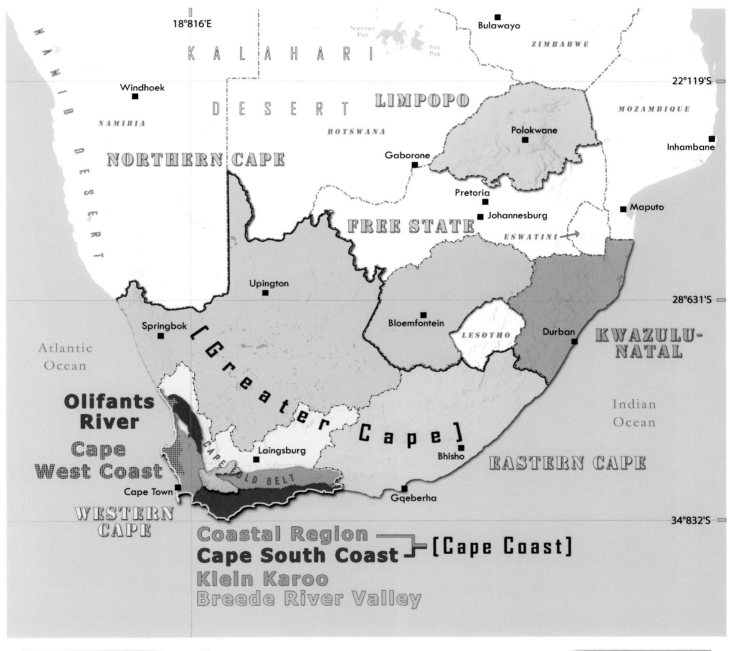

18°816'E

22°119'S

28°631'S

34°832'S

KALAHARI

DESERT

NAMIB DESERT

NAMIBIA

Windhoek

NORTHERN CAPE

Nwetwe Pan

Sua Pan

Bulawayo

ZIMBABWE

LIMPOPO

BOTSWANA

Polokwane

Gaborone

MOZAMBIQUE

Inhambane

Pretoria

Johannesburg

FREE STATE

ESWATINI

Maputo

Upington

Atlantic Ocean

Springbok

Bloemfontein

LESOTHO

Durban

KWAZULU-NATAL

Indian Ocean

Olifants River

Cape West Coast

[Greater Cape]

CAPE FOLD BELT

Laingsburg

Cape Town

Bhisho

EASTERN CAPE

WESTERN CAPE

Gqeberha

Coastal Region — ⌐ **[Cape Coast]**
Cape South Coast —⌐
Klein Karoo
Breede River Valley

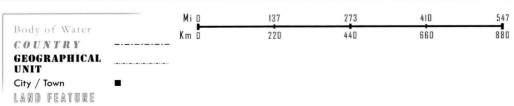

Body of Water

COUNTRY

GEOGRAPHICAL UNIT

City / Town

LAND FEATURE

| Mi | 0 | 137 | 273 | 410 | 547 |
| Km | 0 | 220 | 440 | 660 | 880 |

OUTSIDE OF THE 5 REGIONS
DISTRICT [7]
Ward [16]

Western Cape [District:2 - Ward:6] - Northern Cape [District:3 - Ward:8]
Eastern Cape [Ward:1] - Kwazulu-Natal [District:2] - Free State [Ward:1]

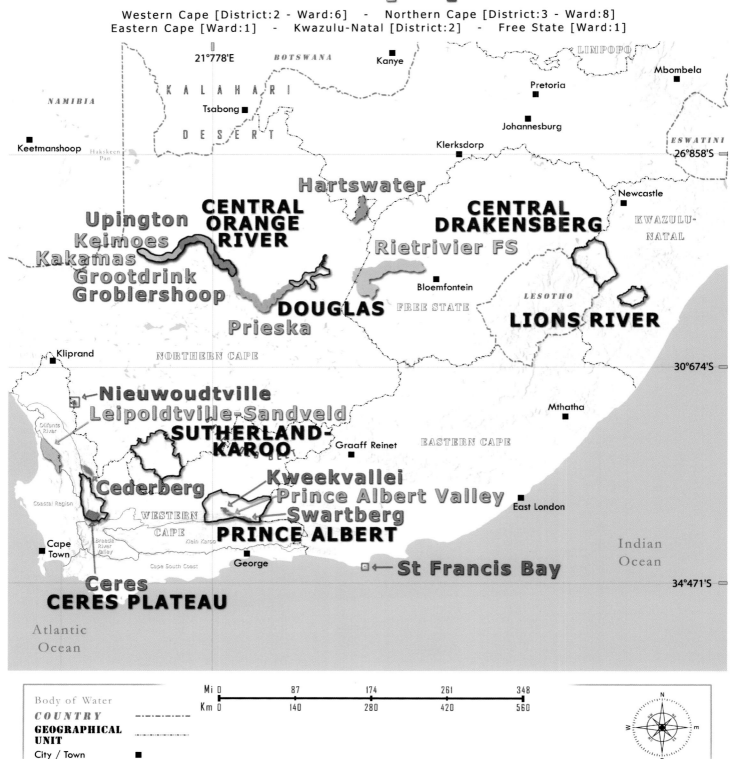

COASTAL REGION
DISTRICT [9]
Ward [32]
CAPE WEST COAST [sub-region]

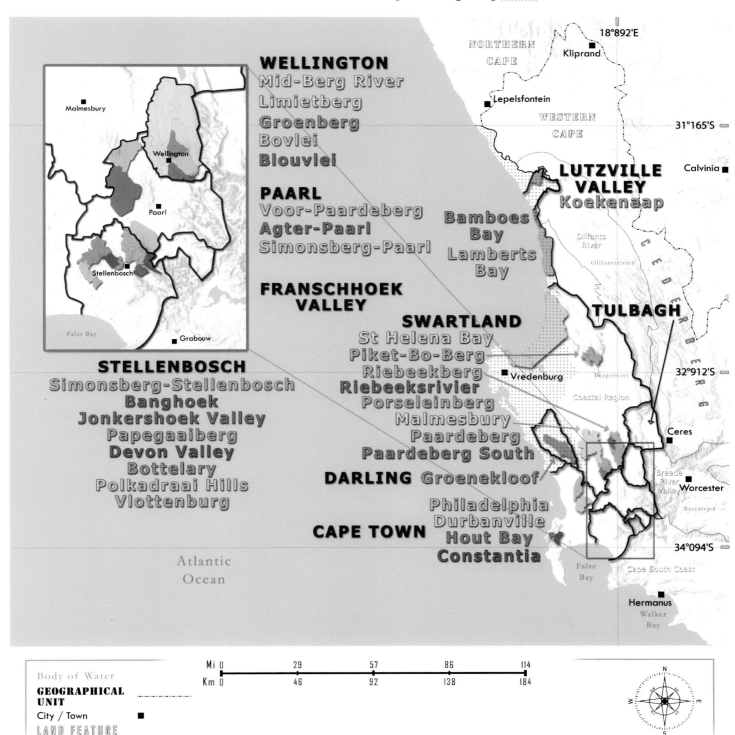

WELLINGTON
Mid-Berg River
Limietberg
Groenberg
Bovlei
Blouvlei

PAARL
Voor-Paardeberg
Agter-Paarl
Simonsberg-Paarl

FRANSCHHOEK VALLEY

STELLENBOSCH
Simonsberg-Stellenbosch
Banghoek
Jonkershoek Valley
Papegaaiberg
Devon Valley
Bottelary
Polkadraai Hills
Vlottenburg

SWARTLAND
St Helena Bay
Piket-Bo-Berg
Riebeekberg
Riebeeksrivier
Porseleinberg
Malmesbury
Paardeberg
Paardeberg South
DARLING Groenekloof

Philadelphia
Durbanville
CAPE TOWN Hout Bay
Constantia

Bamboes Bay
Lamberts Bay

LUTZVILLE VALLEY
Koekenaap

TULBAGH

NORTHERN CAPE
Kliprand
Lepelsfontein
WESTERN CAPE
Calvinia
Olifants River
Olifantsrivier
Vredenburg
Bergsrivier
Coastal Region
Ceres
Breede River Valley
Worcester
Breerivier
False Bay
Cape South Coast
Hermanus
Walker Bay
Atlantic Ocean

Malmesbury
Wellington
Paarl
Stellenbosch
False Bay
Grabouw

18°892'E
31°165'S
32°912'S
34°094'S

Body of Water
GEOGRAPHICAL UNIT
City / Town ■
LAND FEATURE

Mi 0   29   57   86   114
Km 0   46   92   138   184

N
W   E
S

CAPE SOUTH COAST
DISTRICT [7]
Ward [18]

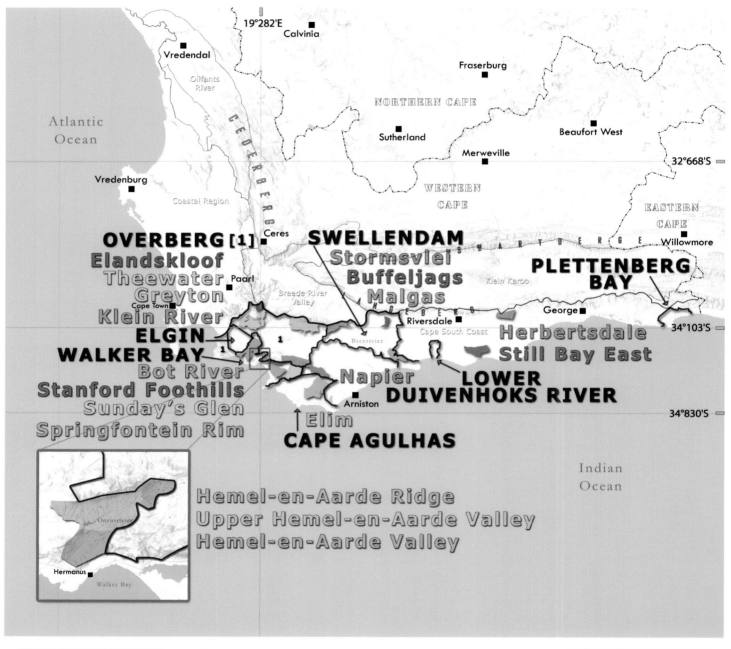

OVERBERG [1]
Elandskloof
Theewater
Greyton
Klein River
ELGIN
WALKER BAY
Bot River
Stanford Foothills
Sunday's Glen
Springfontein Rim

SWELLENDAM
Stormsvlei
Buffeljags
Malgas

PLETTENBERG BAY

Herbertsdale
Still Bay East

Napier
LOWER
DUIVENHOKS RIVER

Elim
CAPE AGULHAS

Hemel-en-Aarde Ridge
Upper Hemel-en-Aarde Valley
Hemel-en-Aarde Valley

Atlantic Ocean

NORTHERN CAPE

WESTERN CAPE

EASTERN CAPE

Indian Ocean

19°282'E
32°668'S
34°103'S
34°830'S

Vredendal · Calvinia · Fraserburg · Sutherland · Beaufort West · Merweville · Vredenburg · Ceres · Paarl · Cape Town · Willowmore · George · Riversdale · Breerivier · Arniston · Hermanus · Onrusrivier · Walker Bay

Olifants River · Coastal Region · Breede River Valley · Cape South Coast · Klein Karoo

Body of Water
GEOGRAPHICAL UNIT
City / Town
LAND FEATURE

Mi 0 · 43 · 86 · 129 · 172
Km 0 · 69 · 138 · 207 · 276

OLIFANTS RIVER & KLEIN KAROO
DISTRICT [4]
Ward [11]

Olifants River [District:2 - Ward:3]
Klein Karoo [District:2 - Ward:8]

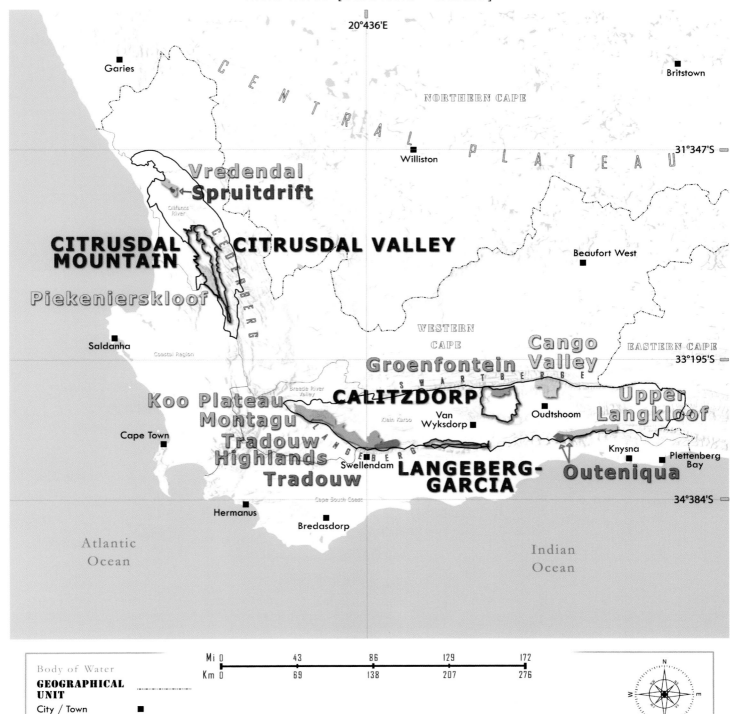

20°436'E

Garies

Britstown

CENTRAL

NORTHERN CAPE

31°347'S

Williston

PLATEAU

Vredendal
Spruitdrift

Olifants River

CITRUSDAL MOUNTAIN

CITRUSDAL VALLEY

CEDERBERG

Beaufort West

Piekenierskloof

Saldanha

Coastal Region

WESTERN CAPE

Cango Valley

EASTERN CAPE

33°195'S

Groenfontein

Breede River Valley

SWARTBERG

Koo Plateau
Montagu

CALITZDORP

Klein Karoo

Van Wyksdorp

Oudtshoorn

Upper Langkloof

Cape Town

Tradouw Highlands
Tradouw

LANGEBERG

Swellendam

LANGEBERG-GARCIA

Knysna

Plettenberg Bay

Outeniqua

34°384'S

Hermanus

Bredasdorp

Cape South Coast

Atlantic Ocean

Indian Ocean

Body of Water

GEOGRAPHICAL UNIT

City / Town ■

LAND FEATURE

Mi 0	43	86	129	172
Km 0	69	138	207	276

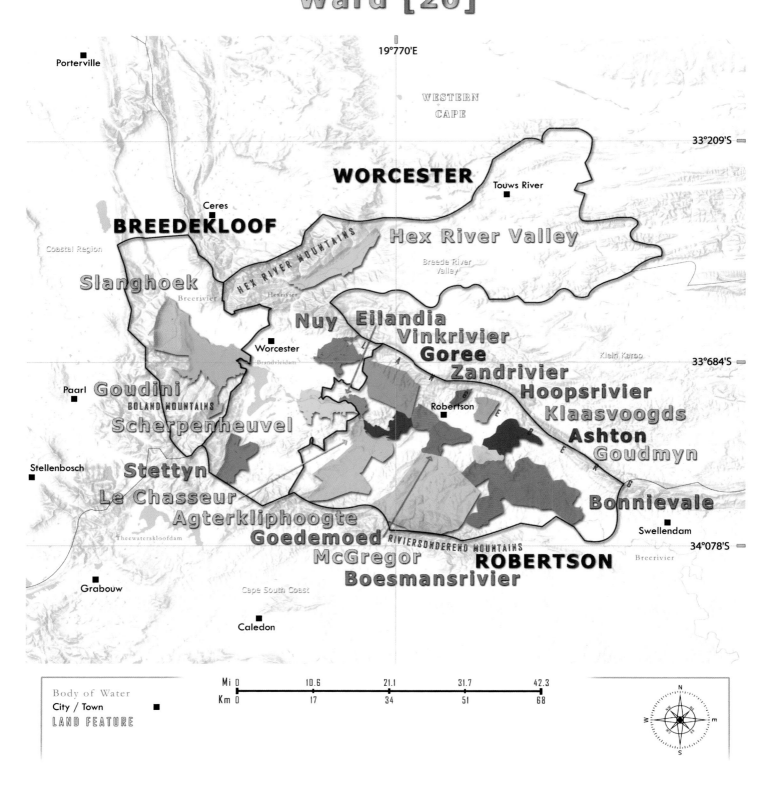

BREEDE RIVER VALLEY
DISTRICT [3]
Ward [20]

19°770'E

WESTERN CAPE

33°209'S

Porterville

WORCESTER

Touws River

Ceres

BREEDEKLOOF

Hex River Valley

Coastal Region

Slanghoek

HEX RIVER MOUNTAINS

Breede River Valley

Breerivier

Hexrivier

Nuy

Eilandia

Vinkrivier

Klein Karoo

Worcester

Goree

Brandvleidam

Zandrivier

33°684'S

Paarl

Goudini

Hoopsrivier

BOLAND MOUNTAINS

Robertson

Klaasvoogds

Scherpenheuvel

Ashton

Goudmyn

Stellenbosch

Stettyn

Le Chasseur

Bonnievale

Agterkliphoogte

Swellendam

Theewaterskloofdam

Goedemoed

RIVIERSONDEREND MOUNTAINS

34°078'S

Grabouw

McGregor

ROBERTSON

Breerivier

Boesmansrivier

Cape South Coast

Caledon

| Mi | 0 | 10.6 | 21.1 | 31.7 | 42.3 |
| Km | 0 | 17 | 34 | 51 | 68 |

Body of Water
City / Town ■
LAND FEATURE

CLASSIFICATION SYSTEM
GI [Geographical Indication]

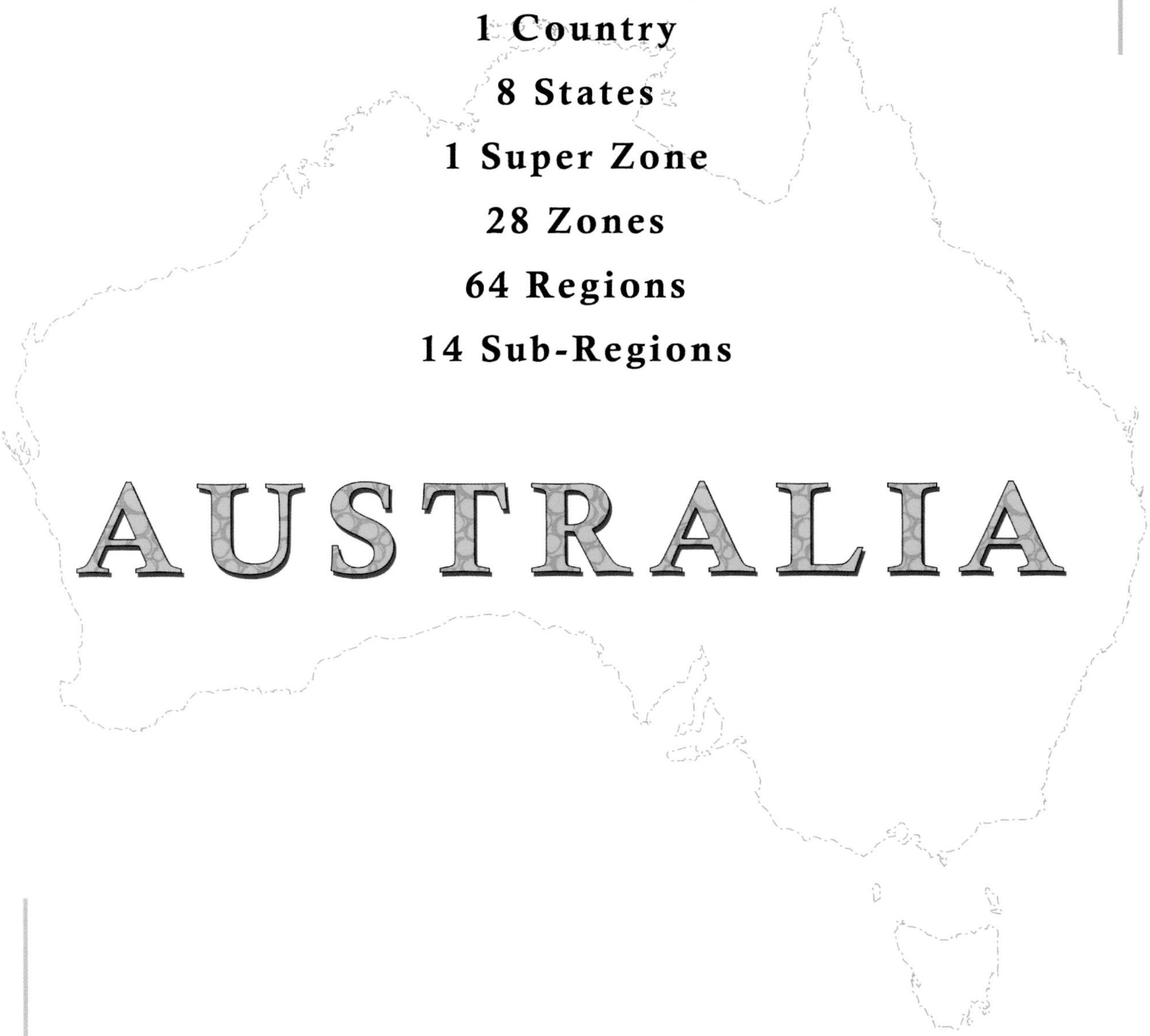

116 TOTAL GI

1 Country

8 States

1 Super Zone

28 Zones

64 Regions

14 Sub-Regions

AUSTRALIA

STATE	ZONE	REGION	EST.	SUB-REGION
Western Australia	Greater Perth	SWAN DISTRICT	1998	Swan Valley (est. 2003)
Western Australia	Greater Perth	PERTH HILLS	1999	
Western Australia	Greater Perth	PEEL	2001	
Western Australia	South West Australia	GEOGRAPHE	1999	
Western Australia	South West Australia	MARGARET RIVER	1996	
Western Australia	South West Australia	BLACKWOOD VALLEY	1998	
Western Australia	South West Australia	MANJIMUP	2006	
Western Australia	South West Australia	PEMBERTON	2006	
Western Australia	South West Australia	GREAT SOUTHERN	1999	Albany, Denmark, Frankland River Mount Barker, Porongurup
Western Australia	Central Western Australia		1996	
Western Australia	West Australian South East Coastal		1996	
Western Australia	Eastern Plains, Inland & North of Western Australia		1996	
South Australia	The Peninsulas		1996	
South Australia	Far North	SOUTHERN FLINDERS RANGES	2003	
South Australia	Lower Murray	RIVERLAND	1998	
South Australia	Mount Lofty Ranges [Adelaide Superzone]	CLARE VALLEY	1996	
South Australia	Mount Lofty Ranges [Adelaide Superzone]	ADELAIDE PLAINS	2002	
South Australia	Mount Lofty Ranges [Adelaide Superzone]	ADELAIDE HILLS	1998	Lenswood, Piccadilly Valley
South Australia	Barossa [Adelaide Superzone]	BAROSSA VALLEY	1996	
South Australia	Barossa [Adelaide Superzone]	EDEN VALLEY	1997	High Eden
South Australia	Fleurieu [Adelaide Superzone]	McLAREN VALE	1997	
South Australia	Fleurieu [Adelaide Superzone]	SOUTHERN FLEURIEU	2001	
South Australia	Fleurieu [Adelaide Superzone]	CURRENCY CREEK	2001	
South Australia	Fleurieu [Adelaide Superzone]	LANGHORNE CREEK	1998	
South Australia	Fleurieu [Adelaide Superzone]	KANGAROO ISLAND	2000	
South Australia	Limestone Coast	MOUNT BENSON	1997	
South Australia	Limestone Coast	ROBE	2006	
South Australia	Limestone Coast	MOUNT GAMBIER	2010	
South Australia	Limestone Coast	COONAWARRA	2003	
South Australia	Limestone Coast	WRATTONBULLY	2005	
South Australia	Limestone Coast	PADTHAWAY	1999	
Victoria	North West Victoria	MURRAY DARLING [shared with New South Wales]	1997	
Victoria	North West Victoria	SWAN HILL [shared with New South Wales]	1996	
Victoria	Western Victoria	HENTY	2000	
Victoria	Western Victoria	GRAMPIANS	1997	Great Western
Victoria	Western Victoria	PYRENEES	2000	
Victoria	Port Phillip	GEELONG	1996	
Victoria	Port Phillip	MORNINGTON PENINSULA	1997	
Victoria	Port Phillip	YARRA VALLEY	1996	
Victoria	Port Phillip	SUNBURY	1998	
Victoria	Port Phillip	MACEDON RANGES	2002	
Victoria	Gippsland		1996	
Victoria	Central Victoria	BENDIGO	2001	
Victoria	Central Victoria	HEATHCOTE	2002	
Victoria	Central Victoria	GOULBURN VALLEY	1999	Nagambie Lakes (est. 2001)
Victoria	Central Victoria	STRATHBOGIE RANGES	2002	
Victoria	Central Victoria	UPPER GOULBURN	2003	
Victoria	North East Victoria	RUTHERGLEN	1997	
Victoria	North East Victoria	GLENROWAN	2003	
Victoria	North East Victoria	KING VALLEY	2007	
Victoria	North East Victoria	ALPINE VALLEYS	1999	
Victoria	North East Victoria	BEECHWORTH	2000	
New South Wales	Western Plains		1996	
New South Wales	Big Rivers	MURRAY DARLING [shared with Victoria]	1997	
New South Wales	Big Rivers	SWAN HILL [shared with Victoria]	1996	
New South Wales	Big Rivers	PERRICOOTA	1999	
New South Wales	Big Rivers	RIVERINA	1998	
New South Wales	Southern New South Wales	TUMBARUMBA	1998	
New South Wales	Southern New South Wales	GUNDAGAI	2002	
New South Wales	Southern New South Wales	HILLTOPS	1998	
New South Wales	Southern New South Wales	CANBERRA DISTRICT	1998	
New South Wales	South Coast	SOUTHERN HIGHLANDS	2002	
New South Wales	South Coast	SHOALHAVEN COAST	2002	
New South Wales	Central Ranges	COWRA	1998	
New South Wales	Central Ranges	ORANGE	1997	
New South Wales	Central Ranges	MUDGEE	2000	
New South Wales	Hunter Valley	HUNTER	1997	Pokolbin (est. 2010) Broke Fordwich (est. 1997) Upper Hunter Valley (est. 2010)
New South Wales	Northern Rivers	HASTINGS RIVER	1999	
New South Wales	Northern Slopes	NEW ENGLAND AUSTRALIA	2008	
Queensland		GRANITE BELT	2002	
Queensland		SOUTH BURNETT	2000	
Tasmania	Tasmania	TASMANIA	1994	
Northern Territory				
Australian Capital Territory				
Multi-States	South Eastern Australia			

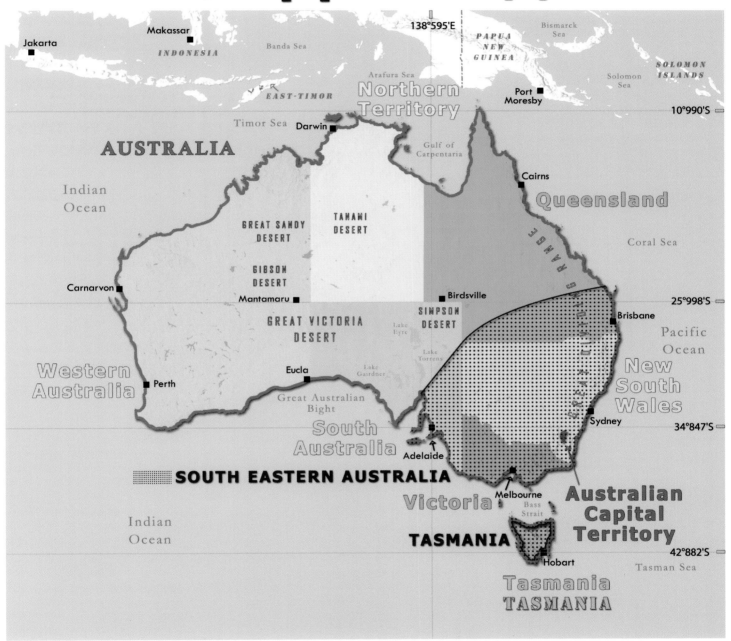

AUSTRALIA
TOTAL GI [12]
COUNTRY [1] State [8]
ZONE [2] REGION [1]

Jakarta

Makassar

INDONESIA

Banda Sea

138°595'E

Bismarck Sea

PAPUA NEW GUINEA

SOLOMON ISLANDS

Arafura Sea

Solomon Sea

EAST-TIMOR

Port Moresby

Northern Territory

10°990'S

Timor Sea

Darwin

Gulf of Carpentaria

AUSTRALIA

Indian Ocean

Cairns

Queensland

GREAT SANDY DESERT

TANAMI DESERT

Coral Sea

GIBSON DESERT

Carnarvon

Mantamaru

Birdsville

25°998'S

GREAT VICTORIA DESERT

SIMPSON DESERT

Brisbane

Lake Eyre

Pacific Ocean

Western Australia

Lake Torrens

New South Wales

Eucla

Lake Gairdner

Perth

Sydney

Great Australian Bight

34°847'S

South Australia

Adelaide

SOUTH EASTERN AUSTRALIA

Indian Ocean

Victoria

Melbourne

Bass Strait

Australian Capital Territory

TASMANIA

42°882'S

Hobart

Tasman Sea

Tasmania
TASMANIA

Body of Water

COUNTRY

City / Town

LAND FEATURE

| Mi 0 | 298 | 597 | 895 | 1193 |
| Km 0 | 480 | 960 | 1440 | 1920 |

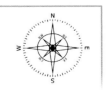

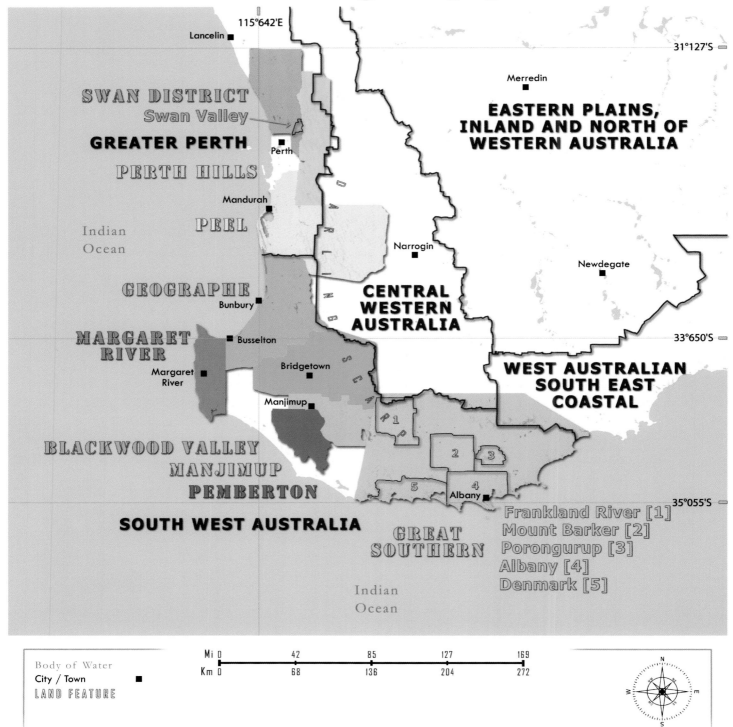

WESTERN AUSTRALIA
TOTAL GI [20]
ZONE [5]   REGION [9]
Sub-region [6]

115°642'E

31°127'S

Lancelin ■

Merredin ■

SWAN DISTRICT
Swan Valley

GREATER PERTH

EASTERN PLAINS,
INLAND AND NORTH OF
WESTERN AUSTRALIA

PERTH HILLS

Perth ■

Mandurah ■

PEEL

Narrogin ■

Newdegate ■

Indian
Ocean

GEOGRAPHE

Bunbury ■

CENTRAL
WESTERN
AUSTRALIA

33°650'S

MARGARET
RIVER

Busselton ■

Margaret
River ■

Bridgetown ■

WEST AUSTRALIAN
SOUTH EAST
COASTAL

Manjimup ■

1

BLACKWOOD VALLEY
MANJIMUP
PEMBERTON

2
3

5
4
Albany ■

35°055'S

SOUTH WEST AUSTRALIA

GREAT
SOUTHERN

Frankland River [1]
Mount Barker [2]
Porongurup [3]
Albany [4]
Denmark [5]

Indian
Ocean

DARLING SCARP

Body of Water
City / Town ■
LAND FEATURE

Mi	0		42		85		127		169
Km	0		68		136		204		272

SOUTH AUSTRALIA
TOTAL GI [29]

ZONE [7]   SUPER ZONE [1]
REGION [18]   Sub-region [3]

FAR NORTH

138°684'E

32°477'S

GAWLER RANGES

Lake Gairdner

Streaky Bay

Whyalla

SOUTHERN FLINDERS RANGES

Scotia

New South Wales

THE PENINSULAS

Spencer Gulf

ADELAIDE

Murray River

LOWER MURRAY

RIVERLAND

Murray River

MOUNT LOFTY RANGES

Auburn

CLARE VALLEY
ADELAIDE PLAINS
ADELAIDE HILLS

Lenswood
Piccadilly Valley

Adelaide

BAROSSA VALLEY
EDEN VALLEY
High Eden

BAROSSA

34°924'S

MCLAREN VALE
FLEURIEU

Gulf St Vincent

Parawa

Murray River
Lake Alexandria

BIG DESERT

Victoria

Lake Hindmarsh

FLEURIEU

LANGHORNE CREEK
CURRENCY CREEK
KANGAROO ISLAND

Keith

Seal Bay

LIMESTONE COAST

Lake Buloke

Litchfield

Great Australian Bight

MOUNT BENSON

ROBE

Naracoorte

Bool Lagoon

Penola

PADTHAWAY

WRATTONBULLY

COONAWARRA

MOUNT GAMBIER

Mount Gambier

38°057'S

Indian Ocean

Portland

Body of Water
City / Town
STATE
LAND FEATURE

Mi 0   42   85   127   169
Km 0   55   109   164   219

VICTORIA
TOTAL GI [28]
ZONE [6] REGION [20] (2 SHARED)
Sub-region [2]

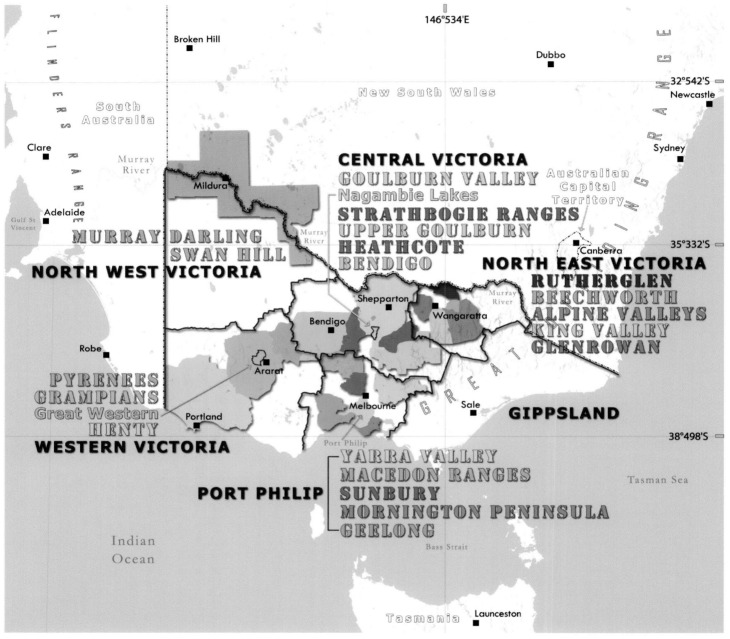

146°534'E

Broken Hill

Dubbo

New South Wales

32°542'S

Newcastle

FLINDERS RANGE

South Australia

Clare

Sydney

Murray River

Adelaide

Mildura

Australian Capital Territory

GREAT DIVIDING RANGE

Gulf St Vincent

MURRAY DARLING
SWAN HILL

NORTH WEST VICTORIA

Murray River

CENTRAL VICTORIA
GOULBURN VALLEY
Nagambie Lakes
STRATHBOGIE RANGES
UPPER GOULBURN
HEATHCOTE
BENDIGO

Canberra

35°332'S

NORTH EAST VICTORIA
RUTHERGLEN
BEECHWORTH
ALPINE VALLEYS
KING VALLEY
GLENROWAN

Shepparton

Wangaratta

Murray River

Bendigo

Robe

PYRENEES
GRAMPIANS
Great Western
HENTY

WESTERN VICTORIA

Ararat

Portland

Melbourne

Sale

GREAT

GIPPSLAND

38°498'S

Port Philip

PORT PHILIP

YARRA VALLEY
MACEDON RANGES
SUNBURY
MORNINGTON PENINSULA
GEELONG

Tasman Sea

Indian Ocean

Bass Strait

Tasmania

Launceston

Legend
Body of Water
City / Town ■
STATE ----
LAND FEATURE

Mi	0	80	159	239	318
Km	0	128	256	384	512

NEW SOUTH WALES
TOTAL GI [27]

ZONE [8] REGION [16] (2 SHARED) Sub-region [3]

QUEENSLAND REGION [2]

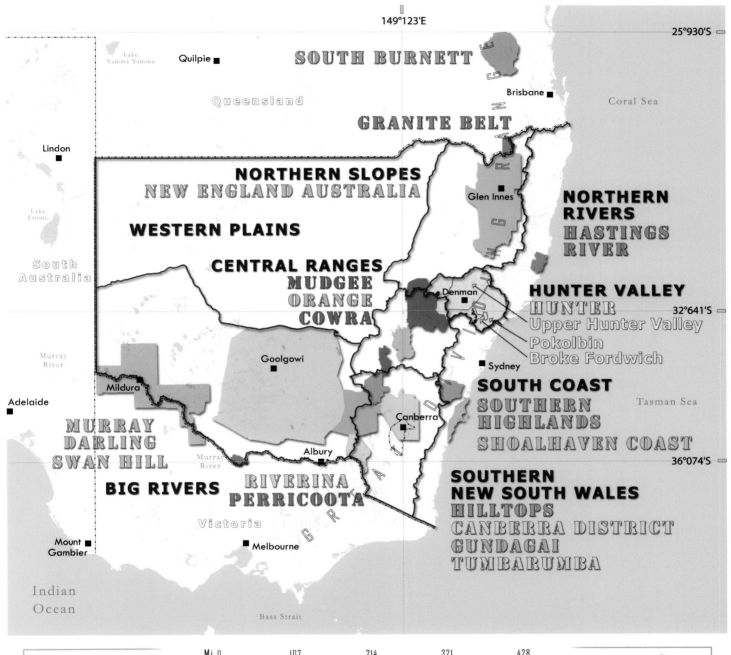

149°123'E

25°930'S

Lake Yamma Yamma

Quilpie ■

SOUTH BURNETT

Queensland

Brisbane ■

Coral Sea

GRANITE BELT

Lindon ■

NORTHERN SLOPES
NEW ENGLAND AUSTRALIA

Glen Innes ■

NORTHERN RIVERS

HASTINGS RIVER

Lake Frome

WESTERN PLAINS

South Australia

CENTRAL RANGES
MUDGEE
ORANGE
COWRA

Denman ■

HUNTER VALLEY

HUNTER
Upper Hunter Valley
Pokolbin
Broke Fordwich

32°641'S

Murray River

Goolgowi ■

Sydney ■

SOUTH COAST

SOUTHERN HIGHLANDS

Mildura ■

Adelaide ■

Canberra ■

SHOALHAVEN COAST

Tasman Sea

MURRAY DARLING SWAN HILL

Albury ■

Murray River

36°074'S

BIG RIVERS

RIVERINA PERRICOOTA

SOUTHERN NEW SOUTH WALES

HILLTOPS
CANBERRA DISTRICT
GUNDAGAI
TUMBARUMBA

Victoria

Mount Gambier ■

Melbourne ■

Indian Ocean

Bass Strait

Mi 0   107   214   321   428
Km 0   172   344   516   688

Body of Water
City / Town ■
STATE ----
LAND FEATURE

CLASSIFICATION SYSTEM
GI [Geographical Indication]

22 TOTAL GI

13 Regions
9 Sub-Regions

NEW ZEALAND

NEW ZEALAND
TOTAL GI [22]
REGION [13]
Sub-region [9]

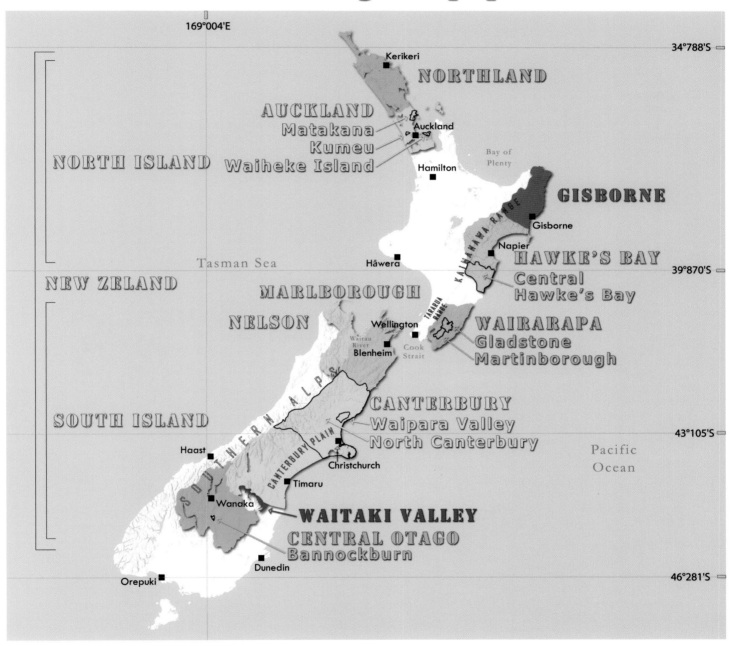

169°004'E

34°788'S

NORTHLAND

Kerikeri

AUCKLAND
Matakana
Kumeu
Waiheke Island

Auckland

Bay of
Plenty

NORTH ISLAND

Hamilton

GISBORNE

Gisborne

KAIMANAWA RANGE

Tasman Sea

Hāwera

Napier

HAWKE'S BAY

39°870'S

NEW ZELAND

MARLBOROUGH

Central
Hawke's Bay

NELSON

Wellington

TARARUA RANGE

WAIRARAPA
Gladstone
Martinborough

Wairau
River

Blenheim

Cook
Strait

SOUTH ISLAND

CANTERBURY
Waipara Valley
North Canterbury

43°105'S

SOUTHERN ALPS

Pacific
Ocean

Haast

CANTERBURY PLAIN

Christchurch

Timaru

Wanaka

WAITAKI VALLEY

CENTRAL OTAGO
Bannockburn

Dunedin

Orepuki

46°281'S

Body of Water
City / Town   ■
LAND FEATURE

Mi 0   99   199   298   398
Km 0   160   320   480   640

OTHER COUNTRIES

LEBANON
REGION [4] Sub-region [4]

ISRAEL
REGION [6] Sub-region [15]

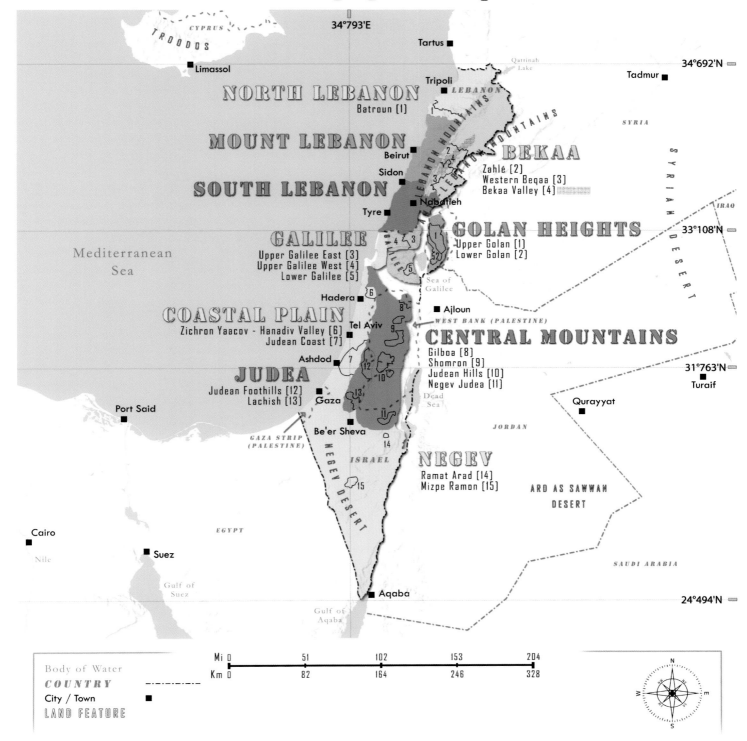

34°793'E

34°692'N

Tartus

Qattinah Lake

Tadmur

Limassol

TROODOS

CYPRUS

LEBANON

Tripoli

NORTH LEBANON
Batroun [1]

AL LEBANON MOUNTAINS

LE BANON Mountains

SYRIA

MOUNT LEBANON
Beirut

Sidon

SOUTH LEBANON

Nabatieh

Tyre

BEKAA
Zahlé [2]
Western Beqaa [3]
Bekaa Valley [4]

SYRIAN DESERT

IRAQ

GALILEE
Upper Galilee East [3]
Upper Galilee West [4]
Lower Galilee [5]

GOLAN HEIGHTS
Upper Golan [1]
Lower Golan [2]

33°108'N

Mediterranean
Sea

Sea of Galilee

Hadera

COASTAL PLAIN
Zichron Yaacov - Hanadiv Valley [6]
Judean Coast [7]

Tel Aviv

Ajloun

WEST BANK (PALESTINE)

CENTRAL MOUNTAINS
Gilboa [8]
Shomron [9]
Judean Hills [10]
Negev Judea [11]

Ashdod

JUDEA
Judean Foothills [12]
Lachish [13]

Gaza

Be'er Sheva

31°763'N

Turaif

Dead Sea

JORDAN

Qurayyat

GAZA STRIP (PALESTINE)

NEGEV DESERT

ISRAEL

NEGEV
Ramat Arad [14]
Mizpe Ramon [15]

ARD AS SAWWAN DESERT

Port Said

Cairo

Nile

Suez

EGYPT

Gulf of Suez

SAUDI ARABIA

Aqaba

Gulf of Aqaba

24°494'N

| Mi 0 | 51 | 102 | 153 | 204 |
| Km 0 | 82 | 164 | 246 | 328 |

Body of Water
COUNTRY
City / Town
LAND FEATURE

N
W   E
S

SLOVENIA
REGION [3] Sub-region [9]
CROATIA
REGION [4] Sub-region [12]

PODRAVSKA
Prekmurje
Štajerska Slovenija

POSAVSKA
Bizeljsko Sremič
Dolenjska
Bela Krajina

PRIMORSKA
Goriška Brda
Vipavska dolina
Kras
Slovenska Istra

SLAVONIA AND DANUBE
Slavonia
Podunavlje

ISTRIA AND KVARNER
Istria
Primorje

CROATIAN UPLANDS
Zagorje-Međimurje
Plešivica
Pokuplje
Prigorje-Bilogora
Moslavina

DALMATIA
Sjeverna Dalmacija
Dalmatinska Zagora
Srednja I Juzna Dalmacija

Munich
Salzburg
GERMANY
AUSTRIA
Bratislava
SLOVAKIA
47°809'N
Budapest
Danube 15°981'E
Neusiedler See
Tisza
HUNGARY
Lake Balaton
Danube
Drava Maribor
Mur
SLOVENIA
Ljubljana
Zagreb
Sava
45°963'N
Timişoara
Trieste
Rijeka
Kupa
Drava
Osijek
Novi Sad
ROMANIA
Slavonski Brod
Lago di Garda
Po
CROATIA
BOSNIA & HERZEGOVINA
Sava
Danube
44°352'N
Kragujevac
SERBIA
San Marino
Florence
Zadar
Split
Mostar
Pristina
42°445'N
MONTENEGRO
KOSOVO
Tiber
Rome
ITALY
Adriatic Sea
Skopje
NORTH MACEDONIA
Tyrrhenian Sea
Bari
Tirana
ALBANIA
GREECE

Body of Water
COUNTRY
City / Town
LAND FEATURE

| Mi 0 | 66 | 133 | 199 | 266 |
| Km 0 | 107 | 214 | 321 | 428 |

ROMANIA
REGION [12]
DOC [33]

POLAND

SLOVAKIA

26°104'E

Ivano-Frankivsk

Vinnytsia

Košice

48°492'N

UKRAINE

MARAMUREŞ

TRANSYLVANIA

MOLDOVA

HUNGARY

CRIŞANA
Crişana

Satu Mare

MOLDOVA

Lechinţa

Botosani

Cotnari
Iaşi
Bohotin

Szolnok

Bistriţa

Oradea

Cluj-Napoca

ZĂRAND
Miniş

APUSENI MOUNTAINS Aiud

Târnave

Bacău

Tiraspol

46°770'N

Huşi
Iana
Dealu Bujorului
Nicoreşti

Odesa

Arad

Alba
Iulia
Sebeş-
Apold

Panciu
Odobeşti
Coteşti

Recaş

Timişoara

SOUTHERNS CARPATHIANS

MUNTENIA
Ştefăneşti

VRANCEA

TIMIŞ

Resita

Brăila

Danube

Sarica
Niculiţel

Banat

Sâmbureşti
Drăgăşani

Buzău

Belgrade

Ploieşti

Babadag
Murfatlar

44°572'N

CARAŞ

SERBIA

Pietroasa
Dealu Mare

DOBROGEA
Adamclisi

Mehedinţi
Banu Mărăcine
Segarcea

Craiova

Olt

Bucharest

Constanţa

Oltina

OLTENIA

Danube

Însurăţei

Black
Sea

DANUBE TERRACES

Nis

Pleven

42°695'N

KOSOVO

Sofia

BULGARIA

Burgas

ALBANIA

Skopje

NORTH
MACEDONIA

CZECH REPUBLIC
REGION [2]   Sub-region [6]
SLOVAKIA
REGION [6]

17°120'E

Warsaw

Cottbus

Elbe

Kalisz

Vistula

51°473'N

Lublin

BOHEMIA

GERMANY

POLAND

Litoměřická

Mělnická

50°448'N

Carlsbad

Kraków

Prague

Elbe

Vltava

CZECH REPUBLIC

MORAVIA

Slovácká

Brno

Zlín

Velkopavlovická

VÝCHODOSLOVENSKÁ

Mikulovská

NITRIANSKA

Košice

Znojemská

48°719'N

Danube

Linz

Danube

Váh

SLOVAKIA

UKRAINE

Munich

Bratislava

Nitra

TOKAJ

Hron

Miskolc

MALOKARPATSKÁ

STREDOSLOVENSKÁ

Neusiedler
See

47°681'N

JUŽNOSLOVENSKÁ

Budapest

AUSTRIA

HUNGARY

ROMANIA

Klagenfurt

Lake
Balaton

Danube

Pécs

Arad

ITALY

SLOVENIA

Venice

Zagreb

CROATIA

SERBIA

Adriatic
Sea

Mi	0		60		119		179		239
Km	0		96		192		288		384

Body of Water

COUNTRY

City / Town

LAND FEATURE

TURKEY REGION [4] Sub-region [4]
BULGARIA REGION [5]
MOLDOVA IGP [3]
CYPRUS ОEOП [5]
UKRAINE REGION [5]
RUSSIA REGION [5]

POLAND
Kyiv
33°431'E
UKRAINE
Dnipro
49°460'N
Lviv
Don
SLOVAKIA
Volgograd
KAZAKHSTAN
ZAKARPATTYA   ODESSA   KHERSON
MYKOLAIV ZAPORIZHIA
HUNGARY
MOLDOVA
Donetsk
RUSSIA
Debrecen
Volga
CODRU
Chişinău
ŞTEFAN VODĂ   Kherson
VALU LUI TRAIAN
Odesa
Sea of Azov
ROMANIA
Sea   ROSTOV
Crimea   STAVROPOL
Danube Olt Bucharest   DAGHESTAN
Danube   KRASNODAR
Sevastopol   CRIMEA
Caspian
Sea
SERBIA   Varna   DANUBE PLAIN
BULGARIA   VALLEY OF THE ROSES   GREATER CAUCASUS
Burgas   STRUMA VALLEY   Nalchik   43°142'N
Sofia   THRACIAN VALLEY   Black
NORTH   BLACK SEA COAST   Sea   GEORGIA
MACEDONIA   LESSER CAUCASUS
GREECE   Tbilisi
Thessaloniki   Istanbul   PONTIC   ARMENIA   AZERBAIJAN
Sea of   MOUNTAINS   MARMARA
Marmara   3   AEGEAN   Yerevan
Ankara   MEDITERRANEAN
1   ANATOLIA
Peloponnese   TURKEY   IRAN
Aegean   3   Elazig
Sea   Mid-Northern [1]
Athens   İzmir   1   2   Mid-Southern [2]   38°078'N
4   Mid-Eastern [3]   Tabriz
South East [4]
T   A   U   R   U   S
Antalya   ZAGROS
Aleppo   MOUNTAINS
Crete   Mediterranean Sea   Nicosia
CYPRUS   SYRIA   35°186'N
LEBANON
Polis   AKAMAS LAONA
Lefka   Akaki   VOUNI PANAYIAS - AMBELITIS
TROODOS   PITSILIA   IRAQ   Baghdad
COMMANDARIA
Paphos   KRASOCHORIA LIMASSOL
Limassol   ISRAEL
Tel Aviv

Body of Water
COUNTRY
City / Town
LAND FEATURE

Mi 0   177   354   531   708
Km 0   285   570   855   1140

293

SERBIA REGION [2] Area [20]
BOSNIE & HERZEGOVINA REGION [6]
MONTENEGRO REGION [2]
ALBANIA REGION [4]
NORTH MACEDONIA REGION [3]

VOJVODINA
Subotički [1]
Bački [2]
Telečka [3]
Potiski [4]
Banatski [5]
Južnobanatski [6]
Sremski [7]

CENTRAL SERBIA
Pocersko Valjevski [8]
Beogradski [9]
Šumadijski [10]
Čačansko–kraljevački [11]
Mlavski [12]
Tri Morave [13]
Niški [14]
Nišavski [15]
Toplički [16]
Leskovački [17]
Vranjski [18]
Negotinska Krajina [19]
Knjaževački [20]

KOZARAC
UKRINA
MAJEVICA
JABLANICA
ŠIROKI BRIJEG
MOSTAR

COASTAL REGION
LAKE SKADAR

COASTAL PLAIN (LOWLANDS)
CENTRAL (HILLY)
EAST (SUBMOUNTAINOUS)
HIGHLANDS

PCINJA-OSOGOVO
POVARDARIE
PELAGONIJA-POLOG

Mi 0   64   128   192   256
Km 0   103   206   309   412

Body of Water
COUNTRY
City / Town
LAND FEATURE

ENGLAND
REGION [6]

LUXEMBOURG
REGION [1] AOC [2]

BELGIUM
REGION [2]   AOC [7]

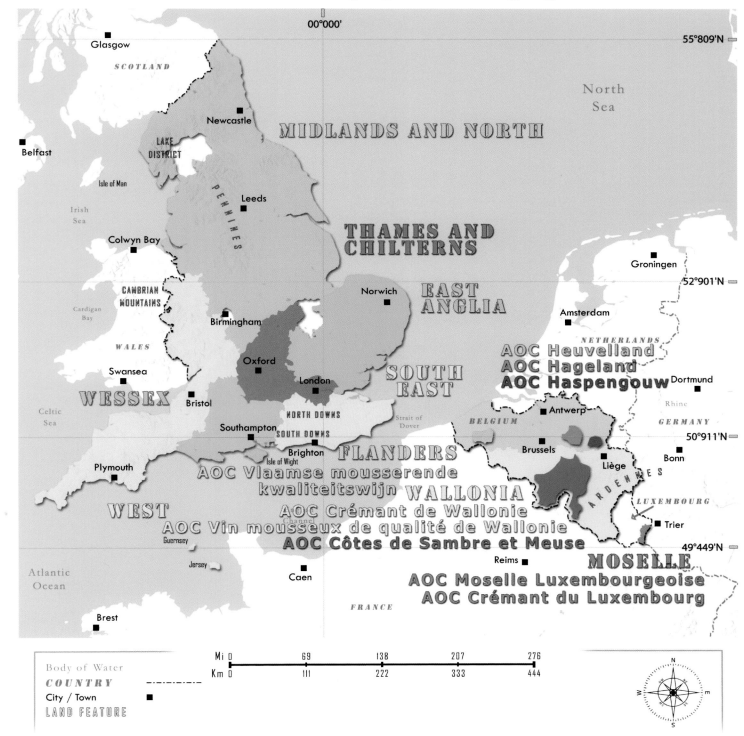

Glasgow

SCOTLAND

North
Sea

55°809'N

Newcastle

Belfast

LAKE
DISTRICT

Isle of Man

MIDLANDS AND NORTH

Irish
Sea

PENNINES

Leeds

Colwyn Bay

THAMES AND
CHILTERNS

Groningen

52°901'N

CAMBRIAN
MOUNTAINS

Norwich

EAST
ANGLIA

Amsterdam

Cardigan
Bay

Birmingham

NETHERLANDS

AOC Heuvelland
AOC Hageland
AOC Haspengouw

Dortmund

WALES

Oxford

Rhine

Swansea

London

GERMANY

WESSEX

Bristol

SOUTH
EAST

BELGIUM

Antwerp

Celtic
Sea

NORTH DOWNS

Brussels

50°911'N

Southampton

SOUTH DOWNS

Liège

Bonn

Plymouth

Brighton
Isle of Wight

Strait of
Dover

FLANDERS

ARDENNES

LUXEMBOURG

AOC Vlaamse mousserende
kwaliteitswijn

WALLONIA

WEST

AOC Crémant de Wallonie

Trier

Guernsey

AOC Vin mousseux de qualité de Wallonie

Channel

Jersey

AOC Côtes de Sambre et Meuse

49°449'N

Atlantic
Ocean

Caen

Reims

MOSELLE

AOC Moselle Luxembourgeoise
AOC Crémant du Luxembourg

Brest

FRANCE

Body of Water

COUNTRY

City / Town

LAND FEATURE

Mi 0   69   138   207   276
Km 0   111   222   333   444

GEORGIA
REGION [10]

ARMENIA
REGION [11]

AZERBAIJAN
REGION [3]

45°206'E

44°918'N

Krasnodar

Stavropol

Kuban

KAZAKHSTAN

Aktau

Reka
Belaya

RUSSIA

Terek River

Black
Sea

Nalchik

Caspian
Sea

Sokhumi

LECHKHUMI
RACHA

Makhachkala

Patara
Enguri

KARTLI
KAKHETI

ABKHAZIA
SAMEGREIO
IMERETI
GURIA
ADJARA
MESKHETI

Rioni   Kutaisi

41°848'N

Batumi

GEORGIA

Tbilisi

CASPIAN
SHORELINE

Mtkvari

Trabzon

Ismailli

SHIRAK
LORI
TAVUSH
ARAGATSOTN
ARMAVIR
KOTAYQ
GEGHARKUNIK

ARMENIA

Ganja

PONTIC MOUNTAINS

Gyumri

GANJA
SHRIVAN
VALLEY

Yerevan

Lake Sevan

Baku

AZERBAIJAN

YEREVAN
ARARAT
VAYOTS DZOR
SYUNIK

Goris

39°508'N

TURKEY

Elazığ

Van Gölü

SOUTHEASTERN TAURUS

Tigris   Batman

Tabriz

Lake
Urmia

Rasht

Sefid-rud
River

36°987'N

ELBURZ MOUNTAINS

IRAQ

IRAN

Bukan

SYRIA

Tigris   Mosul

Great Zab
River

Body of Water

COUNTRY

City / Town

LAND FEATURE

| Mi | 0 | | 84 | | 168 | | 252 | | 336 |
| Km | 0 | | 135 | | 270 | | 405 | | 540 |

C H I N A
REGION [8] Sub-region [6]
J A P A N
REGION [4]

106°372'E

Ob

Angara

RUSSIA

Sea of
Okhotsk

56°362'N

Omsk

SAYAN

Irkutsk

Lake
Baikal

DONGBEI

Lena

Yakutsk

Aldan

Amur

Nur-Sultan

KAZAKHSTAN

Lake
Balkhash

ALTAY MOUNTAINS

XINJIANG

Ürümqi

GOBI DESERT

MONGOLIA

Ulaanbaatar

Hulun
Lake

Jixi

Vladivostok

Sapporo

43°141'N

KYRGYZSTAN

TAKLA MAKAN
DESERT

ALTUN SHAN

HEBEI

NINGXIA

Hulun
Lake

Lanzhou

Beijing

Anshan

NORTH KOREA

Yantai

Pyongyang

Seoul

Sea of Japan

HOKKAIDO
YAMAGATA
NAGANO
YAMANASHI

TAJIKISTAN

KUHLUN MOUNTAINS

GANSU

Handan

Jinari

SOUTH KOREA

Yellow
Sea

Osaka

Tokyo

JAPAN

Pacific
Ocean

PAKISTAN

HIMALAYAS

New Delhi

NEPAL

BHUTAN

SHANXI

CHINA

Yangtze

SHANDONG

East China
Sea

28°574'N

Ganges

INDIA

BANGLADESH

Kunming

YUNNAN

Taipei

Mumbai

MYANMAR

VIETNAM

LAOS

Hong Kong

TAIWAN

Philippines
Sea

Shizuishan
Jinshan
Zhenbeibu
Yuquanying
Qingtongxia
Hongsipu

Bangkok

THAILAND

CAMBODIA

South China
Sea

Manila

PHILIPPINES

← PALAU

HELAN MOUNTAINS

Wuhai

Yinchuan

38°491'N

Wuzhong

Andaman
Sea

Gulf of
Thailand

Ho Chi Minh City

Yellow River

Colombo

SRI LANKA

BRUNEI

MALAYSIA

Celebes Sea

2°020'N

SINGAPORE

Indian
Ocean

INDONESIA

Makassar

Java Sea

Banda Sea

Bismarck
Sea

PAPUA NEW GUINEA

| Mi | 0 | 696 | 1392 | 2088 | 2784 |
| Km | 0 | 1120 | 2240 | 3360 | 4480 |

Body of Water

COUNTRY

City / Town

LAND FEATURE

BRAZIL
REGION [6]

URUGUAY
REGION [6] Department [15]

00°000'

Recife

Porto Velho

Palmas

São Francisco River

10°242'S

VALE DO SÃO FRANCISCO

PERU

Río Madre de Dios

Cusco

BOLIVIA

São Francisco River

Brasília

Cuiabá

BRAZIL

ESPINHAÇO MOUNTAINS

Titicaca

Sucre

Vitória

Pacific Ocean

22°475'S

Antofagasta

Paraná

São Paulo

CHILE

Londrina

Atlantic Ocean

Copiapó

ARGENTINA

Asunción

PARAGUAY

PLANALTO CATARINENSE

Concórdia

Florianópolis

CAMPOS DE CIMA DA SERRA

Lages

NORTHERN RIVERSIDE

San Juan

Paraná

Uruguay River

URUGUAY

CAMPANHA

Rivera

SERRA GAÚCHA
SERRA DO SUDESTE

Porto Alegre

30°036'S

Artigas [1]
Salto [2]
Paysandú [3]

SOUTHERN RIVERSIDE

Santiago

Melo

NORTHERN   Tacuarembó [14]
Rivera [15]

Río Negro [4]
Soriano [5]
Colonia [6]

Montevideo

CENTRAL   Lavalleja [11]
Florida [12]
Durazno [13]

34°902'S

METROPOLITAN   OCEANIC
San José [7]   Maldonado [9]
Canelones [8]   Rocha [10]

Mar del Plata

Mi 0   227   453   680   907
Km 0   365   730   1095   1460

Body of Water
COUNTRY — · — · —
City / Town ■
LAND FEATURE

Index

2

25 de Mayo, 268

9

9 de Julio, 268

A

A l'Ecu, 64
A Vigne Rouge, 82
Aargau, 230
Abadía Retuerta, 160
Abaújszántó, 213, 214
Abbaye de Morgeot, 76
Abkhazia, 296
Abona, 171
Abruzzo, 121, 148
Abymes/Les Abymes, 41
Acél, 223
Aconcagua, 263
Aconcagua Valley, 263
Açores, 175, 178
Adamclisi, 291
Adelaida District, 253
Adelaide, 283
Adelaide Hills, 283
Adelaide Plains, 283
Adjara, 296
Aegean, 293
Aegean Islands, 234
Agáros, 225
Aglianico del Taburno, 151
Aglianico del Vulture, 152
Aglianico del Vulture Superiore, 152
Agneux (M), 80
Agrelo, 269
Agterkliphoogte, 278
Agter-Paarl, 275
Agyag, 214, 219
Ahr, 186, 187
Aiud, 291
Ajaccio, 114
Akamas Laona, 293
Akasztódomb, 224
Alabama, 247
Alaska, 247
Alba, 124
Alba Iulia, 291
Albania, 294
Albany, 282
Albardón, 268
Albarella, 133
Alberta, 239
Albesani, 127
Albignano, 124
Alcamo, 154
Aleatico di Gradoli, 147
Aleatico di Puglia, 150
Alella, 163
Alenquer, 176
Alentejano, 175
Alentejo, 176
Alessandria, 123
Alexander Valley, 251
Alexandria Lakes, 258
Alezio, 150
Alfaraz, 169
Algarve, 175
Alghero, 155
Alicante, 165
Alisos Canyon, 253
Almansa, 166
Almási, 221
Almocadén, 169
Aloxe- Corton, 61
Aloxe-Corton, 62
Alpine Valleys, 284
Alsace, 22, 23
Alsó-Bea, 214
Alsó-Esztáva, 227
Alsó-gát, 226
Alsó-Lete, 214
Alsó-Remete, 219
Alta Langa, 124
Alta Mesa, 254
Altenasso, 134
Altenberg de Bergbieten, 25, 26
Altenberg de Bergheim, 25, 29
Altenberg de Wolxheim, 25, 26
Alto Adige, 137
Alto Valle de Río Negro, 270
Altus, 258
Amandi, 159
Amarguillo, 169
Amarone della Valpolicella, 138
Amboise, 111
Ambonnay, 43

Amelia, 146
Ameugny, 85
Ammerschwihr, 32
Ampuis, 91, 93
Amynteo, 235
Anatolia, 293
Anchialos, 235
Ancient Lakes, 256
Andalucia, 158, 167
Anderson Valley, 249
Andlau, 171
Añelo, 270
Angaco, 268
Angélus, 107
Anjou, 110
Anjou Villages, 110
Anjou Villages Brissac, 110
Anjou-Coteaux-de-la-Loire, 110
Anjou-Saumur, 108, 110
Annapolis Valley, 243
Annunziata, 132
Ansonica Costa dell'Argentario, 142
Antalka, 224
Antelope Valley of the California High
   Desert, 248
Appalachian Foothills, 242
Appalachian High Country, 259
Appalachian Plateau, 242
Appenzell Ausserrhoden, 230
Appenzell Innerrhoden, 230
Applegate Valley, 255
Apremont, 41
Aprilia, 147
Arabako Txakolina, 162
Aragatsotn, 296
Aragón, 158, 162
Aranka-tető, 216
Aranyos, 220
Arany-Patkó, 224
Arany-Sajgó, 221
Ararat, 296
Arauco, 268
Arbin, 41
Arbois, 38
Arborea, 155
Arborina, 132
Archanes, 236
Arcole, 138
Ardillats, 87
Argentina, 264, 266
Arione, 135
Arizona, 247, 257
Arkansas, 247, 258
Arkansas Mountain, 258
Arlanza, 160
Armavir, 296
Armenia, 296
Arribes, 160
Arroyo Grande Valley, 253
Arroyo Seco, 252
Arruda, 176
Artigas, 298
Arvelets, 51
Ascheri, 132
Ashton, 278
Asili, 126
Assisi, 146
Asti, 123, 124
Asturias, 159
Atacama, 263
Atalaya, 169
Atina, 147
Atlantic Region, 266, 270
Atlas Peak, 250
Au Closeau, 52
Au Vignerais, 86
Auckland, 287
Au-Dessus des Malconsorts, 56
Augusta, 258
Ausario, 128
Ausone, 107
Austral, 263
Australia, 279, 281
Australian Capital Territory, 281
Austria, 200, 202
Austrias, 158
Aux Argillas, 58
Aux Beaux Bruns, 54
Aux Boudots, 58
Aux Bousselots, 58
Aux Bouthiéres, 86
Aux Brulées, 56
Aux Chaignots, 58
Aux Chailloux, 86
Aux Champs Perdrix, 58
Aux Charmes, 53
Aux Cheseaux, 53
Aux Clous, 63
Aux Combottes
   Chambolle-Musigny, 54
   Gevrey-Chambertin, 52
Aux Coucherias, 64
Aux Cras
   Beaune, 64
   Nuits-Saint-Georges, 58
Aux Échanges (M), 54
Aux Fourneaux, 63
Aux Gravains, 63
Aux Guettes, 63
Aux Malconsorts, 56
Aux Murgers, 58

Aux Perdrix, 60
Aux Quarts, 86
Aux Raignots, 56
Aux Serpentiéres, 63
Aux Thorey, 58
Aux Vignerondes, 58
Auxey- Duresses, 61
Auxey-Duresses, 71
Avellaneda, 270
Aversa, 151
Avize, 43
Axarquía, 167
Aÿ, 43
Aylés, 162
Ayze, 41
Azay-le-Rideau, 111
Azé, 85
Azerbaijan, 296

B

Babadag, 291
Bábakúta, 224
Bába-völgy, 216
Bački, 294
Bacskai, 218
Badacsony, 212
Badarina, 135
Baden, 186, 196
Badische Bergstrasse, 196
Bagnoli di Sopra/Bagnoli, 138
Bagnols-sur-Cèze, 90
Bairrada, 176
Baja Montaña, 162
Bajusz, 219
Bakonyi, 219
Baksa, 223
Baksó, 219
Balaton, 210
Balatonboglár, 212
Balaton-Felvidék, 212
Balatonfüred-Csopak, 212
Balatonmelléki, 210
Balaton-melléke, 210
Baleyat, 93
Ballard Canyon, 253
Balluri, 127
Bambooes Bay, 275
Banat, 291
Banatski, 294
Bandol, 95
Bandusz, 222
Banghoek, 275
Bangó, 224
Bannockburn, 287
Banu Mărăcine, 291
Bánya, 224
Bányász, 215
Bányi-hegy, 227
Banyuls, 97
Banyuls Grand Cru, 97
Barakonyi, 221
Bárány, 216
Barát, 219
Barbaina, 169
Barbaresco, 124, 125, 126
Barbera d'Alba, 124
Barbera d'Asti, 124
Barbera del Monferrato, 124
Barbera del Monferrato Superiore, 124
Barco Reale di Carmignano, 142
Bardolino, 138
Bardolino Superiore, 138
Barkóczi, 223, 225
Barletta, 150
Barna, 214
Barna-máj, 223
Báró kútja, 225
Barolo, 124, 130, 133
Barossa, 283
Barossa Valley, 283
Barr, 27
Barrancas, 269
Barreal, 268
Barsac, 99, 106
Bartalos, 224
Bártfai, 215
Bartus, 220
Bas de Vermarain à l'Est, 72
Bas des Duresses, 71
Basarin, 127
Bas-Boucharey, 93
Basel-Landschaft, 230
Basel-Stadt, 230
Basilicata, 121, 152
Bas-Rhin, 23
Basses Mourottes, 62
Basses Vergelesses, 63
Basse-Viallière, 93
Bataillère (M), 63
Batailley, 101
Bâtard-Montrachet, 61, 73, 75
Bátori, 215
Batroun, 289
Baudana, 135
Bayerischer Bodensee, 197
Bea, 214

Beamsville Bench, 241
Béarn, 98
Beaujeu, 87
Beaujolais, 22, 87
Beaulieu sur Layon, 110
Beaumes-de-Venise, 89
Beaumont-sur-Vesle, 43
Beaune, 61, 64
Beauregard, 77
Beaurepaire, 77
Beauroy, 48
Beauséjour, 107
Beau-Séjour Bécot, 107
Beblenheim, 30
Becsk, 223
Beechworth, 284
Beine, 47
Beira Atlântico, 175
Beira Interior, 176
Bekaa, 289
Bekaa Valley, 289
Bekecs, 213, 214
Bel Air, 52
Bela Krajina, 290
Bélair Monange, 107
Belén, 267
Belgium, 295
Belgrave, 104
Belissand, 64
Bell Mountain, 257
Bellet, 95
Bellmunt del Priorat, 164
Bellő, 224
Ben Lomond Mountain, 252
Bencsik, 223
Bendecz, 221
Bendigo, 284
Benmore Valley, 249
Bennett Valley, 251
Bennwihr, 31
Beogradski, 294
Berdiot, 48
Bergbieten, 26
Bergeisa, 133
Bergerac, 98
Bergera-Pezzole, 131
Bergheim, 24, 29
Bergholtz, 35
Berkecz, 216
Berlou, 96
Bern, 230
Bernadot, 128
Bernkastel, 189
Berri, 132
Bertholon, 93
Béru, 47
Berzé-la-Ville, 85
Berzé-le-Chatel, 85
Besset, 93
Béton, 94
Betsek, 217
Bettolotti, 132
Beugnons, 48
Beychevelle, 102
Bialka, 225
Bianchello del Metauro, 145
Bianco Capena, 147
Bianco dell'Empolese, 142
Bianco di Custoza, 138
Bianco di Pitigliano, 142
Bielersee, 231
Biella, 123
Bienvenues-Bâtard-Montrachet, 61, 73
Bierzo, 160
Biferno, 149
Big Rivers, 285
Big Valley District- Lake County, 249
Bige, 219
Bikoldal, 224
Binét, 220
Bingen, 192
Binissalem, 170
Bío Bío Valley, 263
Birsalmás, 218
Biscoitos, 178
Bissy-la-Mâconnaise, 85
Bissy-Sous-Uxelles, 85
Bivongi, 153
Bizeljsko Sremič, 290
Bizkaiko Txakolina, 162
Blacé, 87
Black Sea Coast, 293
Blackwood Valley, 282
Blagny, 61
Blanches Fleurs, 64
Blanchot, 49
Blanchot Dessus, 75
Blanot, 85
Blaye, 99
Blienschwiller, 24, 28
Blouvlei, 275
Boca, 124
Bóda, 227
Bodensee, 196
Bodrogkeresztúr, 213, 221
Bodrogkisfalud, 213, 221
Bodrogolaszi, 213, 225
Boesmansrivier, 278
Bogár, 214
Boglyos, 224
Bohemia, 292
Bohomáj, 215

Bohotin, 291
Boiolo, 132
Bois de Chassagne, 76
Bois Roussot, 62
Bojták, 215
Bolandin, 162
Bolgheri, 142
Bolgheri Sassicaia, 142
Bollène, 90
Bombly, 218
Bonarda dell'Oltrepò Pavese, 136
Bonnay, 85
Bonnes Mares, 50
Bonnes-Mares, 53, 54
Bonnezeaux, 110
Bonnievale, 278
Bonnivières, 93
Bons Arrêts, 94
Bonvillars, 231
Bordeaux, 22, 99
Bordeaux Haut-Benauge, 99
Bordeaux Supérieur, 99
Bordini, 127
Borkút, 217
Borzone, 131
Boscareto, 135
Boscatto, 131
Boschetti, 133
Bosco Eliceo, 141
Bosnia & Herzegovina, 294
Boszorkány, 224
Bot River, 276
Bottelary, 275
Botticino, 136
Bouchet, 90
Boudes, 113
Bougros, 49
Bourgogne, 44, 45
Bourgogne Aligoté, 44
Bourgogne Mousseux, 44
Bourgogne Passe-tout-grains, 44
Bourg-Saint-Andéol, 90
Bourgueil, 111
Bourrier, 92
Bouscaut, 105
Bouzeron, 79
Bouzy, 43
Bovlei, 275
Boyd Cantenac, 103
Boyer, 85
Brachetto d'Acqui, 124
Brada, 277
Branaire-Ducru, 102
Brand, 25, 32
Brandini, 132
Brane-Cantenac, 103
Bray, 85
Brazil, 298
Brea, 135
Breede River Valley, 273
Breede River Vallez, 278
Breedekloof, 278
Breganze, 138
Breisgau, 196
Brem, 109
Breri, 131
Bresse-sur-Grosne, 85
Bric Micca, 127
Briccho Chiesa, 132
Bricco Ambrogio, 131
Bricco Boschis, 134
Bricco Cogni, 132
Bricco Delle Viole, 133
Bricco di Neive, 127
Bricco Luciani, 132
Bricco Manescotto, 132
Bricco Manzoni, 133
Bricco Rocca, 132
Bricco Rocche, 134
Bricco S. Giovanni, 133
Bricco San Biagio, 132
Bricco San Pietro, 131
Bricco Voghera, 135
Brico di Treiso, 128
Bricolina, 135
Brindisi, 150
British Columbia, 239, 240
Broglio, 131
Broke Fordwich, 285
Brouilly, 87
Broustet, 106
Bruderthal, 25, 26
Brulhois, 98
Brunate, 132, 133
Brunella, 134
Brunello di Montalcino, 142
Bucelas, 176
Budaházi, 222, 223
Buenos Aires, 266
Buffeljags, 276
Bugey, 22, 39
Buisson, 90
Bükk, 211
Bulgaria, 293
Bullas, 165
Burg Cochem, 189
Burgenland, 202, 205
Burgundy, 22, 44
Burgy, 85
Burnand, 85
Burujena, 169

Bussia, 131, 133
Bussières, 85
But de Mont, 94
Buttafuoco dell'Oltrepò Pavese, 136
Butteaux, 48
Buzet, 98

C

Ca'grossa, 126
Cabardès, 96
Cabernet d'Anjou, 110
Cabrières, 96
Čačansko–kraljevački, 294
Cacc'e mmitte di Lucera, 150
Cachapoal Valley, 263
Cachi, 267
Cadillac, 99
Cafayate - Valle de Cafayate, 267
Cagliari, 155
Cahors, 98
Cailleret, 75
Caillou, 106
Cairanne, 89
Calabria, 121, 153
Calamin, 231
Calatayud, 162
California, 247, 248
California Shenandoah Valley, 254
Calingasta - Valle de Calingasta, 268
Calistoga, 250
Calitzdorp, 277
Calon-Ségur, 100
Calosso, 124
Calouère, 53
Calvi, 114
Camaret-sur-Aigues, 90
Camensac, 104
Campanha, 298
Campania, 121, 151
Campasso, 21
Campi Flegrei, 151
Campidano di Terralba, 155
Campix, 169
Campo de Borja, 162
Campo de la Guardia, 166
Campos de Cima da Serra, 298
Canada, 237, 239
Canadilla, 169
Canary Islands, 158, 171
Canavese, 124
Canberra District, 285
Candia, 236
Candia dei Colli Apuani, 142
Candy Mountain, 256
Canelones, 298
Cangas, 159
Cango Valley, 277
Cannellino di Frascati, 147
Cannonau di Sardegna, 155
Cannubi, 133
Cannubi Boschis, 133
Cannubi Muscatel, 133
Cannubi S. Lorenzo, 133
Cannubi Valletta, 133
Canon, 107
Canon la Gaffeliére, 107
Canon-Fronsac, 99
Canota - Valle de Canota, 269
Canova, 127, 131
Cantabria, 158
Cantarranas, 169
Cantemerle, 104
Cantenac-Brown, 103
Canterbury, 287
Capalbio, 142
Capalot, 132
Capay Valley, 248
Cape Agulhas, 276
Cape Breton Island, 243
Cape May Peninsula, 260
Cape South Coast, 273, 276
Cape Town, 275
Cape West Coast, 273
Cappallotto, 135
Capri, 151
Capriano del Colle, 136
Caramany, 97
Caraş, 291
Carbonnieux, 105
Carcavelos, 176
Carelle Sous La Chapelle, 66
Carema, 124
Carignano del Sulcis, 155
Cariñena, 162
Carmel Valley, 252
Carmignano, 142
Carnuntum, 203
Carpegna, 135
Carrahola, 169
Carrascal, 169
Cars, 126
Carso (Carso-Kar), 139
Casa del Blanco, 166
Casablanca Valley, 263
Casavecchia di Pontelatone, 151
Case Nere, 132
Casorzo, 124

Casot, 128
Caspian Shoreline, 296
Cassis, 95
Castagni, 132
Casteggio, 136
Castel del Monte, 150
Castel del Monte Bombino Nero, 150
Castel del Monte Nero di Troia Riserva, 150
Castel del Monte Rosso Riserva, 150
Castel San Lorenzo, 151
Casteller, 137
Castellero, 133
Castelletto, 131
Castelli di Jesi Verdicchio Riserva, 145
Castelli Romani, 147
Castellina, 144
Castellizzano, 128
Castello, 131
Castelnuovo Berardenga, 144
Castiglione Falletto, 130, 134
Castilla- la Mancha, 158, 166
Castilla y León, 158, 160
Castro Barros, 268
Catalonia, 158, 163
Catamarca, 266
Catoctin, 260
Caucete, 268
Caumont-sur-Durance, 90
Cautín Valley, 263
Cava, 172
Cavanna, 126
Cayuga Lake, 260
Cederberg, 274
Cellatica, 136
Center, 266, 270
Central, 298
Central (hilly), 294
Central Coast, 248, 252, 253
Central Delaware Valley, 260
Central Drakensberg, 274
Central France, 108, 113
Central Greece, 234
Central Hawke's Bay, 287
Central Mountains, 289
Central Orange River, 274
Central Otago, 287
Central Ranges, 285
Central Serbia, 294
Central Valley, 263
Central Victoria, 284
Central Vineyards (Upper Loire), 108, 112
Central Western Australia, 282
Cepre, 227
Cerasuolo d'Abruzzo, 148
Cerasuolo di Vittoria, 154
Cercié, 87
Cerdon, 39
Cerequio, 132, 133
Ceres, 274
Ceres Plateau, 274
Cérons, 99
Cerrati, 135
Cerretta, 135
Cerro de Orbaneja, 169
Cerro de Santiago, 169
Cerro del Pelado, 169
Cerveteri, 147
Cerviano-Merli, 131
Cesanese del Piglio, 147
Cesanese di Affile, 147
Cesanese di Olevano Romano, 147
Chablais, 231
Chablis, 47
premier cru, 48
Chablis (incl 1er Cru), 46
Chablis Grand Cru, 46, 47, 49
Chaines Carteaux, 59
Chaintré, 85
Chalk Hill, 251
Chalone, 252
Chambertin, 50, 52
Chambertin Clos de Béze, 50
Chambertin-Clos de Béze, 52
Chambolle-Musigny, 50, 54
Champ Canet, 73
Champ Chevrey (M), 63
Champ Gain, 73
Champ Nalot, 82
Champ Toizeau, 83
Champagne, 22, 42
Champagny-Sous-Uxelles, 85
Champans, 66
Champeaux, 52
Champlain Valley of New York, 260
Champonnet, 52
Champs Cloux, 80
Champs Jendreau, 76
Champs Pimont, 64
Champtoceaux, 109
Chânes, 85, 87
Chantada, 159
Chantonnay, 109
Chanturgue, 113
Chapadmalal, 270
Chapaize, 85
Chapelle-Chambertin, 50, 52
Chapelle-de-Guinchay, 87
Chapelle-Vaupelteigne, 47
Chapelot, 48
Chapitre, 80
Chardonnay, 85
Charentay, 87
Charlemagne, 61, 62
Charmes, 69
Charmes-Chambertin, 50, 52
Charnay-lès-Mâcon, 85
Chassagne, 75
Chassagne du Clos Saint-Jean, 75
Chassagne-Montrachet, 74, 75, 76
Chatains, 48
Château Gris (M), 59
Château-Chalon, 38
Chateaugay, 113
Château-Grillet, 89
Châteaumeillant, 113
Châteauneuf-de-Gadagne, 90
Châteauneuf-du-Pape, 89
Château-Thébaud, 109
Chatelon, 93
Châtillon-en-Diois, 89
Chaume de Talvat, 48
Chautagne, 41
Chavaroche, 93
Chazelle, 83
Chehalem Mountains, 255
Chemilly-sur-Serein, 47
Chénas, 87
Chenonceaux, 111
Cherasco, 130, 131
Cherbaudes, 52
Chevagny-lès-Chevrières, 85
Cheval Blanc, 107
Chevalier-Montrachet, 61, 73
Cheverny, 111
Cheyres, 231
Chianti, 142, 143
Chianti Classico, 142, 144
Chichée, 47
Chiclana de la Frontera, 168
Chignin, 41
Chignin-Bergeron, 41
Chile, 261, 263
Chilecito, 268
Chiles Mountain, 250
Chimbas, 268
China, 297
Chinon, 111
Chipiona, 168
Chiroubles, 87
Chissey-lès-Mâcon, 85
Chitry, 45
Choapa Valley, 263
Chorey-lès-Beaune, 61
Chouilly, 43
Chozas Carrascal, 165
Chubut, 266
Chusclan, 90
Cienega Valley, 252
Cigales, 160
Cigány, 221
Cilento, 151
Cinque Terre, 140
Ciocchini, 132
Ciocchini-Loschetto, 131
Circeo, 147
Cirkáló, 226
Cirò, 153
Ciróka, 224, 226
Cisterna d'Asti, 124
Citrusdal Mountain, 277
Citrusdal Valley, 277
Clairette de Bellegarde, 89
Clairette de Die, 89
Clairette du Languedoc, 96
Clare Valley, 283
Clarksburg, 254
Claro Valley, 263
Clavaillon, 73
Clear Lake, 249
Clements Hills, 254
Clerc-Milon, 101
Clessé, 85
Climat Du Val, 71
Climens, 106
Clisson, 109
Clos Arlot (M), 60
Clos Baulet, 53
Clos Berthet (M), 62
Clos Blanc, 65
Clos Chareau, 76
Clos Charlé, 82
Clos de Forêts Saint-Georges (M), 60
Clos de la Baraude, 82
Clos de la Barre (M), 66
Clos de la Bousse-d'Or (M), 66
Clos de la Boutiére (M), 78
Clos de la Cave des Ducs (M), 66
Clos de la Chapelle (M), 66
Clos de la Commaraine, 65
Clos de la Feguine (M), 64
Clos de la Fussiére (M), 78
Clos de la Garenne, 73
Clos de la Maréchale (M), 60
Clos de la Mouchére (M), 73
Clos de la Mousse (M), 64
Clos de la Perriére (M)
Fixin, 51
Vougeot, 55
Clos de la Roche, 50, 53
Clos de la Rougeotte, 66
Clos de l'Audignac, 66
Clos de l'Ecu (M), 64
Clos de Paradis, 81
Clos de Réas (M), 56
Clos de Tart (M), 50, 53
Clos de Tavannes, 77
Clos de Verger, 65
Clos de Vougeot, 50, 55
Clos des 60 Ouvrées (M), 66
Clos des Argilliéres, 60
Clos des Avaux, 64
Clos des Barraults, 81
Clos des Chênes, 66
Clos des Corvées (M), 60
Clos des Corvées Pagets, 60
Clos des Ducs (M), 66
Clos des Epeneaux (M), 65
Clos des Grandes Vignes (M), 60
Clos des Grands Voyens (M), 81
Clos des Lambrays, 50, 53
Clos des Maréchauds (M), 62
Clos des Montaigus, 81
Clos des Mouches, 77
Clos des Myglands (M), 81
Clos des Ormes, 53
Clos des Perrières (M), 69
Clos des Porrets- Saint-Georges (M), 59
Clos des Toisiéres (M), 70
Clos des Ursules (M), 64
Clos des Varoilles (M), 52
Clos du Cellier Aux Moines, 82
Clos du Chaigne, 80
Clos du Chapitre, 62
Clos du Chapitre (M)
Fixin, 51
Gevrey-Chambertin, 52
Clos du Château de Montaigu (M), 81
Clos du Château des Ducs (M), 66
Clos du Cras Long, 82
Clos du Roi, 64
Clos Du Val, 71
Clos du Vernoy, 82
Clos du Verseuil (M), 66
Clos Faubard, 77
Clos Fourtet, 107
Clos Haut-Peyraguey, 106
Clos Jus, 82
Clos Marceaux (M), 82
Clos Marcilly (M), 81
Clos Marole, 82
Clos Napoléon (M), 51
Clos Pitois (M), 76
Clos Prieur, 52
Clos Rousseau, 77
Clos Saint-Jacques, 52
Clos Saint-Jacques (M), 80
Clos Saint-Jean, 75
Clos Saint-Landry (M), 64
Clos Saint-Marc (M), 60
Clos Salomon (M), 82
Clos Sorbé, 53
Clos St-Denis
Côte de Nuits, 50
Morey-Saint-Denis, 53
Vosne-Romanée, 56
Clos Tonnerre, 81
Clos Voyens, 81
Clos-Saint-Paul (M), 82
Clos-Saint-Pierre (M), 82
Cloux, 80
Coastal Plain, 289
Coastal Plain (lowlands), 294
Coastal Region
Montenegro, 294
South Africa, 273, 275
Codana, 134
Codolet, 90
Codru, 293
Cognet, 93
Colares, 176
Colchagua Valley, 263
Cole, 126
Cole Ranch, 249
Collan, 47
Collaretto, 135
Collet, 94
Colli Albani, 147
Colli Altotiberini, 146
Colli Aretini, 143
Colli Asolani (Asolo Prosecco), 138
Colli Berici, 138
Colli Bolognesi, 141
Colli Bolognesi Classico Pignoletto, 141
Colli del Trasimeno, 146
Colli della Sabina, 147
Colli dell'Etruria Centrale, 142
Colli di Conegliano, 138
Colli di Faenza, 141
Colli di Luni, 140, 142
Colli di Parma, 141
Colli di Rimini, 141
Colli di Scandiano e di Canossa, 141
Colli d'Imola, 141
Colli Etruschi Viterbese, 147
Colli Euganei, 138
Colli Euganei Fior d'Arancio, 138
Colli Fiorentini, 143
Colli Lanuvini, 147
Colli Maceratesi, 145
Colli Martani, 146
Colli Orientali del Friuli Picolit, 139
Colli Perugini, 146
Colli Pesaresi, 145
Colli Piacentini, 141
Colli Romagna Centrale, 141
Colli Senesi, 143
Colli Tortonesi, 124
Collina Torinese, 124
Colline di Levanto, 140
Colline Joniche Tarantine, 150
Colline Lucchesi, 142
Colline Novaresi, 124
Colline Pisane, 143
Colline Saluzzesi, 124
Colline Teramane Montepulciano d'Abruzzo, 148
Collio Goriziano, 139
Collioure, 97
Colombaro, 135
Colón, 270
Colonia, 298
Colonia Caroya, 270
Colorado, 247, 257
Columbia Gorge, 255, 256
Columbia Valley, 255, 256
Combe au Moine, 52
Combsville, 250
Commandaria, 293
Conca, 132
Conca de Barberà, 163
Condado de Huelva, 167
Condado do Tea, 159
Condrieu, 89
Conegliano Valdobbiadene Prosecco, 138
Cònero, 145
Confluencia, 270
Connecticut, 247, 260
Constantia, 275
Contea di Sclafani, 154
Contessa Entellina, 154
Controguerra, 148
Coonawarra, 283
Copertino, 150
Copiapó Valley, 263
Coquimbo, 263
Corbières, 96
Corbières-Boutenac, 96
Córdoba Argentina, 266
Corent, 113
Cori, 147
Corini-Pallaretta, 131
Cornas, 89
Cornevent, 83
Corps de Loup, 94
Corrèze, 98
Corse, 22, 114
Cortambert, 85
Cortese dell'Alto Monferrato, 124
Cortevaix, 85
Corti Benedettine del Padovano, 138
Cortijo de Guerra, 169
Corton, 61, 62
Cortona, 142
Corton-Charlemagne, 61, 62
Cos d'Estournel, 100
Cos Labory, 100
Costa d'Amalfi, 151
Costabella, 135
Coste della Sesia, 124
Coste di Rose, 133
Coste di Vergne, 133
Costers del Segre, 163
Costières de Nîmes, 89
Cosumnes River, 254
Côte Blonde, 93
Côte Bodin, 93
Côte Brune, 93
Côte Chalonnaise, 44, 45, 79
Côte de Beaune, 44, 61
Côte de Beaune-Villages, 61
Côte de Bréchain, 48
Côte de Brouilly, 87
Côte de Cuissy, 48
Côte de Fontenay, 48
Côte de Jouan, 48
Côte de Lèchet, 48
Côte de Nuits, 44, 50
Côte de Nuits-Villages, 50
Côte de Rouffach, 24
Côte de Savant, 48
Côte de Vaubarousse, 48
Côte des Blancs, 43
Côte des Prés-Girots, 48
Côte d'Or, 45
Côte Rotie, 53
Côte Rozier, 93
Côte Saint-Jacques, 45
Côteaux Bourguignons, 44
Coteaux Champenois, 42
Coteaux d'Aix-en- Provence, 95
Coteaux d'Ancenis, 109
Coteaux de Bassenon, 94
Coteaux de Die, 89
Coteaux de la Vézère, 98
Coteaux de l'Aubance, 110
Coteaux de Tupin, 94
Coteaux- de-Saumur, 110
Coteaux du Cap Corse, 114
Coteaux du Giennois, 112
Coteaux du Haut-Koenigsbourg, 24
Coteaux du Layon, 110
Coteaux du Loir, 111
Coteaux du Lyonnais, 88
Coteaux du Quercy, 98
Coteaux du Vendômois, 111
Coteaux Varois en Provence, 95
Côte-Rôtie, 89, 91, 92, 93, 94
Côtes d'Auvergne, 113
Côtes d'Auxerre, 45
Côtes de Barr, 24
Côtes de Bergerac, 98
Côtes de Blaye, 99
Côtes de Bordeaux, 99
Côtes de Bordeaux Blaye, 99
Côtes de Bordeaux Cadillac, 99
Côtes de Bordeaux Castillon, 99
Côtes de Bordeaux Francs, 99
Côtes de Bordeaux Ste-Foy, 99
Côtes de Bordeaux-St-Macaire, 99
Côtes de Bourg, 99
Côtes de Duras, 98
Côtes de Millau, 98
Côtes de Montravel, 98
Côtes de Provence, 95
Côtes de Sambre et Meuse, 295
Côtes de Toul, 37
Côtes du Couchois, 45
Côtes du Forez, 113
Côtes du Jura, 38
Côtes du Marmandais, 98
Côtes du Rhône, 89
Côtes du Rhône méridionaux, 89, 90
Côtes du Rhône septentrionaux, 89
Côtes du Rhône-Villages, 89, 90
Côtes du Roussillon, 97
Côtes du Roussillon-Villages, 97
Côtes du Vivarais, 89
Côtes Roannaises, 113
Côtes-de- l'Orbe, 231
Coteşti, 291
Cotnari, 291
Cotta', 127
Couhins, 105
Couhins-Lurton, 105
Coulanges-la-Vineuse, 45
Coulée de Serrant, 110
Cour-Cheverny, 111
Courgis, 47
Coutet, 106
Covelo, 248
Cowra, 285
Craipillot, 52
Cramant, 43
Crauzot, 82
Crêches-sur-Saône, 85
Creek Shores, 241
Crémant d'Alsace, 23
Crémant de Bordeaux, 99
Crémant de Bourgogne, 44
Crémant de Die, 89
Crémant de Limoux, 96
Crémant de Loire, 108
Crémant de Savoie, 40
Crémant de Wallonie, 295
Crémant du Jura, 38
Crémant du Luxembourg, 295
Crémillons, 82
Crépy, 41
Crest of the Blue Ridge Henderson County, 259
Creston District, 253
Crete, 234
Creux de Beaux Champs, 83
Creux de la Net, 62
Crimea, 293
Criots-Bâtard-Montrachet, 61, 75
Crişana, 291
Crişana, 291
Croatia, 290
Croatian Uplands, 290
Croizet-Bages, 101
Cros Parantoux, 56
Crosia, 133
Crozes-Hermitage, 89
Cruet, 41
Cruz del Eje, 270
Cruzille, 85
Csadó, 221
Csáki, 221, 222
Csatorna, 215
Csemege-tábla, 216
Cserepes, 214
Cserfás, 216
Cserőczi, 216
Csető, 224
Csicsiri, 216
Csicsiri alja, 216
Csillagdomb, 225
Csirke-máj, 221
Csongrád, 211
Csonka-tető, 215
Csontos, 222
Csopak, 212
Csuka, 222
Cuadrados, 169
Cuartillo, 169
Cucamonga Valley, 248
Cumberland Valley, 260
Cumelle, 92
Cuneo, 123
Curicó Valley, 263
Curra', 127
Currency Creek, 283
Curtefranca, 136
Curtil-Sous-Burnand, 85
Cuyo, 266
Cyprus, 293
Czech Republic, 292
Czeke, 219

D

d'Arche, 106
d'Armailhac, 101
d'Issan, 103
d'Olivier, 105
d'Yquem, 106
Dafnes, 236
Daghestan, 293
Dahlenheim, 26
Dahlonega Plateau, 259
Dalmatia, 290
Dalmatinska Zagora, 290
Dambach-la-Ville, 28
Damiano, 135
Dancka, 218
Danszállás, 223
Danube Plain, 293
Danube Terraces, 291
Dão, 176
Darling, 275
Darnó, 226
Dauzac, 103
Davayé, 85
De Fieuzal, 105
de Malle, 106
Deák, 219
Dealu Bujorului, 291
Dealu Mare, 291
Debrői Hárslevelű, 211
Dehesa del Carrizal, 166
Dehesa Peñalba, 160
Delaware, 247
Delia Nivolelli, 154
delle Venezia, 137, 139
Delle Venezie, 138
Délrefekvő-Sulyom, 214
Denicé, 87
Denmark, 282
Dent de Chien, 75
Dereszla, 221
Derriére Chez Edouard, 72
Derriére la Grange, 54
Derriére la Tour, 72
Derriére Saint-Jean (M), 65
Desmirail, 103
Dessewffy, 220
Deux-Montagnes, 242
Devon Valley, 275
Dézaley, 231
Dézaley-Marsens, 231
Dezső, 222
Diablo Grande, 248
Diamond Mountain District, 250
Diano d'Alba, 130, 131
Dió-kút, 223
Distrito Medrano, 269
Disznódélő, 223
Do Tejo, 176
Dobai, 219
Dobó, 220
Dobra, 225
Dobrogea, 291
Dogliani, 124
Doisy Daëne, 106
Doisy Dubroca, 106
Doisy Védrines, 106
Dolcetto d'Acqui, 124
Dolcetto d'Alba, 124
Dolcetto d'Asti, 124
Dolcetto di Diano d' Alba, 124
Dolcetto di Ovada, 124
Dolcetto di Ovada Superiore, 124
Dolenjska, 290
Domaine de Chevalier, 105
Domazan, 90
Dominio de Valdepusa, 166
Donáth, 220
Dongbei, 297
Dongó, 215, 222
Dorgó, 215, 217
Dőri, 216
Dörzsike, 227
Dos Rios, 248
Douglas, 274
Douro, 176
Drăgăşani, 291
Druca', 133
Dry Creek Valley, 251
Du Tertre, 103
Duché d'Uzès, 89
Ducru-Beaucaillou, 102
Duhort-Milon, 101
Dukát, 215
Duna, 211
Dunántúl (Transdanubia), 210
Duna-Tisza Közi, 210
Dundee Hills, 255
Dunnigan Hills, 248
Durazno, 298
Durbanville, 275
Durfort-Vivens, 103
Duriense, 175

E

Eagle Foothills, 255
Eagle Peak Mendocino County, 249
East (submountainous), 294
East Anglia, 295
Eastern Cape, 273
Eastern Connecticut Highlands, 260
Eastern Plains, Inland and North of Western Australia, 282
Echaille, 72
Echézeaux, 50, 56
Echézeaux du Dessus, 56
Eden Valley, 283
Edna Valley, 253
Eger, 211
Eguisheim, 33
Eichberg, 25, 33
Eichhoffen, 27
Eilandia, 278
Eisenberg, 205
El Corchuelo, 169
El Dorado, 254
El Duque, 169
El Flamenco, 169
El Hierro, 171

El Inglés, 169
El Lloar, 164
El Paraíso, 269
El Pomar District, 253
El Puerto de Santa María, 168
El Terrerazo, 165
El Vicario, 166
Elandskloof, 276
Elba, 142
Elba Aleatico Passito, 142
Elgin, 276
Elim, 276
Elkton Oregon, 255
Előhegy, 219, 224, 225
Elő-hegy, 216
Eloro, 154
Elqui Valley, 263
Elstertal, 199
Émeringes, 87
Emilia-Romagna, 121, 141
Empordà, 163
En Cailleret, 75
En Caradeux, 62
En Charlemagne, 62
En Chevret, 66
En Choué, 82
En Créot, 72
En Ergot, 52
En France, 86
En Genêt, 64
En la Perriére Noblot (M), 58
En la Ranché, 72
En Largilliére, 65
En L'orme, 64
En Montceau, 72
En Naget, 62
En Orveaux, 56
En Remilly
    Chassagne-Montrachet, 75
    Saint-Aubin, 72
En Servy, 86
En Veau, 82
En Virondot, 76
En Vollon à l'Est, 72
Encostas d'Aire, 176
Engelberg, 25, 26
England, 295
Entraygues-Le Fel, 98
Entre-Deux-Mers, 99
Entre-deux-Mers Haut-Benauge, 99
Eola-Amity Hills, 255
Epineuil, 45
Epirus, 234
Erbaluce di Caluso/Caluso, 124
Erdőbénye, 213, 223
Erdőhorváti, 213, 225
Eresztvény, 223
Erice, 154
Es Champs, 72
Escaladei, 164
Escondido Valley, 257
Esino, 145
Est! Est!! Est!!! di Montefiascone, 147
Estaing, 98
Estézargues, 90
Estournelles- Saint-Jacques, 52
Etna, 154
Etrigny, 85
Etyek-Buda, 212
Extremadura, 158, 166
Ez Crets, 75
Ez Crottes, 76

Fair Play, 254
Falanghina del Sannio, 151
Falerio, 145
Falerno del Massico, 151
Falletto, 135
Famatina, 268
Far North, 283
Fara, 124
Farkas, 219
Farkas-dűlő, 221
Faro, 154
Faset, 126
Faucon, 90
Faugères, 96
Fausoni, 127
Faye d'Anjou, 110
Fehér-kút, 223
Fekete-hegy, 219, 227
Felipe Varela, 268
Felső-Bea, 214
Felső-Esztáva, 227
Felső-gát, 226
Felső-Lete, 214
Felső-Magyarország, 210
Fennville, 258
Ferenc diák, 223
Ferrere, 128
Ferriére, 103
Fiano di Avellino, 151
Fiasco, 134
Fiddletown, 254
Fiefs Vendéens, 109
Figari, 114
Figeac, 107
Filhot, 106
Finca Élez, 166
Finger Lakes, 260
Fitou, 96

Fixin, 50, 51
Flanders, 295
Fleurie, 87
Fleurieu, 283
Fleys, 47
Floc de Gascogne, 98
Florida
    Uruguay, 298
    Usa, 247
Florimont, 25, 32
Fongeant, 93
Fontanafredda, 135
Fontenay-près-Chablis, 47
Fonteny, 52
Forêts, 48
Forrás, 219
Fort Ross-Seaview, 251
Fossati, 132, 133
Fountaingrove District, 251
Four Mile Creek, 241
Fourchaume, 48
Fourvier, 93
France, 10, 22
Francemont, 76
Francia, 135
Franciacorta, 136
Frangy, 40
Franken, 186, 195
Frankland River, 282
Frankstein, 25, 28
Franschhoek Valley, 275
Frascati, 147
Frascati Superiore, 147
Fraser Valley, 240
Fredericksburg in the Texas Hill
    Country, 257
Free State, 273
Freisa d'Asti, 124
Freisa di Chieri, 124
Fréjus, 95
Frémiets, 66
Frémiets-Clos de la Rougeotte (M), 66
Fribourg, 230
Friularo di Bagnoli, 138
Friuli, 139
Friuli Annia, 139
Friuli Aquileia, 139
Friuli Colli Orientali, 139
Friuli Grave, 139
Friuli Isonzo, 139
Friuli Latisana, 139
Friuli-Venezia Giulia, 121, 139
Froehn, 25, 30
Fronsac, 99
Fronton, 98
Fuissé, 85
Fúló-hegy, 214
Fürdős, 226
Fürstentum, 25, 31

Gabiano, 124
Gabutti, 135
Gadagne, 90
Gaia Principe, 127
Gaillac, 98
Gaillac Premières Côtes, 98
Gaiole, 144
Galagonyás, 214, 224
Galambos, 217, 227
Galatina, 150
Galicia, 158, 159
Galilee, 289
Galina, 132
Gallaretto, 131
Gallega, 169
Gallina, 127
Galluccio, 151
Galuska, 215, 224
Galyagos, 215
Gambellara, 138
Ganja, 296
Gansu, 297
Garai, 220
Garassino, 128
Garda, 136, 138
Garda Colli Mantovani, 136
Gárdony, 216
Garretti, 131
Gattera, 132
Gattinara, 124
Gavi (Cortese di Gavi), 124
Gazsó, 214
Geelong, 284
Gegharkunik, 296
Geisberg, 25, 29
Gelencér, 214
Gellért, 224
Genazzano, 147
General Alvear, 269
General Conesa, 270
General Lamadrid, 268
General Roca, 270
Geneva, 230
Genevrières, 69
Geographe, 282
Georgia, 247, 259, 296
Gerendás, 216
Gerine, 93
German Swiss, 230
Germany, 179, 186

Getariako Txakolina, 162
Gevrey-Chambertin, 50, 52
Ghemme, 124
Giachini, 132
Giacone, 128
Giacosa, 128
Gianetto, 135
Gibalbín, 169
Gigondas, 89
Gilányi, 224
Gilboa, 289
Ginestra, 131
Ginter, 222
Gioia del Colle, 150
Gippsland, 284
Girò di Cagliari, 155
Gisborne, 287
Giscours, 103
Givry, 79, 82
Gladstone, 287
Glarus, 230
Glenrowan, 284
Gloeckelberg, 25, 29
Góböly, 221
Godoy Cruz, 269
Goedemoed, 278
Golan Heights, 289
Golden Mile Bench, 240
Goldert, 25, 34
Golfo del Tigullio- Portofino, 140
Golop, 213, 214
Gombos-hegy, 226
Gomboska, 215
Göndörke, 225
Goose Gap, 256
Görbe, 215, 221, 223
Görbe-Baksó, 219
Goree, 278
Gorges, 109
Goriška Brda, 290
Goudini, 278
Goudmyn, 278
Goulaine, 109
Goulburn Valley, 284
Goumenissa, 235
Graciosa, 178
Gramolere, 131
Grampians, 284
Gran Canaria, 171
Grance Senesi, 142
Grand Auxerrois, 44, 46
Grand Clos Fortoul (M), 81
Grand Clos Rousseau, 77
Grand Puy Lacoste, 101
Grand River Valley, 259
Grand Roussillon, 97
Grand Taillis, 93
Grand Valley, 257
Grandes Places, 93
Grands-Echézeaux, 50, 56
Granite Belt, 285
Gratallops, 164
Graubünden, 230
Gravina, 150
Graves, 99
Graves de Vayres, 99
Graves Supérieures, 99
Great Southern, 282
Great Western, 284
Greater Perth, 282
Greco di Bianco, 153
Greco di Tufo, 151
Greece, 232, 234
Green Valley of Russian River Valley,
    251
Grenouilles, 49
Grés de Montpellier, 96
Grésigny, 80
Greve, 144
Grevilly, 85
Greyton, 276
Grifféres (M), 81
Grignan-les-Adhémar, 89
Grignolino d'Asti, 124
Grignolino del Monferrato Casalese,
    124
Grinzane Cavour, 130, 131
Griotte-Chambertin, 50, 52
Groblershoop, 274
Groenberg, 275
Groenekloof, 275
Groenfontein, 277
Grootdrink, 274
Gros Plant du Pays Nantais, 109
Grottino di Roccanova, 152
Gruaud-Larose, 102
Guaymallén, 269
Gueberschwihr, 34
Guebwiller, 35
Guenoc Valley, 249
Guerchére, 76
Guijoso, 166
Guiraud, 106
Gulf Islands, 240
Gundagai, 285
Guria, 296
Gustava, 131
Gutturnio, 141
Gyaka-lyuk, 226
Gyepföld, 217
Gyertyános, 221
Gyopáros, 224
Győr mester, 223
Györgyike, 222
Győri, 215
Győri-tető, 216

Hageland, 295
Hajós-Baja, 211
Halas, 221
Halasi, 222
Halastó, 215
Hamasberg, 221
Hames Valley, 252
Hangács, 217
Happy Canyon of Santa Barbara, 253
Haragos, 225
Haraszt, 222
Harcsa, 217
Harcsa-tető, 217
Harsad, 223
Hartswater, 274
Haspengouw, 295
Hastings River, 285
Hasznos, 214, 215
Hatalos, 217
Határi, 222, 223
Határszüg, 225
Hatschbourg, 25, 34
Hattstatt, 34
Haut-Bages-Libéral, 101
Haut-Bailly, 105
Haut-Batailley, 101
Haut-Brion, 104, 105
Hautes Côtes de Beaune, 45
Hautes Côtes de Nuits, 45
Hautes Mourottes, 62
Haut-Médoc, 99, 104
Haut-Montravel, 98
Haut-Poitou, 110
Haut-Rhin, 23
Haw River Valley, 259
Hawaii, 247
Hawke's Bay, 287
Heathcote, 284
Hebei, 297
Hegyfark, 216
Hegyfarok, 221
Hegymege, 214
Hegymegi, 217
Hemel-en-Aarde Ridge, 276
Hemel-en-Aarde Valley, 276
Henderke, 224
Hengst, 25, 33
Henty, 284
Henye, 221
Herbertsdale, 276
Herceg, 217
Hercegkút, 213, 226
Herczeg, 223
Hermann, 258
Hermitage, 89
Hervelets, 51
Hessische-Bergstrasse, 186, 194
Hetény, 215
Hétszőlő, 220
Heuvelland, 295
Hex River Valley, 278
High Eden, 283
High Valley, 249
Highlands, 294
Hilltops, 285
Hintós, 218
Hokkaido, 297
Hold-völgy, 217, 218
Hongsipu, 297
Hoopsrivier, 278
Hornillo, 169
Horse Heaven Hills, 256
Hosszú-földek, 227
Hosszú-hegy, 226
Hosszú-Kötelek, 218
Hosszú-máj, 221
Hosszú-mály, 221
Hout Bay, 275
Howell Mountain, 250
Huasco Valley, 263
Hudson River Region, 260
Hunawihr, 30
Hungary, 206, 210
Hunter, 285
Hunter Valley, 285
Hurigny, 85
Huşi, 291
Húza-dűlő, 221

I Terreni di Sanseverino, 145
Iana, 291
Iaşi, 291
Idaho, 247, 255
Igé, 85
Iglesia, 268
Ile des Vergelesses, 62
Illésházy, 217
Illinois, 247, 258
Indiana, 247, 259
Indiana Uplands, 259
Ingersheim, 32
Inwood Valley, 248
Ionian Islands, 234
Iowa, 247, 258

Irancy, 46
Irouléguy, 98
Irpinia, 151
Ischia, 151
Isle St. George, 259
Israel, 289
Issarts (M), 52
Isten-hegy, 217
Isten-hegy alja, 217
Istria, 290
Istria and Kvarner, 290
Italy, 115, 121
Itata Valley, 263
Izdenczi, 220
Izsáki Arany Sárfehér, 211

Jablanica, 294
Jáchal, 268
Jahant, 254
Janet, 93
Japan, 297
Jasnières, 111
Jerez de la Frontera, 168
Jerez- Xérès-Sherry, 167
Jerez-Xérès-Sherry, 168, 169
Jinshan, 297
Johannisberg, 190
Jónap, 215
Jongieux, 41
Jonkershoek Valley, 275
Jonquières, 90
Judea, 289
Judean Coast, 289
Judean Foothills, 289
Judean Hills, 289
Jugy, 85
Juharos, 218
Jujuy, 266
Juliénas, 87
Jullié, 87
Jumilla, 165, 166
Junín, 269
Jura, 22, 38, 230
Jurançon, 98
Južnobanatski, 294
Južnoslovenská, 292

Kácsa, 216
Kácsárd, 226
Kaefferkopf, 25, 32
Kaiserstuhl, 196
Kakamas, 274
Kakas, 214, 218, 221
Kakheti, 296
Kalap, 225
Káli, 212
Kamptal, 203, 204
Kanawha River Valley, 259
Kangaroo Island, 283
Kansas, 247
Kanzlerberg, 25, 29
Kapi, 222
Kaposi, 223
Kärnten, 202
Kartli, 296
Kásás, 222
Kassai, 219
Kassai Hasznos, 215
Kassaváros, 214
Kassi, 221
Kastelberg, 25, 27
Kastély-tábla, 221
Katzenthal, 32
Keimoes, 274
Keleti-Sulyom, 214
Kelsey Bench-Lake County, 249
Kentucky, 247, 259
Képések, 219
Kerek-domb, 215
Kerek-domb alja, 215
Kerék-tölgyes, 217
Kereszt-dűlő, 226
Kertész, 216
Kessler, 25, 35
Két út közi, 215
Kherson, 293
Kientzheim, 31
Kincsem, 224
Kincsem alja, 224
King Valley, 284
Kintzheim, 29
Király, 218
Király-gát, 219
Király-hegy, 226
Kirchberg de Barr, 25, 27
Kirchberg de Ribeauvillé, 25, 29
Kirwan, 103
Kis-Boglyoska, 227
Kis-Garai, 220
Kis-Hasznos, 215
Kis-hegyek, 218
Kis-Henye, 221
Kis-Köves-hegy, 227
Kis-Messzelátó, 223
Kis-Rohos, 215
Kis-szőlők, 226

Kisvár, 221
Kitterlé, 25, 35
Klaasvoogds, 278
Klein Karoo, 273, 277
Klein River, 276
Klevener de Heiligenstein, 24
Knights Valley, 251
Knjaževački, 294
Kocher-Jagst-Tauber, 197
Kőcsere, 225
Koekenaap, 275
Koldu, 215, 217
Komoróc, 222
Koo Plateau, 277
Kootenays, 240
Kopaszka, 224
Kőporos, 216, 217, 226
Koszorú, 217
Kotayq, 296
Kővágó, 215, 218, 221
Kövesd, 219
Köves-hegy, 215, 216, 227
Kozarac, 294
Közép-hegy, 217, 218
Kozér, 214
Kraichgau, 196
Krakkó, 214
Kras, 290
Krasnodar, 293
Krasochoria Limassol, 293
Kremstal, 203, 204
Kulcsár, 222
Külső-Meszes, 222
Kumeu, 287
Kunság, 211
Kupak, 222
Kútpatka, 224, 226
Kutyafogó, 214
Kutya-hegy, 225, 226
Kwazulu-Natal, 273
Kweekvallei, 274

L'Arsélie, 93
L'Homme Mort, 48
La Bondue, 81
La Bossière (M), 52
La Boudriotte, 76
La Bressande (M), 80
La Brocarde, 93
La Brosse, 93
La Brûlée, 82
La Bussière (M), 53
La Cailloute (M), 81
La Cardeuse, 76
La Carrera, 169
La Chaniére, 65
La Chapelle
    Auxey-Duresses, 71
    Chassagne-Montrachet, 76
La Chapelle Notre-Dame, 45
La Chapuise, 92
La Chassiére, 81
La Chateniére, 72
La Clape, 96
La Combe d'Orveau, 54
La Combe d'Orveau, 54
La Comme, 77
La Condemine du Vieux Château, 83
La Consulta, 269
La Corte, 131
La Corvée, 62
La Côte, 231
La Coutiére, 62
La Croix Rameau, 56
La Dominode, 63
La Fosse, 80
La Frérie, 86
La Fussiére, 78
La Gaffeliére, 107
La Garenne, 73
La Gigotte, 66
La Gomera, 171
La Grande Berge, 82
La Grande Borne, 76
La Grande Montagne, 76
La Grande Piéce, 83
La Grande Rue (M), 50, 56
La Haye Foussaière, 109
La Islas Canarias, 171
La Jaraba, 166
La Jeunellotte, 69
La Lagune, 104
La Landonne, 93
La Levriére, 81
La Londe, 95
La Maladiére, 77
La Maltroie, 75
La Mancha, 166
La Maréchaude
    Aloxe-Corton, 62
    Pouilly-Fuissé, 86
La Matrosse, 82
La Méjanelle, 96
La Micaude (M), 62
La Mignotte, 64
La Mission (M), 81
La Mission Haut-Brion, 105
La Mondotte, 107
La Morra, 130, 132
La Moulliére, 83
La Moutonne, 49

La Palma, 171
La Pampa, 266
La Paz, 269
La Perriére, 52
La Pièce Sous le Bois, 69
La Plante, 82
La Platiére, 65
La Pucelle, 80
La Reféne, 65
La Renarde (M), 80
La Richemone, 58
La Rioja, 158, 161
La Rioja Argentina, 266, 268
La Riotte, 53
La Roche, 93
La Roche-Vineuse, 85
La Romanée
  Chassagne-Montrachet, 76
La Romanée (M)
  Côte de Nuits, 50
  Gevrey-Chambertin, 52
  Vosne-Romanée, 56
La Roquemaure, 76
La Serra, 132
La Servonnière, 92
La Tâche (M), 50, 56
La Taquière, 93
La Taupine, 70
La Toppe au Vert, 62
La Tour Blanche, 106
La Tour Carnet, 104
La Tour Haut-Brion, 105
La Triote, 93
La Truffiére, 73
La Viallière, 93
La Vigna, 131
La Vilella Alta, 164
La Vilella Baixa, 164
La Volta, 133
La-Chapelle-Sous-Brancion, 85
Lachish, 289
Lacrima di Morro d'Alba, 145
Ladoix, 61, 62
Lafaurie-Peyraguey, 106
Lafite Rothschild, 101
Lafões, 176
Lafon-Rochet, 100
Lagarde-Paréol, 90
Lago di Caldaro, 137
Lago di Corbara, 146
Lagoa, 176
Lagos, 176
Lagrange, 102
Lagunetas, 169
Laives, 85
Lajosok, 217
Lake Chelan, 256
Lake Erie, 259, 260
Lake Erie North Shore, 241
Lake Michigan Shore, 258
Lake Saint-Pierre, 242
Lake Skadar, 294
Lake Wisconsin, 258
Lalande-de-Pomerol, 99
Lamberts Bay, 275
Lambrusco di Sorbara, 141
Lambrusco Grasparossa di Castelvetro, 141
Lambrusco Mantovano, 136
Lambrusco Salamino di Santa Croce, 141
Lamezia, 153
Lamole, 144
Lamorinda, 252
Lamothe Despujols, 106
Lamothe Guignard, 106
Lancaster Valley, 260
Lancement, 93
Lancié, 87
Langeberg-Garcia, 277
Langhe, 124
Langhorne Creek, 283
Langoa Barton, 102
Languedoc, 22, 96
Lantignié, 87
Lantos, 219
Lanzarote, 171
Lapis, 221
Lapis-tető, 221
Larcis Ducasse, 107
Las Compuertas, 269
Las Heras, 269
Lascombes, 103
Lassolle, 66
Latour, 101
Latour-de-France, 97
Latour-Martillac, 105
Latriciéres-Chambertin, 50, 52
Laudun, 90
Laudun-l'Ardoise, 90
Laurelwood District, 255
Lavalle - Desierto de Lavalle, 269
Lavalleja, 298
Lavaut Saint-Jacques, 52
Lavaux, 231
Laville Haut-Brion, 105
La-Vineuse, 85
Lazio, 121, 147
Lazzarito, 135
Le Bas de Gamay à l'Est, 72
Le Bas des Teurons, 64
Le Bourg, 93
Le Cailleret, 73
Le Carcan, 93
Le Cas Rougeot, 70
Le Champ Lalot, 82
Le Champin, 93
Le Champon, 93
Le Chapitre, 45
Le Charlemagne, 62
Le Charmois, 72
Le Chasseur, 278
Le Château Gaillard, 70
Le Clos, 86
Le Clos Blanc (M), 55
Le Clos Chaudron, 83
Le Clos de Monsieur Noly, 86
Le Clos de Solutré, 86
Le Clos des Loyéres, 78
Le Clos des Mouches, 64
Le Clos des Rois, 78
Le Clos du Roy, 81
Le Clos Gauthey, 70
Le Clos l'Evêque, 81
Le Clos Micot, 65
Le Clos Reyssier, 86
Le Clou des Chênes, 70
Le Clou d'Orge, 62
Le Cloux, 83
Le Clouzot, 83
Le Combard, 93
Le Corton, 62
Le Coste, 133
Le Coste di Monforte, 131
Le Croix Moines, 78
Le Goutay, 93
Le Médenchot, 82
Le Meix Bas, 51
Le Meix Bataille, 70
Le Meix Cadot, 80
Le Meix Caillet (M), 80
Le Mollard, 93
Le Mont, 92
Le Morera de Montsant, 164
Le Pallet, 109
Le Paradis, 82
Le Peite Berge, 82
Le Petit Prétan, 82
Le Pied de Chaume, 82
Le Pied du Clou, 82
Le Plomb, 93
Le Porusot, 69
Le Porusot Dessous, 69
Le Porusot Dessus, 69
Le Puits, 72
Le Remilly, 92
Le Rognet et Corton, 62
Le Ronceret, 66
Le Truchet, 93
Le Turne, 135
Le Vieux Château, 83
Le Vigron, 82
Le Village
  Côte-Rôtie, 92
  Monthélie, 70
  Morey-Saint-Denis, 53
  Pommard, 65
  Volnay, 66
Lebanon, 289
Lebrija, 168
Lechința, 291
Lechkhumi, 296
Leelanau Peninsula, 258
Legyesbénye, 213, 214
Léhely, 221
Lehigh Valley, 260
Leipoldtville-Sandveld, 274
Leithaberg, 205
Lemnos, 236
Lencsés, 220
Lenswood, 283
Leona Valley, 248
Léoville-Barton, 102
Léoville-Las Cases, 102
Léoville-Poyferré, 102
L'Epaule, 83
Lepény, 223
Les Aigrots, 64
Les Amoureuses, 54
Les Angles, 66
Les Argilliéres, 60
Les Arvelets, 65
Les Aspres, 97
Les Avaux, 64
Les Barbiéres, 70
Les Bassets, 83
Les Baudes, 54
Les Baudines, 76
Les Baux-de- Provence, 95
Les Beauregards, 48
Les Beaux Champs, 83
Les Beaux Monts, 56
Les Beaux Monts Bas, 56
Les Bercheries, 94
Les Bertins, 65
Les Blanchards, 53
Les Boirettes, 76
Les Bois Chevaux, 82
Les Bois Gautiers, 82
Les Bondues, 75
Les Bonneveaux, 83
Les Bordes, 83
Les Borniques, 54
Les Bouchéres, 69
Les Boucherottes, 64
Les Boucherottes (M), 65
Les Bouchots
  Montagny, 83
  Morey-Saint-Denis, 53
Les Bressandes, 64
Les Bréterins, 71
Les Brouillards, 66
Les Brulés, 86
Les Brussonnes, 76
Les Buis, 62
Les Burnins, 83
Les Byots, 81
Les Caillerets
  Meursault, 68
  Volnay, 66
Les Cailles, 59
Les Carrières, 54
Les Castets, 72
Les Cazetiers, 52
Les Cents Vignes, 64
Les Chabiots
  Chambolle-Musigny, 54
  Morey-Saint-Denis, 53
Les Chabœufs, 59
Les Chaffots, 53
Les Chaillots, 62
Les Chalumaux, 73
Les Champlots, 72
Les Champs Fulliots, 70
Les Champs Gain, 75
Les Champs Martin, 81
Les Champs Traversins, 56
Les Chanavaries, 92
Les Chaniots, 83
Les Chanlins-Bas, 65
Les Chaponniéres, 65
Les Charmes, 54
Les Charmes Dessous, 69
Les Charmes Dessus, 69
Les Charmots, 65
Les Charniéres, 63
Les Charriéres, 53
Les Chatelots, 54
Les Chaumées, 75
Les Chaumelottes, 83
Les Chaumes
  Chassagne-Montrachet, 76
  Vosne-Romanée, 56
Les Chaumes de Narvaux, 69
Les Chaumes des Perrières, 69
Les Chenevery, 53
Les Chenevottes, 75
Les Chevriéres, 86
Les Chouacheux, 64
Les Clos, 49
Les Clos Roussots, 78
Les Clous, 70
Les Coéres, 83
Les Combards, 75
Les Combes
  Givry, 82
  Montagny, 83
  Saint-Aubin, 72
Les Combes au Sud, 72
Les Combes Dessus, 65
Les Combettes, 73
Les Combins, 81
Les Combottes, 54
Les Commes, 75
Les Corbeaux, 52
Les Cortons, 72
Les Coudrettes, 83
Les Craboulettes, 83
Les Cras
  Chambolle-Musigny, 54
  Meursault, 68
Les Crâs, 55
Les Crays, 86
Les Crêts, 81
Les Croichots, 81
Les Croix Noires, 65
Les Crots, 59
Les Cruots ou Vignes Blanches, 56
Les Damodes, 58
Les Demoiselles, 73
Les Didiers (M), 60
Les Duresses
  Auxey-Duresses, 71
  Monthélie, 70
Les Ecussaux, 71
Les Embazées, 76
Les Epenotes, 64
Les Épinottes, 48
Les Faconniéres, 53
Les Fairendes, 76
Les Feusselottes, 54
Les Féves, 64
Les Fichots, 62
Les Folatiéres, 73
Les Fourneaux
  Chablis 1er Cru, 48
  Mercurey, 81
  Santenay, 77
Les Fourniéres, 62
Les Fremiéres, 53
Les Fremiers, 65
Les Frionnes, 72
Les Froichots, 53
Les Fuées, 54
Les Galaffres, 82
Les Garchéres, 83
Les Gaudichots, 56
Les Gaudichots ou la Tâche, 56
Les Gémeaux, 52
Les Genavriéres, 53
Les Genevrières Dessous, 69
Les Genevrières Dessus, 69
Les Goulots, 52
Les Gouresses, 83
Les Gouttes d'Or, 69
Les Grandes Ruchottes, 76
Les Grandes Vignes, 82
Les Grands Champs, 71
Les Grands Clos, 76
Les Grands Epenots, 65
Les Grands Prétans, 82
Les Graviéres, 77
Les Graviéres-Clos de Tavannes, 77
Les Grêchons et Foutriéres, 62
Les Gréves, 64
Les Groseilles, 54
Les Gruenchers
  Chambolle-Musigny, 54
  Morey-Saint-Denis, 53
Les Guérets, 62
Les Hauts Doix, 54
Les Hauts Jarrons, 63
Les Hauts Marconnets, 63
Les Hauts Pruliers, 59
Les Jardins, 83
Les Jaroliéres, 65
Les Jarrons, 63
Les Joyeuses, 62
Les Languettes, 62
Les Las, 83
Les Laviéres, 63
Les Lavrottes, 54
Les Loächausses, 56
Les Lurets, 66
Les Lys, 48
Les Macherelles, 75
Les Macles, 83
Les Marconnets
  Beaune, 64
  Savigny-lès-Beaune, 63
Les Maréchaudes, 62
Les Maroques, 83
Les Ménétriéres, 86
Les Millandes, 53
Les Mitans, 66
Les Mochamps, 53
Les Montrevenots, 64
Les Moutonnes, 93
Les Moutottes, 62
Les Murées, 75
Les Murgers des Dents de Chien, 72
Les Narbantons, 63
Les Naugues, 81
Les Noirots, 54
Les Paquiers, 83
Les Pasquelles, 75
Les Paulands, 62
Les Perriéres
  Beaune, 64
  Montagny, 83
  Nuits-Saint-Georges, 59
  Pouilly-Fuissé, 86
  Puligny-Montrachet, 73
  Saint-Aubin, 72
Les Perrières Dessous, 69
Les Perrières Dessus, 69
Les Petites Clos, 76
Les Petites Fairendes, 76
Les Petites Loliéres, 62
Les Petits Epenots, 65
Les Petits Monts, 56
Les Petits Musigny, 54
Les Petits Vougeots, 55
Les Peuillets, 63
Les Pézerolles, 65
Les Pidances, 83
Les Pierres, 80
Les Places, 75
Les Plantes, 54
Les Platiéres, 83
Les Plures, 68
Les Porrets-Saint-Georges, 59
Les Pougets, 62
Les Poulaillères, 56
Les Poulettes, 59
Les Poutures, 65
Les Preuses, 49
Les Procés, 59
Les Pruliers, 59
Les Pucelles, 73
Les Puillets, 81
Les Quartiers de Nuits, 56
Les Ravelles, 69
Les Rebichets, 75
Les Referts, 73
Les Reisses, 86
Les Resses, 83
Les Reversés, 64
Les Richebourgs, 56
Les Riottes, 70
Les Rouges, 56
Les Rouges du Bas, 56
Les Rouvrettes, 63
Les Ruchots, 53
Les Ruelles (M), 81
Les Rugiens Bas, 65
Les Rugiens Hauts, 65
Les Saints-Georges, 59
Les Santenots Blancs, 68
Les Santenots du Milieu, 68
Les Saumonts, 81
Les Saussilles, 65
Les Sceaux, 64
Les Sentiers, 54
Les Seurey, 64
Les Sizies, 64
Les Sorbés, 53
Les Suchots, 56
Les Talmettes, 63
Les Terres Blanches, 60
Les Teurons, 64
Les Toussaints, 64
Les Travers de Marinot, 72
Les Treufféres, 83
Les Treux, 56
Les Tuvilains, 64
Les Vallerots, 59
Les Valoziéres, 62
Les Vasées, 81
Les Vaucrains, 59
Les Velley, 81
Les Vercots, 62
Les Vergelesses, 63
Les Vergers, 75
Les Véroilles, 54
Les Véroilles ou Richebourg, 56
Les Vignes Blanches, 86
Les Vignes Derriére, 83
Les Vignes des Prés, 83
Les Vignes Franches, 64
Les Vignes Longues, 83
Les Vignes Rondes, 70
Lesardes, 93
Leskovački, 294
Les-Mesnil-sur-Oger, 43
Lesquerde, 97
Lessini Durello, 138
Lessona, 124
Lestár, 219
Lete, 214
L'étoile, 38
Leverano, 150
Lewis-Clark Valley, 255, 256
Leyat, 93
Leyda Valley, 263
Leynes, 87
Liget, 223
Lignorelles, 47
Ligny-le-Châtel, 47
Liguria, 121, 140
Lillooet, 240
Limarí Valley, 263
Lime Kiln Valley, 252
Limestone Coast, 283
Limietberg, 275
Limoux, 96
Limpopo, 273
Lincoln Lakeshore, 241
Linganore, 260
Lions River, 274
Lirac, 89
Lirano, 135
Lisboa, 175
Lison, 138, 139
Lison- Pramaggiore, 139
Lison-Pramaggiore, 138
Liste, 133
Listrac-Médoc, 99
Litoměřická, 292
Livermore Valley, 252
Lizzano, 150
Loazzolo, 124
Loché, 85
Locorotondo, 150
Lőcse, 223
Lodi, 254
Loess Hills District, 258
Loire Valley, 22, 108
Lókötő, 222
Lombardia, 121, 136
Lomopardo, 169
Loncomilla Valley, 263
Long Island, 260
Lontué Valley, 263
Lónyai, 219
Loramie Creek, 259
Loreley, 188
Lori, 296
Lorraine, 22, 37
Los Balagueses, 165
Los Carneros, 250, 251
Los Cerrillos, 166
Los Chacayes, 269
Los Olivos District, 253
Los Tercios, 169
Louisiana, 247
Loupiac, 99
Lourinhã, 176
Lournand, 85
Louvois, 43
Lower Duivenhoks River, 276
Lower Galilee, 289
Lower Golan, 289
Lower Long Tom, 255
Lower Murray, 283
Luberon, 89
Lugana, 136, 138
Lugny, 85
Luján de Cuyo, 269
Lunlunta, 269
Lussac-Saint-Émilion, 99
Lutzville Valley, 275
Luxembourg, 295
Luzern, 230
Lynch-Bages, 101
Lynch-Moussas, 101
Lyonnais, 22, 88

M

Macedon Ranges, 284
Macedonia, 234
Macharnudo Alto, 169
Macharnudo Bajo, 169
Mâcon, 84, 85
Mâconnais, 44, 84
Mâcon-Villages, 84
Macvin du Jura, 38
Mád, 213, 218
Madargues, 113
Madeira, 177
Madeirense, 177
Madera, 248
Madiran, 98
Madrid, 158, 166
Magita, 222
Magos-hegy, 225
Mahina, 169
Mailly-Champagne, 43
Maindreieck, 195
Maine, 247
Mainviereck, 195
Maipo Valley, 263
Maipú, 269
Maison Brûlée, 53
Maison Rouge, 94
Maisons Blanches, 94
Majevica, 294
Mák-hegy, 225
Makkos, 217
Makkoshotyka, 213, 226
Makra, 226
Málaga, 167
Malartic Lagraviére, 105
Malay, 85
Maldonado, 298
Malepère, 96
Malescot St-Exupéry, 103
Malgas, 276
Malibu Coast, 248
Malibu-Newton Canyon, 248
Maligny, 47
Malleco Valley, 263
Malmesbury, 275
Malokarpatská, 292
Malomfeli, 220
Malomhegy, 224
Malom-zug, 214
Malvasia Candia, 236
Malvasia delle Lipari, 154
Malvasia di Bosa, 155
Malvasia di Castelnuovo Don Bosco, 124
Malvasia Paros, 236
Malvasia Sitia, 236
Mambourg, 25, 31
Mamertino, 154
Mancey, 85
Manchuela, 166
Mandelberg, 25, 30
Mandrolisai, 155
Mandulás, 219, 224, 226
Manicle, 39
Manilva, 167
Manitoba, 239
Manjimup, 282
Manocino, 135
Mansfelder Seen, 198
Mantinia, 235
Mantoetto, 131
Manton Valley, 248
Manzanilla Sanlúcar de Barrameda, 167
Manzola, 128
Maramureș, 291
Maranges, 61, 78
Marcarini, 128
Marchampt, 87
Marche, 121, 145
Marcillac, 98
Marckrain, 25, 31
Marcorino, 127
Maremma Toscana, 142
Marenca, 135
Marestel, 40
Mareuil, 109
Margaret River, 282
Margaux, 99, 103
Margheria, 135
Margita, 214
Margotés, 80
Mari Hernandez, 169
Marignan, 41
Marin, 41
Marino, 147
Marinot, 72
Mariondino, 134
Marissou, 80
Markgräflerland, 196
Marlborough, 287
Marlenheim, 26
Marmara, 293
Marquesado, 169
Marquis d'Alesme-Becker, 103
Marquis de Terme, 103
Marsala, 154
Marsannay, 50
Marsannay Rosé, 50
Marsanne, 93
Martailly-lès-Brancion, 85
Martha's Vineyard, 260
Martina, 150
Martinborough, 287
Martinenga, 126
Maryland, 247, 260
Masos del Terme de Falset, 164
Massachusetts, 247, 260
Massara, 131
Massif d'Uchaux, 90
Massy, 85
Matakana, 287
Matera, 152
Matino, 150
Mátra, 211
Maule Valley, 263
Maury, 97

Mavrodaphne of Cephalonia, 236
Mavrodaphne of Patras, 235
Mazis-Chambertin, 50, 52
Mazoyéres-Chambertin, 50, 52
McDowell Valley, 249
McGregor, 278
McLaren Vale, 283
McMinnville, 255
Mediterranean, 293
Médoc, 99
Medve, 221
Meggyes, 214, 217
Meggyesek, 215
Megyer, 226
Mehedinţi, 291
Meissen, 159
Meix Rentier, 53
Meleg-föld, 227
Meleg-máj, 219
Meleg-mály, 225
Meleg-oldal, 215, 220, 227
Mélinots, 48
Melissa, 153
Mělnická, 292
Mendocino, 249
Mendocino Ridge, 249
Mendoza, 266, 269
Menetou-Salon, 112
Menfi, 154
Méntrida, 166
Mercurey, 79, 81
Meriame, 135
Mérindol-les-Oliviers, 90
Merlara, 138
Merritt Island, 254
Meruzzano, 128, 129
Mesilla Valley, 257
Meskheti, 296
Mesland, 111
Messenikola, 235
Messzelátó, 221, 223
Mester-völgy, 219
Mészárka, 223
Meszes, 222, 223
Metropolitan, 298
Meursault, 61, 67, 68, 69
Mézes-mály, 219
Mezőzombor, 213, 217
Michigan, 247, 258
Mid-Berg River, 275
Middle Rio Grande Valley, 257
Middleburg Virginia, 259
Midlands And North, 295
Mikulovská, 292
Milly-Lamartine, 85
Mimbres Valley, 257
Minervois, 96
Minervois-La Livinière, 96
Minho, 175
Miniş, 291
Minnesota, 247, 258
Mirabel-aux-Baronnies, 90
Miraflores, 169
Mississippi, 247, 258
Mississippi Delta, 258
Missouri, 247, 258
Mittelbergheim, 27
Mittelburgenland, 205
Mittelhaardt-Deutsche Weinstraße, 193
Mittelrhein, 186, 188
Mittelwihr, 30
Mizpe Ramon, 289
Mlavski, 294
Modena, 141
Moenchberg, 25, 27
Mogyorós, 219
Mogyorósok, 223
Mokelumne River, 254
Moldova, 293
　　Romania, 291
Molesme, 80
Molinos, 267
Molise, 121, 149
Mollans-sur-Ouvèze, 90
Molsheim, 26
Monbazillac, 98
Mondéjar, 166
Mondoha, 223
Mondragon, 90
Monemvasia Malvasia, 235
Monferrato, 124
Monforte d'Alba, 130, 131
Monica di Sardegna, 155
Monnières-Saint-Fiacre, 109
Monok, 213, 214
Monor, 211
Monprivato, 134
Monreale, 154
Monrobiolo di Bussia, 133
Mont de Milieu, 48
Mont Laurent, 83
Montagne de Reims, 43
Montagne-Saint-Émilion, 99
Montagnieu, 39
Montagny, 79, 83
Montagu, 277
Montalbano, 143
Montana, 169, 247
Montanello, 134
Montaribaldi, 126
Montbellet, 85
Montceaux-Ragny, 85
Montcuchot, 83
Montecarlo, 142
Montecompatri-Colonna, 147
Montecucco, 142

Montecucco Sangiovese, 142
Montée de Tonnerre, 48
Montée Rouge, 64
Montefalco, 146
Montefalco Sagrantino, 146
Montefico, 126
Montefioralle, 144
Montello Colli Asolani, 138
Montello Rosso/Montello, 138
Montenegro, 294
Montepulciano d'Abruzzo, 148
Monteregian Hills, 242
Monteregio di Massa Marittima, 142
Monterey, 252
Monterminod, 40
Monterrei, 159
Montersino, 128, 129
Montescudaio, 142
Montespertoli, 143
Montestefano, 126
Monthélie, 61, 70
Monthoux, 40
Monti Lessini, 138
Monticello, 259
Montilla-Moriles, 167
Montlis, 92
Montlouis-sur-Loire, 111
Montmain, 93
Montmains, 48
Montmelas-Saint-Sorlin, 87
Montmélian, 41
Montorge, 83
Montpalais, 85
Montpeyroux, 96
Montrachet, 61, 73, 75
Montravel, 98
Montrecul, 45
Montrose, 100
Monts Luisants, 53
Montsant, 163
Monvigliero, 131
Moon Mountain District Sonoma
　　County, 251
Mór, 212
Moravia, 292
Morein, 48
Morellino di Scansano, 142
Morey-Saint-Denis, 50, 53
Morgeot, 76
Morgon, 87
Morières-lès-Avignon, 90
Mornachon, 93
Mornington Peninsula, 284
Moscadello di Montalcino, 142
Moscatel de Valencia, 165
Moscato di Sardegna, 155
Moscato di Scanzo, 136
Moscato di Sorso Sennori, 155
Moscato di Trani, 150
Mosconi, 131
Mosel, 186, 189
Moselle, 37, 295
Moselle Luxembourgeoise, 295
Moseltor, 189
Moslavina, 290
Mostar, 294
Moulin-à-Vent, 87
Moulis, 99
Mount Barker, 282
Mount Benson, 283
Mount Gambier, 283
Mount Lebanon, 289
Mount Lofty Ranges, 283
Mouton Rothschild, 101
Mouzillon-Tillières, 109
Mt. Harlan, 252
Mt. Pisgah Polk County Oregon, 255
Mt. Veeder, 250
Mudgee, 285
Muenchberg, 25, 28
Mulató, 215, 223, 224
Muncagöta, 126
Muntenia, 291
Murány, 221
Murcia, 158, 165
Murfatlar, 291
Murray Darling, 284, 285
Muscadet Coteaux de la Loire, 109
Muscadet Côtes de Grandlieu, 109
Muscadet Sevre-et-Maine, 109
Muscat de Beaumes-de-Venise, 89
Muscat de Frontignan, 96
Muscat de Lunel, 96
Muscat de Mireval, 96
Muscat de Rivesaltes, 97
Muscat de Saint-Jean-de-Minervois, 96
Muscat du Cap Corse, 114
Muscat of Cephalonia, 236
Muscat of Lemnos, 236
Muscat of Patras, 235
Muscat of Rhodes, 236
Muscat of Rio Patras, 235
Musigny, 50, 54
Mykolaiv, 293
Myrat, 106

Nagy-Bajóka, 223
Nagy-Boglyoska, 227
Nagy-Hasznos, 215
Nagy-hegy, 214
Nagyka, 221
Nagy-kő, 224
Nagy-Kövesd, 219
Nagy-Majos, 214
Nagy-Rohos, 215
Nagy-Somló, 212
Nagy-szőlő, 220
Nahe, 186, 191
Nahetal, 191
Nairac, 106
Nanton, 85
Naoussa, 235
Napa Valley, 250
Napier, 276
Napos, 214
Naramata Bench, 240
Narancsi, 222
Nardò, 150
Nasco di Cagliari, 155
Navarra, 158, 162
Nebbiolo d'Alba, 124
Nebraska, 247
Negev, 289
Negev Judea, 289
Negotinska Krajina, 294
Negroamaro di Terra d'Otranto, 150
Négyszögű, 222, 223
Neirane, 131
Neive, 125, 127
Nelson, 287
Nemea, 235
Nervo, 128
Neszmély, 212
Nettuno, 147
Neuchâtel, 230
Neuquén, 266
Neusiedlersee, 205
Nevada, 247
Nève, 93
New Brunswick, 239
New England Australia, 285
New Hampshire, 247
New Jersey, 247, 260
New Mexico, 247, 257
New South Wales, 281, 285
New York, 247, 260
New Zealand, 286, 287
New Zealand, NZ, 287
Newfoundland and Labrador, 239
Niagara Escarpment, 241, 260
Niagara Lakeshore, 241
Niagara Peninsula, 241
Niagara River, 241
Niagara-on-the-Lake, 241
Nicoreşti, 291
Nidwalden, 230
Niedermorschwihr, 32
Niederösterreich, 202, 203
Nierstein, 192
Nieuwoudtville, 274
Ningxia, 297
Nišk, 294
Nišk, 294
Nišką, 294
Nitrianska, 292
Nizza, 124
Norte, 167
North Canterbury, 287
North Carolina, 247, 259
North Coast, 248, 249, 250, 251
North Dakota, 247
North East Victoria, 284
North Fork of Long Island, 260
North Fork of Roanoke, 259
North Island, NZ, 287
North Lebanon, 289
North Macedonia, 294
North West Victoria, 284
North Yuba, 254
Northern, 298
Northern Cape, 273
Northern Neck George Washington
　　Birthplace, 259
Northern Rivers, 285
Northern Riverside, 298
Northern Slopes, 285
Northern Territory, 281
Northland, 287
Northumberland Shore, 243
Northwest Territories, 239
Nothalten, 28
Noto, 154
Notre-Dame des Anges, 95
Nova Scotia, 239, 243
Novara, 123
Novello, 130, 131
Nuits-Saint-Georges, 50, 57, 58, 59, 60
Nunavut, 239
Nuragus di Cagliari, 155
Nuy, 278
Nyakvágó, 224
Nyergesek, 215
Nyírjes, 215
Nyulas, 219
Nyulászó, 218

Naches Heights, 256
Nagambie Lakes, 284
Nagano, 297

O Rosal, 159
Oak Knoll District of Napa Valley, 250
Oakville, 250
Oberer Neckar, 197
Obermosel, 189
Oberösterreich, 202
Óbidos, 176
Obwalden, 230
Oceanic, 298
Odenas, 87
Odessa, 293
Odobeşti, 291
Offida, 145
Oger, 43
Ohio, 247, 259
Ohio River Valley, 259
Oiry, 43
Oisly, 111
Okanagan Falls, 240
Okanagan Valley, 240
Oklahoma, 247, 258
Ökörtánc, 215
Ökrös, 224
Olaszliszka, 213, 222
Olifants River, 273, 277
Old Mission Peninsula, 258
Ollwiller, 25, 36
Oltenia, 291
Oltina, 291
Oltrepò Pavese, 136
Oltrepò Pavese Metodo Classico, 136
Oltrepò Pavese Pinot Grigio, 136
Omlás, 223
Ó-mogyorós, 222
Ontario, 239, 241
Orange, 285
Orcia, 142
Öreg-Buckler, 222
Öreg-diós, 222
Oregon, 247, 255
Oremus, 227
Orléans, 112
Orléans-Cléry, 112
Ormeasco di Pornassio, 140
Ornato, 135
Orsan, 90
Orschwihr, 34
Orta Nova, 150
Ortenau, 196
Ortona, 148
Ortrugo dei Colli Piacentini, 141
Orvieto, 146, 147
Osorno Valley, 263
Osterberg, 25, 29
Ostuni, 150
Ósz-hegy, 215, 218
Ösztvér, 223
Ottrott, 24
Ötvenhold, 215
Outeniqua, 277
Outer Coastal Plain, 260
Ovello, 126
Overberg, 276
Ozark Highlands, 258
Ozark Mountain, 258
Ozenay, 85

Paardeberg, 275
Paardeberg South, 275
Paarl, 275
Pacheco Pass, 252
Pacherenc-du-Vic-Bilh, 98
Padi-hegy, 217
Padthaway, 283
Pago Calzadilla, 166
Pago de Añina, 169
Pago de Arínzano, 162
Pago de Otazu, 162
Pago de Rui Diaz, 169
Pago de Tizón, 169
Paiagallo, 133
Paicines, 252
País Vasco, 158, 162
Pajé', 126
Pajore', 128
Pajzos, 225
Palandor, 222
Palánkos, 223
Palánta, 215
Palásti, 223
Palette, 95
Palmela, 176
Palmer, 103
Palos Verdes Peninsula, 248
Palota, 214, 215, 220, 224
Pampa el Cepillo, 269
Panciu, 291
Panerole, 131
Panka, 214
Pannon, 212
Pannonhalma, 212
Pantelleria Moscato di Pantelleria
　　Passito di Pantelleria, 154
Panzano, 144
Pápa, 222

Pape Clément, 105
Papegaaiberg, 275
Parafada, 135
Paraje Altamira, 269
Parlag, 223
Paros, 236
Parrina, 142
Parussi, 134
Paso Robles, 253
Paso Robles Estrella District, 253
Paso Robles Geneseo District, 253
Paso Robles Highlands District, 253
Paso Robles Willow Creek District, 253
Passetemps, 77
Pastrana, 169
Patagonia, 266, 270
Patócs, 215
Patras, 235
Patrimonio, 114
Pauillac, 99, 101
Pavie, 107
Pavie-Macquin, 107
Pays Nantais, 108, 109
Paysandú, 298
Pécharmant, 98
Pécs, 212
Pécsi, 220
Pécsi-oldal, 221
Pédesclaux, 101
Peel, 282
Pelagonija-Polog, 294
Peloponnese, 234
Pemberton, 282
Pendics, 214
Penedès, 163
Pengő, 219
Península de Setúbal, 175
Penisola Sorrentina, 151
Pennsylvania, 247, 260
Pentro di Isernia (Pentro), 149
Pénzásó, 224
Percze, 218
Peresek, 223
Pergola, 145
Pernand-Vergelesses, 61, 62
Pernanno, 134
Perno, 131
Perőcz, 219
Péronne, 85
Perréon, 87
Perrières, 69
Perth Hills, 282
Pertuisots, 64
Pessac-Léognan, 99, 104, 105
Petaluma Gap, 251
Péter deák, 219
Petingeret, 75
Petit Chablis, 46, 47
Petit Clos Rousseau, 77
Petit Marole, 82
Petite Chapelle, 52
Petits Cazetiers, 52
Petits Godeaux, 63
Petők, 224
Petrács, 224
Petruska, 224
Peza, 236
Pézenas, 96
Pfaffenheim, 34
Pfalz, 186, 193
Pfersigberg, 25, 33
Pfingstberg, 25, 34
Philadelphia, 275
Pianta', 134
Piave, 138
Piave Malanotte, 138
Pic Saint-Loup, 96
Pichon-Longueville Baron, 101
Pichon-Longueville Comtesse de
　　Lalande, 101
Pico, 178
Picpoul de Pinet, 96
Pied d'Aloup, 48
Piégon, 90
Piekenierskloof, 277
Piemonte, 121, 123, 124
Pierreclos, 85
Pierrefeu, 95
Pierrevert, 95
Pietroasa, 291
Pignoletto, 141
Piket-Bo-Berg, 275
Pillot, 80
Pimotin, 94
Pincesczer, 223
Pine Mountain-Cloverdale Peak, 249,
　　251
Pinerolese, 124
Pinkóczi, 220
Pinot Nero dell'Oltrepò Pavese, 136
Piolenc, 90
Pipiske, 215
Pira, 134
Piroska, 216
Pisapola, 131
Pissotte, 109
Pitangeret, 72
Pitsiia, 293
Pitures Dessus, 66
Pla de Bages, 163
Pla i Llevant, 170
Plan de Dieu, 90
Planalto Catarinense, 298

Planèze, 92
Plany, 92
Plešivica, 290
Plettenberg Bay, 276
Plottes, 85
Poboleda, 164
Pocerski Valjevski, 294
Pocito, 268
Podravska, 290
Podunavlje, 290
Pogány-kút, 226
Poilly-sur-Serein, 47
Poissenot, 52
Poklos, 221
Pokolbin, 285
Pokuplje, 290
Polkadraai Hills, 275
Pomán, 267
Pomerol, 99
Pomino, 142
Pommard, 61, 65
Pontet-Canet, 101
Pora, 126
Porongurup, 282
Porrera, 164
Porseleinberg, 275
Port Philip, 284
Portimão, 176
Porto, 176
Porto-Vecchio, 114
Portugal, 173, 175
Porusot, 69
Posavska, 290
Potiski, 294
Potter Valley, 249
Pouget, 103
Pouilly, 86
Pouilly- Fuissé, 84
Pouilly sur Loire, 112
Pouilly- Vinzelles, 84
Pouilly-Fuissé, 86
Pouilly-Fumé, 112
Pouilly-Loché, 84
Povardarie, 294
Pozo de los Algarrobos, 268
Prabon, 135
Prado de Irache, 162
Praelatenberg, 25, 29
Prapo', 135
Préaux, 80
Preda, 133
Préhy, 47
Prekmurje, 290
Premeaux-Prissey, 57, 60
Premiéres Côtes de Bordeaux, 99
Prieska, 274
Prieuré Lichine, 103
Prigorje-Bilogora, 290
Primorje, 290
Primorska, 290
Prince Albert, 274
Prince Albert Valley, 274
Prince Edward County, 241
Prince Edward Island, 239
Priorat, 163, 164
Prissé, 85
Prosecco, 138, 139
Provence, 22, 95
Pruzilly, 87
Puerto Real, 168
Puget Sound, 256
Puglia, 121, 150
Pugnane, 134
Puisieulx, 43
Puisseguin-Saint-Émilion, 99
Puligny-Montrachet, 61, 73
Pupillin, 38
Puyméras, 90
Puy-Notre-Dame, 110
Pyrenees, 284

Qingtongxia, 297
Quarts de Chaume ["Grand Cru"], 110
Quatourze, 95
Québec, 239, 242
Québec and the Banks of the St.
　　Lawrence River, 242
Quebrada de Humahuaca, 267
Queensland, 281, 285
Quincié-en-Beaujolais, 87
Quincy, 112
Quiroga-Bibei, 159

Rabaja', 126
Rabaja'bas, 126
Rabaud Promis, 106
Rablay sur Layon, 110
Rabourcé, 80
Racha, 296
Raclot, 80
Rácz-dűlő, 216
Radda, 144
Radoska, 224

Rafaj, 223
Rákóczi, 220
Rakottyás, 222
Ramandolo, 139
Ramat Arad, 289
Ramona Valley, 248
Rangen, 25, 36
Rány, 222, 224
Rapel Valley, 263
Rapsani, 235
Rasteau, 89
Rátka, 213, 217
Rattlesnake Hills, 256
Rauzan Gassies, 103
Rauzan Ségla, 103
Ravera, 131, 133
Ravera di Monforte, 131
Raviole, 131
Rawson, 268
Rayne Vigneau, 106
Recaş, 291
Recioto della Valpolicella, 138
Recioto di Gambellara, 138
Recioto di Soave, 138
Red Hill Douglas County, 255
Red Hills Lake County, 249
Red Mountain, 256
Redondón, 169
Redrescul (M), 63
Redwood Valley, 249
Reggiano, 141
Régnié, 87
Régnié-Durette, 87
Regodón, 169
Remete, 215
Remeték, 219
Remeték alja, 219
Remstal-Stuttgart, 197
Reno, 141
Répás, 218
Reugne, 71
Reuilly, 112
Rézló, 224
Rheingau, 186, 190
Rheinhessen, 186, 192
Rhode Island, 247, 260
Rhodes, 236
Rhône, 22, 89
Rías Baixas, 159
Ribbon Ridge, 255
Ribeauvillé, 29
Ribeira Sacra, 159
Ribeiras do Miño, 159
Ribeiro, 159
Ribeiro de Ulla, 159
Ribera Alta, 162
Ribera Baja, 162
Ribera del Duero, 160
Ribera del Guadiana, 166
Ribera del Júcar, 166
Riberiras do Sil, 159
Richebourg, 50, 56
Richelieu River Valley, 242
Riebeekberg, 275
Riebeeksrivier, 275
Riesi, 154
Rietrivier FS, 274
Rieussec, 106
Rigóska, 225
Rio Negro
  Argentina, 266
  Uruguay, 298
Rio Sordo, 126
Rioja, 161
Rioja Alavesa, 161
Rioja Alta, 161
Rioja Oriental, 161
Ripaille, 41
Riquewihr, 30
Ritolas, 93
Riva Rocca, 131
Rivadavia, 268, 269
Rivassi, 133
Rive, 132
River Junction, 248
Rivera, 298
Riverina, 285
Riverland, 283
Rivesaltes, 97
Rivette, 135
Rivetti, 127
Riviera del Brenta, 138
Riviera del Garda Bresciano, 136
Riviera Ligure di Ponente, 140
Rivolet, 87
Rizzi, 128, 129
Roaix, 90
Robardelle, 66
Robe, 283
Robertson, 278
Robola of Cephalonia, 236
Roccalini, 126
Rocche dell'Annunziata, 132
Rocche dell'Olmo, 131
Rocche di Castiglione, 131, 134
Rocche Massalupo, 129
Rocchettevino, 132
Rocha, 298
Roche Aux Moines, 110
Rochefort sur Loire, 110
Rochefort-du-Gard, 90
Rochegude, 90
Rochins, 93
Rockpile, 251
Rocky Knob, 259
Rodasca, 131
Roddi, 130, 131
Rodern, 24, 29
Roere di Santa Maria, 132
Roero, 124
Roggeri, 132
Rogue Valley, 255
Rohály, 225
Roma, 147
Romagna, 141
Romagna Albana, 141
Romanèche-Thorins, 87
Romanée-Conti (M), 50, 56
Romanée-Saint-Vivant, 50, 56
Romania, 291
Rombone, 128
Romer, 106
Romer du Hayot, 106
Roncaglie, 126, 132
Roncagliette, 126
Ronchi, 126
Roncières, 59
Roncières, 48
Roquebrun, 96
Rosacker, 25, 30
Rosalia, 205
Rosazzo, 139
Rosé d'Anjou, 110
Rosé de Loire, 108
Rosé des Riceys, 42
Rosette, 98
Rossese di Dolceacqua, 140
Rosso Cònero, 145
Rosso della Val di Cornia, 142
Rosso di Cerignola, 150
Rosso di Montalcino, 142
Rosso di Montepulciano, 142
Rosso Orvietano, 146
Rosso Piceno, 145
Rostov, 293
Rota, 168
Rouffach, 34
Rousset-les-Vignes, 90
Roussette de Savoie, 40
Roussette du Bugey, 39
Roussillon, 22, 97
Royal Slope, 256
Royer, 85
Rozier, 93
Rubino di Cantavenna, 124
Ruchè di Castagnole Monferrato, 124
Ruchottes-Chambertin, 50, 52
Rudnok, 225
Rue de Chaux, 59
Rue', 133
Rueda, 160
Rufina, 143
Rully, 79, 80
Russel, 269
Russia, 293
Russian River Valley, 251
Ruster Ausbruch, 205
Rutherford, 250
Rutherglen, 284
Ruwertal, 189

S

S. Anna di Isola Capo Rizzuto, 153
S. Lorenzo, 133
Saale-Unstrut, 186, 198
Saar, 189
Sablet, 90
Sachsen, 186, 199
Saddle Rock-Malibu, 248
Saering, 25
Saint Aubin de Luigné, 110
Saint Hippolyte, 24
Saint Lambert du Lattay, 110
Saint-Amour, 87
Saint-Amour-Bellevue, 87
Saint-Andéol, 90
Saint-Aubin, 61, 72
Saint-Bris, 46
Saint-Chinian, 96
Saint-Christol, 96
Saint-Cyr-sur-le-Rhône, 91, 92
Saint-Didier-sur-Beaujeu, 87
Saint-Drézéry, 96
Sainte-Cécile, 90
Sainte-Cécile-les-Vignes, 90
Saint-Émilion, 99
Saint-Émilion Grand Cru, 99, 107
Sainte-Morille, 83
Saint-Estèphe, 99, 100
Saint-Étienne-des-Oullières, 87
Saint-Étienne-des-Sorts, 90
Saint-Étienne-la-Varenne, 87
Sainte-Victoire, 95
Saint-Gengoux-de-Scissé, 85
Saint-Gengoux-le-National, 85
Saint-Georges-d'Orques, 96
Saint-Gervais, 90
Saint-Hippolyte, 29
Saint-Jean-de-la-Porte, 41
Saint-Jeoire-Prieuré, 41
Saint-Joseph, 89
Saint-Julien, 87, 99, 102
Saint-Just-d'Ardèche, 90
Saint-Lager, 87
Saint-Marcel-d'Ardèche, 90
Saint-Marcellin-lès-Vaison, 90
Saint-Martin-d'Ardèche, 90
Saint-Maurice, 90
Saint-Maurice-de-Satonnay, 85
Saint-Mont, 98
Saint-Pantaléon-les-Vignes, 90
Saint-Péray, 89
Saint-Pourçain, 113
Saint-Romain, 61
Saint-Romain-en-Viennois, 90
Saint-Roman-de-Malegarde, 90
Saint-Sardos, 98
Saint-Saturnin, 96
Saint-Saturnin-lès-Avignon, 90
Saint-Symphorien-d'Ancelles, 87
Saint-Véran, 84
Saint-Vérand, 87
Saint-Victor-la-Coste, 90
Saint-Ytages, 83
Saint-Ythaire, 85
Sajgó, 218, 221, 222
Salado Creek, 248
Salaparuta, 154
Salice Salentino, 150
Salles-Arbuissonnas-en-Beaujolais, 87
Salta, 266
Salto, 298
Salurnay-sur-Guye, 85
Salzburg, 202
Sambuca di Sicilia, 154
Sâmbureşti, 291
Samegreio, 296
Samos, 236
San Antonio Valley, 252, 263
San Benito, 252
San Bernabe, 252
San Bernardo, 135
San Blas de los Sauces, 268
San Carlos, 267, 269
San Casciano, 144
San Colombano al Lambro, 136
San Cristoforo, 127
San Donato in Poggio, 144
San Francisco Bay, 252
San Giacomo, 132
San Gimignano, 142
San Ginesio, 145
San Giovanni, 131
San Giuliano, 127
San Javier, 270
San José, 298
San Juan, 266, 268
San Juan Creek, 253
San Julian, 169
San Lorenzo di Verduno, 131
San Lucas, 252
San Luis, 266
San Luis Obispo Coast, 253
San Martín, 268, 269
San Martino della Battaglia, 136, 138
San Miguel District, 253
San Pablo, 269
San Pasqual Valley, 248
San Pietro, 133
San Ponzio, 133
San Rafael, 269
San Rocco, 135
San Rocco Seno d'Elvio, 125, 129
San Severo, 150
San Stunet, 128
San Torpè, 142
San Ysidro District, 252
Sanagasta, 268
Sancerre, 112
Sangue di Giuda dell'Oltrepò Pavese, 136
Sanlúcar de Barrameda, 168
Sannio, 151
Sant' Antimo, 142
Sant'Anna, 132
Santa Clara Valley, 252
Santa Cruz Mountains, 252
Santa Lucía, 268
Santa Lucia Highlands, 252
Santa Margarita Ranch, 253
Santa Margherita di Belice, 154
Santa Maria, 132
Santa María, 267
Santa Maria Valley, 253
Santa Rosa, 269
Santa Ynez Valley, 253
Santenay, 61, 77
Santenots, 66
Santorini, 236
Sárazsadány, 213, 225
Sardegna, 121, 155
Sardegna Semidano, 155
Sarica Niculiţel, 291
Sarkad, 217, 218
Sarmassa, 133
Sarmiento, 268
Sáros, 223
Sárospatak, 213, 226
Sartène, 114
Sas alja, 215
Saskatchewan, 239
Sátor, 214
Sátoraljaújhely, 213, 227
Sátor-hegy, 227
Saumur, 110
Saumur-Champigny, 110
Saussignac, 98
Sauternes, 99, 106
Savennières, 110
Savigny-lès-Beaune, 61, 63
Savigny-sur-Grosne, 85
Savoie, 22, 40
Savuto, 153
Saze, 90
Sazenay, 81
Scarrone, 134
Scavigna, 153
Schaffhausen, 230
Scharrachbergheim, 26
Scherpenheuvel, 278
Scherwiller, 24
Schloss Neuenburg, 198
Schlossberg, 25, 31
Schoenebourg, 30
Schoenenbourg, 25
Schwyz, 230
Sciacca, 154
Searing, 35
Sebeş-Apold, 291
Sécher, 48
Secondine, 126
Segarcea, 291
Séguret, 90
Seiad Valley, 248
Semons, 94
Seneca Lake, 260
Sennecey-le-Grand, 85
Serbia, 294
Serédi, 224
Sérignan-du-Comtat, 90
Serra, 135
Serra dei Turchi, 132
Serra do Sudeste, 298
Serra Gaúcha, 298
Serraboella, 127
Serracapelli, 127
Serradenari, 132
Serragrilli, 127
Serralunga d'Alba, 130, 135
Serranía de Ronda, 167
Serrapetrona, 145
Serrières, 85
Servoisine, 82
Setúbal, 176
Seyssel, 40
Sforzato di Valtellina, 136
Shandong, 297
Shanxi, 297
Shawnee Hills, 258
Shenandoah Valley, 259
Shirak, 296
Shizuishan, 297
Shoalhaven Coast, 285
Shomron, 289
Short Hills Bench, 241
Shrivan Valley, 296
Shuswap, 240
Sicilia, 121, 154
Siebengebirge, 188
Sierra Foothills, 254
Sierra Pelona Valley, 248
Sierras de Málaga, 167
Sigalas Rabaud, 106
Signargues, 90
Sigolsheim, 31
Sigy-le-Châtel, 85
Silio, 132
Siller-oldal, 219
Sillery, 43
Similkameen Valley, 240
Simonsberg-Paarl, 275
Simonsberg-Stellenbosch, 275
Sipos, 215
Siracusa, 154
Široki Brijeg, 294
Sitia, 236
Sizzano, 124
Sjeverna Dalmacija, 290
Skaha Bench, 240
Slanghoek, 278
Slavonia, 290
Slavonia and Danube, 290
Slopes of Meliton, 235
Sloughhouse, 254
Slovácká, 292
Slovakia, 292
Slovenia, 290
Slovenska Istra, 290
Smith Haut Lafitte, 105
Snake River Valley, 255
Snipes Mountain, 256
Soave, 138
Soave Superiore, 138
Sóhajó, 219
Solanes del Terme de El Molar, 164
Solano County Green Valley, 250
Solanotto, 134
Sologny, 85
Solothurn, 230
Soltvadkert Ezerjó, 211
Solutré-Pouilly, 85
Som, 224
Somló, 212
Somlyód, 226
Sommerberg, 25, 32
Sommières, 96
Somontano, 162
Somos, 214, 221, 225
Somszög, 215
Sonnenglanz, 25, 30
Sonoita, 257
Sonoma Coast, 251
Sonoma Mountain, 251
Sonoma Valley, 251
Sopron, 212
Sorano, 131, 135
Soriano, 298
Sós, 217
Sottocastello di Novello, 131
Soultzmatt, 34
Sous Blagny, 69
Sous Frétille, 62
Sous le Dos d'Ane, 69
Sous le Puits, 73
Sous les Feilles, 83
Sous Roche Dumay, 72
South Africa, 271, 273
South Australia, 281, 283
South Burnett, 285
South Carolina, 247
South Coast, 248, 285
South Dakota, 247
South East, 295
South Eastern Australia, 281
South Island, NZ, 287
South Islands, 241
South Lebanon, 289
South Shore, 243
South West Australia, 282
South West France, 98
Southeastern New England, 260
Southern Flinders Ranges, 283
Southern Highlands, 285
Southern New South Wales, 285
Southern Oregon, 255
Southern Riverside, 298
South-West France, 22
Soutomaior, 159
Sovana, 142
Spain, 156, 158
Spiegel, 25, 35
Spoleto, 146
Sporen, 25, 30
Spring Mountain District, 250
Springfontein Rim, 276
Spruitdrift, 277
Squaw Valley-Miramonte, 248
Squinzano, 150
Srednja I Juzna Dalmacija, 290
Sremski, 294
St Francis Bay, 274
St Helena Bay, 275
St Pierre Sevaistre, 102
St. David's Bench, 241
St. Gallen, 230
St. Helena, 250
Sta. Rita Hills, 253
Stags Leap District, 250
Štajerska Slovenija, 290
Stanford Foothills, 276
Starderi, 127
Starkenburg, 194
Stavropol, 293
Ste-Croix-du-Mont, 99
Ştefan Vodă, 293
Ştefăneşti, 291
Steiermark, 202, 205
Steigerwald, 195
Steinert, 25, 34
Steingrubler, 25, 33
Steinklotz, 25, 26
Stellenbosch, 275
Stettyn, 278
St-Georges-Saint-Émilion, 99
Still Bay East, 276
St-Nicolas de Bourgueil, 111
Stormsvlei, 276
Strathbogie Ranges, 284
Stredoslovenská, 292
Strevi, 124
Struma Valley, 293
Suau, 106
Suba, 218
Subotički, 294
Südliche Weinstraße, 193
Südsteiermark, 205
Suduiraut, 106
Suisun Valley, 250
Sujtó, 222
Sulyom, 214
Šumadijski, 294
Sunbury, 284
Sunday's Glen, 276
Sur, 263
Sur Gamay, 72
Sur la Roche, 86
Sur la Velle, 70
Sur le Sentier du Clou, 72
Sur les Gréves, 64
Sur les Gréves-Clos Sainte-Anne (M), 64
Sutherland-Karoo, 274
Suvereto, 142
Suze-la-Rousse, 90
Swan Creek, 259
Swan District, 282
Swan Hill, 284, 285
Swan Valley, 282
Swartberg, 274
Swartland, 275
Swellendam, 276
Switzerland, 228, 230
Syunik, 296
Szár-hegy, 223, 224, 225, 227
Szarka, 220
Szarvas, 219
Szegfű, 226
Szegi, 213, 221
Szegilong, 213, 221
Szekszárd, 212
Szemere, 216, 217
Szemince, 226
Szemszúró, 223, 227
Szent Mihály, 222
Szent Tamás, 218
Szentkereszt, 219
Szentvér, 224
Szenyes, 223
Szepsy, 221
Szerelmi, 220
Szerencs, 213, 216
Szilvás, 216, 218
Szil-völgy, 219
Szirmai, 220
Szőlőshegy, 214

T

Tacoronte-Acentejo, 171
Tacuarembó, 298
Tafí, 267
Taille Pieds, 66
Tajpó, 220
Talbot, 102
Tállya, 213, 215
Táncos, 214
Tarcal, 213, 219
Târnave, 291
Tarquinia, 147
Tarragona, 163
Tasmania, 281
Tauberfranken, 196
Taurasi, 151
Tautavel, 97
Tavel, 89
Tavira, 176
Tavoliere delle Puglie, 150
Távora-Varosa, 176
Tavush, 296
Tehachapi Mountains, 248
Tehéntánc, 226
Teichi-szőlők, 226
Tejo, 175
Tekenő, 215
Telečka, 294
Teleki, 220
Temecula Valley, 248
Templeton Gap District, 253
Templomőrzés, 225
Tennessee, 247, 259
Teno Valley, 263
Teodoro, 135
Terézia, 219
Térhegy, 224
Terlo, 133
Teroldego Rotaliano, 137
Terra Alta, 163
Terra d'Otranto, 150
Terracina (Moscato di Terracina), 147
Terras de Beira, 175
Terras de Cister, 175
Terras do Dão, 175
Terras Madeirenses, 175
Terrasses du Larzac, 96
Terratico di Bibbona, 142
Terre Alfieri, 124
Terre del Colleoni, 136
Terre dell'Alta Val d'Agri, 152
Terre di Casole, 142
Terre di Cosenza, 153
Terre di Offida, 145
Terre di Pisa, 142
Terre Tollesi (tullum), 148
Tête du Clos, 76
Texas, 247, 257
Texas Davis Mountains, 257
Texas High Plains, 257
Texas Hill County, 257
Texoma, 257
Thames And Chilterns, 295
Thann, 36
The Burn of Columbia Valley, 256
The Hamptons, Long Island, 260
The North, 266, 267
The Peninsulas, 283
The Rocks District of Milton-Freewater, 255
Theewater, 276
Thermenregion, 203
Thessaly, 234
Thompson Valley, 240
Thrace, 234
Thracian Valley, 293
Three Lakes, 230
Thunersee, 231
Thurgau, 230
Thüringen, 198
Thurzó, 219
Ticino, 230
Tierra de Estella, 162
Tierra de León, 160
Tierra del Vino de Zamora, 160
Tihany, 212
Timiş, 291
Tinogasta, 267
Tintilia del Molise, 149
Tip of the Mitt, 258
Tirol, 202
Todi, 146
Tokaj
  Hungary, 211, 213, 220
  Slovakia, 292
Tökös-máj, 215
Tókus-tető, 216
Tolcsva, 213, 224
Tolna, 212
Tompa-kő, 227
Tonnerre, 45
Tonton Marcel (M), 76
Toplec, 222
Toplički, 294
Torgiano, 146
Torgiano Rosso Riserva, 146

Torino, 123
Toro, 160
Torres Vedras, 176
Torriglione, 132
Torroja del Priorat, 164
Torrox, 169
Toscana, 121, 142
Touraine, 108, 111
Touraine Noble-Joué, 111
Tournus, 85
Tours-sur-Marne, 43
Tracy Hills, 248
Tradauw, 277
Tradouw Highlands, 277
Traisental, 203
Transmontano, 175
Transylvania, 291
Trás-os-Montes, 176
Travaillan, 90
Tre stelle, 126
Trebbiano d'Abruzzo, 148
Trebujena, 168
Treiso, 125, 128
Trentino, 137
Trentino-Alto Adige, 121, 137
Trento, 137
Tresques, 90
Trevelin, 270
Tri Morave, 294
Trifolera, 126
Trinity Lakes, 248
Troësmes, 48
Troplong Mondot, 107
Trotte Vieille, 107
Truskóczki-szőlő, 214
Tualatin Hills, 255
Tucumán, 266
Tulbagh, 275
Tulette, 90
Tumbarumba, 285
Tuniberg, 196
Tunuyán, 269
Tupin, 94
Tupin-et-Semons, 91, 94
Tupungato, 269
Turckheim, 32
Turkey, 293
Túróska, 215
Tursan, 98
Tutuvén Valley, 263
Twenty Mile Bench, 241

U

Uchaux, 90
Uchizy, 85
Uclés, 166
Ugar, 219
Új-Buckler, 222
Új-diós, 222
Új-hegy, 217
Új-mogyorós, 222
Ukraine, 293
Ukrina, 294
Ullum, 268
Umbria, 121, 146
Umpqua Valley, 255

Umstadt, 194
Upington, 274
Upper Galilee East, 289
Upper Galilee West, 289
Upper Golan, 289
Upper Goulburn, 284
Upper Hemel-en-Aarde Valley, 276
Upper Hiwassee Highlands, 259
Upper Hudson, 260
Upper Hunter Valley, 285
Upper Langkloof, 277
Upper Mississippi River, 258
Úrágya, 218
Urbán, 218
Uri, 230
Urueña, 160
Uruguay, 298
Usa, 244, 247
Utah, 247
Utiel-Requena, 165

V

Vacqueyras, 89
Vagliagli, 144
Vaillons, 48
Vaison-la-Romaine, 90
Val d'Arbia, 142
Val d'Arno di Sopra, 142
Val di Cornia, 142
Val do Salnés, 159
Val Polcàvera, 140
Val Saint Grégoire, 24
Valais, 230
Valandraud, 107
Valcalepio, 136
Valdadige (Etschtaler), 137, 138
Valdadige Terradeiforti, 137, 138
Valdeorras, 159
Valdepeñas, 166
Valdichiana Toscana, 142
Valdinievole, 142
Valdizarbe, 162
Vale do São Francisco, 298
Valeirano, 128
Valençay, 111
Valencia, 158, 165
Valentino, 134
Valgargado, 169
Valle d'Aosta, 122
Valle d'Aosta, 121
Valle de Chañarmuyo, 268
Valle de Güímar, 171
Valle de la Orotava, 171
Valle de Uco, 269
Valle de Zonda, 268
Valle del Pedernal, 268
Valle del Tulum, 268
Valle Fértil, 268
Vallée de la Marne, 43
Vallée Noble, 24
Vallegarcía, 166
Vallegrande, 128
Valles Calchaquíes - Valle Calchaquí, 267
Valles del Famatina, 268
Vallet, 109

Valley of the Roses, 293
Valli Ossolane, 124
Valmur, 49
Valpolicella, 138
Valpolicella Ripasso, 138
Valréas, 90
Valsusa, 124
Valtellina Rosso, 136
Valtellina Superiore, 136
Valu lui Traian, 293
Vámosújfalu, 213, 222
Van Duzer Corridor, 255
Vancouver Island, 240
Várhegy, 221, 224
Városoldal, 215
Váti, 219
Vau de Vey, 48
Vau Ligneau, 48
Vaucoupin, 48
Vaud, 230
Vaudésir, 49
Vaugiraut, 48
Vaulorent, 48
Vaupulent, 48
Vauvry, 80
Vaux Ragons, 48
Vaux-en-Beaujolais, 87
Vauxrenard, 87
Vay, 222
Vayots Dzor, 296
Vecsey, 220
Vedène, 90
Vég-hegy, 225
Velkopavlovická, 292
Velletri, 147
Veneto, 121, 138
Venezia, 138
Venterol, 90
Ventoux, 89
Vera de Estenas, 165
Verbano-Cusio-Ossola, 123
Vercelli, 123
Verde Valley, 257
Verdicchio dei Castelli di Jesi, 145
Verdicchio di Matelica, 145
Verdicchio di Matelica Riserva, 145
Verduno, 130, 131
Verduno Pelaverga, 124
Verebes, 220
Vérenay, 93
Veres Bálint, 222
Veresek, 218
Veres-mogyorós, 219
Vergelesses, 62
Vergisson, 85
Vérmány, 226
Vermentino di Gallura, 155
Vermentino di Sardegna, 155
Vernaccia di Oristano, 155
Vernaccia di San Gimignano, 142
Vernaccia di Serrapetrona, 145
Vers, 85
Vers Cras, 86
Verzé, 85
Verzenay, 43
Verzy, 43
Vesuvio, 151
Vézelay, 46
Vézerance, 92

Vicenza, 138
Vicenziana, 126
Victoria, 281, 284
Vida, 216
Vide Bourse, 75
Vidlám, 224
Vigna Rionda, 135
Vignane, 133
Vignanello, 147
Vigne Blanche, 76
Vigne Derriére, 75
Vigne du Soleil, 83
Vignes Couland, 83
Vignes Moingeon, 72
Vignes Saint-Pierre, 83
Vignes sur le Cloux, 83
Vigneti della Serenissima, 138
Vignolo, 134
Vigyorgó, 214, 219
Villa Ventana, 270
Village, 72
Village de Pernand (M), 62
Villamagna, 148
Villány, 147
Villedieu, 90
Villero, 134
Villié-Morgon, 87
Villy, 47
Vilmány, 218
Vin d'Alsace, 23
Vin de Corse, 114
Vin de Savoie, 40, 41
Vin mousseux de qualité de Wallonie, 295
Vin Santo del Chianti, 142
Vin Santo del Chianti Classico, 142
Vin Santo di Carmignano, 142
Vin Santo di Montepulciano, 142
Vinchina, 268
Vinemount Ridge, 241
Vinho Verde, 176
Vinkrivier, 278
Vinnai, 219
Vino Nobile di Montepulciano, 142
Vinos de Madrid, 166
Vinsobres, 89
Vinzelles, 85
Vióka, 227
Violès, 90
Vipavska Dolina, 290
Viré-Clessé, 84
Virginás, 217
Virginia, 247, 259
Virginia Peninsula, 259
Virginia's Eastern Shore, 259
Virieu-le-Grand, 39
Visan, 90
Vista Flores, 269
Vittoria, 154
Viviers, 47
Vix, 109
Vlaamse mousserende kwaliteitswijn, 295
Vlottenburg, 275
Voegtlinshoffen, 34
Vojvodina, 294
Volnay, 61, 66
Voor-Paardeberg, 275
Vorarlberg, 202

Vorbourg, 25, 34
Vosgros, 48
Vosne-Romanée, 50, 56
Vougeot, 50, 55
Vouni Panayias – Ambelitis, 293
Vouvray, 111
Vrancea, 291
Vranjski, 294
Vredendal, 277
Vulkanland Steiermark, 205
Vully, 231
Východoslovenská, 292

W

Wachau, 203, 204
Wagram, 203
Wahluke Slope, 256
Waiheke Island, 287
Waipara Valley, 287
Wairarapa, 287
Waitaki Valley, 287
Walker Bay, 276
Walla Walla Valley, 255, 256
Wallonia, 295
Walporzheim-Ahrtal, 187
Warren Hills, 260
Washington, 247, 256
Weinviertel, 203
Wellington, 275
Wessex, 295
West
   England, 295
West Australian South East Coastal, 282
West Elks, 257
West Virginia, 247, 259
Western Australia, 281, 282
Western Beqaa, 289
Western Cape, 273
Western Connecticut Highlands, 260
Western Plains, 285
Western Victoria, 284
Westhalten, 34
Weststeiermark, 205
Wettolsheim, 33
White Bluffs, 256
Wiebelsberg, 25, 27
Wien, 202, 203
Wiener Gemischter Satz, 203
Wild Horse Valley, 250
Willamette Valley, 255
Willcox, 257
Willow Creek, 248
Wineck-Schlossberg, 25, 32
Wintzenheim, 33
Winzenberg, 25, 28
Wisconsin, 247, 258
Wisconsin Ledge, 258
Wolxheim, 24, 26
Wonnegau, 192
Worcester, 278
Wrattonbully, 283
Wuenheim, 36
Württemberg, 186, 197
Württembergischer Bodensee, 197
Württembergisches Unterland, 197

Wyoming, 247

X

Xinjiang, 297

Y

Yadkin Valley, 259
Yakima Valley, 256
Yamagata, 297
Yamanashi, 297
Yamhill-Carlton, 255
Yarra Valley, 284
Ycoden-Daute-Isora, 171
Yecla, 165
Yerevan, 296
York Mountain, 253
Yorkville Highlands, 249
Yountville, 250
Yukon, 239
Yunnan, 297
Yuquanying, 297

Z

Zafír, 219
Zagarolo, 147
Zagorje-Međimurje, 290
Zahlé, 289
Zakarpattya, 293
Zala, 212
Zandrivier, 278
Zaporizhia, 293
Záporos, 219
Zărand, 291
Zarzuela, 169
Zellenberg, 30
Zemplén, 210
Zhenbeibu, 297
Zichron Yaacov - Hanadiv Valley, 289
Zinnkoepflé, 25, 34
Zitsa, 235
Znojemská, 292
Zoccolaio, 133
Zomborka, 216, 217
Zonchetta, 133
Zonda, 268
Zotzenberg, 25, 27
Zsadányi, 225
Zsebrik, 214
Zsedényi, 222
Zug, 230
Zuncai, 133
Zürich, 230
Zürichsee, 231

About the Author

Istvan Barczikay

A Certified Sommelier by the Court of Master Sommeliers, Istvan's long standing passion for wine and lifelong love of geography encouraged him to create his first book The Wine Region Atlas.

Born and raised in north-east Hungary, Istvan familiarized himself with the world-renowned wine region, Tokaj.

His knowledge for wine has expanded with his travels, as he has spent time living and working in the United States, Germany, United Arab Emirates, and the United Kingdom, learning more about the industry with each experience.

His travels have given him opportunities to work with various small businesses as well as high-calibre establishments such as St. Regis Saadiyat Island Resort and Savoy Grill.

Outside of work, Istvan has sought out more learning opportunities and had the privilege to go behind the scenes of the 2017 harvest of the Chateau Dereszla winery, and witness the entire process of wine making, from grape to bottling.

He currently lives in London, and when not working and gaining knowledge of the wine industry, Istvan enjoys watching superhero movies, culinary arts, and maintaining good physical health.